accounting and information systems

john r. page
university of new orleans

h. paul hooper
university of virginia

reston publishing company, inc.
a prentice-hall company
reston, virginia

Library of Congress Cataloging in Publication Data

Page, John
   Accounting and information systems.

   Includes index.
   1. Accounting—Data processing. I. Hooper, Paul,
joint author. II. Title.
HF 5679.P25   657'.028'54   78-26610
ISBN 0-8359-0082-7

10 9 8 7 6 5 4 3

Printed in the United States of America

contents

preface

The application of information systems concepts to the accounting process and accounting models is a relatively recent phenomenon. Indeed, the study of information systems is itself new. However, because of the increasing importance of information systems, these areas now are firmly entrenched as an important part of university curriculum in business.

Courses (usually required) in accounting information systems now exist in virtually every business school, and to service this market a substantial number of textbooks of varying focus and depth have been written. It is our desire to offer a new book in this area, which will be significantly different in design and emphasis from those currently available.

Textbooks in the business/management/accounting information systems area have historically been of two types. Those that purport to give an introduction and overview of the field are usually so general in content as to make impossible the operationalization of the ideas presented. Others, which claim a comprehensive coverage have tended toward technical sophistication beyond the background and interests of the major groups of potential users. In addition, these texts have almost universally made no attempt to ground the study of information systems in basic accounting concepts, resulting in an isolation of the field from other accounting study. We have attempted to correct these deficiencies in the literature of accounting systems with this book.

The most important feature of our approach is the integration of information systems concepts into the basic accounting process, and the extension of traditional accounting models to include the systems approach. This integration and extension seems to be the link that students search for in relating their work in this area to other accounting study. Without this link it is difficult to appreciate where accounting systems fit into the "big picture." Additionally, this approach is designed not only for accounting students, but also those interested in systems work and management consulting, including engineers, computer scientists, and business majors, who have had only an introductory exposure to accounting.

It should be noted that the concepts of information systems are introduced only after the student is firmly grounded in the components and procedures of manual accounting systems. Importantly, manual accounting systems are introduced and discussed to give the student an overview of how the accounting cycle flows from the beginning to end, not simply to teach mechanical facility and bookkeeping. Such a background (Part One) is fundamental to under-standing and applying the ideas which follow in the text. Part Two then introduces the basic tools of systems analysis. Part Three illustrates the application of these systems analysis tools in the development of computer-based information systems. Finally, Part Four synthesizes the concepts of accounting systems and information systems in a computer context. Of special use to the beginning student throughout these sections is the development and subsequent use of a sample company with comprehensive supporting documents and illustrative transactions to demonstrate the application of the principles being explained. Two appendices (one using the BASIC language and the other using the COBOL language) illustrate some of the major pro-gramming considerations of computer-based system development.

This book is better because of the time and efforts of many people, including Lloyd Brandt, J. Herman Brasseaux, Michael Dugan and Vincent Messina (all of the University of New Orleans), and James Schmit of Loyola University. In addition we want to mention the careful reviewing and suggestions made by John Kohlmeier, Charles Kriebel, R. Keith Martin, James B. Thies and Myron Uretsky. We would also like to thank the students at the University of New Orleans who used the book in manuscript form and made helpful comments. Manette Sartain typed the manuscript under often trying circumstances and always kept her good spirits. Special thanks go to Ron Thacker of the University of New Orleans for his advice and encour-agement. Finally, the expertise and efforts of Frederick Easter, Executive Editor, and Lucy Cuzon du Rest, Production Editor, of Reston Publishing Company were critically important to the making of this book.

John R. Page
New Orleans, Louisiana

H. Paul Hooper
Charlottesville, Virginia

To
our parents
and
Pam, Lisa, Jody and Jennifer

part I

manual accounting systems

the accounting system

outline

INTRODUCTION

In this chapter we introduce the basic structure and reasoning behind the accounting system. This topic is considered first because we strongly feel that understanding the basic concepts of accounting is absolutely essential to grasping and using the subject matter that comprises most of this book. The ability to apply the principles of information systems to business situations requires a feel for manual recording systems based on fundamental accounting ideas. This chapter and the next three will present basic components of manual accounting systems to provide you with this background.

If the subject matter presented in these chapters is a review for you, we promise an approach you have probably not seen before, and one that should clarify this material in your mind. If you are a newcomer to this material, we feel that you will have sufficient background after Part One to understand what follows.

1.1   INTRODUCTION TO ACCOUNTING SYSTEMS

Many long, complex, and wholly uninformative definitions have been offered to define what accounting is and does. Let us offer a short, easy, and rather clear definition of accounting.

> Accounting is a system for keeping track of the financial events in the life of any individual or organization in a manner that makes it possible for that individual or organization to report on its financial position and activities to anyone who may be interested.

You should remember some points about our definition if you are going to apply it properly:

1. Accounting is concerned with financial events only, which means you cannot rely on the accounting system for all of your information about a business. Information which is not financial in nature is ignored by accounting and, therefore, must be secured from some other source.

    Accounting systems, then, are a subset of information systems. Information systems provide more than financial information and are therefore made up of accounting systems plus other systems.

2. The accounting system is applicable not only to businesses, but also to individuals and to organizations which are not businesses in a profit-making sense, such as governments, hospitals, churches, and universities.

3. During the life of even the smallest business, there are many individuals or groups which may desire some information on the position and activities of that business. Accounting systems must be prepared to serve many different users of information, including at least owners, creditors, certain governmental agencies (IRS, SEC), and management. As a business gets larger many other groups such as labor unions and other governmental regulatory agencies begin to call for financial information about its position and activities. The demands of company management are strongest on the accounting system since this group must direct the progress of the business. Accounting systems must provide information for the decision making, planning, and control of a business.

Basic Assumptions Underlying the Accounting System

Accounting systems are based on certain assumptions about the nature of business, and a logical structure is developed from using basic assumptions. There are six such basic givens on which accounting systems are based. You should study these carefully because they tell you something about the nature of accounting systems and will provide you with guidelines to follow in understanding these systems.

1. *Entity.* We assume that all businesses are separate units (entities) for accounting purposes, and therefore account for each business separately from all others and separately from the owners of the business. Each business is an accounting unit whose affairs should not be mixed with other units.

2. *Going concern.* In the absence of strong evidence to the contrary, we always assume that a business will go on forever and account for it on that basis. This assumption has strong implications for the way accounting systems operate.

3. *Accounting period.* Although the business is usually assumed to have a very long life, most people or groups would like to know how the business is doing at intermediate shorter intervals. Accounting systems break the very long life of the business into shorter, somewhat arbitrary time segments called accounting periods. These accounting periods become the basis for reporting on the position and activities of the business. These periods have, by custom, tradition, and to some extent law, become a year in the United States for most businesses. The year may be calendar (January 1 to December 31) or it may be fiscal (beginning and ending at any other time), but the reports that result are always tentative because the accounting period is short compared to the life of the business.

4. *Monetary.* We need a common denominator for expressing measurements of the different events in which a business engages. That common unit of measure in accounting is the dollar. The accounting system measures everything in dollar terms. This seems reasonable in that the dollar is objective, familiar, and reasonably well understood.

   The use of the dollar, however, does generate two potential problems. First, the more stable the measuring stick the more useful it is. Comparisons must be made between events valued at different times and these comparisons are made more useful by a constant, or relatively constant, unit of measure. Second, if everything is valued by the dollar, then events or things that are not susceptible to dollar valuation must be ignored by the accounting system. Since many important things and events cannot be valued in dollars, the accounting system is not a total information system.

5. *Exchange.* If accounting systems value everything in dollar terms, the question then becomes what amount of dollars to use for each event as it occurs. All events have some exchange value at the moment they take place, such as the cost of a building or the amount borrowed or repaid, and it is this exchange value that the accounting system is interested in. Accounting systems use the exchange value which exists when the event occurs and subsequent movements in value are generally ignored by the system.

6. *Financial Statements.* Some assumption must be made about the kind of information various people or groups interested in a business would like to have. Of all the possible kinds of information the accounting system could generate, how much is enough and what form should the information take? The last assumption says that most users of accounting output would like to have two basic pieces of information. First, it is desirable to have a statement that depicts the financial position of the business, an overall picture of where the business stands at a point in time. This report lists the things a business possesses and the obligations that the business faces. The accounting system produces such a statement, called a *balance sheet.* Second, users want to know whether or not the firm has been successful in its profit-seeking activities since the last financial position report. In other words, they desire a statement which summarizes the results of the business operations for

a period of time, disclosing the various accomplishments and efforts expended by the business during that time period. Such a statement lists accomplishments and efforts, and compares the two to determine whether or not the business is better off from its activities. The *income statement* in accounting does just this. (Accounting systems regularly produce a third financial statement, called a *statement of changes in financial position*. This statement will not be explored further since its information system's significance is relatively small compared to the balance sheet and income statement.)

1.2 ACCOUNTING SYSTEM MEASUREMENTS

At the most abstract level, there is no mystery to what businesses do or the role accounting systems play in the process of business. Every business, large or small, does essentially two major things. First, businesses acquire financial and productive resources from some source; then, these resources are combined and used to create more resources. The basic idea of business activity is to make resources grow. To the extent resources grow, business activity has been, generally speaking, successful. The reverse is true for declining resources.

Assets and the Fundamental Accounting Equation

Accounting systems term the resources businesses acquire from some source and use to create more resources, *assets*. Obviously, in the real world every asset has a source; that is, comes from some individual or organization. We call sources of assets (i.e., places from which a business has acquired its resources), *equities*. Since every financial and productive resource in a business has either been acquired or created, it is always true that for every business at all times in its life

$$\text{Assets} = \text{Equities}$$

This simple equation is the basis for all that is done in accounting. It is the first building block in the structure from which the entire system is built. This equality is called the *basic accounting equation*. Individuals or organizations that supply businesses with assets almost without exception would like those assets or others of equal or greater value returned to them someday. Similarly, if a business has created new assets by its activities, the owners of that business would like ultimately to enjoy the benefits of those assets. This means that equities not only measure sources of assets, but at the same time equities measure claims against the assets of the business. In effect then, the basic accounting equation shows that all the assets of a business have claims against them. These claims may have been created because assets were supplied to the business, or because the business has created its own assets and the owners have a right to enjoy the business success by receiving these assets.

To summarize, everything accounting systems do is traceable directly from the basic accounting equation. The equation is simple, but the concepts underlying it are somewhat complex. The essential meaning of this equation is made clear by noting that the following three expressions are absolutely identical in meaning and may be used interchangeably:

$$\text{Assets} = \text{Equities}$$
$$\text{Assets} = \text{Sources of Assets}$$
$$\text{Assets} = \text{Claims Against Assets}$$

Resources versus Assets

Assets are financial and productive resources; however, not all resources are assets. To be an asset in an accounting system for a particular business a resource must meet three criteria.

1. The resource must possess *future value* for that business.
2. The resource must be under the effective control of that business.
3. The resource must have a dollar value resulting from an identifiable event in the life of that business.

To be an asset, a resource must meet *all* of the above criteria. If any one of the requirements is not met, the resource simply is not an asset in accounting terms, regardless of its physical existence or presence. Let us examine each of these criteria a little more closely.

Future value simply means that there must be some benefit in the future to the company from holding the resource today. Resources exhibit future value either by *exchange value* or by *use value*. Exchange value means the resource can be readily exchanged for other resources which a business may desire. Obviously, the epitome of an exchange value resource is *cash*, which can be exchanged for just about anything. There are, however, other exchange value assets which may not be so obvious. For example, amounts of money owed to a business, often called *accounts receivable* in accounting systems, represent a resource with exchange value. The receivable is collected (exchanged) in cash, which is exchangeable for anything. *Inventory*, which is the term used to indicate goods held by a business for resale to its customers, is also an exchange value resource because the inventory is sold (exchanged) either for cash or for a receivable. These three resources represent the primary exchange value resources; however, there may be many others in the life of a real-world business.

Accounting systems encounter a second type of future value called *use value*. For a resource to possess use value, it must be expected to contribute to a business by its physical use. Resources which businesses actually use up (usually a little at a time) such as buildings, equipment, machines, trucks and cars fall into this category and are the most common use value resources found. Remember, it is the concept of use value and its application that is important.

If a resource exhibits future value, we must then determine if the resource is under the control of the business in question. Effective control and legal ownership are not at all the same thing. Although it is possible for any business to possess ownership without control or vice versa, the usual circumstance for most businesses with respect to its resources is to enjoy both characteristics at once or to have effective control without legal ownership. This control criterion is an important factor in the determination of accounting assets. Air, sunshine, oceans, highways and so on are obviously resources of great value, but are under the control of no particular entity; therefore these resources could never be accounting assets to any business. On the other hand, a business may buy a truck or car on credit and have control over the vehicle while legal ownership rests with the financing bank or credit company. Such a vehicle would meet the control criterion for inclusion as an asset.

The final criterion to be met is rather straightforward in concept and application. The standard unit of measure in accounting systems is the dollar; hence, resources must be susceptible to dollar valuation if they are to be accounting assets. Since the accounting system prefers objectively determinable facts to subjective opinion, this dollar valuation must result from an identifiable event (usually an exchange between independent parties) in the life of the business. It follows, then, that certain valuable resources (a firm's reputation for quality service, products, or favorable location) do not qualify as assets in the normal course of events. Though valuable, they are very difficult to measure in dollars since they do not usually result from one event, but rather are the result of many events and actions over long periods of time.

In summary, to determine whether or not a resource is an accounting asset, simply apply the above criteria. If the resource meets *all three* criteria, the resource is indeed an asset. If any one criterion is not met a resource may exist, but it is not one with which the accounting system is concerned.

Liabilities

Recall that equities are sources of assets and, at the same time, claims against the assets of a business. A business can acquire assets from either (1) its owners, or (2) nonowners, which includes all other individuals or businesses. When persons or groups other than owners supply a business with assets, the claim against the assets that necessarily results usually takes the form of debt. That is, by accepting assets from "outsiders" (i.e., banks, suppliers), the business incurs a legal obligation to return to these outsiders assets of equal or greater value at some time in the future. These sources of assets from nonowners and claims on the assets of a business by nonowners are called *liabilities* in accounting systems. Liabilities represent the debts and legal obligations of a business which have resulted from the business acquiring assets from persons or groups other than the owners. Keep in mind the following three characteristics of liabilities.

1. They generally represent *legal* obligations of a business; that is, if the obligations are not satisfied, the business risks its very existence.

2. The amount of the obligation is generally known with certainty.

3. The point in time at which the obligation must be satisfied is generally known with certainty.

Owner's Equity

Of course, a business may decide to secure assets from its owners instead of outsiders or in addition to outsiders. When the owners supply a business with assets, the claim against these assets that results is called *owner's equity* (sometimes called stockholder's equity if the business is a corporation). Like liabilities, the business incurs an obligation by accepting assets from owners; however, owner's equity represents quite a different sort of claim from that represented by liabilities. Note the following characteristics of owner's equity and compare them to liabilities:

1. Owners' claims against the business are generally *not* legally enforceable; that is, if the claims are not satisfied, the owners usually have no recourse but to give up ownership.

2. The owners' claim is said to be *residual* because the owners of the business may claim all assets not specifically claimed by outsiders. They may claim what is left over, whether it is a lot, a little, or nothing.

3.   There is no specific time in the future when the claim must be satisfied by the business. The claim is *open-ended*.

What we are saying about the owner's equity component of total equities is this: When owners of a business supply that business with assets, a claim against that business is created. Unlike liabilities, however, the business makes no specific promise to return these assets to its owners, and the extent to which these claims are ever satisfied depends upon the company's success. A certain amount of owners' claims against the assets of any business are more or less permanent and will not be satisfied as long as the business continues to operate.

Since equities can be subdivided into two major groups, liabilities and owner's equity, we can rewrite the basic accounting equation as follows

$$Assets = Liaibilities + Owner's\ Equity$$

This expanded version of the basic accounting equation is the basis for the balance sheet, one of the two primary reports produced by the accounting system. The balance sheet is simply an elaboration of the A = L + OE statement for a particular business.

1.3 BALANCE SHEET

When a business lists its assets, usually in some specified order, and does the same with the liability claims and owner's equity claims against those assets, it has prepared a balance sheet. Notice that the title of this financial statement reflects the equality condition always present in the basic accounting equation and that the balance sheet is prepared as of one instant in time. It is a still picture of the business depicting its financial position (status) as of the date it is prepared. Once you are able to recognize and separate assets, liabilities, and owner's equity, you have done most, but not all of the work necessary to the preparation of a balance sheet. For consistency and effectiveness of communication, assets are listed in a prescribed order and classified so that like assets are grouped together and unlike assets are kept apart from each other. The same is true for liabilities and owner's equity. The classification scheme used in balance sheet preparation is important because it conveys something about the nature of individual assets, liabilities, and owner's equities and the intention of the business toward them.

Classification and Valuation of Assets, Liabilities, and Owner's Equity

Current and Noncurrent Assets

For reporting purposes, assets are classified into two major groups called *current* and *noncurrent*. Current assets are those resources which are expected to be converted to cash or used up within the next accounting period. These are the business' most liquid assets and are listed in order of closeness to cash.

Noncurrent assets are those resources which qualify as assets, but are not current. Somewhat more precisely defined, they are resources expected to be of use or benefit to the business for more than one accounting period. In effect, these are assets of long-term significance.

If you study the asset side of any balance sheet carefully you will probably note the following:

1. There are five primary current assets almost always found on a balance sheet, irrespective of the size or type of business. They are cash, receivables, and inventory which we briefly discussed earlier, marketable securities, and prepaid expenses. *Marketable securities* represent short-term temporary investments of cash into some very liquid security such as U.S. government bonds. *Prepaid expenses* are slightly more troublesome in that they represent claims to future services such as insurance protection or advertising which have already been paid for. In this case, the right to the future service is a resource. A sixth current asset frequently encountered on business balance sheets is termed *supplies*, indicating that the business holds incidental resources such as cleaning materials, paper, pens, pencils, and so on to be used up in the near future.

2. Noncurrent assets are usually grouped into several subcategories called investments, plant property and equipment, and other assets. *Investments* represent the long-term commitment of cash to securities by the purchase of stocks and bonds of other businesses. *Plant property and equipment* indicates the businesses' holding of productive assets such as land, buildings, and so on. *Other assets* are obviously a catch-all category for resources which cannot be otherwise classified.

Current Liabilities and Long-term Debt

Consider now the equities side of any balance sheet. First, note the major subdivision into liabilities and owner's equity. Remember that liabilities depict the legal obligations or debts of the business which must be paid or satisfied at some known future date. It is this expected date of satisfaction of the debt that is important in the balance sheet classification of liabilities. If the debt satisfaction or payment is expected to take place within the upcoming accounting period, and will require the use of current assets, the obligation is reported on the balance sheet as a *current liability*. Amounts owed to suppliers for inventory merchandise purchased on credit, taxes owed to the government, and amounts owed to banks and others for short-term borrowings are typical current liabilities. Amounts owed to creditors usually from borrowings, which are expected to be repaid over many years made up most of *long-term debt*, the second major category of liabilities.

Conceptually the most difficult area of the balance sheet to understand is owner's equity. This is true for two reasons: first, because the nature of the owner's claim on assets is quite different from other claims; and second, because it is in the owner's equity section of the balance sheet that the two primary accounting reports (financial statements) interact and come together.

Common Stock, Income, Dividends, and Retained Earnings

Remember that owner's equity represents sources of assets from the owners and, at the same time, measures the owner's claims against the assets of a business. In fact, there are really two ways in which an owner can supply a business with assets. The simplest way is for an owner to directly and voluntarily turn over assets (usually cash) to a business in exchange for ownership interest in that business. This direct and voluntary investment takes the form of a purchase of shares of stock when the corporate form is used. Shares of stock represent ownership interest, and as these are sold the business receives assets, the source being the business owners. Simultaneously, a claim is created against the assets in favor of those holding this ownership interest. In a corporation (the most successful form of business in the United States), sources of assets and claims against assets created by the direct and voluntary transfer of assets by the owners to a business are called *capital stock* or *common stock*.

There is, however, a second way in which owners may supply assets to a business. The process is always indirect and sometimes involuntary. Remember that the essence of successful business activity is making resources which we now know to be assets, grow. If successful operations create assets, then the question is, Who has a claim to them? Recall that with assets *acquired* by the business, the persons or other businesses supplying the assets hold a claim against the business for the return of similar assets. If assets have been *created* by successful operations rather than *acquired*, the source of the assets is the activities of the business itself, not an external person or other business. The increase in a business' assets due to successful operations, is called *income* in accounting systems. Keep in mind the residual nature of the owners' claim, and then you will be able to see that assets created cannot be claimed by anyone external to the business and therefore are claimed by the owners. The fruits of successful operations, which are the assets generated by a business in its profit seeking, belong to its owners. A business' income belongs to its owners.

Since these created assets are claimed by the owners, from time to time the business may want to give the assets directly to them. That is, to keep its owners happy, a business will often disburse some portion of these internally generated assets (usually in the form of cash) to its owners. In a corporation, this disbursement of assets which have been created by successful operations is called a *dividend*. It is very unusual for U.S. corporations, large or small, to distribute to owners all of the assets the business has created in any one accounting period. For reasons of growth and taxes, as well as others, corporations retain some of their internally generated assets in the business. In practical terms, this means that for a successful business, income (assets *created* to which the owners have a claim) is always larger than dividends (assets distributed to satisfy owner claims). Thus, in each accounting period owner claims increase by the difference between the two. In effect, owners are reinvesting in the business by not withdrawing all of the "new" assets which belong to them. Since the owners do not get these assets in the first place, and then consciously decide to return them, the reinvestment is indirect. Since the decision as to how much they actually do receive is often not theirs to make, the reinvestment can be involuntary. Some owners may prefer to get all of the assets to which they are entitled and not reinvest at all. The *cumulative* amount of new assets generated by the business' operations and not distributed to the owners since the business began operating represents a source of assets to the business and an increased claim on the assets by business owners. On corporate balance sheets this second way that owners may supply a business with assets is designated *retained earnings*. As a source of assets, retained earnings is equal to income minus dividends over the life of the business. Keep this in mind as we study the second primary financial statement produced by the accounting system, the *income statement*.

Finally, some fundamental points to remember as you study the equities side of any balance sheet.

1. Although all equities are claims on assets, there is a definite hierarchy or priority of claims based mostly on the law. Claims held by nonowners are considered first priority and therefore liabilities represent higher order claims than do owner's claims. Liabilities are

primary claims and owner's equity residual claims. The order in which these equities appear on the balance sheet reflects this fact.

2.   Whether primary or residual, all equities represent *general* claims against all of the assets of the business rather than specific claims on specific assets in the business. There is seldom a one-to-one relationship between a specific asset and a specific claim or source. Instead, the accounting system views the business as a collection of assets matched and balanced by a set of general claims which are assigned a priority listing in the balance sheet.

1.4 INCOME STATEMENT AND STATEMENT OF RETAINED EARNINGS

The second primary statement which results from the accounting system is called the *income statement*. This report is more of a dynamic statement in that it attempts to summarize the results of a business' operations (profit-seeking activities) for a period of time. The income statement shows the ultimate effect on the business of its profit-seeking activities for a specific accounting period and serves the informed reader as a guide to understanding why the affect came about. The "bottom line" of this statement, called in accounting *net income, net profit, or net earnings,* is the amount by which assets have been increased by successful operations. The income statement is not unrelated to the balance sheet, but rather the two statements very much interact and formally come together at retained earnings.

Expanded Accounting Equation

Study closely the following progression of equations and you should begin to appreciate further the very important relationship and interaction between the income statement and balance sheet. Such an appreciation is critical to understanding how accounting systems work.

The basic accounting equation is

$$A = L + OE \quad \text{where A is Assets}$$
$$\text{L is Liabilities}$$
$$\text{OE is Owner's Equity}$$

but we know that owner's equity can be divided into direct and indirect sources of assets, or claims on assets by the owners, so we can rewrite the equation without changing its meaning as

$$A = L + CS + RE \quad \text{where CS is Capital or Common Stock}$$
$$\text{RE is Retained Earnings}$$

But remember that retained earnings is nothing but net income minus dividends over the life of the business, so the equation can be further expanded as

$$A = L + CS + (NI - D) \quad \text{over the life of the business}$$

which can be rewritten

$$A = L + CS + \Sigma (NI - D) \quad \text{where } \Sigma \text{ is a summation sign indicating the cumulative}$$

Net income is itself the result of combining two very important accounting system measurements called *revenue* and *expense,* so the completely expanded (for our purposes) version of the basic accounting equation is

$$A = L + CS + \Sigma [(R - E) - D]$$

The expression within the parenthesis (i.e., R - E) is equal to net income for an accounting period, while the expression within the brackets (i.e., R - E - D) represents the increase in indirect investment by the owners and, at the same time, the increase in claims against the assets of the business because of this indirect investment. Stated another way, R - E - D measures the amount of assets generated by successful operations during an accounting period, less the amount of those assets distributed to the owners during that accounting period. If this increase in indirect investment is summed (added) up for each accounting period in the business' life, the result is the balance sheet total for indirect investment by owners, which is retained earnings. If this figure is added to the total direct investment by owners (capital stock or common stock), the result is total owner's equity representing the total owner's claims on the assets of the business.

Revenue and Expense

Net income is the accounting system's measure of the success of a business. The determinants of net income are *revenue* and *expense.* In the study of accounting these two measurement ideas are among the most difficult to grasp for two reasons: (1) the concepts underlying them are complex, and (2) we all have some "layman notions" derived from our general experience which tend, unfortunately, to get in the way of precision in this area.

Both revenue and expense are abstract measurement concepts. Both measure in accounting terms movements in assets and/or liabilities, that are caused by the profit-seeking activities of a business within a given time period. Revenue measures increases in or inflows of assets caused by the profit-seeking activities of a business during an accounting period. Note the following very important aspects of this definition of revenue.

1. Revenue is an abstraction which measures "real" movement someplace else. The actual movement takes place among the assets, or liabilities and revenue is the expression we use to measure the amount of inflow.

2. Assets may increase for many reasons in a typical business, but revenue measures only those increases caused by profit-seeking activities.

To elaborate further on the second point, consider the following example: a business may borrow money from a bank with the result being that assets increase. The act of borrowing money is a financing activity, rather than a profit-seeking activity. The profit seeking would occur when the business decided how to use the money it had borrowed. On the other hand, a business may sell some of its products to a customer. Such a sale would most certainly cause assets to increase and would be profit seeking in nature. Both borrowing money and selling products cause assets to increase, but only the latter gives rise to revenue. In accounting, we use revenue to distinguish between asset increases caused by profit-seeking events and all other increases in assets. We want to separate and measure assets created as distinct from assets acquired. In terms of the basic accounting equation; the first event above (borrowing money) causes assets to increase (cash) and liabilities to increase (loans payable to bank) by the same amount, thus equality is maintained. The second event (selling products) causes assets to increase (cash or accounts receivable), but also causes revenue to increase. If you refer to the progression of equations previously discussed, you will find that as revenue increases, so does retained earnings and consequently owner's equity. We then realize that the result of the second event Is quite different from the result of the first. The second event causes assets and owner's equity to increase by the same amount and thus equality is maintained.

Expense is almost the exact opposite of revenue. Expense measures decreases in or out-flows of assets (note the close parallel to the definition of revenue), or increases in liabilities caused by the profit-seeking activities of a business. In other words, when a business consumes or uses up its assets or creates liabilities in the course of seeking a profit, expenses are created. The two important points to remember about revenue made earlier, also apply to expense.

1. Expense is an abstraction which measures "real" movement someplace else. Either the actual consumption takes place among the assets or the increase takes place among liabilities, and expense is the expression of these changes.

2. Assets may decrease or liabilities increase for many reasons in a typical business, but expense measures only those changes caused by profit-seeking activities.

Suppose, for example, a business pays off a bank loan with a resulting decrease in assets. This act simply retires a legal obligation of the business, and therefore its effect on the basic accounting equation would be a reduction of assets and an equal reduction of liabilities. Similarly, a business which borrows money would increase assets and increase liabilities by the same amount. In these events either an asset decreases or a liability increases, but, importantly, no expense is created. Now consider the sale of products to a customer. The sale causes assets to increase, but at the same time an asset (inventory) is consumed as a result of the sale. This consumption is measured and separated from other consumptions by the creation of an expense. Again, referring to the progression of accounting equations, notice that as expense increases (it is a negative factor in the equation), retained earnings and owner's equity decrease. Assets have decreased and the balancing movement is a decrease in owner's equity.

Accrual and Cash Basis Accounting

The idea that a business should recognize accomplishment (revenue) and the related effort (expense) when any asset (not just cash) is created or consumed is the basis for what is termed *accrual* accounting. The idea that revenue and expense should be recognized only when cash is affected is called *cash basis* accounting. Most businesses use an accrual basis accounting system, while most individuals use a cash basis accounting system. This distinction is true for income tax reporting, as well as for other purposes, and is mandated by either law or accounting principles. In our discussions we will focus on accrual basis accounting systems for businesses. Table 1-I should make clear the basic differences between these two revenue-expense recognition guidelines.

TABLE 1-1 GUIDLINES FOR THE RECOGNITION OF REVENUE AND EXPENSE

		Revenue	*Expense*
ACCOUNTING SYSTEM	CASH	Cash is received from profit-seeking events	Cash is paid for profit-seeking events
	ACCRUAL	Any asset is received from profit-seeking events—usually when product is sold or services rendered	Any asset is consumed or liability created from profit-seeking events—usually matched to revenue

Interaction of Income Statement and Balance Sheet

Recall that the balance sheet and income statement actually connect or come together at retained earnings. Net income (the bottom line of the income statement) minus the amount of those assets withdrawn by the owners (dividends) represents the net amount by which retained earnings increase for the period. This interaction between the two major financial statements is so important that most accounting systems produce a simple statement whose sole function is to emphasize this connection. The statement is called a *statement of retained earnings*, and its purpose is to make explicit the effect of income and dividends on the basic accounting equation. The general format of this statement follows the equation progression previously discussed where net income is added and dividends subtracted from beginning retained earnings to determine ending retained earnings.

1.5 ACCOUNTING CYCLE AND DOUBLE-ENTRY BOOKKEEPING

Mechanics of the Accounting Process

Remember that the income statement, retained earnings statement, and balance sheet represent the output of the accounting system and are typically prepared only once each period. Let us turn our attention to the system which makes possible the preparation of these reports. The series of steps any business goes through to produce meaningful financial reports from all of the events that occur in its life is called the *accounting cycle*. This cycle is usually a seven-step process which has as its goal the recording, classifying, summarizing, and communicating of financial information. When this process is carried out by hand or with the aid of mechanical devices, but without the use of computers, it is called a *manual* accounting system. The flow of data through this system is manifested in a typical accounting cycle:

1. *Journalize* the accounting transactions.
2. *Post* the accounting transactions.

3. Prepare a *trial balance.*

4. Journalize and post *adjusting entries.*

5. Prepare an *adjusted trial balance.*

6. Prepare *financial statements.*

7. Journalize and post *closing entries.*

Double-Entry Bookkeeping

If we prepare financial statements only every now and then, a technique is needed to keep track of the events that occur between these financial statements. To record these events in a way that makes financial statements reasonably easy to prepare, we use a technique in accounting systems called *double-entry bookkeeping.* An appreciation of manual accounting systems requires a complete understanding of double-entry bookkeeping.

The Journal and Ledger

The two primary instruments used in double-entry bookkeeping are the journal and the ledger. The *journal* is a device which facilitates the recording of events as they occur in the life of a business. It provides a place for writing things down in an orderly manner. The *ledger* is used to classify these events based on their effect on assets, liabilities, owner's equity, revenue, and expense of the business. Figure 1-1 summarizes double-entry behavior patterns for each of these account classifications.

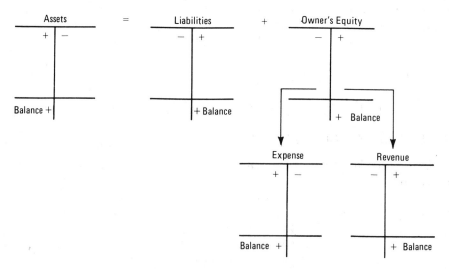

FIGURE 1-1 Double-Entry Behavior Patterns

Accounting Logic

The double-entry bookkeeping rules for these account classifications are simply mechanical reflections of the relationships implied in Figure 1-1. For example, as expense (a negative owner's equity) increases, owner's equity decreases. The logical implementation of this connection in double-entry fashion is that debits cause expense to increase (negatively) and owner's equity to decrease. By the same token, credits to expense (very rare except for closing entries to be discussed later in this chapter) cause them to decrease.

As a business earns revenue, the ultimate effect on the basic accounting equation is an increase in owner's equity. Since this positive connection exists between revenue and owner's equity, it stands to reason that the debit-credit rules should be the same for these accounts. In fact, the rules are exactly the same: credits cause increases in revenue and owner's equity and debits result in decreases in revenue (very rare) and owner's equity. We have already emphasized this tie between these income statement and balance sheet accounts and these double-entry relationships are just a manifestation of this tie-in. For a summary of the logic behind the debit-credit rules for revenue and expense, refer to the definitions of these measurements discussed earlier.

These basic ideas behind double-entry bookkeeping form an internally logical system. There is no situation faced by a business which cannot be handled easily within these rules. As you apply these ideas to business transactions and manual recording systems note the following:

1. Accounting systems are not concerned with all of the events in which a business may engage. Business events which become a part of the accounting system are called *transactions* or *accounting events*. For an event to be considered by the accounting system (recorded, classified, summarized, and communicated), the event must immediately affect one or more parts of the basic accounting equation. Transactions, then, are events which alter in some fashion the A = L + OE equation (do not forget the role of revenue and expense). Transactions are the raw data of accounting systems.

2. Double-entry bookkeeping derives its name from its view of accounting transactions as two-sided events. All transactions have at least two different effects on the basic accounting equation (otherwise equality could not possibly be maintained). For *every* transaction, there is at least one debit effect and at least one credit effect, and the *total* debits *always* equal the *total* credits for each transaction. This is called the *duality* idea in accounting. This idea of two-sidedness for every transaction is one of the excellent self-checks built into the double-entry bookkeeping system. Knowing that every accounting transaction has a debit effect and a credit effect, and that these effects always equal, aids in obtaining accuracy and complete analysis of transactions.

We now are able to state a second version of the basic accounting equation in bookkeeping terms. The following two statements are equivalent in accounting systems. The first equation is the conceptually based basic accounting model of the firm, and the second is a mechanical bookkeeping-oriented statement. Both are always true.

$$\text{Assets} = \text{Liabilities} + \text{Owner's Equity}$$
$$\text{Debits} = \text{Credits}$$

Table 1-2 summarizes the relationships between these two basic statements.

TABLE 1-2 DEBIT-CREDIT RELATIONSHIP

	Debit Balances	Credit Balances
Balance Sheet	Assets	Liabilities and Owner's Equity
Income Statement	Expense	Revenue

1.6 RECORDING AND CLASSIFYING DATA

Beginning the Accounting Cycle—Journalizing Transactions

Now that you understand the basic principles of double-entry bookkeeping, we can examine the beginning of the accounting cycle. The first step in the cycle is journalizing the accounting transactions. The *journal* should be thought of as the book of original entry because all transactions are first written down in the business journal. Actually, most accounting systems use several different types of *journals*; however, we will consider only the general journal, in this chapter. (Several of the other most commonly used journals will be discussed in Chapter 2.) Figure 1-2 is a sample segment of a typical general journal for a manual recording system.

Date		Transaction Accounts	PR	Debit Amount	Credit Amount
1979					
Jan	5	Accounts Payable	10	100	
		Cash	1		100
Jan	20	Accounts Receivable	3	450	
		Sales Revenue	21		450
		Cost of Inventory Sold	25	300	
		Inventory	4		300
Jan	25	Cash	1	200	
		Accounts Receivable	3		200

FIGURE 1-2 General Journal Sample Page

The primary task of journals, no matter the type, is to accomplish the recording function of the accounting process. The idea is to have a place where a business can record the important (accounting) events that occur, as they occur. What we want is a "diary" that gives the chronological history of that business. Additionally, we want to record these transactions in a way that makes it easy to determine the effect of the events on the assets, liabilities, owner's equity, revenue, and expense of the business. You should note the following important specific characteristics of journals:

1. The focus of journals is on the accounting transaction. Each transaction is recorded in the journal as a unit separately from other transactions. In even the smallest of businesses, transactions occur constantly so that recording activity in journals tends to be daily and constant.

2. General journals are numbered by pages and are organized by dates, so that transactions are recorded when, and in the order that they occur.

3. Each transaction is analyzed and recorded in terms of its debit-credit effect (recall that every transaction has a debit *and* credit effect). The specific account or accounts to be debited (increased or decreased) are written down first and against the margin, then the accounts credited as a result of the transaction are entered, usually indented from the left margin.

4. The column headed PR is a Posting Reference column in which the account numbers of debited and credited accounts are written (every ledger account has both a title and a number) as the amounts of the transactions are posted to the ledger. The appearance of the account number in the PR column indicates that the amounts have been posted.

5. Finally, separate amount columns are provided for Debit and Credit amounts, with the *Debit* amounts always written on the left in line with the debit accounts and likewise for credit amounts.

Since it is difficult to intuitively analyze and disclose the effect of perhaps 100 such transactions a day, every day for a year, a rather precise instrument like a journal with a well-known and widely-used format is necessary if a system is to record in a useful way the things that happen.

Posting Transactions—the Ledger

Of course, recording the transactions of a business as they occur (so that they are not forgotten or overlooked) is critical to the accounting system because transactions are the raw data of the system. Recording, however, is only the beginning of the cycle. If we are to produce useful reports about a business at the end of an accounting period, we must be able to determine the cumulative effect that all the period's transactions have on the accounts of the business. This is called classification and it involves use of the second bookkeeping instrument, called the *ledger*. The second step in the accounting cycle, posting, accomplishes this function. A portion of a typical general ledger for a manual system is shown in Figure 1-3.

The primary task of the ledger is to accomplish the classification function of the accounting system. The idea is to separate the components of each transaction and then group together all of the components that affect each individual asset, liability, owner's equity, revenue and expense account. In this manner we can show for each account the cumulative effect of all the transactions which affected that account. You should note the following important specific characteristics of ledgers:

1. The focus of the ledger is on the individual accounts of the business. There may be 50 or 100 or more transactions affecting cash, spread out throughout the journal. The ledger brings together all of these effects in the cash account so that the net change in cash can be determined.

2. Although it is important to know the net effect on all assets, liabilities, owner's equity, revenues, and expenses of a series of events, it is not necessary that the effect of each individual transaction be determined immediately as it occurs. Thus, posting to the ledger need not occur constantly and, in fact, usually takes place only after a number of transactions have occurred, perhaps every week or so.

ASSETS

CASH #1

Date	PR	Debit	Credit	PR	Date
12/31	✓	100			
1979					1979
1/25	J13	200	100	J13	1/5
1/31	✓	200			

ACCOUNTS RECEIVABLE #3

Date	PR	Debit	Credit	PR	Date
12/31	✓	500			
1979					1979
1/20	J13	450	200	J13	1/25
1/31	✓	750			

INVENTORY #4

Date	PR	Debit	Credit	PR	Date
12/31	✓	600			
1979					1979
			300	J13	1/20
1/31	✓	300			

LIABILITIES

ACCOUNTS PAYABLE #10

Date	PR	Debit	Credit	PR	Date
			400	✓	12/31
1979					1979
1/5	J13	100			
			300	✓	1/31

OWNER'S EQUITY

CAPITAL STOCK #15

Date	PR	Debit	Credit	PR	Date
			600	✓	12/31
1979					1979
			600	✓	1/31

RETAINED EARNINGS #17

Date	PR	Debit	Credit	PR	Date
			200	✓	12/31
1979					1979
			200	✓	1/31

REVENUES

SALES #21

Date	PR	Debit	Credit	PR	Date
1979			0		1979
			450	J13	1/20
			450	✓	1/31

EXPENSES

COST OF INVENTORY SOLD #25

Date	PR	Debit	Credit	PR	Date
1979		0			1979
1/20	J13	300			
1/31	✓	300			

FIGURE 1-3 General Ledger for a Manual System

3. Notice that each posting is dated in the ledger with the date the transaction occurred (and was entered in the journal) and that a posting reference indicating the journal and page from which the transaction was taken is included.

4. Finally, posting to the ledger creates no new information; it simply reproduces the information already recorded in the journal, in a way that shows the cumulative effect of the transactions on the individual accounts.

The Trial Balance

You have probably noticed certain numbers in each account in Figure 1-3 exhibit checks (✓) rather than journal and page information in the Posting Reference column. These numbers bring us to the third step in the accounting cycle, called the *trial balance*. Numbers with checks in the PR column indicate the balance in the account at a specific date, given in the Date column. It is important to distinguish between balances and transactions. A *balance* indicates the dollar value of an account at a specific point in time. A *transaction* is a change in an account from an event taking place since the last balance. Balances are arrived at by adding up the debits in the account and subtracting the credits, if the debits are larger than the credits. For example, in Figure 1-3 Accounts Receivable shows a debit balance at 12/31 of $500 which represents the cumulative effect of all the transactions involving Accounts Receivable prior to 12/31. During January, two transactions occurred affecting Accounts Receivable, one causing an increase and one causing a decrease. Since this account is an asset, we expect a debit balance. To determine the dollar value of Accounts Receivable at 1/31 we would simply add $500 + $450 and subtract $200. The number showing the cumulative effect of all transactions involving Accounts Receivable prior to 1/31 is $750; it is the balance in the account.

If the credits in an account are larger than the debits, the process of determining a balance would be the opposite to that described above. Refer to any account expected to show a credit balance in Figure 1-3 (liabilities, owner's equity, or revenue) to observe that the balance is arrived at by adding the credits and subtracting the debits. The zero balances you may have noticed in revenue and expense at the start of the month will be discussed later in this chapter.

Any business needs to know the dollar value of each of its accounts at various times during its life to be assured that the basic accounting equation is still intact (A = L + OE) and to help in the detection of errors. On the other hand, it is not necessary that balances in each account be determined after each posting. As a result, most businesses calculate balances showing the cumulative effect of all prior transactions at various points in its life, but not as frequently as posting takes place. A somewhat informal, internal statement, called a *trial balance*, is usually created when these balances are determined. The trial balance is simply a list of all the accounts used by the business and the appropriate dollar amounts in each account at some date. It is used to *summarize* the effect of all transactions on the business. By periodically making such a statement, we can get an overview of the accounts and amounts and can be sure that Debits = Credits and A = L + OE still hold for the business.

1.7 END-OF-PERIOD PROCEDURES

Adjusting Entries

Every business records in its journal the things that happen to it, usually as they occur. Frequently, businesses then classify the effects of these transactions on their accounts by posting to the ledger, and periodically determine the dollar amount of each account and summarize these balances in a trial balance. All these steps occur constantly, frequently, or at least more than once during an accounting period. There are, however, a very important set of steps in the accounting cycle that occur only once each accounting period. These steps are carried out only at the end of each accounting period and are designated *end-of-period* activities.

External Events

To understand adjusting entries, it is necessary to distinguish two basic types of events in which most businesses engage—external and internal. External events take place between a business and persons or other businesses. These events are rather easy to identify because they occur at discrete points as a business interacts with its environment. Also, there are usually supporting documents (like checks or bills) created by one or both of the parties to the transaction indicating that a transaction has occurred. Examples of such transactions include selling goods, purchasing assets, borrowing money, selling stock, repaying loans, and paying dividends. External events are recorded as they occur in step one of the accounting cycle because (a) they involve outsiders and (b) certain legal relationships are created as a result of the event which require immediate reflection in the accounting system. In fact, external events are the only transactions that require recording in the accounting system as they occur and, therefore, steps one to three of the accounting cycle are concerned *only* with external events. In step one we journalize external events and in step two we post external events. The trial balance of step three results from only those external events recorded in that period and the account balances from the beginning of the period.

Internal Events

There is a second major class of transactions which occur in the life of businesses. These *internal* events are much more subtle and consequently somewhat more difficult to grasp than external events. Essentially, internal transactions take place wholly within the firm; that is, no person or other business is directly involved in the transaction. In addition, these events tend to be continuous in nature in that they occur constantly rather than at specific, identifiable points in time; thus, there is rarely a source document supporting the transaction which alerts the system to its occurrence.

Since these internal events usually do not concern outsiders, there is no necessity that the system record them as they happen. Since they are constantly taking place in any business, it would be very cumbersome (also expensive) to record these in the way we record external events. As a result, internal events are handled quite differently from external events in the accounting cycle.

Since internal transactions occur but are not recorded during an accounting period, the *cumulative* effect of these continuous events must be recorded at the end of the period by a series of entries called *adjusting entries*. Although it is not necessary to record this type of transaction as it happens, it is absolutely essential that all events, external and internal, be properly recorded before financial statements are prepared at the end of the accounting cycle. Adjusting entries are designed to bring the books of a business up-to-date for a group of events ignored during an accounting period. This process requires returning to the journal so that internal transactions can be recorded, then to the ledger so that they can be posted and classified.

Types of Adjusting Entries

The continuous internal transactions recorded in an accounting system can be categorized into four fundamental types of adjusting entries. Remember as we review these basic types of adjustments that they all are recorded *only* at the end of the accounting period. The following basic adjusting entry types are given in order of importance and frequency of occurrence for most businesses. You should notice that most of these adjustments are required because businesses use accrual accounting. If cash-basis accounting were used, most of these adjusting entries would not be necessary.

1. *Internal expiration of assets*. As an accounting period goes by, businesses generally use up some of their assets (usually a little at a time) in the process of seeking a profit. This consumption of assets is wholly internal and goes on more or less constantly. As the business engages in profit-seeking events, supplies and prepaid expenses are consumed, inventory is sold, buildings, machines, trucks, cars, tools and so on are used up. At the end of the period a series of adjusting entries are made to reflect the expiration of these assets. These entries (we might call them Type 1) are all of exactly the same general format, only the specific account titles change: Type 1 adjustments *always* result in an increase in an expense and a decrease in an asset.

$$\text{Expense} \qquad \text{XXX}$$
$$\qquad \text{Asset} \qquad\qquad \text{XXX}$$

In all cases, you must be able to distinguish the acquisition of an asset, which is an external event to be recorded as it occurs, from the use or consumption of that asset, which is internal and recorded as an adjusting entry.

2. *Accruing an expense*. You might remember from our discussion of accrual accounting earlier in this chapter that most businesses recognize expenses when any asset has been consumed or any liability created as a result of profit-seeking events. This means that sometimes an expense must be recognized even though no external transaction has actually occurred or no asset used up. If an event occurs which has as its result the creation of a liability and that event is internal by its nature, we make an adjusting entry to recognize an increase in expense and an increase in liabilities. Remember that these adjustments (Type 2) are concerned with liability-creating events which take place internally near the end of the accounting period. The process of recording these events is called "accruing an expense," and it always takes the following format.

$$\text{Expense} \qquad \text{XXX}$$
$$\qquad \text{Liability (usually a payable)} \quad \text{XXX}$$

There are two primary examples of this type of adjustment: salaries and wages, and interest. If payday for a business' employees does not fall on the same day the accounting period ends, salaries and wages earned during the period, but not paid until the next period (when the payday occurs) must be accrued. Such salaries and wages should be expenses of the period in which the work was actually performed by employees because as of the end of the current period, the business has incurred an obligation to the employees for these yet unpaid amounts. Adjusting entry Type 2 recognizes both the existence of the liability and the creation of an expense for these incurred, but not yet paid salaries and wages. This very same reasoning would also apply to interest which may be owed by a business on amounts borrowed. As time passes, interest accrues on loans; however, most interest is paid only at fixed points in time. If the accounting period ends between these interest payment dates, a Type 2 adjustment is necessary for expenses and liabilities to be properly stated.

Remember that borrowing money and repaying the amount borrowed plus interest are both external transactions, but accruing the interest is an internal event. Also, paying employees is external, accruing their wages is internal.

3. *Accruing a revenue.* Accrual accounting requires that revenues be recognized and recorded as they are earned by a business whether or not an external event occurs. If an asset has been generated (not swapped or acquired) as a result of the profit-seeking activities of a business, then revenue measures the amount of that increase in assets. An internal event may take place which results in an increase in assets and consequently in revenue. If such an event occurs, recognition must be given to it in order for the accounts of the business to be properly stated. This process is called "accruing a revenue." It is exactly the other side of the coin from adjustment Type 2 discussed above, and it always results in an increase in assets and in revenue as follows:

Asset	XXX	
Revenue		XXX

4. *Earning revenue received in advance.* We now know that it is possible to recognize revenue in the absence of an external event or the receipt of cash if the revenue is earned. What happens then if a business receives cash from a customer before performing any service or delivering a product? In this case, an external event has occurred, an asset has increased, and the increase will ultimately be the result of a profit-seeking activity, but at the moment the event takes place, nothing has been done by the business to "earn" the revenue. To record such an external event, the following entry would be made upon the receipt of cash from a customer.

Cash	XXX	
Advances from Customers		XXX
or Deferred Revenue		
or Unearned Revenue		

The account titles given as credits above are interchangeable and all represent a current liability for the business. In effect, the business, by accepting cash from a customer, has obliged itself to deliver a service or product in the very near future, and until the business does so, no revenue has been created. Assets have increased, but so have liabilities. As the product or service is delivered to the customer, the obligation is satisfied and the asset (cash) is earned, resulting in the creation of revenue.

Adjusting entry Type 4, involves the recognition of revenue previously received but unearned when received. Note that the receipt of cash and the resulting liability is an external event; however, the process of earning the revenue by satisfying the liability is a wholly internal adjustment. Thus the basic format of this type of adjustment is as follows:

Liability	XXX
Revenue	XXX

As you might expect, this adjustment is usually rather rare; however, for some types of businesses (those which traditionally collect in advance like magazine publishers, insurance companies, and landlords), this is a very common and important adjusting entry.

The fundamental principles underlying adjusting entries, the internal events on which they are based, and the basic differences between these events and the more straightforward external events are summarized in Table 1-3.

TABLE 1-3   EXTERNAL AND INTERNAL EVENTS

	External	*Internal*
Who	Business and Outsiders	Business Only
When	Discrete Occurrences Identified by Source Documents	Constantly Occurring; May Be No Source Documents

Adjusted Trial Balance

Remember that step four of the accounting cycle (adjusting entries) represents the first in a series of end-of-period procedures that every business must go through. Adjustments bring the accounts of a business up-to-date for those events that were not recorded as they happened and, therefore, are a continuation of the basic summarization function of the accounting process. As you will note from the overview of the cycle presented early in this chapter, a second trial balance is usually prepared after all adjusting entries have been made. This internal statement, called an *adjusted trial balance*, is more complete than the trial balance prepared earlier in the cycle because it includes *all* events (external and internal) in the life of the business. This adjusted trial balance concludes the summarization function.

Closing Entries

Financial statements represent the culmination or goal of the accounting system. They convey meaningful financial information about a business to anyone who may be interested; however, they do not represent the final step in the accounting cycle. Once the communication function is fulfilled by preparation and dissemination of the income statement, retained earnings statement and balance sheet, all that remains at the end of the accounting period is a housekeeping step called *closing the books*. More than anything, this last step in the cycle is designed to prepare the accounts of the business for the new accounting period and thus begin again the cycle. To do so it is necessary to return to the journal to record a series of special entries. These entries are then posted to the ledger and, finally, the accounting cycle for a period is complete.

Note that closing entries have to do only with Revenue and Expense accounts, and the Dividends and Retained Earnings account. No other accounts are affected by this final step. Remember that Revenue and Expense are created as temporary extensions of Retained Earnings to measure movements in assets (and sometimes liabilities) that result from the profit-seeking activities of a business. In effect, at the beginning of each period, we create Revenue and Expense accounts in order to keep track of the results of operations for that period. The amounts in these accounts then make up the income statement for the period, with Retained Earnings eventually increasing by the amount of Net Income and decreasing by Dividends. Once this information has been collected and these statements prepared, the purpose of these accounts for this period is over. When a new period starts, these Revenue and Expense accounts will have to start out at zero if accomplishment and effort information for the new period is to be collected. Each period the accounting system must collect operating results; it cannot carry the operating information from one period to the next or financial statements would be useless. The closing process, then, is designed to accomplish two goals:

1. Closing entries result in the zeroing-out of the balances in all Revenue and Expense accounts of the period just ended. The accounting system begins again to measure operations for the new period.

2. Closing entries transfer the difference between Revenue and Expense (Net Income) to Retained Earnings and the balance in the Dividends account to Retained Earnings.

To accomplish these goals, the accounting system goes through a three-step process as books are closed:

1. Journal entries are made and posted, which cause all Revenue and Expenses to have zero balances. These amounts are transferred to a new account called *Income Summary.*

2. A journal entry is made and posted which causes Income Summary to have a zero balance, and the amount in this account is transferred to Retained Earnings.

3. A journal entry is made and posted which causes the Dividends account to have a zero balance, and the amount is transferred to Retained Earnings.

The following points are important to remember:

1. All Revenues and Expenses carry zero balances into the new period.

2. The Income Summary account is created to temporarily hold income statement information and then it is immediately closed out.

3. All figures which appear in the income statement also appear in the Income Summary account.

4. Retained Earnings goes up by the amount of Net Income for the period and down by Dividends for the period.

5. All figures which appear on the retained earnings statement also appear in the Retained Earnings account.

6. The only balance sheet account affected by the closing process is Retained Earnings. Other balance sheet accounts are *never* closed and consequently are termed *permanent* accounts.

7. Since Revenue, Expense and Dividend accounts are *always* closed, they are called *temporary* or *nominal* accounts.

You have now been through the basic concepts, practicalities, and mechanics of a manual accounting system. Chapter 2 will add some recording sophistications to this accounting system and then the complete cycle will be illustrated through a comprehensive example.

exercises

1-1 Accounting financial statements are commonly used by at least the following groups: (a) management, (b) creditors, such as banks, and (c) owners. For what specific purpose would each of these groups use financial statements? What kind of information from financial statements would be most important to each of these groups?

1-2 The following accounts (which have normal balances) were taken from the records of a retail company. For each account, give the adjusting journal entry probably responsible for the change in that account balance.

Account	Trial Balance	Adjusted Trial Balance
Advances from customers	19,000	13,000
Prepaid insurance	6,000	4,000
Wages payable	2,000	3,500
Interest revenue	600	1,000
Accumulated depreciation	12,000	14,200
Supplies	-0-	500

1-3 The following account balances are taken from the books of the Iberville Corporation on June 30, 1979.

Accounts receivable	17,000
Prepaid expenses	1,200
Inventory	20,000
Notes payable	15,000
Accounts payable	11,500
Investments	6,500
Plant & equipment (net of depreciation)	12,000
Cash	7,500
Wages payable	2,000

Owners' equity at the beginning of the year was $20,000. During the year, the owner, Issac Iberville, made an additional investment of $15,000. He also received $13,000 in cash and $5,000 in inventory as salary. Dividends of $8,000 were paid to the owners, Issac and his mother Ione, during the year.

1. Calculate net income for the year ending June 30, 1979.

2. Is it possible to prepare an income statement? If not, why not?

1-4 Below are the transactions for the Conti Company (a sole proprietorship):

a. Carl Conti invests $10,000 in the company.

b. Inventory of $7,500 is purchased on credit from A-1 Corporation.

c. $15,000 loan is made from the Left Bank on a two-year note.

d. Equipment is purchased for $5,000 on account from P-U Suppliers.

e. Sales of $5,200 are made to the following customers on credit:

> Leroy— $3,000
> Mervin— $2,200

f. $2,500 of accounts payable is paid to A-1.

g. $2,600 of accounts receivable is collected from Leroy.

h. Salaries of $950 are paid to employees, Rob and Roy.

i. $5,000 of sales were made to the following customers:

> Ralph— $2,500 on credit
> Miguel— $2,500 for cash

j. Carl withdrew $1,500 for personal use.

Journalize the above transactions in good general journal form.

1-5

The Royal Corporation
Balance Sheet
December 31, 1979

Cash	-0-	Accounts payable	20,000
Accounts receivable	40,000	Notes payable	15,000
Inventory	60,000	Capital stock	40,000
Plant & equipment	75,000	Retained earnings	100,000
	175,000		175,000

Income Statement
For the Year Ended December 31, 1979

Sales revenue	58,000
Expenses	43,000
Net Income	15,000

1. Could this company pay a cash dividend for the year to its stockholders? If so, how?

2. What do you think is meant by the phrase, "paying dividends from retained earnings"? How do these financial statements illustrate the misunderstandings contained in this phrase?

3. What is the relationship between retained earnings and the asset side of the balance sheet? What are the similarities between retained earnings and other equities?

1-6   The following occurred during the calendar year 1979 for the Toulouse Corporation.

a. Inventory of $72,000 was purchased and freight of $720 was paid on the purchases. Of these purchases, $1,500 of goods was returned to suppliers and discounts of 2 percent were taken as $50,000 was paid to suppliers. Inventory on hand at the beginning of the period was $17,000 and at the end, $32,000.

b. Supplies on hand at January 1 were $1,000. Additional supplies of $1,200 were purchased during the year for cash and a count showed $400 of supplies left at December 31. (Two assumptions are possible with respect to the treatment of supplies purchased.)

c. The company borrowed $40,000 from the bank on April 1, 1979 on a 10 percent one-year note. Principal and interest are to be repaid at the due date of the note.

d. At the end of each month, a carrying charge of 1-1/2 percent is added to all amounts owed to Toulouse by its customers. Accounts Receivable at December 31 were $50,000.

e. On December 1, a major customer made a payment of $30,000 on products to be delivered over the next two months. By the end of the year 40 percent of these products had been delivered and accepted.

1. Journalize the external events included in the above descriptions.

2. Journalize all adjusting entries which would be necessary at December 31, 1979. You should state any assumptions necessary for the determination of these adjusting entries.

1-7 Below are the transactions of the Chartres Company for the month of August, 1979.

a.	Cash sales	10,000
b.	Collections of receivables	5,000
c.	Credit sales	20,000
d.	Payments on account payable	7,000
e.	Credit purchases of merchandise	13,000
f.	Cash from bank loan	15,000
g.	Payment of dividends	2,000
h.	Cash purchases of merchandise	4,000
i.	Payments for salaries	6,000
j.	Payment of bank loan	5,000

Additionally, inventory at the beginning of the month was $14,000 and inventory at the end of the month was $8,000.

1. Determine the total cash receipts, the total cash disbursements, and hence the change in cash for the month.

2. Determine cash basis revenue, cash basis expense and profit on a cash basis for the month.

3. Determine accrual basis revenue, accrual basis expense, and accounting net earnings for the month.

4. Explain the source of difference between each of these net figures.

1-8 John and Paul opened a bar in the French Quarter with an investment of $10,000 each on March 1, 1979. Rent for six months was paid on that date in the amount of $9,600. A complete line of bar equipment was purchased for $10,000, of which $5,000 was on account and $3,000 worth of inventory (liquor, etc.) was purchased for cash. Sales for the first half of the month were $1,800 in cash. To increase sales John and Paul embarked upon an advertising campaign and spent $3,000 of funds borrowed from the bank on radio, television, and newspaper advertisements. In anticipation of increased business, John and Paul purchased an additional $5,000 of inventory on account. Certain friends of the owners immediately established a tab. At the end of the month, the tabs totaled $500. Salaries for the month (not including withdrawals of $750 each by the owners) were paid in cash in the amount of $1,000. Sales in the second half of the month totaled $3,600. The owners paid $2,000 on the amount owed for inventory and $1,500 to reduce the amount owed the bank. Inventory on hand on March 31 was $4000. The owners estimated that $150 of the cost of the bar equipment was used up during the month.

1. Prepare a balance sheet as of March 31, 1979.

2. What was the amount of net income or loss for the month?

1-9   The following represents all of the information pertaining to the activities of the Decatur Corporation as of December 31, 1979.

Cash on hand	$1,200
Amounts owed to suppliers	4,000
Amounts invested by owners	15,000
Expired insurance premiums	1,800
Unexpired insurance premiums	1,800
Amounts owed to banks	9,000
Inventory—January 1, 1979	3,000
Purchases of inventory	21,000
Cash in checking account	2,200
Amounts owed by customers	6,100
Investment in U.S. government bonds	3,800
Lease payment on a truck for next year	3,600
Unexpired cost of building and equipment	23,100
Unused supplies	200
Used supplies	300
Deposit from customer on future delivery of products	1,400
Retained earnings—January 1, 1979	9,800
Total of products sold during the year	30,900
Cash distributed to stockholders	2,000
Income taxes (unpaid as of year-end)	4,400
Inventory—December 31, 1979	4,000

1. Prepare an income statement and a statement of retained earnings for the year in good form suitable for external reporting.

2. Prepare a balance sheet as of December 31, 1979 in good form suitable for external reporting.

1-10 The Bienville Company, Inc., sellers of fine antiques, opened for business on March 1, 1979. The following transactions occurred during the two weeks prior to opening and the two weeks following the opening.

a. February 15: The corporate charter was received from the state and the corporate books were opened with an investment of $15,000 in cash and $175,000 in antiques by the owner, Benny Bienville.

b. February 15: The corporation leased a building for one year and paid $9,000 to Cats Realty for the first six months rent.

c. February 19: Paid $100 for a telephone deposit and $50 for a utility deposit, both of which will be returned after one year of satisfactory bill payments.

d. February 22: Paid $4,680 to Fat Harry Refinishers for cleaning and painting the building. This major overhaul was expected to last three years.

e. February 25: Paid $1,040 for a business sign and interior furnishings to Henry's Fine Signs both of which were expected to last two years. Purchased at auction from Bids Unlimited $10,000 of antiques, to be paid for within fifteen days.

f. February 27: Paid $2,500 to Big Al's Movers for moving antiques into the store and laying out the selling floor.

g. March 2: Paid $1,500 to WINE-TV for one week's ad spots. Returned to Bids Unlimited $2,000 of antiques which were in unsatisfactory condition when received.

h. March 3: By the end of the first week, the company had sold antiques with a cost of $9,500 for $19,000 as follows: Tom—$10,000, Dick—$5,000, Harry—$4,000; all on credit.

i. March 6: Supplies costing $800 were delivered by the Lo-Ball Supply Company to be paid for within thirty days. One-fourth of these supplies were used up during the first two weeks of business. Tom changed his mind about $500 worth of antiques and returned them.

j. March 9: A deposit of $5,000 was received from the Duke of Prunes on a special order of antique Louis XIII furniture to be delivered in April. Paid amount due Bids Unlimited.

k. March 10: During the second week, the company sold antiques costing $15,000 for $32,000 as follows: Bertha—$17,000, Betty—$8,000, Beulah—$7,000; all for cash.

l. March 15: Paid $350 in wages to employees, Peter, Paul and Mary, for the first two weeks of operation. So far, in the third week, the company sold antiques costing $8,000 for $14,000 as follows: Tom—$4,000, Jerry—$10,000; all on credit. Received checks from Tom for $3,000, Dick for $5,000, and Harry for $2,000.

1. Develop a general journal for Bienville and journalize the above external transactions.

2. Post the above transactions to the proper general ledger accounts.

3. Journalize and post all appropriate adjusting entries as of March 15, 1979.

4. Prepare an income statement, statement of retained earnings, and balance sheet.

5. Close the books.

processing accounting transactions

outline

2.1 **Subsidiary Ledgers and Special Journals:** concept and use of subsidiary ledgers in a manual accounting system; subsidiary ledgers and their relationship to the general ledger; purpose of special journals; general discussion of the sales, purchases, cash receipts, and cash disbursements journals.

2.2 **Sales Journal:** illustration and discussion of the special journal for recording credit sales.

2.3 **Purchases Journal:** illustration and discussion of the special journal for recording credit purchases.

2.4 **Cash Receipts Journal:** illustration and discussion of the special journal for recording the cash inflows of a business.

2.5 **Cash Disbursements Journal:** illustration and discussion of the special journal for recording the cash outflows of a business.

2.6 **Comprehensive Example:** a problem illustrating the major concepts and mechanics of manual accounting systems as discussed throughout Chapters 1 and 2.

INTRODUCTION

The accounting cycle we discussed in Chapter 1 represents a complete view of the concepts underlying manual accounting systems for businesses. To take this cycle from the textbook to the real world, however, requires certain additional mechanical recording and classifying devices, as well as an understanding of several basic business documents which are the sources of the data processed by an accounting system. The supplemental devices, termed special journals and subsidiary ledgers, are simply convenient refinements of the basic accounting cycle which allow the efficient processing of repetitive events. Additionally, they provide the information necessary for the management and control of the business.

This chapter introduces special techniques for the mass manual processing of transactions. When you have digested this material, your appreciation of how basic manual accounting systems work should be excellent. We will conclude the chapter with a comprehensive example which should pull together the ideas presented in Chapters 1 and 2.

2-1 SUBSIDIARY LEDGERS AND SPECIAL JOURNALS

Concept and Use of Subsidiary Ledgers

Recall from Chapter 1 that the term *accounts receivable* is used to represent amounts owed to a business by its customers and others, and that *accounts payable* indicates amounts owed by a business to its suppliers and others. In Chapter 1 we created "T-accounts" in a ledger to represent these amounts; that is, one account for all amounts owed to the business and one account for all amounts owed by the business. For balance sheet purposes, this is adequate because all we need to know is the total asset (receivable) and total liability (payable) existing at the balance sheet date. But the management of a business, its customers, and its suppliers expect much more information about receivables and payables. Specifically, management must (1) know the exact amount owed to the business by each individual customer; (2) know when a specific customer has reached his limit of credit; (3) be able to give specific customers credit for payments made; and (4) for control purposes, have a general history of the purchase and payment patterns of each customer. In addition, any business would want to know exact amounts owed to individual suppliers so that purchases can be controlled and payments made on time. Obviously, we cannot possibly get all of this information from one account depicting total receivables and another showing total payables. Even a business with only a few customers and suppliers needs some supplementary breakdown of aggregate amounts owed to and owed by the business. This breakdown must be by individual customer and supplier. As a business gets larger, say 100 or so customers and 15 or 20 suppliers, some mechanical technique for keeping track of exact individual amounts owed to and owed by a business becomes absolutely necessary. The technique used by manual accounting systems is the *subsidiary ledger.*

The General Ledger/Subsidiary Ledger Relationship

Subsidiary ledgers provide a detailed breakdown of the total information which appears in certain general ledger accounts. The subsidiary ledger idea can be applied to any general ledger account; however, the need for this kind of detailed information is most critical in the area of receivables and payables.

Figure 2-1 illustrates the general–subsidiary ledger relationship for accounts receivable using sample data. Notice that the sum of figures in the subsidiary ledgers equals the total given in the general ledger account. Both the general ledger and the subsidiary ledgers present the same accounts receivable information, but from a different point of view. The total of all amounts owed to a business is necessary for balance sheet purposes and a detailed breakdown of this total by customer is necessary for collection and control purposes. It is always true that the information in the subsidiary ledgers is simply a breakdown of the amounts in the general ledger account (in this case Accounts Receivable) and is based on the same transactions as the general ledger account. Because of this, general ledger accounts for which a business keeps this additional, detailed information are called *control accounts*. Accounts receivable and Accounts payable are almost always control accounts for any business.

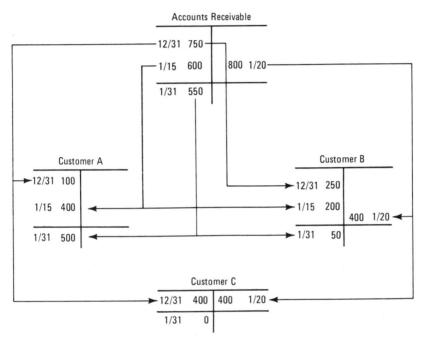

FIGURE 2-1 Accounts Receivable Subsidiary Ledger

Figure 2-2 presents this same type of general–subsidiary ledger relationship for Accounts Payable. Individual supplier balances have been assumed for illustrative purposes. Exactly the same process could be used if business management decided that additional information on inventory, plant and equipment, or any other asset, liability, owners equity, revenue, or expense would be useful for decision-making or control purposes. The basis for such subsidiary ledgers might be type of inventory, kind of plant and equipment, or any other categorization that could provide management with needed (or, at least, desired) information. The subsidiary ledgers presented in Figures 2-1 and 2-2 are in "T-account" form for illustrative purposes. In most manual accounting systems these subsidiary ledgers would probably appear on a file card or a notebook sheet and would contain more detailed information about a customer or supplier. The basic function is the same irrespective of the specific form used.

Purpose of Special Journals

Our discussions of the accounting cycle in Chapter 1 indicated that all accounting transactions are first journalized as a way of recording the event before it is forgotten or its documents lost.

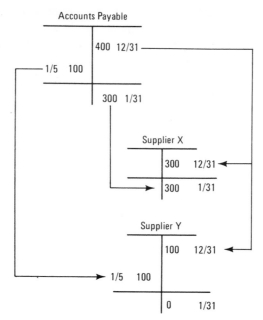

FIGURE 2-2 Accounts Payable Subsidiary Ledger

At that time, the general journal was presented and its form illustrated. For the purpose of understanding the basic flow of data in a manual accounting system, the general journal is both necessary and sufficient. It is, however, not the only journal used in an accounting system, and may actually be the least used recording device in terms of transactions recorded.

Most businesses would very likely use a number of other, supplementary journals, called as a group, *special journals.* It would not be unusual to find four such specialized devices in a manual system—sales journal, purchases journal, cash receipts journal, and cash disbursements journal—in addition to the general journal.

To understand why these special devices are necessary, consider the recording problems of a business. Although the number of events occurring each day might be quite high, most of these transactions are the same kinds of events happening over and over again. The theoretically possible types of events in which most businesses may engage is almost limitless, but, in fact, only a few transactions actually occur with great frequency. The basic recording problem which a manual accounting system must solve then is how to efficiently process repetitive transactions in a manner that allows classification and financial statement preparation. This is exactly what special journals do.

Basically, businesses engage in four major kinds of transactions constantly.

1. *Sell goods to customers*—sales may be made for cash or on credit; this is usually the most frequent event for any business.

2. *Purchase goods from suppliers*—purchases may also be made for cash or on credit; however, most businesses purchase in larger quantities (and consequently less often) than they sell.

3. *Receive cash*—cash inflows usually result from cash sales or collections of receivables, although other types of events may give rise to the receipt of cash.

4. *Disburse cash*—cash outflows for the purchase of goods and payment of accounts payable are most frequent, although other types of payments can occur.

Obviously, businesses can and do engage in other types of transactions; however, if you think about what any business does it should become apparent that the purchase—sell—pay—collect sequence accounts for most of the action. In recognition of this, we create and use in manual accounting systems one specialized recording device for each of these constantly recurring transactions. Each of these special journals is designed to record one basic type of event as efficiently as possible. If a journal is designed specifically for one type of transaction, it will certainly allow for quicker and more accurate processing of that transaction than the general journal, which is general enough in format to accommodate any event. That, of course, is the idea behind special journals.

Types of Special Journals

A good manual recording system should include the following:

1. *Sales Journal.* This is usually a very simple, straightforward journal because it records only *one* sort of event—the *credit* sale of goods to customers—and that event can only affect two different general ledger accounts.

2. *Purchases journal.* This journal is usually reserved for the *credit* purchases of goods for resale (inventory) and supplies, although the credit purchase of any asset could be recorded here. Since many different kinds of credit purchases can occur and several general ledger accounts are affected, this journal is somewhat more complex than the sales journal.

3. *Cash receipts journal.* *All* receipts of cash, no matter what the source, should be entered in this journal and, as a result, a number of general ledger accounts may be affected by the transactions recorded here. Notice that a cash sale represents both a "sale" and a "cash receipt"; however, such an event is always recorded in the cash receipts journal. Reasons for this treatment have to do with the subsidiary ledger ideas discussed earlier and the control of cash.

4. *Cash disbursements journal.* *All* disbursements of cash, no matter what the reason, should be recorded here; thus, potentially, many general ledger accounts could be affected. In this situation (similar to the one discussed above), note that a cash purchase of goods or supplies is always recorded in the cash disbursements journal.

5. *General journal.* Although this journal is capable of handling all types of transactions, its format is somewhat cumbersome. As a result, most manual systems use the general journal to record *only* those transactions which do not fit into one of the special journals described above. You might think of the general journal as the "journal of last resort." If a transaction is of the type covered by one of the special journals, it should be recorded there. Remember that every event is journalized only *once* and no event would ever be divided and entered into more than one journal.

    The exact format and make-up of these special journals depends on the particular accounts affected by the purchase—sell—collect—pay transactions of a certain business;

therefore, the specific journal designs differ somewhat from business to business. None-theless, the common ingredients and functioning of these special journals can be illustrated and discussed.

2.2 SALES JOURNAL

Figure 2-3 is an example of a typical sales journal. You should notice the following about its design and use.

Date		Source Document #	Customer Account	PR	Amount
1979 January	2	201	Customer A	✓	50
		202	B	✓	200
	4	203	C	✓	600
	8	204	D	✓	150
	15	205	C	✓	75
	30	206	A	✓	750
	31	—	Balance	3/21	1825

FIGURE 2-3 Sales Journal

1. Since every credit sale results in a debit to Accounts Receivable and a credit to Sales Revenue, it is not necessary for the sales journal (which records only this type of trans-action) to have separate columns for these general ledger accounts. Whenever posting takes place in the system, the total of the Amount column is posted to the Accounts Receivable and Sales Revenue accounts. At the same time, individual sales amounts are posted directly to the accounts receivable subsidiary ledgers for each customer. The check (✓) in the PR column indicates that the amount was posted to a subsidiary ledger account, while the account numbers (3/21) show that total credit sales were posted to the general ledger. Naturally, the sum of the subsidiary ledger postings must equal the receivable total.

2. Notice that these posting references would be filled in as the amounts are posted to the ledger, not when the events are originally journalized. This provides an effective cross-check that everything has been properly posted and leaves a trail through the system, from the original transaction to the financial statements.

3. As in all journals, the sales journal is organized by date of transaction; and each sales event is recorded by the specific customer to whom the sale was made.

4. A special column is provided for the number of the source document which results from the sale and is the basis for the journal entry. This is particularly important for control purposes so that all transactions can be traced back to the original documents created when the event occurred, or information from these documents can be traced forward to the financial statements. The source document may be an invoice, sales slip, or some other piece of paper.

As you can see, the sales journal is simply a convenient listing of all credit sale transactions for a period. This listing makes the recording and classifying of this repetitive event much easier because the format of the journal is specifically designed to record credit sales, and posting is facilitated by having all the information in one place.

2.3 PURCHASES JOURNAL

Figure 2-4 is an illustration of a typical purchases journal in a manual accounting system. The design of this journal is sufficiently broad so that all acquisitions on credit—inventory, supplies, or any other asset—may be easily and properly recorded. Since the journal illustrated here can record all invoices (bills) in one place, it is often called an *invoice register*. Other, more restrictive journal formats, which record only inventory and supplies purchases are possible.

The following transactions have been recorded in the purchases journal in Figure 2-4:

1. An inventory purchase of $1000 together with freight-in of $50 from Supplier X.

2. A purchase of supplies (goods to be used up in the course of business, rather than resold) from Supplier Y of $600.

3. An additional purchase of inventory from Supplier X in the amount of $900 on which no freight was to be paid.

4. Equipment was acquired from Supplier W for $2000 on credit.

Date			Supplier Account	PR	Accounts Payable	Debits					
						Purchases	Freight-In	Supplies	Account	PR	Amount
1979											
January	6		Supplier X	✓	1,050	1,000	50				
	15		Supplier Y	✓	600			600			
	20		Supplier X	✓	900	900					
	21		Equipment								
			Supplier W	✓	2,000				Equipment	54	2,000
	31		Balance	98	4,550	1,900	50	600	—	—	2,000
						(26)	(27)	(31)			

FIGURE 2-4 Purchases Journal

You have probably noticed that the purchases journal is somewhat more elaborate in format than the sales journal. This is because the purchases journal records several different kinds of purchase transactions, each of which may affect several general ledger accounts. Remember that the sales journal is designed to handle only credit sales of inventory where only two general ledger accounts are affected. The purchases journal, however, is not complex and is very easy to use once you understand it. As you look over Figure 2-4, keep in mind these characteristics of the purchases journal:

1. Most credit purchases by a business, irrespective of the assets acquired, result in an increase in total accounts payable for the business, but also result in the creation of a specific liability to a particular supplier. Whenever posting takes place from the purchases journal to the ledger, the total Accounts Payable column is posted to general ledger (control) Accounts Payable, while the specific amount owed each individual supplier is posted to the appropriate Accounts Payable subsidiary ledger. The check (✓) in the PR indicates that the

amount was posted to a subsidiary ledger account, and the account number (98) shows that the total was posted to Accounts Payable Control. Of course, the sum of the subsidiary ledger postings equals the Accounts Payable total.

2. Remember that these (and all other) posting reference numbers or symbols are filled in as posting takes place, so that we can tell when posting is complete and establish cross-references throughout the accounting system.

3. The purchases journal, like all journals, is organized by date of transaction. Each purchase is recorded by the specific supplier from whom the purchase was made.

4. Since this journal is designed to handle all credit purchases of assets on account, several different debits may result from the kind of events to be recorded. Most often, however, the debits will involve purchases and freight-in related to inventory and supplies because these are the most constant and frequent activities of most businesses.

    To facilitate recording these repetitive events, special Debit columns have been provided which require writing only the amounts involved in each transaction. Then, only the total amounts for a period need be posted to the general ledger for each of these accounts. The numbers in parenthesis represent the posting reference numbers for each of these accounts. These are, of course, the account numbers for each of the accounts involved.

5. In addition to the inventory and supplies transactions which make up most of the activity in a purchases journal, a business will from time to time purchase other assets on account. Since the other assets which could be purchased are extremely varied and since these other purchases are relatively infrequent, no special columns are provided for these acquisitions. Instead three generalized columns appear in the journal so that the particular asset account affected, its account number for posting reference purposes, and the amount of the transaction can be recorded. Because many different accounts may appear in these columns during an accounting period, posting must be done individually by each specific account. It would make no sense to post the Amount column in total, since the individual accounts affected are all different; thus, no posting reference is provided in that column.

It may appear at first glance that we are needlessly complicating a neat little recording process when we add these special devices and instruments. In fact, nothing could be further from the truth. In the context of a textbook or classroom where only a few illustrative transactions are presented, the use of only a general journal may seem sufficient and subsidiary ledgers unnecessary. Consider, however, the problems of recording 50 to 100 transactions a day, every day, in the general journal, and then individually posting each of these transactions to the ledger. What about keeping track of amounts owed to a business by, say, 25 customers and amounts that business owes to another 25 suppliers? Without special journals which are streamlined to record the most repetitive transactions efficiently and aid in classification by reducing the posting burden, manual accounting systems could simply collapse under their own weight. Likewise, without some form of organized, detailed information in the accounting system on specific amounts owed to and owed by a business, efficient and accurate collection and payment would be impossible. These refinements of the basic accounting system are absolutely necessary for manual systems to work in the real world.

2.4 CASH RECEIPTS JOURNAL

The most important and most repetitive transactions a business engages in are those involving the inflow (receipt) and outflow (disbursement) of cash. The frequency of occurrence of cash transactions coupled with the nature of cash itself makes this asset the most difficult for a business to control. The recording and classifying procedures involving cash must be the most carefully designed and monitored in the accounting system. The devices most used for this purpose are the cash receipts journal and the cash disbursements journal. We will focus our attention first on the cash receipts journal.

Remember that the exact design of a cash receipts journal as well as all other special journals, in practice, will depend upon the particular kinds of transactions a business may engage in and the information needs of business management. The following transactions have been recorded in the cash receipts journal in Figure 2-5:

1. On January 4, an owner supplies the business with cash by purchasing $10,000 of corporate stock directly from the firm.

2. Customer A makes a $500 payment on his account on January 5.

3. Cash sales of merchandise for the first week are recorded. Some businesses record all cash sales daily, others weekly or biweekly depending on the size, and information and control requirements of the business. In this example cash sales are recorded at the end of each week.

4. On January 16, the business makes a loan from a bank in the amount of $2,000.

			Debit		Credits			Other Accounts			
						Acc. Receivable					
Date			Cash	Sales	PR	Amount	Account	PR	Debit	Credit
1979							Capital			
January	4	Owner Investment	10,000				Stock	100		10,000
	5	Customer A	500		✓	500				
	6	Cash Sales								
		Week 1	750	750						
	13	Cash Sales								
		Week 2	1,000	1,000						
	16	Bank Loan	2,000				Notes Pay	99		2,000
	19	Customer B	800		✓	800				
	20	Cash Sales								
		Week 3	1,200	1,200						
	25	Customer C	100		✓	200	Sales			
							Return	22	100	
	27	Cash Sales								
		Week 4	1,100	1,100						
			17,450	4,050	—	1,500	—	—	100	12,000
			(1)	(21)		(3)				

FIGURE 2-5 Cash Receipts Journal

5. The business receives $800 as payment in full of the account of Customer B on January 19.

6. Customer C settles his account in full with a $100 payment and a return of merchandise for credit in the amount of $100 on January 25.

As you study the general format of the cash receipts journal and the manner in which these sample events are recorded, you should take note of the following:

1. *All* receipts of cash, no matter the source, should be recorded in the cash receipts journal. The design of this journal is sufficiently broad so that any transaction resulting in an inflow of cash can be accommodated.

2. Although cash may be increased for a number of different reasons, most businesses find that cash inflows occur primarily because of two repetitive events; sales of merchandise for cash and collections of amounts owed (accounts receivable) because of previous credit sales. Since a cash receipt most likely can be traced to one of these two constantly recurring events, the cash receipts journal establishes special columns for Cash Sales and Accounts Receivable Credits so that only numbers need be written in when these accounts are affected.

3. To record all transactions that result in a cash increase, an "Other Accounts" group of columns is provided in which any account title may be written. Note that provision is made for a debit *or* credit to be made as required since a cash inflow could result from events which include other debit effects in addition to cash.

4. If a transaction increases cash at all, even though it may affect many other accounts also, it must be recorded in the cash receipts journal (note event #6 explained above and recorded on January 25). This is true without regard to whether the cash effect is major or minor in light of the total transaction. Remember that for control purposes all cash receipts *must* appear in this journal and that no transaction may be split among journals. All transactions must be recorded in their entirety in the most appropriate journal and no single event should ever appear in more than one journal.

5. The cash receipts journal is organized chronologically and an Explanation column is provided so that brief elaborations or necessary additional information (such as specific customer names) may be supplied.

6. Notice that Cash (Account #1) is posted in total whenever postings are made in the system (monthly here) and the same is true for Sales (#21). Accounts Receivable is posted in total to the *control* account (#3) and each specific collection is posted individually to the appropriate *subsidiary* account (✓) so that the totals equal. Finally each entry listed in the "Other Accounts" columns must be posted individually to the proper general ledger account.

The orderly recording of all cash inflows in one place is the major goal of the cash receipts journal. The format illustrated in Figure 2-5 allows for the efficient mass processing of this very frequent event in a manner that makes classification (posting) easy to perform and, at the same time, contributes to the control of cash.

2.5 CASH DISBURSEMENTS JOURNAL

Inflows of cash, although probably the most important event in the life of most businesses, represent only one side of the cash-related activity of business. The other side of the coin is cash outflows (disbursements) which are almost as constantly recurring as inflows and are at least as important from a control perspective. The cash disbursements journal is specifically designed to record *all* disbursements of cash in one place so that classification of these transactions can be carried out efficiently. In addition, by coupling this journal with the cash receipts journal, a business may effectively control its cash assets in a manual accounting system.

A typical cash disbursements journal appears in Figure 2-6. Keep in mind that design flexibility in meeting a particular business' needs is an important aspect of any special journal. The following transactions have been recorded in this Journal:

1. On January 5, $1,000 owed to Supplier X as a result of a purchase of inventory is satisfied by a payment of $980 and a discount of $20 is taken. Note that the contra account, Purchase Discounts, is created when the account is paid (if it is paid within the discount period) rather than when the goods are actually purchased. You might relate this transaction to the credit purchase transactions recorded in the purchases journal earlier in this chapter.

2. Inventory of $500 is purchased for cash on January 10 (a periodic recording system is assumed). Notice that cash purchases of inventory are properly recorded as cash disbursements while credit purchases are recorded in the purchases journal.

3. On January 15, rent for January is paid in the amount of $300.

4. $150 owed to Supplier Y from an earlier purchase is paid on January 20. No discount was available for the transaction.

5. A truck is purchased for $5,000 on January 25, with a cash down payment of $1,000 and a promissory note given for the balance. Because part of this transaction included a disbursement of cash, the entire event must be recorded in the cash disbursements journal. In this case two accounts other than Cash are affected by the transaction and both appear in the "Other Accounts" area of the journal (one Debit and one Credit).

6. Advertising for the month of February is paid for on January 30. Since this $100 payment involves services to be consumed in the future, an asset is created. At the end of February an adjusting entry will be made to record the consumption of these advertising services.

7. On the last day of the month our company's three employees are paid. Notice that three checks have been issued (one for each employee) and several different accounts are effected by the event. Payroll is one of the most recurring of cash disbursements and therefore must be subject to close control and careful procedures. It can also be one of the most important disbursements because it is an area permeated by government regulations and requirements which must be met by every business.

As in our previous discussions of special journals, there are certain important points you should know about the structure and use of cash disbursements journals.

Date	Check #	Explanation	Credit Cash	DEBITS Acc. Payable PR	DEBITS Acc. Payable Amount	DEBITS Wage Expense	CREDITS Purchase Discounts	CREDITS Fed W/ Payable	CREDITS Soc Sec Payable	CREDITS St. W/ Payable	Other Accounts Account	Other Accounts PR	Other Accounts Debit	Other Accounts Credit
1979														
January 5	98	Supplier X	980	✓	1,000		20							
10	99	Purchase inv.	500								Purchases	26	500	
15	100	Paid rent	300								Rent exp	143	300	
20	101	Supplier Y	150	✓	150									
25	102	Purchased Truck	1,000								Truck	55	5,000	
											Note pay	99		4,000
30	103	Pd. Advert.	100								Prepaid Advertising	51	100	
31	104–106	Payroll	1,470			2,000		300	120	110				
			4,500		1,150	2,000	20	300	120	110	—	—	5,900	4,000
			(1)		(98)	(140)	(29)	(85)	(86)	(87)				

FIGURE 2-6 Cash Disbursements Journal

1. *All* disbursements of cash, no matter the reason, should be recorded in the cash disbursements journal. This journal is designed so that all transactions involving an outflow of cash, even though there may be several other aspects to the event, can be recorded in one place.

2. Since all cash expenditures (with the possible exception of those from a petty cash fund) should be made by check, a special column for check number is provided as a cross-reference back to the source document and forward from the source document through the accounting system.

3. Although cash may be paid out for many reasons, most businesses find that cash expenditures occur primarily because of two repetitive events—payment of amounts owed to suppliers (Accounts Payable) and payments to employees for services (Salaries and Wages). Because most cash outflows are likely traceable to one of these two constantly recurring events, the cash disbursements journal establishes special columns for Accounts Payable and Wage Expense Debits. Likewise, special Credit columns appear for payroll-related liabilities since these are usually created when employees are paid as a part of the basic payroll entry. These events can now be easily recorded by simply writing in the appropriate amounts.

4. In a manner similar to the cash receipts journal, an "Other Accounts" group of columns is provided in which any account title may be written. Also, a provision is made for a Debit or Credit (or both) to be made in this group of columns since a cash outflow could result from transactions which include either or both effects.

5. Remember that all cash disbursements *must* appear in this journal, even though the cash component of the transaction may be minor in light of the total transaction (note event #5 explained above and recorded on January 25). Every transaction must appear in one journal only.

6. Like all journals, the cash disbursements journal is organized chronologically and an Explanation column is provided so that brief elaborations or necessary additional information (such as specific supplier accounts) may be written in.

7. Note that the Cash column (account #1) is posted in total whenever postings are made in the system (monthly here); the same is true for Wage Expense (#140), Purchase Discounts (#29), and the three payroll-related liabilities (#85, #86, #87). Accounts Payable is posted in total to the control account (#98), and each specific payment is posted to individual supplier subsidiary accounts (✓). Each entry in the "Other Accounts" columns must be posted individually to the proper general ledger account.

Our discussion of the special journals and subsidiary ledgers necessary for the mass processing of transactions in a manual accounting system is now complete. That each of these journals is specifically designed to handle one basic type of transaction makes possible the recording and classification of large numbers of transactions without huge expenditures of time and money. At the same time these journals together with subsidiary ledgers play a major part in controlling and monitoring the activities of a business.

2.6 COMPREHENSIVE EXAMPLE

We have discussed the basic concepts and relationships underlying accounting systems, the series of steps necessary to make the accounting system operational, and certain recording refinements which must be understood and used if manual accounting systems are to work in the real world. We will conclude this chapter with an example which illustrates the major concepts and mechanics discussed in Chapters 1 and 2. This example, together with a suggested solution, follows:

Two recent college graduates decide to open a sporting goods store devoted exclusively to selling ice hockey equipment. They feel that their chances of success are good since they will have the only ice hockey equipment store in Miami Beach, Florida. The store, called Puck & Stick, Inc., opened on June 1, 1979. The following transactions occurred during June:

June 1: Each owner deposited $10,000 of personal funds into a business bank account and received 1,000 shares of stock in Puck & Stick in exchange.

June 4: Hockey equipment was ordered and delivered from Puck & Sons. The invoice cost was $3,000 and a freight cost of $100 was added to the cost. The terms of the purchase are 2/10, n/30. Display equipment was purchased from A-1 Suppliers on 90-day credit terms for $2,400, and a company car was purchased for $4,500 with a $500 (check #1) down payment and a bank loan for the remainder. Utilities were turned on and a deposit of $100 (check #2) was paid. This deposit will be returned after one year if all bills are paid on time.

June 8: Hockey equipment in the amount of $500 was sold to the Bahama Flashers hockey team on credit.

June 12: Purchased $500 of hockey sticks from Crooked Stix, Inc. for cash with check #3.

June 13: Returned $100 worth of defective pucks from the June 4 purchase and was given credit against the amount owed.

June 14: Mailed check #4 to Puck & Sons for the amount due less the appropriate discount.

June 15: Cash sales for the first half of the month were $2,500.

June 18: Additional purchases of merchandise from Crooked Stix, Inc. for $4,000 were made on credit terms of 2/15, n/30.

June 20: Sold to the Equator Eskimos $2,800 of merchandise on credit.

June 21: Supplies costing $200 were purchased on credit from B-2 Suppliers.

June 25: Received a check from the Bahama team settling their account in full.

June 28: Received a check from the Equator Eskimos for $2,3000

June 29: Paid salaries of $500 (checks #5 and #6) to each of the owners. Amounts withheld for each were as follows: $50 for federal income taxes, $10 for state income taxes, and $30 for social security. In addition to matching social security the company contributes $40 per month for each owner to an insurance plan (check #7).

June 30: Cash sales for the last half of the month were $3,000.

The following additional information is available:

1. The display equipment is expected to last 10 years and the company car three years. Both are expected to be worthless at the end of their useful lives. Straight-line depreciation is used by the company.

2. Interest on the bank loan accrues at the rate of 1 percent of the unpaid balance at the end of each month.

3. An interest charge of 1 percent is added to all amounts owed to Puck & Stick, Inc. unpaid as of the end of the month.

4. A physical count of inventory reveals that $350 of merchandise is still on hand on January 30.

Puck & Stick, Inc. uses a sales, purchases, cash receipts, and cash disbursements journal as well as a general journal in their accounting system. Also, subsidiary ledgers are maintained for receivables and payables. It is the intention of the owners to adjust and close the accounts, and prepare financial statements monthly.

You should accomplish the following for Puck & Stick, Inc. for the month of June, 1979.

1. Journalize all transactions for the month in the proper journals.

2. Post all journals to the appropriate ledgers at the end of the month.

3. Adjust the accounts.

4. Prepare financial statements.

5. Close the accounts.

It would be very beneficial for you to work through all of the month's events and actually complete the five requirements before looking at our solution. Otherwise you will not derive the maximum benefit from this example of a manual accounting system at work.

The chart of accounts for this company follows. Charts of accounts provide guidelines for the recording and classification of all events in the accounting system by giving the asset, liability, owner's equity, revenue, and expense account titles and numbers to be used by the business. They can also be management control devices.

Account	Number	Account	Number
Cash	1	State withholding payable	56
Accounts receivable	5	Social security payable	57
Inventory	10	Bank loan payable	60
Purchases	11	Interest payable	61
Freight-In	12	Capital stock	101
Purchase returns	13	Retained earnings	105
Purchase discounts	14	Sales revenue	125
Supplies	20	Interest revenue	130
Equipment	25	Cost of goods sold	151
Accumulated depreciation,		Salary expense	155
equipment	26	Payroll taxes	156
Car	30	Insurance expense	157
Accumulated depreciation,		Advertising expense	165
car	31	Depreciation expense	170
Accounts payable	51	Interest expense	175
Federal withholding payable	55	Income summary	199

You may add any new accounts you feel are necessary to properly reflect the month's transactions. Our suggested solution follows:

Figures 2-7 through 2-11 give the special and general journals for Puck & Stick, Inc. for the month's events.

PUCK & STICK, INC. SALES JOURNAL				
Date	*Source Document #*	*Customer Account*	*PR*	*Amount*
1979 June 8	—	Bahama Flashers	✓	500
20	—	Equator Eskimos	✓	2,800
30			5/125	3,300

FIGURE 2-7 Sales Journal

PUCK & STICK, INC. PURCHASES JOURNAL									
	Supplier		*Accounts*	*DEBITS*					
Date	*Account*	*PR*	*Payable*	*Purchases*	*Freight-In*	*Supplies*	*Account*	*PR*	*Amount*
1979 June 4	Puck & Sons	✓	3,100	3,000	100				
4	A–1	✓	2,400				Equipment	25	2,400
18	Crooked Stix	✓	4,000	4,000					
21	B–2	✓	200			200			
30		—	9,700	7,000	100	200	—	—	2,400
			(51)	(11)	(12)	(20)			

FIGURE 2-8 Purchases Journal

PUCK & STICK, INC. CASH RECEIPTS JOURNAL									
			CREDITS						
		Debit			*Acc. Receivable*		*OTHER ACCOUNTS*		
Date	*Explanation*	*Cash*	*Sales*	*PR*	*Amount*	*Account*	*PR*	*Debit*	*Credit*
1979 June 1	Owner investment	20,000				Capital Stock	101		20,000
15	Cash sales 1–15	2,500	2,500						
25	Bahama Flashers	500		✓	500				
28	Equator Eskimos	2,300		✓	2,300				
30	Cash sales 16-30	3,000	3,000						
30		28,300	5,500	—	2,800	—	—		20,000
		(1)	(125)		(5)				

FIGURE 2-9 Cash Receipts Journal

PUCK & STICK, INC. CASH DISBURSEMENTS JOURNAL

			Credit	DEBITS Acc. Payable			Salary	Purchase	Fed. W/	Soc Sec	St. W/	OTHER ACCOUNTS			
Date	Check #	Explanation	Cash	PR	Amount		Expense	Discounts	Payable	Payable	Payable	Account	PR	Debit	Credit
1979 June 4	1	Car Purchase	500									Car	30	4,500	
												Bank Loan Payable	60		4,000
4	2	Deposit	100									Rec. from Utilities	8	100	
12	3	Crooked Stix	500									Purchases	11	500	
14	4	Puck & Sons	2,940	✓	3,000			60							
29	5	Payroll	410				500		50	30	10				
29	6	Payroll	410				500		50	30	10				
29	7	Insurance	80									Insurance Expense	157	80	
30			4,940	—	3,000		1,000	60	100	60	20	---		5,180	4,000
			(1)		(51)		(155)	(14)	(55)	(57)	(56)				

FIGURE 2-10 Cash Disbursements Journal

PUCK & STICK, INC. GENERAL JOURNAL				p. 1
Date	*Transactions Accounts*	*PR*	*Debit Amount*	*Credit Amount*
1979				
June 13	Accounts payable—			
	Puck & Sons	51/✓	100	
	Purchase returns	13		100
29	Payroll taxes	156	60	
	Social security			
	Payable	57		60
	Adjusted entries			
June 30	Depreciation expense	170	145	
	Accumulated			
	depreciation—			
	equipment	26		20
	Accumulated			
	depreciation—			
	car	31		125
30	Interest expense	175	40	
	Interest payable	61		40
30	Accounts receivable—			
	Equator Eskimos	5/✓	5	
	Interest revenue	130		5

PUCK & STICK, INC. GENERAL JOURNAL				p. 2
Date	*Transactions Accounts*	*. PR*	*Debit Amount*	*Credit Amount*
June 30	Cost of goods sold	151	7,090	
	Inventory	10	350	
	Purchase returns	13	100	
	Purchase discounts	14	60	
	Purchases	11		7,500
	Freight-In	12		100
	Closing entries			
June 30	Sales revenue	125	8,800	
	Interest revenue	130	5	
	Income summary	199		8,805
30	Income summary	199	8,415	
	Cost of goods sold	151		7,090
	Salary expense	155		1,000
	Payroll taxes	156		60
	Insurance expense	157		80
	Depreciation expense	170		145
	Interest expense	175		40
30	Income summary	199	390	
	Retained earnings	105		390

FIGURE 2-11 General Journal

Figure 2-12 gives the general ledger for the business with the ledger accounts in abbreviated form, and Figures 2-13 and 2-14 display the subsidiary ledgers for receivables and payables.

The accounts receivable and accounts payable subsidiary ledgers presented in this example are more realistic in format and information content than those illustrated earlier in the chapter. Note that the adjusting and closing entries for the month appear in the general journal and are posted to the general ledger.

Finally, Figures 2-15 and 2-16 illustrate the financial statements for the company. The statement of changes in financial position has been omitted.

CASH #1

1979					1979
6/30	CR1		4,940	CDI	6/30
		28,300			
6/31	✓	23,360			

ACCOUNTS RECEIVABLE #5

1979					1979
1979			2,800	CD1	6/30
6/30	S1	3,300			
6/30	J1	5			
6/31	✓	505			

RECEIVABLE FROM UTILITY #8

1979			
6/4	CR1	100	
6/31	✓	100	

INVENTORY #10

1979			
6/30	J1	350	
6/31	✓	350	

PURCHASES #11

1979					1979
6/30	P1	7,000			
6/30	CD1	500	7,500	J1	6/30

FREIGHT-IN #12

1979					1979
6/30	P1	100	100	J1	6/30

PURCHASE RETURNS #13

1979					1979
6/30	J1	100	100	J1	6/30

PURCHASE DISCOUNTS #14

1979					1979
6/30	J1	60	60	CD1	6/30

SUPPLIES #20

1979			
6/30	P1	200	
6/31	✓	200	

EQUIPMENT #25

1979			
6/4	P1	2,400	
6/31	✓	2,400	

CAR #30

1979			
6/4	CDI	4,500	
6/31	✓	4,500	

ACCUMULATED DEPRECIATION— EQUIPMENT #26

				1979
			20	J1	6/30
			20	✓	6/31

ACCUMULATED DEPRECIATION—CAR #31

		125	J1	6/30
		125	✓	6/31

ACCOUNTS PAYABLE #51

1979					1979
6/13	J1	100	9,700	P1	6/30
6/30	CD1	3,000			
			6,600	✓	6/31

FIGURE 2-12 General Ledger

FEDERAL WITHHOLDING PAYABLE   #55

			1979
	100	CD1	6/30
	100	✓	6/31

STATE WITHHOLDING PAYABLE   #56

			1979
	20	CD1	6/30
	20	✓	6/31

SOCIAL SECURITY PAYABLE   #57

			1979
	60	J1	6/29
	60	CD1	6/30
	120	✓	6/31

BANK LOAN PAYABLE   #60

			1979
	4,000	CD1	6/4
	4,000	✓	6/31

INTEREST PAYABLE   #61

			1979
	40	J1	6/30
	40	✓	6/31

CAPITAL STOCK   #101

			1979
	20,000	CR1	6/1
	20,000	✓	6/31

RETAINED EARNINGS   #105

			1979
	390	J1	6/30
	390	✓	6/31

SALES REVENUE   #125

1979					1979
			3,300	S1	6/30
6/30	J1	8,800	5,500	CR1	6/30

INTEREST REVENUE   #130

1979					1979
			5	J1	6/30
6/30	J1	5			

COST OF GOODS SOLD   #151

1979					1979
6/30	J1	7,090	7,090	J1	6/30

SALARY EXPENSE   #155

1979					1979
6/30	CD1	1,000	1,000	J1	6/30

PAYROLL TAXES   #156

1979					1979
6/29	J1	60	60	J1	6/30

INSURANCE EXPENSE   #157

1979					1979
6/29	CD1	80	80	J1	6/30

ADVERTISING EXPENSE   #165

0	

DEPRECIATION EXPENSE   #170

1979					1979
6/30	J1	145	145	J1	6/30

INTEREST EXPENSE   #175

1979					1979
6/30	J1	40	40	J1	6/30

INCOME SUMMARY   #199

1979					1979
6/30	J1	8,415	8,805	J1	6/30
6/30	J1	390			

FIGURE 2-12 General Ledger (continued)

PUCK & STICK, INC. ACCOUNTS RECEIVABLE SUBSIDIARY LEDGER

BAHAMA FLASHERS #A/R - 1

Street Address			Credit Limit - $XXX		
City, State Zip Code					

Date		Transactions	Debit	Credit	Balance
1979					0
June	8	Credit sale - S1	500		500
	25	Cash receipt - CR1		500	0

EQUATOR ESKIMOS #A/R - 2

Street Address			Credit Limit - $XXX		
City, State Zip Code					

Date		Transactions	Debit	Credit	Balance
1979					0
June	20	Credit sale - S1	2,800		2,800
	28	Cash receipt - CR1		2,300	500
	30	Interest - J1	5		505

FIGURE 2-13 Accounts Receivable Subsidiary Ledger

PUCK & STICK, INC. ACCOUNTS PAYABLE SUBSIDIARY LEDGER

PUCK & SONS #A/P - 1

Street Address			Terms: 2/10, n/30		
City, State Zip Code					

Date		Transactions	Debit	Credit	Balance
1979					0
June	4	Credit purchases - P1		3,100	3,100
	13	Return goods - J1	100		3,000
	14	Cash payment - CD1	3,000		0

CROOKED STIX, INC. #A/P - 2

Street Address			Terms: 2/15, n/30		
City, State Zip Code					

Date		Transactions	Debit	Credit	Balance
1979					0
June	18	Credit purchase - P1		4,000	4,000

FIGURE 2-14 Accounts Payable Subsidiary Ledger

PUCK & STICK, INC. ACCOUNTS PAYABLE SUBSIDIARY LEDGER

A-1   #A/P - 3

	Street Address City, State Zip Code		Terms: 90 day	
Date	*Transactions*	*Debit*	*Credit*	*Balance*
1979				0
June 4	Equipment - P1		2,400	2,400

B-2   #A/P - 4

	Street Address City, State Zip Code		Terms:	
Date	*Transactions*	*Debit*	*Credit*	*Balance*
1979				0
June 21	Supplies - P1		200	200

FIGURE 2-14 Accounts Payable Subsidiary Ledger (continued)

PUCK & STICK, INC.
INCOME STATEMENT
FOR THE MONTH OF JUNE, 1979

Revenues:		
Sales revenue	$8,800	
Interest revenue	5	$8,805
Expenses:		
Cost of goods sold	7,090	
Salary expense	1,000	
Payroll taxes	60	
Insurance expense	80	
Depreciation expense	145	
Interest expense	40	8,415
Net Income		$ 390

STATEMENT OF RETAINED EARNINGS

Retained earnings - June 1, 1979	$ 0
Net income for the month	390
Dividends	0
Retained earnings - June 31, 1979	$ 390

FIGURE 2-15 Income and Retained Earnings Statement

PUCK & STICK, INC.
BALANCE SHEET
JUNE 30, 1979

Current Assets		
Cash	$23,360	
Accounts receivable	505	
Receivable from utility	100	
Inventory	350	
Supplies	200	$24,515
Noncurrent Assets		
Equipment	2,400	
Accumulated depreciation—		
equipment	(20)	2,380
Car	4,500	
Accumulated depreciation—car	(125)	4,375
Total Assets		$31,270
Current Liabilities		
Accounts payable	$ 6,600	
Federal withholding payable	100	
State withholding payable	20	
Social security payable	120	
Bank loan payable	4,000	
Interest payable	40	$10,880
Owners Equity		
Capital stock	$20,000	
Retained earnings	390	$20,390
Total Equities		$31,270

FIGURE 2-16 Balance Sheet

exercises

2-1 The functions of the bookkeeper are often confused with those of the accountant. Distinguish between the roles of the accountant and the bookkeeper and state which steps of the accounting cycle are likely to be performed by each.

2-2 Explain the term *double-entry* as it is used in double-entry bookkeeping. Would a single-entry system be possible? If so, give an example of a single-entry record-keeping system.

2-3 Distinguish the relationship of a special journal to a general journal from the relationship of a subsidiary ledger to a general ledger. What functions do special journals and subsidiary ledgers serve in manual accounting systems? Are these devices absolutely necessary?

2-4 The concept of special journals and subsidiary ledgers can be applied to many areas in accounting other than those named in this chapter. Name three areas where the idea of special journals can be applied and name three areas where the idea of subsidiary ledgers can be applied beyond those already discussed.

2-5   Chapter 2 presents subsidiary ledgers as T-accounts which contain detailed breakdowns of the receivables and payables general ledger accounts. In fact, subsidiary ledgers may take any one of a number of possible other forms depending on the information needs of the business.

1. What information should be kept on each credit customer of a small department store?

2. What information should be kept on each supplier of a small department store?

3. Prepare a sample accounts receivable subsidiary ledger for one customer and a sample accounts payable subsidiary ledger for one supplier, as they might actually appear in this department store.

2-6   For the following types of businesses, name the journals that each would use in recording its accounting events.

a. Doctor's office where patients pay upon leaving.

b. Department store.

c. Hot dog vendor.

d. Doctor's office with customer billing.

e. Gift shop with cash and major credit card sales only.

2-7   Refer to the transactions for the Conti Company given in Exercise 1-4. Journalize those transactions in good form, using the sales journal, purchases journal, cash receipts journal, cash disbursements journal, and general journal. Post these transactions to the appropriate general and subsidiary ledger accounts.

2-8   For each of the following accounting transactions, indicate whether the transaction should be recorded in the sales journal (SJ), purchases journal (PJ), cash receipts journal (CRJ), cash disbursements journal (CDJ), or general journal (GJ). If the recording of any transaction would depend upon the design of the special journals, give two alternative treatments of that transaction.

a. Cash sale.

b. Credit purchase of inventory.

c. Purchase of truck with down payment and note.

d. Sales return by customer.

e. Correction of incorrect posting of customer payment.

f. Credit sale.

g. Sale—25 percent down and balance in one month.

h. Withdrawal of cash by owner.

i. Depreciation.

j. Transfer of net income figure to retained earnings.

k. Purchase of equipment on account.

l. Purchase discount.

2-9 The Esplanade Company (a sole proprietorship) has not maintained its records on a double-entry basis since its inception in 1951.[1] The following is all the information you could determine from the "books" of Esplanade.

a. The assets and equities as of December 31, 1978 were:

	Debit	Credit
Cash	$ 5,175	
Accounts receivable	9,816	
Fixtures	3,130	
Accumulated depreciation		1,110
Prepaid insurance	158	
Prepaid supplies	79	
Accounts payable		4,244
Accrued misc. expenses		206
Accrued taxes		202
Merchandise inventory	19,243	
Notes payable		5,000
Roberts, capital		26,839

b. A summary of the transactions for 1979. as recorded on the checkbook, showed:

Deposits for the year (including redeposit of $304)	$83,187
Checks drawn during the year	84,070
Customers checks charged back by the bank	304
Bank service charges	22

c. The following information was available concerning accounts payable:

Purchases on account during year	$57,789
Returns of merchandise allowed as credits against accounts by vendors	1,418
Payments of account by check	55,461

d. Information pertaining to accounts receivable showed the following:

Accounts collected	$43,083
Balance of accounts on December 31, 1979	11,921

---

[1] Adapted from the AICPA examination.

e. Checks drawn during the year included checks for the following items:

Salaries	$10,988
Rent	3,600
Heat, light, and telephone	394
Supplies	280
Insurance	341
Taxes and licenses	1,017
Withdrawals by owner	6,140
Miscellaneous expense	769
Merchandise purchases	2,080
Notes payable	3,000
	$28,609

f. Merchandise inventory on December 31, 1979, was $17,807. Prepaid insurance amounted to $122 and supplies on hand to $105 as of December 31, 1979. Accrued taxes were $216 and miscellaneous accrued expenses were $73 at the year-end.

g. Cash sales for the year are assumed to account for all cash received other than that collected on accounts. Fixtures are to be depreciated at the rate of 10 percent per year.

1. Prepare a cash basis income statement for the calendar year 1979.

2. Prepare an accrual basis income statement for the calendar year 1979.

3. Prepare a balance sheet as of December 31, 1979.

2-10 Refer to the transactions for the Bienville Corporation given in Exercise 1-10. Journalize those transactions in good form using the sales journal, purchases journal, cash receipts journal, cash disbursements journal and general journal. Post these transactions to the appropriate general and subsidiary ledger accounts. Would any changes in adjusting entries, financial statements, and closing entries result from the addition of these special journals and subsidiary ledgers? If so, make any necessary changes.

internal control in manual accounting systems

outline

3.1 **Accidental and Deliberate Errors**: detecting accidental errors; the problem of embezzlement; profile of typical embezzler.

3.2 **Defalcations of Cash**: embezzlement techniques involving cash disbursements, petty cash, and cash receipts.

3.3 **Detection and Prevention of Mistakes**: auditor's orientation; techniques designed to prevent or detect errors involving cash or inventory; four-column bank reconciliation.

3.4 **Elements of Internal Control in a Manual Environment**: general concept of internal control; basic elements of internal control.

INTRODUCTION

In earlier discussions we concentrated on fundamental accounting concepts and the related practical techniques used to put these concepts to work. Our basic focus centered on how we could accomplish the necessary accounting tasks in the most efficient manner possible. In this chapter our attention turns to the darker side of accounting systems.

The problem is that despite the best system in the world, we still might not get the proper answers, namely proper reflection in the accounts of the transactions to date. Assuming the system can work and is capable of handling all transactions, improper answers are the result of improper processing of transactions. These improper processings of transactions divide neatly into two types: those done accidentally and those done intentionally.

3.1 ACCIDENTAL AND DELIBERATE ERRORS

Detecting Accidental Errors

Accidental improper processings of transactions are, of course, simply mistakes. Certainly, people will always make some errors and no system can possibly prevent them all. However, the system should point out the existence of an error as soon as possible. In fact, the typical accounting system we have dealt with in the first two chapters contains a number of features designed to detect errors:

1. The most important error-detecting feature is the double-entry method itself. The constant requirement that debits equal credits will point out numerous mistakes, since rarely will an error on the debit half of an entry be exactly compensated by an equivalent error on the credit half. The opposite also applies—an error in the credit entry will almost surely not be balanced by an equal error in the debit entry. The balancing of the special journals prior to posting, the taking of the trial balance, and the taking of the adjusted trial balance are all examples of attempts to catch errors as soon as possible. Of course, just because debits equal credits does not mean there are no mistakes.

2. The second most important error-detecting feature is the audit trail. You remember from our discussion in earlier chapters that we can go from the figures in the financial statements to their supporting documents. The figures in the financial statements come from ledger balances. The ledger accounts indicate by their posting reference the journal source of all the debits and credit. Thus, by checking the journals we can see the original entries and hence find the supporting documents. Similarly, we can go from the source documents forward through the ledger to their appearance on the financial statements by using the posting reference in each journal. This audit trail is absolutely essential for error detection. Whenever an error is discovered in an accounting number, we must be able to go back to see where the record came from to determine the source of the mistake. Suppose we take the balance in an asset account, such as inventory, and compare it with the result of a physical check of the inventory. If the two do not balance, we must be able to go back through the accounting records to see where the balance in the records came from and where the accounting records went wrong. (Note: we are here assuming that the inventory is correct, and the accounting records are wrong. Possibly, the records are correct and some inventory is missing—we will discuss this later in the chapter.) Even if an error is small in amount, it may be a symptom of a larger problem, the start of a growing problem, or the result of major (but offsetting) errors. Because of this, we always must be able to get to the root of a problem—hence the audit trail.

3. Another error-detecting device is the bank reconciliation. Accounting depends a great deal on judgment and two different accountants could derive two somewhat different figures for net income for the same firm for the same period. Cash, however, is as objective as we get in accounting. Certainly, what the bank states is our cash balance should reconcile with

what our books indicate is our cash balance; any discrepancy should be explainable as timing differences in the recording of cash transactions. A good bank reconciliation is an effective test that: (a) all checks were recorded properly; (b) all deposits were recorded properly; and (c) miscellaneous charges, such as bank service charges and checks returned NSF (i.e., not sufficient funds), were properly incorporated into the accounts.

4. A fourth error-detecting feature is the use of subsidiary ledgers. Notice that the control accounts in the general ledger for accounts receivable and accounts payable should always equal the total of the individual accounts in the respective ledgers. If the control does not agree with (or in accounting terminology, balance to) the total of the subsidiary ledger accounts, there is an error somewhere. It is quite possible for these totals not to agree. If a cash receipt on accounts receivable is entered properly in the cash receipts journal, but is not posted to the individual account in the subsidiary ledger, the accounts receivable control account will be correct while the subsidiary ledger will not be correct. Also, if a sales return is recorded in the general journal, it may be that only one of the two necessary postings (i.e., to the control account and to the subsidiary ledger) will be made.

5. An additional error-detecting feature is the use of billing statements for credit customers. It is certainly possible (in fact, it often happens) that a cash receipt on account or a credit sale is posted to the wrong individual account. Observe that both the control total and the total of the subsidiary ledger will be correct. It is the individual accounts that will be incorrect; one account will be overstated by some amount, while another will be understated by the same amount. Since these two errors cancel each other out when totaling the subsidiary ledger, balancing is not effective in detecting this error. It is extremely likely, however, that if we send statements of account to our customers, they will let us know if something is incorrect. Of course, the customer whose balance due is higher than it should be is more likely to contact us than the customer whose balance is too low. However, since there cannot be one without the other (or else the subsidiary ledger would not balance to the control), this should not overly concern us.

6. The final error-detecting feature we will discuss here is communication with our vendors. We do not send statements to our vendors as we do to our customers; nevertheless, the vendors will let us know if we have not paid them enough. Suppose, for example, we paid one of the vendors, Fireplaces Unlimited, but debited the account of Fireworks Unlimited. Note that the total of the subsidiary ledger will be correct: one balance will be understated, but another will be overstated by an equivalent amount. We will thus not pay Fireworks because we thought we paid them. However, they will let us know that we have not paid them. And if we pay Fireplaces again, it is at least possible that they will inform us that we have overpaid them and will send us a refund check. Thus, communication with our vendors helps to clear mistakes we may have made.

Table 3-1 briefly summarizes our discussion of the basic error-detecting features of a manual accounting system.

TABLE 3-1   BASIC ERROR-DETECTING FEATURES OF A MANUAL ACCOUNTING SYSTEM

Double-entry Method	Points up errors, since rarely will an error in one-half of an entry be exactly offset by an equivalent error in the other half
Audit Trail	Allows the accountant to track backwards through the accounting records to the source of an error
Bank Reconciliation	Provides an independent check that all checks, deposits, and miscellaneous charges were recorded properly
Subsidiary Ledgers	Provides cross checks of the general ledger control account with the subsidiary ledger
Customer Statements of Account	Provides independent check of accounts receivable subsidiary ledger account balances
Communication With Vendors	Provides an independent check of accounts payable subsidiary ledger account balances

The Problem of Embezzlement

Our attention now turns to the more sinister side of this area—deliberate mistakes. Writers discussing this topic generally employ euphemisms, or inoffensive language, for what is really stealing. Stealing through the manipulation of accounting records does not usually involve physical violence, but it does involve the betrayal of trust. Two words are used commonly in this context—embezzlement and defalcation. In fact, they mean the same thing, namely, the fraudulent appropriation to one's own use of property entrusted to one's care. You should not think that this sort of thing cannot happen to you or your firm. A defalcation was disovered in an international CPA firm which involved the stealing of large sums from travel and expense money over a period of years by a bookkeeper in the main office. This fraud at the heart of the CPA's own business was discovered when the bookkeeper confessed to wrongdoing and gave herself up.

It is, of course, impossible to determine the amount of embezzlement precisely—much is never discovered. But estimates place white collar crime at well over ten billion dollars per year, truly an astonishing figure. Understandably, cash and inventory are the main targets of dishonest employees. Cash can buy almost anything. Inventory can either be used by the thief, or in many cases be readily converted into cash. On the other hand, prepaid expense may be an asset, but there is nothing to steal. A CPA firm study bears this reasoning out—88 percent of their client's defalcations which were uncovered involved cash, with the remainder involving inventory. For cash embezzlements, it is important to note that the majority of individual incidents involved cash receipts, but the vast majority of dollar amounts (80%) involved cash disbursements.

The Embezzler

We must next be concerned with the people who do the embezzling. Contrary to what you might think, the embezzler is only rarely a dyed-in-the-wool thief. Generally speaking, the embezzler is a trusted employee who has been with his firm a long time. For one group of embezzlers studied, the people were employed an average of six and a half years before they started to steal. In fact, we have enough information about the embezzler to draw a general sketch.

The embezzler usually finds eventually that it is impossible for him to live on his salary or that his salary is otherwise inadequate. This is due to two basic factors: (1) living around and associating with people wealthier than he; or (2) a feeling that he is discriminated against, put upon, or otherwise treated unfairly by the company. Thus, the employee eventually convinces himself he either needs the money or at least deserves it. Notice, however, that the embezzler can often convince himself that the stealing is only temporary; he will repay the money when needs are not quite so pressing. The needs only increase, so the embezzler is trapped in a never-ending cycle to avoid detection.

3.2 DEFALCATIONS OF CASH

We will first discuss the potential losses from improper cash disbursements, involving both petty cash funds and the bank-checking account. Unless manual accounting systems and how they work in practice are very familiar to you, we suggest you review the material in Chapter 2, especially the discussion of the cash disbursements journal.

Defalcations of Cash Disbursements

Cash disbursements is usually the area of greatest dollar loss, so this subject should have particular emphasis. Consider the following techniques for embezzling from cash disbursements.

Preparing Checks Payable to Real or Fictitious Companies

A bookkeeper might prepare checks payable to other firms, so that the checks appear to be normal payments on account. After the checks are signed, he can divert the funds to himself by either: (1) forging the endorsement of the check and then cashing it or (2) using a bank account which he created to deposit the funds into. The problem is then getting an authorized signature on the checks. Techniques for doing this would depend upon whether he: (1) created the payee firm or (2) used an existing and real firm. If he created the firm, he must also create false invoices from it as well as any supporting documents which might be required for signature. If he used a real vendor, he could simply resubmit invoices which have already been paid. However, he would then have the problem of two checks tying to the same invoice. This problem can then be solved by intercepting the second, fraudulent check when it returns from the bank and destroying it. The number and date of the original check can then be changed and substituted for the fraudulent check.

Padding the Payroll

Padding the payroll is another method of issuing checks to others and then appropriating them. In this method, an employee might either: (1) keep paying checks for people after they have quit or been fired or (2) add fake employees to the payroll. Notice that padding can be accomplished by a number of people besides the bookkeeper. If the foreman distributes paychecks, he might "forget" to inform the office that an employee has quit and appropriate the check. Similarly, the person who adds employees might add a brother-in-law or cousin.

Embezzler Prepares Checks Payable to Himself

Another possibility is for the embezzler to prepare checks to himself using either a check that was not prenumbered or a prenumbered check from the back of the checkbook. He can get the check signed by either forging an authorized signature or by using checks which have been signed in blank (i.e., with the date, payee, and amount not yet filled in). Then he must intercept or control the bank statement so that the checks can be destroyed when the bank returns them. Notice the cash balance per bank would be reduced by the cleared check, but the general ledger balance has not been reduced to keep them in balance. This can be done by increasing the recorded amount for another check and then changing the check when the bank returns it. You recall that part of the process of balancing the special journals prior to posting involved adding up the totals of the various columns. Developing a sum total of a column of figures is called *footing*. Underfooting is then the misadding of a column to get too small a total, while overfooting is, of course, the opposite. Thus, the embezzler can overfoot the cash column of the cash disbursements journal to reduce the general ledger cash balance. However, credits will then exceed debits in the journal. He must then either decrease credits by under-footing purchase discounts or increase debits by overfooting expenses.

Overpaying Vendors

The last manipulation of cash disbursements we will discuss is overpaying the amount due a vendor. At first glance, this does not seem to help the embezzler much, but some vendors will send the firm a refund check for the amount overpaid. The embezzler can then appropriate this refund check. Note that the books are perfectly in balance: some asset or expense is simply overstated. This technique, however, does not often work since most vendors will carry a debit balance and not refund the money.

Defalcations of Petty Cash

Though disbursements should generally be made by check, almost all companies require cash to pay for items like postage due. For this reason, most firms have a small amount of cash on hand to pay for these items (this amount is called *petty cash*). Generally speaking, defalcations of petty cash are particularly easy since they simply involve taking cash from the petty cash fund. For most systems you can just leave it at that—there can be little effective detection.

Because of this risk of loss, many companies use an imprest petty cash system. In such a system, a certain amount (say $100) is set as the amount for petty cash. The petty cash fund begins with a $100 check drawn to petty cash. The journal entry would be:

Petty cash	100	
Cash		100

Petty cash is thus set up as an asset account. After the check is cashed, the petty cash fund is established.

To get cash out of the fund, a voucher is prepared, where the voucher states the reason for and the amount of the cash needed. After approval by a responsible official, the voucher is placed with the petty cash fund and the cash is withdrawn. Thus, the total of all the vouchers plus the cash still on hand should always total $100.

When the cash in the fund becomes too low, another check is drawn to petty cash in the amount of the total of all vouchers. The vouchers are then removed from the petty cash fund and the cash added (the cash should then again total $100). The journal entry should debit the expense (or possibly asset) accounts affected by the cash payments supported by the vouchers.

To continue our above example, suppose vouchers totaled $70 and cash was $30 in the petty cash fund. Petty cash would be replenished by a $70 check drawn to petty cash, but the journal entry would be:

$$\text{Expense accounts} \qquad 70$$
$$\text{Cash} \qquad\qquad\qquad\qquad 70$$

Thus, the petty cash account in the general ledger will always remain $100, and the only journal entries will occur when the petty cash fund is replenished.

With an imprest system, control over petty cash is greatly improved. However, stealing is not ruled out; it is simply that under an imprest system, false vouchers must be prepared. This can be done by: (1) increasing the amount of a voucher that has already been approved, (2) creating vouchers and forging the necessary signatures, or (3) submitting vouchers twice by changing the date of the voucher.

Defalcations of Cash Receipts

Cash Sales

If the embezzler takes cash from cash sales, he can keep the books in balance by simply not recording the transaction or recording an amount smaller than the actual sale. (If a cash register or sales slip is part of the system, either can be used improperly. A situation such as a bar comes immediately to mind, where the cash register need not be used at all.) Or consider the case of a movie theater where tickets are serially prenumbered. The cashier can get around the system by selling the same ticket twice and pocketing the amount. If ten tickets are resold at $3.50, that is $35.00 per night. The cashier can get used tickets back from the ticket taker. If the taker must tear the tickets and return half to each customer, he can take one of a couple's two tickets, tear it, and give the two halves back to the people. A complete ticket is then available for reuse. Of course, the cashier will have to split the take with the ticket taker, and some conspiracy is necessary for this to work.

Cash Collections on Accounts Receivable

A major technique for stealing collections on accounts receivable is called *lapping*. Lapping consists essentially of stealing Paul's payment, but then paying Paul's account by using the next receipt, say that of Peter. Peter's account is then paid by the next receipt and the process continues indefinitely. Some people cannot believe this is a prevalent practice because it is a process which never ends. But remember many embezzlers feel their theft is only temporary; they will then put the money back and everything will be covered.

Another possibility is to bill for a sale at the total amount due, while recording the sale at some lower amount. The embezzler can then appropriate the difference when the customer pays his bill.

A bolder method involves taking the cash, but then recording the collection as usual in the cash receipts journal. Notice that the bank balance and the general ledger balance will not agree because the books have "too many debits." This shortage in the bank can be covered by manipulating the bank reconciliation so the books and bank statement appear to balance. Alternatively, the embezzler can improperly use the cash receipts journal by simply underfooting the cash column, but keep debits equal to credits by overfooting the sales discount column. If a payment does not take a discount because the discount period has come and gone, the embezzler can still record the receipt incorporating the discount and take the discount himself.

Finally, the embezzler may not record the cash receipt at all. Since the person involved might complain of an incorrect bill, the embezzler must then intercept the statement of account and any dunning letters which might follow. Notice that the debit balance simply continues on the books. To reduce the balance, a credit must be obtained. The embezzler can get this desired credit by either creating a credit memo or by writing off the debt as uncollectible.

Table 3-2 summarizes these potential defalcations of cash.

3.3 DETECTION AND PREVENTION OF MISTAKES

Auditor's Orientation

We will now go into further detail on how to detect and prevent mistakes in the processing of accounting transactions. But before we discuss this topic, it is important to distinguish our orientation from that of independent auditors. Our approach is essentially that of management concerned with the operation of the firm. Ideally we would like to develop a system which would detect and correct any errors, accidental or deliberate, and do so in an inexpensive manner.

It is important to realize that the independent auditor only attests to the company's financial statements. The financial statements are prepared by the company, not the auditor, and the responsibility for the financial statements ultimately lies with management. The auditor's purpose is to provide an independent check that the financial statements are presented fairly in accordance with generally accepted accounting principles. The auditor cannot be responsible for the proper processing of all transactions; that is the responsibility of management.

Specifically we have the following differences in perspective from auditors:

1. We wish to detect errors as soon as possible. The auditor is also interested in detecting errors, but he is mainly concerned with whether or not they are ultimately detected. When they are detected makes little difference to his examination. We, on the other hand, want to reduce as much as possible the potential for making bad decisions based upon incorrect information.

2. We are more concerned with errors than is the auditor. The auditor is basically concerned with whether the financial statements are presented fairly in accordance with generally accepted accounting principles. However, the financial statements can present fairly while containing a certain amount of error; it is enough that the amounts are roughly correct. We take a more particular attitude toward these errors because potentially they can grow out of control.

TABLE 3-2   DEFALCATIONS OF CASH

Area of Defalcation	How To Obtain Cash	How To Cover In Accounting Records
Cash Disbursements	A. Issue checks to others, appropriate the checks	1. Create false invoices 2. Use invoices twice for support 3. "Pad" the payroll 4. Pocket unclaimed wages and dividends
	B. Issue check to yourself	1. Incorrectly foot the cash disbursements journal 2. Increase recorded amount of another check
	C. Overpay vendor, appropriate refund	1. Allow asset or expense to remain overstated
Petty Cash	A. Remove cash from petty cash fund	1. Increase amount on vouchers 2. Create false vouchers 3. Submit vouchers twice 4. Allow fund to remain short
Cash Receipts	A. Take cash from cash sales	1. Record no amount 2. Record less than was received
	B. Take cash payments on accounts receivable	1. Lapping 2. Bill for full amount, but record sale at lower amount 3. Record cash receipt, but manipulate bank reconciliation 4. Record cash receipt, but incorrectly use the journal 5. Do not record cash receipt, but intercept statements of account 6. Do not record cash receipt, but create credit memo or write off the amount 7. Pocket payment on an account which has been written off

3. As a corollary to the second comment, we are more interested in detecting fraud than is the auditor. The auditor disclaims responsibility for detecting fraud, unless the fraud materially affects the financial statements. He asserts that the necessary audit procedures to detect fraud would be too expensive for the possible benefit. The auditor is only concerned with fraud if it is so gross that it makes the financial statements materially misstated. Management is naturally more interested in detecting all fraud.

4. We are more concerned with the trade-off between the costs of increased controls and their benefits. Auditors will be pleased with any additional features or procedures that will provide further assurance of accuracy. We, however, must keep in mind that any additional steps in the system will cost us in terms of dollars, irritation, and increased time. We have to trade off these costs with the potential benefits.

5. Finally, we have to be more jealous of management time than are the auditors. The auditor will often see his area of concern as more important than management may believe it to be. Thus, he will make more demands on the time of management than management feels is justified. Our system should not and cannot eliminate the role of management in maintaining accuracy and reliability. Nonetheless, we should try to keep demands on management time to a minimum.

Techniques Designed to Prevent or Detect Errors

We now want to consider exactly what should be done in particular business situations to detect mistakes and to help prevent their occurrence. We must keep in mind that effective error detection and prevention is possible even in small businesses, despite claims to the contrary. For example, some companies use cash receipts to cover disbursements when it is convenient. In other words, the company might use cash sales to pay for a delivery. The company will try to justify this inexcusable practice by saying the company is too small to prevent or detect mistakes or that such mistakes do not occur.

Procedures Involving Cash

All businesses can afford to have a reasonably good control system. The system should consist of at least the following:

1. All cash disbursements should be made with prenumbered checks, with the exception of petty cash. Using checks for all major cash disbursements ensures that: (1) the disbursement is authorized and (2) there is a permanent receipt. The check should be prenumbered to ensure that it is accounted for properly. This procedure helps to prevent the issuance of a check which is not recorded in the cash disbursements journal.

2. If someone makes a mistake preparing a check and the check must be redrawn, the bad check should be voided before preparing a new one. The voided check should then be (1) altered to prevent its use; (2) kept to make sure *all* prenumbered checks are accounted for; and (3) filed with other checks for a permanent record.

3. Someone should reconcile the bank statement to the accounting records on a monthly basis. This is essential to determine if any unauthorized checks were issued or receipts stolen. Thus, if the bank reconciliation is to be effective, it should be performed by

someone other than the person who controls the checkbook. Even in the smallest business, this division of labor is possible; the owner can and should reconcile the bank statement. Of course, to make this process effective, the bank statements must be unopened when the person responsible for the reconciliation receives it.

4. The system should utilize a cash register to record any cash transactions which occur over the counter. The cash register makes two records of all transactions which it records; one is kept internally and one is given to the customer. Thus, in order to make a receipt for the customer, the operator must make a record which the machine retains. Then, daily checks should be made of the cash register totals to ensure that all cash receipts per the cash register balance to the journal and to the bank deposits. In situations such as bars, where no receipt is given the customer and no receipt is expected, it is not uncommon for cash to be pocketed and no record made.

5. Daily cash receipts should be deposited intact. This is essential to ensure that cash receipts are not being taken. If disbursements are made from cash receipts, the system will lose control; it will be difficult or impossible to distinguish proper from improper disbursements.

6. Check signing should be the responsibility of management who have no access to the accounting records. This step is necessary to ensure that the accounting records accurately reflect the checks written. Of course, in a small company, this rule must be relaxed, at least as far as the owner is concerned.

7. Checks should only be drawn if there is proper support for them. This support should consist at least of (1) a proper invoice, (2) evidence that the goods or services were received, and (3) evidence that the purchase transaction was properly authorized in the first place. We must do this to ensure we pay only properly authorized and justified expenditures.

8. Any supporting documents should be cancelled once a disbursement is made. This is necessary to prevent paying the invoice twice, which is not desired for even proper expenditures.

9. All checks should be mailed promptly and directly to the payee. This step ensures that the payee and only the payee receives the disbursement. Otherwise, an employee may appropriate the check.

10. The system should use an imprest petty cash fund with one custodian. The imprest fund involves replenishing petty cash only when properly approved vouchers are presented justifying all expenditures. For accountability, one person must be in charge of the fund.

11. Invoices should be prenumbered. There must be physical control over invoices so that they cannot be improperly used. Prenumbered invoices help ensure that all invoices will be accounted for.

12. When the mail is opened, a list of collections should be made. A responsible official should then compare the list with the journal record and the bank deposit. This procedure helps ensure that all mail collections are retained by the firm.

13. Management (in a small company, the owner) should review monthly comparative financial statements. These statements ought to be sufficiently detailed to allow detection of any unusual revenue, expense, asset, or liability amounts.

14. All general journal entries should be properly approved. Since these entries can affect all ledger accounts, they must be adequately supervised.

The techniques which we have discussed so far are summarized in Table 3-3. Even though these are basic control techniques, they are certainly not all that could, or even should be used in any particular situation. You will have to use your judgment to determine exactly what a particular system should contain. The important point is not the memorization of long lists of procedures, but rather to understand the basic concepts and needs of a control system.

TABLE 3-3 GENERAL CONTROL TECHNIQUES

Techniques	Reason for Techniques
1. Use only prenumbered checks for disbursements	Ensure all checks are accounted for
2. Alter but keep voided checks	Ensure voided checks are not used
3. Reconcile bank statements monthly	Ensure all checks are authorized and recorded and receipts deposited
4. Use cash register, check register daily	Ensure all cash receipts are recorded
5. Deposit cash receipts intact	Ensure all cash receipts are deposited
6. Check signing by management with no access to records	Ensure accounting records accurately reflect checks written
7. Have proper support for checks	Only pay properly authorized and justified expenditures
8. Cancel supporting documents when paid	Only pay once even for proper expenditures
9. Mail check directly to payee	Ensure that payee and only payee receives disbursement
10. Use imprest petty cash fund with one custodian	Establish authority over petty cash and review periodically
11. Use prenumbered invoices	Ensure all invoices are accounted for
12. List mail collections, compare with journal	Ensure all mail collections are retained by firm
13. Review monthly comparative financial statements	Check any unusual revenue, expense, asset, or liability amounts
14. Approve all entries to general journal	Ensure only authorized and proper journal entries are made

Procedures Involving Inventory

Many small businesses, such as real estate firms and doctor's offices are, basically service oriented and thus do not have significant amounts of inventory. As a result, the above discussion did not include inventory procedures because it was designed to apply essentially to all businesses. But merchandising firms (such as retail stores and wholesalers that have significant amounts of inventory), must have procedures to protect these valuable assets. There are three basic areas of concern with inventory—purchasing, custody, and record keeping.

Purchasing

Purchasing is the important task of buying the inventory the company needs at the best price possible. This area of responsibility should be centralized under a responsible official usually called the *purchasing agent*. Since inventory purchase is one of the primary areas of the firm's operations, proper support for checks and the cancellation of the support after payment is made become even more important (see # 7 and # 8 above). Purchase returns then become a major item and must be supervised to ensure that proper credit is obtained for the returned merchandise. Finally, if an operating department requests that inventory be purchased, the department should fill out a requisition form and have it approved to ensure that all purchases are properly authorized.

Custody

Custody of the inventory involves receiving, storing, and eventually transferring the merchandise. Purchasing and receiving should be performed by different employees, so that each can provide a check upon the other. Similarly, receiving and storekeeping should be independent operations to provide additional checks. Further, there should be a physical inventory count taken on a regular basis by employees who are not in charge of the inventory; it is essential that the firm periodically check its inventory to make sure that the amount is reasonable given the levels of purchases and sales. Finally, there should be physical control of the inventory. Of course, the value of the inventory should dictate the amount of physical control—unset one-carat diamonds require more control than twopenny nails. Locks, keys, guards, and authorization for withdrawal should be used as appropriate.

Record Keeping

Record keeping is the task of keeping track of the amount in inventory. The person in charge of inventory should not also keep the books. If the same person does both, then a loss of merchandise could be covered in the books. When merchandise is moved from the storeroom to the sales department, vouchers should be prepared to assign responsibility, and the sales clerk should sign them to indicate receipt of the goods. Just as in the case of checks, all documents should be prenumbered to ensure their physical control. If practicable, a *perpetual* inventory system should be used. A perpetual system involves constantly keeping track of the receipts and withdrawals of each item of inventory as they occur. Thus, if the system is operated properly, the accounting records will always be up-to-date and should agree with the physical realities of inventory. Table 3-4 summarizes our discussion of inventory control techniques.

TABLE 3-4 INVENTORY CONTROL TECHNIQUES

Purchasing	1. Centralize under a responsible official 2. Attach purchase invoices to checks for payment 3. Cancel support when check is paid 4. Supervise all returned purchases 5. Use requisitions to initiate purchases
Custody	1. Separate purchasing from receiving 2. Separate receiving from storekeeping 3. Take physical inventory regularly 4. Use independent employees for physical inventory 5. Physically control access to inventory
Record Keeping	1. Separate record keeping from custody 2. Use vouchers on merchandise moved to sales area 3. Require all documents to be prenumbered 4. Use a perpetual system, if possible 5. Compare results of physical inventory to records

Four-Column Bank Reconciliation

We will turn our attention now to an elaborate control-oriented form of bank reconciliation. This is the four-column bank reconciliation, often referred to as a *proof of cash*. You are perhaps familiar with the usual form of bank reconciliation, where the balance per bank is reconciled to the balance per books at one particular date. The four-column bank reconciliation checks the bank records with the accounting records for a period of time. This period is usually a month but it could be any other time period. There are four goals of this reconciliation, one for each column:

1. To reconcile the balance per bank to the general ledger amount at the beginning of the period.

2. To reconcile the deposits for the period with the cash receipts journal to see if all deposits were recorded and if all recorded cash receipts were deposited.

3. To reconcile the withdrawals of the period with the cash disbursements journal to see if all recorded checks were paid and if all paid checks were recorded.

4. To reconcile the balance per bank to the general ledger amount at the end of the period.

We will go over this reconciliation in some detail because it provides an excellent indication of what is actually happening in the control of cash. The reconciliation checks all recorded cash transactions for an entire period and thus is an excellent method of comparing recorded cash receipts and disbursements with the bank records. However, we must be clear on what the reconciliation does not do. The reconciliation does not help when checks are made for an improper amount or when cash receipts are stolen before being deposited and recorded.

Figure 3-1 gives a simple four-column bank reconciliation for one month for a sample corporation. Each of the five major elements of the reconciliation are numbered to correspond to the following discussion:

TYPICAL CORPORATION, INC.
FIRST NATIONAL BANK AND TRUST
BANK RECONCILIATION FOR AUGUST, 1979
SEPTEMBER 10, 1979

	Balance 7/31/79	—August— Deposits	Withdrawals	Balance 8/31/79
1. Balance, per bank	$4300	$2150	$2800	$3650
2. Deposits in transit				
on 7/31	550	(550)		
on 8/31		875		875
3. O/S checks				
drawn before 7/31	(1200)		(1050)	(150)
drawn after 7/31			650	(650)
4. NSF check redeposited		(125)	(125)	
5. Balance, per books	$3650	$2350	$2275	$3725
	G/L	CRJ	CDJ	G/L

FIGURE 3-1 Four-Column Bank Reconciliation

1. The first element consists of the beginning balance, deposits, withdrawals, and ending balance as indicated by the bank statement. A summary of all transactions giving these four numbers should appear on the statement. If only the beginning and ending balances and a list of transactions are given, then it is necessary to add all deposits and all withdrawals separately.

2. The second element consists of the deposits in transit. Notice that the deposits in transit as of 7/31 are credited to our account by the bank during August. Thus, the 7/31 balance per books has to be $550 *greater than* the balance per bank because the $550 has been recorded on the books but the bank has not yet credited us. But, during the month, the deposits per books must then be $550 *less than* the deposits per bank because the $550 was previously recorded. A somewhat similar treatment follows for deposits in transit as of 8/31, totalling $875 in this example.

3. The third element consists of the outstanding checks (abbreviated O/S by accountants). There were checks totaling $1200 which were outstanding as of 7/31; thus, the balance per books must be $1200 *less than* the balance per bank. Some of these checks (totaling $1050) cleared during the month, leaving $150 still outstanding at the end of the month. Thus, the withdrawals per books must be $1050 *less than* withdrawals per bank for the period because the withdrawals were previously recorded. Then, the $150 must be subtracted from the balance per bank to get the balance per books because the amount is still outstanding. A similar treatment follows for checks which were written during the period, but were outstanding at the end of the period, totaling $650 in this example.

4. The fourth element consists of checks that were returned and stamped *not sufficient funds* (i.e., NSF). We assume in this example that a check of $125 was returned, but that the $125 was then redeposited without making an accounting entry. Thus, the deposits per

books would be $125 *less than* deposits per bank because the check was only recorded once in the books.

A similar adjustment is necessary for withdrawals. The withdrawals per books would be $125 less than withdrawals per bank because there was no $125 withdrawal in the books, while there was a $125 debit memo for the NSF check. Note that the $125 check appears three times on the bank statement: once for its original deposit; once as a debit memo when the check is returned; and once for the redeposit.

5. The fifth element consists of the beginning balance, receipts, disbursements, and ending balance as given by the accounting records. The beginning balance and ending balance come from the general ledger cash balance at those dates. The receipts figure comes from the cash receipts journal for the period, while the disbursements figure comes from the cash disbursements journal. Naturally, these amounts should reconcile with the figures from the bank statement.

After you work a few examples, you should get a feel for this reconciliation and an idea of where errors are likely to arise.

3.4 ELEMENTS OF INTERNAL CONTROL IN A MANUAL ENVIRONMENT

General Concept of Internal Control

Earlier in this chapter we discussed a number of methods and procedures designed to detect errors and correct them. We further discussed how companies might prevent or at least help protect against embezzlement. Let us now see if we can draw some general conclusions and focus on the essential concepts, which unfortunately have a way of getting lost in the mass of details.

Basically, all these procedures have two major aims;

1. To protect assets (especially cash and inventory) from being lost or stolen.
2. To ensure that the accounting records are accurate and complete.

Thus, when you design, operate, or analyze an accounting system, you should always keep these aims in mind. It is not sufficient for a system to be simple, efficient, and provide management with the information it requires. The system must also accomplish the two aims given above: (1) the system must protect the assets with which it deals and (2) the system must protect itself from errors and ensure the accuracy of its records.

In fact, these aims are so important that the techniques, methods, and procedures which help accomplish these goals are given a special name, *internal control*. Internal control is then the total collection of means we employ to accomplish the objectives stated above. Earlier in this chapter we reviewed a number of internal control procedures, such as bank reconciliation and separation of duties between those who handle cash disbursements and those who handle the related accounting.

The name internal control makes a good deal of sense if you think about it. These are control techniques which are contained in the system; that is, control which is internal to the system. You must realize that an accounting system will not automatically be accurate. The accounting records live in a world of their own, separate from the actual asset operations of the business. The goal, of course, is for the accounting records to accurately reflect what is going on in the "real world" of asset operations. The important point is that the accounting records may not accurately reflect what is going on. Errors, both accidental and deliberate, will inevitably occur, and unless control is applied the system will just as inevitably go "out of control" and no longer reflect accurately the facts of asset operations.

Certainly, a system can have external controls as well as internal controls. External controls would include outside auditors, the police, or the FBI. The goals of these external controls are the prevention of misleading financial statements, in the case of auditors, or the prevention of theft, in the case of the police and FBI. A minute's reflection, however, will convince you that these external controls will necessarily be ineffectual, except in special situations. There are simply so many transactions in even a small business that they can never be all checked to determine that they were processed correctly. If a system is to be protected from errors, the system must protect itself from errors. Internal control is the way a system protects itself from error.

Actually, internal control has taken on a more expansive meaning due to the increase in scope of many business activities. Large companies, such as General Motors, have hundreds of thousands of employees located all over the world. In fact, the chairman of the board of Textron was able to claim at his confirmation hearing as head of the Federal Reserve System that he was a small businessman; his company had sales less than the profit of IBM and his company only had 65,000 employees.

The problem, of course, is that with such a vast number of employees, top management cannot supervise (in any direct sense) all of the workers. As a result, controls must be developed to see to it that top management's policies and directives are carried out. Thus, in addition to the two objectives listed above, internal control has the following further objectives:

3.   To promote efficient operations by reducing waste and duplication of effort.

4.   To encourage the following of company policies and procedures.

We generally distinguish the first two objectives of internal control from the last two. The first two are the area of accounting controls, whereas the last two are the area of administrative controls. The situation is illustrated in Table 3-5.

Let us give some examples of administrative controls to point up the difference between accounting controls and administrative controls. Personnel methods and procedures designed for hiring, training, and retaining employees are administrative controls; they promote efficient operations but do not protect assets or ensure record accuracy, at least directly. Other administrative controls would include:

1.   Quality controls to help guarantee that only high quality merchandise will be sold to customers.

2.   Guidelines for determining whether salesmen are visiting an appropriate number of customers per day.

3.   Ratios and other statistics (such as inventory turnover) developed by operating departments to check if operations are running to form.

TABLE 3-5   OBJECTIVES OF INTERNAL CONTROL

Objectives of Accounting Controls	1.	Protect assets from being lost or stolen
	2.	Ensure that the accounting records are accurate
Objectives of Administrative Controls	3.	Promote efficient operations
	4.	Encourage the following of company policies

Basic Elements of Internal Control

It is impossible to memorize enough lists of internal control procedures and techniques to handle every situation. You have to be able to keep the general concepts in mind and then be able to apply these concepts in particular situations. The following elements of internal control should be part of any system. To the extent any are missing, the system is deficient in internal control.

1. Employees must be honest and capable. Certainly, any system is critically dependent on the people who use it. If the people are dishonest or incompetent, even the finest system in the world cannot perform properly. In contrast, honest and capable employees can function even in a situation where the other five elements of internal control are sadly lacking.

    However, even with honest and able employees, the system must have effective internal control. As discussed earlier, the embezzler is usually basically honest, but the lure becomes too strong to resist. The following suggestions may prove helpful in deterring employee dishonesty:

    a. The firm should require annual vacations of employees to make sure they are aware that any fraud that requires their constant attention will be found out.

    b. Employees should be bonded. A fidelity bond is essentially insurance protecting the company from loss resulting from employee dishonesty. In other words, if the company suffers a loss from employee dishonesty, the insurance company will cover the loss. Thus, the firm should bond employees in positions of trust in order to provide an outside check on its people and protect against loss.

    c. The firm should have a stated conflict of interest policy to prevent potential abuse.

2. There should be a clear delegation and separation of duties. For a system to work properly, the employees must know what they are to do and what others are to do. This can be partly accomplished by an organization chart, but that is not always sufficient. Job descriptions may be necessary for proper delegation.

    Even more important is the clear separation of duties. Custody of assets must be separated from the record keeping for those assets. For example, if someone is in charge of inventory and keeps the inventory records, he may cover the stealing of inventory by manipulation of the accounting records. He may cover stealing even if he is not the one stealing because he does not want to point out his failure to protect the assets.

    Authorizing transactions must be separated from recording the transactions in the journals, and both must be separated from posting the transactions to the ledgers. The discussion earlier in the chapter about cash defalcations gives a number of potential abuses if this rule is not followed.

Finally, for inventory it is important to separate the purchasing function from the receiving function. This was discussed at greater length earlier in the chapter.

3. Proper procedures for the processing of transactions are essential. These must start with proper authorization. Although a corporation's board of directors has ultimate authority, the day-to-day operating authority is delegated to top management with specific guidelines to follow (for example, the maximum amount to be borrowed without authorization by the directors). In turn, top management might allow others to give the authorization for credit sales to customers as long as a credit limit is not exceeded. This delegation of authority is necessary, but it must be suitable under the circumstances, and there should be a check that the guidelines are followed.

    Other specific procedures were discussed earlier in the chapter, but some of the most important are: to ensure proper support before signing any checks; to approve all noncash entries on returns, discounts, and write-offs; and to review all past due or uncollectible accounts as a check to see if they are properly accounted for.

4. There should be suitable documents and accounting records. Certainly the documents should be: (1) as simple and easy to use as possible to help cut down on error; (2) prenumbered to make it easier to keep physical control over the documents; (3) as few in number as possible to minimize confusion and form cost; and (4) designed to ensure that they will be properly filled out, by providing, for example, blocks for necessary approval signatures.

    As discussed earlier in the chapter, the financial statements should be comparative. The following discussion of necessary accounting documents will provide a basis for comparison for the present period's accounting results.

    a. A specific document which should always be used to encourage consistency in the *chart of accounts*. The chart of accounts should contain of course a list of the account numbers and names for all asset, liability, owner's equity, revenue and expense accounts. However, it should additionally contain a description of each account and guidance on when each should be used.

    b. The chart of accounts and the procedures to be followed should be documented in a *procedures manual*. This manual is necessary to train new employees in the operation of the system and to ensure that the same types of transactions will always be handled in the same way.

    c. Another useful document is the *budget*. This gives the anticipated results of operations and financial position. Actual results can be compared with the budgeted amounts to point out areas of deficiency or problems.

5. There should be adequate physical control over assets and accounting records. Of course, the specific assets and accounting records will dictate what adequate physical control is—diamonds are treated differently than nails.

    Specifically, inventory should be kept in a stockroom, under the custody of one man to allow the assignment of responsibility. Additionally, critical paper such as cash, certificates of deposit, marketable securities, accounting journals, and accounting ledgers should be stored in fireproof safes.

You should always consider the cost and time of reconstructing documents or accounting records. If the risk of their loss is great enough, copies may be justified. A related problem is then the need for reasonable record retention and storage. You must consider the needs of the firm, the volume of the records to store, and the relevant state and federal rules on records.

Earlier in the chapter we discussed a number of specific examples of physical control. These include depositing cash receipts intact on a daily basis and keeping all voided checks.

6. There should be an independent verification of performance. Certainly, no one is able to verify or evaluate his own performance very effectively. Thus, the verification must be done by someone independent of the subject and the system, definitely not a subordinate who would then be in an untenable position.

As time passes, procedures become sloppy and people get careless. Additionally, both accidental and deliberate errors can always potentially occur. Thus, independent verification of performance is periodically necessary to help ensure that the system works properly. Important means of independent verification were discussed earlier. Some examples in-

TABLE 3-6   ELEMENTS OF INTERNAL CONTROL

Honest and capable employees	1.	Hire qualified people with good references
	2.	Require annual vacations
	3.	Bond employees in positions of trust
	4.	State conflict of interest policy
Clear delegation and separation of duties	1.	Develop organization chart
	2.	Separate record keeping from custody of assets
	3.	Separate authorization from record keeping
	4.	Separate purchasing from receiving
Proper procedures for processing of transactions	1.	Ensure proper authorization of transactions
	2.	Sign checks only with proper support
	3.	Approve all noncash entries on returns, discounts, write-offs
	4.	Review past due and uncollectible accounts
Suitable documents and accounting records	1.	Prenumber important documents
	2.	Develop comparative financial statements
	3.	Describe accounting methods in manuals
	4.	Prepare budget of anticipated results
Adequate physical control over assets and records	1.	Limit access to inventory
	2.	Safeguard all important records
	3.	Deposit cash receipts intact daily
	4.	Keep all voided checks
Independent verification of performance	1.	Reconcile bank statement independently
	2.	Prelist cash receipts
	3.	Take complete inventory regularly
	4.	Have an annual audit by a CPA firm

clude: (1) the bank reconciliation if done by a person other than the one who controls cash or the related accounting records; (2) a list of cash receipts made when the mail is opened; (3) the physical counting of inventory to compare with perpetual inventory records; and (4) two separate groups counting inventory (an independent verification of an independent verification so to speak). Perhaps the most common and best known independent verification is an audit by an outside CPA firm at periodic intervals.

Table 3-6 gives the basic elements of internal control. You will never be able to memorize enough to handle every situation you will encounter. Use the detailed examples discussed earlier in the chapter as a reference, learn the basic elements of internal control, and then be able to apply these concepts in particular situations.

exercises

3-1   The Galliano Company, a client of your firm, has come to you with the following problem.[1] It has three clerical employees who must perform the following functions:

a. Maintain general ledger.

b. Maintain accounts payable ledger.

c. Maintain accounts receivable ledger.

d. Prepare checks for signature.

e. Maintain cash disbursements journal.

f. Issue credit memos on returns and allowances.

g. Reconcile the bank account.

h. Handle and deposit cash receipts.

'Assuming that there is no problem as to the ability of any of the employees, the company requests that you assign the above functions to the three employees in such a manner as to achieve the highest degree of internal control. It may be assumed that these employees will perform no other accounting functions other than the ones listed and that any accounting functions not listed will be performed by persons other than these three employees.

1. State how you would distribute the above functions among the three employees. Assume that, with the exception of the nominal jobs of the bank reconciliation and the issuance of credit memos on returns and allowances, all functions require an equal amount of time.

2. List four possible unsatisfactory combinations of the above listed functions.

3-2   Jerome Paper Company engaged you to revise its internal control system.[2] Jerome does not prelist cash receipts before they are recorded and has other weaknesses in processing collections of trade receivable, the company's largest asset. In discussing the matter with

---

[1] Adapted from the AICPA examination.

[2] Adapted from the AICPA examination.

the controller, you find he is chiefly interested in economy when he assigns duties to the 15 office personnel. He feels the main considerations are that the work should be done by people who are most familiar with it, capable of doing it, and available when it has to be done.

The controller says he has excellent control over trade receivables because receivables are pledged as security for a continually renewable bank loan, and the bank sends out positive confirmation requests occasionally, based on a list of pledged receivables furnished by the company each week. You learn that the bank's internal auditor is satisfied if he gets an acceptable response on 70 percent of his requests.

1. Explain how prelisting of cash receipts strengthens internal control over cash.

2. Assume that an employee handles cash receipts from trade customers before they are recorded. List the duties which that employee should not do, to withhold from him the opportunity to conceal embezzlement of cash receipts.

3. What are the implications to the bank, if during the bank auditor's examination of accounts receivable, some of a client's trade customers do not respond to his request for positive confirmation of their accounts?

3-3   The Patrick Company had poor internal control over its cash transactions.[3] Facts about its cash position at November 30, 1979 were as follows:

a. The cash books showed a balance of $18,901.62, which included undeposited receipts.

b. A credit of $100 on the bank's records did not appear on the company's books.

c. The balance per bank statement was $15,550.

d. Outstanding checks were: No. 62 for $116.25; No. 183 for $150.00; No. 284 for $253.25; No. 8621 for $190.71; No. 8623 for $206.80; and No. 8632 for $145.28.

The cashier abstracted all undeposited receipts in excess of $3,794.41 and prepared the following reconciliation:

Balance, per books, November 30, 1979		$18,901.62
Add: Outstanding checks:		
8621	$190.71	
8623	206.80	
8632	145.28	442.79
		$19,344.41
Less: Undeposited receipts		3,794.41
Balance per bank, November 30, 1979		15,550.00
Deduct: Unrecorded credit		100.00
True cash, November 30, 1979		$15,450.00

---

[3] Adapted from the AICPA examination.

1. Prepare a supporting schedule showing how much the cashier abstracted.

2. How did he attempt to conceal his theft?

3. Taking only the information given, name two specific features of internal control which were apparently missing.

3-4 Discuss briefly what you regard as the more important deficiencies in the system of internal control in the following situation; in addition, include what you consider to be a proper remedy for each deficiency.[4]

> The cashier of the Easy Company intercepted customer A's check payable to the company in the amount of $500 and deposited it in a bank account which was part of the company petty cash fund, of which he was custodian. He then drew a $500 check on the petty cash fund bank account payable to himself, signed it, and cashed it. At the end of the month, while processing the monthly statements to customers, he was able to change the statement to customer A so as to show that A had received credit for the $500 check that had been intercepted. Ten days later he made an entry in the cash received book which purported to record receipt of a remittance of $500 from customer A, thus restoring A's account to its proper balance, but overstating cash in bank. He covered the overstatement by omitting from the list of outstanding checks in the bank reconcilement, two checks, the aggregate amount of which was $500.

3-5 Henry Brown is a large independent contractor.[5] All employees are paid in cash because Brown believes this arrangement reduces clerical expenses and is preferred by his employees. You find in the petty cash fund approximately $200, of which $185 is stated to be unclaimed wages. Further investigation reveals that Brown has installed the procedure of putting any unclaimed wages in the petty cash fund so that the cash can be used for disbursements. When the claimant to the wages appears, he is paid from the petty cash fund. Brown contends that this procedure reduces the number of checks drawn to replenish the fund and centers the responsibility for all cash on hand in one person inasmuch as the petty cash custodian distributes the pay envelopes.

1. Does Brown's system provide proper internal control of unclaimed wages? Explain fully.

2. Because Brown insists in paying wages in cash, what procedures would you recommend to provide better internal control over unclaimed wages?

3-6 The Billou Company has an employee bond subscription plan under which employees subscribe to bonds and pay in installments by deductions from their salaries.[6]. The cashier keeps the supply of unissued bonds in a safe together with the records showing each employee's subscription and payments to date. The amounts of unissued bonds in the hands of the cashier and the balances due from employees are controlled on the general ledger,

---

[4] Adapted from the AICPA examination.

[5] Adapted from the AICPA examination.

[6] Adapted from the AICPA examination.

another department. However, the employees may, if they desire, pay any remaining balance to the cashier and receive their bonds.

When an employee makes a prepayment, the cashier notes the amount on his account, delivers the bond, and receives a receipt from the employee for the amount of the bond. The cashier deposits bond cash received in an employee bond bank account and submits a report showing the transaction to the general ledger department; this report is used as a basis for the necessary adjustments of the control accounts. Periodic surprise counts of bonds on hand are made by independent employees, who check the amounts of unissued bonds and employees' unpaid balances with the control accounts.

During the cashier's lunch hour or at other times when he is required to be absent from his position, another employee, with keys to the safe in which unissued bonds and employee bond payment records are kept, comes in and carries out the same procedures as enumerated above.

1. Point out the deficiencies in internal control and describe the errors or manipulations which might occur because of each weakness.

2. Recommend changes in procedures to eliminate those weaknesses.

3-7 Internal control is so important that accounting systems often contain methods, procedures, or a division of duties which appear wasteful to an outsider. For each of the following, explain why it is very important:

a. Having two financial officers, a treasurer and a controller.

b. Budgeting expenses and capital expenditures.

c. Requiring that every customer be given a cash register tape of their purchase.

d. Requiring cash disbursements be made by check when cash receipts for the day could be used.

e. Not allowing the bank to cash checks payable to the company, even when the company needs cash on hand.

f. Keeping voided checks even though they cannot be used and they take up space.

g. Reconciling the bank statement, even though the bank almost never makes a mistake.

h. Making a separate list of mail collections, even though the bank deposit slip will contain a breakdown of the cash received and deposited.

i. Approving all general journal entries, even though they are almost always routine.

j. Requiring prenumbered checks and sales invoices rather than simply stacks of available forms.

3-8 You have been recently engaged by the Alaska Branch of Far Distributing Company.[7] This branch has substantial annual sales which are billed and collected locally. As a part of your review you find that the procedures for handling cash receipts are as follows:

---

[7]Adapted from the AICPA examination.

a. Cash collections on over-the-counter sales and C.O.D. sales are received from the customer or delivery service by the cashier. Upon receipt of cash the cashier stamps the sales ticket "paid" and files a copy for future reference. The only record of C.O.D. sales is a copy of the sales ticket which is given to the cashier to hold until the cash is received from the delivery service.

b. Mail is opened by the credit manager's secretary and remittances are given to the credit manager for his review. The credit manager then places the remittances in a tray on the cashier's desk. At the daily deposit cut-off time the cashier delivers the checks and cash on hand to the assistant credit manager who prepares remittance lists and makes up the bank deposit which he also takes to the bank. The assistant credit manager also posts remittances to the accounts receivable ledger cards and verifies the cash discount allowable.

c. You also ascertain that the credit manager obtains approval from the executive office of Far Distributing Company, located in Chicago, to write off uncollectible accounts, and that he has retained in his custody as of the end of the fiscal year some remittances that were received on various days during last month.

1. Describe the irregularities that might occur under the procedures now in effect for handling cash collections and remittances.

2. Give procedures that you would recommend to strengthen internal control over cash collections and remittances.

3-9 The Generous Loan Company has 100 branch loan offices.[8] Each office has a manager and four or five subordinates who are employed by the manager. Branch managers prepare the weekly payroll, including their own salaries, and pay employees from cash on hand. The employee signs the payroll sheet signifying receipt of his salary. Hours worked by hourly personnel are inserted in the payroll sheet from timecards prepared by the employees and approved by the manager.

The weekly payroll sheets are sent to the home office along with other accounting statements and reports. The home office compiles employee earning records and prepares all federal and state salary reports from the weekly payroll sheets.

Salaries are established by home office job-evaluation schedules. Salary adjustments, promotions, and transfers of full-time employees are approved by a home office salary committee based upon the recommendations of branch managers and area supervisors. Branch managers advise the salary committee of new full-time employees and terminations. Part-time and temporary employees are hired without referral to the salary committee.

Based upon your review of the payroll system, how might funds for payroll be diverted?

3-10 The following information is available to you, and you can assume the November reconciliation is correct.[9]

---

[8] Adapted from the AICPA examination.

[9] Adapted from the AICPA examination.

Reconciliation November 30, 1979

Cash per general ledger	$ 2,631.74
Less—cash on hand	210.89
	2,420.85
Less—bank service charge for November	9.00
	2,411.85
Add—outstanding checks	991.00
Balance per bank	$ 3,402.85

Cash Receipts for December, 1979

December 1	Balance from 11/30	2,631.74
1	Received on accounts	403.25
2	Received on accounts	1,366.40
3	Received on accounts	974.86
4	Received on accounts	4,322.47
5	Received on accounts	5,201.89
7	Received on accounts	7,310.75
8	Received on accounts	6,195.18
9	Received on accounts	8,884.46
10	Received on accounts	10,227.55
11	Received on accounts	6,698.89
12	Received on accounts	210.20
14	Received on accounts	1,426.46
16	Received on accounts	400.00
17	Received on accounts	700.00
18	Received on accounts	2,709.82
21	Received on accounts	850.00
23	Received on accounts	1,100.00
27	Received on accounts	911.35
29	Received on accounts	3,875.50
		$65,300.77

Cash Payment Record for December 1979

December 1	Nov. service charge	9.00
3	Checks	5,236.50
5	Checks	3,645.21
8	Checks	16,394.89
10	Checks	15,873.42
12	Checks	3,123.47
14	Checks	475.42
17	Checks	1,250.00
19	Checks	3,622.83
22	Checks	3,692.09
26	Checks	3,456.45
31	Checks	4,201.25
Balance—December 31		4,311.24
		$65,300.77

Cash on hand December 31 amounted to $100. The transactions per the December bank statement, which are correctly recorded by the bank, show that deposits amounted to $62,870.92; checks paid amounted to $57,952.03; service charges for the month were $10; and a charge of $100 was made against the account because of the return unpaid of a customer's check. Neither the service charges nor the returned check were recorded on the client's books. The total of outstanding checks as of December 31 was found to amount to $4,110.50.

1. Prepare a four-column bank reconciliation for the month of December.

2. Include any explanations you consider necessary.

basic systems case

Outline

INTRODUCTION

In this chapter we introduce a sample company to illustrate the basic accounting system discussed in the preceding chapters and to serve as the framework for many of the discussions throughout the remainder of the book. It is important that you become very familiar with the sample company's organization, its employees and their duties, as well as the company's basic information flow. To the extent you do this now, much time will be saved later and the application of fundamental principles will come easier.

4.1 COMPANY BACKGROUND

In November, 1973, John Paul Pooper and his wife Pamela opened the Pooper Audio Center in New Orleans, Louisiana. The company was organized as a corporation with 2,000 shares of no-par common stock ($10 stated value), 1,200 shares of which were owned jointly by John Paul and his wife Pamela. The remainder of the shares were unissued. Pooper Audio Center (hereafter PAC-1) is a retail store selling a complete line of audio equipment, ranging from small and inexpensive radios to professional level components and systems. In addition, supporting equipment such as stereo headphones, needles, records, tapes, and cassettes account for a major share of PAC-1 sales volume.

So successful was PAC-1, that in June, 1976, J. P. and Pamela opened a second store designed to sell audio equipment plus a full complement of home appliances. This new store, called Pooper Appliance Center (hereafter PAC-2), also proved to be an immediate success primarily because of the substantial sales volume generated by the marketing of stoves, refrigerators and freezers, washing machines and dryers, dishwashers, air conditioners and televisions. The Poopers believe that the success of their stores is due to the courteous and knowledgeable staff and the friendly and efficient service for which the Pooper Centers are known. Prices at both stores on all merchandise are competitive, but not lower than those of competing stores.

For the fiscal year ended June 30, 1978, the company showed net sales of $1,800,000 and net income of $92,000. Although audio and appliance retail trade had become fiercely competitive in the past few years, both stores continued to increase sales volume at a remarkable rate. Sales per month for the remainder of this fiscal year are expected to be $60,000–$70,000 for PAC-1 and $130,000–$140,000 for PAC-2, with projected net income of $100,000–$110,000 for the fiscal year. PAC-1 sales have steadily been 75 percent cash and 25 percent credit while sales at PAC-2 have been consistently 75 percent credit and 25 percent cash. The firm has carried between 50 and 100 accounts receivable representing credit granted directly by the stores and regularly uses 15 to 20 different major suppliers of inventory items.

4.2 COMPANY ORGANIZATION

The Pooper Centers, Inc. employ twenty-one people including Mr. Pooper, who acts as president and general manager of the firm. Each store is supervised by a manager and, because both stores are open from 10:00 A.M. to 10:00 P.M. six days a week, there are two shifts of employees at each location. A shift at PAC-1 consists of two salespersons, with the most senior salesperson on each shift acting as assistant manager. At PAC-2, where sales volume is greater and customers expect more attention and time, a shift requires four salespersons. Here also, the most senior salesperson doubles as assistant manager. In all cases at both stores the assistant manager supervises the store in the absence of the manager.

All of Pooper's purchasing, accounting, and inventory control are centralized. A full-time buyer and a full-time accountant handle these functions. The accountant supervises a bookkeeper and inventory stock clerk. In addition, a janitor cleans and straightens both stores from 11:00 P.M. to 7:00 A.M. on Sunday through Friday evenings.

Mr. Pooper, the managers of PAC-1 and PAC-2, the buyer and the accountant form what J. P. likes to call his "management group." This group seems to get along quite well together and, at Pooper's insistence meet once a week, usually at lunch on Friday afternoons, to discuss company activities and plans. These meetings are very important to J. P. as a vehicle for making his feelings known to his key people and as a feedback mechanism enabling him to keep in touch with what is going on in the stores on a day-to-day basis. They also serve as a social event for the group. There is a good deal of talk and curiosity about and interest in these weekly meetings by other employees of the Pooper Centers.

4.3 COMPANY OPERATIONS

Pooper Centers, Inc. maintains a manual accounting system and information flow. In addition to a general journal, the company keeps a sales journal, purchases journal, cash receipts journal, and cash disbursements journal. Also, a subsidiary ledger system for receivables and payables is used. Transactions are recorded as the various supporting documents are received by the accountant's office, usually the day after the event occurs. Posting takes place at the end of each week. Company books are adjusted and closed and financial statements prepared for J. P. and Pamela Pooper monthly.

Documents typically used by the firm include checks (incoming and outgoing), cash register tapes, sales slips, purchase orders, shipping reports, and debit and credit memos. The creation and flow of these documents and the roles of each of the employees in this flow is described below.

J. P. Pooper prefers assigning himself a minimum of specific duties in the firm. Since beginning his organization, he has enjoyed becoming involved in all aspects of company activities as the mood strikes him and that continues today. J. P. has always been an audio buff, however, and still feels more comfortable in this end of the business, particularly when dealing with people. He is thirty-two years old and Pooper Centers, Inc., which he started with a trust fund received upon graduation from college, has been his only business venture of any consequence. John Paul Pooper delegates authority easily, expects responsible performance by his employees, and is generally well liked by those who work for him.

Because of his love for "sound" and the "people" end of the business, J. P. is probably personally closest to the firm's buyer and the manager of PAC-1. Both are young and enjoy the complete confidence of the owner, but must often accept large amounts of advice from him on how best to do their jobs. The buyer is responsible for all merchandise purchases made by both stores and he makes all decisions relating to which vendor or supplier to use. What to purchase, the timing of purchases and reorder points are established by constant discussions between the buyer, PAC-1 manager, PAC-2 manager, accountant and sometimes Pooper himself. The discussions are informal and in the final analysis the buyer's decisions prevail on all purchasing matters. When a purchase of merchandise has been decided upon, the buyer prepares a purchase order of the type illustrated in Figure 4-1. An original and three copies are prepared, with the original going to the vendor, the buyer keeping one copy, and the accountant receiving the other two. As a matter of practice, the buyer forwards all major purchase orders to J. P. for his perusal before they are finalized. The buyer spends a good deal of time in each store checking inventory quantities and discussing sales patterns with store managers. He makes it a practice to be present, along with the inventory stock clerk, when major shipments of merchandise arrive and often personally checks the goods and compares the shipping report accompanying the goods to his purchase order. The buyer is known around the firm and among vendors to be very careful (some even say picky) about the goods he accepts. When merchandise is deemed unacceptable for one reason or another, it is physically separated, and the buyer prepares a four-copy debit memorandum as shown in Figure 4-2. The buyer retains one copy, which is

PURCHASE ORDER
POOPER CENTERS, INC.

			No. _____
To: _____		Date _____	
_____			
_____			
_____		Shipping Instructions: _____	
		_____	
Ship To:			
_____			
_____		Terms: _____	
_____		_____	

Quantity	Description	Unit Price	Total

Ordered By: _____

FIGURE 4-1 Sample Company Purchase Order

forwarded to the accountant after verification by the supplier, the original is immediately forwarded to the vendor, one copy stays with the goods to be returned, and the accountant receives one copy. Some travel is required of the buyer, but most purchases are made through catalogs and personal contacts in the industry which have been developed by hard work.

The store managers have approximately the same duties, although their personal styles and approach to their jobs are quite different. The PAC-2 manager is much the older of the two and possesses substantial experience in appliance sales as appliance manager of a major department store. He is much less interested in the audio equipment component of PAC-2 merchandise and feels that the people at PAC-1 are better equipped to handle this kind of product. He is also more autocratic in style and considerably less close to the salespersons in his store than is the PAC-1 manager. Of the people in the management group, the PAC-2 manager gets along best

DEBIT MEMORANDUM
POOPER CENTERS, INC.

Date: _____

To: _____

_____

_____

_____

Purchase Order No. _____

Quantity	Description	Unit Price	Total

Returned By: _____

FIGURE 4-2 Sample Company Debit Memorandum

with the accountant. Each manager in his own way supervises his store; evaluates the performance of his salespersons; approves all customer checks and returns of merchandise; is responsible for the layout and display of merchandise; oversees the movement of goods from the stockroom to the sales floor; and occasionally waits on special customers or helps out if the store is particularly busy. Each manager must also see to it that all documents generated in his store are forwarded to the accountant by the day following their creation, and that cash sales receipts are deposited intact in the bank twice each work day.

Documents originating in the stores themselves include cash register tapes, some customer checks, sales slips, and credit memos. All sales employees have access to all store cash registers while on duty. Cash registers have special keys which all salespersons use to record the quantity sold, the stock number of the item, the unit price and total price of the items, and the total amount of the sale, in addition to a code to identify the person entering the transaction for each cash sale and each cash refund made. One copy of the tape goes to the customer as a receipt while a second internally stored copy automatically keeps a cumulative total of cash sales and cash refunds. Twice a day, first thing each morning and late in the afternoon, store managers remove these internally stored tapes from all registers together with cash and checks except for $100 in small bills and change. The store managers prepare bank deposit slips from the tapes and deposit intact the cash and checks from the registers into the bank. One copy of the deposit slip together with the cash register tapes is brought to the accountant's office twice daily.

Sales slips in three copies, as illustrated in Figure 4-3, are prepared only for credit sales. Credit sales made on charge accounts already opened and in good standing are handled by the

SALES SLIP
POOPER CENTERS, INC.

No. _____

Salesperson	Date / /	Store
Account No.		Approval Code
Name		Telephone No.
Address		
City	State	Zip
Delivery Instructions:		

Quantity	Stock No.	Description	Unit Price	Total

X _____
Customer Signature

FIGURE 4-3 Sample Company Sales Slip

salesperson if the total amount of the sale transaction is under $50. If a credit sale amounts to $50 or more, the salesperson must receive approval from the accountant's office or, if that is not possible, from his store manager. Lists of accounts not in good standing or over their credit limit are prepared each week and sent to each store.

The initial credit application for all new accounts must be approved by the accountant and a credit limit set. Credit sales slips and supporting information on new account customers are collected at the store and forwarded to the accountant for credit approval before merchandise is released to the customer. All copies of approved credit sales slips are returned to the store manager usually within one week. All copies of disapproved credit sales slips are retained by the accountant. One copy of each sales slip is given to the credit customer; the original and one copy are delivered to the accountant twice daily.

On January 1 of this year Pooper Centers began accepting a major credit card for sales in both stores. For all credit card sales, telephone approval for the charge is secured by the salesperson from the credit card agency. The credit card customer gets one copy of the Pooper sales slip and one copy of the credit card sales slip. The original of both is stapled together and forwarded to the accountant; the third copy of both is sent to the credit card agency. A fee of 5 percent of the total gross credit card sales is charged by the credit card agency for billing and servicing these accounts. Pooper Centers always receives from the credit card agency 95 percent of its credit card sales in cash within three to four weeks of reporting the sales to the agency. Major credit card sales are recorded by Pooper each week.

Credit memos must be prepared for all goods returned, either for cash or to reduce an account balance, and all returns must be approved by the store manager. If the return is for cash, the transaction appears on the cash register tape and copies of the credit memo go to the accountant. When the return involves a reduction in the customer's account balance, one copy of the credit memo goes to the customer and one copy to the accountant. Figure 4-4 shows the form of a credit memo for Pooper Centers, Inc.

The firm's information flow and all supporting documents eventually converge on the office of the accountant where each type of document is filed separately by the date of the transaction and, if more than one copy has been received by the accountant, by customer or supplier also. The accountant is very experienced in small businesses and manual accounting systems and took this job with Pooper Centers, Inc. at the time PAC-2 was opened. He is a hard worker, but sees his current position as low pressure compared to earlier jobs. Since both he and the PAC-2 manager joined the firm at the same time and are considerably older than the other three members of the management team, they have become very close within the company and socially.

The accountant supervises a bookkeeper, the inventory stock clerk, and the janitor. The bookkeeper records all transactions and events from source documents which reach the accountant's office. From the buyer come purchase orders and debit memos; from the store managers come cash register tapes, sales slips, and credit memos. One copy of each purchase order is kept by the bookkeeper and one copy is given to the inventory stock clerk to be matched against the shipping report when the goods arrive. The inventory stock clerk has become something of a protégé of the buyer, carefully observing his style and technique in evaluating merchandise and, at the suggestion of the buyer, studying catalogs, product comparisons, and pricing structures. The clerk obviously admires the buyer's skill, is ambitious, and wants to learn as much as possible from his job. A primary duty of the stock clerk is to be present when all shipments of goods arrive (there is usually one shipment per week) to help the

CREDIT MEMORANDUM
POOPER CENTERS, INC.

No._____

Salesperson		Date / /	Store
Account No.		Approval Code	
Name		Telephone No.	
Address			
City		State	Zip

Quantity	Stock No.	Description	Unit Price	Total

Approved By _____

FIGURE 4-4 Sample Company Credit Memorandum

buyer check the shipment. If the shipment is accurate and merchandise is in good shape, the shipping report accompanying the goods is attached to the clerk's copy of the purchase order and both are returned to the accountant. If inaccuracies or damaged goods materialize, debit memos are prepared by the buyer.

✔ The clerk is also responsible for keeping order in the stockrooms, which are located in the rear of each store, and assists in the movement of inventory on to the sales floor of the stores at the direction of the store managers. Occasionally, the clerk moves goods from one store location to the other or picks up specially shipped goods from nearby locations. The buyer has come to appreciate the clerk's energy and abilities and makes considerable informal use of his familiarity with the inventory of both stores.

The bookkeeper actually records all transactions under the guidance and supervision of the accountant. She feels overworked and feels that she could do the entire job alone for less money than the accountant is currently being paid. Some support has been given these feelings by the manager of PAC-1 with whom the bookkeeper has formed a relationship. At any rate, most incoming documents physically go to the bookkeeper for checking and recording. Bank deposit slips and cash register tapes are recorded and held to be compared by the bookkeeper to the bank statement received each month and then discarded if there are no discrepancies in the bank reconciliation. Discrepancies are immediately reported to the accountant and the deposit slips and cash register tapes are held to clear discrepancies. Debit memos, sales slips representing completed sales, and credit memos are also recorded as received and filed by day.

The accountant handles on a continuing basis only sales slips which require initial credit approval, and incoming and outgoing checks. For credit purposes he analyzes supporting information on the customer, follows up on the information where necessary, and uses standard credit rating agencies for additional information. If credit is approved, the store manager is notified and sales slips are returned to the store. The sale then goes through the normal sales slip processing cycle. The monthly billings to customers and incoming checks from customers are both processed personally by the accountant, so that the chance of an error in a customer's account is absolutely minimized.

It is the policy of the accountant, with total support from J. P. Pooper, that the firm take all available discounts on purchases. Since this had not been a common practice prior to the opening of PAC-2, the accountant views this policy as a major contribution to the company's financial health. All outgoing Pooper Centers, Inc. checks, no matter the purpose or amount, must be signed by both the accountant and J. P. Pooper.

The work force at Pooper Centers, Inc. has been very stable over the years primarily because the employees feel that they are well paid and that J. P. and the other management people are fair and evenhanded. J. P. Pooper in the past fiscal year took a salary of $50,000 for himself; the buyer, managers and accountant are paid $20,000 per year each; and the bookkeeper, stock clerk, and janitor earn $800, $600, and $500 per month respectively for 40-, 40-, and 48-hour work weeks. Salespersons at each store average $1,200 per month, and assistant managers average $1,400 per month on a compensation plan that includes a small base salary ($200 for salespersons and $400 for assistant managers) and a commission on sales. The accountant together with the bookkeeper manually calculate amounts due to salespersons from an analysis of their individual sales totals. In fact, the accountant handles the entire payroll and issues paychecks to all employees.

The newest employee in the firm is a secretary hired by J. P. Pooper to handle the typing of all company correspondence including company checks, purchase orders, and debit memos. In addition, she has responsibility for filing all company documents, opening mail, and various other office duties. It is clear to everyone in the firm that the secretary works directly for J. P. and she will do no typing other than that discussed above for anyone else. She earns $600 per month for 40 hours work each week.

Pooper Centers, Inc. has grown so rapidly during the past several years that J. P. has become concerned about the ability of the firm's current organizational structure and manual accounting system to serve the needs of the company. As of January, 1979, certain operational and control problems had begun to surface which seemed to threaten the success of the company. An overall review of the basic structure, information flow, and accounting procedures used by the firm appears to be in order.

4.4 COMPANY BOOKS

Following is the chart of accounts and post-closing ledger balances for the company as of year-end, 1978.

Pooper Centers, Inc.
Schedule of General Ledger Accounts
December 31, 1978

	Account	Balance
100	Cash	$ 35,000
110	Accounts receivable	80,000
111	Allowance for bad debts	4,000
120	Inventory—appliances	150,000
121	Inventory—audio	80,000
122	Inventory—other	10,000
130	Supplies	1,000
140	Prepaid insurance	4,000
141	Prepaid advertising	6,000
160	Furniture and fixtures	30,000
161	Accumulated dep.—F & F	15,500
170	Station wagon	6,000
171	Accumulated dep.—SW	3,100
200	Accounts payable	122,329
220	Income taxes payable	—
230	Interest payable	—
231	Federal withholding payable	4,441
232	FICA payable	2,630
233	Federal unemployment payable	—
234	State unemployment payable	—
300	Common stock	12,000
310	Paid in capital in excess of par	48,000
350	Retained earnings	190,000
390	Income summary	—
400	Cash sales	—
401	Credit sales	—
410	Sales returns	—
450	Interest revenue	—
500	Purchases	—
501	Purchase returns	—
502	Purchase discounts	—
503	Transportation—In	—
505	Cost of goods sold	—
510	Bad debts expense	—
515	Supplies expense	—
520	Insurance expense	—
525	Advertising expense	—
530	Depreciation expense	—
535	Income tax expense	—
540	Salaries expense	—
545	Commission expense	—
550	Payroll tax expense	—
555	Utilities expense	—
560	Rent expense	—
565	Interest expense	—
570	Miscellaneous expense	—

Amounts owed to Pooper Centers, Inc. by individual customers at year-end were:

	Account	Balance
11001	Uptown Const. Co.	$ 50,000
11002	Lil' Pig Laundermat	21,200
11007	Wrigley Wright	1,000
11019	Akbar Ikbar	700
11031	Harold Shadrack	900
11044	Marvin Meshack	500
11045	Bruce Abendigo	1,200
11046	Iona Carr	1,500
11069	I. M. Woman	1,200
11081	Sterling Silver	800
11082	Cherry Herring	1,000

Amounts owed by Pooper Centers, Inc. to individual suppliers at year-end were:

	Account	Balance
20001	Mardi Gras Distributors	$ 8,329
20020	Panasonic	12,000
20022	Sony	15,000
20045	Westinghouse	40,000
20049	General Electric	47,000

50 Sunbeam.

4.5 COMPANY TRANSACTIONS FOR A MONTH

During January, Pooper Centers, Inc. engaged in the following transactions and events. The date given for each occurrence represents the day on which that transaction or event took place.

January 2 Issued check number 469 to Zingblat Realtors in the amount of $15,000 for January rent on both stores.

3 Recorded cash sales for January 2 of $3,000. Issued check number 470 to Sony, Inc. for amount owed less 2 percent discount. Received check from Marvin Meshack settling his account in full. Purchased office supplies from Staff of Life, Inc. with check number 471 in the amount of $250.

4 Recorded cash sales for January 3 of $3,200. Prepared and mailed purchase order to Mardi Gras Distributors for records and tapes in the amount of $5,000. Received check from Lil' Pig for $5,300.

5 Recorded cash sales for January 4 of $2,900. Received shipment of small appliances from Sunbeam; the shipping report was included in the amount of $4,700, with terms 2/10 net 30. Received bill from the Post-Times-Dispatch-Courier-Journal for newspaper advertising of $3,500. Credit sales for the week were as follows:

Akbar Ikbar	$ 700
Uptown Construction	10,000
Major Credit Cards	14,500

change to A/P and adv. prepaid

8   Recorded cash sales for January 5 of $4,100 and January 6 of $5,500. Mr. Ikbar returned $200 of defective audio equipment and received credit for that amount. Received $200 from Cherry Herring and $50 from I. M. Woman.

9   Recorded cash sales for January 8 of $2,700. Returned defective audio equipment to Panasonic; issued debit memo in the amount of $150. Purchased from Honest Arnold Auto Sales a delivery truck for $10,000 with check number 472. The truck's useful life was expected to be 5 years with a $500 salvage value. The company plans to utilize double-declining balance depreciation on the truck.

10   Recorded cash sales for January 9 of $3,350. Received check from Uptown Construction of $15,000. Sent check number 473 to General Electric for December purchases totaling $10,000 less 2 percent discount. Issued check number 474 to Westinghouse for December purchases totaling $12,000 less 2 percent discount.

11   Recorded cash sales of $2,975 for January 10. John Paul arranged a line of credit of $100,000 with the Blank Bank & Trust and immediately used the line of credit to borrow $50,000. Included in cash sales of January 9 was a check for $500 from Iona Carr that was intended to be a payment on her account.

12   Recorded cash sales of $3,100 for January 11. Received checks on account from Harold Shadrack for $200. Also, received check from Bruce Abendigo for $350. Issued check number 475 to Sunbeam for amount due. Credit sales for the week were as follows:

Trip the Lite Fantastik Disco	$10,000
Lil' Pig Laundermat	1,600
Major Credit Cards	16,300

15   Recorded cash sales for January 12 of $3,900 and January 13 of $5,600. Issued check number 476 to the Big Brother Bank to pay the amounts due on federal withholding and FICA which appear as liabilities. Paid the bookkeeper, stock clerk, secretary and janitor with checks 477 to 480. Each earns one-half of a month's salary and is paid that amount less deductions. Deductions for each individual are 10 percent of gross pay for federal withholding and 6 percent for FICA. Additionally, the company records its share of the FICA tax as payroll tax expense at this time.

16   Recorded cash sales for January 15 of $2,825. Received a call from Mardi Gras Distributors that notified us that merchandise amounting to $500 on the purchase order of January 4 was out of stock and will require one month to deliver; the remaining goods are in-transit, F.O.B. destination. Issued check 481 to Staff of Life for $150 of office supplies and $225 of store supplies.

17   Recorded cash sales for January 16 of $2,900. Received check from Mr. Ikbar for $700. Received shipping report for audio equipment (dated 1/10/79) from Sony.

The amount was $40,000 for merchandise and $425 for transportation. Terms were 1 percent discount if paid within 30 days. Issued check 482 to the Post Office for $100 of stamps.

18 Recorded cash sales for January 17 of $3,250. Determined $750 worth of merchandise was not included in the shipment from Sony. Accordingly, a debit memorandum was prepared. Received check from Uptown Construction for $15,000.

19 Recorded cash sales for January 18 of $3,100. Sold the station wagon to the stock clerk for $1,000. Pooper Centers' policy is to take a full month's depreciation on assets purchased in the first half of the month or sold in the last half. No depreciation is taken for the month if the sale occurs in the first half or the purchase occurs in the last half. The station wagon had been depreciated on a straight-line basis at the rate of $100 per month. Credit sales for the week were:

Uptown Construction	$12,000
Wrigley Wright	500
Major Credit Cards	14,100

22 Recorded cash sales for January 19 of $4,400 and January 20 of $5,200. Borrowed another $40,000 from the Blank Bank & Trust on our line of credit. Issued check number 483 to Westinghouse and check number 484 to General Electric to pay our account in full.

23 Recorded cash sales for January 22, of $2,975. Received shipping report for merchandise of $4,500 from Mardi Gras Distributors. Shipment was in satisfactory condition and there was no freight charge. Returns of merchandise for cash by customers amounted to $50.

24 Recorded cash sales for January 23 of $3,105. Received call from Mardi Gras Distributors requesting immediate payment of balance in full. Prepared purchase orders for General Electric and Westinghouse for merchandise in the amounts of $23,000 and $21,500 respectively. Issued check number 485 to Natural Gas of the South, Inc. in the amount of $4,600 for utilities for the month.

25 Recorded cash sales for January 24 of $3,225. Paid the Post-Times-Dispatch-Courier-Journal in full with check number 486. Received shipment from Westinghouse on a December purchase order in the amount of $45,000 for merchandise with related freight of $2,100. Received check for $250 from Sterling Silver.

26 Recorded cash sales for January 25 of $2,910. Credit sales for the week were:

I. M. Woman	$ 300
Major Credit Cards	11,000
House of Pleasure Apartments	16,000

V Received a bill from the Hard Rock Cafe for four weekly lunches for the management group for $246. Issued check number 487 to pay bill in full.

29 Recorded cash sales for January 26 of $4,300 and January 27 of $4,900. Issued check number 488 to Superdome Sewerage and Water Board for $130. Issued check number 489 to South Central Taco Bell for telephone service for $690. Issued check number 490 to Oxbow Oil Company for $210 for gasoline and maintenance on delivery vehicles. Received reimbursement of credit card sales for the week ending January 5, less 5 percent credit card company service fee.

30 Recorded cash sales for January 29 of $2,800. Issued check numbers 491 to 494 to the bookkeeper, stock clerk, secretary, and janitor for the second semimonthly pay period. Data for this pay period are the same as that given for January 15. Paid J. P. Pooper, buyer, accountant, and both store managers with check numbers 495 to 499. Each earns one-twelfth of a year's salary and is paid that amount less deductions. Deductions for each individual are 20 percent of gross pay for federal withholding and 6 percent for FICA. Each salesman and assistant manager earned $1,000 in commissions plus his base salary; deductions were then 15 percent of gross pay for federal withholding and 6 percent for FICA. Issued check numbers 500 to 511 for the salesmen and assistant managers. Additionally, the company records its share of the FICA tax as payroll tax expense at this time. State unemployment is 2.7 percent of the first $4,200 of salary and commissions for each employee and federal unemployment is 0.5 percent of the same amounts. The amounts are recorded at the end of the month as payroll tax expense.

31 Recorded cash sales for January 30 of $2,975. Discovered defective merchandise from Sunbeam shipment in the amount of $500. Prepared debit memo with request for cash refund. House of Pleasure Apartments returned $2,000 of stoves and refrigerators as defective.

February 1 Recorded cash sales for January 31 of $3,125. Credit sales for the last days of the month were:

Wrigley Wright	$ 800
I. M. Woman	200
Wo Fat Construction Co.	8,200
Major Credit Cards	9,500

Additional information as of the end of January, 1979:

1. The accountant estimates that 2 percent of credit sales would never be collected by Pooper.

2. Ending inventories are calculated on a LIFO periodic basis. A physical count of inventory showed the following cost of merchandise on hand:

Appliances	$95,000
Audio	90,000
Other	4,500

3. Supplies on hand are $1,200.

4. Prepaid insurance is $2,000.

5. Prepaid advertising is $2,500.

6. Furniture and fixtures are estimated to last 5 years with no salvage value. Straight-line depreciation is used.

7. Carrying charges of 1 percent per month multiplied by the accounts receivable balance at the beginning of the month are added to all accounts receivable outstanding at the beginning of the month which are not paid-in-full during the month. Partial payments and new purchases during the month do not affect the interest calculation.

8. The bank loan carries an interest rate of 10 percent annually. Interest will be accrued each month on the loan although a payment is not due until July 1, 1979.

9. Pooper Centers, Inc. pays corporate taxes at an annual rate of 22 percent on the first $50,000 of taxable income and 48 percent for the excess.

exercises

4-1 Develop a sales journal and an accounts receivable subsidiary ledger for Pooper Centers. Journalize all sales journal transactions and post them to the appropriate general and subsidiary ledger accounts.

4-2 Develop a purchases journal and an accounts payable subsidiary ledger for Pooper Centers. Journalize all purchases journal transactions and post them to the appropriate general and subsidiary ledger accounts.

4-3 Develop a cash receipts journal for Pooper Centers. Journalize all cash receipts journal transactions and post them to the appropriate general and subsidiary ledger accounts. (Note: you will have to use the accounts receivable subsidiary ledger developed in Exercise 4-1 above.)

4-4 Develop a cash disbursements journal for Pooper Centers. Journalize all cash disbursements journal transactions and post them to the appropriate general and subsidiary ledger accounts. (Note: you will have to use the accounts payable subsidiary ledger developed in Exercise 4-2 above.)

4-5 Notice that many cash disbursements are related to payroll. Note also that these payroll transactions are almost identical each time they occur. Because of the repetitive nature of payroll-related cash disbursements, many businesses find it useful to separate these transactions from other cash disbursements by creating a special payroll journal called a *payroll register.* Develop a payroll register for Pooper Centers as you think it should be designed and journalize all payroll transactions in this special journal. Foot and balance this new payroll journal. Redevelop the cash disbursements journal without payroll-related cash disbursements, eliminating any columns which are now unnecessary.

4-6 Develop a general journal for Pooper Centers. Journalize all external transactions appropriate to this journal and post them to the general and subsidiary ledger accounts.

4-7   Incorporating all of the information recorded and classified in Exercises 4-1 through 4-6, prepare a trial balance for Pooper Centers as of January 31, 1979.

4-8   Journalize and post all end-of-period adjusting entries for Pooper Centers and prepare an adjusted trial balance as of January 31, 1979.

4-9   Prepare an income statement, retained earnings statement, and balance sheet, all in good form, for Pooper Centers. Keep in mind that these statements are intended primarily for J. P. Pooper's information and use, and design them accordingly. ~~Close the books for the period and prepare them for February's activities.~~

4-10 Using your knowledge of the organization structure, personalities, and accounting system at Pooper Centers, discuss five specific internal control problems which currently exist in the firm. For each of these areas of internal control difficulty make a recommendation as to how the problem might be solved.

part II

systems analysis

systems analysis techniques

outline

5.1 **Organization charts**: levels of authority in the organization; common organization chart errors.

5.2 **Introduction to flowcharting**: standard symbols and basic conventions of flowcharting.

5.3 **Flowchart of a sales system**: processing sales through a company from the original customer order to the beginning of the accounts receivable system; system flowchart; importance of the six-part invoice.

5.4 **Flowchart of an accounts receivable system**: processing accounts receivable and cash receipts; importance of flowcharts.

5.5 **Other systems analysis techniques**: documents flowcharts; decision tables and internal control questionnaires.

INTRODUCTION

In earlier chapters you were introduced to accounting concepts and their implementation. You became familiar with the complete accounting cycle from the original journal entry to the financial statements, with the necessity of internal control, and with some of the details of internal control techniques. In Chapter 4 you applied this material to a realistic example. Thus, to this point everything has been given to you, and you, in effect, have been told: this is the way it is.

In this and the next chapter we adopt a more critical or analytical approach. The problem we are now concerned with is the following:

> Suppose we are given a specific system. Our task is to determine how well the system accomplishes its objectives. If there are any deficiencies or omissions, we would like to point them out. Finally, we want to make specific recommendations to improve the system to better accomplish its objectives.

This task is called *system analysis.* The term system analysis is appropriate because that is exactly what we are doing—analyzing a system. Certainly, system analysis is interesting in its own right, but it is done primarily as the first step toward a larger purpose. This larger purpose might be:

1. *To undertake a new activity.* This would include, for example, the establishment and use of a perpetual inventory system in a firm which has only used a periodic system.

2. *To expand an existing activity.* This might include the extension of a perpetual inventory system to include a larger percentage of inventory or the addition of a new branch store.

3. *To take advantage of technological changes.* The availability of a new type of cash register may make it possible for a retail store to utilize an entirely different method of checkout or price markings.

4. *To correct mistakes in an existing system.* No system is perfect, but sometimes a major deficiency is identified which should be corrected.

Before we would act in any of the above situations, we would want to know exactly what is now being done. Only then can we put our actions in proper perspective and determine how they affect the organization and the present system.

You will probably not be surprised, then, to learn that people who do this work are called *systems analysts.* Actually, systems analysts do more than systems analysis. If the system under analysis is so bad or so out-of-date that it cannot be corrected, the systems analyst is often asked to develop a new system. The design of new systems is then also the task of systems analysts. However, we will defer consideration of systems design until Part Three. In this chapter and the next, we will be exclusively concerned with systems analysis.

Before we go further, we should discuss the basic steps of systems analysis to show where this and the next chapter fit into the overall picture. The five basic steps of systems analysis are then:

1. *Determine the system to be analyzed* and the objectives of the system. In other words, decide what system we are going to look at and what that system is supposed to accomplish. Actually, this is often the most difficult or creative step in systems analysis. For the moment, however, we will be dealing with standard systems and will assume the objectives of the system are to accomplish the standard goals in the most efficient manner possible.

2. *Understand the system* and fully document its operation. Here we wish to comprehend how the system works. An important question to keep in mind is: How does this company make a dollar? We also wish to have in writing a complete discussion of all system procedures, control techniques, documents, and forms. This documentation is necessary for (a) communication with others, (b) assurance that the work is complete, and (c) backup for the later steps presented below.

3. *Analyze the present system* and discern any deficiencies and omissions. At this point you must bring to bear your knowledge of accounting theory, accounting systems, and internal control to identify weaknesses in the system under analysis. These weaknesses might include improper accounting treatment of transactions (such as not capitalizing assets appropriately), poor document or form design, lack of timeliness in report generation, inadequate internal control, as well as many others.

4. *Develop cost-effective recommendations* that the company can implement to correct any system deficiencies. Of course, all your recommendations should be cost effective. In other words, the benefits of the recommendations should exceed their implementation costs; otherwise, the effort will not be worthwhile. Keep in mind, however, that the present system might be so bad that its correction or modernization would not be worth the trouble. Thus, the only recommendation possible might be to scrap the old system after developing a new one.

5. *Prepare a report* which documents and supports all the materials and work done in the four earlier steps. You must communicate your results to others who are in a position to implement your recommendations. This communication will be in part oral presentation and verbal discussion, but will be primarily in written report form. Since many people will only see the report, the report must sell your analysis and your recommendations. If the report is a mere collection of facts, it is inadequate. The report must have a theme and must build in a coherent manner to the recommendations. We will discuss this further in the next chapter.

We will focus now on basic techniques: the organization chart, the flowchart decision tables and questionnaires; these will prove invaluable in systems analysis. In the next chapter, we will use all we have learned (including these techniques) to perform a specific systems analysis of Pooper Centers. But in order to do that you must become completely familiar with the organization chart and flowchart. Both are based upon the same concept: draw a picture of the situation to better understand it. You are familiar, of course, with all the cliches about pictures being worth a thousand words. Also, as you may know, the first step in physics, engineering, or applied mathematics problems is usually to draw a picture prior to analysis and problem solution. The purposes of the two techniques can then be stated:

1. The organization chart is designed to portray the structure of responsibility and authority in the company; that is, who is in charge of what and who reports to whom.

2. The flowchart is designed to show the procedures and document flow of the accounting system; in other words, who does what and what they do it with.

5-1 ORGANIZATION CHARTS

Levels of Authority

An example of an organization chart for a hypothetical firm, French Quarter Company, Inc. appears in Figure 5-1 and shows the lines of authority and areas of responsibility in a trading corporation. The highest level of authority is the board of directors, and it is represented by the highest box. The president is hired by the board of directors and serves at its pleasure. For this reason the box representing the president lies below that of the board of directors and a vertical line connects them. Similarly, there are a number of people reporting to the president. In this company they are the sales manager, the secretary-treasurer, the controller, and the general manager. All of these people have approximately comparable areas of responsibility, and since they all report to the president, their relationship to him is represented by vertical lines. The chart gives a more understandable appearance if the lines flow either horizontally or vertically and not at an angle. Figure 5-1 shows the preferred schematic representation of the relationship between the president and those who report to him.

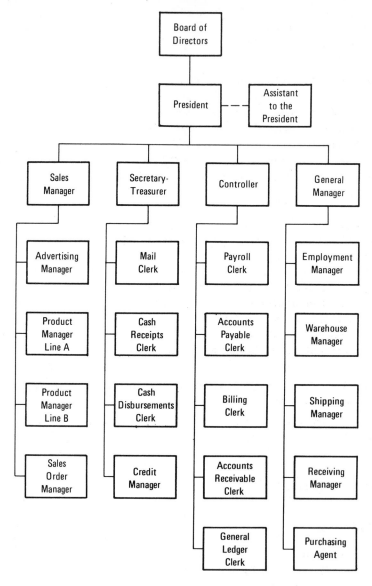

FIGURE 5-1 Sample Organization Chart

There are a number of people who are not strictly in this organizational chain of command. These people are the staff, such as executive assistants, administrative assistants, and advisors of various sorts. We represent people in these positions by putting them on the same "level" as the person to whom they report and by connecting them with horizontal, dotted lines. One example appears in Figure 5-1, the assistant to the president.

As noted above, the way the president is connected to the sales manager, the secretary-treasurer, the controller, and the general manager is the preferred method of connecting one level of authority to the next. However, this method is not always practical because the material becomes too cumbersome and difficult to condense in this manner. In Figure 5-1, the advertising manager, the product manager of line A, the product manager of line B, and the sales order manager all report to the sales manager. Similarly, four people report to the secretary-treasurer and five people each to the controller and to the general manager. As you can see, if we continued in our pyramid fashion, the pyramid would rapidly become huge. One approach then would be to put each subpyramid on a separate chart; thus, there would be an individual organization chart for the sales manager, the secretary-treasurer, the controller, and the general manager. Our approach is slightly different because we wish to put the whole chart in one picture, so the entire situation can be comprehended in a glance. Everyone reporting to each of these four officers is put under the appropriate officer in the chart. The connecting lines, however, are drawn to show the levels of authority. To return to the sales manager, the chart shows the advertising manager, the managers of product lines A and B, and the sales order manager are all the same level of authority and all report to the sales manager.

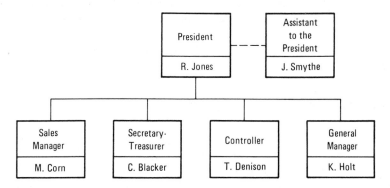

FIGURE 5-2 Named Organizational Chart

A slightly different approach is shown in Figure 5-2, where the name of the person occupying each of the positions is put in the box along with the title of the position. You would need such specific identification when developing an organization chart for the first time, since people would not be used to titles, just personalities. Or if you were proposing a new organization structure it would be helpful to see where each person would fit into the overall picture and where new people would need to be hired.

Common Organization Chart Errors

Several mistakes are commonly made in drawing organization charts. The first appears in Figure 5-3. As you see, the assistant to the president is drawn at the same level as the managers and financial officers. This is understandable, since the assistant also reports to the president. However, you should remember the organization chart also gives the chain of command and the

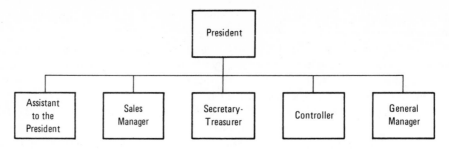

FIGURE 5-3 Organization Chart Error

assistant is not really part of the chain of command. Thus, as we discussed above, the assistant is drawn out to the right of the president. The second mistake appears in Figure 5-4. In this chart, everyone who reports to the president is connected by a separate line. This approach makes the chart hard to read and should not be used. The third mistake appears in Figure 5-5. In this chart everyone who reports to the secretary-treasurer is drawn under him. Unlike the approach of Figure 5-1, however, there is simply one line drawn down through all the boxes. Unfortunately, this is extremely misleading; it appears that the mail clerk reports to the secretary-treasurer, the cash receipts clerk reports to the mail clerk, the cash disbursements clerk reports to the cash receipts clerk, and the credit manager reports to the cash disbursements clerk.

It is important that you review Figure 5-1 because we will illustrate system flowcharting using this organizational pattern.

5-2 INTRODUCTION TO FLOWCHARTING

As we discussed earlier in the chapter, a flowchart is a picture which shows the processing steps and document flows of a system—a picture of how the system works. You may have been exposed to flowcharting in a computer science or programming course. However, we distinguish here between a *program flowchart*, which is the flowchart of an individual computer program,

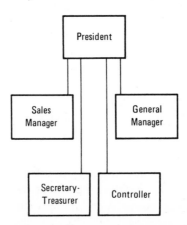

FIGURE 5-4 Organization Chart Error

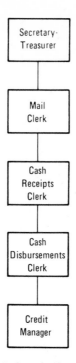

FIGURE 5-5 Organization Chart Error

and a *systems flowchart*, which is the flowchart of the entire system including manual processing and document flows.

The flowchart should be developed in as standard a way as possible for three reasons: (1) every person drawing a flowchart should not have to generate his own method (i.e., reinvent the wheel); (2) different flowcharts developed by different people should be roughly comparable; and (3) if a person can understand one flowchart, he should be able to understand all flowcharts.

Standard Flowchart Symbols

The only way to develop standard flowcharts is to use standard symbols and use them in a standard way. Figure 5-6 provides the standard symbols we need for flowcharting. But before introducing these symbols and discussing their application to a simplified sales system, some brief introductory comments describing this sales system may prove helpful. Then, we will go over the flowchart of the system. The system begins with the customer, who sends in a written order. The sales department then takes this order, prepares a six-part invoice, and files the order by customer name. The invoice set then goes to the credit department for a credit check, comparing that customer's present balance and proposed sale with his credit limit. If the credit is rejected, the customer is informed, the invoice is filed by customer name, and the system is finished. If the credit is approved, the six copies of the invoice are used in a variety of ways: one copy goes to the customer as an invoice, another is filed by invoice number, a third is filed by customer name, one copy goes to the customer with the goods as a packing slip, one is

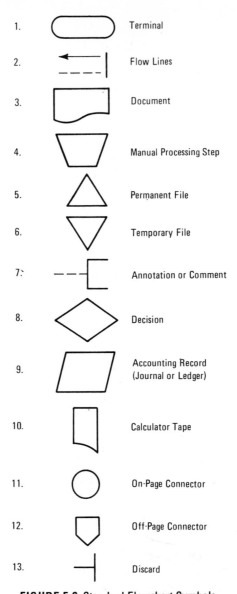

1.	Terminal
2.	Flow Lines
3.	Document
4.	Manual Processing Step
5.	Permanent File
6.	Temporary File
7.	Annotation or Comment
8.	Decision
9.	Accounting Record (Journal or Ledger)
10.	Calculator Tape
11.	On-Page Connector
12.	Off-Page Connector
13.	Discard

FIGURE 5-6 Standard Flowchart Symbols

filed by billing date, and finally, one goes to the customer as an acknowledgement of the order. Of course, many of the steps in a real system have been left out here, but this simplified system will serve to illustrate the flowchart symbols and concepts.

1. The first symbol is the oval, which stands for a terminal in the system—either a beginning or an end. The terminal generally shows something coming from outside the system in or shows something going from inside the system out. Thus, if a sale begins with a customer, the flowchart begins at an oval labelled *CUSTOMER*. Notice that in Figure 5-7 the beginning oval is at the top of the chart; a well-drawn flowchart reads from top to bottom.

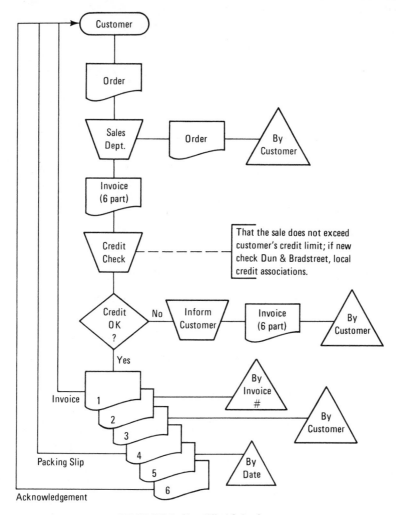

FIGURE 5-7 Simplified Sales System

2. The second symbol is the flow line. The solid flow line indicates a document flow, while the dashed line indicates an information flow without a document. Thus, if a person makes out a form or mails in a form, you would use the solid line. An example would be the customer who generates an order. This is illustrated in Figure 5-7, with the order essentially flowing out of the customer. If, on the other hand, a foreman makes a verbal requisition (i.e., request for parts), this would be shown as a dashed line. This information flow is illustrated in Figure 5-8.

Since we are all used to reading English, which flows from top to bottom and left to right, a flowchart should flow in the same manner to make it as easy to read as possible. The flow lines not only indicate a flow, they also indicate the direction of the flow. However, an arrow is not always necessary to indicate direction of flow, because we can make the assumption that unless otherwise indicated, the flow lines go from top to bottom and left to right. In Figure 5-6, the dashed line is flowing from left to right, and the vertical

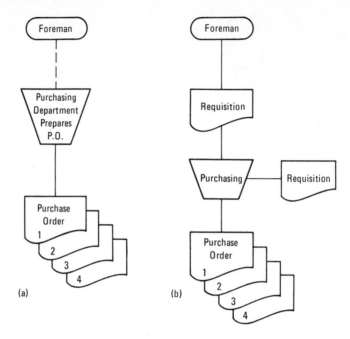

FIGURE 5-8 Verbal and Written Requisitions

line is flowing from top to bottom. Sometimes a flow must go the other way and in those cases, we use an arrow to indicate the direction. Therefore, the horizontal document flow in Figure 5-6 is from right to left. Figure 5-7 also illustrates several types of flows.

3.   The third symbol is the document. This symbol represents any document, form, or report utilized by the system. Figure 5-7 illustrates the use of this symbol in a number of ways. At this point, we will only mention its first use; that is, to show that the customer generates an order. Since this is a written order, we use the solid (i.e., document) flow line and the document symbol for the order.

4.   The fourth symbol is the manual processing step. This symbol is a trapezoid and it indicates any filling out of forms or adding up of numbers. You can then see in Figure 5-7 that the customer order goes to the sales department, which prepares a six-part invoice. The next processing step is a credit check. Thus, the processing step box indicates any standard steps performed at any point in the system.

5.   The fifth symbol is the permanent file. After the sales department prepares the six-part invoice, the sales department still has the customer order. Figure 5-7 shows the customer order disappearing into the permanent file. But it is not enough just to know that something is filed, it is also important to know how the document is filed. The filing sequence should therefore be indicated within the file triangle.

6.   The sixth symbol represents the temporary file; that is, documents only reside there for an interim period, or until a specific event occurs. A file may always exist, but if documents only remain in the file for a temporary period, then that is a temporary file. For example, a file in the shipping department may contain a copy of an invoice which serves as a control

on open orders which have not yet been shipped. The document will be removed from the file when the goods are shipped. Notice that the temporary file symbol is on its point whereas the permanent file rests on its base.

7. The seventh symbol is the annotation or comment. This symbol is used to provide further explanation as necessary. For example, in Figure 5-7, the space in the symbol for the credit check is insufficient to explain the complete processing step. To provide a better explanation, the symbol for comment is used out to the side to provide further details.

8. The eighth symbol is the decision. This important symbol is used for steps in the flowchart where alternative paths are taken based upon some decision. An example appears in Figure 5-7 where the decision is whether or not the credit of the customer is OK. Notice there are two possible results—yes or no—and a different processing path is taken depending on the result.. If the result is no, the customer is informed, the invoice is filed, and the system is over. If, on the other hand, the result is yes, the credit is OK, the six parts of the invoice are then processed in different ways.

9. The ninth symbol is the accounting record. Remember that an accounting record is a journal or a ledger. Thus, for Pooper Centers the only accounting records are: (1) general journal, (2) cash receipts journal, (3) cash disbursements journal, (4) purchases journal, (5) sales journal, (6) general ledger, (7) A/R subsidiary ledger, and (8) A/P subsidiary ledger. The accounting record has a symbol separate from documents because it is not necessary to show the filing of an accounting record. The flowchart will simply assume the accounting records exist as complete entities in and of themselves. (A number of examples using this symbol appear later in this chapter.) A note of caution: worksheets and financial statements are not part of the accounting records and should be represented by the document symbol.

10. The tenth symbol is the calculator tape or adding machine tape. This symbol is used when compiling a total, for example, from a batch of sales slips. Figure 5-9 depicts the preparation of a tape of the accounts receivable subsidiary ledger. The tape symbol is used in essentially the same way as the document symbol.

11. The eleventh symbol is the on-page connector. It sometimes happens that it is impossible to connect all parts of a flowchart with flow lines without making the chart look like a maze. You then use the on-page connector to indicate the point at which the flowchart is being left off and another connector to indicate where it is being picked up again. Figure 5-9 shows the use of an on-page connector. Another connector would be placed elsewhere on the flowchart to pick up what happens when the tape total equals the general ledger control.

12. The twelfth symbol is the off-page connector. As we will see in later parts of the chapter, we often have situations where the flowcharts of different systems are on different pages and these systems must be tied together. The off-page connector is used to show where and how the flowcharts fit together.

13. The thirteenth symbol is the discard symbol. There are three possible end results for every document processed by the system: (1) to be sent out of the system, symbolized by the oval; (2) to be filed, symbolized by the triangle; and (3) to be thrown away as no longer important, symbolized by the discard symbol. Figure 5-9 shows how to indicate the discard of a tape after it is no longer useful.

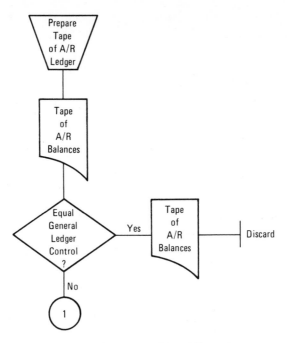

FIGURE 5-9 Tape and Discard Example

Recall that the dashed flow line represents information flow, rather than the document flow illustrated by a solid flow line. Figure 5-8 illustrates these concepts, but we are now in a position to see what Figure 5-8 is really telling us. In (a) there is a verbal request by the foreman for some product or products. Upon receiving this *verbal* request, the purchasing department will prepare a four-part purchase order and the system will continue from there. In (b) there is a written requisition prepared by the foreman and given to the purchasing department. Upon receiving this *written* request, the purchasing department prepares a four-part purchase order and files or otherwise takes care of the requisition.

It is very common in business systems to use multipart forms or to generate multiple copies of one report. There are three basic ways to show this in a flowchart, as exemplified by Figure 5-10. Flowcharts (a) and (b) are similar in that they show the six copies to make it visually apparent (even without reading) that there are multiple copies of the form. This presentation has the advantage that lines can be drawn from each copy of the form to show where each goes. Whether you use presentation (a) or presentation (b) is strictly a matter of taste. Flowchart (c), on the other hand, is a more compact presentation, which is useful when the set of forms is transported or used as a group rather than individually. You will have to use your judgment concerning the most appropriate presentation for any particular flowchart.

There is one final, related topic of flowcharting which we must cover in this introductory discussion: the flowchart must show the final disposition of every document, form, or report utilized by the system. Remember our flowchart in Figure 5-7 of the simplified sales system: the order is filed by customer name; copies 1, 4, and 6 of the invoice go out of the system back to the customer; copy 2 is filed by invoice number; copy 3 is filed by customer name; and copy 5 is filed by date. Thus, all documents are accounted for. You should then make sure that every

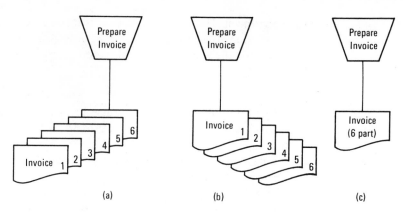

FIGURE 5-10 Alternatives for Multipart Forms

document in your flowchart is: (a) sent out of the system, which is represented by an oval; (b) filed permanently, which is represented by a stable triangle; or (c) discarded, which is represented by the vertical line and the word *discard*.

5.3 FLOWCHART OF A SALES SYSTEM

To tie together our knowledge concerning the different flowchart symbols we will actually flowchart a sales system. This sales system will be for a company with the organization structure given in Figure 5-1. We will first describe the system and how it works. Then we will go through a flowchart of the same system and see how the flowchart can describe the system in pictures.

Processing Sales

The system begins with a customer order, which is either sent to the sales order department or obtained over the phone by the sales order department. The sales order department then prepares a six-part copy of an invoice. The second copy of the invoice goes to the credit department for approval of credit terms. When the credit copy returns from the credit department, the copies are distributed: copy 1 (invoice copy) and copy 3 (ledger copy) go to billing; copy 2 (credit copy) is filed with the order; copy 4 (packing slip) goes to shipping; copy 5 (stock request copy) goes to the warehouse; and copy 6 (acknowledgement copy) goes to the customer to confirm the order. The sales order department thus originates the invoice, but it does not have custody of the assets and does not record the transaction. The warehouse releases the goods upon receipt of the stock request copy. Thus, the goods only leave with an approved stock request. The goods go with the stock request copy to shipping, where the stock request is matched with the packing slip. The goods then go to the customer along with the packing slip. The stock request copy then goes to the billing department indicating that the goods have been shipped, and it is now time to bill the customer. The billing department then matches the invoice copy, the ledger copy, and the stock request copy, checks the prices and extensions, and completes the invoice. The invoice and ledger copies thus act as a control on orders which have not yet been shipped. The invoice copy goes to the customer as a bill. The ledger copy goes to the accounts receivable department. The stock request copy is filed by customer. Daily, the billing department runs a tape of all invoices, which is sent to the general ledger department for entry in the sales control account and the accounts receivable control account.

System Flowchart

Notice that the flowchart is divided into columns, for ease of comprehension (see Figure 5-11). Thus, for the sales system we have separate columns for the Customer, Sales Order, Credit, Billing, Accounts Receivable, General Ledger, Warehouse, and Shipping. The flowchart then shows everything that occurs in a department in that department's column. This arrangement makes it easier to see where documents come from and where they go.

The flowchart begins in the top left-hand corner with a customer order. Since the flowchart is in columns, we need only write ORDER on the document symbol to make clear it is a customer order. This order goes to the sales order column, indicating a document flow to this department. We then have a processing step for invoice preparation and show that copy 2 of the invoice (the credit copy) goes to credit for their approval and then returns. (Notice here that for sake of clarity, it may not be possible to show every tiny step in the process; you will have to use your judgment). After the invoice preparation, there are seven documents—six invoice copies and the customer order. The invoice (copy 1) and the ledger copy (copy 3) go together to billing where they are placed in the temporary file which provides a control on orders not shipped. The credit copy (copy 2) and the customer order are filed together by invoice number in a permanent file. This provides physical control over invoices; any gap in the sequencing shows an invoice is missing. The packing slip (copy 4) is sent to shipping where it goes into a temporary file pending arrival of goods from the warehouse. The stock request (copy 5) goes to the warehouse where it triggers another processing step, the release of goods. The stock request (copy 5) goes to shipping along with the goods. The related packing slip (copy 4) is then removed from the temporary file. Then the next processing step occurs: the documents are matched and the goods are shipped. The packing slip (copy 4) goes with the goods to the customer to show what should be in the shipment. The stock request (copy 5) goes to billing to trigger the billing process. Billing takes the invoice (copy 1) and ledger copy (copy 3) out of the temporary file. Billing then performs the following processing step: (a) the three copies of the invoice (1, 3, and 5) are matched; (b) the invoice (copy 1) is sent to the customer; (c) the ledger copy (copy 3) goes to the accounts receivable system, which is continued on a later flowchart; (d) the sale is recorded in the sales journal, (e) the stock request (copy 5) is put into a permanent file of invoice copies sequenced by date, and (f) a daily total of all billings is sent to general ledger. Because there is often a delay in shipping orders, the sales order department mails an acknowledgement copy of the invoice (copy 6) to the customer when all the copies of the invoice are distributed to the different departments.

Importance of the Six-part Invoice

It is important not to just passively flowchart the system; you must also try to understand why it is the way it is. Let us use the sales system as an example: the system uses a six-part invoice, but is that the proper number of copies? Is that too few? Is that too many? To understand why this system has six copies, let us review where each one goes and what purpose it serves:

#1   goes to the customer as his invoice.

#2 is filed by invoice number in the sales order department to maintain physical control over invoices and to make sure no invoices are missing.

#3 goes to accounts receivable to update the customer account with the purchase, where it is filed by customer name.

#4 goes to the customer as a packing slip accompanying the goods to show what the shipment should contain.

#5 is filed by date in the billing department to back up the total billings for the day sent to the general ledger department.

#6 goes to the customer as an acknowledgement of the receipt of his order.

Only by reference to the actual situation is it possible to determine whether the system is appropriate. There is no one perfect system which can be applied in all situations and each copy should be scrutinized to determine whether it is actually necessary. As an example, let us consider the acknowledgement copy, number six. In many cases, it takes a long time for a company to fill a customer order: some furniture companies take over three months to deliver, and some computer companies take over a year to deliver on certain models. In situations like these, it is essential that the customer receive an acknowledgement to show him that the order is being processed and he has not been forgotten or ignored. Suppose, however, the firm can generally ship goods to the customer very soon after an order is received because of an extensive inventory. In that case, an acknowledgement would not be necessary because the invoice would reach the customer at essentially the same time as the acknowledgement. Thus, in every situation, you must judge what is necessary or appropriate.

We would now like to place a seed for thought. Remember there are six copies of the invoice: three go to the customer and we retain three. But all three copies we retain have the same information on them, so the question arises: Is it not wasteful to keep three copies of the same thing? The answer is that all three copies are necessary because the firm must access the same information in three different ways:

1. One copy must be filed by invoice number to provide (a) physical control over invoices and (b) quick access to the invoice by its identifying number.

2. One copy must be filed by customer name to provide backup for the statement of account. Thus, if a customer calls or writes about his bill, all relevant documents should be grouped together for convenient access.

3. One copy must be filed by date of billing. The total billed in a day is entered in the sales journal as sales for the day. To maintain a proper audit trail, the firm must be able to go to the source documents backing up the journal entry. In this case, the source documents are the invoices; to back up a journal entry, the firm need only go to the batch of invoices for that day.

Thus, there are good reasons for keeping multiple copies of the same information in a manual system. You might be thinking, however, about the impact of the computer on this. One of our main interests in the use of computers will be to store information once and then to use the capabilities of the computer to access the information in many different ways.

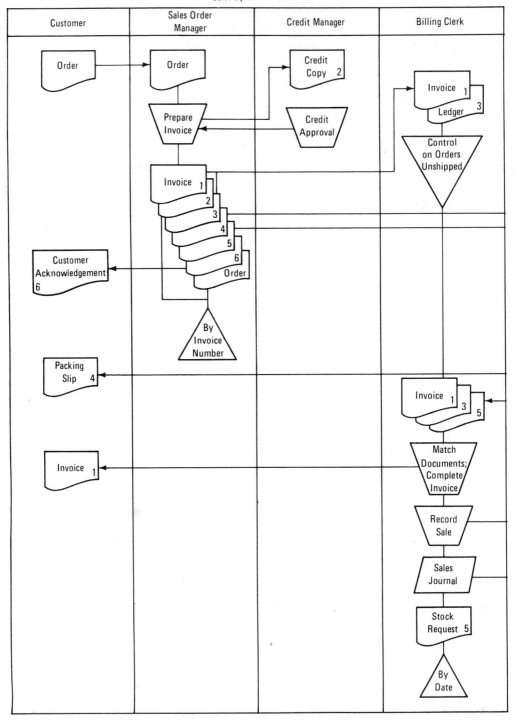

FIGURE 5-11 Sales System Flowchart

French Quarter Company, Inc.

Sales System Flowchart

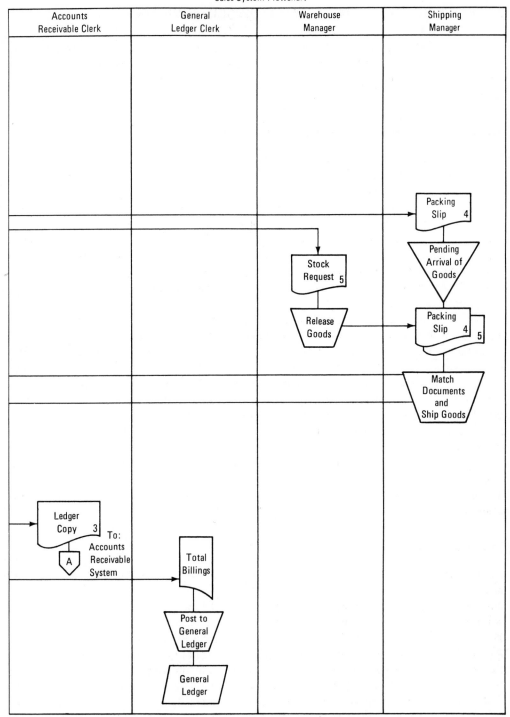

FIGURE 5-11 Sales System Flowchart (Continued)

5.4 FLOWCHART OF AN ACCOUNTS RECEIVABLE SYSTEM

In this part of the chapter we develop the accounts receivable and cash collections systems for the French Quarter Company discussed earlier and the sales system we have just gone through. Notice the Notes column in Figures 5-12 and 5-13 that further explains the material in the flowchart.

Processing Accounts Receivable and Cash Receipts

The ledger copy (copy 3) is then sent to accounts receivable where it is used to post the accounts receivable subsidiary ledger.

The customer will then sometimes return goods. When the goods arrive, receiving prepares a sales return receiving slip. This slip goes to credit, which approves sales returns. The sales return receiving slip then goes to the billing department which prepares a two-part credit memo. One copy of the credit memo goes to accounts receivable, where it is posted to the accounts receivable subsidiary ledger. The second copy is filed in billing by credit memo number to provide physical control over credit memos; any missing credit memos are apparent from the gap in the sequence. On a daily basis, the total credit memos go to general ledger for recording in the control accounts.

The customer mails in a check and it is received by the mail room. Some customer checks will come with a remittance advice (the detachable portion at the bottom of a voucher check, for example); if so, the remittance advice is detached by the mail room. If a remittance advice is not provided, the mail room prepares one. The remittance advice is sent to accounts receivable for posting to the accounts receivable subsidiary ledger. The check then goes to cash receipts, which records the transaction in the cash receipts journal and prepares two copies of a deposit slip. The check and the two copies of the deposit slip go to the bank. A total of all cash receipts goes to general ledger to post to the control accounts. After the bank processes the deposit, it returns the second copy of the deposit slip to cash receipts where it is filed by date.

Thus, accounts receivable gets: (1) invoices (ledger copy) from billing, (2) remittance advices from the mail room, and (3) credit memos from billing—all of which are posted to the accounts receivable subsidiary ledger. On a monthly basis, accounts receivable prepares statements of account which are sent to the customers.

Importance of Flowcharts

At this point you should be able to see the tremendous advantages of flowcharts and their use, primarily in (a) ensuring completeness and (b) displaying clearly the essence of the situation. When you get a narrative description of a system and how it works, it is impossible to tell whether or not the description is complete just by reading it. However, when you begin to flowchart the system from the narrative you quickly begin to perceive any gaps or omissions. As for displaying the essence of a situation, the flowchart not only can describe the procedures followed but can also display the separation of duties for internal control purposes. As you recall from Chapter 3, one of the elements of good internal control is a proper separation of duties. The flowchart, especially one divided into columns by department or by person, can lay out the separation of duties so the analyst can determine if the actual separation is appropriate. Thus, in our example system, we have the following separation of duties concerning cash receipts on accounts receivable:

1. The mail room receives the cash and prepares a remittance advice if necessary.

2. The cash receipts clerk records in the cash receipts journal and deposits the check.

3. The accounts receivable clerk uses the remittance advice to post the accounts receivable subsidiary ledger.

This system appears to have good internal control; no one person has control over both custody and record keeping for the important asset, cash. Notice that the cash receipts clerk both records the receipts and has custody of those assets, but the accounts receivable clerk has an independent check. Any differences would become apparent in the balancing of the accounts receivable subsidiary ledger to the general ledger control total.

5.5 OTHER SYSTEMS ANALYSIS TECHNIQUES

Document Flowchart

To this point we have discussed system flowcharts. These flowcharts have included not only the documents used by the system, but also the procedures and processing steps involved in the system. However, in many situations a complete procedure flowchart may not be necessary or even desirable. For example, in the first step of a systems analysis, the analyst may want to get a general overview of the information-processing flow by determining where each document goes. In another situation, the processing steps may be relatively obvious and thus the processing detail is an unnecessary distraction upon reading the flowchart. A final example would be an attempt to inventory the forms a company uses and their purposes; to ensure completeness the analyst might want to flowchart the flow of documents.

A document flowchart is often the answer to problems such as these. In a document flowchart, all processing steps are omitted and only the flow of documents is shown. It is important to understand the distinction between the document flowchart and the procedure flowchart. Figure 5-14 is a document flowchart for our familiar accounts receivable system of the French Quarter Company, Inc. You see, of course, that a great deal has been left out, namely what is done with each of the forms in each department. However, you can also see that the document flowchart gives a good overview of the information processing, uncluttered by a lot of detail. Often, by using your experience and common sense, it is fairly clear what must occur at each stage of the system.

Decision Tables and Internal Control Questionnaires

As useful and as important as flowcharts are, there are some additional techniques which have also been developed to aid in the task of system analysis. Two techniques we will go over in some depth are:

1. *Decision tables*, which give a concise summary of often complicated decision rules.

2. *Internal control questionnaires*, which help ensure that important areas are not overlooked.

French Quarter Company, Inc.

Accounts Receivable System Flowchart

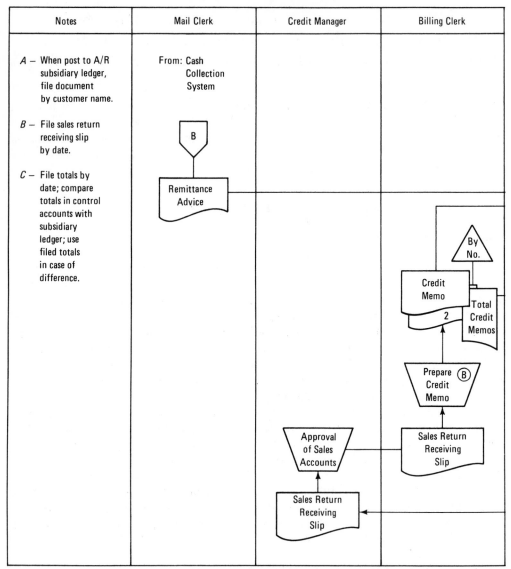

FIGURE 5-12 Accounts Receivable System Flowchart

French Quarter Company, Inc.

Accounts Receivable System Flowchart

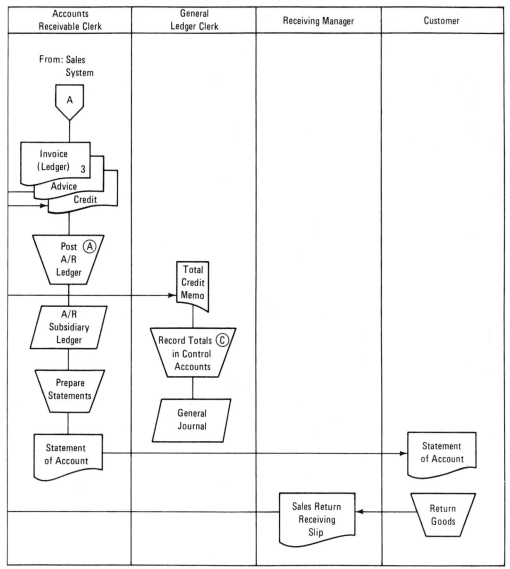

FIGURE 5-12 Accounts Receivable System Flowchart (Continued)

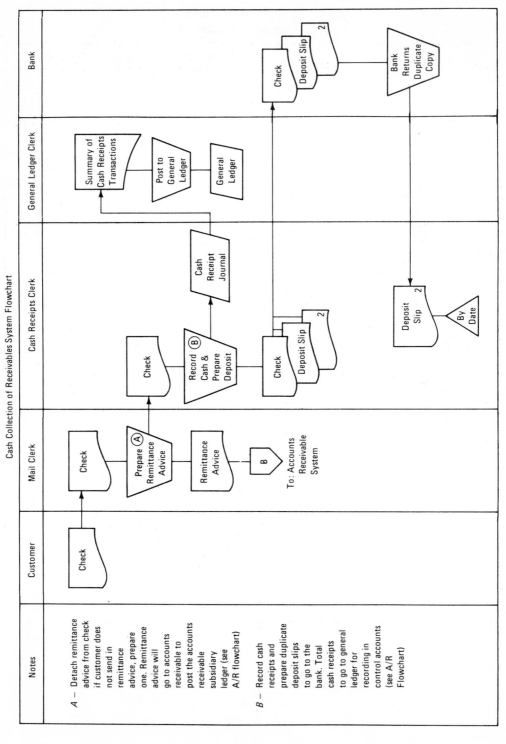

French Quarter Company, Inc.
Cash Collection of Receivables System Flowchart

FIGURE 5-13 Cash Collection of Receivables System Flowchart

122

French Quarter Company, Inc.
Accounts Receivable System Document Flowchart

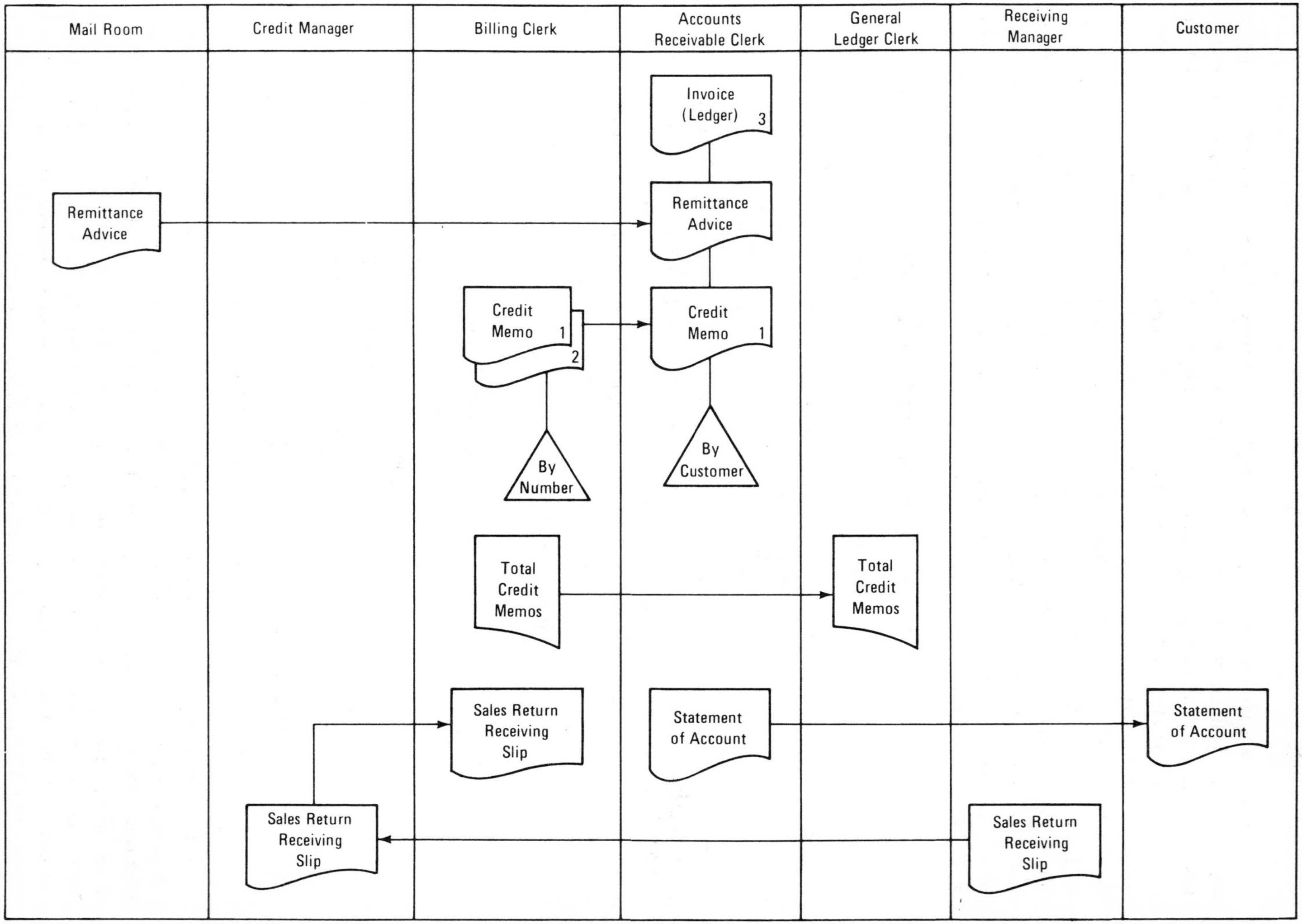

FIGURE 5-14 Document Flowchart

Decision Tables

Decision tables lay out the logic to be followed in decision making and are most valuable when presenting a situation where many different factors all combine to determine the result. Thus, the decision table can quickly summarize a complicated decision situation and make our task of system analysis easier. The decision table is then a complement to a well-drawn system flowchart; the flowchart is at its best with the typical yes/no decisions of business data processing, whereas the decision table is at its best with complicated decisions.

Table 5-1 provides the basic structure for this systems analysis technique. The condition stub is a list of possible conditions which might hold. The action stub is a list of possible actions which might be taken. The entry side of the decision table is then divided into different rules, and for each possible set of conditions there is a separate rule which details the action to be taken given those conditions.

TABLE 5-1   BASIC DECISION TABLE COMPONENTS

If . . .	Condition Stub	Condition Entries
Then . . .	Action Stub	Action Entries

Let us consider a basic check-cashing decision, such as Pooper Centers might face: When people want to pay by check, when do we accept the check and when do we refuse the check? Suppose that the firm decides to only accept checks from local banks. Also, the firm decides to only accept checks when the person has a picture identification. This situation is shown in Table 5-2, where the following codes are used

Condition entries: Y   = yes, that condition is met

N   = no, that condition is not met

—   = it is not relevant to the decision whether the condition is met or not

Action entries: X   = take that action

(blank) = do not take that action

This example then has two possible conditions—a local bank check and a picture identification—and two possible actions—either accept the check or refuse the check. There are then three rules: Rule 1 says that if the customer has a local bank check and if the customer has a picture identification, then accept the check; Rule 2 says that if the customer has a local bank check, but does not have a picture identification, then refuse the check; Rule 3 says that if the customer does not have a local bank check, it does not matter whether the customer has a picture identification; the check will always be refused.

TABLE 5-2   BASIC CHECK-CASHING RULES

	1	2	3
Local Bank	Y	Y	N
Picture Identification	Y	N	—
Accept Check	X		
Refuse Check		X	X

As you can see, the decision table quickly and concisely sums up the information concerning this decision. In addition, the decision table can easily be extended to handle more complicated situations. As an example, suppose the firm required the store manager to approve all checks over $10.00, and the manager is given the authority to decide what identification is appropriate. Table 5-3 shows these expanded check-cashing rules.

TABLE 5-3   EXPANDED CHECK-CASHING RULES

	1	2	3	4
Local Bank	Y	Y	Y	N
Picture Identification	Y	—	N	—
Manager Approval	—	Y	N	—
Accept Check Over $10		X		
Accept Check Not Over $10	X			
Refuse Check			X	X

Internal Control Questionnaires

Internal control questionnaires are a method of ensuring that all important internal control problem areas are at least considered. The questionnaire is a series of questions designed so that a *no* answer to any question indicates a potential area of difficulty. Figure 5-15 provides a sample internal control questionnaire for petty cash. Additional questionnaires would then be necessary for cash receipts, cash disbursements, accounts receivable, inventory, and all the other areas of internal control problems. Of course, for these more complicated areas, the questionnaire would have to be much more extensive; a complete questionnaire might then run fifty pages. Further, there would have to be different questionnaires for different types of firms, since the internal control problems of an international airline would be quite different from those of a real estate broker.

Thus, the internal control questionnaire provides some basic information which is needed, but it may fail to give you the entire picture. Necessarily, the questionnaire will be made up of standard questions that are applicable in most situations in most companies; the questionnaire is almost surely not going to be applicable in every situation in all companies. Finally, though the questionnaire can help identify an area of difficulty, it does not give an overall view of the system or even review the system as a process.

As a final note, we must mention that because of the importance of the task of system analysis, techniques to assist this task are still in a vigorous state of development. The goals of

INTERNAL CONTROL QUESTIONNAIRE

Petty Cash	*N/A*	*Yes*	*No*
1. Are all petty cash disbursements made from an imprest petty cash system?	_____	_____	_____
2. Is the petty cash fund under the custody of one person?	_____	_____	_____
3. Is the cash balance periodically checked by people independent of the custodian?	_____	_____	_____
4. Is the custodian of petty cash denied access to the accounting records?	_____	_____	_____
5. Is the balance kept in petty cash reasonable given the needs of the business?	_____	_____	_____
6. Is the petty cash custodian bonded?	_____	_____	_____
7. Is a proper voucher or receipt available for each disbursement?	_____	_____	_____
8. Is each voucher cancelled after payment is made?	_____	_____	_____
9. Is each voucher signed by the person receiving the cash?	_____	_____	_____

FIGURE 5-15

the new techniques include ease of use, better methods for making changes, and the incorporation of the computer to assist with the documentation details. As with many computer-related activities, these techniques are often identified by acronyms: ADS (Accurately Defined System by NCR) and SOP (Study Organization Plan by IBM). This area is one of continual change, with new approaches constantly appearing.

exercises

5-1 Below is a narrative description of the lines of authority and responsibility for data processing and accounting matters in a medium-sized firm. From this material, prepare an organization chart in good form.

Both the data processing manager and the controller report to the president. The data processing manager is in charge of operating the already existing systems and developing new systems as necessary. The controller is in charge of the accounting for the company. The data processing manager has five people reporting to him: (a) the data control supervisor who is in charge of detecting and correcting errors in the computer's input data; (b) a systems programmer who is responsible for the computer system software; (c) an application programming manager who is in charge of developing programs for new systems and maintaining old programs; (d) a data librarian who is responsible for physical control over the tapes and disks used in the system; and (e) an operations supervisor who is in charge of the computer's operations. The data control supervisor has three clerks who work for her. The application programming manager supervises four programmers. The data librarian has one assistant. The operations supervisor has two operators who work for him. Four people report to the controller: (a) a systems accountant, who is responsible for developing new accounting-related systems; (b) the chief accountant, who is responsible for accounting records; (c) the budget manager, who develops budgets and monitors performance relative to budget; and (d) the internal auditor, who provides an independent verification of performance. Five clerks report to the chief accountant, one for each of the following areas: general ledger, accounts payable, accounts receivable, billing, and payroll.

5-2   This question refers to the organization chart of Tulane University pictured in Figure 5-16. Answer each of the following specific questions concerning the organization chart.

1.   How many people report to the president?

2.   What is the relationship between the board of visitors and the board of administrators?

3.   What is the relationship between the board of administrators and the board of governors of Tulane Medical Center?

4.   To whom does the vice-president for health affairs report?

5.   Briefly describe the areas of responsibility of the dean of students.

6.   To whom does the director of administrative services (Medical Center) report?

7.   Why might there be an accounting section under the director of administrative services (Medical Center) as well as a chief accountant under the business manager?

8.   Do the activities and responsibilities of the director of admissions make it more desirable for him to be under the provost rather than the dean of students?

9.   What is the role of the university senate?

10.   It is unusual for the director of computing to report directly to the president. Where might the head of the computer center be placed?

5-3   For this exercise, use the information given in 5-2 above.

1.   One of the primary activiites of university administrators is academic administration. These administrators do not primarily teach or do research, but they hire, supervise, and fire those who do. From the flowchart, give a narrative description of the lines of authority and responsibility in the academic administration of the university.

2.   Another important area of university administration is the management of business affairs. Give a narrative description of the lines of authority and responsibility in the business administration of the university.

5-4   Charting, Inc. processes its sales and cash receipts documents in the following manner:[1]

1.   *Payment on account.* The mail is opened each morning by a mail clerk in the sales department. The mail clerk prepares a remittance advice (showing customer and

---

[1] Adapted from the AICPA examination.

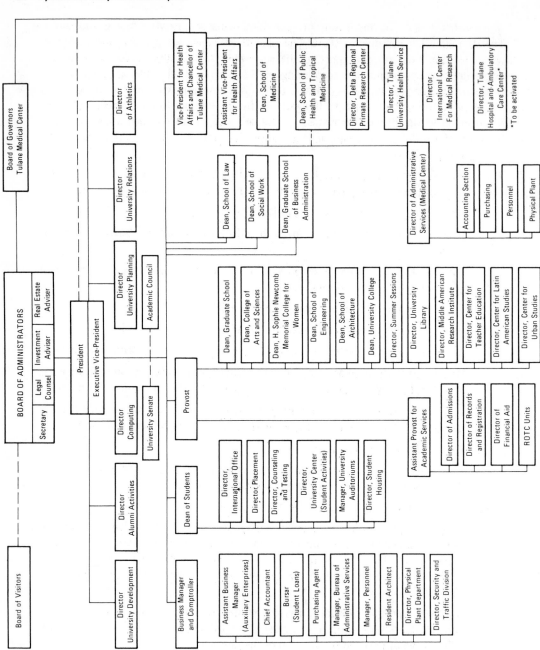

FIGURE 5-16 Tulane University Administrative Organization

amount paid) if one is not received. The checks and remittance advices are then forwarded to the sales department supervisor who reviews each check and forwards the checks and remittance advices to the accounting department supervisor.

The accounting department supervisor, who also functions as credit manager in approving new credit and all credit limits, reviews all checks for payments on past due accounts and then forwards the checks and remittance advices to the accounts receivable clerk who arranges the advices in alphabetical order. The remittance advices are posted directly to the accounts receivable ledger cards. The checks are endorsed by stamp and totaled. The total is posted to the cash receipts journal. The remittance advices are filed chronologically.

After receiving the cash from the previous day's cash sales, the accounts receivable clerk prepares the daily deposit slip in triplicate. The third copy of the deposit slip is filed by date, and the second copy and the original accompany the bank deposit.

2. *Sales.* Sales clerks prepare sales invoices in triplicate. The original and second copy are presented to the cashier. The third copy is retained by the sales clerk in the sales book. When the sale is for cash, the customer pays the sales clerk who presents the money to the cashier with the invoice copies.

A credit sale is approved by the cashier from an approved credit list after the sales clerk prepares the three-part invoice. After receiving the cash or approving the invoice, the cashier validates the original copy of the sales invoice and gives it to the customer. At the end of each day the cashier recaps the sales and cash received and forwards the cash and the second copy of all sales invoices to the accounts receivable clerk.

The accounts receivable clerk balances the cash received with cash sales invoices and prepares a daily sales summary. The credit sales invoices are posted to the accounts receivable ledger and then all invoices are sent to the inventory control clerk in the sales department for posting to the inventory control cards. After posting, the inventory control clerk files all invoices numerically. The accounts receivable clerk posts the daily sales summary to the cash receipts journal and sales journal and files the sales summaries by date.

The cash from cash sales is combined with the cash received on account to comprise the daily bank deposit.

3. *Bank deposits.* The bank validates the deposit slip and returns the second copy to the accounting department where it is filed by date by the accounts receivable clerk. Monthly bank statements are reconciled promptly by the accounting department supervisor and filed by date.

You recognize that there are weaknesses in the existing system and belive a chart of information and documentation flows would be beneficial in evaluating this client's internal control. After reviewing the symbols shown in Figure 5-17, complete the flow chart for sales and cash receipts of Charting, Inc. (Figure 5-18) by labeling the appropriate symbols and indicating information flows. The chart is complete as to symbols and document flows.

5-5 Anthony, CPA, prepared the flowchart shown in Figure 5-19 which portrays the purchasing function of one of Anthony's clients, a medium-sized company, from the preparation

FLOW CHART SYMBOLS   Permanent file of documents

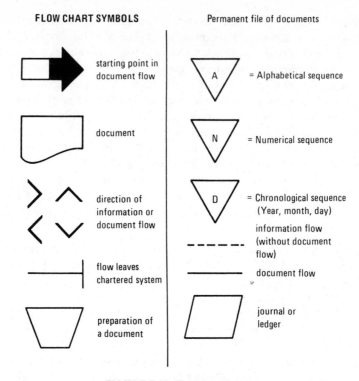

FIGURE 5-17 Flowchart Symbols

of initial documents through the vouching of invoices for payment in accounts payable.[2] The flowchart was a portion of the work performed to evaluate internal control.

1.   Identify and explain the systems and control weaknesses evident from the flow-chart.
2.   Include the internal control weaknesses resulting from activities performed or not performed. All documents are prenumbered.

5-6   The organization chart given in Figure 5-1 and the flowcharts in Figures 5-11, 5-12, and 5-13 all pertain to the French Quarter Company, Inc. Flowchart the payroll system for this company given in the narrative below.

When a person is hired, the employment manager prepares an employment and rate authorization form and a deductions slip which are forwarded to the payroll clerk. Each week employees turn in timecards showing hours worked to the payroll clerk. Every two weeks the payroll clerk computes earnings and deductions for each employee and payroll taxes for the company. This detailed information is then forwarded to the cash disbursements clerk who (a) prepares paychecks, (b) enters the payroll transactions in the cash disbursements journal, and (c) sends paychecks back to the payroll clerk. Employee year-to-date earnings and deductions are then updated by the payroll clerk and checks are distributed to employees.

---
[2] Adapted from the AICPA examination.

5-7   Flowchart the purchases system for the French Quarter Company, Inc. given in the narrative below.

      The purchasing agent prepares a three-part purchase order and sends the first two copies to the vendor. Acknowledgement of the order by the vendor is obtained when the vendor returns copy 2 to the purchasing agent. Copy 2 is kept by the purchasing agent and copy 3 is sent to the accounts payable clerk. The vendor sends the goods accompanied by a packing slip to the receiving manager and a two-part invoice to the purchasing agent. The receiving manager verifies the accuracy of the packing slip and forwards it to the accounts payable clerk. The purchasing agent determines that the invoice accurately reflects the order and sends the received invoice to the accounts payable clerk, who compares it to the verified packing slip. The accounts payable clerk approves the invoice for payment and sends the purchase order, verified packing slip, and approved invoice to the cash disbursements clerk and records the purchase in the purchases journal. Each week, the accounts payable clerk posts from the purchases journal to the accounts payable subsidiary ledger. Each month, the accounts payable clerk prepares summary total information on purchases, which goes to the general ledger clerk.

5-8   Flowchart the cash disbursements system (for purchases) for the French Quarter Company, Inc. given in the narrative below.

      The cash disbursements clerk receives the supporting documents from the accounts payable clerk and prepares checks for vendors which are signed by the secretary-treasurer. These checks are entered in the cash disbursements journal and sent directly to the vendor. Each week, the accounts payable clerk posts from the cash disbursements journal to the accounts payable subsidiary ledger. Each month, the cash disbursements clerk prepares summary total information on cash disbursements which goes to the general ledger clerk. The bank statement goes to the controller, who compares it to the cash receipts journal, cash disbursements journal, and the general ledger.

5-9   For each of the systems given in problems 5-6, 5-7, and 5-8, prepare a document flowchart.

5-10   A hardware store has three cash registers that are constantly in use. There are usually five salespersons on duty, each of whom has access to every cash register. Prepare an internal control questionnaire for cash sales in such a situation.

CHARTING, INC,
FLOW CHART FOR SALES AND CASH RECEIPTS

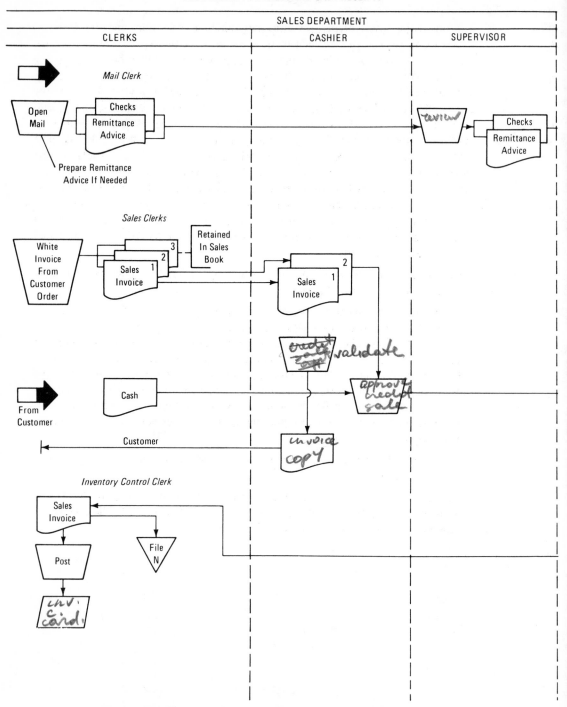

FIGURE 5-18 Flow Chart for Sales and Cash Receipts

CHARTING, INC,
FLOW CHART FOR SALES AND CASH RECEIPTS

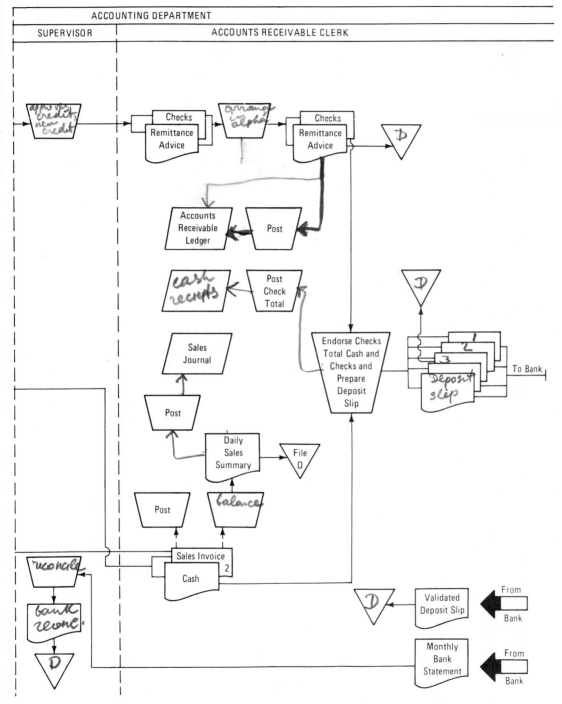

FIGURE 5-18 Flow Chart for Sales and Cash Receipts (Continued)

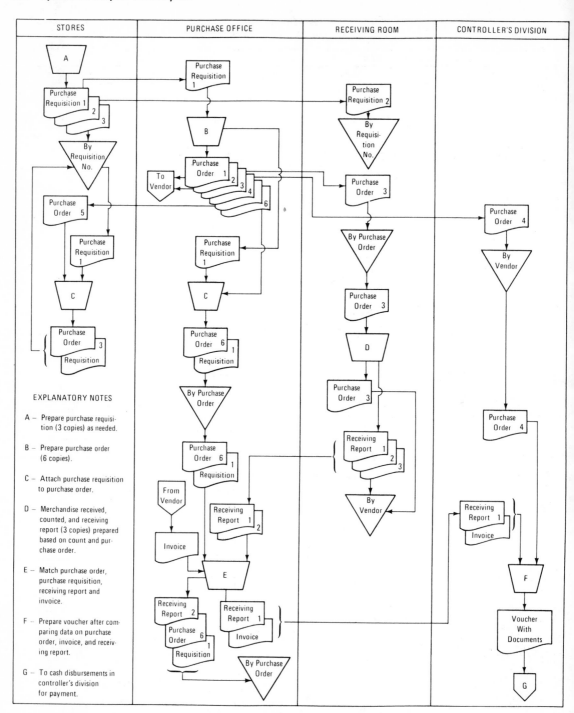

FIGURE 5-19

systems analysis application

outline

6.1 Structure of a Systems Analysis Report: report components; supporting report recommendations.

6.2 Systems Analysis Report For Sample Company: Concepts discussed earlier in the chapter are made concrete by showing the precise form of one report.

INTRODUCTION

In this chapter we will apply the general concepts of systems analysis and the flowcharting technique to the sample company introduced in Chapter 4, Pooper Centers, Inc. One of the most important areas of analysis will be internal controls. By performing this systems analysis, you will enhance your understanding of the fundamental principles and concepts discussed thus far.

Many people believe that systems analysis is necessarily related to the computer and computer systems, but this is a misconception. Systems analysis is necessary as a first step for the development of computer-based systems; however, systems analysis can also be used effectively in a purely manual system. Therefore, in this chapter we will present a systems analysis in a manual system so that understanding the basic systems analysis concepts will not be complicated by the presence of a computer. Later, we will use systems analysis in the context of the computer and computer-based systems.

As you recall from Chapter 5, systems analysis consists of the following steps: (1) determine the system to be analyzed, (2) understand the system, (3) analyze the present system, (4) develop cost-effective recommendations, and (5) prepare a report. This chapter will then consist of two major parts; the first will be a discussion of a general approach to a systems analysis report and where and how to get the necessary information; the second part of the chapter will be an actual report concerning the specific situation at Pooper Centers.

6.1 STRUCTURE OF A SYSTEMS ANALYSIS REPORT

Report Components

The structure of a systems analysis report is shown in Figure 6-1. Since this is a general structure, it may not be entirely applicable in every case in exactly the same form and you must use your judgment in applying this material in particular cases. As you can see, the report consists of the following components:

1. *Title page*—names the report and identifies the system and company analyzed and the group preparing the report.

2. *Letter of transmittal*—provides an overall conception of the report, including the reason for its preparation and major results.

3. *Table of contents*—lays out the structure of the report and how the material is presented.

4. *General background*—sets the report in context and describes the environment of the system.

5. *Organization structure*—describes how the company is structured and where authority and responsibility lie.

6. *Job descriptions*—describe each position, its duties, its areas of responsibility and its necessary qualifications.

7. *Documents*—inventory all the documents, forms, and reports which the system uses, both in blank and filled out.

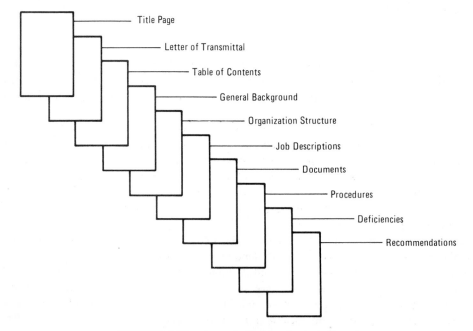

FIGURE 6-1 Structure of a Systems Analysis Report

8. *Procedures*—provide both a narrative description and system flowcharts of the activities in the system.

9. *Deficiencies*—pinpoint areas of difficulty or areas where important elements are missing.

10. *Recommendations*—specify exactly what the company should do about the deficiencies.

Let us now go over each of these components in more detail. The title page is almost self-explanatory; it gives the name of the company studied, the title of the report, the name of the company or group preparing the report, and the date of the report. The letter of transmittal follows, which gives an overall view of the report. The letter should be addressed to the company official in charge of the project and should highlight the report, because few, especially managers, will read the entire report. When you write this letter, keep in mind the following question: What should this manager learn from this report, assuming he reads only this one-page letter? Certainly you will have to simplify, even oversimplify, but this is necessary for communication. (You cannot assume the person will read the entire report.) Following the letter of transmittal is the table of contents, which should lay out the structure of the report; that is, how the report is organized and in what order.

We will need to cover the remaining components of the report in somewhat more detail. (Refer to Figure 6-2 and to the summary in Table 6-1.)

1. *General background.* This should discuss the company's lines of business, its size, its history, its place in the market, and its present financial position and future status. The

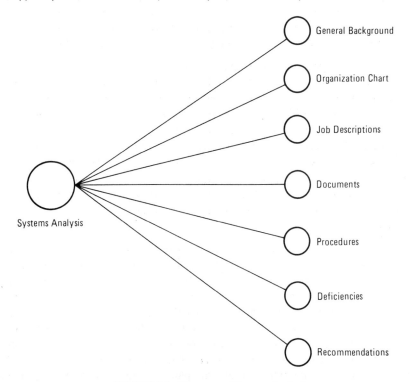

FIGURE 6-2 Elements of System Analysis

TABLE 6-1   SYSTEM ANALYSIS SUMMARY

GENERAL BACKGROUND	Context and environment of both the system and the report
ORGANIZATION CHART	The lines of authority and the areas of responsibility
JOB DESCRIPTIONS	The duties and necessary qualifications for each job position
DOCUMENTS	Forms and reports used or generated by the system
PROCEDURES	Description and flowchart of system processing steps
DEFICIENCIES	Errors or areas where improvement could be made
RECOMMENDATIONS	Suggestions on the steps to be taken to correct the deficiencies

purpose of this section is primarily to allow the reader to get a "feel" for the company—where it has been, where it is, and where it is going. The intended users would include technical people who may not have a clear understanding of this aspect of the business. Additionally, this section should provide important information to the system analyst about the extent of flexibility needed: Is the company growing very rapidly? Acquiring new business? Branching into new areas? If so, the proposed system will have to be far more sophisticated than one designed for a mature company growing very slowly, if at all.

2.   *Organization chart.* The organization chart is a pictorial representation of the way in which the firm is structured. The chart shows the hierarchy of authority at the firm and who reports to whom. If properly drawn, the organization chart will show the area for which each individual is responsible and the people he supervises. The analyst should begin by asking to see the company's present organization chart. Many companies do not have an organization chart; everyone "knows" who is in charge of what and who reports to whom. Even if the company has its own chart, it is typically out of date or incorrect. Remember also that the official attitude about the organization structure may not be correct; the real relationships may not be what management believes them to be. It is important to get past the official line by talking to the employees and checking and cross-checking what each person tells you.

3.   *Job descriptions.* You should prepare a job description for each significant position. The job description should contain the title, the position which supervises this one, the positions which this one supervises, a narrative of the duties, the salary, and a list of the necessary educational and experience requirements. Obtaining this information can be a very delicate endeavor—if you simply ask people direct questions, they may be afraid because they feel you are out to eliminate their job or they may want to make you believe their job is more than it is. Generally, the best approach is to follow one function, say purchasing, from its beginning to end and see what each individual person does. Then do the same for the other functions and put the pieces together about the people and their duties. Finally, when you have each job description at least sketched out, talk to the individual involved and clear up misunderstandings or loose ends.

4. *Documents, forms, and reports.* An important step is to collect an example of every document, form, or report used by the company in the area of study. If possible, pre-printed forms should be both blank and filled in to show what information is recorded and how it is recorded. For example, a purchase order form should appear both unused and filled in with typical information. Importantly, there are two goals: (1) to inventory present forms and reports for possible elimination or reduction and (2) to determine what information is now collected, processed, and generated. This section should show where each copy of each form goes and what reports or forms each individual receives. This step is especially important when analyzing a computer-based system. If anything, people are often overloaded with excessive reports, few of which are ever used.

5. *Documentation of procedures.* The next step is to flowchart and describe the firm's proce-dures. The flowchart gives a pictorial description of the procedures to provide at a glance the overall picture of the system under study. The flowchart should tie to a narrative description which explains in further detail exactly what happens and which steps are followed. This documentation is absolutely essential to an understanding of the present system and to developing a reasonable, workable system.

6. *Deficiencies and omissions.* After the initial review and documentation of the present system, the analyst should isolate any deficiencies and omissions. Deficiencies would in-clude wasted effort, duplication of effort, excessive cost, overstaffing, poor policies, and inadequate control. Omissions would include ineffective supervision, lack of clear company policies, and important information which is unavailable.

7. *Recommendations.* Finally, the analyst must commit to specify recommendations for im-provement. Certainly, if there is no need for improvements in the present system, then the firm should not consider the development of a modified system. If, on the other hand, the system needs improvements, the nature of these improvements determines the type of new system procedures necessary. Of course, the analyst should identify possible improvements which will be acceptable to management and practical. Do not go overboard with wildly extravagant proposals.

Supporting Report Recommendations

You must realize, however, that you should not simply develop part one of the report, then part two, then part three, and so on until the report is complete. The first step is to sketch out the entire report, developing the necessary material for each section. The second step is to make a final selection of recommendations you wish to include in the report. The third, and final step, is then to go back and write the report keeping your recommendations in your mind at all times. Just like a historian, you cannot simply list facts in your report: you must have an under-lying, unifying theme. Your theme is the necessity of adopting the proposed recommendations and your report should build toward these recommendations; that is, the recommendations should flow directly from the report. If someone reads the entire report, the recommendations should seem inevitable from what has come before. They should not seem to come out of no-where or seem to be simply a standarized set of recommendations plugged into the report.

In addition to reading well "forwards," the report should also read "backwards," so to speak. Most readers will read the letter of transmittal to understand the overall conception of the report and will then skip directly to the recommendations. For these readers, the rest of the report should back up the recommendations. They should be able to turn to the deficiencies section for further discussion of the deficiencies the recommendations are designed to correct. They should then be able to turn to the appropriate section—background, organization structure, job descriptions, documents, or procedures—to back up the claim of deficiency if challenged. The report should thus document the present situation to back up the claim of deficiency, not simply as an interesting subject in its own right.

6.2 SYSTEMS ANALYSIS REPORT FOR SAMPLE COMPANY

We will now present a sample system analysis for Pooper Centers to make the discussions earlier in the chapter more concrete. Before going over this material, however, you should at least sketch out the material you would include in each section. You can then compare your thoughts to those of the authors.

Pooper Centers, Inc.
Analysis of Accounting Systems

Friendly & Wise
Certified Public Accountants
March, 1979

FRIENDLY & WISE
CERTIFIED PUBLIC ACCOUNTANTS
1000 Bourbon Street
New Orleans, Louisiana

March 14, 1979

Mr. John Paul Pooper, President
Pooper Centers, Inc.
1000 Canal Street
New Orleans, Louisiana

Dear John Paul:

We have completed our engagement to prepare an analysis
of your firm's accounting systems. The results of our work
are included in the attached report.

The primary objective of our engagement was to determine
if your accounting systems should be improved to deal with
your recent problems and to handle your expected future
growth. We have made a number of recommendations which
we believe are realistic and will meet the information and
control needs of management.

The secondary objective was to involve management more deeply
in the operation of the accounting systems, We feel that this
objective has been accomplished. There is now a general appreciation
of the importance of good accounting controls and the assistance
accounting reports can provide management.

At this time, we would like to express our appreciation for
having been given this opportunity to conduct this study.
We believe this analysis has provided your company with a
means of improving its operating efficiency. Finally, we
would like to express our thanks to each employee of your
company who participated in this study.

Very truly yours,
FRIENDLY & WISE

Jack R. Friendly

Jack Friendly

JRF/ms

Table of Contents

1.0 General Background

Pooper Centers, Inc. began as an audio equipment store in November, 1973. John Paul and Pamela Pooper opened this store on their own and continue to be the sole shareholders. The success of the company led the Poopers to open a second store in June, 1976. Both stores have proven successful, but recent problems with profitability and cash flow have called for an analysis of their accounting systems.

The original store started and continues to specialize in retail audio sales. The store sells equipment ranging from small and inexpensive radios to professional level components and systems. Also sold are audio accessories and related equipment, such as stereo headphones, needles, records, tapes, and cassettes. This original store is called the Pooper Audio Center and is referred to as PAC-1.

The second store also carries audio equipment, but concentrates on the sale of appliances. These appliances include stoves, refrigerators, freezers, washing machines, dryers, dishwashers, air conditioners, and televisions. Thus, the second store is called the Pooper Appliance Center and is referred to as PAC-2.

Until early 1979, both stores have enjoyed increasing sales and profits. Despite intense competition, the Pooper Centers stores have done well because of its excellent reputation based on its efficient, courteous staff. However, the company has recently experienced a number of operational and control problems. Specifically, despite continually increasing sales, there has recently been a marked reduction in profitability. Also, a cash flow problem has developed, which has caused increased borrowing from the bank to make payments to suppliers and employees. These problems led Pooper Centers to ask an outside firm to review its accounting system with a view toward correcting the problems.

2.0 Organization Structure

The organization structure at Pooper Centers is not a rigidly defined hierarchy. The people are closely knit and get along at all levels and between levels. However, there is a structure to the organization, and this section of the report will develop this structure (see Fig. 6-3). Further details on each position are given in the next section of the report (i.e., 3.0 Job Descriptions).

John Paul and Pamela Pooper are the sole stockholders, and, in addition, John Paul serves as the president of the firm. There is then a management group, which meets weekly to set policies for the company and guide its growth. In addition to the president, the management group consists of the accountant, the buyer, the manager of Pooper Audio Center (PAC-1) and the manager of Pooper Appliance Center (PAC-2). These four all report to the president.

The accountant then supervises the bookkeeper, the stock clerk, and the janitor. The buyer supervises no one directly, but does use the stock clerk informally in his work. Each manager has two assistant managers which report to him, one for each shift. At PAC-1, there is additionally one salesman in each shift. At PAC-2, there are additionally three salesmen in each shift.

3.0 Job Descriptions

There are essentially ten separate job positions at Pooper Centers. In this section we give a description of each of these positions as they now exist. Section 7.0, Recommendations, then suggests a number of changes to these positions.

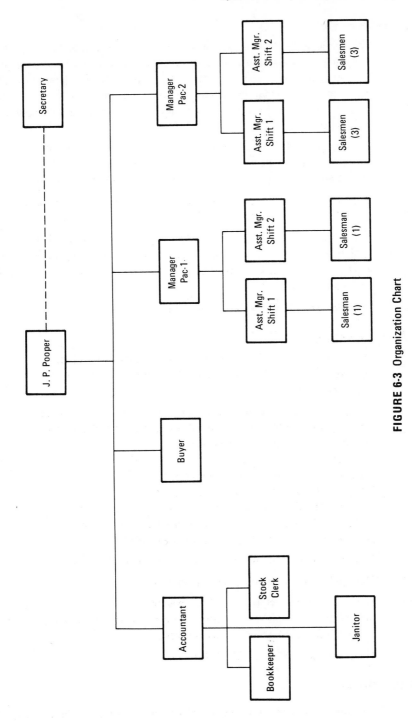

FIGURE 6-3 Organization Chart

3.1 Job Title: President

Duties:
The president is also the general manager and hence supervises all aspects of the company's activities. He also provides guidance and long-range planning for the company, with the attendant duties of arranging financing and planning investments. He keeps up with the activities in both stores by personal visits and informal meetings with employees. In addition, the president:

(1) approves all major purchase orders before they are mailed.
(2) signs all checks.
(3) attends and chairs weekly meetings of the management group.

Supervises:
The president supervises the accountant, the buyer, and the manager of each store.

Qualifications:
The president needs detailed knowledge of the audio equipment and appliance business; he also needs experience with the full range of business activities, including bank financing, advertising, merchandising, and dealing with employees.

Salary
The president receives $50,000 annually.

3.2 Job Title: Accountant

Duties:
The accountant is in charge of the record-keeping end of the business and is responsible for the design and operation of all accounting systems. Specifically, he:

(1) approves credit applications for potential customers on account.
(2) prepares monthly statements of account for credit customers.
(3) processes all incoming checks.
(4) signs all outgoing checks.
(5) issues payroll checks to employees.
(6) prepares monthly financial statements.
(7) assists bookkeeper with bank reconciliation as necessary.
(8) assists bookkeeper with calculation of commission due salesmen.
(9) attends weekly meetings of the management group.

Supervises:
The accountant supervises the bookkeeper, the stock clerk, and the janitor.

Supervised by:
The accountant is supervised by the president.

Qualifications:
The accountant needs a college degree in accounting plus experience supervising a complete accounting system. Experience in small business and manual accounting systems is also necessary.

Salary:
The accountant receives $20,000 annually.

3.3 Job Title: Buyer

Duties:
The buyer purchases all products for sale by the company. Specifically, he:

(1) monitors inventory quantities.

(2) confers with the other members of the management group concerning timing and quantity of purchases.

(3) decides on suppliers to use.

(4) prepares purchase orders, with review by the president for major purchase orders.

(5) receives goods when they arrive and checks both their quantity and quality.

(6) prepares debit memos for rejected goods which are returned to the vendor.

(7) attends weekly meetings of the management group.

Supervised by: The buyer is supervised by the president.

Qualifications: The buyer should have a detailed knowledge of both audio equipment and appliances; he should also have an eye for details because the reputation of the firm depends on the quality of product. An engineering background is desirable.

Salary: The buyer receives $20,000 annually.

3.4 Job Title: Manager

Duties: The manager is the day-to-day supervisor of the store. There is a separate manager for each of the two stores and each is a member of the president's management group. As a member of the management group, the managers must report to the president weekly on the business of their stores. These discussions include sales trends, employee relations, and other activities of the store. Specifically the manager:

(1) meets informally with the buyer to give input on what inventory his store needs, the timing of the purchases, and the establishment of reorder points; he also assists the buyer in checking inventory quantities and discussing sales patterns.

(2) evaluates performance of assistant managers and salesmen.

(3) approves returns of merchandise.

(4) sets up the layout and display of merchandise.

(5) oversees the movement of inventory from the stockroom to the sales floor.

(6) waits on special customers or helps out when the store is busy.

(7) makes sure that all documents generated in his store are forwarded to the accountant by the day following the transaction.

(8) sees that cash sales receipts are deposited intact in the bank twice each work day.

(9) approves checks of cash sales customers.

Supervises: The manager of PAC-1 supervises two shifts of employees consisting of one assistant manager and one salesman per shift. The manager of PAC-2 supervises two shifts of employees consisting of one assistant manager and three salesmen per shift.

Supervised by: The managers are supervised by the president.

Qualifications: The manager should have as much knowledge about either audio equipment or major appliances (depending on which store) to effectively be able to make a sale to any customer. Some experience in management with good recommendations from former employers would also be necessary.

Salary: The managers each receive $20,000 annually.

3.5 Job Title: Assistant Manager

Duties: The assistant manager serves in the place of the manager when the manager is not in the store. At that time, he assumes the manager's duties, such as approving checks; otherwise he serves as a regular salesman. (Detailed duties are listed under "Salesman.")

Supervises: When acting as the assistant manager, he supervises the other salesmen in the store.

Supervised by: The store manager supervises the assistant manager.

Qualifications: The assistant manager is the senior salesman of the store and should have the same qualifications as the other salesmen.

Salary: The assistant managers receive a salary base of $400 per month plus commissions. The average annual salary has been $16,800.

3.6 Job Title: Salesman

Duties: The task of the salesman is to make sales. Depending on the store, the salesman sells either the audio equipment or the major appliance inventories. Specifically, the salesman (either PAC-1 or PAC-2):

(1) sells the goods available in the store.
(2) fills out the proper forms for credit sales or puts information properly into the cash register for cash sales.

Supervised by: The manager at each of the stores supervises all the sales personnel. In the absence of the store manager, the assistant manager has temporary authority to supervise the sales staff.

Salary: Each salesman receives a $200 base salary per month plus commissions. The average annual salary has been $14,400.00.

3.7 Job Title: Bookkeeper

Duties: The bookkeeper aids the accountant in maintaining the books of the manual accounting system. The bookkeeper also:

(1) records all transactions from source documents which reach the accountant's office.
(2) reconciles the bank statement received monthly.

(3) helps the accountant calculate commissions due to store personnel from an analysis of sales.

(4) posts general ledger, accounts receivable and accounts payable ledgers.

Supervised by: The bookkeeper is under the supervision of the accountant.

Qualifications: Though no college education is required of the bookkeeper, either business school training or sufficient experience is required.

Salary: The bookkeeper receives $800 per month or $9,600 annually.

3.8 Job Title: Stock Clerk

Duties: The stock clerk is responsible for the stockrooms and manually handles the storage and moving of inventory for the two stores. Specifically, the stock clerk:

(1) is present when all shipments of merchandise arrive.

(2) moves goods from the stockroom to the sales floor of each store.

(3) helps the buyer check goods received from vendors and sends his copy of the purchase order with the shipping report to the accountant.

(4) keeps order in the stockrooms located in the rear of each store.

(5) moves goods from one store location to the other or picks up specially shipped goods from nearby locations.

Supervised by: The stock clerk is supervised by the accountant; however, he also follows the directions of the buyer and store managers when he is helping them.

Qualifications: The stock clerk should have a driver's license and be in good health. No formal education is required.

Salary: The stock clerk receives a monthly salary of $600 or an annual salary of $7,200.

3.9 Job Title: Secretary

Duties: The secretary types and performs general office duties. Specifically, the secretary:

(1) types all of the company's correspondence, including company checks, purchase orders, and debit memos.

(2) files all of the company's documents.

(3) opens the mail.

(4) answers the phone.

Supervised by: The secretary is supervised by the president.

Qualifications: The secretary should be able to type, file, and handle ordinary office procedures. College is not required but either business school training or practical experience is necessary.

Salary: The secretary receives a monthly salary of $600 or an annual salary of $7,200.

3.10 Job Title: Janitor

Duties:	The janitor is responsible for keeping the stores clean. He removes the dirt and trash which accumulate during the day. The janitor cleans and straightens both stores between 11 P.M. and 7 A.M., Sunday through Friday.
Supervised by:	The janitor is supervised by the accountant.
Qualifications:	The janitor does not require formal education, but must be stable, honest, and reliable.
Salary:	The janitor receives a monthly salary of $500 or annual salary of $6,000.

4.0 Documents, Forms, and Reports

This section of the report details the documents, forms, and reports which are used or generated by the Pooper Centers accounting system.

4.1 Sales Slip

Sales slips are prepared for all credit sales. If the sale is on a major credit card, telephone approval for the charge is secured by the salesman from the credit card agency. In all cases, one copy of the sales slip is given to the customer and the original and one copy is placed in a folder kept near the cash register. These credit sales slips are delivered to the accountant twice daily.

If the sale is for a new account to be carried by Pooper Centers, Inc., the credit sales slip, together with supporting information on the customer, are forwarded to the accountant for credit approval. One copy of each approved credit sales slip is normally returned to the store manager within a week, and the merchandise is then given to the customer.

Sales slips representing completed sales are recorded as received at the accountant's office and filed by day.

The salesman fills out the sales slip with the following information:
(1) the sales slip number
(2) the name of or code identifying the salesman making the sale
(3) the date of the sale
(4) the store where the sale was made
(5) the customer's account number
(6) the approval code
(7) the customer's name, address, city, state, ZIP code, and telephone number
(8) the delivery instruction specified by the customer
(9) a detailed description of each of the goods sold:
    (a) the quantity or number sold
    (b) the stock number of the item
    (c) a description of the item
    (d) the unit price of the item
    (e) the total extension of the item (unit price × quantity)
    (f) the final total price of all items
(10) The customer signs the sales slip in the space provided at the bottom of the sales slip.

4.2 Credit Memorandum

Credit memorandums are prepared in duplicate for all sales returns by customers, either for cash or for credit. All returns must be approved by the store manager. If the return is for cash, the transaction appears on the cash register tape, and the copies of the credit memorandum go to the accountant. Where the return reduces the customer's account balance, one copy of the credit memorandum goes to the customer and one to the accountant.

When received by the accountant's office, the credit memorandums are recorded as received and filed by day.

The salesman fills out the credit memorandum with the following information:

(1) the credit memorandum number
(2) the name of or code identifying the salesman handling the transaction
(3) the date and the store where the transaction took place
(4) the customer's account number
(5) the customer's name, address, city, state, ZIP code, and telephone number
(6) detailed information about the items returned:
    (a) the quantity of each item
    (b) the stock number of each item
    (c) the description of each item
    (d) the unit price of each item
    (e) the extension of the item (unit price x quantity)
    (f) the total price of the goods returned
(7) The person who approves the merchandise return (usually the store manager) signs the form at the space provided at the bottom of the form.

4.3 Purchase Order

The buyer prepares a purchase order to purchase merchandise. He prepares an original and three copies; the original goes to the vendor, the buyer keeps one copy and the accountant receives the other two. All major purchase orders are forwarded to the president for his approval before they are mailed.

The accountant gives one copy of the purchase order to the stock clerk to compare with the shipping report when the goods arrive.

When the goods arrive, the shipping report accompanying the goods is compared to the stock clerk's copy of the purchase order. The purchase order is then sent to the accountant if all is in order. The bookkeeper then records the transaction in the purchase journal.

The buyer fills out the following information:

(1) the purchase order number
(2) the vendor and his address
(3) the date of the purchase order
(4) where the goods are to be shipped
(5) the shipping instructions on how the goods are to be shipped
(6) the terms of the purchase
(7) the specifics of the items purchased:
    (a) the quantity ordered of each item

    (b) the description of each item
    (c) the unit price of each item
    (d) the extension of each item
    (e) the total price of all items
(8) the buyer then signs the bottom of the purchase order.

4.4 Debit Memorandum

The buyer prepares a debit memorandum when he receives unacceptable merchandise from a vendor. There are four copies of the debit memorandum: the buyer retains one copy, the original is sent to the vendor, one copy is shipped with the returned goods, and one copy goes to the accountant.

Debit memorandums are recorded when received at the accountant's office but are held to be matched against confirmations from suppliers that the goods have been returned and appropriate adjustments have been made.

The buyer fills out the debit memorandum with the following information:

(1) the date the debit memo is prepared
(2) the purchase order number to which the debit memo relates
(3) the vendor to whom goods are being returned
(4) a detailed description of the goods returned with:
    (a) the quantity of each item returned
    (b) the description of each item returned
    (c) the unit price of each item
    (d) the extension of each item returned (unit price x quantity)
    (e) the total price of all goods returned
(5) the buyer then signs the bottom of the debit memorandum.

4.5 Cash Register Tapes and Bank Deposit Slips

Cash registers have special keys which all salesmen use to record (1) the quantity sold, (2) the stock number of the item, (3) the unit price, (4) the total price of the items, (5) the total amount of the sale, and (6) a code to identify the person making the cash sale. Each cash refund is similarly recorded.

The total amount of the transaction is computed by the register and entered on the tape. One copy of the tape goes to the customer as a receipt while a second, internally stored tape, automatically keeps a cumulative total of cash sales and cash refunds. Twice a day, first thing each morning and late in the afternoon, store managers remove these internally stored tapes from all registers together with cash and checks except for $100 in small bills and change. The store managers prepare bank deposit slips from the tapes and deposit intact the cash and checks from the register into the bank. One copy of the deposit slip together with the cash register tapes goes to the accountant's office twice daily.

Bank deposit slips and cash register tapes are recorded and held to be compared by the bookkeeper to the monthly bank statement. Discrepancies are immediately reported to the accountant.

4.6 Shipping Report

The shipping report is the request for payment that the vendor sends us for the goods we receive.

A shipping report arrives with ordered goods and the buyer and stock clerk compare it to its related purchase order.

The shipping report is sent to the accountant's office with the clerk's copy of the purchase order if all merchandise is acceptable. When unacceptable merchandise is received, a debit memorandum is attached to the shipping report and the purchase order for returned goods before being sent to the accountant's office.

4.7 Financial Statements

Monthly, the accountant prepares a set of financial statements. These financial statements include the standard income statement and balance sheet. The statements also include schedules of accounts payable and accounts receivable. The schedule of accounts payable is a listing of all amounts owed to our vendors; the total of this list then balances to the control total of Accounts Payable in the balance sheet. The schedule of accounts receivable is a listing of all amounts owed to us by our customers; the total of this list then balances to the control total of Accounts Receivable in the balance sheet.

5.0 Accounting Procedures

This section provides narrative descriptions and flowcharts for the company's accounting system procedures.

5.1 Credit Sales

The salesman prepares a three-copy sales slip. If it is a major credit card purchase, the salesman must call the credit card agency for approval. If the sale is based on an account to be carried by Pooper, the salesman must determine whether this customer has an already established account, or if it is an initial credit purchase.

If this is an initial credit purchase, all credit sales slips are sent to the accountant with supporting information on the customer. The accountant uses standard credit-rating agencies to assist him in making his decision. The merchandise is not released to the customer until credit is approved.

Upon giving his approval, the accountant sends one copy of the sales slip back to the store manager, within one week, which is given to the customer when the merchandise is released. The other two copies are sent to the bookkeeper.

If the purchase is on an already established account or a major credit card purchase, one copy of the sales slip is given to the customer, and the original and one copy are put into a folder near the cash register. Twice daily, the store manager sends the sales slips to the accounting office.

In the accounting office, the bookkeeper checks the sales slips and records the transaction in the sales journal. From the journal, the bookkeeper posts weekly to the general ledger and the accounts receivable subsidiary ledger.

The secretary files the sales slips by day in a temporary file. They will later be used by the bookkeeper and accountant to determine commissions for the salesmen. (See Figure 6-4.)

5.2 Cash Sales

The salesman rings the transaction into the cash register. The register is equipped with special keys to record (1) quantity sold, (2) the stock number of the item, (3) unit price, (4) total price, and (5) salesman number on the tape. One copy of the tape is given to the customer as a receipt, while the other is internally stored in the cash register. The machine keeps a cumulative total of cash sales and cash refunds. Twice daily, the store manager prepares a two-copy deposit slip. He sends one copy with the cash to the bank, while the other copy is sent to the accounting office with the tape.

In the accountant's office, the bookkeeper checks over the documents and the tape and compares the tape with the deposit slip. The bookkeeper records the transaction in the cash receipts journal and posts weekly to the general ledger. The deposit slip and tape are filed temporarily and are compared with the bank statement when it arrives. The cash register tape is temporarily filed by day, to be used later to determine commissions. If any discrepancies appear in the bank reconciliation, they are reported to the accountant. (See Figure 6-5.)

5.3 Sales Returns and Allowances

The salesman prepares a two-copy credit memo, which is sent to the store manager for his approval. If the return is for cash, the transaction is entered into the cash register and appears on the cash register tape. The customer is given the cash and tape, while both copies of the credit memo are sent to the accountant's office.

If the return is for credit on the customer's account, one copy of the credit memo goes to the customer and the other is sent to the accountant's office.

When received, the bookkeeper checks the credit memo and records the transaction in the general journal and then posts weekly to the general ledger. The secretary files the credit memo permanently by day. (See Figure 6-6.)

5.4 Cash Receipts

The secretary opens the mail and sends all customer checks to the accountant. He records all customer payments in the cash receipts journal and prepares a two-part deposit slip. One copy goes to the bank with the checks and the other is held to compare with the bank statement when it arrives. This comparison with the bank statement is discussed in 5.2 Cash Sales.

The bookkeeper posts weekly from the cash receipts journal to both the general ledger and the accounts receivable subsidiary ledger. (See Figure 6-7.)

5.5 Purchasing

The Buyer, with suggestions from the managers of both PAC-1 and PAC-2, the accountant, and J. P. Pooper, decides to purchase and prepares a four-part purchase order. If it is a major purchase, then it goes to J. P. Pooper for his approval.

The original purchase order is sent to the vendor. One copy is held by the buyer and the other two go to the accountant's office.

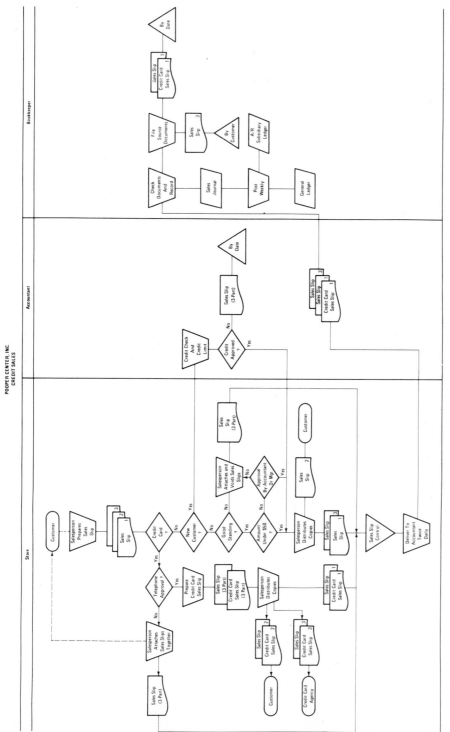

FIGURE 6-4

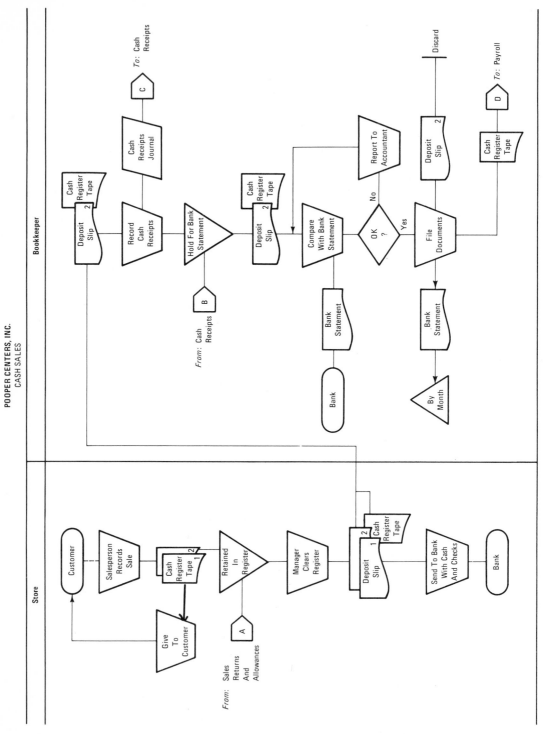

POOPER CENTERS, INC.
CASH SALES

Store

Bookkeeper

To: Cash Receipts

From: Cash Receipts

From: Sales Returns And Allowances

To: Payroll

FIGURE 6-5

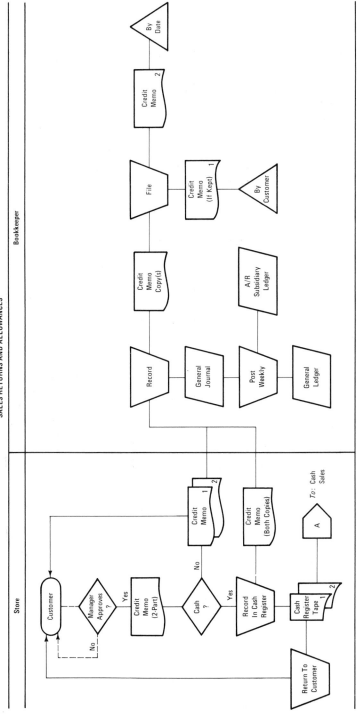

POOPER CENTERS, INC.
SALES RETURNS AND ALLOWANCES

FIGURE 6-6

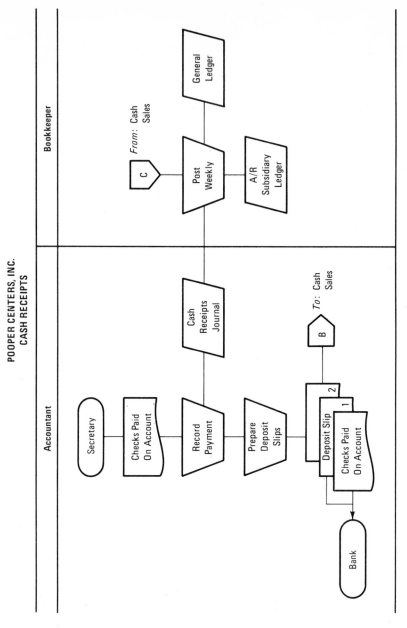

POOPER CENTERS, INC.
CASH RECEIPTS

FIGURE 6-7

One copy of the purchase order is filed by the bookkeeper in a temporary file to be matched later with the shipping report. The second copy goes to the stock clerk.

The stock clerk uses this purchase order to help the buyer check over the shipment. The buyer makes the decision whether or not to accept the shipment. If the shipment is acceptable, the purchase order and shipping report are sent back to the accountant's office. The bookkeeper matches the shipping report and the purchase order and records the transaction in the purchases journal; weekly, she posts to the general ledger and accounts payable subsidiary ledger. The buyer takes his copy of the purchase order and compares it with the shipment along with the stock clerk. Then the buyer refiles the purchase order.

If the shipment is not acceptable, the buyer prepares a four-copy debit memo. One copy is sent to the vendor, one to the bookkeeper, one to the stock clerk to be put with the goods, and one is kept by the buyer. The bookkeeper records this return transaction in the general journal and posts weekly to the general ledger. The secretary temporarily files the debit memo which is held to be matched against the vendor's confirmation. The stock clerk keeps his copy of the purchase order for the next shipment. (See Figure 6-8.)

5.6 Cash Disbursements

The accountant prepares all outgoing checks and gathers all support for the checks. This support includes purchase orders, and shipping reports for payments to vendors, invoices from the utility, etc. The accountant believes in taking all available discounts. The secretary types the checks and both J. P. Pooper and the accountant sign them. The accountant mails the checks to vendors and creditors.

The check support is given to the bookkeeper who records the transactions in the cash disbursements journal and posts weekly to the general ledger and the accounts payable subsidiary ledger. The secretary files the supporting documents. (See Figure 6-9.)

5.7 Payroll

The accountant, with the assistance of the bookkeeper, calculates the amount of commission due to the salesman from sales slips and the cash register tape. The bookkeeper, stock clerk, secretary, and janitor are paid semimonthly. All other employees are paid monthly. The other payroll items computed include: federal withholding, FICA, and federal and state unemployment. The company share of FICA is computed and recorded at each payroll. Unemployment tax is recorded once a month. The secretary types the payroll checks from the supporting information given to her by the accountant. Then both J. P. Pooper and the accountant sign the checks. The accountant then distributes the checks to the employees.

The supporting payroll documents, from which the checks are typed, are sent to the bookkeeper to be recorded in the cash disbursements journal and posted weekly to the general ledger. The supporting documents are filed by the secretary. (See Figure 6-10.)

6.0 Deficiencies and Omissions

This analysis uncovered a number of deficiencies and omissions in Pooper Centers' accounting system. This section will discuss each of these items and briefly indicate why it might be a problem. The next section of this report will lay out recommendations for improvement.

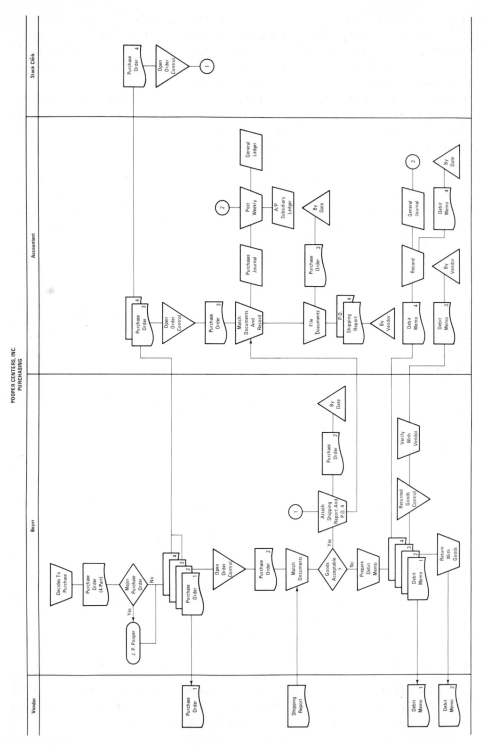

FIGURE 6-8

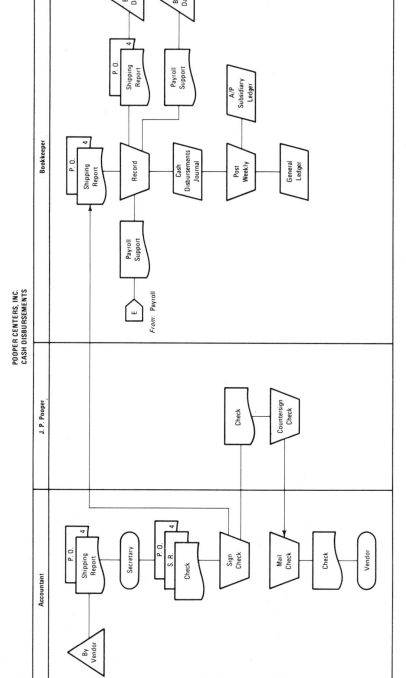

POOPER CENTERS, INC.
CASH DISBURSEMENTS

FIGURE 6-9

POOPER CENTERS, INC.
PAYROLL

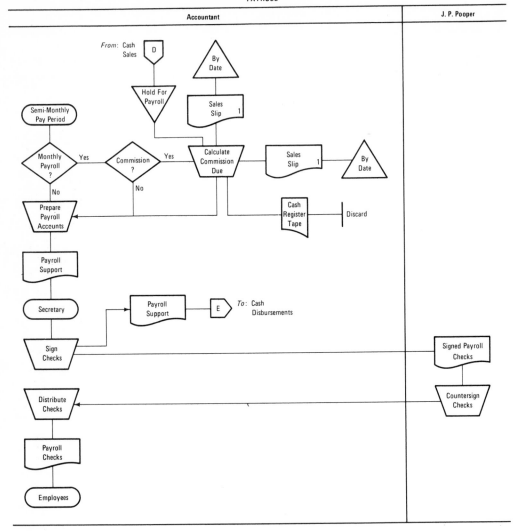

FIGURE 6-10

1. Pooper Center employees, including those who handle large amounts of cash and inventory, are not bonded. This practice exposes the company to a substantial risk.

2. There are a number of areas where the company policy or required procedure is left unnecessarily vague. These areas include: (a) conflicts of interest or dealing with related firms by, for example, salesmen of professional audio systems or large appliances; (b) the definition of a major purchase order which the president must approve; (c) a chart of accounts to detail precisely which accounts to use in specific cases; (d) a basis of comparison to judge good or bad performance—as it is, there is no budget with which to compare actual performance, nor do the monthly financial statements provide any comparative

figures; and (e) the procedure for determining uncollectible accounts (i.e., those accounts from which we will never receive payment, either due to bankruptcy or some other reason).

3. There are a number of points where employees' duties are not consistent with accepted practice and thus present internal control problems. These areas include: (a) the concentration of both custody of inventory (which is handled by the stock clerk) and the related recordkeeping (which is handled by the bookkeeper) under one person, the accountant; (b) the concentration of duties whereby the bookkeeper both records transactions in the journals and posts them to the ledgers; (c) the concentration of duties whereby the accountant approves credit customers, sends out customer statements, and receives payments on account; (d) the lack of a record of cash received in the mail which is independent of those processing the receipts; (e) a perhaps excessive closeness of the PAC-1 manager and the bookkeeper; (e) the concentration of duties where the bookkeeper both records cash disbursements and reconciles the bank statement; (f) the lack of an independent record of the sales slips sent to the bookkeeper for credit sales; and (g) the lack of an independent record, such as a perpetual inventory system, on the inventory moved and controlled by the stock clerk.

4. There are a number of areas where procedures are weak and leave the company open to excessive risk. Paid invoices are not perforated or cancelled and thus, potentially, could be used more than once. The invoice does not accompany the check for signing and thus there is inadequate support for the checks. The documents—purchase order, debit memorandum, sales slip, and credit memorandum—are not prenumbered; this practice allows the possibility that documents could be lost or misplaced without that fact becoming apparent. Important accounting records, such as the accounts receivable subsidiary ledger, are not kept in a safe and could be lost in a fire or other accident. Too many people have access to cash in the stores' cash registers; since all salesmen have equal access to the registers, it is impossible to assign specific responsibility for any discrepancies in the cash figure. The cash is left in the cash registers overnight; this leaves the firm open to considerable risk of loss, especially since the janitor has access to both stores overnight.

5. There is no audit of the financial statements by an independent CPA firm. There is therefore no independent check that the company's financial statements are fairly presented and that generally accepted accounting principles are applied.

7.0 Recommendations

This section details the recommendations the company should implement in order to have a more controlled, more efficient accounting system. These recommendations are:

1. The company should bond employees who handle cash and inventory. Experience has shown that bonding provides a psychological deterrent and another independent check on backgrounds in addition to protection in case of loss.

2. The company should develop a policies and procedures manual to provide guidance and direction to employees in their duties. The manual would additionally have the benefit of providing easier training for new employees. This manual should detail company policy concerning conflicts of interest, amount of paid vacation, sick leave, maternity leave, hiring

and firing of employees, the length of time to keep records, issuing credit, accepting personal checks, and writing off uncollectible accounts. The manual should also detail company procedures, as well as guidelines for transaction processing. This should include a chart of accounts which will detail the appropriate use of each account. The manual should also detail the duties and responsibilities of employees and the procedures which should be followed. (Sections 3.0, 4.0, and 5.0 of this report could provide a start for this manual.)

3. The company should divide the duties of the employees differently, to promote efficiency and provide more effective internal control.

    a. The secretary should continue to open all mail (except the bank statement), but should make a list of cash received. This list should then be compared to the entry in the cash receipts journal and the bank statement.

    b. The bank statement should go unopened to Mr. Pooper, who should prepare the bank reconciliation.

    c. The bookkeeper should continue to record the transactions in the journals, but the accountant should post the transactions to the ledgers.

    d. The bookkeeper should prepare the customer statements of account.

    e. Mr. Pooper should receive the checks for signing along with the supporting invoice or shipping report. After signing the check, he should perforate or otherwise cancel the supporting documents.

    f. All duties concerning custody of inventory should be assigned to the buyer and separated from the accountant's record-keeping function.

4. The company procedures should be changed in a number of areas. These changes should provide increased efficiency and improved internal control:

    a. The financial statements should provide a comparison of this month's and this year's performance to those of last year. Also, there should be a separate profit and loss statement for each store. When the company becomes more stable, the company should develop budgets.

    b. The monthly financial statements should include an aged trial balance of accounts receivable instead of a simple schedule. This should indicate the collectibility of these accounts.

    c. The documents—purchase order, sales slip, credit and debit memorandums—should all be prenumbered to allow better physical control.

    d. Important documents should be kept in a safe for better physical control.

    e. Cash deposits should be made nightly upon closing rather than being left in the store overnight.

    f. There should be one cashier at each store who would not function also as a salesperson. The cashier would have sole responsibility for the cash register and the handling of cash in the store.

    g. All credit sales should be recorded on the cash register tape to provide an independent record of the sales slip sent to the bookkeeper.

h. The company should implement a perpetual inventory system to keep better track of the location and quantity of the inventory.

5. The company should have an audit by an independent CPA firm.

exercises

6-1 System analysis is the first step in correcting systems which are not working properly, as well as in the creation of new systems. This is true no matter the nature of the system. Give three specific examples of systems you have come into contact with which should be analyzed with the purpose of improving the system or determining what is preventing effective operation.

6-2 Following are elements of system analysis. Arrange these elements into the order in which they would be performed.

7 *a.* Write summary of findings.

5 *b.* Flowchart system operation.

6 *c.* Determine internal control difficulties.

2 *d.* Discuss system with top management.

1 *e.* Determine areas to be reviewed.

4 *f.* Collect examples of documents.

8 *g.* Sketch out suggestions for improvement.

3 *h.* Discuss system with employees.

6-3 Following are components of a system analysis report. Arrange these components into the order in which they would appear.

a. Detailed steps to be taken by management.

4 *b.* Examples of documents processed by the system.

c. Explanation of weaknesses.

d. Summary of report and conclusions.

3 *e.* Job description.

5 *f.* Description of procedures.

1 *g.* Place the system in its context.

2 *h.* Determine lines of authority and responsibility.

6-4 The recommendations at the end of the system analysis report are the goal of the entire system analysis process. However, these recommendations must consider the political environment of the firm and must be acceptable to management.

1. In the sample report for Pooper Centers, items were mentioned in the section on deficiencies which were not followed by specific recommendations. Identify these deficiencies and state why recommendations might not have been made for each of them.

2. Give three examples of recommendations which may seem called for in Pooper Centers, but which would probably not be made because they are impractical or unrealistic.

6-5 In determining job descriptions and what tasks employees actually perform, the system analyst often does not get a clear picture from discussions with the particular employee involved. Discuss three approaches which might be used in addition to conversations with the affected employee to determine the real nature of the job.

6-6 Following is a list of deficiencies and omissions often discovered as a result of system analysis. Give one example of each of these deficiencies and omissions which might be found in an accounts receivable system.

a. Wasted effort.

b. Duplication of effort.

c. Excessive cost.

d. Overstaffing.

e. Poor policies.

f. No clear policies.

g. Ineffective supervision.

h. Important information not available.

6-7 Give an example of each of the deficiencies and omissions listed above in Exercise 6-6 which might be found in an accounts payable system.

6-8 The system analysis report for Pooper Centers given in the chapter included a recommendation that a policy and procedure manual be developed. Such a manual would include a chart of accounts consisting of the number, name, and guideline for use for each asset, liability, owner's equity, revenue, and expense account. Develop a chart of expense accounts for Pooper Centers providing the number, name, and guideline for use for each expense account.

6-9 The system analysis report for Pooper Centers given in the chapter included a recommendation that the duties and responsibilities of several positions be altered. Rewrite job descriptions for the accountant, bookkeeper, and buyer consistent with the findings of the report.

6-10 The system analysis report for Pooper Centers given in the chapter included a recommendation that separate profit and loss figures be developed for each store. Develop a new chart of accounts which would make possible the generation of profit and loss figures by store. This chart of accounts should include only account number and account name (guidelines for use may be omitted). How would you handle the salaries of those employees who work for both stores?

computer hardware
and software

outline

7.1   Basic Computer Concepts: components and functions of hardware devices; software components.

7.2   Input and Output: the primary types of input devices and media used in business data processing; types of output devices and media.

7.3   Processing and Storage: the basic functions of a central processing unit/the concepts of memory and storage; various types of data storage and their characteristics.

7.4   Batch to Real-Time Hardware Configurations: fundamental advantages and basic requirements of computer system design; sequential versus interactive systems.

7.5   Computer Software: primary programming languages; relationship of instructions to computer hardware and the source to object language translation process.

INTRODUCTION

In this chapter, we introduce the basic characteristics of computer systems. The physical attributes of computers are perhaps the most confusing and frustrating aspect of information systems. Much of the confusion, we feel, can be traced to attempts to present extremely technical material in a simplified and superficial manner. Since it is not necessary to understand all of the complex inner workings of a computer in order to use the capabilities of the system, such technical discussions have been kept to a minimum in this chapter. Instead, we focus on the characteristics (physical and otherwise) of computer systems which are important if you are to effectively use these systems.

7·1 BASIC COMPUTER CONCEPTS

The components of a computer system can be conveniently thought of as falling into two major categories—hardware and software. All computer systems are made up of both hardware and software, although the relative importance of one or the other may vary depending upon the particular system and the perspective of the system user.

The term *computer hardware* generally refers to the machines that make up the system. In fact, most people mean hardware when they use the terms *computer* or *computer system*. Because the machines are tangible and easy to see they tend to get more attention (particularly from the casual observer) than the software components of a system. *Computer software* generally refers to the entire set of instructions which direct and control the activities of the hardware. Together they make up (in most cases) a viable, functioning computer system.

To understand how these major system components function, consider the simple pocket calculator. For a calculator to be useful a problem must exist which can be solved by carrying out a series of steps. These steps can be converted into a set of instructions (software) and data which must somehow be given to the calculator (hardware). Some part of the calculator should be designed to receive these instructions (input) so that the machine can carry out the instructions on the data supplied. In a calculator the keyboard of numbers and mathematical functions represent the input component of the hardware. All instructions must pass through this hardware component. As the instructions are passed through the keyboard, they must be stored and then processed by the other hardware components. Instructions are actually carried out in a calculator by the electronic circuits inside the machine (processing unit) and then the result or answer conveyed (output) to the person with the problem. The output portion of a calculator is the visual display of numbers which represents the solution to the problem at hand. Figure 7-1 illustrates these relationships in a simple situation.

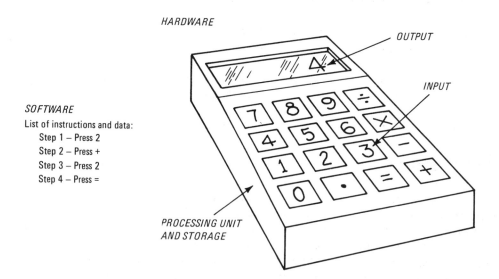

FIGURE 7-1 Components of the Pocket Calculator

Hardware devices/components/functions

We can generalize, then, about the required hardware components of any computer system. There must always be a hardware device(s) to accomplish each of the following functions:

1. *Input.* These devices have the task of receiving the instructions to be performed by the computer, and receiving the data (numbers, names, symbols, and so on) on which these steps should be carried out.

2. *Storage.* Even in the simplest problem, some processing steps must be remembered by the computer so they can be performed repeatedly. Also, some basic data must be retained for the same purposes. Storage devices accomplish these functions.

3. *Processing.* The central processing unit (CPU) actually carries out the instructions on the data provided. Since executing the desired instructions is the most important and difficult responsibility of any computer system, the CPU is the most complex hardware unit.

4. *Output.* These devices convey the results of the processing (in effect, the answer to the processing problem), to those with the need or desire to know these results. Processing solutions are received from the computer through these output devices.

Software Components

It is slightly more difficult to generalize about the required software components of a computer system. We can, however, be sure that there will always be at least the following software components:

1. A set of internally stored general instructions which control and coordinate the activities of the various hardware devices (input, storage, processing, and output). These instructions as a group are often called *master programs* or *control programs* and are, generally speaking, supplied by the hardware vendor. Thus, some software comes with the hardware as a combined package from the vendor.

2. A set of specific instructions to the processing unit to perform certain actions on certain specific data and the location of this relevant data. It is these instructions, usually called *application programs* because they do a specific set of processing toward a desired result or solution, that we normally think of when programming or computer programs are discussed. These instructions (i.e., the application programs) may be written by the user or purchased from companies called *software vendors.* Many different programming languages can be used to write these application programs and we will discuss the most common of these languages later in this chapter.

7·2 INPUT AND OUTPUT

Before any of the advantages of computer processing can be realized a link must be provided between the computer (CPU) and the person with a problem to be solved. Input-output devices provide this link. The task of these devices is to efficiently transfer instructions (programs) and data (names, numbers, symbols) from people to machines and then return the results of this processing to the users. Input devices are the path of entry to the processing unit and output devices represent the path of exit from it. Although there are some machines which are either exclusively input or exclusively output, most can serve both input and output functions. That is, many of the devices we will discuss are used to provide entry of instructions and data to the computer and for the exit of results. In addition, many input-output devices and media also serve a data storage function for processed information. These latter input-output devices are sometimes called *file devices* because their storage capacity makes possible the retention of large files of data within the system.

Types of Input Devices and Media

The four most common types of input devices and media used in business processing are discussed below:

1. *Punched card.* This is the oldest form of input media, and one that actually predates electronic computers (punched cards were used as early as 1890 with purely mechanical machines). The punched card rèmains a widely used input media in business processing today although its use is on the decline. Instructions and data are entered onto punched cards by a keypunch machine which inserts holes in the cards at the instruction of an operator. When all instructions and data have been transferred to cards, these cards can then be passed through an input device called a *card reader* which reads the holes in the cards and transfers this information to the computer for processing. Some features of punched cards with which you should be familiar are:

    a.   Although card readers are now very fast (up to 2,000 cards per minute) relative to earlier models, they are still slow compared to many other input devices.

    b.   The transmission of instructions and data to punched cards by keypunching can be done away from the computer and without computer help or using computer time, however, the process of keypunching is extremely slow and fraught with the possibility of error.

    c.   The cards themselves are bulky and somewhat hard to handle in large quantities, and are easily folded, spindled, or mutilated. Some manufacturers have begun to move toward a smaller, much more compact punched card, about one-third the size of a conventional card, to cure some of these problems. Even if this smaller punched card becomes widespread (something that is not at all certain) storage of instructions and data will still be a problem.

2. *Terminals.* These input devices come in many styles and designs, but they are all essentially keyboards of one sort or another similar to a typewriter, and a visual screen or printing capability for output. Figure 7-2 shows two basic types of terminal equipment. An operator sits at the terminal and enters instructions and data through the keyboard. The basic idea behind terminals is not new, although there have been many sophistications of the basic design. The use of these devices in business data processing is relatively recent and rapidly expanding. Some important points about terminal devices are:

    a.   Even the fastest of terminal designs are very slow compared to other input devices, consequently, transmitting very large amounts of data may pose a problem.

A. Teletype Model 33 ASR Data Terminal

B. Teletype® Model 40/2 Keyboard Display Printer

FIGURE 7-2 Terminals (Courtesy of Teletype Corporation)

b.   The problem of speed is further compounded by the extreme slowness of the terminal operator when compared to the speed of the CPU. Since most terminals are in contact with or have direct access to the central processing unit, data and instructions may be entered while the processor is idle, thus decreasing system efficiency.

c.   Terminals allow for the instant editing of instructions and data as input is taking place because of their direct contact with the CPU.

d.   Terminals are easy to use and are inexpensive, but provide no storage capacity.

3.   *Magnetic tape.* This input media has been a staple in business processing since its inception and remains very widely used today. Magnetic tape is similar to that used in home tape recorders or cassettes, except that characters and numbers are entered in the place of music or voices. A device called a *tape drive* equipped with special reading and writing heads is able to (1) scan the tape and transmit the instructions and data from the tape to the processing unit, and (2) enter new information on the tape. Keep in mind the following characteristics of magnetic tape:

a.   With tape drives, input devices move into the very fast category. Magnetic tape can be read and information transferred at rates of 80,000 to 800,000 characters each second, which equates to 1,000 to 10,000 punched cards a second.

b.   Magnetic tape possesses enormous storage capacity in addition to its speed advantage. A typical reel of tape (only slightly larger than an ordinary home tape recorder reel) can hold up to 20 million characters of information. The media is rather well suited for storing files of permanent and semipermanent instructions and data.

c.   Computers are able to read information from and write to magnetic tape through tape drives without human assistance once the tapes are actually on the tape drives. Human action is necessary for the placing of reels of tape onto the tape drives and changing them at appropriate times.

d.   Although magnetic tape is very inexpensive, the tape drives are considerably more expensive than either card readers or terminals and somewhat more complex to use because information on magnetic tape is not man-sensible without translation using other devices.

4.   *Disks.* This is the most advanced and widely used input device in business applications. You might think of this media as similar to a phonograph album or a number of phonograph albums stacked on top of each other with only space for a small arm between them. On each of these "albums" information is recorded in a series of circles. Each of the arms is equipped with a reading head so that the disk can be scanned and instructions and data transmitted to the processing unit and a writing head so that new information can be entered on the disk. Disks are placed on machines called *disk drives* which move the disks and the read-write arms. You should note the following about disks in general:

a.   Disk speed equals that of magnetic tape with the transfer of information being about as fast as tape.

b.   Like tape, disks possess capacity to store very large quantities of information in a very small area and thus are ideal for storing files of instructions and data. One advantage of disks over tape is that the availability of information to the CPU is not affected by the location of the information on the disk. All information on disks is available in about the same time, while information at the end of a reel of magnetic tape is considerably less accessible than information at the beginning.

c. Like tape, computers are able to read information from and write to disks without human intervention, although human assistance may be needed if *disk packs* (groups of individual disks in a removable package) must be removed or replaced on disk drives.

d. Disks and disk drives represent the most expensive input media and devices of those we have discussed. The difference in cost can be significant and the operation more complex when compared to tapes and tape drives. Of course, like magnetic tape, information contained on disks is not understandable by humans without translation through other devices.

e. Direct human input to both magnetic tape and disks is possible through the use of *key to tape* and *key to disk* devices. These input devices, which are similar in principle to the keypunch machine, allow data and instructions to be entered directly on tapes and disks without interaction with or help from the CPU or other devices.

Types of Output Devices and Media

Input devices and media make possible human to computer communication. Output devices and media reverse this process and allow the computer to transmit the results of processing. Computer processing would be to no avail if we could not get the solutions to problems from the computer in man-sensible form or in a form suitable for storage for later use. Output devices and media are designed to provide either immediately usable or efficiently storable results of processing.

Of the four primary input devices and media used in business applications, three also function as output. The storage problems and lack of readability associated with punched cards has resulted in their not being a viable output media except in cases where the output from one processing run will be used as input to another subsequent run. In this case, the punched card becomes a turn-around document. We will introduce an additional device which functions exclusively as output, thus providing four primary output devices and media.

1. *Terminals.* Modern terminals have the capacity to deliver immediately usable, man-sensible computer results in several different forms. Some transmit output in printed form, others are able to display results on a visual screen, and still others may do both (see Figure 7-2). Generally, the major characteristics of terminals as input devices apply as well to their use as output. The ability of terminals to perform both input and output functions and their contact with the CPU allows for a give-and-take between people and computers which can produce more precise and useful processing results. Use of these devices in business systems is on the increase.

2. *Printers.* This device is ideal for printed reports and other output which must be understood by people and for which a hard copy is desired. If output must be disseminated to various users or if a permanent record is necessary, the printer is usually used. Although printed output from a printer can resemble output from a printing terminal, printers are

usually much faster (up to 2,000 or so lines per minute), and the output can take almost any form desired by the user (from computer paper to bills). Printers are output devices only and can perform no other function. Figure 7-3 illustrates a typical small printer.

3. *Magnetic tape and disks.* If man-sensible output is not immediately required and is to be stored until needed, or if computer results are to be used in further processing, tapes and/or disks are very useful output devices. Both are fast and can hold large amounts of information in small spaces, so that output which must be stored for long periods of time or stored and periodically used can best utilize these devices. Data on customer or supplier accounts or payroll are examples of information which must be stored and periodically processed at reasonable speeds.

Figure 7-4 is an illustration of a small computer system which contains most of the input-output devices and media we have been discussing. It will help you to see how they physically fit together in a typical small system and how the appearance and function of these hardware devices relate. As you study Figure 7-4 reflect back to our calculator illustration in Figure 7-1. Both "systems" have the same basic components; however, as we move from the calculator to the small computer system, the components themselves become more prominent and physically (although not electronically) separated. These same hardware components would be present in even the largest computer systems and would differ only in sophistication and combination rather than basic function.

7·3 PROCESSING AND STORAGE

The central processing unit (CPU) is the computer in a computer system and is the most important and complex component of the system. In spite of this prominent role, the CPU is among the least noticeable physical components of a system. Popular media tend to show computer systems as the more "glamorous" and easily recognizable terminals, video screens, and tape drives. The processor (CPU) usually sits off to one side like a box with nothing to give

FIGURE 7-3 Printer
(courtesy of Digital Equipment Corporation, Commercial Group)

FIGURE 7-4 IBM 5110 Business Computing System
(courtesy of IBM Corporation)

away its true function. If you return to our typical small system in Figure 7-4, you will find the CPU on the table top within the same unit as the terminal and therefore not noticeable at all.

Throughout our discussion of input-output, we mentioned the relative speeds of these devices and media. Our purpose was to indicate what "fast" really is in computer terms and thus help you develop an appreciation for the major speed differences between devices. Some of the speeds may seem incredibly fast and indeed they are, but real speed, in computer terms, is encountered when the CPU begins to function. Processing units perform basic operations in something called *nanoseconds*. A nanosecond is one thousandth of a millionth of a second. It is very hard to think of a second divided into a million parts, and then one of these parts further divided into one thousand parts, but that is the time frame in which processors operate. In the half second or so it would take your pencil to hit the floor if you dropped it, a large computer could (if the instructions and data were in the proper form) perform millions of basic operations. Even the very fastest input-output devices are very slow when compared to the incredible speed of the CPU.

Basic Functions of a Central Processing Unit/Memory and Storage

Processing units perform three major functions. Common to all CPUs is (1) a control unit, (2) an arithmetic and logic unit (ALU), and (3) a storage unit. The control unit does no processing, but directs the activities of the entire system. The other units of the CPU respond to commands from the control unit as do the other major components of the computer system. The control unit gets its instructions from humans via the computer program which details the processing steps necessary to solve a problem. In effect, we communicate through our computer programs to the control unit of the processor which, in turn, issues directions to the other units of the CPU and the other components of the system to carry out the processing task.

When an arithmetic calculation or comparison, or any other comparison is required the data necessary for the calculation or comparison is transferred to the arithmetic and logic unit where these functions are carried out. The ALU is peculiar because it has no permanent storage capacity. Data is transferred into the ALU at the direction of the control unit; calculations and comparisons are made, then the data is immediately removed to other storage. This other storage represents the third function of the processing unit. CPUs have their own storage capacity usually called *main memory* or *primary storage*. The information stored here is accessible to the processor without intervention by humans. This primary storage is very small compared to other types of storage and is usually reserved for master programs which exercise overall control of the system and the program and data for the particular processing application currently being "run" on the system. In fact, one of the commonly accepted measures of CPU capacity and sophistication (and consequently price) is the size of primary storage.

Figure 7-5 depicts the relationship between these three functions of the central processing unit in terms of the flow of instructions and data.

Since the CPU is the focal point of any computer hardware system, the relationships of the other hardware components to the CPU is important in hardware system design. Generally it is important to distinguish those devices and media in direct contact with the processor at all times without human assistance, from those devices and media whose contact with the CPU is one-way and intermittent. The same distinction can be made with respect to data transmitted or stored by these devices. The terms *on-line* and *off-line* are used to describe the relationship of computer hardware devices to the CPU as well as the accessibility of data to the CPU.

On-line and off-line, then, may be applied to hardware components or to data in a computer system. A hardware device is said to be on-line if the device is in constant contact with the processor and interchange is possible. The same on-line description can be applied to data transmitted or stored in a system that is accessible to the processor at all times without

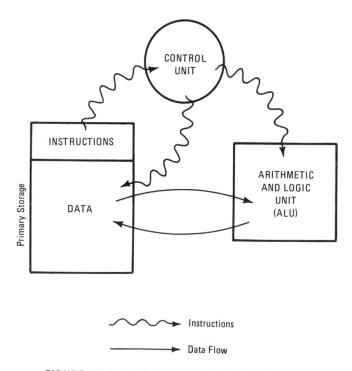

FIGURE 7-5 Instruction and Data Flow in the Computer

intervention by humans. Computer terminals and disks are generally on-line devices, consequently, data transmitted or stored by these devices is also on-line. Hardware devices and data whose accessibility to the CPU is intermittent and requires some human action are described as off-line. Card readers and tape drives are said to be off-line because the contact of these devices with the CPU is generally one-way (no give-and-take interchange is possible), and human action is necessary for the data transmitted and stored by these devices to be accessible to the CPU.

Types of Data Storage and Their Characteristics

On-line and off-line distinctions are most important in system design when applied to data storage in a computer system. Large amounts of information (files) must be stored, processed, and then stored again, so business processing systems must be able to provide for extensive storage capacity beyond the processing unit. This storage is often called *external, secondary,* or *peripheral* and almost always takes the form of magnetic tape or disk storage. (These are the file devices we discussed earlier.) Secondary storage may be on-line or off-line, and it may be direct access or sequential. Generally, magnetic tape storage is off-line because there may only be a relatively few tape drives compared to the reels of tape on which information is stored, and these reels must be placed on the tape drive to be within the reach of the processor. Disk storage is usually on-line; however, with removable disk packs this type of storage may also be off-line.

The direct access vs. sequential idea is a different matter. *Direct access* (sometimes referred to as random access) simply means that the time it takes for the computer to retrieve instructions or data is not affected by the exact position of the information on the media. On direct access storage devices like disks each piece of information is equally accessible regardless of its location on the disk. All disks are necessarily direct access by their design. Sequential storage exhibits the opposite characteristic. The location of the information on the media very much affects the time it takes for the processor to retrieve the information since all instructions and data on the beginning of the media must be passed through in order to get to that information stored at the end. Obviously, magnetic tape is always going to exhibit sequential storage. Table 7-1 gives the major characteristics of the computer system storage we have discussed.

We have now been through all of the major hardware components of a computer system. Figure 7-6 illustrates a major computer system consisting of all of the components presented earlier. Compare this system to the pocket calculator presented in Figure 7-1 and the small computer system presented in Figure 7-4. Note that all systems exhibit the same basic components and functions. Only the size, sophistication, and number of components differ.

TABLE 7-1 CHARACTERISTICS OF DATA STORAGE

	Availability	*Accessibility*
Primary storage	On-line	Direct Access
Disk storage	On-line or off-line	Direct Access
Magnetic tape storage	Off-line	Sequential

FIGURE 7-6 NCR V-8580 Computer System
(courtesy of NCR Corporation)

7·4 BATCH TO REAL-TIME HARDWARE CONFIGURATIONS

Fundamental Advantages/Basic Requirements of Computer System Design

Let us now put these hardware components together to make a computer system. Since there are so many different types of hardware devices and media, there are many possible combinations of input-processing-storage-output components. A basic approach or guideline to the design of computer hardware systems will be presented in the remainder of this chapter, but first, two general, overriding considerations of computer system design must be kept in mind.

These considerations are (1) the fundamental advantages computer systems offer over alternative methods of processing data and (2) the basic requirements of a business data processing system. First, what kinds of things are computers and computer systems able to do better than any other processing alternatives? If you think back over the characteristics of the various hardware components of a system, three distinct advantages of these devices should come to mind.

1. *Computer system hardware* (particularly the CPU) is *very* fast. Extraordinary speeds, by human standards, are commonplace for all these devices. In the speed of calculations, decisions, and input *and* output no processing alternative can match a computer system.

2. *Computer systems* possess incredible memory. Storage devices and the processing unit are able to keep extremely large amounts of data accessible in very small spaces without ever forgetting any of it.

3. *Computer hardware* does exactly what it is told to do. Since instructions are *always* followed without deviation and without complaint, computer systems do not make mistakes in their own right. On the other hand, hardware devices must be given instructions in

minute detail, will do everything they are told to do (no matter how silly it may seem), and apply no perception, reasoning, initiative or common sense to their activities.

Second, what must business data processing systems be able to do if they are to be effective and efficient?

Recall the basic nature of business processing systems as discussed in Part One of this book. All business processing systems exhibit the following characteristics:

1. *The generation of large amounts of data.* All businesses create significant amounts of data in the course of their operations. There is a definite need (sometimes legal) for this information about business activities to be processed accurately. In addition, some of these data must be retained for long periods of time; while other data must be digested into some form of useable output (statements and reports).

2. *Simple processing of repetitive events.* Although businesses may engage in all sorts of different kinds of events, in fact they experience the same common transactions repeatedly. Business processing time is spent mostly on a few (perhaps a dozen or so) basic events, and the calculations and decisions required to process these events are very simple.

Business systems must have the capacity to receive, store, and output very large amounts of data quickly and accurately, and do very simple (for a computer) and repetitive processing of this data. Since CPU speed, even for complex calculations and decisions, is well in excess of the speed of other hardware, the obvious emphasis in the design of a business computer system must be on the input-output and data storage components of the system. Here is where bottlenecks and inefficiencies can occur in business processing systems. Contrast this situation to scientific processing where small amounts of data input and output might be required in a processing problem and where relatively little or no permanent storage is necessary, but where unique, complex decisions and calculations are made. In scientific systems, the emphasis must be placed on the processor in the system.

Computer systems are made up of a set of components which are extremely fast, possess an excellent memory, and follow instructions perfectly, but which are not very bright and have no imagination or initiative. In business processing we have problems which require the simple, but fast and accurate processing of very large amounts of repetitive data. The advantages of computer systems could not be better suited to the needs of business processing.

The actual design of a computer system to take full advantage of this suitability depends upon the particular information needs of a business, its most repetitive and important processing problems, and many other factors including cost. We will discuss four basic configurations used in business processing systems. These approaches represent discrete examples of successful hardware combinations for particular information and processing needs which have been selected from an almost continuous scale of possibilities. The possible configurations which could be used in business data processing are almost endless. Hardware system design is limited only by the imagination of the user.

Sequential versus Interactive Systems

The first decision to be made in establishing a hardware configuration is the basic orientation of the system. There are two such basic orientations available—*sequential* or *interactive.*

In sequential processing systems, data is stored and processed in a specified order and at specified discrete times. Generally, data is accumulated and stored for a certain period of time or until a certain quantity of data is accumulated. Then, processing of all data accumulated takes place at once, and output is generated from all of the data. This approach is called *batch* processing, and is ideal if information needs are such that timely, immediate processing results are not necessary. Data, however, must be organized on some numerical (sequential) basis for batch processing to be efficient. Data storage in sequential systems may be off-line since processing takes place only at predetermined times and data needs are known well in advance. The most useful sequential storage media is magnetic tape, and most sequential systems are built around magnetic tape storage, although data may be organized and processed sequentially from disk storage. The capabilities of disk storage are such that either sequential or interactive processing is possible. Magnetic tape, on the other hand, is purely a sequential media.

Refinements of the sequential batch-processing approach can be made in the process of conversion of source documents data to machine input form and in the methods of transmission of this converted data to the computer for processing. Consider the brief descriptions of two sequential batch approaches in Table 7-2 and note the differences in data conversion and transmission. Remember, however, that both descriptions represent the batch approach to processing and require that (1) data be susceptible to sequential organization and processing; (2) data be processed at discrete times in groups of similar transactions or events; and (3) that management needs for timely or special information do not require that each transaction be processed individually as it occurs and immediate results generated. Sequential orientation and batch processing represent the oldest approach to computer hardware system design and may still be the most widely used approach in business. On computers specifically designed for batch processing, it is the simplest and least expensive approach to processing business data.

Interactive processing systems are characterized by data storage in direct access, easily accessible media, and by processing which can take place immediately as transactions occur. In the interactive approach to hardware system design the data is processed individually and continuously as transactions take place and output is generated instantly. Since processing in interactive systems takes place in any order as events occur or information is needed, data storage must be in on-line, direct-access form. Disks are the most widely used on-line, direct-access storage, and most interactive systems are built around this media.

Basic approaches to interactive systems can differ in the extent to which processing can be initiated from remote locations as transactions occur. Table 7-3 describes two interactive systems which differ in the degree that continuous processing is allowed from remote data-gathering locations. As you study this figure keep in mind that the interactive approach to processing requires that (1) data be always available in direct-access storage; (2) some processing be initiated from remote locations away from the computer system; and (3) management needs for timely information make it impossible for processing to wait while significant data accumulation takes place. In summary, interactive processing must make fast, up-to-date information constantly available.

Which particular system orientation a company may choose will depend, of course, on its overall processing problems and applications and its information needs. Generally, however, the necessity for up-to-date accurate information must be balanced against the extra cost and complexity of interactive systems. Also important in basic hardware design is the level of flexibility in the system. The capacity of the system for change and growth as business processing

TABLE 7-2 TWO APPROACHES TO BATCH PROCESSING

Sequential Orientation	
Basic Batch	*Batch With Remote Data Transmission*
1. Source documents are gathered and manually transferred to computer site.	1. Source documents data is converted to machine input form at various remote data collection points.
2. All data is converted to machine input form at computer site.	2. At certain predetermined times the data is electronically transferred to the computer site to be stored for processing.
3. Processing takes place in batches at predetermined times.	3. Processing takes place in batches at predetermined times.
4. Output is generated at the computer site and then manually transferred to users.	4. Output is generated at the computer site and may be electronically transferred to remote points to users.
5. The various specific input and output devices and media would be a matter of weighing relative data recording costs and speed against the volume requirements of the processing. Punched cards for input and printers for output would not be unusual in such a system.	5. Input and output devices and media would probably be a combination of those used in basic batch plus some remote devices such as terminals or remote card readers and printers.
6. Data storage would likely be on magnetic tape for files of permanent or semi-permanent data.	6. Data storage would likely be on magnetic tape for files of permanent or semi-permanent data.
7. This is the simplest and least expensive large system to operate.	7. Better turnaround and accuracy would likely result as compared to basic batch, since some manual functions are eliminated. Costs of this system would be higher than basic batch.

needs and circumstances change is a critical dimension of any hardware configuration. Clearly observable in the world of business data processing systems is a general trend toward quick response (interactive) systems as competition and customer demands accelerate and hardware costs decrease.

Computer Cost

One final note on the cost of computer hardware systems. Nothing seems as certain in the world of computer hardware as the fact that prices of hardware components will continue to fall at a dramatic rate. Computer systems are still relatively expensive but technology has been such that very powerful and sophisticated systems now cost about what medium systems cost a few years ago and a good medium-sized system falls in the cost category of a small system of five to ten years ago.

The most dramatic of these cost decreases are now occurring in the area of small interactive systems. These systems are not simply a smaller version of older-type computers, but rather involve a completely new approach to data processing. Older computers, such as most second and third generation machines, were designed for batch processing. With a tremendous addition of time, cost, and complexity, these computers can work in a direct-access mode; however, they

TABLE 7-3 TWO APPROACHES TO DIRECT-ACCESS PROCESSING

Interactive Orientation	
Direct Access—Inquiry/Response Only	*Direct Access With Real-Time Processing*
1. Direct interaction with the computer is possible through remote terminals (I/O devices) for questions and answers.	1. Direct interaction with the computer is possible through remote terminals (I/O devices) for questions and answers as in the previous system, but also for the processing of data.
2. Normal processing is interrupted as questions come in and the CPU searches data stored in on-line, direct access devices (disks) to answer questions.	2. Normal processing is initiated from remote input-output devices as transactions occur with data stored in on-line, direct access devices (disks).
3. No processing is done from remote input-output devices, only a question and answer dialogue is possible, and questions are answered using the data available.	3. Since normal processing is continuous there is no time lag between the occurrence of a transaction and the reflection of that transaction in the stored data of the computer system. This is called a *real-time* system.
4. Normal processing is accomplished at the computer site at fixed times using input-output devices and media similar to that used in sequential systems.	4. Unless errors occur, information is constantly accurate and up-to-date because computer system data instantly reflects events as they occur.
5. This approach provides much more timely information than batch processing (at a greater cost, of course). The information is still not precisely up-to-date because processing is not continuous and some time lag is necessary between the occurrence of an event and its reflection in the data files of the system.	5. This is a very costly and complex system to implement and operate; however, the movement in computer system hardware has been toward this design.

are not designed for it and do not do it well. The new small systems, on the other hand, are designed from the ground up to be direct access systems. Thus, in contrast to the older systems, it is actually easier to use the new systems in an interactive, direct-access way than in a sequential processing mode. In fact, these small systems are so inexpensive that essentially all business firms can now afford the computer hardware they need.

If you have a little trouble with this idea of increasing capacity with dramatically decreasing costs consider the pocket calculator we discussed at the very beginning of this chapter. Calculators of ten years ago were twenty times as large as current ones with probably one-half to one-tenth the processing capabilities and a cost as much as ten times that of today's models. Now almost everyone has a pocket calculator and we take them for granted. The situation with computer hardware is somewhat similar. So much so that "personal" computer systems are now becoming available at reachable prices. Figures 7-7 and 7-8 illustrate two such personal computer systems with substantial processing capability which are currently available at reasonable costs. Who knows, someday soon we might all have such a system at home for our personal data processing needs.

FIGURE 7-7 Personal Computer System PCS-80/30
(courtesy of Imsai Manufacturing Corporation)

FIGURE 7-8 The Digital Group System 7
Under $5,000 Assembled and Tested
(courtesy of The Digital Group)

7·5 COMPUTER SOFTWARE

Remember from our general discussion at the beginning of this chapter that computer software normally consists of two primary components. A set of hardware-oriented instructions which control the overall interaction of the machines, called *control* programs, are usually acquired along with the hardware system from the computer vendor. This component of software is usually a package with the hardware. Of more interest to most system users is the second component of computer software, called *application* programs. These programs are more user oriented because they are designed to instruct a hardware system on how to accomplish some specific processing task desired by the user and produce some output. It is these application programs which are written in programming languages. Writing such an application program is generally called *programming* the computer.

Primary Programming Languages

As computer use has become more widespread many programming languages have been developed, with each language being designed to accomplish some specific task or meet some perceived need. Three programming languages have emerged as most significant, however, because they are much more widely used in data processing than the others. FORTRAN, BASIC, and COBOL are the most successful of programming languages because each has filled a general need of system users well.

FORTRAN is a scientific-oriented language which was designed for ease of problem solving in complex mathematical models. The focus and strength of FORTRAN is in its ability to manipulate numbers and equations. The input and output capabilities of FORTRAN are limited and somewhat cumbersome to implement if elaborate data or report structures are a part of the processing task. In response to the complexities and limitations of FORTRAN, the BASIC programming language was created. The motivation behind BASIC was the desire to create a simple language which beginning computer students could understand quickly, thereby reducing the lag time in actually getting students to the computer. BASIC was conceived as an instructional language which could be learned and quickly used to solve problems. It is related to FORTRAN, but simplifies many of the input and output complexities of that language. Although BASIC is the easiest to learn and use of the three primary languages, it is fairly powerful and is used in its own right in many business data processing applications on small computer systems.

The primary business-oriented programming language in use today is COBOL. COBOL was created as a part of an attempt to standardize the writing of business application programs and is specifically designed to meet the needs of business data processing. The language makes use of commands and syntax which are very much like ordinary English and focuses on the massive input and output requirements which exist in most business data processing problems. COBOL is designed to facilitate the input and output of large amounts of data and can accommodate elaborate data or report structures. The English-like syntax of the language makes the straightforward processing required in business problems easy to program.

Relationship of Instructions to Computer Hardware—The Translation Process

We have now discussed the basic hardware and software components of a computer system. All that remains is to tie these components together by a discussion of how machines and instructions actually combine to carry out a particular processing task. System users have a processing need or problem and desire to use computer hardware to fill the need or solve the problem. Humans would prefer to communicate the necessary steps to solve a problem in their own language (such as English), but computers only understand their own language, which is a series of "0's" and "1's" used in various combinations. For human-computer communication to take place, human language instructions must be translated into machine language instructions to be carried out by the hardware. This translation process involves three steps.

1. The use of a programming language rather than a natural language is the first step in the translation process. All natural languages contain ambiguities which require inference and contextual translation and thus would be impossible for a machine to translate in an exact manner. Programming languages require humans to issue instructions in a precise format

using commands, syntax, and structure in a rigidly fixed manner. Although programming languages may be based on a natural language, the ambiguities are removed and a precise structure is substituted which allows for unambiguous translation. An application program written in a programming language is called a *source program*, and the language is often called a *source language*.

2. Even programming languages, however, are not understood by computers, so that they must undergo a translation into machine language. The rigid syntax and structure of programming languages makes them susceptible to translation by a special software component called a *compiler*. The compiler is itself a program which is designed to accept a source program and convert it instruction by instruction into machine language. Obviously, each programming language must have its own unique compiler which is based on the structure of the language. Compilers are most often acquired, along with control programs, from the computer vendor as a package with the hardware system.

3. The original set of instructions translated into machine language is called the *object program*. It is the object program that is understood by the control unit of the CPU. The control unit interprets each machine language instruction and issues directions to the other units of the CPU as well as the other hardware components of the system to carry out the processing.

This chapter has presented the major computer hardware and software technology, characteristics and relationships which are necessary to the understanding and use of computer-based information systems. Chapter 8 will introduce the basic data organization and file concepts which are necessarily based upon the ideas presented in this chapter. That chapter will add data to our package of hardware and software.

exercises

7-1 A basic communication problem exists between people and computer hardware: people prefer to communicate in their natural language (such as English), while computer hardware only understands 0's and 1's. Thus, in order for human-computer communication to exist, some translation process must take place. Describe the components of this translation process and how the process works in terms of the hardware and software components of a system.

7-2 Each of the three primary programming languages has been developed to meet a particular kind of processing need. For each of the following programming applications, give the programming language which would likely be used:

a. Bank processing of customer transactions.

b. Mathematical modelling of bridge design.

c. Hospital processing of patient charges.

d. Real estate investment analysis on personal computer.

e. Solving complex equations.

f. United States government payroll.

    g. Billing of customers by major department store.

    h. Demonstration introductory program for beginners.

7-3   Consider the system used by the Internal Revenue Service to process annual income tax returns. The taxpayer mails his return, supporting documents, and check to a regional office where the information is converted and input to a computer system for basic accuracy checks. Computer-sensible data on what each taxpayer has filed is then manually forwarded to the national computer center in Maryland for further analysis and comparison with previous years' returns. From this analysis and comparison, the computer generates lists by region of returns with high probabilities of fraud or negligence; these lists go back to the regional offices for audit purposes. As a by-product of this processing, data are generated and stored in the central computer system. These data are used to immediately answer general statistical and policy questions about income and taxes for all taxpayers. Specify the input, file, and output hardware devices which would likely be used in each regional computer system. Explain the data flow through each of these devices in the regional computer systems.

7-4   Using the data presented in Exercise 7-3 above, specify the input, file, and output hardware devices which would likely be used in the national computer system. Explain the data flow through each of these devices in the national computer system.

7-5   Following is a list of information which might be input to, stored by, or generated from a computer system. For each item, specify the hardware device(s) which would process or transmit it in a batch system.

    a. Data on year-to-date earnings for each employee.

    b. Current pay period hours worked for one employee.

    c. Monthly department store billing statement.

    d. Amounts of inventory on hand for immediate response to customer questions.

    e. Payroll check.

    f. Customer payment on account.

    g. Invoice for credit sale.

    h. General journal entry.

7-6   For each item listed in Exercise 7-5 above, specify the hardware device(s) which would process or transmit it in an interactive system.

7-7   One important consideration in computer hardware is whether the system will have a sequential, batch orientation or a direct access interactive orientation. For each of the following processing areas, state whether a batch or an interactive orientation would be most appropriate and why.

    a. Airline reservations.

    b. Bank generation of monthly statement.

    c. Payroll.

    d. Telephone company generation of monthly bills.

e. Holiday Inn reservation.

f. Inventory in a retail store.

g. Financial statements.

h. Student registration.

7-8 Suppose a medium size retail firm wants to computerize the billing of its customers and the receipts of cash from them, as well as the payment of bills from suppliers.

1. Describe a hardware configuration which could accomplish this processing in batches at specific predetermined times. Give the flow of data through these devices.

2. Describe a hardware configuration which could accomplish this processing if up-to-date information on customers and suppliers is desired at all times. Give the flow of data through these devices.

7-9 Suppose a wholesale firm wants to computerize its processing of sales orders from retailers and purchases of inventory from manufacturers.

1. Describe a hardware configuration which could accomplish this processing in batches at specific predetermined times. Give the flow of data through these devices.

2. Describe a hardware configuration which could accomplish this processing, if up-to-date information on inventory levels is desired at all times. Give the flow of data through these devices.

7-10 A typical retail firm is characterized by a large number of relatively small sales which take place within the store. A wholesale firm, on the other hand, usually engages in relatively few but large sales which may originate long distances from the business. How would input devices for these types of businesses differ as a result of these different demands? Would there be any differences in file or output devices as a result of these demands?

data files and data bases

outline

INTRODUCTION

At this point you should be comfortable with the computer concepts of hardware and software. You may even have some experience writing computer programs in a particular computer programming language to accomplish a wide variety of tasks.

Our concern now turns to the following problem: How do we process the vast quantities of information with which business data processing deals? It is not uncommon for a bank to have over 10,000 customers; certainly, it is necessary for the bank to keep track of all the names, addresses, and transactions for all these customers. An airline deals with thousands of flights and ticket reservations. Again, keeping track of all the necessary information is a monumental task.

In this chapter we introduce the means of handling these problems and a simple accounts receivable system for illustration. The basic concepts we will discuss are widely applicable to business data processing.

8.1 PROGRAM VERSUS DATA

There is an important distinction to be made between the program, which is the series of instructions for the computer, and the data, which are the pieces of information upon which various operations are performed. For example, consider a program which computes the square of a given number. The program consists of instructions which tell the computer to:

1. Print out a question.

2. Accept a number from the keyboard.

3. Print out certain letters and certain numbers. These numbers are derived from the number accepted in Step 2.

The data upon which these instructions operate consist in this case of simply the number input from the keyboard. Notice that the instructions are the same no matter what number is input from the keyboard. A symbol stands for whatever number the instructions are carried out upon.

Remember that the program is separate from the data. We write the program and check it for correct form without regard to the particular data to be used. We can then apply our program to whatever data we want and is appropriate. When the computer executes the program, it brings the data and the program together and the instructions are carried out on the data. Thus, the data are not incorporated into the program until execution.

In this chapter, we will be dealing with programs which may be difficult to visualize. To make the concepts more concrete and the discussion more easily comprehensible we will provide a flowchart of the programs. The concepts in this chapter are independent of any particular programming language, so we prefer not to tie the discussion to any one language. The concepts are used in the programs in the Appendices; if you wish, you can refer to those programs to see how some of our discussion could actually be carried out. Figure 8-1 provides the basic program flowchart symbols; we are familiar with system flowcharting from Chapters 5 and 6 and here we extend the same concept to the preparation of "pictures" giving the structure of the program.

Suppose we had a program to (1) read from the keyboard the number of numbers to follow, (2) read in the numbers, (3) add up their total, (4) calculate the average, (5) read the data in again, (6) count the number above the average, (7) calculate the percentage above the average, and (8) print out the average and the percentage above the average. (See program flowchart, Figure 8-2.) Certainly, this approach is very inefficient because the same data are input twice. This causes double work, and also provides the opportunity for error. Thus, the program would be written where the data are input and stored in a list (i.e., a vector or one-dimensional array) for future use. This has two advantages over the approach given above. First, the data are input only once, thus cutting the input work in half. Second, the program eliminates the chance of putting different numbers in the second time, which would be potentially a source of error.

However, the approach of storing the data in a list for future use cannot be used in general for two major reasons:

1. The data can only be used by this one program. When the program is finished and the area is returned to the computer, we can no longer access the data—they are lost to our use.

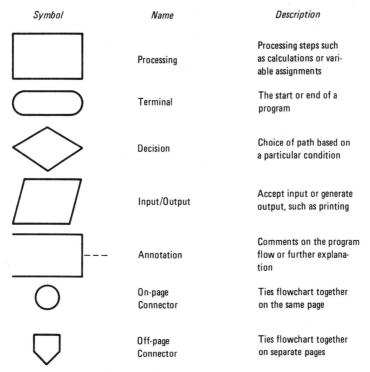

Symbol	Name	Description
	Processing	Processing steps such as calculations or variable assignments
	Terminal	The start or end of a program
	Decision	Choice of path based on a particular condition
	Input/Output	Accept input or generate output, such as printing
	Annotation	Comments on the program flow or further explanation
	On-page Connector	Ties flowchart together on the same page
	Off-page Connector	Ties flowchart together on separate pages

FIGURE 8-1 Program Flowchart Symbols

2. There is not enough computer memory space to use this approach in realistic programs to process a bank's customer accounts or an airline's ticket reservations.

Thus, we need a way to store data separately from the program(s) that use it, but such storage must meet two criteria:

1. The method must allow the data to be used by several different programs.

2. The method must allow for the storage of vast quantities of data.

8.2 CONCEPT OF FILES

There is a way to store data which satisfies these criteria; that is, by using *files*. A file (in the sense we use the term in computer science) is a collection of information stored on a secondary storage device such as disk or tape, rather than stored in main computer memory (i.e., primary storage). A file in the computer science sense is thus very similar to a manual file, except that our computer file is machine-readable while our manual file is man-readable.

Record/File/List Relationship

Our file is somewhat like a list in that both lists and files are collections of building blocks, where each building block has a similar nature. In the case of a list, for example, the list P is

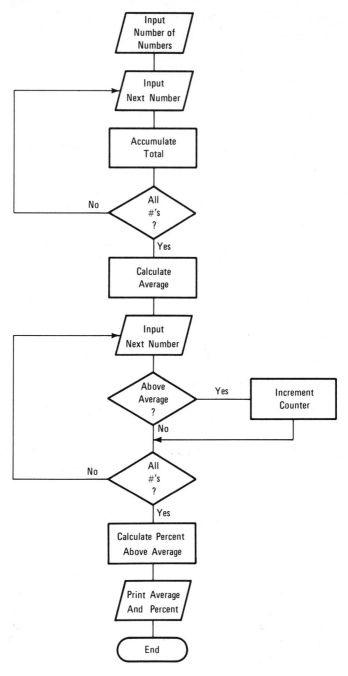

FIGURE 8-2 Program for Percent Calculation

built up from the individual elements P(1), P(2), P(3), etc. In the case of a file, the file is built up from individual records. A record is then the basic building block of the file, and each building block or record is similar to every other.

We can visualize this with Figure 8-3. The file is the collection of all the records and is built up of many similar building blocks. Note how much the file is like the list. In fact, at this point the main differences between the file and the list is that (1) the file will exist on the disk while the list will exist in the computer's main memory, and (2) the file will continue to exist after the program is over while the list will no longer be available.

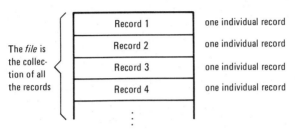

FIGURE 8-3 Record/File Relationship

In Figure 8-4, a file of numbers, note that each number is in an individual record. In other words, each record consists of one number. We will discuss more complicated situations later on, where each record consists of more than one number, but this will do for now.

In our earlier flowchart (Figure 8-2), we calculated the average of a series of numbers; and then we calculated the percentage of those numbers which which exceeded the average. Suppose we wish to create a file of these numbers and then process them with a program that gets the data from the file, rather than having the data input by the operator. This process will require two steps:

1. A program to load the numbers onto the data file.

2. A program to process these numbers, calculate the average, and calculate the percentage above the average.

First, we must flowchart the first program. This flowchart is shown in Figure 8-5. We will see later that this structure, simple as it seems, is the basic structure of all file creation programs, no matter how complex the files become.

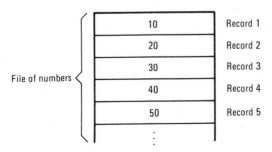

FIGURE 8-4 File of Numbers

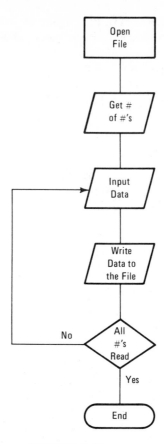

FIGURE 8-5 Flowchart

Figure 8-6 helps us to visualize the process. Before the program execution begins, the file did not exist. After the program opens the file, the file is created, but no information is in it. It appears as in (a). After the first number (we will assume 10) is written to the file, the number 10 will have been loaded on the file. Note that the program automatically begins writing at the beginning of the file. When the write statement is executed the second time, the 20 will be written following the 10, so it will go in the second record as shown in (c). Note that the

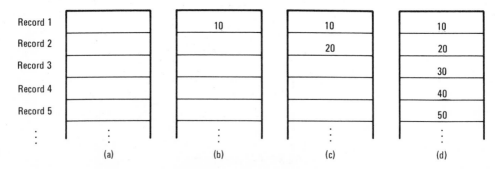

FIGURE 8-6 The Stages of the File

program automatically remembers where it last wrote to the file and writes just after that. After the computer executes the write statement five times, the five numbers have all been written to the file, as shown in (d).

Now that we have the numbers for analysis, we have to write a program that accepts the numbers from the file, calculates the average, and calculates the percentage above the average. Note that this second program must use the file created by the first; this important connection between the two programs is made by using the same file name in both programs.

The program flowchart might appear as in Figure 8-7. Note that the program begins by opening the file created by the earlier program. The program then consists of two loops similar to those in our earlier program in Figure 8-2. The first loop accumulates the total of all numbers and then calculates the average. The second loop then computes the percent above average. Finally, the program prints out the answer and stops.

Sequential and Direct Access

One interesting fact about the file program we have dealt with in the Figures 8-5 through 8-7 is that the information on the file is accessed sequentially. In other words, each time we used the program we began at the beginning of the file and accessed (i.e., read or wrote) the first record, then the second, and so on until we reached the end of the file. Further, we either wrote all the way through the file or we read all the way through the file—we did not mix reading records with writing records. Thus, program 8-5 wrote record one, then record two, up to record five; while program 8-7 read record one, then record two, up to record five, and then went back to the beginning of the file and went through the entire file again.

This use of the file is called *sequential access* (i.e., the file is accessed sequentially). Sequential access is often used in business data processing. For example, suppose a company were writing payroll checks. A reasonable approach is to access the file sequentially, thus checking everyone on the file and paying all employees who should be paid.

However, useful though sequential access is in some situations, it is simply not always adequate for effective data processing. Take, for example, the case of payments on accounts receivable. When we receive a payment, we may want to be able to jump directly to the record for that customer in the file, without checking all the other (unaffected) records. Jumping directly to the desired record is called *direct access*, because we jump directly to the desired record. Thus, the computer could directly read a record, update it with new information, and then write it back out in its corrected form.

Fortunately, direct access is available on modern computers. In fact, the main use of disk storage in most computer systems is the storage of data files which are accessed randomly. This brings up the main distinction between tape and disk: files on tape can only be accessed sequentially whereas files on disk can be accessed both sequentially and randomly. Because of this versatility (and despite its higher cost), disks are in general supplanting tapes on new computer systems.

Let us consider an example of a program utilizing direct access of a file. Suppose we had a class of 25 students and we wanted to store each student's name in a separate record. The simplest way to do this is to assign each student a unique number between 1 and 25 and store the student's name in the corresponding record of the file. Thus, student number 1 would have his (or her) name stored in record 1 and student 15 would have his name stored in record 15; a similar approach would be used to store the other names. Figure 8-8 shows a flowchart for such a program.

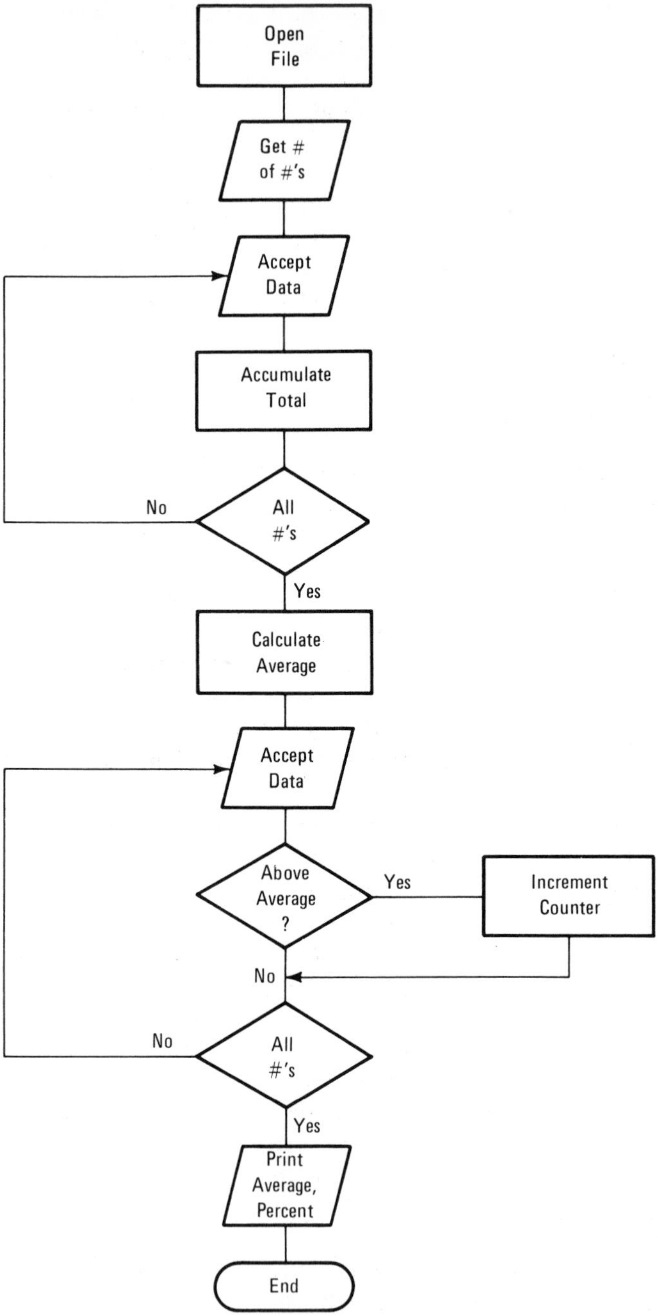

FIGURE 8-7 Flowchart

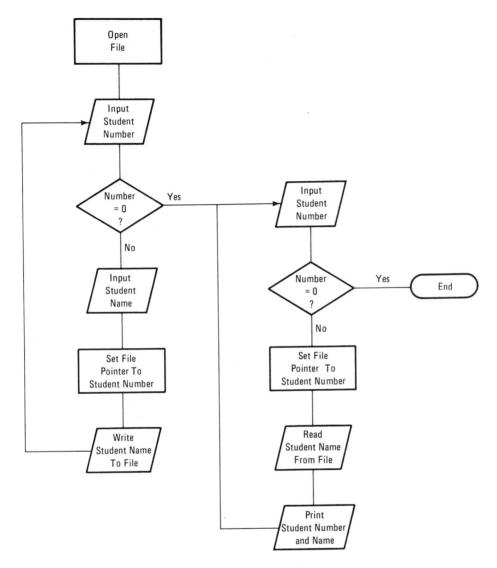

FIGURE 8-8 Student Name Program

End of File Marker and File Pointer

This program naturally brings up the related topics of the end of file marker and the file pointer. The end of file marker gives the location of the furthest record written onto the file. The file pointer, on the other hand, points to the record on the file where the next record will be read from or written to. (See Figure 8-9.)

After the file is opened, the file is established on the disk. We can envision the file as potentially unlimited in length; there are, of course, physical limits, but these are so large they

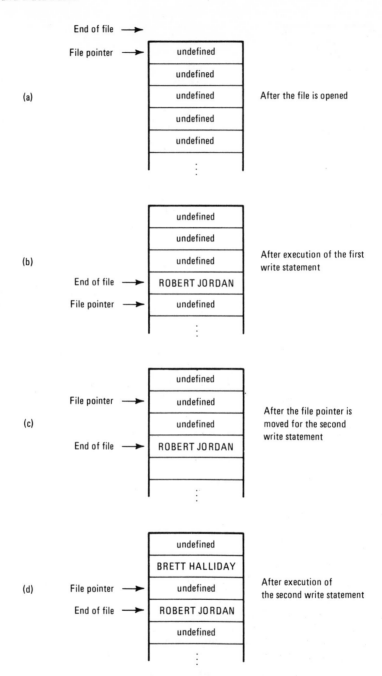

FIGURE 8-9 File Pointer and End of File

will not affect us here. When the file is established, the end of file marker is 0 because nothing has been written on the file. The file pointer is 1 because the first record to be written will normally be the first record. However, the program can change the file pointer if desired. Suppose student number 4 with the name ROBERT JORDAN is input. The program will first move the file pointer to record 4, while the end of file marker remains at 0 because nothing has yet been written to the file. When the write statement is executed (a) the name ROBERT JORDAN is written out to the file, (b) the end of file marker is moved to record 4 because it is the last record written, and (c) the file pointer is moved up by one to record 5, so it will be pointing to the next record on the file.

Suppose student number 2, with the name BRETT HALLIDAY is now input. Then the program will move the file pointer to record 2. After execution of the write statement, two things will change: (a) BRETT HALLIDAY will be put in record 2 and (b) the file pointer will automatically move to record 3. Note that the end of file marker does not move here because we have not written further into the file. Record 4 is still the last record written on file.

Now you can better understand the earlier programs in Figures 8-5 and 8-7. When the file is opened, the end of file marker is set to 0 and the file pointer is set to 1. Each time we read or wrote to the file the file pointer was automatically moved up. Thus, everything was taken care of automatically when the program read sequentially or wrote sequentially. In our later program in Figure 8-8, we wished to jump around in the file. Thus, in that case we needed to set the file pointer.

Checking Record Number Validity

We also want to point out the importance of checking the record number we wish to access to make sure it is valid. The end of file marker indicates that there is no information stored past it. Thus, attempting to read past the end of file marker is invalid because there can be no information there; hence, attempting to read past the end of file marker will generate an error message. Writing past the end of file marker is normal in extending the length of the file.

8.3 DATA-BASE APPROACH

Batch Processing and Its Disadvantages

In an earlier discussion, we went through the processing of the accounting transactions of a firm where one clerk handled all the books. This bookkeeper took each transaction from the initial recording in the books of original entry all the way to the preparation of the financial statements. This mode of operation has the significant advantage that the information is up-to-date and the files and balances are current. Thus, if a customer or supplier had to know the status of his account, the information would be available and would be current.

However, this approach is impossible to implement *manually* for large volumes of transactions because one person is simply not capable of doing that much work. Historically, this has led to the division of the work into groups of transactions called batches. Thus, transactions were not processed as they occurred, but were rather divided into separate batches, such as a cash receipt batch, credit sale batch, and so on. Then, after a certain size batch had been accumulated or a certain time limit exceeded, the system would process all the transactions in the batch. This processing of all the transactions by groups (i.e., *batch processing*) adapts directly to punched-card equipment and the earliest sorts of computers. As a result of its economy, batch processing is the standard means of processing accounting transactions even to the present day.

Unfortunately, batch processing has tremendous drawbacks:

1. The information kept by the system is no longer current. The time between occurrence of a transaction, its accumulation in a sufficient batch, and its subsequent processing can be quite substantial. During that time lag, the balances in the accounts affected by these transactions are no longer current. This leads to the now common frustration of dealing with credit departments of hospitals, department stores, and the like which do not know current balances of accounts.

2. Separate files for each batch-processing application seems to be an inevitable result of this approach. This is rather difficult to explain to someone unfamiliar with data processing. However, what seems to happen is the following. Each batch application, such as accounts payable or accounts receivable, receives machine assistance when it reaches a certain size. This machine assistance usually includes setting up computer files and the use of computer programs. However, each application is developed independently of other applications, so the files and programs of separate applications are unrelated to one another. Thus, even though it does not have to be true, batch processing generally results in separate files for each application.

3. Correction of errors is a problem with batch processing. There is a lag between the time the source document is recorded and the time the batch is processed. As a result, if a transaction is rejected by the computer, it becomes necessary to go back several days to try to determine the source of the error. For example, suppose a hospital records a patient charge which includes a doctor code of 35. If the computer processes the charge a day or so later and determines that doctor code 35 is invalid, the computer will reject the transaction. Then the user will have to go back and decide whether the code should have been 55, 33, or 53 or some other number.

4. Management often needs information which spans departments. For example, when analyzing the introduction of a new product line, information would be needed from both sales and distribution. In these circumstances, the data is not simply needed for the processing of specific applications; the data is an important resource in its own right and is necessary for all sorts of decisions.

Concept of Data-Base and Related Terminology

We are thus led to the concept of a *data-base*. A data-base is a collection of interrelated information stored independently of the programs and applications which use it. Unfortunately, a certain amount of jargon is necessary to the understanding of a data-base. The first term we need is data-item. A *data-item* is the smallest unit of information which has meaning to users. In this sense, users mean ultimate users of the data-processing output, such as managers, rather than the actual machine users, such as programmers. Examples of data-items might then be a customer name or a price for an item of inventory. Notice that to the programmer, every letter of the name may have meaning. However, since only the whole name has meaning to the ultimate users, the name is the data-item.

Related data-items are then grouped to form *records*. A record is then a set (i.e., a collection) of related data-items. An example might be a customer record: the record would contain a data-item for name, another for the account balance, and perhaps several for the address. The concept of a record is particularly important because computer programs usually read and write records. In other words, the computer reads in a record from storage, processes it, and then writes it back out onto storage once it has been updated. Suppose, then, that we wanted to change a customer name, either due to an earlier error or to marriage. The program would then read in the entire record for that customer, not just the particular data-item for update (the customer name). The customer name would then be corrected and the entire customer record written back out onto storage.

Let us look at Figure 8-10. This should help make these concepts somewhat more concrete. Figure 8-10 is a picture of five general ledger account records. There are three data-items in each record: the account number, the account name, and the account balance. These three data-items combine to form one record, one record for each general ledger account.

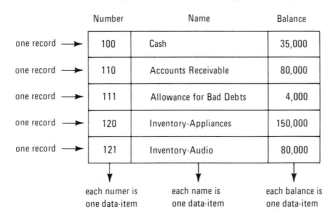

FIGURE 8-10 Pooper Centers, Inc.
General Ledger Accounts

We must give each data-item a unique name, so that we may refer to every data-item without ambiguity. In our example, Figure 8-10, account number would not be a good data-item name because there could be confusion over whether account number refers to customer account number, supplier account number, general ledger account number, or whatever. To eliminate this ambiguity, we might refer to this data-item by the following name: GENERAL-LEDGER-ACCOUNT-NUMBER.

Needless to say, for any corporation the number of data-items necessary for all the myriad accounting, recording-keeping, and analysis functions is quite large. Thus, to keep its data-base coherent, the corporation must form a dictionary to specify each of the different data-items: the dictionary includes all variables used by all the programs.

Simple and Complex Data Items

We should make a distinction here between simple data-items and complex data-items. Simple data-items are essentially simple facts (like a supplier number or an invoice date). These items are fixed and solid; they stand by themselves. Complex data-items, on the other hand, are built up from simple data-items. Complex data-items might include the amount of unearned discounts taken by a customer so far this year or the number of deliveries by a supplier which have been late this year. This kind of information would be important in determining which of our customers were trying to get by with slightly shady dealings and which of our suppliers were giving good service and which were giving bad service.

Purpose of the Data-Base Approach

We now come to the basic purpose behind the data-base approach. This is simply to have one set of uniquely defined data-items; then all computer applications use the same data-items. Typically, a company has one set of prices for materials which is used by inventory control for costing issues, and still another set of prices in purchasing for determining from whom to purchase. These different sets of prices are all updated at different times by different people from different information. Needless to say, they are never in agreement, even though they supposedly represent the same thing. Rather than this, the data-base approach is to have one set of prices for materials and then have each application use the same information.

An example of this would be the data-item, supplier number. Certainly, every company must have a way of uniquely identifying its suppliers. With the data-base approach, each supplier would have a supplier number which would be used by each application, such as ordering, accounts payable, and inventory.

Costs

Of course, the data-base approach is not without its costs. The main cost of the data-base approach is the necessity of coordination and cooperation. If the same number will uniquely identify a particular supplier in the ordering system, the accounts payable system, and the inventory system, someone or some group must coordinate the design of these systems. Thus, the corporation cannot allow separate groups to develop systems independently of everyone else; however, the price of coordination and cooperation is higher than many firms will pay. There is another, less important, cost. Since each system is not designed by itself, certain compromises must be accepted in each individual system design so that the systems will fit together. Thus, each system will not be optimal for that particular task. However, this should only disturb those who are more interested in optimizing one specific subsystem, such as inventory, than in optimizing the overall company's operations.

In a sense then, we have come full circle. At the beginning of the book we went through the operation of the accounting cycle by one person. One person handled all the books and kept files and balances up-to-date. The data-base approach then implies that the computer will become superbookkeeper and, with its incredible speed, keep unimaginably vast files current for all users.

Importantly, however, the computer's function as superbookkeeper is not its most valuable contribution to the firm. Its most valuable contribution is the analysis it can perform once the data is in machine-readable form. Suppose John Paul Pooper wanted to know the average sale for the month of January, the total number of sales in the month, the largest sale, or the smallest sale. Suppose he wanted to know how sales varied by day (i.e., how Thursday sales compared to Monday's sales and so forth). This information is all available with the manual system, but the time, trouble, and effort of extracting that kind of result would be large. With a computer system, on the other hand, the information is already in machine-readable form so it is a small task to write a program to access the data to obtain the desired reports. This sort of analysis and the improved management and control it can provide is the real promise and use of a computer system.

8-4 MASTER FILE—TRANSACTION FILE DATA STRUCTURE

Common Programming Problems

We will now use our expanded concept of record by developing the program(s) and files for a small (but somewhat realistic) system. Consider a simple example at first: suppose we wanted to keep track of a customer's name and the balance he owes us. Each record in the file would consist of:

1. The name of the customer.
2. The balance owed by the customer.

We will keep the situation simple by using one program to handle two tasks: (a) load the name and initially zero the balance owed and (b) process transactions to update the balance owed. The program appears in Figure 8-11.

1. The first part opens the file AR. This file will contain both the alphabetic information (such as the name) and the numeric information (such as the balance).
2. The second part loads names onto the file AR. This section is similar to earlier programs (e.g., Figure 8-8). However, there is a new twist. Each new customer when loaded to the file will begin with a zero balance; any balance must be loaded by a transaction (see below).
3. The third part processes transactions by the following means: (a) get the customer number, (b) read the customer record off the file, (c) input the amount of the transaction and whether it is a debit or credit, (d) update the balance, increasing the balance if it is a debit transaction and decreasing the balance if it is a credit transaction, (e) print the new balance, (f) write out the updated information on the file. This process is repeated until customer number 0 is input, and the program then ends.

This program is very similar in structure to many business data-processing programs. Of course, the typical program will deal with more data-items, such as address and phone number, for each customer, but the basic structure is essentially the same. As a result, you can now see what is basically wrong with most business data-processing programs:

1. *There is no audit trail.* Note that the program keeps a current balance, but that the transactions are lost. Thus, there is no backup to the balance and it is impossible to determine from the files where the balance came from. If you have been through the material in Parts one and two, you should be aware of the problems which result from the lack of an audit trail.

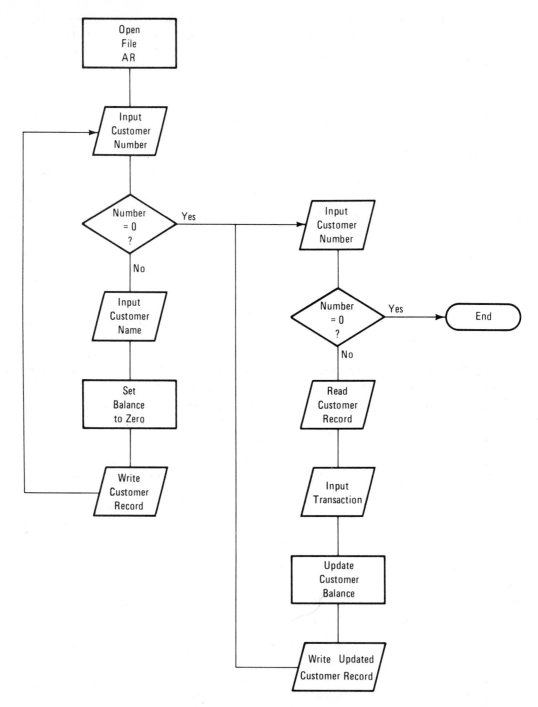

FIGURE 8-11 Simple File Program

2. *There are no checks for valid input.* When a customer number is input the program does not check it for validity. Also, the program does not ensure that the amount of the transaction is nonnegative, which it must be.

Masterfile—Transaction File Relationship

Our task is then to rewrite the program, eliminating these faults. This will require a new concept—the transaction file vs. the master file. The master file contains the name, address, phone number, and other data-items which are relatively permanent (see Figure 8-10). The transaction file, on the other hand, contains the transactions which have developed the ending balance; thus, the transaction file can provide an audit trail. Our new approach will be to process the transaction (updating the master file) but then to also store the transaction in the transaction file. If you compare the files to the accounts receivable subsidiary ledger, you see that the master file is the top part of each ledger account and that the transaction file is the collection of the individual lines of the ledger account.

Basic Types of Business Data Processing

To put these final two programs into perspective, we will now discuss the four basic types of business data processing:

1. *File creation.* A file creation program initially loads information onto the file so it can be used by other programs. As an example, a file creation program would initially load a customer's name and address and establish a customer's record when a new customer's account is established.

2. *File maintenance.* A file maintenance program keeps the master file current, except for transactions. If a customer changed names (due to marriage, for example), a file maintenance program would update the customer record.

3. *Transaction processing.* A transaction processing program does all necessary steps with each transaction as it occurs. The transaction-processing program would handle a customer payment on account or a credit sale; it would update the master file and then add the transaction to the transaction file.

4. *Report writing.* Report writer programs take the information off the data files (created and updated by the earlier types of programs) and then generate printouts analyzing the information. Thus, an aged trial balance is a report which is simply a printout and analysis of the information already on file about the customer and the amount he owes.

Examples/File Creation and Transaction-processing Programs

Examples of a file creation program and a transaction-processing program appear in Figures 8-12 and 8-13. The file creation program begins with the opening of the file named AR. Four balances will be kept for each customer: (a) the beginning balance, (b) the total debits for the period, (c) the total credits for the period, and (d) the current balance. Note that we store all four totals as a check; this way if any total gets inadvertently modified, it will be apparent. If

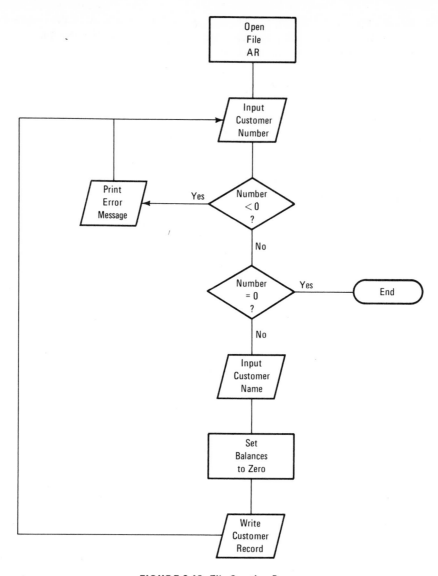

FIGURE 8-12 File Creation Program

only three were stored, we could compute the fourth from the other three (assuming they were all correct). However, if one of the totals was disturbed, there would be no way to detect this. Note also that the computer checks the customer number and will not accept a negative customer number.

Figure 8-13 is a file transaction program. Its basic structure is:

1.   Open both necessary files, the master file (AR) and the transaction file (TRANS).

2.   Input customer number.

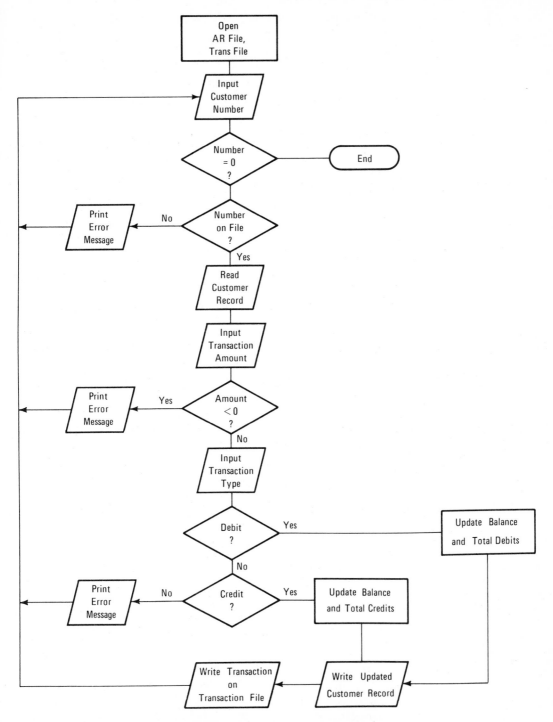

FIGURE 8-13 File Transaction Program

3. Check customer number for validity.

4. End program with customer number 0.

5. Read current content of customer record.

6. Input transaction amount and ensure the amount is nonnegative.

7. Input type of transaction and direct flow differently if it is a debit than if it is a credit. Note that if it is neither a debit nor a credit, the program will not accept the transaction. Increase the current balance with a debit and increase the total amount of debits or decrease the current balance with a credit and increase the total amount of credits.

8. Write the updated record back to the master file.

9. Add a transaction to the end of the transaction file. The program writes out the customer number, the transaction amount, and the type of transaction.

Basic Approach/File Maintenance and Transaction Programs

Thus, the basic approach of all file maintenance and transaction programs is:

1. To read the information from the master file into the computer's main memory.

2. To update this information in the main memory with the maintenance and/or file balance transaction.

3. To write the updated information back onto the master file in the same place it was originally found.

It is important to realize that when the information is read off the master file, the information on the master file is not lost or changed in any way; all that occurs is that a *copy* of the information is transferred into the computer's main memory. Because of this, if the updating in steps two and three above does not occur, the information on the master file will remain as it was and will not be lost. This is important because the updating will often not occur; some examples might be that the transaction is rejected because it is invalid or does not match the information on the master file. As a further example, suppose the transaction was for an inactive customer; when the master file record was read in, the transaction could be rejected, but not before, because the information necessary for rejection was not available. Note that some transactions can be rejected offhand (such as a credit sale of $1,000,000,000), but others must be checked with information on the master files.

Storing Transactions

There is no one way to store the transactions on the transaction file. Figures 8-14, 8-15, and 8-16 give three possibilities. Figure 8-14 has the transactions stored sequentially on the transaction file; in order to access the transactions for a particular customer it would be necessary to read all the transactions on the file and pick out those transactions which match the desired customer. In this situation, when a new transaction is processed for *any* customer, it is simply added to the end of the transaction file. Figure 8-15 has the transactions stored in a similar fashion, but with a pointer added to each master file record and each transaction file record.

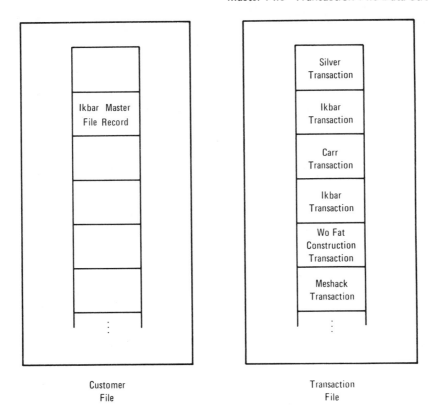

FIGURE 8-14 No Pointers

The pointer in the master file record points to the position on the transaction file of the first transaction processed for *that* master file record. That transaction then points to the next transaction processed for that record; this process continues until the last transaction is found. Note that in a large transaction file, this set of pointers will speed up access to all of the transactions for a particular master file record. However, when a new transaction is processed, the pointers have to be updated to make sure they now point eventually to this newest transaction. That generally means following the chain of pointers from the master file record out to the last transaction for that record; the latest transaction is then added to the end of the chain. If there are many transactions for a particular record, this process can be quite slow. Figure 8-16 shows one way around this problem; that is, pointers in both directions. Thus, the pointers in the master file record point not only to the first transaction, but also to the last transaction for that record. Adding a transaction to the chain is then speeded up because the pointer will direct the program immediately to the end of the chain, without having to follow the chain of pointer to pointer.

At this point the following question may arise: Why not have the information in the master file *and* the transaction file all in the same file? This is basically because different master file records will have differing numbers of transactions and because we do not usually know the maximum number of transactions per master file record. These facts lead to the following conclusions:

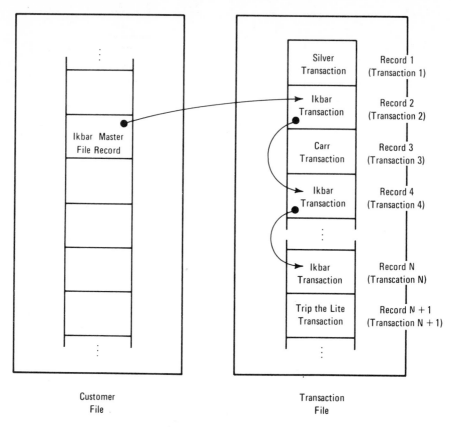

FIGURE 8-15 Forward Pointers

1. Since different master file records have differing numbers of transactions, the file layout will have to leave room for the maximum number in every record, thus leading to tremendous wasted space in those records which do not have the maximum number of transactions.

2. However, even if wasted space were not a problem, we still do not know how much space to leave since we do not know the maximum number of transactions. If we make a guess and leave too little room, a record might fill up making it impossible to process another transaction for that record without reorganizing the entire file, making every record that much bigger.

For these reasons, it is far better to design files so that each record has the same number of data-items, and thus usually each record has the same length. It is true that some languages (such as COBOL), will allow variable-length records; however, the variable-length record is best used to handle data-items which are of variable length (such as names and addresses), rather than a variable number of data-items. Thus, with a separate master file and transaction file, the master file record can contain the information which will always be kept for every master file record (such as name and current balance), while the transaction file will contain every transaction for every master file record. In this way, additional transactions merely add to the length of the transaction file, which is easily handled.

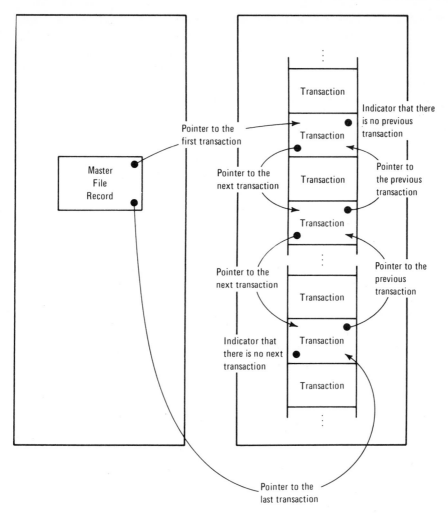

FIGURE 8-16
Pointers in Both Directions

8.5 FURTHER DATA-BASE CONCEPTS

Entity/Attribute

To this point we have concentrated on the example of an accounts receivable system, with a customer master file and a related transaction file. We realize, however, that there could be a master file for general ledger accounts, vendors, for a particular business, students at a university, employees of a company; we are limited only by our imagination. Thus, in all cases, the file is storing information about something; the something about which the information is stored is then called an *entity*. We therefore have a convenient term for all our discussions about files: we can discuss files in general by using the term "entity" without tying the discussion to any specific type of file. For each entity the file stores various *attributes* of that entity, such as name, address, or current balance. Thus a specific accounts receivable file may have entities which are customers. The attributes stored for each entity might then be the customer number, name, address, and credit limit, among others. The data-items then represent the attribute. The specific information stored in the record for an entity would then be specific values of those attributes. For example, in an accounts receivable system for Pooper Centers, the attribute might be *name* and one particular attribute value would be Akbar Ikbar.

Primary and Secondary Keys

As we have discussed, each record in the master file is distinct and applies to a separate entity. Thus, in different applications an entity might be a general ledger account, a customer, or a vendor. This then creates the problem of indicating to the computer exactly what record we want to refer to. For example, in ordinary conversation we may refer to a customer's name or a vendor's name. However, when dealing with the computer this is not adequate: we need a unique entity identifier which unmistakably picks out one and only one master file record. Such an identifier is called a *key*, or more precisely a *primary key*. In most situations, this key will be an identifying number, such as the general ledger account number, the customer number, or the vendor number. It is possible, however, to have an alphabetic key, such as a name, to uniquely identify the master file record. The main difficulty of an alphabetic key is that it must generally be spelled exactly right for the computer to easily find the proper master file record. Sophisticated systems can get around this problem by providing a dialog with the terminal operator where the computer provides the user the keys "closest" to the key the operator used and gives the operator a "menu" of possible choices; the operator is then given the opportunity to choose the exact entity which he had in mind.

Often, a master file record contains data-items that identify the record, but do not *uniquely* identify the record. These data-items are called *secondary keys*. For example, consider a customer file: the primary key would probably be a customer number, which would allow the computer to answer the question, What is the information stored on customer number X? A possible secondary key would be the ZIP code. Generally speaking, there will be more than one customer for any one ZIP code and thus the ZIP code could certainly not be used to uniquely identify a customer record. The ZIP code, however, could be used to answer the following question: What customers have their address in a particular ZIP code? Despite the fact that the question will in general have multiple answers, the ZIP code still identifies the record (though not uniquely) and thus is a secondary key. In a university's student file the primary key would almost certainly be a student number. Secondary keys would then probably include grade in school and declared major. These secondary keys could then be used to answer questions such as: How many junior accounting majors does the university have?

Coding

The task of assigning a primary key is often referred to as *coding*. In Part one we briefly discussed the chart of accounts and the assignment of account numbers to the various general ledger accounts. You can see now that this assignment of account numbers is only one example of the problem of assigning primary keys; other examples of coding would include assigning inventory item numbers, vendor numbers, customer numbers, and employee numbers. There is a trade-off between the complexity of the code (i.e., primary key) and the complexity of the file. In some cases it is useful to have a complex code which conveys information in the code itself. An example would be the coding of general ledger accounts: the 100 accounts might be assets, the 200 accounts might be liabilities, and so on. This type of coding will probably result in fewer errors in the use of the code as well as make financial statements and other reports from the general ledger file easier to generate. Note that in a customer file all records are basically equivalent and their information is manipulated in the same way. In the general ledger file, however, the various types of records (assets, liabilities, owners' equity, revenue, and expenses) all get printed out quite differently in the financial statements. Another example of complex coding would be the assignment of an inventory item number where one digit indicated color, another part of the number indicated size and so on. We see from our previous discussion, however, that the information, such as color or size, which could be conveyed in the item number would be better stored as an attribute in the record. If the information is stored in the record, there are two advantages: first, the code is shortened and simplified; and second, there need not be a conversion process in the programs to convert from the code to the information it is trying to convey. Generally speaking, therefore, it is better to make the code or primary key as simple as possible and store all information in the record. Thus, the code will only uniquely identify the record and will convey no information by itself. Codes can then be assigned in a sequential manner; every time a new entity is added to the file, it is simply assigned the next higher code number.

File Organization

We now know that the primary key uniquely identifies the record for a particular entity. Our next concern is determining how to find the record corresponding to a given primary key. The method by which we order the records in the file and provide access to those records is called the *file organization*. There are four basic types of file organization:

1. *Serial organization.* The records are placed in the file in no particular order. Access to a particular record is provided by reading through the file until the value on a record matches the given primary key. For very large files, this method of access is extremely slow, but it is easy to program, and for small files the time to read even all the records in a file is not very long.

2. *Sequential organization.* The records in the file are sequenced by the primary key. Again, access is provided by reading through the file until a match is found for the primary key. Because the file is sequenced, however, multiple access to the file can be made much more efficiently than in the case of serial organization.

3. *Direct organization.* The primary key for the record is the storage address on the disk drive or other direct-access device on which the file is stored. Access is then provided by reading the storage area given by the primary key.

4. *Indexed sequential organization.* Records are stored sequentially by primary key, but in addition there is a separate *index file* which stores all the primary keys for all the records on the file; this index file also contains the location on the file for the record matching that primary key. Access is then provided by searching the index file for a match of the primary key and then accessing the master file at the given location. Since the index file is quite

small and the master file is generally quite large, a search of the index file is much faster than a sequential search of the master file.

More Sophisticated File Structures

Let us try to generalize about the *structure* of the data on the file, rather than the specific data we will store. For this, we will begin with a file structure that we have already gone over to some extent; the customer master file and the related invoices for that customer. As we know there will be one master file record for each customer, but there will be multiple invoices (generally speaking). The diagram in Figure 8-17 represents this file structure. Such a representation of file structure is called a *schema*. Note that the same type of structure will also apply for general ledger accounts and the multiple entries that affect that account, as well as basic accounts payable and payroll. However, the file structure can be much more sophisticated than this (relatively) simple schema. A more complex example of a schema is shown in Figure 8-18.

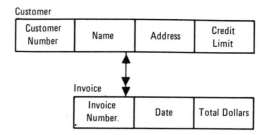

FIGURE 8-17 Sample Schema

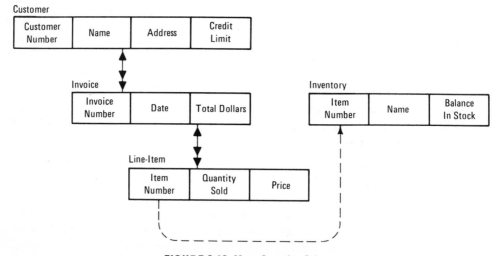

FIGURE 8-18 More Complex Schema

In this schema, there is not only a multiple set of invoices for each customer, but also a multiple set of line items for each invoice. Thus, our file will keep track of the individual items in the invoice, not just the total amount as in less sophisticated systems. Each line-item will contain the part number of that item, and that item number will give the system a cross-reference to the inventory master file record for that item. But every programmer and every program that uses this set of files need not be interested in all the data in all the files; they may be only interested in a small portion of the data. For this reason they may be only interested in a *subschema*, as illustrated in Figure 8-19. Note that the subschema extracts a small part of the overall data which might be of interest in one particular program—printing invoices, for example. There is a further complication that must be considered in some situations. Even the complex schema in Figure 8-18 had only one "parent" customer for each invoice and only one "parent" invoice for each line item: this is called a *tree structure.* Figure 8-20 gives an example where each invoice has two "parents"; one for customer so we can tell how many invoices we have for each customer, and one for salesman so we can tell how many invoices we have for each salesman. Note that in general, each customer's invoice is associated with a different salesman and each salesman's invoice is associated with a different customer. This is called a *network structure.*

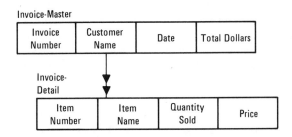

FIGURE 8-19 Sample Subschema

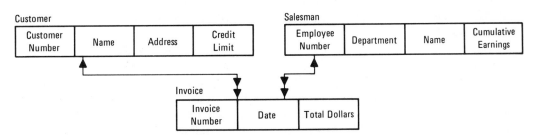

FIGURE 8-20 Sample Network Structure

Data-Base Management Systems

There are two important conclusions to be drawn from our earlier discussions in this chapter:

1. The programming to handle these very complicated file structures will itself be very complicated.

2.   The same file structure will be useful in many apparently different situations.

Because of these important facts, very complicated, generalized software packages have been developed by many different organizations to allow the user to specify the file structure he wants, while the software package handles much of the attendant programming chores. These software packages are called *data-base management systems* because they handle the task of managing the data-base. All major computer equipment vendors provide data-base management systems (often abbreviated DBMS); these include: IMS (Information Management System) from IBM, which was originally developed with Rockwell International; IDS (Integrated Data Score) which was begun by General Electric and further developed by Honeywell; and IMAGE from Hewlett-Packard. DBMS are also sold by independent software vendors; these include TOTAL from Cincom Systems and IDMS from Cullinane Corporation. This last system, IDMS, is the only DBMS which is really a CODASYL-type DBMS (see below). TOTAL is the DBMS provided with NCR and Varian computers, and Varian is now owned by Sperry-Univac, which provides its own DBMS for the larger systems. Finally, IDMS is the DBMS provided with Digital Equipment Corporation computers. Each of these different systems has its own advantages and disadvantages. They range from the easy to use (TOTAL) to the very complex (IMS). They also range in approach from the hierarchical approach of IMS to the network approach of IDMS.

CODASYL is an acronym for the Conference on Data Systems Languages, and stands for a national organization composed of industry, university, and government representatives. CODASYL originally developed the COBOL language at the instigation of the United States government. In response to the widespread interest in data bases, CODASYL created a Data-Base Task Group (DBTG) which in 1971 proposed a standard for the development of DBMS. This proposed standard has made a major impact on data-base thinking and data-base management systems. The proposed standard, however, has not been universally accepted; in fact, the two most widely used DBMS, TOTAL from Cincom Systems and IMS from IBM, are not compatible with the standard proposed by the CODASYL DBTG. It is beyond the scope of this text to go into the intricacies of this standardization effort and the relative advantages and disadvantages of the different possible data-base management approaches, but this material is widely available.

This chapter has discussed the basic concepts of data files and data bases. These concepts are absolutely essential to the effective use of the computer in business data processing because data processing primarily is involved with the updating of information and the analysis of accumulated information. It is not uncommon for the first data-processing course to introduce the computer and simple computer programming. Unfortunately, the programming is often a simple mathematical calculation. As a result, the student still cannot effectively use the computer to solve business problems because he does not have the basic tool of files and their capabilities.

You should now have a grasp of files and how they might be used in an accounting or an information system. DBMS and other tools will continue to make the use of files easier and more effective, but it is absolutely necessary for you to understand the basic concepts even if you are not to be involved in the actual computer programming. In order to make these concepts more concrete, the Appendices give some basic examples of file processing (including file maintenance, transaction processing, and report writing) using both the BASIC and COBOL languages. Though the exact techniques will vary with different languages and even different computers, the same basic concepts will apply. You should now be ready to undertake the task of system development, the topic of Part III, where we put together the accounting and system analysis knowledge in order to create an improved or entirely new system.

exercises

8-1 Widespread use of computers in business data processing has led many observers to predict that computers will ultimately replace accountants. Based on your knowledge of computers and accounting, do you believe this is true? Why, or why not? How does your answer here compare to your answer to Exercise 1-2?

8-2 The distinction between programs and data is fundamental to understanding the use of computers in data processing. This distinction is important because programs are not necessarily tied to one particular data file and data are not necessarily processed by only one program.

1. Give three specific examples from business data processing of one file being used by more than one program.   A/P file

2. Give three specific examples from business data processing of one program utilizing both a master file and a transaction file.   A/P update

3. Can you think of a program that might use more than one master file?   A/P update   A/P file and GL

8-3 Computer data processing is based upon the logical organization of data into files, records, and data-items. For each of the following, state whether it is a file, a record, or a data-item.

a. All information on one customer.

b. Accounts receivable subsidiary ledger.

c. Employee number.

d. Amount owed a particular vendor.

e. List of all inventory items on hand.

f. General ledger.

g. Accounts payable subsidiary ledger.

h. Information on a particular vendor.

i. The name of one vendor.

j. All information on one inventory item.

8-4 In Chapter 7 there was an extended problem on the IRS and its method for processing taxpayer income tax returns. Review this material and give the files which would likely be used in the regional offices and the files which would likely be used in the national office in Maryland. (Be sure to include the files used to answer the inquiry questions.) Also, for each file, give the organization of files into records and the data-items to be included in each record.

8-5 The St. Charles Company is in the midst of converting to a new computer-based information system. A critical step in the conversion process is the design and specification of each file necessary for the processing. One of the areas to be included in the new system is accounts payable. Processing accounts payable requires that information on each vendor be kept and that purchase invoices, payments to vendors, and debit memos be handled. Determine the files required, the organization of the files into records, and the data-items to be included in each record.

8-6 Suppose the St. Charles Company were interested in including in the new system the processing of payroll. Processing payroll requires that information on each employee be kept and that earnings and all related payroll deductions, as well as all necessary government reports be handled. Determine the files required, the organization of the files into records, and the data-items to be included in each record.

8-7 Suppose the St. Charles Company were interested in including in the new system the processing of accounts receivable. Processing accounts receivable requires that information on each customer be kept and that sales invoices, collections from customers, and credit memos be handled. Determine the files required, the organization of the files into records, and the data-items to be included in each record.

8-8 Suppose the St. Charles Company were interested in including in the new system the processing of inventory. Processing of inventory requires that information on each inventory item be kept and that purchase orders, sales orders, receipts of inventory, shipments of inventory, and adjustments be handled. Determine the files required, the organization of the files into records, and the data-items to be included in each record.

8-9 Suppose the St. Charles Company were interested in including in the new system general ledger record-keeping and financial statement preparation. These activities require that information on each general ledger account be kept and that all debits and credits for the period be handled. Determine the files required, the organization of the files into records, and the data-items to be included in each record.

8-10 For each of the applications described in Exercises 8-5 through 8-9, identify the entity, the primary key and any secondary keys.

part III

systems development

overview of system development

outline

9.1 **System Analysis:** importance of proper background analysis prior to any system developmental work; basic approaches to system development; basic elements of a background study.

9.2 **Statement of Objectives:** importance of management involvement; components of the statement of objectives.

9.3 **System Design:** important goals; elements of system design.

9.4 **System Specification:** important goals; component steps.

9.5 **Programming:** major programming steps/program testing/proper run documentation.

9.6 **Implementation:** employee response; component steps.

9.7 **Evaluation:** difficulty encountered in reviewing the system implementation; basic steps in the postimplementation review.

INTRODUCTION

You should now have an understanding of how an accounting system fits together, a knowledge of the tools of systems analysis, and some experience with the file and data-base concepts necessary for computer-based systems. We now need to put this knowledge together in the development of a computer-based system; that is what we will do in this part of the book. We will first discuss the overall conception of what it is to develop a computer-based system in order to give you a framework within which to function during the development of any specific system. Of course, any system will have to be adapted to the specific circumstances in which it is to function, but the general framework will remain the same. After discussing the conceptual framework, we will apply this framework to the development of a complete new system for our sample company, Pooper Centers. This new system will be an accounts receivable system, utilizing the computer to provide more effective billing and collection procedures. Because of the computer's incredible speed, the new system will be able to bill more efficiently and furnish management with vastly increased information about potential delinquent accounts. These improvements will therefore provide increased cash flow and improved profitability.

In actual fact, however, the path of system development does not always run smoothly; often it is a road to disaster. This results from the system being designed by either accountants who know little about the computer or computer people who know little about accounting. Accountants who know little about the computer usually use it to automate some mechanical, clerical tasks. However, because the accountant knows little about the computer's capabilities, the computer is grossly underutilized, and the major result is increased rigidity in the system since the computer must be served instead of a clerk. Additionally, because the accountant knows little of computer technicalities, the system takes far longer to develop and install than anticipated. On the other hand, computer people who know little about accounting try to utilize the computer's capabilities, but wind up ignoring the legitimate needs of accounting. As a result, the developed system lacks adequate controls and possibly even an audit trail because the computer person ruthlessly eliminates checks and redundancies as inefficient. This inevitably leads to user dissatisfaction, excessive errors, and tremendous difficulty in backing up final figures from source documents. Understanding the ideas presented in this text will allow you to avoid both types of errors.

Approaches to Computer Potential

The question might arise: If systems development is so difficult and fraught with danger, why should we bother with it? Why not simply use the manual systems with which we are familiar and not bother with the computer and its problems? The nonhuman nature of the computer is the key to these questions. The computer cannot show initiative; it can only do what it is told. This becomes extremely frustrating, as every little detail must be laid out. However, the computer does what it is told unfailingly, consistently, and with incredible speed; these are tremendous advantages.

There are then two major ways of looking at the potential of computers and computer-based system development: the way of resignation and the way of hope. The way of resignation is appropriate because the computer is inevitable. Consider the following facts: the cost of labor is *increasing* at up to 10 percent per year and the cost of electronic systems is *decreasing* at up to 25 percent per year. Couple this with the fact that $200 billion or 20 percent of this country's gross national product is yearly spent on "office" functions, much of which could be automated and you can see the simple economics of it all. The computer has only begun to make its impact on American business and if you hope to be part of business, especially accounting, in the years to come, you had better get used to the computer. On the other hand, the way of hope is a far better approach. In an era of cries for zero economic growth because of supply shortages, the computer offers the chance for economic growth by more efficiently using the materials we have available. The potential for savings in production and distribution in the American economy are staggering. Additionally, the computer represents an opportunity to use the capabilities of millions of people more effectively by relieving them of mechanical burdens which do not allow them to use their human capacity for creativity and judgment.

Overall System Development Process

Suppose we are now convinced of the desirability, or at least the inevitability of computer-based systems. How do we go about developing one? There are seven basic steps in this process. These are diagrammed in Figure 9-1.

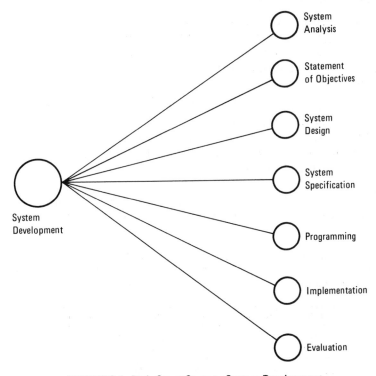

FIGURE 9-1 Basic Seven Steps to System Development

1. *System Analysis.* In this step the analyst becomes familiar with the process or task to be studied. He then prepares documentation in the form of written descriptions and flow charts of the present system in order to identify the information-processing flow.

2. *Statement of objectives.* This step identifies the overall purpose and specific objectives of the proposed system; in other words, what the proposed system will try to accomplish. The analyst will have to determine the output necessary to accomplish these objectives and the data-base necessary to generate this output.

3. *System design.* Once the system objectives have been approved, the analyst must specify the system requirements more precisely. Then the analyst must define the basic modules that will satisfy these system requirements and arrange these modules into a functional design. The entire system must then be analyzed on a cost/benefit basis.

4. *System specification.* The analyst now details the system and how it will work. This includes the exact software and hardware environment, the exact appearance of input forms and output documents, the program flowcharts, and the complete details of the files to be maintained and their structure. The manual procedures are now totally spelled out.

5. *Programming.* At this point, the specifications detail precisely what the individual programs are to do and the flowcharts of how the programs are to work. The tasks of the programmer are then to (1) write the computer programs in the agreed language, (2) develop test data, (3) test the programs to ensure they are working, and (4) prepare documentation on the program and how to use it.

6. *Implementation.* After the system is designed and the programs are working, the job is then to get the new system working in place of the old. This step consists of installing the new hardware, if any, writing detailed procedures, orienting people to the new system including any necessary training, converting files to the new format, and then operating the old and new systems in parallel.

7. *Evaluation.* After the new system has been shaken down and has been in operation for a reasonable period of time (such as six months), independent observers should evaluate the progress and status of the new system. This review should include the documentation, the general acceptance by users, and an analysis comparing the actual costs and benefits as opposed to the anticipated costs and benefits of the system.

To help you remember these seven steps more easily they are summarized in Table 9-1. This oversimplifies things somewhat, but it should be useful in keeping things clear in your

TABLE 9-1   BASIC STEPS OF SYSTEM DEVELOPMENT

SYSTEM ANALYSIS	What is done now. What the present system is.
STATEMENT OF OBJECTIVES	What we will try to accomplish.
SYSTEM DESIGN	How we will accomplish those objectives. Whether it will be worth it.
SYSTEM SPECIFICATION	Precisely how the system will work.
PROGRAMMING	Development of the computer programs necessary for the system.
IMPLEMENTATION	Getting the new system in operation in place of the old.
EVALUATION	How well the new system is working. What we can learn from our experience.

mind despite all the overwhelming detail. Unfortunately, these seven steps are more prescriptive (telling the way it should be done) than they are descriptive (telling the way it is done).

Another set of seven steps of system development appears in Table 9-2. This set of pitfalls should be remembered as a warning.

TABLE 9-2 PITFALLS OF SYSTEM DEVELOPMENT

Uncritical Acceptance
Wild Enthusiasm
Dejected Disillusionment
Total Confusion
Search for the Guilty
Punishment of the Innocent
Promotion of Nonparticipants

9.1 SYSTEM ANALYSIS

In the system analysis or background stage, the analyst prepares documentation on the present system and how it works. This documentation will include both written descriptions and system flowcharts designed to picture the present information-processing flow. A proper background study will include a brief description of the firm and its future prospects, a chart of the company's organizational structure, samples of documents, forms, and flowcharts of procedures. The study should then identify any deficiencies and recommend improvements.

Note that this system analysis is exactly what we covered in Chapters 5 and 6. You can now see how the material in Part two fits into the overall pattern of system development.

Importance of Proper Background Analysis

The background study is absolutely critical to the development of new systems. To understand why this is so, however, we must briefly mention the three basic approaches to system development:

1. The first approach is to apply a standard package or an approach which has been successful elsewhere to the problem at hand. The advantages of this approach are clear: (1) we know the new system can work, since it has already worked and (2) we can become fairly familiar with the system either by observing it in operation or by studying its documentation. The disadvantage is that it may not fit the present situation. This approach, generally speaking, is the one followed by computer people who know little about accounting. In this way, they do not need to understand the present system; they need only implement the new system.

2. The second approach is to use the computer to automate the present system directly. Thus, if a clerk now extends prices and adds up a column of figures, the new system will utilize the computer for the computations. Similarly, if a typist generates a specific report, the new system will have the computer print the same report. The advantage of this approach is that the present system is familiar and the new system will be essentially the same as the old, with the computer simply relieving some of the clerical burden. The disadvantages are: (1) the new system does not utilize the capabilities of the computer to any real extent and (2) the company loses the opportunity to rethink its mode of operation and use the computer to operate more efficiently. Again, generally speaking, accounting people who

know little about the computer take this approach. In this way, they do not really have to understand the computer; they need only use the computer as a fast adding machine and printer.

3. The third approach is to really understand both the present system and the objectives it is to accomplish and then to utilize the computer to more efficiently and effectively meet those objectives. The computer has tremendous advantages—especially vast memory and incredible speed. However, these advantages cannot be utilized properly unless the entire system is rethought. In fact, this rethinking of the system can be as important or even more important than the use of the computer. It is not unknown for a new computer system to be given credit when a redesigned manual system would have generated equal or greater savings. For example, one organization paid some people daily, some weekly, some every two weeks, some semimonthly, and some monthly. The question was posed: Why not pay everyone every two weeks? There was no reason not to. Apparently, the present system had just grown up and no one had ever stopped to rethink the problem. The advantage of this third approach to system development is that potentially the organization will obtain the greatest benefits. The disadvantages of this approach are: (1) it requires more time *initially*, though it will usually save time in the long run (unfortunately, most people do not have time to do it right, though they later have time to do it over); (2) it requires more knowledge, discipline and creative thought to do well.

The text included earlier discussions of manual accounting systems and system analysis to present the knowledge necessary to carry out this third approach. Unfortunately, this approach is not used as often as it should be.

Basic Elements of a Background Study

Notice that the third approach is the only one which requires the system analysis; in both of the other approaches it would be either a hindrance or irrelevant. But the background study is absolutely essential to successful use of this third approach. The question then becomes: What information is necessary for a proper background study? Certainly, there is no definitive answer which will work for all occasions. However, we will recall at this point the basic seven steps of system analysis presented in Chapter 6. These seven steps are diagrammed in Figure 9-2 and include the following:

1-1. *General background*—a discussion of what the company does and where the company is going.

1-2. *Organization structure*—an organization chart and narrative which describe how the company is structured and who reports to whom.

1-3. *Job descriptions*—a description of who does what, including a discussion of individual people's duties.

1-4. *Documents*—an inventory of the forms used now and the reports now generated.

1-5. *Procedures*—a description in flowcharts and narrative of what procedures are now done and why they are done.

1-6. *Deficiencies*—a summary of what is wrong with the present system, both what is done poorly and what has been left out.

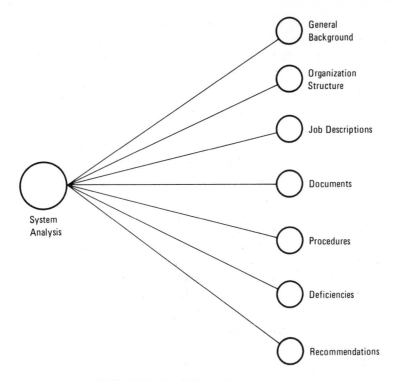

FIGURE 9-2 Seven Steps of System Analysis

1-7. *Recommendations*—a list of what could be done better; details the changes which are necessary to correct the deficiencies.

9.2 STATEMENT OF OBJECTIVES

In his first letter to the Corinthians, Paul tells us, "For if the trumpet give an uncertain sound, who shall prepare himself to the battle." Two thousand years later, this statement is as true now as it was then. For our purposes here, the trumpet is the statement of objectives and the battle is the system development. The statement of objectives proposes that we develop a system to accomplish certain goals. Its purpose is to make as specific as possible exactly what it is we are trying to do. The overall concept is to (1) present a report in management terms which details the goals of the new system and (2) have this report approved and signed by the affected management.

Importance of Management Involvement

Over and over, studies and personal experience confirm that one of the major reasons for disasters in system development is the lack of top management involvement in the project. The statement of objectives helps to solve this problem by requiring the signature of top management on the report signifying approval. If top management is not interested enough to sign the report, we can stop early and avoid potential disasters later.

The most important task for the analyst is to develop a proper set of objectives for the system. A common mistake is to simply take what the present system provides, add a wish-list put together by asking individual managers what they want, and then to collate this to obtain a statement of objectives. You should always keep the following precepts in mind:

1. *Managers need useful information, not simply more and more information.* If anything, many managers have too much information—a state we call information overload. In this state, managers have more information than they know what to do with. They need information that will help them to make better decisions, but a fat computer printout that is not read or used is a waste of resources. Do not simply provide additional information.

2. *Managers do not necessarily know what they need.* Certainly, the analyst must talk with managers about what they want. However, managers may not know the capabilities of the computer (i.e., what the computer could do for them). Also, the manager may be too used to the present system to think of other approaches. The analyst must sift through (1) the information the present system provides and (2) the manager's desires and must help determine the information the manager needs. Thus, the need is for a creative partnership between the analyst and the manager. The analyst should not function simply as a clerk and write down what the manager needs. But, by the same token, the analyst must not dictate to the manager how to run the business.

3. *Even if the system provides the manager needed information, his performance will not necessarily improve.* A common assumption, though not always stated outright, is that a manager will use needed information and improve his decision making. This is not necessarily so. You must determine how well the manager can use the information. If he cannot use the information well, one of the objectives must be to determine decision rules for proper use of the information.

4. *The system should let the managers know how well they are doing.* In the jargon of systems talk, the system should provide "feedback." A manager cannot improve his decision making if he does not know how well or how poorly his past decisions have turned out. If, however, the system provides that information (i.e., gives him feedback), he will be able to isolate areas of difficulty and improve performance.

5. *System goals follow from company goals.* It is impossible to develop the goals for any particular system independently of the overall company goals. For example, in developing a general ledger system, the analyst must keep in mind the centralization/decentralization philosophy of management. The system must report budgeted and actual financial results by the organizational unit to which management has assigned the related authority and responsibility.

Components of the Statement of Objectives

As in the case of system analysis, the statement of objectives is also broken down into seven steps:

2-1. *Overall purpose*—the basic reason for the system and what we are really trying to accomplish.

2-2. *Specific objectives*—the specific tasks and goals necessary to accomplish the given overall purpose.

2-3. *Required output*—the reports and information management needs to accomplish the objectives.

2-4. *Required data*—the data necessary to produce those reports and where the system will obtain that data.

2-5. *Necessary controls*—the controls the system needs to ensure the accuracy and reliability of its data.

2-6. *New policies or procedures*—any changes to corporate policies or procedures as a result of the new system.

2-7. *Signature of management*—agreement by affected management that the given system objectives are those desired by them.

These steps are diagrammed in Figure 9-3 and are discussed further in Chapter 10, where an application is then made to an accounts receivable system for Pooper Centers.

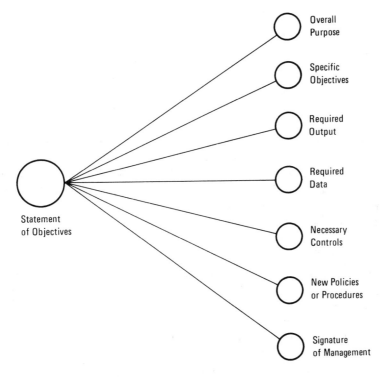

FIGURE 9-3 Seven Steps of the Statement of Objectives

9.3 SYSTEM DESIGN

After we document and understand the present system in the background phase and after we lay out the goals of the new system in the statement of objectives, we must create the new system (at least conceptually) in the system design. The system design will discuss, at a conceptual level, how the new system will work. This discussion will show where and how the system collects data, the flow of data, and the disposition of system outputs.

Designing the new system is certainly the most creative part of system development. The analyst must understand what the present status and future prospects of the company are, understand the goals of the new system, and then create a new system which is appropriate for that company, with those goals. Thus, we should not worry ourselves about creating the perfect system: no system is ever perfect, we can always improve upon it. We should therefore strive for a very good, even excellent system, but we must be prepared to compromise. Remember that in a sense "the best is the enemy of the good," because in our striving for the best we may not be satisfied with something that is perfectly adequate for its purposes.

Important Goals

There are several, often conflicting, goals which we should keep in mind in the development of new systems. Of course, how well we balance these goals is a measure of how well we do:

1. *The system should be as simple as possible.* This is known as the KISS principle. Keep It Simple, Stupid. Certainly, overly complicated system design has been the most common reason systems have exceeded their budgets and had innumerable operational problems. If your design starts to get too complicated, something has gone wrong somewhere; stop and rethink your design.

2. *The system should handle the present and the foreseeable future.* Certainly the system should be able to process the transactions of the firm at the time the system is developed. However, a certain amount of common sense is necessary here. If a system is developed in the off-season for a seasonal business, the designer should keep in mind the volumes which will be processed in the busy season. Also, let us remember that the first step in the background study is to determine not just where the firm is now, but where it is going. Thus, if the firm is growing slowly or is growing fast, that should be taken into consideration. It is absurd, but not uncommon, to design a system, with related hardware where the program flexibility and file sizes were barely able to handle the present volume of transactions, much less the future.

3. *The system should be easily modified.* No one can anticipate the future and there is no way a system can be adequate forever. We must anticipate change, not by guessing what changes will occur, but by designing systems so they can be easily adapted to changing circumstances. In fact, as data processing matures in an organization, an increasing percentage of the total effort is spent on the maintenance of existing systems and a decreasing percentage is spent on the development of new systems. A schematic of this relationship is shown in Figure 9-4. It is obvious that certain things are going to change, such as tax rates. Other changes which may or may not occur, such as future integration of separately developed systems, should also be provided for. A good system design at the time will save a great deal of work later.

4. *The system should be cost effective.* It is important to always keep the cost of obtaining information in mind. For example, it may be possible to keep some information always

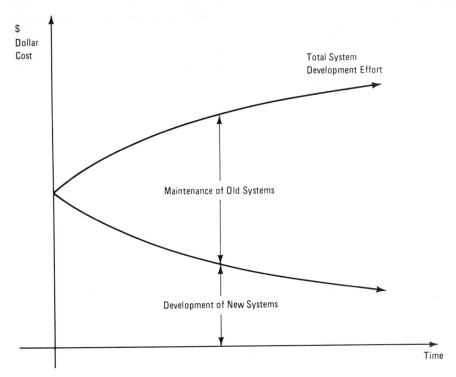

FIGURE 9-4 Breakdown of System Development Effort

current, with on-line real-time processing. However, other approaches may make that information available only on a daily, weekly, or monthly basis, but for a much smaller cost. Only if the current information is worth its cost should that approach be taken.

Elements of System Design

Again, the system design is broken down into seven steps:

3-1. *Scope and boundaries*—a description both of what the system will do and what the system will not do.

3-2. *Specific requirements*—the reports, files, and data necessary for the system.

3-3. *Conceptual design*—how the system (both manual operations and computer programs) will fit together into an overall functional design.

3-4. *Resource requirements*—the amount of money, manpower, and contracted services necessary to develop the system.

3-5. *Tangible benefits*—the "hard dollar" savings from reduction of direct operating expenses.

3-6. *Intangible benefits*—the important but hard to quantify results of improved service or better information.

3-7. *Cost/benefit analysis*—comparison of anticipated costs and benefits, and whether the system will be worth what it costs.

These seven steps are diagrammed in Figure 9-5. A more detailed discussion appears in Chapter 11 along with an application to Pooper Centers.

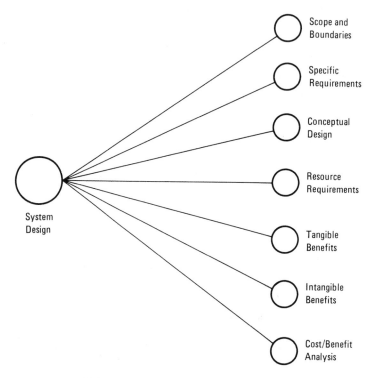

FIGURE 9-5 Seven Steps of System Design

9.4 SYSTEM SPECIFICATION

Once you develop the system design and everyone agrees that this is the way for the system to operate, the next step is to detail the system specifications. This will include all the details of how the procedures and the programs will work, and exactly what the files and output will look like.

The system specification is the most important and difficult technical step in the entire system development process. Prior to this step, everything is somewhat conceptual, or even vague. After this step, the computer programming should actually be a fairly mechanical task if the specifications are done properly. The task, then, is to translate the system design into a workable system.

Important Goals

As in other situations, to be good the translation must remain faithful to both the spirit and the letter of the original. However, there is no one single way to translate a system design into specifications. Thus, it is important to keep the following goals in mind during the process.

1. *The programs and files should be as simple as possible.* The goal should be simplicity not sophistication. The file structure should be easy to understand. The programs should be easy to read, with clear logic paths.

2. *The programs and files should be easy to modify.* Even though it is not clear what will later have to be modified, you can be sure the files will eventually have to accommodate more and different types of data. Also, the programs will have to be changed to handle more and different situations. You should provide for this essentially inevitable change by allowing room for growth.

3. *The programs and files should be machine independent.* Programs and files can easily become essentially tied to one particular computer or one particular computer company. This can often be avoided by choosing wisely before programming begins. Data storage should be done in a way that would work on a wide variety of computers. Do not choose a nonstandard storage technique even if it is more efficient for a particular computer; the technique might be more efficient in a narrow sense for the moment, but it will lock you into a particular computer. When more attractive alternatives become available from other vendors, you may not be able to take advantage of the fact because you are stuck with a tremendous investment in a nonstandard approach. Similarly, you should use programming languages in their standard forms. Computer manufacturers often offer "extensions" of standard languages. Do not use them. Use standard languages in a standard way and the task of converting to another computer will be much easier.

4. *The programs should be easy to test.* This implies establishing separate programs to accomplish identifiable tasks. Thus, we create the entire system from building blocks. Each building block is a program which does a reasonably small number of tasks. In this manner we can test each program separately, as it is written. Further, if the system malfunctions, it is easier to identify the problem area. The alternative approach is to use giant programs that handle "everything." This approach makes the resulting programs hard to test because there are so many more possibilities to test.

Component Steps

System specification is broken down into seven component steps:

4-1. *Control section*—approval of the report by users and management as well as all authorized later changes.

4-2. *System description*—a narrative in management terms of what the system will do and how the system will do it.

4-3. *System flowchart*—a picture of how the system will fit together.

4-4. *Computer system requirements*—the hardware and software packages necessary for the system.

4-5. *Data management summary*—exact description of the input data, the files maintained by the system, and the system output.

4-6. *Individual module design*—narrative and flowchart of each manual operation and computer program utilized by the system.

4-7. *Implementation schedule*—the timetable describing how the system should develop and be implemented.

These seven steps of system specification are diagrammed in Figure 9-6 and discussed further in Chapter 11.

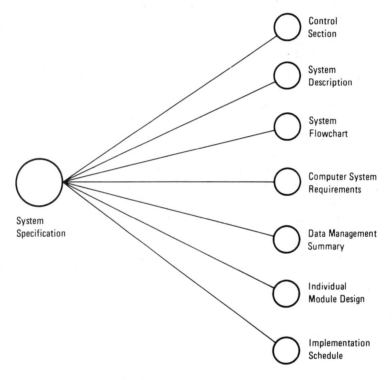

FIGURE 9-6 Seven Steps of System Specification

9.5 PROGRAMMING

After the system specifications are made final and approved, we may now start the actual programming, or writing the computer programs necessary for system operation. It may seem a waste of time to wait until the complete system specifications are finished in order to start programming. The temptation is to start programming even if all the details of the system specification are not completely spelled out. This is a mistake. One of the main reasons for delays in programming projects is the changing of system design or system objectives, thereby wasting large amounts of programming effort.

If the system specifications are properly spelled out, the programming of the system is actually the easiest, most mechanical part of system development. The goal of the system specification step should be to provide enough detail so that the task of programming the system can be turned over to professional programmers. Ideally, we should not have to expect the programmers to know anything about accounting or the system's application area. The system specifications should be complete and self-contained and the programmers should be able to get everything they need from the specifications. In addition, with the development of more and more sophisticated software tools and computer languages, the programming task is becoming easier and easier. More precisely, the programming can now be done by the accountant, if necessary, a prospect totally out of the question as late as the sixties.

Those who work in large companies or who otherwise have access to professional programmers may ask if they should spend time, trouble, and effort learning how to write computer programs when they can have this done for them by people with more experience and knowledge of computers. The answers are: (1) you need some exposure to and experience with computer programming in order to fully appreciate what computer-based systems can and cannot do, and (2) the more you know about computer programming the better and more accurate will be your system designs and system specifications.

Major Programming Steps

Programming basically involves four major steps. Of course, every program is different and has its own unique aspects, but the general approach should be roughly the same:

1. *Determine the program's major logic paths.* This should be available from the flowcharts in the system specification. For example, a file maintainence program may have four major paths:

   a. Add a master file record.

   b. Delete a master file record.

   c. Modify an existing master file record.

   d. End the program.

   These paths will be programmed one by one; we will get one working, then the next, and so on until they all work.

2. *Choose an unwritten path and prepare test data for it.* One of the most important steps is to determine what data are necessary to test whether or not a program logic path works. Ideally, the data should be completely representative; if the program works with that data, we should be able to assume it will work in practice. Of course, if the program fails to work with this data, there are certainly bugs in the program. However, even if the program works for this data, we cannot be positive there are no additional bugs.

3. *Program and test this logic path.* The next step is then to actually write the program steps for this logic path. This step involves the repetition of the following procedures: (a) run the program, (b) identify errors, (c) correct the bugs, and (4) go back to (a) and repeat until there are no more errors which you can identify.

4. *Repeat steps 1 to 3 until the program is complete.* If all logic paths are completed, the program is tentatively finished. If, however, a path is left undone, the next step is to go back to step 2 and repeat the process for the next path. Notice that we build the program in layers, only adding the next layer when the one below is complete. The advantage of this approach is that if something is in error for one level, we can at least tentatively assume the prior levels are correct.

The documentation of programming breaks down into seven basic steps:

5-1. *Narrative description*—explanation of the purpose and uses of the individual program.

5-2. *User instructions*—step by step description of exactly how to use the program.

5-3. *Sample input*—concrete example of the type of input desired by the program.

5-4. *Sample output*—concrete example of the printout generated by the program.

5-5. *Test data*—data with known results which check the proper operation of the program.

5-6. *Operator instructions*—any separate instructions necessary for the computer operator.

5-7. *Program listing*—printout of the program statements.

These system programming steps are diagrammed in Figure 9-7 and discussed more fully in Chapter 12.

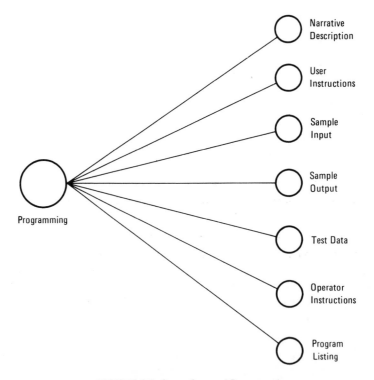

FIGURE 9-7 Seven Steps of Programming

9.6 IMPLEMENTATION

Employee Response

> It must be considered that there is nothing more difficult to carry out, nor more doubtful of success, nor more dangerous to handle, than to initiate a new order of things. For the reformer has enemies in all those who profit by the old order, and only lukewarm defenders in all those who would profit by the new order, this lukewarmness arising partly from fear of their adversaries, who have the laws in their favor; and partly from the incredulity of mankind, who do not truly believe in anything new until they have had actual experience of it.
>
> Niccolo Machiavelli,
> *The Prince*

System implementation is the difficult and time-consuming task of replacing the old system with the new system. Certainly, the central problem is the people problem. All systems are only computer-based and thus can only work through people, not to the exclusion of people. However, the people will be familiar with the old system and its operation and will be thus very likely to resent or at least dislike the trauma of moving to a new system and learning new procedures. Additionally, most people do not have a strong ability to conceptualize and thus really cannot understand the concepts of a new system until it is actually in operation—which is exactly what we are trying to do. Often, once a system is operational, the people like it and would not do without it; however, it was extremely difficult to implement the same system with those same people. As a result, a good sense of humor and an ability to get along well with others are in an important sense more critical than the technical aspects we will discuss later.

When planning for the implementation of a new computer-based system and in actually implementing the system, it is important to remember that there will be both unreasonable as well as reasonable opposition to the new system. Any resistance based upon specific problems with the new system design should have been mentioned and dealt with in the earlier stages of system development. Thus, at the implementation step opposition will be primarily a generalized resistance to the computer and computer-based systems. As a result, the following should be kept in mind during the system implementation:

1. *Employees may have had bad experiences with the computer in the past.* Long-term employees may still remember an earlier ill-fated attempt to automate in the company. Also, employees may have worked at other companies with poor computer-based systems. Therefore, it is important to create a positive attitude about the computer: the employees must believe the computer can work and can make a positive contribution. Any previous poor attitudes about the computer must be overcome.

2. *Managers may subvert system implementation while trying to appear cooperative.* Not all opposition will be verbal and clearly visible. Often, the major obstacles are managers who are opposed to the computer or the new system for personal reasons. One very real fear of managers is the future impact of computers on the manager's job. Even if the system to be implemented is not a direct threat, the manager may see a potential reduction in his prestige, power, or usefulness. Another major difficulty can be that managers may not understand the new system and thus cannot identify with or commit to its successful implementation.

3.   *The person in charge of implementation should have a business orientation.* As mentioned above, the main problems of implementation will be people problems. The employees will want to know how the new system fulfills a business purpose and how the new system fits into the overall operation of the firm. They will be definitely less interested in the technical aspects of the system and how it works. As a result, the implementation must be led by someone with the same orientation as that of the employees so he can communicate with them to motivate the use of the new system.

4.   *Top management must be involved in system implementation.* One of the primary reasons to involve top management in the system development process from the beginning is to have management support in the implementation stage. Employees will get their attitude toward the new system from management. If management is enthusiastic and involved, the employees will be also. If management is not very interested and does not get involved, then the employees will not be interested and the implementation will fail.

Component Steps

Implementation breaks down into seven steps:

6-1.   *Hardware installation*—getting any new equipment in place and properly operating.

6-2.   *Procedure writing*—developing step by step instructions for each job position which is part of the system.

6-3.   *Personnel orientation*—introduce employees to the computer; stress the positive impact of the new system.

6-4.   *Training*—instruct employees in the new procedures and operations they must perform in the new system.

6-5.   *Testing*—utilizing the new system and checking that the results generated are correct.

6-6.   *File Conversion*—changing the data in the files of the old system to the format of the new system.

6-7.   *Parallel operation*—use of the new system at the same time as the old system to compare the results.

These implementation components are diagrammed in Figure 9-8 and discussed further in Chapter 12.

9.7 EVALUATION

After the new system has been in operation long enough for the initial difficulties to be shaken down (say six months), we should stop and take stock of our experience to that date. This evaluation process should include a review of how the system is operating and a comparison of the actual costs and benefits compared to the anticipated costs and benefits. The evaluation report should conclude with recommendations for improvement in system design or operating efficiency.

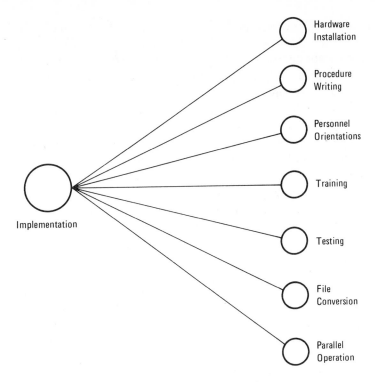

FIGURE 9-8 Seven Steps of Implementation

Potential Difficulty

This process is in fact very difficult to do well, especially if it is done by the people who designed the system or the people who operate the system. Writing some four thousand years ago, Confucious said that he had "yet to meet a man who, on observing his own faults blamed himself." As a result, the postimplementation evaluation should be done, if possible, by independent reviewers. However, even if the review is undertaken by people involved in the system, it will be a valuable exercise, showing how the system concepts are applied in practice.

An independent audit is a form of evaluation and can substitute for an evaluation in some situations, especially in basic accounting systems. Auditors prepare a *management letter* which, if done well, has basically the same information as our evaluation.

When evaluating a new system, you must keep in mind that the system is not either a complete success or a total failure; it will be somewhere within this range. As a result, there will always be something wrong or less than perfect about the system. In addition, it is important not only to determine what is wrong, but also to determine why it went wrong: we must know both these things in order to not make the same mistakes again. There are four major reasons for difficulty in system operation:

1. *The system attempted to do too much.* A standard problem is the creation of a system which is too complex or too ambitious to work properly. One possible reason for this is

that the computer hardware is inadequate for the processing asked of it. A more common reason is simply an excessive scope of the project or overly ambitious objectives. System development must be performed in reasonable, digestible pieces, without excessive reaching.

2   *The system attempted to do too little.* Another common problem is the development of a new computer-based system which is simply a replacement for the previous manual system. As mentioned above, it is important to limit the scope of the new system to manageable proportions. However, if the scope is reduced essentially to that of the manual systems, there is no benefit to be had in developing the computer-based system. The computer-based system may turn out to be simply a more expensive way to do the same thing.

3.   *The employees withdrew psychologically from the system.* When the computer is used extensively for decision making, this results in less scope for action on the part of many employees, especially middle management. Additionally, with computer-based systems information is often available to higher management much faster and thus they can become involved in what had previously been the responsibility of others. In these situations, the employees begin to have less concern for the system, its accuracy, and its effectiveness.

4.   *The employees opposed the system development and the system implementation.* If the employees who must work with and use the system are opposed to it, the system will not work. The employees will simply not trust the system: (1) if the system has inadequate internal controls and is inaccurate; (2) if the new system is incompatible with or does not balance to other old systems; or (3) if the new system is not fully explained or is otherwise incomprehensible to them. Less legitimate opposition is caused by dissenting internal factors who are opposed to the system for personal reasons.

Component Steps

Evaluation breaks down into seven steps:

7-1.   *Documentation review*—analysis of the system documentation, its completeness, accuracy, and adequacy.

7-2.   *Cost analysis*—comparison of the anticipated costs in the system design to the actual costs incurred.

7-3.   *Benefit analysis*—comparison of the anticipated benefits in the system design to the actual benefits obtained.

7-4.   *Acceptance of users*—review of the degree of enthusiasm with which the users have reacted to the system.

7-5.   *Internal controls*—review of the internal controls of the new system, to determine whether they are in use and if they are adequate.

7-6.   *Deficiencies*—the weaknesses and omissions of both the new system and the system development process.

7-7.   *Recommendations*—specific steps to be taken to improve the new system or improve the system development process.

The seven steps of evaluation appear in Figure 9-9 and are discussed in detail in Chapter 12. As you can see, system development is a process of systematically refining our conceptions, making them more and more specific and definite until we finally have a completed, imple-

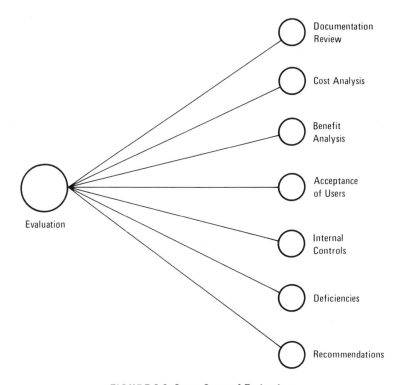

FIGURE 9-9 Seven Steps of Evaluation

mented system. The process is similar to that of painting: the artist begins by sketching the overall conception of the painting; then, gradually he adds more and more detail to the painting until it is complete.

In our system design, we begin with our overall objectives. We then develop a general system flowchart which gives the overall picture of the entire system and how it fits together. Next, we specify exactly what the outputs will contain, the data-base the system will maintain in order to produce these outputs, and the necessary inputs to generate this data-base. Following this, we flowchart the individual programs and detail the exact forms and procedures the system needs. After this we write the individual programs, test them, and put them into practice. Finally, we evaluate the results of the new system and compare the actual costs and benefits to those anticipated. (See Figure 9-10.)

It is impossible for a painter to start and completely finish one small segment of a painting; then start and finish another small segment; and continue in this fashion until the painting is complete. Each individual piece might be acceptable, but the entire work would not fit together. Similarly, it is impossible to jump directly to the programming of even a small section of a system until the entire system has been sketched in the system design and the system specification steps.

It is however, a matter of judgment to determine how many major preliminary sketches, so to speak, must be made for any particular system development. In vast and complicated systems, of course, the process must be more deliberate, with more intermediate stages. In extremely simple situations, we might only need a rough sketch before constructing an especially simple program. Therefore, the rule to keep in mind is: though you must go through the seven

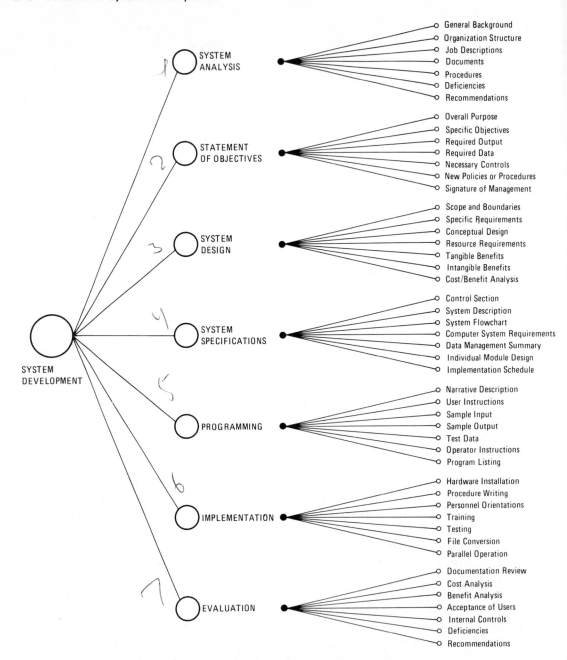

FIGURE 9-10 Overview of System Development

stages of system development given in this chapter you do not always have to go through them in seven completely separate steps. There can be more steps or fewer steps, as the occasion requires.

There is another step which is often included in the system development process, called the *feasibility study*. The feasibility study is often the first step of the development of a large-scale system and is a preliminary review of the entire system development project. The system development process is very time consuming and expensive; the system analysis stage alone can easily cost tens of thousands of dollars, and the system development effort can take five years or more. For these reasons, management is understandably reluctant to simply start on a new system development effort; hence the feasibility study. The feasibility study reviews the potential of a new system development effort and tries to determine if the potential benefits make it worthwhile to proceed. Thus, for large-scale systems, the feasibility study is a very important first step. (However, we did not include the feasibility study as a basic step because (1) it is not always necessary, especially in small systems and (2) it is essentially an application of the same basic principles, since a feasibility study is really a mini-system analysis/statement of objectives/system design.)

The following three chapters provide more detail on each stage of system development and show the development of an accounts receivable system for our sample company, Pooper Centers, Inc. Again, this is a *sample* system development and you will not be able to force every system into this mold. However, this should give you a firm idea of how a system should be developed and provide a general structure within which you will be able to work.

exercises

9-1 Following is a list of important factors, each of which must be considered in the overall system development process. For each of these factors, state the phase of system development in which it would be considered and briefly mention how the factor affects that phase.

   a. Privacy protection.

   b. Capacity for growth.

   c. Program flowcharting.

   d. Employee concern about change.

   e. Reliability.

   f. Future problems.

   g. System flowcharting.

   h. Flexibility.

   i. Choice of programming language.

   j. Current problems.

   k. Cost.

9-2 Listed below are ten background and personal characteristics of system development personnel. For each phase of system development, state the two characteristics which will most likely contribute to success in that phase.

  a. Technical computer background.

  b. Extensive auditing experience.

  c. Familiarity with company operations.

  d. Effectiveness in written communication.

  e. Effectiveness in oral communication.

  f. Ability to focus on larger issues.

  g. Thoroughness.

  h. Systems point of view.

  i. Rigorous logical approach.

  j. Rapport with employees.

9-3 Accountants often view computer-based systems as simply extensions of the processing capabilities of manual systems. Computer technicians often are not aware of the record-keeping and control needs of accounting. Distinguish between the use of the computer as a processing tool and as an analytical tool. Give three specific examples of the use of the computer as a processing tool and three examples of the use of the computer as an analytical tool. Your examples should be taken from a business information system.

9-4 Managers may become so accustomed to receiving only certain kinds of information that they fail to realize that additional needed information could be provided by a computer-based system. Give two specific examples of information which could easily be provided by a computer-based system but which is not normally available from a manual system for each of the following areas.

  a. Accounts receivable.

  b. Accounts payable.

  c. Payroll.

  d. Financial statements.

  e. Sales.

9-5 Computer-based information systems are capable of providing the data necessary for good performance evaluation of managers and employees. Give two specific examples of information which would be useful in the performance evaluation of each of the following positions.

  a. Credit manager.

  b. Purchasing agent.

  c. Salesmen.

  d. Sales manager.

  e. President.

9-6 Table 9-2 presents seven possible pitfalls which may be encountered in system development. State how you would overcome the problems exhibited by each of these pitfalls.

system objectives

outline

10.1 **Elements of the statement of objectives**: importance of clearly defined objectives; components of the statement of objectives.

10.2 **Computer acquisition**: basic elements of the computer system; computer vendor alternatives; computer acquisition specification sheet.

10.3 **Application to sample company**: general concepts are made concrete with sample company.

INTRODUCTION

In the last chapter, our discussion was designed to give a general overview of the system development process. In this chapter we begin a more detailed discussion of each of the steps of system development and will illustrate the entire process using Pooper Centers.

10.1 ELEMENTS OF THE STATEMENT OF OBJECTIVES

To review, there are seven basic steps in system development:

1. system analysis
2. statement of objectives
3. system design
4. system specification
5. programming
6. implementation
7. evaluation

The first step, systems analysis, was extensively illustrated in Chapter 6. Thus, even though the systems analysis is critical to success in systems development, we need not go over that material again here. But, for ease in reference, a schematic of systems analysis is provided in Figure 10-1.

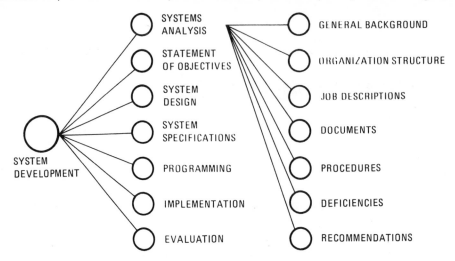

FIGURE 10-1 Elements of the Systems Analysis

The next step is then the statement of objectives. The basic structure of the statement of objectives appeared in Chapter 9, but, for ease of reference, a schematic of the elements of the statement of objectives appears in Figure 10-2.

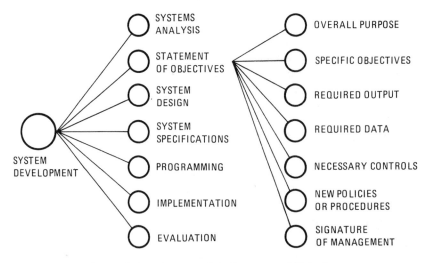

FIGURE 10-2 Elements of the Statement of Objectives

Importance of Clearly Defined Objectives

The primary distinctive feature of the systems approach is its intense focus on objectives. The problem, however, is that determining the system objectives and making them operational is far easier to say than to do, because of often conflicting objectives and because real objectives are often masked. For example, when college presidents go to the legislature for increased funds, they usually talk about quality education, community service, and similar topics. Careful studies have shown, however, that often the *real* objective of those same colleges is to grant the maximum number of degrees. Similarly, a corporation president will generally talk about the maximization of profits. In fact, his real objective often is the maximization of the company's size along with steady growth in, though not necessarily a maximization of, profits.

Components of the Statement of Objectives

A properly developed statement of objectives should contain the following information:

1. *Overall purpose*. The first step is to set out why we are trying to develop the system at all. For example, the overall purpose of an accounts payable system could be "to increase profitability by ensuring the obtaining of all discounts and the delaying to the extent possible, of all payments." Note that we are only interested in how much we owe as a means to other ends. If the overall purpose is merely to make the bookkeeping easier, the system should be rethought. Again, the overall purpose of an accounts receivable system might well be to encourage faster payment by customers of amounts due, to improve internal control over receivables and cash collections, to provide management with better information, or any combination of these goals. Thus, to repeat, the overall purpose is the ultimate goal we are trying to reach or the basic reason for the system.

2. *Specific objectives*. As discussed above, the overall purpose must be identified to give us our underlying rationale. However, this overall purpose must be made operational, and the specific objectives section does exactly that. For example, let us use the accounts payable system discussed above; we must make the overall purpose (i.e., to increase profitability by ensuring the obtaining of all discounts and the delaying, to the extent possible, of all payments) operational by detailing how this goal will be accomplished. Specific objectives of the system might then be:

   a. Preparation on demand of a printout detailing which invoices are due, by their due date. This printout would tell management how much cash is needed on each day to pay suppliers and thus allow time to arrange financing as necessary.

   b. Preparation of the checks to suppliers for all invoices due before a specific date. This would be a convenient way of paying all invoices due and would relieve the clerical staff of a huge burden of typing checks.

      Let us take another example: a payroll system for a school board. Suppose the payroll system's overall purpose is not merely to pay the employees, but also to analyze pay-expense to determine the cost of each school activity. We must then make this overall purpose operational by determining specific objectives. We may want or need to know costs by type of school (elementary, junior high, senior high), and that would become a specific objective: determine costs by type of school. Similarly, we may want to know costs by type of activity (math, French, etc.). This would be another objective. We may then want to know what the costs are by type of school *and* type of activity (e.g., what is the cost of math in junior high school, the cost of French in senior high school). This would be an additional specific objective.

The main point here is that we must specify exactly what the objectives of the new system are because the rest of the system development process depends critically upon these objectives. Certainly, the more objectives and the more complicated the objectives are, the more complicated the system must be and the more expensive the system will be.

3. *Required output.* Once we have the specific objectives of the system determined, the next step is to determine precisely what output the system should generate. If at all possible you should develop a sample or picture of the output, exactly as it will be printed by the computer. This step is extremely important for three reasons. First, most people simply do not have a good capacity for conceptualization and are not capable of getting a good mental image of what the system can do for them. For this reason, you must prepare a picture so the person can visualize the results of the system and so he can develop a "feel" for what the system can do. Second, this picture will be a given goal for the system. Thus, a user must concentrate on the proposed output and determine whether or not that is what he wants out of the system because that is exactly what the system will generate. If he wants something different later, it will be clear he changed his mind, and the responsibility for delays and increased costs will be pinpointed. Third, many technically small differences (which are nonetheless extremely important to the user) can often be quickly cleared up by the use of a picture. For example, the user might want to delete one column, or add one column, or perhaps switch the position of columns; these sorts of changes can be extremely important to the user even though they are almost trivial from a systems or programming standpoint.

4. *Required data.* We continue in this step to move "backwards," so to speak. We went from the overall purpose, to the specific objectives to accomplish that purpose, to the required reports needed to meet those objectives, and now we must determine the data necessary to develop those reports. Certainly if we wish the computer to generate names on a report, these names must have come from some source, fed into the computer, stored in a file on the computer, and made available to a program for report generation. Similarly, if we wish the system to be able to generate an audit trail printout of all transactions which have affected an account balance, these transactions must have been captured at the time of file updating and stored for later recovery.

Let us look again at the accounts payable system discussed earlier, where we want a report to give us the amount we need to pay out suppliers, for any given day. In this case, it will not be adequate to simply record an invoice when it arrives as a particular amount owed to a particular vendor. The system must capture, in addition to the gross amount owed, the total potential discount and the due date after which we lose the discount. If the system does not record and store this information, the computer will not be able to generate the required report. Note, however, that the net amount payable by the due date need *not* be stored in the computer system because it can easily be computed from the gross amount owed and the discount (net = gross–discount).

This step of determining the information necessary and the source of that information is absolutely essential for eliminating unpleasant surprises later in the system development process. For example, consider a general ledger system. As part of a reasonably sophisticated general ledger system it is quite possible to generate comparative financial statements (i.e., comparing this month's results to the results of the same month last year). It is necessary to simply store an additional twelve data-items (one for each month of last year) in each general ledger account record. The technical part is not a tremendous problem. What *is* a problem, however, is the source of that data. If the chart of accounts is substantially changed, the data from last year will not be comparable to the data for this year. Short of reclassifying and reprocessing every transaction of the previous year, it may not be possible to generate last year's results to compare with this year's.

5. *Necessary internal controls.* By this point, you should be thoroughly familiar with internal controls and their importance in all accounting systems. As you are aware, internal controls are absolutely necessary to ensure the accuracy and reliability of the accounting data and accounting reports.

   The importance of internal control is not reduced in a computer-based system. In fact, in many ways, internal control is even more important when using the computer. However, we will defer to Chapter 16 a detailed discussion of internal control in computer-based systems. Suffice it to say that the basic elements of internal control—honest and capable employees, clear delegation and separation of duties, appropriate documents, proper procedures, adequate physical control, and independent verification are all required here.

   Thus, in an accounts payable system, one necessary control might very well be a separation of duties, whereby the person who enters an invoice for payment into the computer does not also authorize payment by the computer. Similarly, prenumbered documents, such as checks, are also necessary controls for even a computer-based system. As a final example, it may be necessary to limit access to the computer or computer terminal to have adequate physical control over the accounting records now on the computer.

6. *New policies or procedures.* The next step is to determine the impact of the new system on the organization. Often, to fully utilize the capabilities of the new system, there must be changes made to long-standing policies or procedures of the company. These changes should be made visible and apparent as soon as possible for two reasons: (a) to see if the proposed changes are acceptable to management, since it is absurd to develop a system which assumes certain policy changes which will never be accepted; and (b) to give the organization enough time to get used to the changes if they are inevitable.

   Let us consider a specific example to make these concepts more concrete. In one bank, a new system was to involved the "cycling" of bank statements. In other words, instead of everyone (individuals, corporation, etc.) receiving their statements at the end of the month, some customers would receive their statements as of the tenth, some customers would receive their statements as of the twentieth and some would receive theirs at the end of the month. When presented with this proposal, management absolutely rejected it, despite evidence that such "cycling" had worked well in other banks. Management was adamant that their customers would not accept such practices and that cycling was out of the question. Certainly, in such a case, the systems analyst must defer to management and design as good a system as possible, given the constraints.

   It is important to realize that technical questions are often left to the technical experts, but if the new system affects company policy, management must participate in and accept policy changes.

7. *Signature of management.* As you perhaps recall, we mentioned in the last chapter that one of the major reasons for systems development disasters is lack of top management involvement. This concept is so important that it cannot be repeated too often.

Let us consider, in more detail, why this is. It is critical to realize that no one in the organization will be as interested in new systems and their success as the systems development people. Thus, even though you may be developing a system for the controller, he will not be as interested in the system as you are. The controller has other, pressing things to do and people to supervise. Thus, even though he may work on or be interested in what he will consider to be *your* new system, *your* new system will tend to fall to the bottom of his list of priorities. If both systems and the controller are on the same level they represent the same level of authority. Thus, systems cannot tell the controller anything; systems can only suggest. Note, however, that both systems and the controller report to the president. If the president is interested in the project, he will see that *his* new system is made a priority by the controller and that the necessary work gets done.

The basic problem is then to get the president interested and the best place to start is with the statement of objectives. You should give the statement of objectives to the president, make any changes he deems necessary, and then ask him to sign the statement to indicate his approval. If the president signs it, fine, you have made an excellent start in involving top management in the project. If the president does *not* sign it, this is also fine, since you now know he will not back the project and it is best to forget it.

Note, however, that top management's signature on the statement of objectives does *not* mean they have signed off on the project: management must continue to be deeply involved in the project until completion.

Table 10-1 summarizes the concepts we have discussed in this chapter thus far.

TABLE 10-1 ELEMENTS OF THE STATEMENT OF OBJECTIVES

OVERALL PURPOSE:	basic reason for the system, and why we are interested in the system at all
SPECIFIC OBJECTIVES:	a list of goals making the overall purpose operational; gives what the system will accomplish
REQUIRED OUTPUT:	exactly what the output of the system will be like, details of what the user will get
REQUIRED DATA:	the necessary data files to generate the above output and the source of that data
NECESSARY CONTROLS:	the internal controls to ensure the accuracy and reliability of the accounting data
NEW POLICIES OR PROCEDURES:	the impact of the proposed system on the organization; lists needed changes in company policy
SIGNATURE OF MANAGEMENT:	approval in writing by higher management, signifying their willingness to see the project through to completion

10.2 COMPUTER ACQUISITION

The simple economics of computer technology imply that most new systems and all major new systems will include a computer as part of the system in some fashion. Assuming that, the next step we must consider is that of determining what computer we should obtain to incorporate into the system.

We discuss computer acquisition here because we wish to keep our options open, so to speak, for the system design. A common approach is to design the system and then to request proposals for computers to fit that design. We feel, however, that this approach closes off too early entirely different designs which actually may be more appropriate. As we will see later in this chapter, there are a tremendous number of computer vendor alternatives, and these vendors will often take radically different approaches to the same problem. As a result, it is often better to formulate only the system objectives (not the system design) and ask various vendors for their proposals on the proper equipment and system design. Once the vendor is selected, the system design can then be developed.

Basic Elements of the Computer System

When we wish to incorporate a computer into a system, we need more than a piece of equipment. We need four basic elements:

1. *Hardware*—the actual computer equipment and what most people think about when they think about computers.

2. *Software*—the collection of application and supervisory programs which tell the computer hardware what to do. Though software is not always considered, it is becoming the dominant expense of a computer system.

3. *Maintenance*—the continuing process of keeping the equipment working. This includes the necessary spare parts and the technician(s) capable of keeping the equipment in operation. Maintenance is important for all computer systems, since equipment (no matter how advanced) will sometimes break. However, different users will place differing emphasis on maintenance. In the case of an on-line system such as an airline reservations, computer failure puts the entire system out of operation; thus, maintenance is critical. In the case of a small business computer used for accounting purposes, a delay of one day in fixing the equipment might not be excessive. In the case of an electrical engineer or computer hobbyist, the user could fix the machine himself and maintenance is not as important.

4. *Operations*—the actual turning on of the machine, paying electricity bills, mounting tape drives, buying paper and other supplies, and replacing disk drives. Simple computers can be operated by their users—their operation is relatively straightforward. Large computer systems require, on the other hand, a separate operations staff to handle all the tape drives, printers, etc.

A summary of the above discussion appears in Table 10-2.

TABLE 10-2   ELEMENTS OF A COMPUTER SYSTEM

HARDWARE	The physical computer equipment
SOFTWARE	The instructions to tell the equipment what to do
MAINTENANCE	The process of keeping the equipment working
OPERATIONS	The operating of the tapes, disks, and printers

Computer Vendor Alternatives

As we have just discussed, when we get a computer system we must get all four necessary elements—hardware, software, maintenance, and operations. These four elements are not, however, available from four neat, separate sets of vendors. Some vendors offer only one element, whereas some offer a combination of elements. Let us now go over the computer vendor possibilities (for convenience they are summarized in Table 10-3).

TABLE 10-3   COMPUTER VENDOR ALTERNATIVES

Type of Company	Type of Product or Operation
Mainframe Computer Manufacturers	large-scale systems for large-scale processing, such as airline reservations
Mainframe Replacement Copies	substitutes for IBM mainframe computers at lower cost
Minicomputer Manufacturers	smaller computers for small networks of terminals for transaction processing
Programmable Calculator Manufacturers	stand alone units for one user and one application at a time
Microcomputer Manufacturers	"computer on a chip" for word processing and small business systems
OEM Systems Packager	complete package of hardware (and often software) for end user
Service Bureau	receives input from customer, does all processing off-site and returns results
Time-sharing Services	provides terminals and access to a large-scale central computer for processing
Computer Leasing Companies	purchases computer from manufacturer and leases to the end user
Used Computer Brokers	buys surplus hardware and then resells to others
Peripheral Equipment Manufacturers	"plug-compatible" replacements for the peripherals of the computer manufacturers
Facilities Management Firms	operates computer system for customer, hires employees, often provides software
EDP Consultants	provides advice, guidance, system designs and programming for clients
Software Vendors	programming package to satisfy the common goals of many users

1. *Mainframe computer manufacturers.* These companies make the large-scale systems with which most people are familiar. These companies include IBM, Burroughs, and Sperry Univac. Their products are the most powerful computers available and range up to the Cray machines costing approximately $10 million each. These machines are most useful for large-scale computation or, for business purposes, the maintenance of huge data files. Thus, these machines are ideal for banks, insurance companies, and others who have to maintain records for vast numbers of customers or policyholders. The manufacturers of mainframe computers also provide supervisory software and perform any necessary maintenance for their equipment. This equipment is so expensive and generally so important to the company

using it that maintenance is good. Operation of these machines is difficult and requires a separate operations staff.

2. *Mainframe replacement copies.* These companies make equipment which substitute for the computers made by others, particularly IBM. These companies include National Semiconductor and Amdahl. Their products simply substitute for some particular model IBM system. Because they use more advanced technology and because they are in large measure copying rather than developing, these replacement machines are much smaller and less expensive than the IBM equivalent. These companies then use IBM software for their machines, but they have to provide maintenance. Operation is essentially the same level of difficulty as that of the replaced equipment.

3. *Minicomputer manufacturers.* These companies make equipment with a wide range of abilities. The equipment is often used for recording measurements (attached to pipelines, for example). For business purposes they are mainly used for small to medium-scale transaction processing, such as an inventory system which must be continually updated by transactions as they occur. The main minicomputer manufacturers include Digital Equipment Corporation (DEC is its common acronym), and Data General. These companies also provide software and maintenance, as do the mainframe manufacturers, but the software and maintenance is not nearly as extensive—the user is much more on his own. Operation is not as much a problem, and a separate operations staff is generally not required.

4. *Programmable calculator manufacturers.* These companies make calculators which can be directed by computer programs, often written in BASIC. The capabilities of these systems are so extensive that larger models overlap the small end of minicomputers. The distinction between minicomputers and programmable calculators is that the minicomputer can be the heart of a small network of terminals whereas the programmable calculator is best used for one particular application and one user at a time. These companies include Wang, Hewlett-Packard, and Olivetti. Supervisory software is eliminated by the programmable calculator, thus reducing flexibility but at the same time greatly simplifying operation, which is easily accomplished by the user. Maintenance for programmable calculators is generally equivalent to that of minicomputers.

5. *Microcomputer manufacturers.* These companies make complete central processing units for extremely low prices, but these CPUs are sold by themselves, without any input or output devices. The microcomputer can be important in business applications, especially for word processing (i.e., automatic typewriters and text editors which allow the user to correct only the typing mistakes without having to retype the entire page). The machine incorporates changes to the text and then can automatically retype the manuscript. The microcomputer is also extremely effective for small, stand-alone transaction processing, such as a small business accounting system. However, since the microcomputer must be combined with input and output devices to form a complete system, most microcomputers used for business come in packages put together by a packager from different companies' products (see below). The microcomputer manufacturers include Intel and Motorola; generally speaking, they provide little, if any, software, and maintenance is simply a matter of replacing defective chips.

6. *OEM system packager.* OEM stands for Original Equipment Manufacturer. This means that the packager buys different components direct from different factories and then puts together a complete computer system. Most microcomputers and many minicomputers for

business are purchased from the system packager. The packager generally provides three services for his customer: (a) he puts together a compatible collection of equipment which works together; (b) he usually provides software to help accomplish the user's goals; and (c) he exists as one entity where the user can come for assistance in case of hardware or software difficulty. Thus, unless you are technically expert, which most business users are not, the packager is extremely important. Operation is the responsibility of the user, but the packager keeps the operation as simple as possible.

7. *Service bureaus.* These companies take input from their customers, process the data, and then return the results. Thus, the service bureau buys the equipment (hardware), develops the software, and has the burden of maintenance and operation of the computer. The user need only prepare data for input. Generally, the service bureau receives the data, processes it overnight, and then returns the resulting printout. Service bureaus are thus used most often for applications like payroll, where the service bureau will pick up timecards and then return payroll checks, a payroll register, and the necessary government forms like W-2's. The user is thus relieved of the burdens of computer ownership and operation, but at the cost of reduced timeliness of information. Most communities have several local service bureaus.

8. *Time-sharing services.* These companies try to combine the benefits of service bureaus with the responsiveness of computer ownership by providing their users with a computer terminal and access to their large computer. The user need only be concerned with his terminal operation; the time-sharing company owns and operates the central computer. For many years, time sharing was considered the "wave of the future" but recent advances in microcomputers and continuing problems with reliability and cost of communicating to the central computer have limited its use. Time sharing is most useful when performing large numbers of computations with limited output. General Electric and Control Data both have extensive time-sharing networks.

9. *Computer leasing companies.* Many computer users want a large system but do not wish to (or cannot) purchase the system. The manufacturer will lease the computer system to the user, but the charges are high. The computer leasing company buys the computer system from the manufacturer and then leases it to the user at a reduced charge (at least, reduced from the manufacturer's charge). The leasing company can reduce the price by: (a) requiring a lower return on equity than does the manufacturer, and (b) locking the user into a longer-term lease and reducing his flexibility in changing machines. This business used to be a favorite of Wall Street and was viewed as a great growth industry. However, obsolescence of installed equipment when new machines are introduced by the manufacturers has reduced their performance. The computer leasing companies include Itel. But to show you how complicated the situation is getting, Itel now also leases a mainframe replacement copy made by National Semiconductor, a microcomputer manufacturer.

10. *Used computer brokers.* These companies buy used computers from users getting new equipment and then resell the used equipment to others. An example of this type of company is American Used Computer Corporation. Most computer manufacturers will help their customers contact potential purchasers of their present equipment when they get new equipment. However, the manufacturer will generally not buy back their older equipment or accept it as a "trade in." The used computer broker thus provides an important service in buying surplus equipment. Purchase of used equipment should not be attempted by the

novice computer user because the manufacturer treats older equipment as a stepchild. Used computers are most important as a backup for similar or identical equipment a company already owns or has used for some time.

11. *Peripheral equipment manufacturers.* The mainframe computer manufacturers also provide all necessary peripheral equipment, such as tapes, disks, and printers. Peripheral equipment manufacturers make substitutes for these peripherals which simply plug in as replacements. Because of lower overhead and less needed development, these companies can offer peripherals which are less expensive and give better performance. The classical difficulty with these products is that in a mixed vendor environment, if anything goes wrong, the "finger-pointing" starts and each vendor points to another as the source of difficulty. Storage Technology and Memorex are among the peripheral equipment manufacturers.

12. *Facilities management firms.* The operation of a large-scale computer installation is a complicated and often tedious task. Employees of widely varying capabilities (highly educated systems designers to high school graduate operators) must be hired and fired; supplies must be purchased; and deadlines must be met. Additionally, in organizations like city and state governments with fixed salary scales, it may be almost impossible to attract qualified people. As a result, facilities management firms will (for a fee, of course) operate the computer installation for their customer. The customer owns the equipment, the facilities management firm simply operates it for him. Also, in situations with detailed and specialized programming requirements, such as hospitals, the facility management firm provides appropriate software. Computer Sciences Corporation provides facilities management for state and federal agencies, whereas Medicus Systems works for hospitals.

13. *EDP consultants.* The world of computer systems is so new and strange to many users that an electronic data processing (EDP) consulting business has developed to provide assistance. Consulting firms range in quality, of course, and range in size from independent consultants to international CPA firms, such as Arthur Andersen, employing several thousand professionals. Consultants provide a wide range of services, from advice in computer acquisition, to systems design, to programming. Unfortunately, consultants are often not called in until a disaster has occurred and they are then asked to straighten out the situation. Consultants are best used in the beginning of an acquisition or project to make sure everything is planned properly, not after the fact when the mistakes have been made.

14. *Software vendors.* Programming is a large and growing aspect of a computer system. However, there is often a sufficient similarity in the needs of different users that the same software can be used by many different people or firms. The software vendor puts together a complete package to accomplish certain objectives and then sells the package to users with those needs.

Computer Acquisition Specification Sheet

As you can see from this discussion, the question of computer acquisition can be overwhelming, simply because of the vast number of possibilities. This is the reason many firms have difficulty in this area. The firm decides it needs a computer and then goes to several vendors. The firm then asks the vendors what it should do and then proceeds to be overwhelmed with the vastly differing proposals and suggestions by all the different vendors.

The proper approach, then, is not to go to the vendors and ask, "What should I do?" Instead, you should develop a statement of objectives that you wish to achieve and then go to the vendors and ask, "How can you best help me accomplish my objectives?" This difference in approach can make the difference between confusion and clarity and between success and failure.

An immediate reaction might then be to develop the system analysis and statement of objectives and to present them to the vendor. This material would have the information necessary for the vendor to develop a proposal adequate for those needs. Unfortunately, this approach will not work for two reasons. First, the material is too detailed and complex for the vendor to assimilate and comprehend (you must remember salesmen, not technical experts, will be trying to sell you). Second, the material does not provide enough guidance for the vendor's proposal; as a result, the proposals from different vendors will not be comparable and will not contain important information.

The proper approach is to prepare a specification sheet for the vendors. The systems analysis (background study) and statement of objectives are to clarify the situation for you, the user. This material must then be translated for the vendor and guidance provided to get comparable proposals from different vendors. The specification sheet should concentrate on what you want the system to accomplish; all the material backing up those goals and detailing why you want and need them accomplished can be omitted from the specification sheet. Remember: the vendor does not really care about your problems, he only cares about selling you equipment.

What should be done, then, is the preparation of a computer acquisition specification sheet containing the following basic elements:

1. *Background*—giving the vendor a description of the company, its present situation and future prospects. The background section should also describe the present accounting system and present automated equipment, if any, that the company is using. Importantly, this section should give the vendor an idea of the company's timetable for action—in other words, how soon will the company make a decision and how soon will the company want to buy any equipment. This is only fair to the vendor, and if the company is planning to act quickly the vendor will be much more enthusiastic than if the company were merely "looking."

2. *Automated applications*—giving the vendor a description of the areas for automation in roughly the order of priority. This section should discuss for each area the volume of transactions, the report requirements, and any necessary potential for future growth. This material will give the vendor information to help decide what type of equipment is required and the applicability of any available software packages. Any "requirements specifications" such as performance or cost constraints should be mentioned here. An example would be a requirement that the computer respond within some set time limit in order for the equipment to be acceptable.

3. *Proposal format*—giving the vendor a description of the type of proposal required. A standard proposal format is absolutely essential to compare proposals from different vendors. This section should give the place where the proposal should be mailed and the deadline for proposal submission (three weeks is generally a minimum time to give vendors time to prepare an adequate proposal; for very complicated situations, more time would of course be

necessary). This section should require the following of all proposals: (1) a detailed descrip-tion of all proposed equipment; (b) a cost breakdown for all equipment, comparing pur-chase and lease alternatives (if a lease is available); (c) any physical planning considerations such as additional air conditioning and raised floors; (d) any systems and programming assistance which the vendor will provide; (e) the availability of service facilities and the time required to receive a service call; and (f) the availability of any software packages which satisfy the firm's requirements.

10.3 APPLICATION TO POOPER CENTERS

We will now use the material from the earlier parts of this chapter and apply it to Pooper Centers. This should make the concepts more concrete. Of course, as we have mentioned before, you will have to use your judgment in applying this material in any particular case.

We first present a specification sheet

FRIENDLY & WISE
CERTIFIED PUBLIC ACCOUNTANTS
1000 BOURBON STREET
NEW ORLEANS, LOUISIANA

March 30, 1979

Computer Systems Vendor

Dear Sirs:

This letter is an invitation for proposals concerning a computer system for Pooper Centers, Inc. This request for proposals has been submitted to computer service bureaus, time-sharing services, and small-scale computer system equipment vendors. We recognize the basic approach to the various application areas will vary by vendor and request that each company submit specifications for each application that best utilize the capabilities of its equipment, services, and/or any combination of them.

The rest of this letter consists of three parts. First is the background, which is a brief description of the company. Second are the automated applications, which are the areas of potential automation. Third is the proposal format, which is the material that must be covered in your proposal.

Background

In February, 1979, the CPA firm of Friendly & Wise initiated a study of the accounting systems of Pooper Centers. As a result of that study, Pooper Centers decided to investigate the feasibility of converting the existing manual systems in order to utilize current EDP technology.

Pooper Centers, Inc. operates two stores, the Pooper Audio Center (PAC-1) and the Pooper Appliance Center (PAC-2). PAC-1 sells a complete line of audio equipment and related acces-sories, while PAC-2 stresses home appliances, but also sells audio equipment. Both stores have been successful, but there are no immediate plans for expansion. The company now employs 21 people, including the owner, Mr. Pooper, who serves as president. Sales for the company now approach $2 million annually.

Based upon the study, the following areas are potential candidates for automation:

1. Accounts receivable

2. Inventory

3. Payroll

4. Accounts payable

5. General accounting

Automated Applications

As a result of the study, the following functions were selected as being practical and economically feasible areas for the application of automated data processing. All proposed systems *must* provide detail listings of all master file update transactions, including file maintenance transactions; an adequate audit trail is essential.

1. Accounts receivable would include the application of cash on a balance forward basis. All necessary billing information will be contained on the sales slip. All charges are currently being manually priced. This pricing function could be automated if the recommended equipment has the capacity to do so; however, this is not an absolute requirement of any system to be proposed. There are up to 50 open accounts at any one given time, but this should grow to several hundred as the stores continue to grow. The system should be capable of producing a complete, detailed aged trial balance listing, a report describing the current status of delinquent accounts, and monthly detailed customer statements. These reports will generally be issued on a scheduled basis; however, capability must be provided to issue these reports on a request basis.

2. The current inventory system is on a periodic basis and is based upon a monthly physical inventory for both stores. This information is sufficient for the preparation of the present financial statements; however, there are no reports to assist inventory management for the several hundred items the stores sell. The new system must be capable of issuing inventory status reports, reorder reports by item for all products which get too low, and usage reports. The system should be able to produce a monthly cost usage report by store, using the cash register tapes and sales slips as input.

3. The payroll is paid on a bimonthly and a monthly basis. The monthly payroll consists of five salaried management people. The bimonthly payroll includes four salaried employees and twelve salesmen who work on a base salary plus commission basis. The information for commission computations is available from the sales slips. The payroll system must be capable of producing all required government reports, the information necessary for the preparation of payroll checks, and the required expense distribution for the general accounting system.

4. The accounts payable system must be capable of providing the information necessary for check preparation as well as expense distribution data that would be utilized in the general

accounting system. The system should provide a schedule of all invoices and a cash requirements report which details the invoices due by a specific date, in order to ensure the taking of all discounts. The company processes approximately 50 invoices per month, representing 40 expense account entries. Each month the company issues approximately 35 checks and the company has approximately 50 active vendors and suppliers.

5. The present general accounting system only provides one income statement for the entire company. The proposed system must provide a separate income statement for each store, along with an overall income statement. The system should provide for posting all journal entries (approximately 100 per month) to the approximately 200 various general ledger accounts. This information will be used in the preparation of trial balances and will also be used in preparation of audit trail printouts on demand.

Proposal Format

Send the original copy of the proposal to:

> Mr. Israel H. Wise
> Friendly & Wise
> Certified Public Accountants
> 1000 Bourbon Street
> New Orleans, Louisiana

Any questions regarding the specifications should be directed to Mr. Wise at the above address. If necessary, he can be reached at (504) 561-0000. If Mr. Wise is not in the office, leave word and he will contact you directly.

All proposals are due in New Orleans no later than April 21, 1979. Mr. Wise will pick up a second copy of the proposal when he meets with each company the week of April 23, 1979.

Under no circumstances should the vendor contact Pooper Centers directly. Failure to comply with this request will automatically eliminate that vendor from further consideration.

The proposal must include the following specifications:

1. A detailed description of the recommended equipment and any peripheral equipment. Where alternatives are indicated, the relative order of these alternatives should be indicated. Where other than on-site facilities are recommended, a detailed description of the remote facility should be made.

2. A breakdown of costs for each item of hardware. Where applicable, maintenance or service charges shall be listed. Terms of all purchase or lease agreements (including alternative costs) shall be presented in detail.

3. A statement on physical planning considerations, such as space requirements, temperature and humidity limitations, and electrical outlets. The reliability of the equipment (percent downtime), the recommended preventative maintenance schedule, and the availability of back-up facilities will be stated.

4. A statement giving the location of service facilities and the availability of maintenance, including the maximum time between notification of a problem and arrival of a service technician.

5. A detailed description (such as a systems manual) of any relevant applied systems and program packages available through the proposing firm.

6. An explicit statement of what, if any, systems or programming assistance the proposing firm will furnish. Where applicable, each separate application should have its own separate cost for systems and programming assistance.

7. A list of facilities available for education, testing, and preinstallation operation.

8. The name, address, and telephone number of the representative responsible for the preparation and submission of the proposal.

All proposals and correspondence submitted to Friendly & Wise will be retained; however, these proposals will be disclosed only to Pooper Centers management. We look forward to receiving your proposal.

Very truly yours,

Israel H. Wise

IHWise
ms

The next step is to show a particular statement of objectives for Pooper Centers.

Sample Company
Statement of Objectives

FRIENDLY & WISE
CERTIFIED PUBLIC ACCOUNTANTS
1000 BOURBON STREET
NEW ORLEANS, LOUISIANA

May 1, 1979

Mr. John Paul Pooper
President
Pooper Centers, Inc.
1000 Canal Street
New Orleans, Louisiana

Dear John Paul:

We have completed our engagement to lay out a statement of objectives for your new accounts receivable system. This letter gives the results of our study.

Overall Purpose

The overall purpose of the new system is to improve profitability and speed up cash flow by (1) improving internal control over credit sales, receivables, and cash collections; (2) providing better information to management concerning credit sales; and (3) encouraging timely collection of accounts.

Specific Objectives

Specifically, the objectives identified to accomplish the above goals are:

1. To ensure that all transactions relating to the creation of and collection of receivables are recorded correctly and in a prompt and timely manner.

2. To eliminate extension of credit to customers when their balance exceeds an established credit limit or when their payment on account is past due.

3. To spotlight accounts which are past due and prompt management attention.

4. To separate, to the extent feasible, the duties of receiving payments on account, recording payments, authorizing credit sales, recording credit sales, authorizing credit memos, recording credit memos, and preparing statements of account.

5. To produce monthly statements on a balance-forward basis, which will be sent to customers to solicit payment.

Report Requirements

To accomplish these objectives the system needs two basic reports:

1. *Aged trial balance.* This report will extend the material in the schedule of accounts receivable and will replace that report. The aged trial balance will generate one line of output for each customer. Each line will contain the customer's name and balance due. In addition, the balance due will be broken down into the portion that is current, the portion that is over 30 days old, and the portion that is over 60 days old. Finally, the report will total the amount due and the amounts that are current, over 30 days and over 60 days. This report will be invaluable in identifying accounts which are past due and must be acted upon. It will also prevent extension of credit to those who are already past due.

2. *Statement of account.* This report will appear on a monthly basis for every customer. The statement will give the customer's name, address, and the balance due at the beginning of the period. Then the report will detail each transaction (credit sale, cash payment, or adjustment) of the period and conclude with the balance due at the end of the period. This report is essential in providing an audit trail backing up the balance due for each customer. The report also will encourage timely payments on account.

Required Data

To generate these reports, the system needs two basic data files:

1. *Customer master file.* This file will contain the basic data on each customer. This information will include the customer's name, address, credit limit, and balance.

2. *Accounts receivable transaction file.* This file will contain the necessary audit trail information backing up each transaction. For each transaction, the file will contain the type of transaction (whether credit sale, cash payment, or adjustment), the customer number, the date, and the amount.

The basic data for creation of the customer master file is available from the accountant when the credit is initially granted. There are then three types of transactions: (1) credit sale information is available from the sales slip; (2) cash payment information is available from the checks received in the mail; and (3) adjustments by credit memo are available from the credit memo the salesman fills out.

Necessary Controls

The following internal control techniques and procedures are recommended to ensure the accuracy and reliability of the accounting data:

1. All sales slips and credit memos will be prenumbered to maintain physical control of the forms and pinpoint any lost or mislaid forms.

2. The secretary will make an independent record of all incoming checks. This record will be compared to the accounts receivable postings, the bank deposit, and the cash receipts journal to ensure no amounts have been recorded in error.

3. Credit sales, in addition to cash sales, will have to be rung up on the cash register. This independent record will be compared by the accountant to the totals generated by the bookkeeper from the sales slips.

New Policies and Procedures

The following new policies and procedures will be necessary for the proper functioning of the new systems.

1. The accountant will establish credit limits for each customer when he initially grants credit to that individual or company. This will help ensure that no customer exceeds his ability to pay.

2. Sales clerks will verify the credit status of each customer before processing a credit sale. This will be accomplished by a phone call to the bookkeeper and will ensure that credit is not granted when the customer already exceeds his credit limit or when his account is past due.

3. Sales clerks will total sales slips and attach an adding machine tape before transmitting to the bookkeeper for processing. This total should be compared with the cash register total of credit sales to ensure all credit sales have been recorded.

4. The accountant will use the aged trial balance on a monthly basis to contact customers whose payments are slipping. This will help speed up cash flow and encourage timely payment by customers.

If the above statement of objectives is acceptable, please sign below and date your signature.

Yours very truly,

Jack R. Friendly

JRFriendly
ms

Approved: _____ Dated: _____
John Paul Pooper, President

Approved: _____ Dated: _____
Accountant

Approved: _____ Dated: _____
Manager PAC-1

Approved: _____ Dated: _____
Manager PAC-2

exercises

10-1 Consider the development of a new payroll system for a retail firm.

1. Give the overall purpose of such a system and state five objectives which are necessary to accomplish this overall purpose.

2. Are any of these specific objectives conflicting? Discuss how trade-offs may be made between these objectives.

3. Might there be any unstated objectives which should be considered in the system development?

10-2 Consider the development of an inventory control system for a wholesale firm.

1. Give the overall purpose of such a system and state five objectives which are necessary to accomplish this overall purpose.

2. Are any of these objectives conflicting? Discuss how trade-offs may be made between these objectives.

3. Might there be any unstated objectives which should be considered in the system development?

10-3 Internal control is an important consideration in computer-based system development. In fact, internal control may be more significant in computer-based systems than in manual systems. Give three specific internal control problems of computer systems which are not significant problems in manual systems.

10-4 Full utilization of the computer's capabilities may require changes in long-standing company policies and procedures. Consider the situation of a retail store developing a new billing system that is designed to bill customers every two weeks rather than once a month.

1. Summarize the potential advantages and disadvantages of this new approach.

2. Suppose the company wanted to measure customer reaction to this new billing system by a questionnaire. List five questions which should appear on the questionnaire.

10-5 Computer services can be acquired from any of several alternative sources. Each source has its own advantages and disadvantages. For each of the following computer vendor alternatives, discuss a situation where that alternative would be most appropriate.

a. Mainframe computer manufacturer.

b. Minicomputer manufacturer.

c. Programmable calculator manufacturer.

d. Service bureau.

e. Time-sharing.

f. Facilities management.

10-6 If a company wants computer capability, it can be obtained by buying the equipment, leasing the equipment, accessing time-sharing equipment, or using a service bureau. For each of the following, state whether it is most characteristic of buying, leasing, time-sharing, or service bureau use.

a. Telephone cost.

b. High salary cost.

c. No in-house systems capability.

d. Data processing staff.

e. Large initial cost.

f. No maintenance cost.

g. Software development.

h. Necessarily batch oriented.

i. Long-term commitment to specific hardware.

j. Generally interactive.

system design

INTRODUCTION

We now come to the system design and system specifications steps in our system development process. These steps are critical, for they translate the concepts of the statement of objectives into a complete, workable, and cost-effective system. Of course, after the system design and system specification, the system still only exists on paper. Thus, the last three steps of system development serve to get the system working in practice, not just on paper.

In this chapter we will deal with the translation of the concepts into a complete system. We break this translation process down into two basic parts:

1. *System design.* This design is a general look at the different approaches we can take (on-line *vs.* batch, multiple small computers *vs.* one large computer, etc.). It discusses the costs and benefits of each approach and then selects one approach to take.

2. *System specification.* Once the design is selected, the next step is to detail the exact components of the design and how it might work. Thus, the system details are worked out only for the one system selected in the system design.

As we have mentioned before, you will have to use your judgment about applying this material in any particular situation. Certainly, it would be possible in many situations to have only one step in the "translation process." In that case there would only be one report, a combined system design and specification. This combined report could be an efficient step, because, as you will see later, there is necessarily a good deal of overlap between the system design and system specification.

The two step process, system design–system specification, is most useful when it is unclear at the start exactly what design approach should be taken. Also critical is the intimacy with which top management is involved in the system development process. The trade-off is between potential repetition if too many steps are taken and potential waste of effort if too few steps are taken. The classical danger to avoid is deviating too far from management's desires and having to throw out a great deal of work. If you adopt a system design, proceed to specify it in detail, but then have the design rejected by management, all the work specifying the system is then wasted. It is better to check the design and get it approved prior to going to the trouble of specifying the details of the system. For example, a consulting firm spent a great deal of time and effort designing a cost accounting system for a small manufacturer. The system was based upon a central figure, a new cost accountant, the first cost accountant in the history of the company. The company president rejected the entire system without reviewing it. He insisted the company would not hire a cost accountant: the company did not need one and he would not hire one. The consulting firm then had to completely redesign the entire system from scratch. Fortunately, the writing of procedure manuals and other details had been deferred until the design was approved. Otherwise, all the detail work would have been wasted.

Therefore, the best time to economize is when the new system is an extension of an old system or otherwise fits into an established framework. In cases such as these, the system approach is essentially given, since the new system must tie in with previously established, accepted systems. Again, you will have to use your judgment.

11.1 ELEMENTS OF SYSTEM DESIGN

We are now at the point of system design. We know the design of the present system from the systems analysis. Also, we know the objectives the new system will try to accomplish—these goals are detailed in the statement of objectives. We now must use this information and our knowledge of computer systems and computer capabilities to design a new system in place of the old.

Our task is not an easy one and, in fact, is not even primarily a technical task. Our task is primarily conceptual (i.e., what approach we should take, how the system will fit together). There are five basic conceptual topics to consider in each system design:

1. The first topic is whether to use a computer at all. Although this section of this text is titled system development and focuses on computer-based system development, this does not mean that the computer is always useful in every situation. Already in the late1970's a partner at Arthur Andersen could say that *every* new system they work with involves the computer in some way. But, because of Arthur Andersen's size and fee structure, the company is involved in large, complex systems which are natural for the computer. Only because of space limitations, we could not separately discuss manual system development, despite its importance.

The question is: When should you *not* use a computer? The easy answer is: When it is not worth it. If the computer costs more in terms of difficulty in conversion, expense of training, and expense of programming, than it delivers in benefits, the computer is simply not worth it. Let us consider some of the characteristics of situations where a computer may not be worthwhile. One characteristic is the impossibility of eliminating the source documents, and the necessity of recording information manually because of tradition or legal requirements. In this case double work must be performed—once to manually record the information and again to load the information onto the computer. This double work load may outweigh any advantages the computer might have. A second characteristic is the combination of the availability of many clerical workers and the desire to get as many involved as possible. For example, a charity or church may have many volunteers who would like to address envelopes (for instance). It would be absurd to eliminate these jobs, since there would be no benefit and a good deal of cost, both out-of-pocket for the computer and psychic for the now unwanted volunteers. Certainly, one of the problems in less-developed countries is the use of advanced technology which eliminates jobs in the face of massive unemployment. A third characteristic is the presence of a low-paid (and hence prone to high turnover) clerical staff. In this situation it is necessary to get new employees as quickly up to speed as possible. It will, therefore, often be more convenient to use as much as possible the skills the new employee already has from high school or business school. These skills rarely include using the computer, and the presence of the computer might scare off potential new employees. A fourth characteristic is a management which will not or can not use the information the computer can provide. As we have discussed earlier, a computer cannot often be justified on simply the grounds of reduced clerical costs—the real promise is the analysis of the information. If management, because of limited education or psychological barriers, is uninterested or incapable of using the information, perhaps a computer is not called for.

2. If you decide to utilize a computer, the next topic is whether the system will be batch or on-line. As discussed previously, batch systems collect transactions (in a batch) and then process all accumulated transactions when the batch reaches a certain size or when specified times for processing occur. On-line systems, on the other hand, process transactions as they occur. Generally speaking, on-line systems are more complex and expensive since they must be able to drop whatever they are doing (so to speak) to process the transaction as it occurs. Batch systems are most useful in situations like payroll where transactions need not be processed instantly and where check preparation takes place on a scheduled basis. On-line systems are most useful in situations like inventory, where it is necessary to keep track of material on hand to determine if orders can or cannot be filled. Additionally, some business systems are a hybrid of batch and on-line. Inquiry of names, addresses, current balances, and the like are performed on-line, whereas the actual processing of transactions to update balances is done in batch (usually at night). For example, one utility company has a system which can call up a customer's current status on a CRT screen; this screen contains the customer's name, address, payment history, and current balance as of the transactions processed the previous night. Payments and charges are processed on a batch basis each night. Similarly, many banks can inquire about a customer's account on an on-line basis, but process deposits and withdrawals in batch every night. This sort of hybrid system is most useful when transaction processing requires extensive controls which are impossible in that situation to implement for on-line processing.

3.   You must next determine the degree of centralization that your design will involve. One central computer which processes every transaction and which maintains all data files for the system has been the standard approach to data processing until the late 1970's. Note that this centralized approach can work with either a batch system or an on-line system: with a batch system all sources documents are transmitted to the computer center, while with an on-line system all terminals are connected to the central computer. A centralized system makes it easier to establish and maintain standards. However, a great deal of the detailed data processed by a centralized system will only be of interest to local management, while higher management will only be concerned with summary information. For this reason, there has been a trend to *distributed data processing*. The concept of distributed data processing is to place computing power in the organization at the appropriate level so that data entry, inquiry and initial processing occur where the data originate and where the data are used. Then, only summary information is sent to the central computer system. In the case of Sears, each cash register/terminal at a store is connected to the store's minicomputer, which performs local processing tasks, such as checking credit status of customers and keeping track of the store's inventory levels. Each night, the regional computer center dials the store's minicomputer and receives a summary of transactions for the day; this information is then used for such tasks as analysis of regional sales trends. This information is then summarized still further before it is transmitted to the national computer center. Unfortunately, distributed data processing makes it difficult to maintain standards and consistency when processing occurs at many different sites.

4.   The next topic to consider is the nature of the source documents and audit trail which the new system requires. To repeat a fundamental point: every system requires an audit trail. However, there is no one way to incorporate an effective audit trail. As you recall from the manual system, the audit trail always went back to a source document, which was signed to indicate authorization by an appropriate person. In a computer system, material can be input directly into the computer rather than creating a source document. This approach can be very efficient, but the design of the system must, in some other way, ensure proper authorization of all transactions and a useful audit trail which will point back to the origin of each transaction. Some system designers provide an audit trail by generating huge volumes of printout. Analyzing an account then becomes a tedious process of poring over stacks and stacks of computer output. This approach ignores the importance of the audit trail, its necessity, and its utility. Since computer systems can process such large volumes of transactions, the system design must incorporate the use of the computer in the analysis of transactions in the audit trail.

5.   The final major topic to consider is the capability of the present set of employees. If the employees are stable and enthusiastic about the computer, then it would perhaps be worthwhile to try to incorporate the computer into the company's operation. The employees could then utilize the computer in their daily activities to make better decisions and to operate more efficiently. However, this approach requires extensive orientation to the new system and training in the use of the computer. An easier approach to implement is to keep the computer in the background, so to speak, to keep any necessary records and perform analyses of the available information. In this approach, the only people who will require orientation to the new system will be the record-keeping (i.e., accounting and bookkeeping) personnel. For example, let us consider a system for scheduling students in

classes. One approach would be to schedule students on-line; however, this approach would require training people in the use of the on-line terminals and the procedures for scheduling. Another approach would be to schedule students on a batch basis; all the workers would have to do is hand out class cards. The results of the second approach would not be as satisfactory, but it would be much easier to implement in certain situations. The amount of sophistication the organization can handle will be a matter of judgment for the system designer.

Our next concern is the presentation of the system design. There are seven basic elements of a system design. These basic elements are given in a schematic diagram in Figure 11-1.

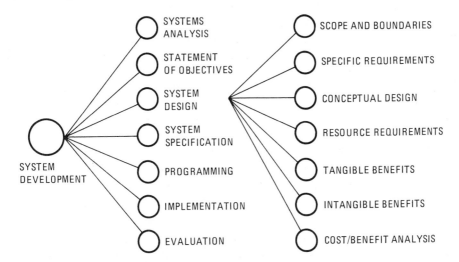

FIGURE 11-1 Elements of System Design

1. *Scope and boundaries of the system.* The first step is to clearly lay out exactly what the system will and will not do. Of course, the scope of the system should be broad enough to ensure that the new system will be a significant contribution. However, the scope should be narrow enough to ensure that the system will be manageable. Certainly the worst possible approach is to try to design the total information system, one big system which handles everything. We must take bite-sized chunks and develop our overall information system one step at a time. It is therefore important that we clearly distinguish the boundaries of the system. One difficult aspect of system design is that the project continues to grow and grow. Let us consider an accounts receivable system. Certainly the system must keep track of our customers and the balance they owe. To keep the balance up-to-date the system must process sales. But sales affect inventory and salesmen's commissions so the temptation is then to include those aspects of the company's operations. But then sales could be analyzed by product, period, store, salesman, etc., so the system could be extended to include these elements. The system can thus grow until it processes everything. As you became aware in Part one, every aspect of the accounting system interrelates eventually with all other aspects. Thus, it is essential to detail exactly where the system being designed stops—(i.e., what are its boundaries).

2. *More specific system requirements.* The statement of objectives lays out the sort of information which the new system will require and will provide. The system design has to be more precise about these items. First, the design should include the outputs to be produced. This should consist of schematics of exactly what the report will look like. Most users cannot conceptualize computer output; to get their useful cooperation you must provide a specific output and ask, "Is this what you want?" The user can then respond and tell you, for example, to drop the third column and interchange the fourth and fifth columns. Second, the design should detail exactly what files the system will require. The files would be those, such as a customer master file or a vendor master file, which would always exist, though their contents would be constantly updated. At this point the design should specify the content of each file—exactly what data will be kept in each file. For example, a customer master file for an accounts receivable system must contain at least the customer's name and address, but it may contain a credit limit, a Dun and Bradstreet number, or any of a vast range of possible data-items. Third, the design should detail the input to the system, exactly what source documents or sources of information will provide the raw data. Fourth, the design should detail the data volumes for the master files and transactions. It is important to the design whether there are 100 customers (such as a small store) or 100,000 customers (such as a major oil company). It is also important to the design whether there are 10 transactions to process each day or 10,000 transactions. The average transaction load is important, but also critical are the "peaks": the system must not overload when the peak volumes occur. Additionally, the design should indicate system-timing considerations (i.e., how fast must the system respond).

3. *Conceptual design.* The next step is to define the basic modules that will satisfy the system requirements and then to arrange these modules into a functional design. It is sufficient here to refer to a computer program to accomplish a given task; it is not necessary to explain exactly how the computer program would work. In essence, then, this is a conceptual design, not a detailed design. We explain here the way the system will fit together without detailing every step in the process. For example, an accounts receivable system may require a credit check for any credit sale. The conceptual design should indicate whether the salesman will use a computer terminal to check credit or whether the salesman will call the bookkeeper. It would not be necessary at this point to describe exactly how the computer program would check the credit—that detail could be deferred until the conceptual design has been approved. Of course, you should be able to detail the design: there should be no question of whether the detail could be worked out, just when.

It is important to realize here that *modularity* is an important design goal. Modularity in system design means that the overall system is broken down into smaller building blocks, called *modules.* Each module can then, if necessary, be further broken down into submodules. The goal is to make the modules fit together in a natural fashion: each module can be developed independently and then fitted together to create the overall system. When future changes or modifications are made to the system (if all goes according to plan), only the affected module need be changed; the effect on the overall system is localized in that module.

4. *Resource requirements.* The next step is to estimate the resource requirements necessary to implement, convert to, and operate every module. Implementation consists of the

system design, system specification, and programming necessary to get the module working. Conversion consists of getting data from the present system into the new module and making the information available to the new system. Operation consists of the day-to-day running of the system.

Each of these steps of implementation, conversion, and operation will have its own resource requirements. These resource requirements will include: (a) manpower, the people necessary to get each job done; (b) computer and other hardware, the equipment necessary for each step; (c) contracted services, such as outside consultants or programming services, and (d) purchased or leased software.

Note that there is often a possible trade-off between these various resources. For example, it may be possible to hire fewer people and use more contracted services. Similarly, it may be possible to purchase software and by spending more money there, less money need be spent for manpower or contracted services.

5. *Tangible benefits.* These benefits include the reduction of direct operating expenses and are the "hard dollar" savings many people prefer to see. Many years ago in the aerospace industry, vast rooms were filled with clerks who performed large volumes of mathematical computations. A computer was able to eliminate all those clerk jobs—a dramatic, tangible benefit. Generally speaking, however, the reduction of clerical costs is one of the most elusive of computer benefits. What usually happens is that the computer eliminates some clerical jobs, but the computer can generate such volumes of newly available information that new clerical positions are required to analyze and use the information. In fact, tangible benefits are so elusive that if the system must depend on clerical salary reduction for its justification, it is probably a good idea to rethink the entire system.

6. *Intangible benefits.* These benefits are the real justification and promise of computer systems. Unfortunately, these benefits are the most difficult to get a handle on and are especially hard to put a dollar value on. One important intangible benefit is capacity—the system's ability to easily handle increasing volumes of transactions; manual systems often require extensive hiring and training of new personnel to process an increased volume of transactions. A second intangible benefit is timeliness; a well-designed computer system can often generate results faster, which can help improve decisions since better (more current) information is available. A third intangible benefit is reliability or accuracy. A standard problem in manual systems is errors in computation, such as incorrectly extending price times quantity for invoices. Such errors reflect poorly on the company and may lead customers to suspect they are being cheated. The computer can perform such tasks easily, without fear of error. A fourth intangible benefit is improvement of service. For example, a manual sales (or order-entry) system typically requires filling out various forms, mailing them to the company, processing the forms, and so on. A computer system can eliminate such delays and speed goods to customers days or even weeks earlier. A fifth intangible benefit, which is by far the most important, is additional or improved information. In the data collected and processed by the company, there is a wealth of information. However, the task of digging out the important nuggets is vast because of the overwhelming detail. The computer is ideally suited to this laborious work. As mentioned above, putting a dollar value on these intangible benefits is difficult, but at least some assessment of their impact should be made.

7. *Cost/benefit analysis.* The final step is to subject this resource configuration to an economic analysis. This work can be obscured by technicalities, but essentially the question is: Is this new system worth what it costs? This is an important step because it should prevent extensive resources being directed toward inappropriate areas. It is important to realize here we are not trying to develop a perfect system or even the best possible system. The perfect system is constantly out of reach because new products are available essentially on a weekly basis. In an attempt to make the system "the best," it would have to be continually reworked to incorporate the latest equipment. This becomes a never-ending cycle which leads to countless delays. IBM worked for years on what it called the Future System, or FS. This system had such lofty goals it never worked and was ultimately abandoned.

The goal, then, is to have a good, even excellent system that satisfies the organization's objectives at a reasonable cost. If you take that perspective you will not constantly be haunted by the fact, "Well, if we waited just one more year, prices would be down 25 percent...." Your attitude should be: costs will be down later, but this system project is worth what it costs, so it should be done.

Unfortunately, there are numerous examples of systems not meeting even the most simple tests of cost effectiveness. For instance, one university decided to get a new computer costing several hundred thousand dollars, primarily because it could then buy extensive software for its admissions, students records, and alumni needs. The business manager then stated that the present clerk positions would have to be upgraded and their salaries raised because of the new computer system. When questioned what the new system would provide that the old one did not, it turned out there was nothing added. In other words, with the expenditure of several hundred thousand dollars for a computer, plus almost $100,000 for software, plus upgrading clerks, plus raising salaries, there was no advantage to the school.

Table 11-1 summarizes our discussion of the elements of system design.

TABLE 11-1   THE ELEMENTS OF SYSTEM DESIGN

SCOPE AND BOUNDARIES	Brief description of what the system will and will not try to do
SPECIFIC REQUIREMENTS	List of the output, data files, and input necessary for the system
CONCEPTUAL DESIGN	Basic module and functional design which will satisfy the system requirements
RESOURCE REQUIREMENTS	The people, equipment and dollars necessary to get each module working
TANGIBLE BENEFITS	Reduction in direct operating expenses anticipated from the new system
INTANGIBLE BENEFITS	Other anticipated benefits of the new system, such as improved information
COST/BENEFIT RATIO	Comparison of the costs versus the benefits of the proposed new system

11.2 ELEMENTS OF SYSTEM SPECIFICATION

We now get to the first highly technical step in system development, the specification of the system design. This specification spells out in detail exactly how the system will work. This detail primarily includes complete descriptions of data used, flowcharts of required computer programs, and a schedule for programming and implementation. (See Figure 11-2.)

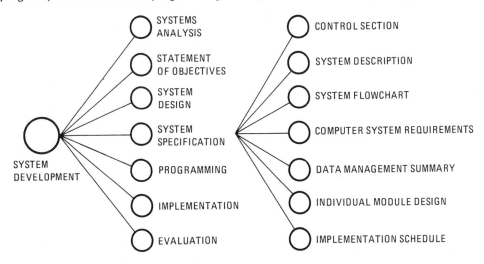

FIGURE 11-2 Elements of System Specification

This system specification step is absolutely necessary, in all cases, before beginning to program anything. If the programs are not first flowcharted and the files completely described, wasted effort, constant revisions, and incompatible programs are the inevitable results. Of course, as mentioned in Chapters 7 and 10, it is possible to buy software—in that case much of this step can be skipped.

Though the specification of the system design is necessary, it need not be done at the same level of detail in all cases. Suppose the people who are developing the specifications are going to later also do the programming. In this case it is not so critical that every step in each program be completely detailed as long as they can fill in the necessary steps. However, if another group, such as outside programmers, were to do the programming, the flowcharts necessarily must be more detailed to avoid both real and claimed misunderstandings.

We should now go over the basic content of a system specification. Keep in mind that this amount of detail is not always necessary. You will have to use your judgment, experience, and common sense to keep the proper balance in each particular situation. There are seven basic elements of a system specification:

1. *Control section.* The control section has two main purposes. The first is to record approval of the specifications by the four major groups whose approval is necessary: management, the users, the system design group, and the programmers. Management and the users will approve the system if it will do the necessary job and satisfy their requirements. Of course, the system designers should approve their own work. Approval by the programmers shows

they feel the system has been sufficiently specified that they can program directly from the information in the report; the flow charts are acceptable and the files have been well laid out. The second main purpose is to help ensure all revisions are handled properly. In many system development projects, there may be five, ten, or more notebooks of system specifications. No matter who develops the specifications and no matter how good they are, there will inevitably be revisions and modifications during the programming and implementation process. It is then absolutely critical to ensure that all notebooks are updated consistently. This control section keeps a record of all modifications after initial approval and the authorization for that modification. Thus, the notebook can be quickly checked to ensure that all necessary changes have been made.

2. *System description.* This description should be in management terms and give an overall view of the system. Management people must read and approve the system specifications, but they are simply not going to read (or understand if they do read) all the technical details. It is therefore essential that a discussion be provided which provides management with a reasonable basis for making a decision on the specifications. The overriding concern should be to provide the information a manager needs to determine if the system meets his requirements at a reasonable cost. The description should begin with an overview of the entire system, placing it in context, and then detailing its objectives and scope. There should then be a discussion of the alternative designs that were considered for adoption to accomplish those objectives. Next should be a narrative describing the operation of the new system. Following this will be an economic analysis of the system design justifying the expense. Additionally, the report should describe the intangible benefits of the system and also its limitations, since no system can do everything. Finally, there should be a discussion of how the system interfaces with other systems. No system stands alone, and the details of how this system will work with others should be developed in advance of programming and implementation.

3. *System flowchart.* The next section of the report should show a flowchart of the entire system, describing its document flow and operation. As a practical matter, this flowchart can largely be taken over from the system design and was treated in more detail earlier in the chapter. However, when the specifications are developed for a system design, many aspects and deficiencies of the design become apparent. Thus, the system flowchart developed for the system design will almost surely have to be refined and modified for inclusion in the system specification.

4. *Computer system requirements.* This part of the report should describe the requirements of the system design for both hardware and software. The hardware requirements would include the necessary computer and main memory for the system. It is important to focus here on exactly what the system needs, not simply what is available. If a company's computer has a huge amount of main memory available, but a new system requires only a small part of it, this should be made clear. Thus, if the company were to get another computer, the demands of this system would be clear. Other hardware requirements would include peripheral equipment, such as the number and capacity of any required printers, disks, or tapes. Additional hardware requirements would perhaps include terminals and other data communication devices. There may even be further hardware needs for off-line auxiliary equipment, such as bursters which separate computer printout into individual sheets.

Software requirements are also important. These include any required operating system. There may also be requirements for software packages from outside vendors. Finally, there are often requirements for a particular subroutine library or set of preprogrammed routines.

5. *Data management summary*. The next step in the system development process is the technically tedious but important task of detailing the precise nature of the data the system will use. The contents of this section can be categorized as input data, files to be maintained, or output reports.

The input data discussion should detail the source of all data. Then the name and the content of the input data should be given. Following this should be the data entry requirements and restrictions. Finally, there should be a projection of the volume of data which will need be input.

There should then be a discussion of each file to be maintained by the system. This should begin with the type of file, either direct access or sequential. Following should be the content of the file and the particular record layout to be used. There should be a discussion of retention cycles, namely how long a copy of the file will be kept before it is scratched or replaced. The exact file name or label should be given. Next should be the file maintenance requirements; how often must the file be updated and how current must the file be kept. A projection of the volume of records in each file and the rate each will grow should be given. Finally, the report should detail the backup requirements, namely how often should a copy of the file be made and where different copies of the file should be retained for protection.

The output summary should present each report or other output of the system. This should contain the name and a discussion of the report. There should then be a sample report showing the format and appearance of the report. Next should be a discussion of the distribution of the report and the necessary control over each copy to prevent unauthorized access. Following this will be the frequency of the report or how often it will be generated (daily, monthly, on-demand, etc.). Finally, there should be a projection of the report volume—how many pages will be printed.

6. *Individual module design*. The report should provide a detailed description of each individual system module. These modules will include manual procedures, electro-mechanical operations, and computer programs.

Each manual procedure should have a narrative description and be assigned to the organization unit which will perform it. The staff designation and classification for those who perform the procedure should be detailed. There should then be a description of tasks in the sequence to be performed. Each source document, form, and report which is required for the procedure should be given. Finally, the frequency and number of times the procedure will be performed should be projected.

Electro-mechanical operations will be those which require the use of devices such as the burster (which separates computer output into individual pages), the decollator (which separates multiple-part output into individual copies), keypunch machines, or keypunch replacements (such as key-to-tape or key-to-disk machines). These should have a narrative description of the operation and a mention of the number and location of the devices. Next should be a description of the required tasks, in sequence. Each source document should be mentioned and any messages or displays the device generates should be described. Finally, there should be a rate and volume projection of the usage of the device.

The discussion of each computer program should begin with a narrative description. There should then be a flowchart of the program, giving its basic structure. There should be a summary of the input and output for the program and a list of file requirements. Any necessary edit and validity checking features should be described. Additionally, any error conditions should be explained; the cause of the error and proper correction procedures should be given. Finally, there should be a discussion of checkpoint/restart or other technique whereby long programs which are interrupted need not be rerun from the beginning.

The program flowcharts must be done well in order to create reliable programs which are easy to modify as circumstances change and which are inexpensive to develop. *Structural programming* is a disciplined approach to program design which uses only the following three control structures in the program flowchart:

a.   Sequence. This simplest control structure provides for sequential processing of statements.

b.   Condition. This control structure tests a condition and executes one of two statements depending upon whether the condition is true or false.

c.   Loop. This control structure executes a statement as long as a given condition is true.

Notice that: (1) each of these structures has only one entry point and only one exit point; (2) each of the statements in the structures can be extended to contain any of the three structures; and (3) the GOTO statement can thus be eliminated from the conceptual flowchart. (Unfortunately, in some porgramming languages, such as BASIC and FORTRAN, you may not actually be able to eliminate the GOTO statement in the source program because the necessary control structures are not available.) If this design discipline is followed, the resulting programs will be easily written, easily tested, easily changed, and easily understood.

7.   *Implementation schedule.* The final section of the report should detail the implementation schedule, namely how we will get from the system on paper in the system specification to

TABLE 11-2   ELEMENTS OF SYSTEM SPECIFICATION

CONTROL SECTION	Record approval and ensure all revisions are handled properly
SYSTEM DESCRIPTION	Give an overall view of the system written in management terms
SYSTEM FLOWCHART	Show a flowchart of the entire system, describing document flow and operation
COMPUTER SYSTEM REQUIREMENTS	Describe the hardware and software requirements of the system design
DATA MANAGEMENT SUMMARY	Detail the precise nature of the input, data files, and output used by the system
INDIVIDUAL MODULE DESIGN	Provide a detailed description of each individual system module
IMPLEMENTATION SCHEDULE	List the sequence of tasks to be performed and the relationships of those tasks

the working system. This schedule should include the sequence of tasks to be performed and the interrelationships of those tasks. It is critical to know what tasks must be completed before other tasks can even begin. For each task there should be a specific assignment of responsibility to ensure that it gets done, or to determine why it does not. There should then be estimates of both the time and the cost necessary for each of these tasks. Finally, these tasks should be arranged for clear comprehension.

Table 11-2 summarizes our discussion of the elements of system specification.

11.3 APPLICATION TO SAMPLE COMPANY

As we discussed at the beginning of the chapter, the two-step process, system design–system specification, is most useful when there are several alternative design approaches and management is not deeply involved in the system design process. In this situation it is advisable to get formal approval of the system design prior to further detail work.

Since much of the system specification and programming work is specific to a particular programming language and even the particular version of the language for the actual computer, we have segregated this material in two Appendices. These appendices give the specifics of program development for the BASIC language and the COBOL language. Certainly, other languages are possible and even desirable.

It is important to realize that even though much of this material appears merely technical, management must nonetheless remain deeply involved in the system development process to ensure that both management's desires are carried out and that the system is effectively pushed to operation.

POOPER CENTERS, INC.
Accounts Receivable System
System Design

Friendly & Wise
Certified Public Accountants
May, 1979

FRIENDLY & WISE
CERTIFIED PUBLIC ACCOUNTANTS
1000 Bourbon Street
New Orleans, Louisiana

May 15, 1979

Mr. John Paul Pooper, President
Pooper Centers, Inc.
1000 Canal Street
New Orleans, Louisiana

Dear John Paul:

We have completed our engagement to design your new accounts receivable system. This system is based upon the objectives for the system which we presented in our report of April 30, 1979, and which you approved. After careful analysis of your present and future information needs, we have designed a simple but efficient system to meet those needs.

Since this is your and your firm's first experience with a computer-based system, we have deliberately designed the system to be as simple to use as possible. Importantly, however, the system can be expanded and extended when you become comfortable with this sytem and wish to expand into other application areas. Please indicate your approval of this design by signing this letter below.

Finally, we would like to express our appreciation for the opportunity to work on this engagement. We, of course, stand ready to assist you in the implementation process in any manner you desire. Please call us if we can be of further assistance.

Very truly yours,
FRIENDLY & WISE

Jack R. Friendly

Jack R. Friendly

JRF/ms

APPROVED: _____ Date: _____
John Paul Pooper, President

APPROVED: _____ Date: _____
Accountant

APPROVED: _____ Date: _____
Manager, PAC-1

APPROVED: _____ Date: _____
Manager, PAC-2

TABLE OF CONTENTS

Letter of Transmittal

1.0 System Description

After an intensive analysis of the entire Pooper Centers accounting system, it was determined that accounts receivable processing was the first priority for revision and computer assistance. This proposed new accounts receivable system will be computer-based. However, the new system will integrate with the rest of the company's accounting system, which will remain manual.

1.1 Narrative description

Credit purchase on account. Credit customers may purchase merchandise in either retail store on open account. The salesman prepares a prenumbered sales slip in duplicate which contains the date; customer name; customer address; salesman's name; the description, quantity, unit price, and extension of each item purchased; and the total price of sale. The salesman then phones the bookkeeper for credit approval. The bookkeeper compares the proposed sale to the credit available for the customer as printed on her copy of the file status report. If the sale is acceptable, the bookkeeper makes a memo note of the sale to prevent another purchase before the file gets updated. The bookkeeper then informs the salesman of the decision. If credit is rejected, the sales slip is marked *void* and the customer is informed. If credit is approved, the customer signs the sales slip and receives the original as a merchandise receipt. The credit sale is then rung up by the cashier on the cash register for totaling purposes, despite the fact that no cash was received. In any case, the sales slips are filed numerically by sales slip number. At the end of the day, the manager assembles the sales slips and runs a calculator tape on them. This total is compared by the manager to the cash register total from the cash register tape. The sales slips and attached calculator tape, along with the adding machine tape, are sent to the bookkeeper. (See Figure 11-3.)

Credit purchase with credit card. For major credit card sales, the salesman will fill out the sales slip in the same fashion as for a purchase on account. Then, using the customer's card, the salesman will fill out the credit card sales slip. If the amount exceeds that credit card company's threshold, the salesman must then phone the credit card company for approval. If approved, the approval code is entered onto the credit card sales slip; the customer is then given his copy of both the Pooper Centers sales slip and the credit card sales slip. The credit sale is then rung up on the cash register and the Pooper Centers sales slip is filed numerically. The two copies of the credit card sales slip are filed next to the cash register until the end of the day, when they go to the bookkeeper. If credit is not approved by the credit card company, both sales slips are marked *void* and filed. (See Figure 11-4.)

Payments on account. All payments on account are made through the mail by check. The secretary opens all mail (except the bank statement) and sorts it. The secretary assembles all payments and runs a calculator tape on them. This information is recorded in the cash payments log by entering the date, initials, and total amount of payments. (See 2.0 Data Management.) This log will then be used by John Paul Pooper as a check with the bank reconciliation. The checks and attached tape are then sent to the bookkeeper. Upon receipt of the checks, the bookkeeper prepares a bank deposit slip and sends the checks and bank deposit slip to the bank for deposit into the firm's checking account. (See Figure 11-5.)

Credit memos. When a customer returns merchandise, the salesman records the customer name, customer address, date, and merchandise description on a prenumbered credit memo form. The credit memo must then be approved by the store manager. One copy goes to the

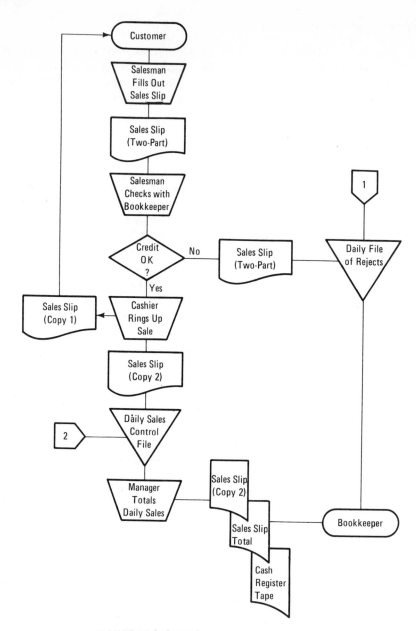

FIGURE 11-3 Credit Purchase on Account

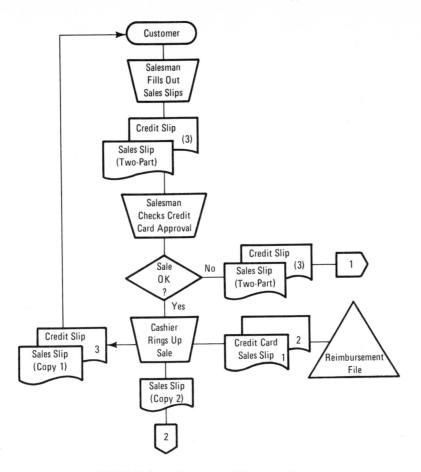

FIGURE 11-4 Credit Purchase With Credit Card

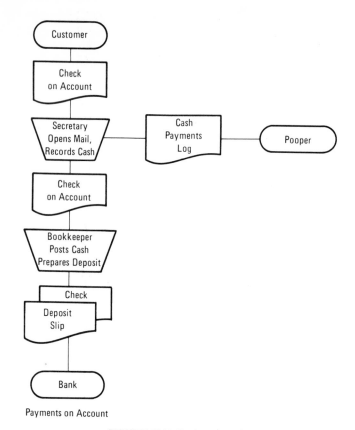

Payments on Account

FIGURE 11-5 Payments on Account

customer; the second copy is kept next to the cash register and is sent to the bookkeeper at the end of the day. (See Figure 11-6.)

Record keeping. The sales slips, checks, and credit memos are then input documents for the computer system. The bookkeeper enters the data into the system using a terminal. The computer system will keep updated all balances owed by Pooper Centers' customers. The total on cash payments is used for an entry in the cash receipts journal. The total on the sales slips is used for an entry in the sales journal. The credit memos are used for individual entries in the general journal. The total of the interest charges is used for a general journal entry. (See Figure 11-7.)

At month-end, the accountant foots and rules all journals and posts entries to the general ledger. At that time a balance will be struck in the accounts receivable control account in the general ledger. The bookkeeper will then utilize the computer system to generate an aged trial balance and this will be compared to the total in the control account. When the subsidiary ledger and control account balance, the bookkeeper then uses the system to generate the statements of account which are mailed directly to the customers.

2.0 Data Management

This section of the report will detail the input data for the system, the files to be maintained by the system, and the output which will be generated by the system.

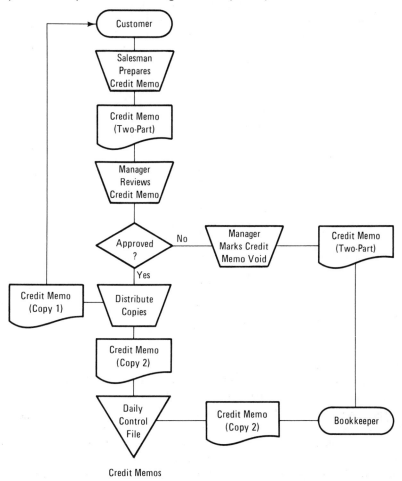

Credit Memos

FIGURE 11-6 Credit Memos

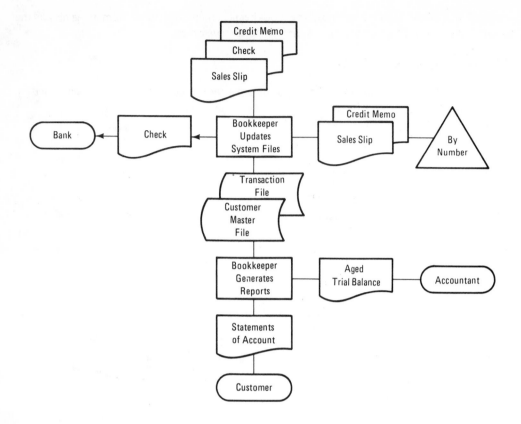

FIGURE 11-7 Record Keeping

2.1 Input

Sales slip. Basically, the same sales slip will be used in the new system as was used by the old system. The only difference is that now the sales slips will be prenumbered. This will allow better physical control and ensure that no sales slips have been lost or misplaced. The book-keeper will use the sales slip to input all credit sales.

Checks. A second basic input document is the check the customer sends in as payment on account. The bookkeeper uses the check to input all cash payments.

Credit memo. The same credit memo will be used, except that the credit memos will now be prenumbered. The prenumbering will allow better physical control and will indicate all lost or misplaced credit memos. The bookkeeper uses the credit memo as input for all merchandise returns.

Cash payments log. See Figure 11-8. Used for bank reconciliation.

2.2 Files

The system will require two basic files, the customer master file and the transaction file.

The *customer master file* contains one record for each customer. Each customer record then contains the basic information for each customer. This information will include:

```
┌─────────────────────────────────────────────────────────────────────┐
│                        POOPER CENTERS, INC.                           │
│                         Cash Payments Log                             │
│                                                                       │
│                        Month of _____                           │
│                                                                       │
│                                                                       │
├──────────────┬────────────────────────────────┬─────────────────────┤
│     Date     │          Recorded By           │       Amount        │
├──────────────┼────────────────────────────────┼─────────────────────┤
│              │                                │                     │
│              │                                │                     │
│              │                                │                     │
│              │                                │                     │
│              │                                │                     │
│              │                                │                     │
├──────────────┴────────────────────────────────┼─────────────────────┤
│              Total Cash Payments               │                     │
└────────────────────────────────────────────────┴─────────────────────┘
```

FIGURE 11-8 Cash Payments Log

a. Name.
b. Address.
c. Credit limit.
d. Beginning balance for the period.
e. Total debits for the period.
f. Total credits for the period.
g. Ending balance for the period.

The *transaction file* contains one record for each transaction which has updated any customer record. Each transaction record then contains the basic information for one transaction for one customer. This information will include:

a. Customer number.
b. Transaction type.

   c.   Date of transaction.

   d.   Amount of transaction.

Every time the system processes a transaction, it accomplishes two separate steps:

1. The system goes to the appropriate customer's record and updates the ending balance and either the total debits or total credits as necessary. For each customer, the following equation should always hold true:

$$\text{Ending balance} = \text{beginning balance} + \text{total debits} - \text{total credits}$$

2. After updating the customer's record, the system then adds a transaction record to the transaction file. There is, therefore, an audit trail kept in the transaction file—every transaction which has updated any customer record will be kept in the transaction file.

2.3 Output

The system will generate three basic outputs, the aged trial balance, the statement of account, and the file status report.

Aged trial balance. This report replaces and extends the present schedule of accounts receivable. Like the schedule of accounts receivable, this report lists every credit customer, the balance each individually owes, and the total balance owed by all customers. This total then balances to the control total in the general ledger. In addition, the aged trial balance determines the portion of each customer's balance which is current, the portion which is over 30 days old, and the portion which is over 60 days old. These amounts are then totaled. This information then indicates the customers whose accounts are getting old and potential uncollectible accounts. A schematic of the aged trial balance appears as Figure 11-9.

POOPER CENTERS, INC.
1000 CANAL STREET
NEW ORLEANS, LOUISIANA

AGED TRIAL BALANCE				
NAME	TOTAL	CURRENT	OVER 30	OVER 60
Sample 1	XXXX	XXX	XX	XX
Sample 2	XXXX	XXXX		
Sample 3	XXXX	XXX	XX	
Sample 4	XXXX		XXXX	
TOTALS	XXXXX	XXXX	XXXX	XX

FIGURE 11-9 Aged Trial Balance

Statement of account. There is one statement of account for each customer. The statement of account includes the name of the customer, his address, and the amount due. There is then a detailed analysis of the transactions which generated that amount due. The report first lists the balance due at the beginning of the period, and then a separate line for each transaction giving the transaction date, the type of transaction, the amount of the transaction, whether it was a debit or credit, and finally a running balance. After the last transaction is printed, the running balance should then equal the amount due. This statement of account goes to each customer at the end of every month to request payment. See Figure 11-10.

POOPER CENTERS, INC.
1000 CANAL STREET
NEW ORLEANS, LOUISIANA

SAMPLE CUSTOMER

ADDRESS

AMOUNT DUE $ XXXX

DATE OF TRANS	TYPE	DEBIT	CREDIT	BALANCE
	Beginning Balance			XXX
XX/XX/XX	Credit Sale	XXX		XXX
XX/XX/XX	Payment		XXX	XXX
XX/XX/XX	Credit Memo		XXX	XXX
	Amount Due			XXX

FIGURE 11-10 Statement of Account

File status report. The file maintenance program generates a report which details the current file status for each customer. The report gives, for each customer, the name, address, credit limit, beginning balance, total debits, total credits, ending balance and amount of credit available. This report is used by the bookkeeper to determine if credit should be extended on a potential credit sale. Figures 11-11 gives a sample of the printout generated for each customer.

1. Customer Name	Ralph Flax
Account is Active	
2. Customer Address	1000 Flood Street
3. Credit Limit	500
4. Beginning Balance	0
5. Debits for Period	410
6. Credits for Period	350
7. Ending Balance	60
8. Credit Available	440

FIGURE 11-11 File Status Report

3.0 Computer Programs

The new system will include four computer programs. These four programs perform the four fundamental tasks of: (1) maintaining the customer file with additions, deletions, and modifications; (2) updating the data files with transactions; (3) printing the aged trial balance; and (4) printing the statements of account.

File maintenance program. This program enables the system to continually update the information in the customer master file. There are three types of changes to the file: additions, deletions, and modifications. For all types of changes, the program checks the input customer number to make sure it is valid. If it is not valid, the program prints an error message and asks for another customer number.

Additions add new customers to the file after their credit is approved by the accountant. The user must input the customer number, the name, the address, and the credit limit. The program then initially creates that customer record and makes the beginning balance, debits, credits, and ending balance all zero.

Deletions remove customers from the file. This would be necessary if the customer declared bankruptcy or moved out of town. The program will not let the user delete a customer with a nonzero balance, the account would first have to be written off. Even if a valid customer number is input for deletion, the program will first print out the status of that customer's account to help ensure that only the desired customers are deleted.

Modifications are changes to the customer's name, address, or credit limit. The program will first print out the current status of the customer's account. The program will then ask what data-items the user would like to change. The user cannot change the balances with this program; balances can only be changed by the transaction program.

This program also generates the file status report.

Transaction processing program. This program processes the four basic types of transactions—credit sales, cash payments, and credit and debit memos. The input will be directly from the documents described earlier (see section 2.0 Data Management). This input will consist of the type of transaction (1 = credit sale, 2 = cash payment, 3 = credit memo, and 4 = debit memo), the customer number, the date of the transaction, and the dollar amount of the transaction. The program accepts individual transactions and updates the appropriate record on the customer master file. The program then adds the transaction at the end of the transaction file to act as an audit trail. Finally, the program updates the totals of all transactions which are kept as the last four records on the transaction file.

Aged trial balance program. This program generates the aged trial balance, previously described in detail (see section 2.0 Data Management). The only input by the user to the program is the date the program is run. This date is then used by the program to determine how old each balance is. For each customer, the program reads that customer's name from the customer master file. The program then reads all the transactions on the transaction file. Thus, for each customer, the program reads every transaction off the transaction file. Each transaction is first checked if it is a transaction for that customer. If it is not, then the transaction is ignored and the next transaction read. If the transaction is for that customer, then the balances owed (i.e., current, over 30 days old, or over 60 days old) are updated. When all transactions have been read, the final balances are printed for the customer. When all customer balances have been printed, the program prints a final total for all customers.

Statement of account program. This program generates a statement of account for each customer. The statement of account is described in detail in section 2.0 Data Management, of this report. This program works in a way somewhat similar to the aged trial balance program. For each customer, the program reads that customer's name, address, and current balance due off of the customer master file. This information is then printed out. The program then reads every transaction off the transaction file. If the transaction does not match this customer, the transaction is ignored and the next transaction read. If the transaction matches, then the line is printed for that transaction. Also, for each line (and hence each transaction) a running balance is kept. Totals of each type of transaction are then printed for that customer.

exercises

11-1 Most computer-based systems are designed to process data in either an on-line interactive fashion or in discrete batches. Describe three processing applications which would be most appropriate for an on-line design and three applications which would be most appropriate for a batch design.

11-2 All data processed by a manual system can be traced back to properly authorized source documents, thus providing a built-in audit trail. However, in a computer system, data can be entered directly through terminals (eliminating many source documents) and this built-in audit trail no longer exists.

1. What specific control procedures can be built into the system design to ensure the proper authorization of all processed transactions?

2. How can an audit trail be established through a computer system in the absence of source documents?

11-3 A computer-based accounts payable system can provide both tangible and intangible benefits to a firm. These intangible benefits are often the most important advantages of the new system. List five specific intangible benefits which an accounts payable system should provide.

11-4 A computer-based general ledger and financial statements system can also provide tangible and intangible benefits. List five specific intangible benefits which a general ledger and financial statements system should provide.

11-5 Computer system design is based in part upon the desired frequency of output reports. The following is a list of some typical output reports. For each of these reports, state whether it should be generated on-demand, daily, weekly, once an accounting period, or never.

a. Trial balance.

b. Income statement and balance sheet.

c. Schedule of accounts receivable.

d. Individual customer balance.

e. Schedule of accounts payable.

f. Amount owed particular supplier.

g. Payroll register.

h. W-2 forms.

i. Inventory on-hand report.

j. Breakdown of sales by salesman.

11-6 Proper system design entails performing numerous tasks, some of which depend upon the prior completion of others. Arrange the following items in the order they would likely be performed in the system design and system specification. Note those which would be performed simultaneously.

a. Flowchart the programs.

b. Flowchart the system.

c. Estimate intangible benefits.

d. Develop input forms.

   e. Specify output reports.

   f. Estimate resources required.

   g. Assign tasks to organizational units.

   h. Organize data files.

   i. Determine limits of system.

   j. Establish the framework for getting system working.

system implementation

outline

INTRODUCTION

We have gone through the process of establishing the system objectives and we have created a system design which will accomplish those objectives. At this point the new system exists only on paper. We now must be concerned with system implementation, the process of getting the system design actually working in operation.

Certainly, all three system development components—objectives, design, implementation—are critically important and must be done well. It is important to realize, however, that the balance between concepts and details changes as we progress through this cycle. The system objectives step is primarily conceptual, with few required details; the focus is on the overall viewpoint and what we are trying to accomplish. The system design step is balanced between concepts and details; the structure of the new system must be constructed, but the details of costs, files, and computer programs must be worked out. The system implementation step, by contrast, is primarily detail work, with little required conceptual work. The concepts have been developed, the task is to put them into practice, and this will necessarily involve many details.

This is not to say, however, that any of these steps is harder or easier to do well than others. It is simply that the tasks are different. In fact, in many ways system implementation is the hardest step, because conceptual difficulties become apparent and have to be corrected.

Certainly, it is most obvious and most vivid when the system implementation does not go well. If system objectives are poorly chosen, this fact can often be obscured and the objectives approved without incident. If the system design is poorly done, this fact can often be lost in thick reports and flowcharts. During system implementation, however, these suppressed flaws come to light and must be dealt with. This is why some consulting firms often prefer that their client does not implement a system design they developed; the consultants get paid for a system design, but they do not have to risk failure by actually trying to get the system working in practice.

This balance between concepts and details is important, however, for deciding who will do what tasks in the overall system development. The conceptual decisions are of critical importance, but do not require many hours of work. Thus, the conceptual tasks of setting objectives and laying out the design of the system are those most suited to the capabilities (and fee structure) of outside consultants. The detail tasks of specifying the system and implementing it are more suited to permanent employees, since they will work with the system. As a result, consultants frequently lay out the objectives and broad design of the system and then help monitor the progress of the permanent staff in specifying and implementing the system. Unfortunately, even good designs have resulted in failure utilizing this approach because the permanent staff have proven incapable of even implementing a well-conceived and well laid out design. Of course, as we have emphasized before, you will have to use your judgment in a particular situation when deciding between the use, if any, of outside consultants and the use of permanent employees.

12.1 ELEMENTS OF PROGRAMMING

Programming is the next step in the process of system development. Certainly, if the computer programs do not work, the computer-based system cannot work. There is, however, no one way to develop the programs. Some companies have a staff of permanent computer programmers who do this work; this is probably the most common approach in medium and large-scale computer installations. Other companies (even large ones) have found greater success by contracting with software houses. The software company will contract to write programs meeting the given system specifications for a fixed fee. Using software houses free the company from the task of hiring, training, and retaining highly mobile computer programmers. Smaller companies sometimes use their EDP (electronic data processing) consultant to also write the programs. This is wasteful in the sense that the consultant is more qualified and demands a higher fee than is required for programming; however, it can be less expensive in the long run because there is no need to write a full system specification in order to communicate with a separate programmer. Finally, many companies utilize software packages, which are generalized programs to handle a particular application area. Thus, the user company can buy the programs "off the shelf" to use in the system.

Programming is not that hard and is becoming easier and easier. Beginning programmers often get overwhelmed and feel that programming is tremendously difficult. In fact, programming simply requires some experience, after which time it becomes very straightforward, even natural. Experience is necessary: an experienced programmer could easily write a program in one afternoon which would take a student who has taken one programming course an entire semester to write. Facility with programming, then, comes with practice.

Many people confuse program development with system development. Program development is the writing of computer programs to satisfy set system specifications. System development is the overall process—objectives, then design, then implementation. Unfortunately, it is not uncommon for companies to advertise for and hire programmers when they need system developers. Not surprisingly these companies have problems because the programmers do not have the necessary accounting and systems background to develop a complete system.

Basic Components of Programming

Let us now go over the seven elements of programming. A schematic presentation appears in Figure 12-1.

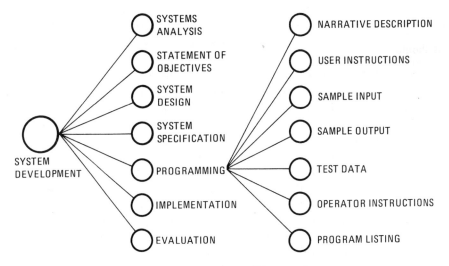

FIGURE 12-1 Elements of Programming

1. *Narrative description.* This discussion should present the purpose of the program and an overview of what the program does. The discussion should be from the user's point of view. In other words, you should describe what the program can do for the user and why he or she should adopt it. The discussion need not go into where the program fits into the overall system design; this has already been covered in the system specification. Let us use an accounts receivable file maintenance program as an example to illustrate this difference in approach:

> System point of view—"this program maintains the master file, etc."
> User point of view—"you would use this program to add customers, etc."

The user ought to be able to read the description and know when to use the program and when not to use the program.

2. *User instructions.* This discussion should explain to the user exactly how to operate and deal with the program. The instructions should be laid out in excruciating detail—nothing should be left to the person's imagination. Always remember that the person using the

program will not be a computer expert and, in fact, will generally not have any prior exposure to the computer. It is therefore not acceptable to say as part of the user instructions, "Answer the questions the program asks you." You must tell the user exactly what questions the computer will ask and exactly how to answer each one. These instructions must clearly indicate the difference between the number 0 and the letter O, between the number 5 and the letter S, between the number 1 and the lower case letter l, and between the number 2 and the letter Z. The instructions should also indicate exactly what buttons to push: if the user needs to type in the letter *A* and then press the RETURN button, then state it

> Type: *A*
> Press: RETURN

As we stated above, be explicit and leave *nothing* to the imagination.

3. *Sample input.* It is difficult for many people to conceptualize the input for the computer from pages of detailed instructions on program use. For all the basic types of input, you should give an example of what a complete set or package of input would look like. This will make the instructions concrete by providing a point of reference.

4. *Sample output.* Most people are primarily interested in the computer program output. Thus, the best way to explain the purpose of a program is to present a sample output. This sample output should be a selected, representative printout which the program generates. This should be a representative sample, so do not include a huge stack of output which no one will be able to read or understand: select carefully. Importantly, you should also provide a description of the sample output. Remember that people with little exposure to the computer are simply baffled by a computer printout and cannot decipher it. Also, in order to get all the information on one sheet of output, often abbreviations must be used. These abbreviations are clear to the programmer; they are rarely clear to the user. Finally, guidance is necessary for the analysis of the computer output, namely what this output means to the user. For all these reasons, it is absolutely necessary to explain what the output says, what each column of output or number means, and what the output means to the user.

5. *Test data.* Test data should be selected to check if the program is working. You have to keep in mind two distinct testing problems. First, the program has to be tested when it is working to make sure it is correct, (i.e., that it processes the data in the manner anticipated by the system specifications). Second, the program must be tested in the future when it is modified or extended. One of the constants of system development is that the programs will later be modified to adapt to new or changing circumstances. However, when the program is extended or changed, it must then be checked to make sure that it still processes the old data in the same old way. For both these reasons, test data must be developed. These will be data for which the results are known. The data can then be processed by the newly developed or recently modified program and the results compared to what they should be. Certainly, if the results are not correct, you know there is something wrong with the program. Unfortunately, even if the results are correct, you can still not be absolutely positive there are no errors in the program. An old saying in programming is that a working program is one with only undiscovered bugs.

Ideally, the test data should be chosen to test or exercise every major logic path of the program. Thus, if there are four types of transactions which can be processed, the test data should include at least examples of each transaction type.

6. *Operator instructions.* You will remember that on larger computer systems there is a distinction between the user and the operator. The user interacts with the program, develops necessary input, and uses any generated output. The operator, on the other hand, is concerned with the care of the hardware. The operator will mount any necessary tapes on tape drives, will put paper as required into the printer, and do other related tasks. The operator instructions should detail exactly whattapes to use with the program and where to find those tapes, where to find any specific disks required, and where to distribute the generated output. In smaller systems, where the user and operator are the same person, the user instructions should include any required discussions of physical tapes, disks, or paper. There should not be a separate discussion of these tasks—the separation would simply be confusing.

7. *Program listing.* The last stage is the actual listing of the program and what it looks like. This listing has both a short-term and a long-term use. The short-term use is for the programmer's supervisor to review. The supervisor should go over the program to ensure that the program is written in the standard way, that all specifications are met and that a proper error-detecting code is included. Under pressure of deadlines, it is not uncommon for programmers to omit needed (but not immediately obvious) steps. These "time savers" will have a high price later, so they should be prevented, if possible. The long-term use is for later modifications to the program. Even after the program is written and works, it does not remain static. There will be future changes required, and a convenient listing of the latest version of the program is extremely helpful for reference purposes.

You will notice that the common theme of both long-term and short-term uses of the program listing is that people other than the programmer will look at the listing. Thus, the listing should be as easy to read as possible and should be self-documenting. In other words, the listing should explain itself with sufficient comments to make the program comprehensible. (See the Appendices for examples of programming in BASIC and COBOL.)

Table 12-1 summarizes the seven programming elements.

TABLE 12-1 Programming Elements

Element	*Summary*
1. Narrative description	brief discussion of the purpose of the program and what it does
2. User instructions	the steps to follow in order to use the program
3. Sample input	an example of acceptable program input
4. Sample output	an example of what the program output looks like
5. Test data	data that provides a reasonable check that the program works
6. Operator instructions	description of tasks a separate operator must do, such as mount tapes
7. Program listing	source language statements of the actual computer programs

12.2 ELEMENTS OF IMPLEMENTATION

Selling the System to Employees

We now come to the implementation of the new system (i.e., getting the new system working in place of the old). In fact, if the system design, specifications, and programming have been done properly, the system implementation is primarily a people problem. As you are aware, the computer part of a computer-based system is only one fraction of the overall system. To actually accomplish something, the system must work through people. People, however, often have ambivalent feelings toward the computer and computer systems. The computer is often perceived as a threat, either to jobs or to the "humanity" of the work place. Even if the computer is not considered a threat, many people are afraid of it, the normal human reaction to something unknown. Finally, many employees simply resent any intrusion into or disruption of their established routine. They are settled into a comfortable routine and installing new equipment and changing procedures is a traumatic shock. Thus, the main task of implementation is selling the system to the employees who must make the system work.

Basic Components of System Implementation

There are essentially seven basic components of a typical system implementation. Of course, any specific system implementation will have to be an adaptation of this basic structure for the particular situation involved. Figure 12-2 is a schematic diagram of these seven basic components.

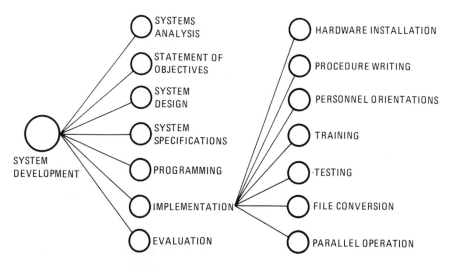

FIGURE 12-2 Elements of Implementation

1. *Hardware installation.* Often the new system will simply use the equipment available to the firm at the time. In that case, there is no need to install new hardware, and that problem is disposed of. However, a new system will sometimes require new equipment; in this case, the nature and timing of hardware installation becomes extremely important. It is our experience that many people look for their first small computer and want it working

for them in a month. That is fine, except that delivery time with small computers is about three months. Delivery on some equipment is twelve or even eighteen months. All this has to be taken into consideration and properly planned for. Additionally, computer equipment is sometimes very sensitive to its environment, and you might then have to provide for special air conditioning or humidity controls. Finally, raised floors, special wiring, and even special plumbing (some large IBM computers are water-cooled!) are sometimes necessary, though less so now than in recent years.

2. *Procedure writing.* You remember that in the system design we outlined the manual procedures and that in the system specification we detailed exactly what would be done. However, even this is not adequate in many situations for three reasons:

-   First, the procedures are not segregated and specified by person or by job position. As a result, employees would have to read all the procedures in order to find out exactly their tasks.

-   Second, the procedures are not written in language appropriate to the actual employee who will do the job. Thus, the system reports may assume more knowledge than reasonably can be expected of the employee.

-   Third, the procedures are not written in the organization's standard way and thus are not directly comparable to the procedures for other system. This will make updating more difficult and cause employees to have to unnecessarily shift mental gears in going from one system to another.

As a result, the procedures have to be written down by job in a simple, easy-to-follow manner and in the organization's standard way. In short, a procedures manual must be written which will fit together with the organization's other policy and procedures manual(s).

3. *Personnel orientations.* As we discussed above, there are many possible employee attitudes toward the computer and toward new systems in general. You simply cannot assume that these attitudes will be positive. Often they will not be positive and, in fact, will usually range from fearful to actively hostile. You will therefore have to sell the system to the employees through personnel orientations. At these orientations you should stress the benefits of the new system and explain how it will make their jobs easier by eliminating drudgery and mechanical burdens. You should also reassure them that the computer will not make them obsolete nor cause them to lose their jobs. You should also mention how the new system benefits the overall organization (*not* mentioning any possible reduction in staff). However, you should realize that vague, company-wide benefits are not very important to most employees; you must bring the benefits of the system to them personally.

4. *Training.* Even after the personnel are oriented to and understand the basic concepts of the new system, there is the next step of training the people in the operation and use of the new system. Often, there is a trade-off here between the possibility of hiring outside people with any necessary training (who then do not understand the company) and the possibility of using present employees who understand the company (but who then need to be trained). In any case, training is often necessary and the kind of training varied. For example, training is often required in computer programming, computer operation, and the use of terminals. Also, training is often required in data preparation, new procedures, or the analysis of system output. This training is generally done by one of three groups: in-house or permanent staff, the computer hardware vendor, or the outside consulting organization which designed the system. Thus, a great deal of work done by many of the large public accounting firms involves training client personnel in system operation and use.

5. *Testing.* It is hardly possible to overstress the importance of testing in system development. Everything to this point has been conceptual. It has not been brought down to earth, so to speak, by actually using the new system on the company's actual data and seeing the result. Testing is so important that a useful rule of thumb is that one-third of the time should be spent on program design, one-sixth of the time should be spent on coding the program statements, and fully one-half of the time should be spent on testing the programs once they have already been written. No matter how much thought and foresight goes into system development, it is a basic fact that not every aspect has been considered, and unforeseen difficulties will arise. Unfortunately, program testing with even a wide range of actual data is not sufficient to determine every *bug* or error in the programs. However, such testing is necessary to have any confidence that the programs are adequate.

6. *File conversion.* Once the programs have been extensively tested, the next step is then to convert the files from the old system to the new format. Certainly, you should not convert any files prior to extensive program testing, because subsequently discovered errors and modifications may require redoing a great deal of work. This file conversion often consists of going from manual records and files to computer records and files. As a result, there may be a huge one-time effort to convert all the present information to a machine-readable form. Since this conversion is so much greater an effort than normal operation, it does not make sense for the organization to permanently staff for this work. In situations such as these, the work is often contracted to service bureaus. In fact, huge conversions to a machine-readable form sometimes are air-freighted to Taiwan or other Southeast Asian countries because of the lower labor costs and greater accuracy for keypunch-like work.

7. *Parallel operation.* Parallel operation is the process of using both the old system and the new system at the same time—and then comparing the results. Certainly, the new system

TABLE 12-2 Implementation Elements

Element	Summary
1. Hardware installation	schedule for, prepare for, and then actually install new equipment
2. Procedure writing	develop procedure manual to follow in operating new system
3. Personnel orientation	introduce people to the new system and their relationship to the system
4. Training	give employees the tools and techniques to operate and use the system
5. Testing	ensure that the computer programs properly process the data
6. File conversion	load the information in the present files onto the new system's files
7. Parallel operation	use the new system at the same time as the old to make sure results are correct

should generate the same results as the old system does. If the results are not the same, the new system is probably in error, though you should also investigate the possibility that the old system has been in error all along. This parallel operation is not as simple or easy as it may at first appear. Notice that the organization has to process everything twice; once with the old system and then again with the new system. Thus, in addition to the operation of the old system (which presumably kept everyone busy before), there is the added burden of another (and completely new, at that) system. This burden of parallel operation always tempts organizations to eliminate this step. Some actually succumb to this temptation and rationalize that the system has been sufficiently tested. This is a mistake! The organization should go to the trouble and expense because there are always unforeseen circumstances which only appear during parallel operation.

A summary of the seven elements of system implementation appears in Table 12-2.

12.3 ELEMENTS OF EVALUATION

We now come to the final step in the process of system development, evaluation. Evaluation is the important activity of stepping back from the system after it has been implemented and has operated for a period of time in order to get an overview of the entire process that the organization has gone through. There are two reasons for this evaluation step:

First, you should analyze the system in operation to determine if the system can be improved.

Second, you should analyze the system development process to see if any lessons can be learned from the company's experience.

Focusing on the Individual System and the System Process

Our focus should be on both the individual system *and* the overall system process. Needless to say, this double focus is often hard to maintain, but it is absolutely necessary.

If you only focus on the one system in question, you may miss important overall lessons which will be very valuable in the development of many future systems. Overall lessons would include a decision that the system development was rushed or that system development proceeded in too leisurely a manner. Another important overall lesson might be that top management was not sufficiently involved in the system project or that management got too involved in system details. Significant changes such as these could be extremely helpful in future systems projects.

On the other hand, if you only focus on the overall questions, you lose the chance to make significant changes to this specific system. Clearly, the overall information system is built up from specific systems. Important results about this specific system would include the decision that important internal controls are missing, that costs are excessive, or that the users of the system are dissatisfied with system performance.

Basic Components of Evaluation

There are seven basic elements of the post-implementation evaluation. Figure 12-3 gives a schematic diagram of this breakdown.

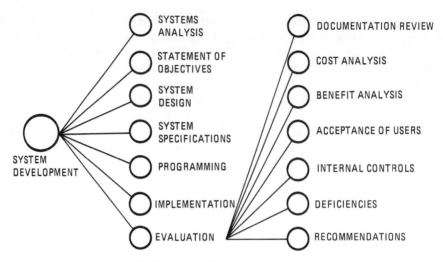

FIGURE 12-3 Elements of Evaluation

1. *Documentation review.* Documentation describing the system and how to operate it is far more important in computer-based systems than in manual systems. A manual system is visible and can thus be reviewed visually by following the audit trail: the manual system is in a sense self-documenting because you can see it. A computer-based system, on the other hand, is largely electronic and hence invisible. Documentation is therefore critical to understanding, operating, and modifying a computer-based system.

   Unfortunately, under the pressure of deadlines it is not uncommon for the persons responsible for documentation (especially programmers) to let it slide because the lack of documentation is not immediately obvious. This is such a standard problem that companies have assigned a separate group solely with the responsibility for system documentation. This approach does not work well, however, because the separate group is not in a position to know enough to write complete documentation. In fact, the people who develop the system must document their own work.

   The documentation review is then an independent review of the work done to date on systems documentation. The review first checks the completeness of the documentation and then reviews the quality of this work. Any necessary corrections and additional documentation can then be laid out.

2. *Cost analysis.* As you remember from the preceding chapter, the system design contains a discussion of the costs of the new system. At the time of the system design, however, these costs are projections and estimates. The task here is to analyze the actual costs and compare them to the costs anticipated in the system design. Human nature being what it is, it is not unknown for people to "sandbag" a new system proposal by estimating costs at an unrealistically low figure. This approach can get a new system design accepted, but at a great cost to the organization later on. Also, in essence it is possible here to evaluate the process used to estimate future costs by checking the results of the estimating process with actual results. Major differences may imply that the cost estimation process is seriously deficient. Actually, one of the most common deficiencies is not the determination of a poor cost figure, but rather the complete omission of important costs.

3. *Benefit analysis.* As were the costs of the new system, the anticipated benefits were laid out in the system design. These anticipated benefits generally include reduction in clerical costs, improved service to customers, and faster and better information for management. However as we have discussed earlier, some of these benefits (especially the reduction in clerical costs) often prove elusive. One important task of the evaluation process is then to compare the actual benefits, if any, to those anticipated by the system design. Also, it is not uncommon to have *un*anticipated benefits which are more important than the actually anticipated benefits. For example, the system may point up unexpectedly some particularly wasteful practice.

4. *Acceptance by users.* It can scarcely be stressed too strongly that the system does not consist solely of the computer programs. The system also consists of manual procedures and human use of the printed or displayed output. Thus, the system can only work through people. This, of course, implies that if the people do not like or will not use the system, then it cannot work. It is therefore an important task of the evaluation process to determine the level of acceptance by users of the system. There are many possible reasons for user dissatisfaction, but two of the most important and common are:

> First, lack of confidence in the system. It is not uncommon for the system to fail to provide adequate error-detecting and error-correcting techniques. When this occurs, excessive errors creep into the system and the system output is no longer useful. The users then stop relying on the system and start keeping their own private system to help them in their work.

> Second, excessive errors and rejected transactions. If the system finds a large percentage of transactions in error and rejects them, the system can collapse under the burden of correcting and re-entering all those transactions in addition to the new transactions.

The human element is absolutely critical to system success and must be specifically reviewed.

5. *Internal controls.* Internal controls are just as important in computer-based systems as they are in manual systems in order to protect the system from both accidental and deliberate errors and to ensure the accuracy and reliability of the system output. We will defer a complete discussion of internal control in computer-based systems to Chapter 16. However, it is important to realize that the same basic elements of internal control are required in computer systems as were required in manual systems. It is simply that the means of implementing these basic elements of internal control will be different because of the addition of the computer to the system.

As part of the postimplementation evaluation process, there should be a specific review and evaluation of the system's internal controls. This review should include the adequacy of the design of the controls, but should also stress how the controls are working out in practice: Are the policies and procedures being followed? Are the controls effective?

The internal control review can not merely concern itself with the way things should be; it should also review the way things actually are. People are often content that certain internal controls are supposed to be in effect. This review should go beyond this and determine whether the controls are in effect. An often useful means of determining this is to test the controls:

> If access to computer terminals is supposed to be limited, an unauthorized person should attempt to use the terminals.

If the computer is supposed to reject unreasonable transactions, an attempt should be made to process an unreasonable transaction, such as a payroll check for 100 hours of overtime or a credit sale of $1,000,000.

Even if the computer system should have the best possible internal controls built into it, they will do no good if they are not used.

6. *Deficiencies.* The report documenting the work done for the preceding five steps of evaluation will doubtlessly be quite extensive. Actually, however, this material is not just of interest in and of itself. It is mainly interesting as a basis for analyzing any deficiencies of either the specific system under evaluation or the entire system development process. You might review here the parallel discussion of deficiencies in Chapter 6 on the topic of system analysis. The thrust and emphasis is the same here: What are the weak points of the system? What areas should be looked at more closely?

7. *Recommendations.* This recommendations section is the goal of the evaluation process. Certainly, if the organization did not change anything as a result of the evaluation, then the evaluation was of limited benefit. The recommendations should answer the following questions: What should the organization do now to improve performance? What should the organization do differently in the future to avoid some of the problems which have occurred? You might review the material and example of recommendations given in Chapter 6 on system analysis. The emphasis here is the same—give the manager guidance on what he should do now. Of course, the recommendations should be realistic and cost effective.

Table 12-3 summarizes the seven elements of the postimplementation evaluation.

TABLE 12-3 Evaluation Elements

Elements	Summary
1. Documentation review	look over the documentation and determine if it is adequate
2. Cost analysis	compare the actual costs of the system with the anticipated costs in the system design
3. Benefit analysis	compare the actual benefits of the system with the anticipated benefits in the system design
4. Acceptance by users	analyze whether the system is being used and whether the users like the system
5. Internal controls	evaluate internal controls to see if they are adequate and if policies are being followed
6. Deficiencies	detail any deficiencies in the system as it is actually operating
7. Recommendations	suggest improvements to the design or ways the system could operate more efficiently

12.4 MANAGEMENT OF SYSTEM DEVELOPMENT

Problems

To this point we have discussed the way system development should proceed: the basic seven steps and the further breakdown of each basic step into seven substeps. Consider, however, the problems associated with actually getting these steps accomplished.

First, there is the wide range of topics which must be dealt with, ranging from the very conceptual (such as the overall purpose in the statement of objectives) to the very technical (such as the data management of the system specification).

Second, there is the related problem of dealing with a wide range of people, including management, technical specialists, clerical employees, outside consultants, and computer salesmen.

Third, there is the extensive time scale, since the entire system development process takes weeks, months, and even years.

Fourth, there is the large number of steps, all taking different amounts of time, done by different people at different locations, and some of which are dependent upon earlier steps.

It is one purpose of this text to give you the information necessary to deal with the first two problems listed above. The third and fourth difficulties bring up again the importance of continuing top management involvement in the system development process. You must remember that most people's concerns will concentrate on their immediate problems rather than the long-term payoff of system development. Top management must keep people oriented to the system process or they simply will not do the work.

GANTT Charts and PERT/CPM Networks

However, in addition to top management involvement, it is necessary to keep the entire process straight—with so many steps and so many people it is easy for the project to become confused and disorganized. Because of this, techniques have been developed to help with this potential difficulty. Two of the most useful techniques are:

GANTT charts, which show the different tasks to be performed and their time frames for accomplishment.

PERT/CPM networks, which show the different tasks to be performed, but which also show the interrelationships of those tasks.

GANTT Charts

GANTT charts are very straightforward, which is one of their great advantages. Figure 12-4 gives an example of a GANTT chart for a ten-week implementation schedule in a small business. Of course, every implementation will be different and in the implementation of many large systems each of these steps might take several months.

The chart breaks down into two basic parts; on the left are the required steps and on the right is the time frame in which the steps will be performed. In this case, there are eight steps, ranging from programming to parallel operation with each step represented by a different line. The time frame is ten weeks, but certainly, if desired, the chart could have whatever number of

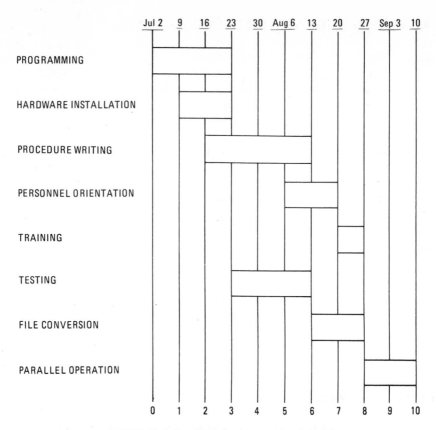

FIGURE 12-4 Ten-Week Implementation Schedule

weeks would be most appropriate. Also, the time frame could be broken down into any units desired (such as years, months, days, hours, or even minutes).

Since there are ten weeks, there are eleven vertical lines, from 0 (the beginning of the first week) to 10 (the end of the tenth week). Each line is numbered twice: the actual date at the top of the line and the relative date at the bottom of the line. Let us look at the middle line; it is marked August 6 at the top and 5 at the bottom, meaning that the end of the fifth week occurs on August 6.

For each step a mark is made in the time frame which gives the (in this case) weeks in which that step is performed. For example, programming takes three weeks and will be done in the first three weeks. Similarly, parallel operation occurs during weeks nine and ten.

Therefore, in a convenient form the GANTT chart gives the steps to be performed and the time frame for their performance. Notice also that the chart gives us what is done in each week. For example, the chart tells us that in week 6 the following things will be going on: procedure writing, personnel orientations, and testing.

Unfortunately, there is one important piece of information that the GANTT chart can not give us: the interrelationships between tasks. In our example chart, both training and testing begin after programming is completed, but we do not know whether programming has to be finished before training can begin, before testing can begin, or before both can begin, or whether or not it is even related to them. As another example, file conversion begins just after procedure writing ends, but we do not know if there is a connection; that is, whether procedure writing must be finished before file conversion can begin.

In some cases, these interrelationships are not particularly important or are so few in number that they can easily be handled. However, in more complicated situations, these inter-relationships can be extremely important, primarily because they imply that delay in completing one task may have far-reaching consequences. In other words, some tasks are critically important to the entire project because later tasks depend upon their completion, while other tasks essentially stand alone. What we would like is a method to show these relationships in a clear and easily used fashion.

PERT/CPM Network

There is a well-inown and well-developed technique for this task—the PERT/CPM network. In fact, this network approach will work with any project that:

First, consists of a well-defined collection of tasks, which, when completed, mean that the project is completed.

Second, has tasks which have to be performed in sequence (e.g., the file conversion must be complete before parallel operation can begin).

The original PERT (or Project Evaluation Review Technique) network approach was developed for project management of the construction of the Polaris submarine for the U.S. Navy. The CPM (or Critical Path Method) network approach was originally developed independently for building construction projects. There are slight differences in the two approaches. PERT is oriented to the uncertainty associated with the time estimate given for each task (e.g., the programming may take more or less time than the three weeks estimated), while CPM is oriented to the trade-off between cost of completion and time of completion for each task (e.g., it may be possible to complete the file conversion in one week rather than two weeks by spending more money). However, for our purposes in this text, the two approaches are identical. If you wish to read further on this topic, the literature on these techniques is vast and widely available.

We begin the PERT/CPM network approach by drawing a picture. The network is then a picture of the implementation schedule where activities are represented by arrows and events are represented by nodes. Figure 12-5 gives a first sketch of the implementation schedule in a network form. The node on the far left represents the event of starting the implementation schedule. There are then four activities which begin from that point: programming, hardware installation, personnel orientation, and procedure writing. The next event is the completion of *both* programming and hardware installation; when that event occurs, the activity testing can begin. Similarly, when both personnel orientation and procedure writing are complete, the activity training begins. After testing is complete, file conversion can begin and, finally, after both file conversion and training are complete, parallel operation can begin. Parallel operation is the final activity and hence, when it is complete, the entire project is finished. You will notice that next to each activity there is a number; it represents the number of weeks that are necessary to complete that activity.

Unfortunately, this network representation is not particularly appropriate for our future analysis. It will be much more convenient if we only have one arrow (i.e., activity) going

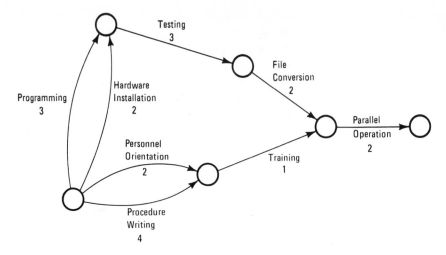

FIGURE 12-5 Network Sketch of the Implementation Schedule

between any two nodes (i.e., events). For this reason we introduce a dummy activity taking zero time just so this formal requirement can be met. Figure 12-6 shows the network after these dummy activities have been added. Notice that there are now eight events and ten activities; the regular eight activities and the two added dummy activities. Node 1 (or event 1) represents the start of the implementation schedule and node 8 (or event 8) represents the end of the implementation schedule. Hardware installation is now the activity between events 1 and 2; programming is now the activity between events 1 and 3; and the dummy activity between events 2 and 3 indicates that hardware installation must be completed before event 3 has occurred. A similar process was carried out for personnel orientation and procedure writing. Personnel orientation is the activity between events 1 and 4, while procedure writing is the activity

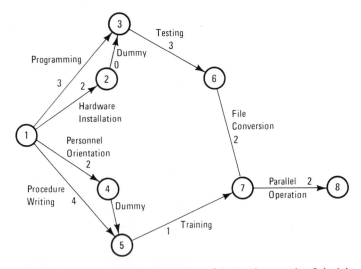

FIGURE 12-6 Network Representation of the Implementation Schedule

between events 1 and 5. Again, a dummy activity was added between events 4 and 5 to indicate personnel orientation must be completed before training can begin.

We must now introduce the concept of a path. A path is a string of events and activities stretching from the start, node 1, to the end, node 8. In our example problem there are four paths through the network. One path is from node 1 to node 3 to node 6 to node 7 to node 8. The four paths through the network are:

Path	Nodes
1	$1 - 3 - 6 - 7 - 8$
2	$1 - 2 - 3 - 6 - 7 - 8$
3	$1 - 4 - 5 - 7 - 8$
4	$1 - 5 - 7 - 8$

Let us consider each path in order. Suppose path 1 were the entire network, that is, assume that the network did not contain any nodes or arrows not on path 1. How much time would it take to go from node 1, the start, to node 8, the end? For path 1 it would take 3 weeks to go from node 1 to node 3 (i.e., programming takes 3 weeks), it would take 3 weeks to go from node 3 to node 6 (i.e., testing), it would take 2 weeks to go from node 6 to node 7 (file conversion), and it would take 2 weeks to go from node 7 to node 8 (parallel opesation). Thus, path 1 would take 10 weeks. If we repeated this process for each of the other 3 paths, we would find that path 2 would take 9 weeks, path 3 would take 5 weeks, and path 4 would take 7 weeks. Path 1 is thus the longest path and is therefore called the *critical path*. The critical path is so named because if any activity on the critical path is delayed, then the entire project is delayed. The entire implementation schedule is thus supposed to take 10 weeks, but if any activity on the critical path (programming, testing, file conversion, or parallel operation) takes longer than expected, the entire project will be correspondingly delayed. Note, however, that the same is not true of all activities in the network. If training took 2 weeks instead of 1, then path 3 would take 6 weeks rather than 5 and path 4 would take 7 weeks rather than 6, but the overall project would still be completed within 10 weeks. Thus, some activities are more critical to the timely completion of the entire project than others, namely those on the critical path.

In a complicated situation, there may be hundreds of nodes and thousands of paths, so we need a standard, unambiguous procedure for determining the critical path; in other words, we need an *algorithm* for determining the critical path. Let us illustrate the standard algorithm using Figure 12-7. This algorithm is based on two concepts, the *earliest time* and the *latest time* for each activity. The earliest time is the soonest that activity could be completed, while the latest time is the latest that activity could be completed without delaying the entire project. Then, those activities which have no difference between these two different times are the activities on the critical path. In other words, if the actifity on the critical path is delayed beyond the earliest it could be completed, then that will delay the entire project. Figure 12-7 therefore has three numbers for each activity—the time necessary for completion, the earliest time, and the latest time. These numbers are presented in the following format:

Time for Completion (Earliest Time, Latest Time)

The earliest times are computed by going through the network "forwards" and the latest times are computed by going through the network "backwards."

The earliest time calculations begin with node 1. Programming, hardware installation, procedure writing, and personnel orientation all have no activities before them and thus the

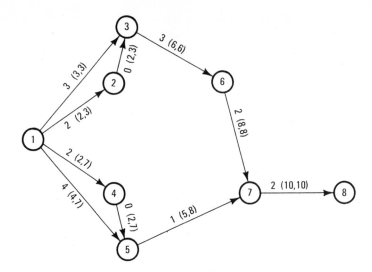

FIGURE 12-7 Earliest Time and Latest Time Calculations

earliest any of them can be completed is the time necessary for their completion. The dummy activities take no time and thus their earliest time is the same as that of their predecessor activity. Testing and training are more complicated because they both require that two activities be completed before they can even begin. Thus, the earliest testing can even begin is the maximum of the two earliest times of its predecessor activities. Testing can not begin for 3 weeks and then takes 3 weeks to complete, thus making the earliest time for completion for that activity 6 weeks. Similarly, the earliest time for training is 5 weeks. It is then straightforward to determine that the earliest time for file conversion is 8 weeks and the earliest time for parallel operation is 10 weeks. All these figures for earliest time appear in Figure 12-7.

The latest time calculations begin with node 8, the end. We know that the earliest completion for the project is 10 weeks. We now must go back through the network to determine how late an activity can be completed without delaying the entire project. Certainly, parallel operation must be completed by 10 weeks to keep from delaying the project. We then come to file conversion and training, but since parallel operation takes two weeks, they must both be completed before 8 weeks and thus their latest times are both 8. Since file conversion takes 2 weeks, the latest time for testing is 6. Then, the latest time for both activities going to node 3 is 3 because testing takes 3 weeks. By the same token, the latest time for both activities going into node 5 is 7 because training takes 1 week. Since both dummy activities take no time, the latest time for hardware installation is then 3, while the latest time for personnel orientation is then 7.

The final concept we must introduce is *slack time*. This is the difference between the earliest time and the latest time. Thus, this amount is the time that activity could be delayed without delaying the entire project. The activities on the critical path are then those activities with zero slack time. The above computations are summarized in Table 12-4. You will note that those activities with zero slack time—programming, testing, file conversion, and parallel operation—are exactly those activities on the critical path.

The network representation of the project has the advantage of picking out the critical path: those activities which should be most closely watched because the project most directly

TABLE 12-4 Network Calculations

| | Nodes | | Times | | |
Activity	Begin	End	Earliest	Latest	Slack
Programming	1	3	3	3	0
Hardware Installation	1	2	2	3	1
Dummy	2	3	2	3	1
Procedure Writing	1	5	4	7	3
Personnel Orientation	1	4	2	7	5
Dummy	4	5	2	7	5
Training	5	7	5	8	3
Testing	3	6	6	6	0
File Conversion	6	7	8	8	0
Parallel Operation	7	8	10	10	0

depends upon them. However, the network approach has another tremendous advantage, namely the conceptual picture it provides of the entire project and the interrelationships between the activities which make up the project. The network makes clear the overall picture and how the various activities fit together.

Chapter 12 has thus provided a discussion of the elements of programming, implementation, and evaluation, the last three steps of the basic seven steps of system development outlined in Chapter 9. Unfortunately, the difficulties of actually carrying out these activities in a real business can not be effectively duplicated on paper and thus we are unable to illustrate our discussion with an application to Pooper Centers, as we did in the previous two chapters. However, we have included Appendices which give the steps of program development using the BASIC language and the COBOL language; this can provide some insight into the types of programs necessary in business data processing. The chapter concluded with a discussion of the problems of managing a system development project and two important techniques for coping with these problems, the GANTT chart and the PERT/CPM network.

Part three has then discussed the full range of steps involved in the development of computer-based systems. These steps were illustrated with an application to Pooper Centers. You should now be comfortable with the problems of developing a new system.

exercises

12-1 In a large organization many different individuals might be associated with the system development process. In which steps of system development might each of the following people be involved and what form would that involvement take?

a. Computer programmer.

b. Data entry clerk.

c. Systems analyst.

d. Top management.

e. Board of directors.

f. Accountant.

g. Bookkeeper.

h. Outside consultant.

    i. Auditors.

    j. Data processing manager.

12-2 In a small firm only one person may be associated with the system development process. Suppose you are the accountant/bookkeeper for such a business and your employer wants to acquire a new computer-based system. In which steps of systems development might you be involved and what form would that involvement take?

12-3 Proper system implementation entails performing numerous tasks, some of which depend upon the prior completion of others. Arrange the following items in the order they would likely be performed in a system implementation. Note those which could be performed simultaneously.

    a. Reorganize data.

    b. Determine actual system cost.

    c. Hire data-processing staff.

    d. Review written descriptions of system.

    e. "Sell" system to employees.

    f. Determine actual system benefits.

    g. Ensure programs work.

    h. Both old and new systems running.

    i. Explain how to use system.

    j. Receive computer equipment.

12-4 Once system specifications have been set, actual programs to meet those specifications can be obtained in four basic ways. Discuss each of these sources of programs and give the general advantages and disadvantages of each.

12-5 Suppose your firm were considering the development of a new payroll system which would include the on-line collection of data on hours worked by each employee. A permanent identification card, unique to each employee, would be placed in a data collection terminal as employees entered and left each work area. This system would replace time cards which were punched in and out as employees arrived and departed work; these time cards were collected and processed every two weeks.

    1. What are the advantages for the company of the new on-line approach over the older system?

    2. Why might employees react unfavorably to the new system? Give five actions you would take to overcome this negative attitude.

12-6 Listed below are several possible findings which might be turned up by a postimplementation evaluation. For each of these possible findings give three different circumstances which could have brought about that result and state generally how you would go about uncovering the true reason for that result.

a. Continuing employee hostility.

b. Errors in system output.

c. Higher than anticipated costs.

d. Inadequate program documentation.

e. Tangible benefits not fully realized.

part IV

computer-based information systems

financial accounting and control systems

outline

13.1 **Information Flow in a Computer-based System**: major computer-based information systems used in business data processing and how these systems interact.

13.2 **Components of a Financial Accounting and Control System**: specific processing applications which make up this information system; general ledger, financial statements and budgeting; information flow between this and other processing systems.

13.3 **Output Requirements**: man-sensible output reports generated by this system including the managerial control and audit trail significance of the reports.

13.4 **Data Organization and Input**: necessary permanent and transaction files of data which must be maintained for this system; techniques of data input.

INTRODUCTION

Recall that in earlier chapters we introduced the basic principles and mechanics underlying the processing of business data and demonstrated how these principles are carried out in manual accounting systems. Subsequent discussions centered on the techniques of systems analysis, the tools fundamental to computer-based systems, and the concepts of computer system design and implementation. In a real sense, we now return to the basic principles of business data processing. Chapters 13–16 will demonstrate how these principles can be carried out by a computer-based information system using the tools, techniques, and concepts introduced since Part One. The basic processing ideas will be the same as those discussed earlier, the way they are carried out will be different.

We will present three computer-based systems which commonly make up a business "information system." These systems will track the manual processing techniques introduced in Chapters 1 and 2, but will improve and extend these techniques with the aid of the computer.

The final chapter of the book is concerned with the application of the basic internal control ideas and principles introduced in Chapter 3 to computer-based information systems.

13.1 INFORMATION FLOW IN A COMPUTER-BASED SYSTEM

A business information system is simply the sum of all the tools, techniques, and procedures used by the business to process data. Such a system accepts input data about a business and generates required or desired output information. These tools, techniques, and procedures may be carried out manually or by a computer. In fact, most information systems are made up of smaller component systems which are designed to process data in specific areas of business activity. Remember that this is just what we did in Part One when we discussed manual accounting and its special systems for processing sales and purchases, cash receipts and disbursements, as well as its general journal which handles all data not processed by these special systems. Any business information system, then, can be divided into smaller, processing systems of narrower scope which accept input data, process it, and interact with each other to produce output information.

These same ideas apply to both computer-based systems and to manual systems. Indeed, the component parts of computer-based systems should parallel those of manual systems since the goals of both are fundamentally the same. It is convenient to view the activities and data of most businesses as falling into three major categories; general financial accounting including budgeting, sales, and purchases, and cash inflows and outflows. It is logical then to view a computer-based information system as consisting of three processing systems which are identifiable and distinguishable, but not isolated from each other. Each of these systems processes data from a certain area of business activities; however, each depends upon the other, and information must flow between them for the computer-based system to work.

Figure 13-1 illustrates these relationships and the logical flow of information between processing systems. It deserves your careful study because it is the "big picture" on which this chapter and the following two are based. As you examine this figure, consider the following important points:

1. The entire figure represents a computer-based business information system. It is composed of three distinct, but interrelated processing systems which are represented by the large curved shapes.

2. The primary (but not necessarily the only) major components of an information system are:

    a.   A financial accounting and control system.

    b.   A cash receipts and disbursements system.

    c.   A sales and purchases system.

3. Each major component, in turn, consists of three specific processing applications or packages which are represented by the rectangular figures. It is these applications which are the basic building blocks of an information system.

4. It is very important to note that information flow between applications within a system, as well as between applications of different systems, is absolutely necessary in a computer-based information system. The arrows indicating information flow which intersect the curved shapes demonstrate that all systems interact with each other.

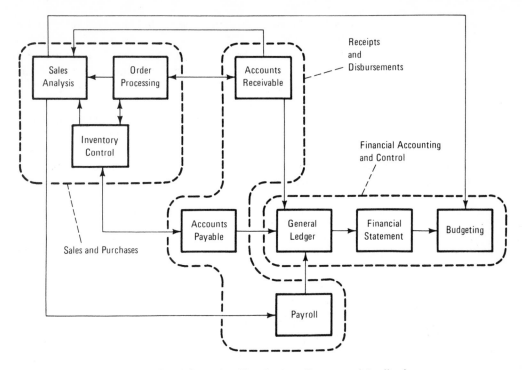

FIGURE 13-1 Information Flow Between Systems and Applications

5. The conceptual differences between computer-based information systems and manual accounting systems should become readily apparent from careful study of Figure 13-1. Remember from Chapter 1 that accounting systems process only certain kinds of events, which we call transactions, because of the basic assumptions on which accounting is based. Information systems, on the other hand, are capable of processing any information which is useful to management or any other user of the system. Information systems, then, process accounting transactions plus many other kinds of data and events which ordinarily are beyond the scope of accounting systems. Many of the arrows indicating information flow in Figure 13-1 represent important information or events which are not accounting transactions and thus would not be available in an accounting system.

Two significant conclusions about computer-based systems can be drawn from the relationships depicted in Figure 13-1.

1. The flow of information between applications and systems makes it unlikely that any individual application, or even any component system, can successfully stand alone or operate independently. Each of these parts provide the necessary "environment" for the other. To think, for example, of an accounts receivable or an order entry application without regard for the interaction of the processing package with its environment simply misses the point of a computer-based information system. To think about the "whole" is an important lesson of the systems approach.

2.   Many processing applications use the same basic data as input, but require that the data be organized or accessed slightly differently. By the same token, the output of some applications may be used as input for applications in other component systems. This commonality of data needs makes it possible for a computer-based system to create a basic set of data which is available to all processing applications and can be referenced by these applications in many different ways. Such a set of data within reach of all processing applications for their use is called a data base. Instead of each application package organizing and storing all of its own data (which would necessarily result in repetition and duplication throughout the system,) the data base concept extracts data that is common to many processing applications and makes it accessible to all. Only with the aid of a computer's speed and memory is this possible, thus implementation of the data base idea in a manual system is not feasible.

Now that we have an overview of the important relationships and flows in a computer-based information system, we will turn our attention to understanding how the major component systems and the specific applications which make them up actually work.

13.2 COMPONENTS OF A FINANCIAL ACCOUNTING AND CONTROL SYSTEM

This is the most basic of the processing systems. It should be designed to handle the bookkeeping and accounting cycle events for a business, from journalizing transactions to the production of period-end financial statements, and the comparison of results to budgeted (expected) figures. Figure 13-2 illustrates the information flow in a financial accounting and control

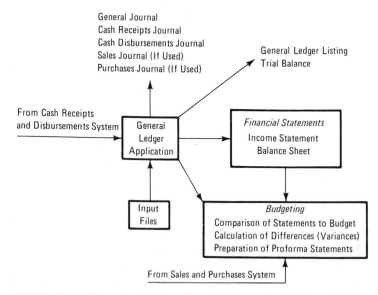

FIGURE 13-2 Information Flow in a Financial Accounting and Control System

system. In this figure, we are focusing in on the lower right curved shape in Figure 13-1 to examine the flow within this system.

Notice that the cash receipts and disbursements system provides input to the general ledger application of the financial accounting and control system. This is necessary because the accounts receivable, accounts payable, and payroll applications provide much of the data necessary for the creation of the cash receipts and cash disbursements journals, as well as the sales and purchases journals. Direct system input to the general ledger application would involve those transactions and data which do not fit into the other processing systems. These transactions would usually be found in the company's general journal. Periodically, a listing is produced of all general ledger accountsand beginning balances, together with a summary of the debit and credit activity in each account and the ending balances. Of course, a general ledge produced by a computer system would not be of the familiar "T-account" form, but would probably consist of a series of lines on a printed sheet. A trial balance could then be produced proving the equality of debits and credits in the system. Finally, at the end of each period the traditional accounting financial statements can be produced according to any format specified by the system user.

An important part of a financial accounting and control system is the control aspect. Budgeting is an important part of any control system and can be accomplished as an extension of financial statement preparation. The master budget for most businesses (a primary control tool) consists of a projected income statement (sometimes called a profit plan), a statement of projected cash needs, and a projected balance sheet. These *pro forma* statements constitute the standard or benchmark against which actual results can be compared. The system can produce budgeted statements in the same format as period-end financial statements so that departures from expected results in any important revenue, expense, or other category can be determined by the system and highlighted for management analysis. The evaluation of variances and the subsequent corrective action which results from the evaluation is management control. Of course, the computer can do neither of these things, but the computer-based financial accounting and control system can, as a matter of course, provide the information which makes these actions by humans possible. Simultaneously, a master budget of pro forma statements which will serve as the benchmark for the following period can be generated.

In addition to this, the system should have the capacity to produce detailed listings of all transactions, together with posting references, so that an audit trail through the system in either direction can be established.

Keep in mind this overview of the financial accounting and control system, as we turn our attention to the input and output requirements of the processing applications which make up the system.

13.3 OUTPUT REQUIREMENTS

The financial accounting and control system must generate several man-sensible output reports in addition to updating permanent files of data stored for further processing. The production of output is, of course, the primary goal of this, as well as any other, system. We will concentrate first on the man-sensible output reports generated by the financial accounting and control system. Then the data organization and file-updating aspects of the system will be presented.

Output Reports

The format of output reports can and does vary in actual application, but these reports must contain certain basic information, and the information must be presented in an easy-to-understand form if the financial accounting and control system is to be useful. Format is mostly a matter of user choice, however, to illustrate what output documents ought to be produced by a financial accounting and control system and what they might look like, we have chosen a series of reports which are included in a general ledger package supplied by IBM Corporation for its System/34. These are good examples of the kind of printed man-sensible output which should be produced by a financial accounting and control system. As you examine each of these figures, you might refer back to Figure 13-2 which listed the basic documents to be generated by this system.

Journals

Following the information flow depicted in Figure 13-2, the first reports printed in a financial accounting and control system are the company's journals. Recall the general journal and special journals of a manual accounting system in Part One; you will find the journals illustrated in Figures 13-3 through 13-7 to be very similar. These journals are, of course, created by a computer-based system, but the principles (although not the mechanics) underlying them are exactly the same. This is an important lesson to learn; that is, the basic underlying concepts of business data processing do not change as computer-based information systems replace manual accounting systems. That is why a firm grounding in fundamental accounting concepts and procedures is so important. If you remember your basics, much of the mystery of computer-based information systems disappears.

You should note the following about each of these journals:

1. *General journal* (Figure 13-3). This journal is generated from data entered directly into the financial accounting and control system from source documents. Although the format of this computer-based journal is slightly different from the manual system general journal, both contain the same information. Notice that most of the transactions journalized use only one line primarily because this approach takes advantage of the processing and storage capabilities of a computer system. The format and content of this journal can be made clear by examining any one of the entries. The journal reference number for each transaction is assigned by the system as entries are made to preserve the sequence of events and provide an audit trail. Also assigned is the transaction source, which is basically the date of the event. A brief description of each transaction is provided, then the general ledger debit account number and amount, and credit account number amount. Account titles are not used in the journal because account numbers are faster and easier for the computer to handle. This does mean, however, that the company's chart of accounts (which is a list of every asset, liability, owner's equity, revenue, and expense title used by the business and the number assigned to each account) must be used to read each entry. The first entry in the journal is a correction of an earlier period (June) entry requiring a debit to #1525 (Office Equipment) and a credit to #1300 (Inventory). The other entries follow the same basic format.

GATEWAY IND   CO NO 02   *** GENERAL JOURNAL ***   RUN DATE 7/15/77   PERIOD 07

JOURNAL REFERENCE NUMBER	TRANSACTION SOURCE	TRANSACTION DESCRIPTION	G/L DEBIT	DEBIT AMOUNT	G/L CREDIT	CREDIT AMOUNT
GJ07-0001	JE07-01	CORRECT JUN ERR	1525	7,500.00	1300	7,500.00
GJ07-0002	JE07-02	NEW TRUCK L7943	1300	5,837.98	1050	375.70
GJ07-0003	JE07-02	CHK# 4078			2500	4,962.28
GJ07-0004	JE07-02	EST CITY-78/49			1200	73.15
GJ07-0005	JE07-03	AR CORRECT-279	104000	73.15	1555	2,500.00
GJ07-0006	JE07-04	DEPR-BLDG	107255	2,500.00	1565	850.00
GJ07-0007	JE07-04	-OFFICE	107265	850.00	1550	700.00
GJ07-0008	JE07-04	-LAND IMPRV	107250	700.00	1570	1,200.00
GJ07-0009	JE07-04	-AUTO,TRUCK	107270	1,200.00	1555	5,000.00
GJ07-0010	JE07-04	-BLDG	207255	5,000.00	1565	2,500.00
GJ07-0011	JE07-04	-OFFICE	207265	2,500.00	1550	1,500.00
GJ07-0012	JE07-04	-LAND IMPRV	207250	1,500.00	1570	975.00
GJ07-0013	JE07-04	-AUTO,TRUCK	207270	975.00		
GJ07-0014	JE07-12	INV THRU 6-8	1200	19,953.49	104000	3,879.53
GJ07-0015	JE07-12	6-1			104000	4,213.42
GJ07-0016	JE07-12	6-5			104000	4,479.83
GJ07-0017	JE07-12	6-6			104000	3,943.52
GJ07-0018	JE07-12	6-7			104000	3,437.19
GJ07-0019	JE07-12	6-8	104120	86.04	104100	422.59
GJ07-0020	JE07-17	A/P EXPENSE ADJ	104130	336.55		
GJ07-0021	JE07-17	A/P EXPENSE ADJ	1290	350.00		
GJ07-0022	JE07-18	ALLOW BAD DEBT			207600	350.00
		** JOURNAL TOTAL		49,362.21		49,362.21
		*** FINAL TOTAL		49,362.21		49,362.21

FIGURE 13-3 General Journal (courtesy of IBM Corporation)

2.   *Cash receipts journal* (Figure 13-4). This journal results from input provided by the accounts receivable application of the cash receipts and disbursements system, and the input is used for control account (general ledger) purposes only. Individual customer accounts (subsidiary ledgers) are updated by accounts receivable. The format and content of this journal is somewhat different from the cash receipts journal we discussed in Part One because this journal focuses on cash receipts from the collection of receivables, leaving other cash receipts (primarily cash sales) to be recorded elsewhere. This difference is by design in the system and is not unusual in computer-based systems. The necessity that all cash receipts be recorded in one journal so important for control purposes in a manual accounting system is not critical in a computer-based information system. The speed and memory capabilities of a computer system allow control over cash transactions to be exercised in other ways. Notice that each entry in this journal contains a deposit number (203) indicating that all cash was deposited in the bank intact as received, an important control and audit trail feature. Summaries and totals are provided, as always, in these computer-based journals.

3.   *Cash disbursements journal* (Figure 13-5). The accounts payable application of the cash receipts and disbursements systems furnishes the input for this journal. It is the accounts payable application that updates (posts) the individual supplier accounts as cash is disbursed. Similar to the orientation of the cash receipts journal, the focus is on the disbursements for the payment of accounts payable, with other cash outflows appearing in the general journal (see the new truck purchase with a partial cash payment in entry #2 of the general journal). The reasons for this departure from the organization of journals in manual systems can be traced to the processing and control capabilities within computer-based applications. Note the important cross-reference to the purchases journal by use of that journal's system assigned reference number as a part of the cash disbursements journal.

4.   *Sales journal–invoice register* (Figure 13-6). This journal presents a record of all sales invoices, both cash and credit, created by the business during the processing period. It is closely related to the cash receipts journal, and together they present a whole picture of the general ledger effects of sales and collections of receivables. The accounts receivable application records the sales invoice and the subsequent collection of the account thus, input for the cash receipts and sales journals comes from the accounts receivable application of the cash receipts and disbursements system. Invoices are always sequentially numbered so that a journal which lists all invoices, both cash and credit, as the sales journal does, is a logical step given the way data is organized and transmitted in a computer-based system. A significant amount of data is provided by the journal on each sale, including the invoice number, order number, customer number, and salesman number, all for control and cross-reference purposes. Remember the importance of being able to trace data through the system. In addition, by using data which is input to the accounts receivable application from the sales and purchases system, the cost and profit associated with each invoice is available and can be printed. Notice again the summary information printed.

5.   *Purchases journal* (Figure 13-7). This journal is closely related to the cash disbursements journal because it records all incoming (purchase) invoices as they are received. As these invoices are later paid, they will, of course, appear in the cash disbursements journal. Both recording the invoice and subsequently paying it are accomplished in the accounts payable

DATE 10/25/77

GATEWAY IND.　　NO. 02　　A/R CASH RECEIPT AND ADJUSTMENT TRANSACTION REGISTER　　　　AMR401　　　　PAGE　1

DEPOSIT NUMBER	CUSTOMER NUMBER	CUSTOMER NAME	CHECK/ ADJ NO	ADJUSTMENT AMOUNT	UNAPPLIED CASH/ADJ	A/R AMOUNT	DISCOUNT ALLOWED	AMOUNT RECEIVED	INVOICE NUMBER	SLSM NO	TRANS TYPE
203	101700	PERFECTION PRODUCTS	1677			496.00	9.92	486.08	551		PMT
203	130700	CENTRAL STATES, INC	P-120	966.30-					497		ADJ
203	130700		437113			2,618.50		2,618.50	553		PMT
203	135801	AMERICAN FASTENER	16332			3,876.45	38.50	3,837.95	1005		PMT
203	184100	PEERLESS, INC				36.50		36.50	552		PMT
203	260100	R R FOSTER COMPANY	27361			39.60		39.60	558		PMT
203	260100		27361			1,203.00		1,203.00	627		PMT
203	332000	HAVCO	5783			415.00		415.00	604		PMT
203	400000	WALTON PRODUCTS	3623			100.00		100.00	591		PMT

BATCH TOTALS

TRANSACTION TOTALS　　　　　　　　　COUNT

　　A/R CREDITS　-　　8,785.08-　　8
　　DISCOUNTS　-　　　　48.42
　　CASH RECVD　-　　8,736.63
　　ADJUSTMENT　-　　　966.30　　　1

FIGURE 13-4 Cash Receipts Journal
(courtesy of IBM Corporation)

GATEWAY IND   CO NO 02   CASH DISBURSEMENTS JOURNAL   RUN DATE 7/15/77   ENTRY DATE 7/15/78

JOURNAL REFERENCE	VENDOR NAME	PAY SEL NUMBER	INVOICE NUMBER	PURCHASE JOURNAL	GROSS	DISCOUNT	NET	G/L ACCOUNT	AMOUNT	CHECK NBR
CD01-0001	APENTHAL	14	G256	PJ01-0034	15,137.00	300.00	14,837.00	2000	15,137.00	
CD01-0002			CHECK TOTAL		15,137.00	300.00	14,837.00	1050	14,837.00CR	100
CD01-0003			DISCOUNT TAKEN					8300	300.00CR	
CD01-0004	ARK.INSTR.	5	1983-51	PJ01-0011	4,350.00	87.00	4,263.00	2000	4,350.00	
CD01-0005	ARK.INSTR.	11	1679-43	PJ01-0026	14,250.00	285.00	13,965.00	2000	14,250.00	
CD01-0006	ARK.INSTR.	12	1573-06	PJ01-0028	2,900.00	56.00	2,744.00	2000	2,900.00	
CD01-0007	ARK.INSTR.	18	1679-43	PJ02-0009	78.00-		78.00-	2000	78.00CR	
CD01-0008			CHECK TOTAL		21,322.00	428.00	20,894.00	1050	20,894.00CR	101
CD01-0009			DISCOUNT TAKEN					8300	428.00CR	
CD01-0010	CHRIS CO	4	A736	PJ01-0009	1,110.00	3.25	1,106.75	2000	1,110.00	
CD01-0011			PREPAID CHECK					1050	1,106.75CR	1936
CD01-0012			DISCOUNT TAKEN					8300	3.25CR	
CD01-0013	CHRIS CO	10	A563	PJ01-0024	3,025.00	121.00	2,904.00	2000	3,025.00	
CD01-0014			CHECK TOTAL		3,025.00	121.00	2,904.00	1050	2,904.00CR	102
CD01-0015			DISCOUNT TAKEN					8300	121.00CR	
CD01-0016	HUGHEY	15	V10047	PJ02-0002	157.00		157.00	2000	157.00	
CD01-0017			PREPAID CHECK					1050	157.00CR	21457

```
COMPANY TOTAL:   GROSS AMOUNT        107,550.36

                 PREPAID DISCOUNT          3.25

                 PAYMENT DISCOUNT      2,810.74

                 PREPAID AMOUNT        1,263.75

                 PAYMENT AMOUNT      103,472.62

                 JOURNAL AMOUNT      107,628.36

                 NUMBER OF CHECKS            5

NOTE: MAXIMUM CHECK AMOUNT EXCEEDED
```

FIGURE 13-5 Cash Disbursements Journal
(courtesy of IBM Corporation)

DATE 10/25/77   NO. 02   INVOICE REGISTER   AMR451   PAGE   1
GATEWAY IND.

INV NO.	ORDER NO.	CUSTOMER NUMBER	NAME	SLSMN NUMBER	P.O. NUMBER	INV DATE	SALES AMOUNT	SPECIAL CHARGES	FREIGHT	DISCOUNT	TOTAL TAXES	INVOICE TOTAL	INVOICE COST	INVOICE PROFIT	PROFIT PERCNT
			HARVEY SPECIALTY PRODUCTS												
1031	00274	92000	Z01400	7		10/15/77	262.50	.00	12.00	12.50	10.00	272.00	230.00	32.50	12.3
			DIXIE INDUSTRIES												
1032	00243	106500	PT1090	20		10/15/77	405.00	.00	10.30	.00	.00	415.30	295.60	109.49	27.0
			M C P SALES												
1033	00251	135802	ZI04A	5		10/15/77	266.00	.00	.00	.00	.00	266.00	191.52	74.48	28.0
			**** OVER CREDIT LIMIT **** CUSTOMER- 135802												
			CREATIVE PRODUCTS												
1034	00244	260200	12769	24		10/15/77	1,106.00	.00	.00	.00	.00	1,106.00	1,139.08	33.08-	2.9-
			PULKMFTER PRODUCTS												
1035	00258	270000	90643	2		10/15/77	800.00	.00	.00	.00	.00	800.00	632.00	168.00	21.0
			THE DELP CORPORATION												
1036	00271	322300	200HD	41		10/15/77	181.60	1.15-		5.45	.00	175.00	119.80	61.80	34.0
			SCLEN PRODUCTS												
1037	00254	351100	3142	24		10/15/77	2,060.00	.00	.00	.00	.00	2,060.00	1,689.20	370.80	18.0
			WALTON PRODUCTS												
1038	00256	400000	70268	2		10/15/77	646.00	.00	.00	.00	.00	646.00	503.00	143.00	22.1

FINAL TOTALS
INVOICES

```
SALES       -  5,727.10
SPECIAL     -      1.15-
FREIGHT     -     22.30
DISCOUNT    -     17.95
TAX 1       -     10.00
TAX 2       -       .00
TAX 3       -       .00
TAX 4       -       .00
INVOICES    -  5,740.30
COST        -  4,800.20

GROSS PROFIT  AMOUNT  -    926.90
              PERCENT -     16.1
```

FIGURE 13-6 Sales Journal (Invoice Register)
(courtesy of IBM Corporation)

GATEWAY IND   CO NO 02   PURCHASE JOURNAL   RUN DATE 7/15/77   ENTRY DATE 7/15/77

JOURNAL REF NO.	VEND NO.	ASSIGNEE NUMBER	INVOICE NUMBER	INVOICE DESCRIPTION	G/L DEBIT NO.	G/L DEBIT AMOUNT	G/L CREDIT NO.	G/L CREDIT AMOUNT	DUE DATE	PAY SEL NO.
PJ01-0001	02900		853-16	WINTER PRODUCTS SHOVELS	4100	21,178.00		21,178.00		
PJ01-0002		MAR. TOOLS		* INVOICE TOTAL		21,178.00	2000	21,178.00	9/03/78	1
PJ01-0003	02900		653-728	CLEANING EQUIP BROOMS & PANS	4100	2,247.00				
PJ01-0004				CLEANING SOLUTION	4100	1,267.00		3,514.00		
PJ01-0005		MAR. TOOLS		* INVOICE TOTAL		3,514.00	2000	3,514.00	8/21/78	2
PJ01-0006	02900		5 8-432	MISC TOOLS	4100	5,980.00		5,980.00		
PJ01-0007		MAR. TOOLS		MISC TOOLS * INVOICE TOTAL		5,980.00	2000	5,980.00	9/04/78	3
PJ01-0008	00700		A736	TENNIS BALLS	4100	1,110.00 [** CHECK NO. 1936 1,110.30]		1,110.00		
PJ01-0009		CHRIS CO		TENNIS BALLS * INVOICE TOTAL		1,110.00	2000	1,110.00	8/10/78	4
PJ01-0010	00200		1983-51	TV PARTS	4100	4,350.00		4,350.00		
PJ01-0011		ARK.INSTR.		TV TUBES * INVOICE TOTAL		4,350.00	2000	4,350.00	8/10/78	5
PJ01-0012	02900		82254	CARPENTERS SUPPLIES	4100	5,127.40		5,127.40		
PJ01-0013		MAR. TOOLS		CARPENTERS SUPPLIES * INVOICE TOTAL		5,127.40	2000	5,127.40	6/30/78	6
PJ01-0032	00150		G256	FALL FASHION LINE FREIGHT-IN	4120	137.00				
PJ01-0033				CLOTHING	4100	15,000.00		15,137.00		
PJ01-0034		APENTHAL		* INVOICE TOTAL		15,137.00	2000	15,137.00	6/15/78	14
				** JOURNAL TOTAL		112,933.66		112,933.66		

NUMBER OF INVOICES   14

CONTROL TOTALS: OPEN PAYABLES   111,823.66
                  PREPAID INVOICES   1,110.00
                  CONTROL   112,933.66

FIGURE 13-7 Purchases Journal
(courtesy of IBM Corporation)

application of the cash receipts and disbursements system. This information is then passed as input to the financial accounting and control system for generation of these journals. Notice that incoming purchase invoices are numbered, but not necessarily sequentially or even on the same number scheme. These invoices come from the suppliers of goods and each of these other firms will maintain its own invoice numbering system. A purchaser of goods has no control over the numbering of invoices he receives. The due date of each invoice (an important piece of information) and a payment selection order based on criteria established by the user can be printed by the system. Finally, the journal is designed so that prepaid invoices or cash purchases can be recorded in the purchases journal. The result is that all purchases invoices are listed in one place, just as all sales invoices were listed in the sales journal. Note the special summary listing for these items, along with the other control totals.

Period-End Reports

Once the transactions of a period (one month in the case of these sample documents) have been recorded and the journals printed, the next major output from the financial accounting and control system is a series of period-end reports beginning with a trial balance of the general ledger accounts and ending with formal financial statements. It is important to understand that this trial balance is the adjusted trial balance we discussed as Step 5 of the accounting cycle in Part One. All adjusting entries are entered as direct input to the general ledger application before any of these journals are produced and appear as part of the general journal. This is consistent with the adjusting entries in a manual system, except that in computer-based systems all journals are produced (printed) at once as they are required. In a manual system the journals are constantly available, while in a computer system journal information is stored but the journals themselves are not automatically produced.

Figures 13-8 through 13-11 depict the end-of-period output reports which should be generated by the financial accounting and control system. A quick reference to Figure 13-2 for the "big picture" of the system will help you reestablish the information flow in the system and the place of these documents in that flow. Remember also that, although the form of these reports might be slightly different from those of a manual accounting system, the basic concepts and ideas are exactly the same.

Keep in mind the following important characteristics about each of these computer-based reports:

1. *General ledger trial balance* (Figure 13-8). This statement is considerably more comprehensive than a manual system trial balance in that it shows for each general ledger account (1) the balance at the beginning of the period; (2) the individual debits and credits during the period; (3) the total of debits and credits for the period; (4) the net change for the period; and (5) the balance at the end of the period. Remember that a manual accounting system trial balance shows only the balance in each account at the date of the statement. Producing this comprehensive trial balance requires the transaction information contained in the journals plus input from a permanent file of data on the balances of each general ledger account from the previous period. Listing all of this information in an output report makes possible extensive cross-checking of transactions for completeness and correctness before the permanent general ledger master file is updated for the period.

GATEWAY IND   CO NO 02   **** GENERAL LEDGER TRIAL BALANCE ****   DATE 7/15/77
PERIOD 07

G/L ACCOUNT	GENERAL LEDGER ACCOUNT DESCRIPTION	TRANSACTION SOURCE	TRANSACTION DESCRIPTION	JOURNAL REFERENCE NUMBER	DEBIT AMOUNT	CREDIT AMOUNT	NET CHANGE
104100	PURCHASES		* PREVIOUS BALANCE		228,123.00		
		1 MO TRANS		GJ06-0002	21,497.84	20,497.84	
		1 MO TRANS		GJ06-0004			
		1 MO TRANS		GJ06-0005	20,497.84		
		JE07-17	A/P EXPENSE ADJ	GJ07-0020		422.59	
			* PERIOD TOTAL		41,995.68	20,920.43	21,075.25
			** ACCT BALANCE		270,118.68	20,920.43	249,198.25
104110	PURCHASE DISCOUNTS	1 MO TRANS		GJ06-0003		197.42	
			* PERIOD TOTAL			197.42	197.42CR
			** ACCT BALANCE			197.42	197.42CR
104120	FREIGHT IN		* PREVIOUS BALANCE		5,823.00		
		1 MO TRANS		GJ06-0006	849.84		
		JE07-17	A/P EXPENSE ADJ	GJ07-0020	86.04		
			* PERIOD TOTAL		935.88		935.88
			** ACCT BALANCE		6,758.88		6,758.88
104130	INVENTORY CHANGE		* PREVIOUS BALANCE		215,941.00		
		1 MO TRANS		GJ06-0007	17,842.79		
		JE07-17	A/P EXPENSE ADJ	GJ07-021	336.55		
			* PERIOD TOTAL		18,179.34		18,179.34
			** ACCT BALANCE		234,120.34		234,120.34

FINAL PERIOD TOTAL   157,485.41   157,485.41
*** COMPANY TOTAL   4,641,821.41   4,641,821.41

FIGURE 13-8 General Ledger Trial Balance
(courtesy of IBM Corporation)

2. *General ledger listing* (Figure 13-9). If the general ledger trial balance proves to be complete and correct, the general ledger listing can be printed and the general ledger master file updated. This listing is an important report for managerial planning and control purposes because of the detailed comparisons made possible by the format of the statement. The report allows the user to (1) compare the actual results for the reporting period (one month here) to the budgeted (expected) results for the period *and* to the actual results for the same period of the previous year; and (2) make the same comparisons for actual year-to-date results. These comparisons allow departures from planned results and/or past results to be evaluated by management and actions taken to correct these deviations. Also, future plans and budgets may be altered based on the results of current activities.

3. *Financial statements* (Figures 13-10 and 13-11). The income statement and balance sheet are traditional in format and content. Both statements, however, contain much information relevant for managerial decision making, planning, and control not often found in financial statements from a manual accounting system. This information is particularly important in interim statements (monthly or quarterly) because immediate feedback to management on the results of operations and activities can be used to spot and correct negative deviations before it is too late. The most important of these "extra" features are:

   a. The income statement and the balance sheet present the current period results of operations and financial position, as well as those of the previous period in both absolute and (for the income statement) percentage terms. Importantly, the variance between periods on each statement item is produced by the system in percentage terms also.

   b. A complete income statement with all of the features described above can be produced for each "profit center" (department, store, product line) which helps trace operating results to those responsible for decisions and actions.

   c. Both statements can be presented in any format and detail specified by the user. A financial accounting and control system should offer flexibility so that the income statement and balance sheet can be tailored to the information needs and particular circumstances of the user.

These are the primary man-sensible reports which should be produced by a financial accounting and control system. You can see that there is no mystery at work here. The output a user should expect from a computer-based accounting system is fundamentally no different from that needed from a manual accounting system. The difference in these reports can be traced to the additional information available and basically improved control procedures which are the result of those computer advantages of speed, memory, and ability to follow instructions. Now we will examine the data organization and input necessary for a financial accounting and control system to function.

GATEWAY IND   CO NO 02   **** GENERAL LEDGER LISTING ****   DATE 7/15/77
PERIOD 07

G/L ACCOUNT	ACCOUNT DESCRIPTION	BUDGETED PERIOD	SAME PERIOD LAST YEAR	CURRENT PERIOD	BUDGETED Y-T-D	PREVIOUS Y-T-D	CURRENT Y-T-D
2250	UNION DUES WITHHELD		9,233.00CR			9,233.00CR	840.00CR
2255	INS. PREMIUM WITHHELD						3,040.00CR
2260	UNITED FUND WITHHELD						8,000.00CR
2270	SAVINGS BONDS WITHHELD						
2280	GARNISHMENT WITHHELD						3,150.00CR
2290	CREDIT UNION WITHHELD						1,570.00CR
2300	FED. INCOME TAXES PAYABLE		46,090.00CR			46,090.00CR	144,000.00CR
2320	STATE INC. TAXES PAYABLE						30,500.00CR
2500	NOTES PAYABLE - BANKS		222,500.00CR	4,962.29CR		222,500.00CR	284,402.28CR
2510	NOTES PAYABLE - OTHER						15,280.00CR
2550	BONDS PAYABLE		6,000.00CR			6,000.00CR	150,000.00CR
2600	DEFERRED TAX PAYABLE		3,000.00CR			3,000.00CR	3,000.00CR
2700	OTHER LONG TERM LIABILITY		39,000.00CR			39,000.00CR	4,000.00CR
3000	COMMON STOCK		275,000.00CR			275,000.00CR	400,000.00CR
3020	PREFERRED STOCK						150,000.00CR
3040	ADDIT. PAID IN CAPITAL		175,000.00CR			175,000.00CR	350,000.00CR
3100	TREASURY STOCK		50,000.00CR			50,000.00CR	100,000.00CR
3200	RETAINED EARNINGS		100,182.00CR			100,132.00CR	118,020.00CR
104000	SALES - OPERATIONS	83,333.33CR	77,476.37CR	102,908.28CR	1,082,331.33CR	1,007,192.83CR	1,077,903.28CR
104050	SALES RETURNS AND ALLOW.				20,400.00		21,640.00
104100	PURCHASES	20,833.33	18,538.80	21,075.25	270,833.33	241,004.34	249,198.25
104110	PURCHASE DISCOUNTS	2,083.33CR	115.59CR	197.42CR	983.33CR	1,502.70CR	197.42CR
104120	FREIGHT IN	666.67	437.89	935.83	8,666.67	5,692.46	6,758.88
104130	INVENTORY CHANGE	16,666.67	17,548.81	18,179.34	216,666.67	228,134.47	234,120.34
104140	ACCOUNTS PAYABLE CHANGE					117,457.28	
105000	SALARIES - SALES	12,000.00	9,035.18	11,875.00	152,000.00		11,875.00
	*** COMPANY TOTAL	35,807.68	536,170.47CR	.00	341,527.68	601,900.10CR	.00

FIGURE 13-9 General Ledger Listing
(courtesy of IBM Corporation)

```
                    G A T E W A Y   I N D .   C O   N O   0 2
                             NEW YORK, N.Y.
                         STATEMENT OF INCOME
                 FOR YEAR-TO-DATE ENDING JULY 31,1977          PREPARED   7/15/77

                                  ------C U R R E N T------    %      ------L A S T   Y E A R------    %      VAR-%
```

	CURRENT	%	LAST YEAR	%	VAR-%
DEPARTMENT 01					
SALES	1,056,265.28	100.00	1,007,192.83	100.00	.05
COST OF GOODS SOLD -----					
PURCHASES	249,198.25	23.59	241,004.34	23.92	.03
PURCHASE DISCOUNTS	197.42	.01	1,502.70	.14	.87-
FREIGHT IN	6,758.83	.63	5,692.46	.56	.19
INVENTORY CHANGE	234,120.34	22.16	228,134.47	22.65	.03
ACCOUNTS PAYABLE CHANGE					
***** TOTAL COST OF GOODS SOLD -----	489,880.05	46.37	473,329.57	46.99	.03
***** GROSS PROFIT/LOSS FROM SALES *****	566,388.23	53.62	533,863.26	53.00	.06
SELLING EXPENSES -----					
SALARIES AND COMMISSIONS	144,250.00	13.65	117,457.28	11.66	.23
BENEFITS	842.00	.07			100.00
ADVERTISING	1,248.00	.11	16,650.83	1.65	.93-
TOTAL SELLING EXPENSES -----	146,340.00	13.85	134,108.11	13.31	.09
***** NET PROFIT FROM SALES *****	420,048.23	39.76	399,756.15	39.69	.05
GENERAL AND ADMINISTRATIVE -----					
SALARIES	138,250.87	13.08	134,349.26	13.33	.03
BENEFITS	9,094.77	.86	8,749.65	.86	.04
OUTSIDE SERVICE EXPENSE	144,752.59	13.70	142,231.05	14.12	.02
MATERIALS AND SUPPLIES	31,798.87	3.01	30,950.24	3.07	.03
DEPRECIATION AND AMORTIZATION	13,006.00	1.23	4,494.21	.44	1.89
RENTS AND UTILITIES	6,427.00	.60	6,156.03	.61	.04
INTEREST					
TAXES	3,025.00	.28	2,297.82	.22	.32
OTHER	200.00	.01	961.16	.09	.79-
TOTAL GEN. AND ADM. EXPENSE -----	346,543.30	32.80	330,189.42	32.78	.05
***** NET PROFIT/LOSS FROM OPERATIONS *****	73,504.93	6.95	69,566.73	6.90	.06
NON-OPERATING INCOME & EXPENSE -----					
MISCELLANEOUS INCOME	6,579.00DR	.62	2,616.25	.25	3.51-
MISCELLANEOUS EXPENSE	5,456.41CR	.51	2,193.25	.21	3.49-
GAIN ON DISPOSITION OF FIXED ASSETS					
TOTAL OTHER INCOME -----	1,122.59DR	.10	423.00	.04	3.65-
***** NET PROFIT/LOSS BEFORE TAXES *****	72,382.34	6.85	69,989.73	6.94	.03
INCOME TAXES -----					
***** NET PROFIT AFTER TAXES *****	26,762.00	2.53	32,354.66	3.21	.17-
	45,620.34	4.31	37,635.07	3.73	.21
PROVISION FOR PROFIT OR LOSS -----					
** DEPARTMENT 01 NET PROFIT AND LOSS **	45,620.34	4.31	37,635.07	3.73	.21

FIGURE 13-10 Income Statement
(courtesy of IBM Corporation)

```
G A T E W A Y   I N D.   C O   N O   0 2
              N E W   Y O R K,   N. Y.
              B A L A N C E   S H E E T
              A T   J U L Y   31, 1977                    PREPARED  7/15/77
```

ASSETS	-----CURRENT-----	-----LAST YEAR-----	VAR-%
CURRENT ASSETS -----			
CASH	117,624.30	76,445.00	.54
ACCOUNTS RECEIVABLE			
SHORT TERM INVESTMENTS	170,000.00	70,000.00	1.43
ACCOUNTS RECEIVABLE – CURRENT	733,280.34	165,174.00	3.44
NOTES RECEIVABLE	1,000.00	395.00	1.53
LESS – ALLOWANCE FOR DOUBTFUL ACCTS	5,650.00	2,610.00	1.16
ACCOUNTS RECEIVABLE	898,630.34	232,959.00	2.86
INVENTORY	822,337.98	159,894.00	4.14
PREPAID EXPENSES			
INSURANCE	5,000.00	1,332.00	2.75
TAXES AND LICENSES	1,750.00	465.00	2.76
RENT	1,880.00	452.00	3.16
SUPPLIES		200.00	1.00–
TRAVEL ADVANCES	2,000.00	800.00	1.50
OTHER			
PREPAID EXPENSES	10,630.00	3,249.00	2.27
TOTAL CURRENT ASSETS -----	1,849,222.62	472,547.00	2.91
FIXED ASSETS -----			
LAND AND BUILDINGS	189,006.00	82,000.00	1.30
EQUIPMENT	321,710.00	46,700.00	5.89
LESS – DEPRECIATION	181,425.00	44,062.00	3.12
TOTAL FIXED ASSETS -----	329,291.00	84,638.00	2.89
INVESTMENTS -----			
SUBSIDIARIES	160,000.00	80,000.00	1.00
LONG TERM INVESTMENTS	8,100.00	4,730.47	.71
CASH VALUE OF LIFE INSURANCE			
TOTAL INVESTMENTS -----	168,100.00	84,730.47	.98
OTHER ASSETS -----			
DEPOSITS			1.00–
MISCELLANEOUS	1,450.00CR	500.00	100.00–
TOTAL OTHER ASSETS -----	1,450.00CR	500.00	3.90–
***** TOTAL ASSETS *****	2,345,163.62	642,415.47	2.65

FIGURE 13-11 Partial Balance Sheet
(courtesy of IBM Corporation)

13.4 DATA ORGANIZATION AND INPUT

To generate the output reports discussed and illustrated in the previous section, the financial accounting and control system must have access to certain input data, and this data must be organized so that processing can be done efficiently. Of concern here is the kind and source of data input necessary and how this input is transmitted to the system.

Permanent and Transaction Data Files

Basically, the input to any system can be thought of as falling into three categories:

1. Relatively permanent data which is used over and over as input to processing applications, but is not altered by the processing and is infrequently changed externally. This data may consist of constants, such as tax rates and limits, exemption amounts, deduction percentages, and so on, or headings and titles to be used in output reports (financial statements, for example). Many business processing applications use one or more of these types of input organized into permanent files. These kinds of data are usually organized into *Constant or Report Files.*

2. Semipermanent data of a cumulative nature which is input, then processed and changed by the processing (this is usually called updating), and finally becomes output to be updated again in later processing. An example of this kind of input data in a financial accounting and control system is balances in general ledger accounts. This data is kept in a file and at the end of each period the balances are updated for all of the transactions (debits and credits) which occurred during the period. The ending balances in each account would then be stored and become input to the next period's processing. All business processing applications require at least one file of this kind of data. Files of this kind are called *Master Files.*

3. Current data pertaining to activity of the present period which must be processed and then may or may not be stored. This current data represents the basis for the updating of cumulative files. An example, consistent with the master cumulative file discussed in (2) above, is the accounting transactions which take place during an accounting period whose effect must ultimately be reflected in general ledger balances. All business processing involves this kind of data input because without current activity there would be no processing. Files of current activity data are called *Transaction Files.*

Now let us consider all of the input data necessary to a financial accounting and control system, and then organize that data into the above types of input files. The number of files required and the content and design of each of the files will vary according to the basic orientation and hardware configuration of the system, the sophistication of the processing, the kinds of output reports desired or needed, the size of the business, and the preferences of the user. Most importantly, however, file design should depend on the other processing applications to be implemented and the interaction between these applications. A business' data base is its collection of stored data. Good data base management techniques require that this collection of stored data be organized so that all processing applications which require the same basic data input (although perhaps in slightly different form) can access and use the same files of input data.

The financial accounting and control system we have been discussing in this chapter would likely require several files of data input in order to be functional. We have suggested a data organization which we feel would be effective for this sort of processing. Following are the major files necessary for the general ledger application:

1. General ledger master file. This file would contain one record for each general ledger account in the chart of accounts used by the company. Each record would consist of at least the following data elements:

    a. Account number.

    b. Account description.

    c. Account classification (asset, liability, owner's equity, revenue, or expense).

    d. Current year balances—by month.

    e. Previous year balances—by month.

    f. Budgeted balances—by month.

    This file is updated with each processing, then stored, and used again as input. It is, therefore, both an input and an output file and is the basis for the end-of-period output reports and statements discussed earlier.

2. Current month transaction file. This file would consist of one record for each detailed and verified accounting transaction which occurred during the current month. Input data from this file would be used to update the general ledger master file and would also be added to the permanent transaction file discussed below. The current transaction file is an input file only and is the basis for the journals discussed earlier.

3. Permanent transaction file. This is a transaction file also; however, it represents a cumulative listing of all the monthly transaction files. This file, unlike the current transaction file, is retained and contains all the detailed and verified accounting transactions for the year. This is a critical input and output file for both legal and audit trail purposes. The file is input to each processing, added to, and then stored for the next processing period. It is the "book of original entry" or the chronological history of the business which supports all reports, and to which all information in the system should be traceable. It is also important backup to other financial accounting and control system files.

Remember also that summarized transaction files from the accounts receivable, accounts payable, and payroll processing applications are passed on to the financial accounting and control system and added to the current month's transaction file so that the general ledger master file and the permanent transaction file can be updated for the data processed by these applications.

In a sequential, batch-oriented hardware system the general ledger master file and permanent transaction file would likely be stored on magnetic tape and the current transaction file would probably be input on punched cards. A direct access, interactive design would use disks for the permanent files and would probably use an on-line terminal device to input current transactions. Figure 13-12 is an illustration of the visual screen of a terminal with a typical accounting journal entry as it would appear in an interactive system upon being entered by an

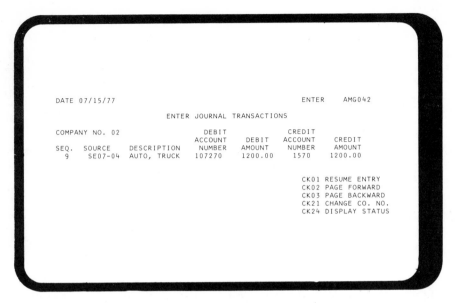

```
   DATE 07/15/77                                           ENTER     AMG042

                             ENTER JOURNAL TRANSACTIONS

   COMPANY NO. 02                    DEBIT            CREDIT
                                    ACCOUNT   DEBIT   ACCOUNT   CREDIT
   SEQ.  SOURCE    DESCRIPTION       NUMBER   AMOUNT  NUMBER    AMOUNT
     9   SE07-04  AUTO, TRUCK       107270   1200.00   1570    1200.00


                                                 CK01 RESUME ENTRY
                                                 CK02 PAGE FORWARD
                                                 CK03 PAGE BACKWARD
                                                 CK21 CHANGE CO. NO.
                                                 CK24 DISPLAY STATUS
```

FIGURE 13-12 Display of Accounting Journal Entry Input
(courtesy of IBM Corporation)

operator. Of course, the output documents discussed earlier would all be generated by the system printer or printing teletype.

An important final feature of all computer-based files is that all stored data may be accessed and processed or printed selectively at will. Quite unlike manually maintained data files, computers give a user ability to immediately access important segments of data, as well as group that data by various criteria, which may be useful for decision making, planning, or control. For example, all transactions affecting cash for a given period could be pulled from the permanent transaction file and printed in report form with little difficulty. This information would be very difficult and time consuming to retrieve from a manual system.

Techniques of Permanent Data Input

There is one other point we would like to discuss briefly before closing this chapter. As you examined the financial statement examples produced by the financial accounting and control system presented earlier in this chapter, you probably wondered how the system could get the computer to produce those elaborate headings, titles, subtotals, and totals. There are really two basic approaches to accomplishing this sort of elaborate title and formatted printing. The simplest approach to getting the output report form and content a user may desire is to maintain a different computer program for each report to be printed, and to make headings, titles, subtotal and total format a part of the program. This approach does, however, require that the program be changed if a different report format is desired. Given that program debugging is often a major step in system design and implementation, this approach has some significant potential problems. The other basic approach to report printing is considerably more sophisticated and difficult to understand, but does make it possible to change the form and content of reports almost at will without the necessity for altering the computer programs of a system. This approach also makes possible the printing of any number of statements using only one program. It involves the creation of a permanent input file which specifies the headings, titles, subtotal, and total format for each output report. Such a file is often called a *report format file* or a *report generator file* and can be quite complex to conceive and generate. In the first approach, financial statement format is a part of the program which generates the statement; in the second, format is a part of the input data on which the program operates. We have assumed in the data organization and file specification presented earlier in this chapter that the first and simplest approach to printing output reports has been used. The same assumption will be made in the two chapters to follow as we explore cash receipts and disbursements systems and sales and purchases systems.

exercises

The following three questions pertain to the information flow concepts presented in Figure 13-1.

13-1 A firm's total information system can be broken down into three component subsystems, each of which is represented in Figure 13-1 by a large curved shape. Think for a moment about the kinds of activity each of these subsystems would handle. Give three examples of major types of activity processed by each subsystem.

13-2 Each component subsystem can then be broken down into three application areas.

1. For each of the following application areas, give two specific examples of the activity processed by them:

    a. Order processing.

    b. Inventory control.

    c. Sales analysis.

    d. Accounts receivable.

    e. Accounts payable.

    f. Payroll.

    g. General ledger.

2. What are the purposes of the financial statement and budgeting application areas?

13-3 In any information system, there must be information flow between application areas. For each of the arrows depicted in Figure 13-1, give a specific example of the information exchanged between these application packages.

13-4 The basic steps a business goes through to process data in a manual accounting system is called the accounting cycle. As presented in Chapter 1, the accounting cycle has seven steps. Are these seven steps accomplished in the computer-based financial accounting and control system depicted in Figure 13-2? Is the order of the steps the same? If not, explain why.

13-5 For each of the data-items stored in the general ledger master file, explain why such information is important in a computer-based system. Also, for each data-item, give the output report(s) in which the information is used. Which of these data-items would normally be updated with each processing run?

13-6 Some accounting events are not processed by either the cash receipts and disbursements or sales and purchases component subsystems. These events enter the information system directly through the general ledger application of the financial accounting and control system. Give eight specific examples of events which enter the system this way.

13-7 For each of the following six fundamental accounting transactions, state in which special journal the transaction would appear in a manual accounting system and in a computer-based financial accounting and control system.

a. Cash sale.

b. Collection of account receivable.

c. Cash received from financing activity.

d. Cash purchase of inventory.

e. Payment of account payable.

f. Payment for a truck.

g. Prepaid purchase invoice.

If any of the above transactions would appear in a different special journal in a computer-based system than in a manual system, explain why.

13-8 At the bottom of the cash receipts journal (Figure 13-4) and the cash disbursements journal (Figure 13-5), there are totals which summarize the effects of all the transactions listed in the report. For each total, explain its significance and where it might be used.

13-9 At the bottom of the sales journal (Figure 13-6) and the purchases journal (Figure 13-7), there are totals which summarize the effects of all the transactions listed in the report. For each total, explain its significance and where it might be used.

13-10 The general ledger trial balance and the general ledger listing are both organized by general ledger account number and present basically the same information. There are, however, some significant differences in the information content of these reports:

1. What information is contained in the general ledger trial balance that is not available in the general ledger listing? Why is this information useful?

2. What information is contained in the general ledger listing that is not available in the general ledger trial balance? Why is this information useful?

cash receipts and disbursements systems

INTRODUCTION

Although the financial account and control system is the most fundamental (and probably most complex) of business processing systems, it is not the only such system. We discovered in Chapter 13 that the financial accounting and control system must interact with other business processing systems. If you refer back to Figure 13-1, which is the "big picture" of computer-based information systems, you will see that important information flow takes place between the general ledger and the cash receipts and disbursements system. In fact, this flow is essentially one-way from the processing applications of the cash receipts and disbursements system to the general ledger application of the financial accounting and control system. This chapter is concerned with the functioning of the cash receipts and disbursements system, the specific applications which make it up, and the information flow between it and other systems.

14.1 INFORMATION FLOW THROUGH THE SYSTEM

The processing applications of this system are probably the most well-known computer-based packages. They are usually the first processing applications to be computerized because they are relatively easy to convert and represent highly visible and active areas in most businesses. Figure 14-1 illustrates the information flow between a cash receipts and disbursements system and other systems. In this figure we are focusing in on the middle curved shape of the total information flow depicted in Figure 14-1.

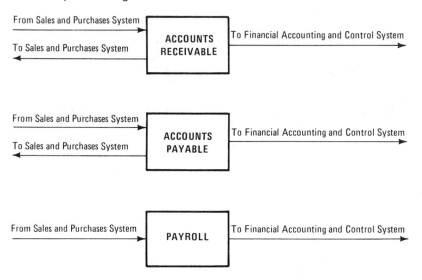

FIGURE 14-1 Information Flow in a Cash Receipts and Disbursements System

Notice the large amount of information flow to and from this central system. The cash receipts and disbursements system stands between (in an information flow sense) the other two major processing systems. The accounts receivable and accounts payable applications receive input from the sales and purchases system and provide output to that system. Since accounts receivable are usually a factor in both sales and cash receipts, and accounts payable a factor in purchases and cash disbursements, this interaction is not surprising. In addition, the receivables and payables applications produce essential output information on these transactions for inclusion in the general ledger by the financial accounting and control system. The payroll application is interesting because it represents the closest thing to a stand-alone application available in computer-based systems. Payroll applications can and sometimes do exist as the sole computerized area of business activities since no input from other systems may be necessary for the package to work. However, as sales or other activity-related variables become important factors in the determination of salaries and wages, data from the sales and purchases system may become either very desirable or absolutely necessary input to the payroll package. The most common example of this kind of situation is a company with a large sales payroll where sales pay is based primarily on commissions. Here, input from a sales analysis package would be essential to a payroll application since, at the very least, a breakdown of sales by salesman is needed for the payroll calculation. At any rate, payroll processing does generate output information to be included in the general ledger. The cash receipts and disbursements system, then, is very active in terms of information interchange with other systems. In the remaining sections of this chapter we will examine how each of the processing packages of this system work, the output to be generated, and the data organization and input required for each.

14.2 ACCOUNTS RECEIVABLE COMPONENT

Often the most important variable in the success of a business is cash flows. Control of cash flows is absolutely essential to the short- and long-term stability of any business. The most important sources of operating cash inflows are sales and collections of receivables. The accounts receivable application is designed to monitor these cash inflows and provide information which will, to the extent possible, reduce the amount of cash tied up in receivables. Basically, we would like this processing package to provide information on (1) who owes us money, (2) how much, (3) for how long, and (4) past receivables collection experience. The focus of the accounts receivable application is on cash inflows from operations and the idea is to process receivables so that attention can be directed where it will do the most good in terms of controlling and accelerating these inflows. Figure 14-2 summarizes the information flow into and from an accounts receivable processing application. Because receivables necessarily interface with so many other applications, the information flow is rather heavy. In the rest of this section we will examine these flows in detail. Careful study of this figure will help you understand the discussion to follow.

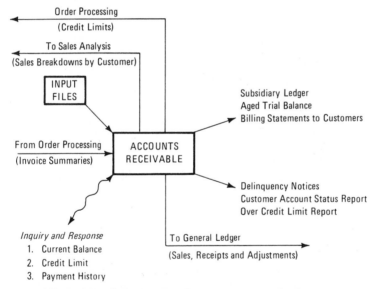

FIGURE 14-2 Information Flow in an Accounts Receivable Application

Output Reports

Let us start with the output which should be generated by this package. Although the number and content of man-sensible output reports from a computer-based receivables application can vary to meet a company's particular information needs, the six printed reports outlined in Figure 14-2 are probably typical. The frequency of these reports could also vary, but monthly would not be unusual.

1. *Subsidiary ledger* (Figure 14-3). Recall the relationship between the general ledger account for receivables and subsidiary ledgers from our manual system discussion in Part One. We know that the general ledger account is called a control account because it gives only the total amount owed by all customers at a specific point. In a computer-based system this account is produced by the financial accounting and control system with other general ledger accounts. The total amount owed by all customers is sufficient for external financial reporting, but is woefully inadequate for actually monitoring the collection of these amounts. The detailed information necessary to do this monitoring and collection is contained in the subsidiary ledger accounts for each customer. The data for this ledger is produced by the accounts receivable application where the individual transactions are actually processed and control over accounts is exercised. This computerized subsidiary ledger is exactly the same in concept and use as those presented in Part One, only the form is different. Individual transactions are listed (sales, returns, customer payments) and totaled to show the amount owed by each customer. Note that the third to last transaction for International Widgit, Inc. is a credit memo resulting in a reduction of the amount owed.

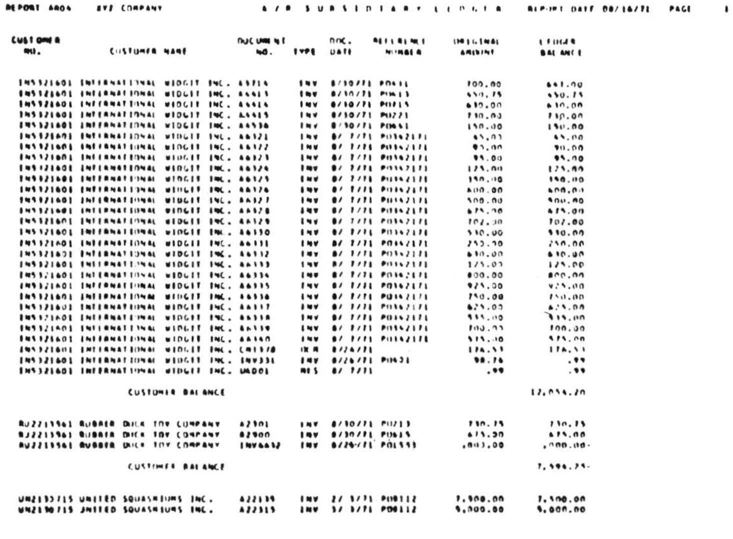

FIGURE 14-3 Accounts Receivable Subsidiary Ledger
(courtesy of McCormack & Dodge Corporation)

2. *Aged trial balance* (Figure 14-4). Prior to producing billing statements for customers, an aged trial balance is printed for management analysis and audit purposes. This output report provides a complete listing of amounts owed by each customer for each invoice outstanding and in total as of the statement date. Also, each amount is classified by the length of time outstanding so that payment patterns and overdue and delinquent accounts are immediately apparent. Summaries at the bottom of the statement show the total amount due from customers and break down this total into amounts due in each of the aged categories chosen by the user. Also, the percentage of total accounts receivable each of these aged categories represent is shown. The statement could also easily summarize the

GATEWAY IND. NO. 02   AGED TRIAL BALANCE REPORT   DATE 10/31/77   PAGE 1   AMR821

CUSTOMERS WITH A MINIMUM BALANCE OF   2,000.00

Account	Customer	TOTAL DUE	CURRENT	OVER 30	OVER 60	OVER 90	OVER 120
00013300	AMSTAN PRODUCTS	2,864.95	656.65	1,863.30	345.00		
00050500	TIOGA INDUSTRIES	3,493.69		2,167.13	1,273.80	52.76	
00092000	HARVEY SPECIALTY PRODUCTS	4,108.98	1,117.20	268.73	68.75	2,654.30	
00101700	PERFECTION PRODUCTS	2,193.60	496.00	1,697.60			
00106530	DIXIE INDUSTRIES	4,540.46	600.30	2,173.90	1,415.00	351.26	
00130700	CENTRAL STATES, INC	5,198.75	1,412.80	3,785.95			
00135801	AMERICAN FASTENER	8,386.80	1,274.00	5,112.80	2,000.00		
00135802	M AND P SALES	3,741.56	597.00	895.76	1,833.60	415.20	
00172000	SELLER ENGINEERING	2,293.40			2,175.30	118.10	
00184100	PEERLESS, INC.	18,311.57	1,283.77	15,156.70	1,871.10		
00185200	DUHOFF AND SONS	5,995.10	2,430.00		1,533.80	1,215.45	815.85
00220100	DECTRON AUTOMATIC PRODUCTS	2,969.58	881.50	1,268.78	819.30		
00225400	YOUNG SUPPLY COMPANY	19,050.72	7,700.50	5,866.15	3,618.00	1,866.07	
00235500	FARMERS UNION CENTRAL	6,053.50	1,776.00	3,066.00	596.30	615.20	
00260200	CREATIVE PRODUCTS	3,720.60	3,687.00	33.60			
00270000	DULKMETER PRODUCTS	6,904.75	2,676.00	2,215.90	2,012.85		
00311100	ASTRO INDUSTRIES	2,603.20	613.00	1,315.00	639.80	35.40	
00320700	BROMFIELD BROTHERS	4,829.85	1,017.00	1,790.00	2,017.60	5.25	
00322300	THE DELP CORPORATION	9,780.59	3,308.15	3,071.44	1,966.00	1,435.00	
00351100	SCALLAN PRODUCTS	10,092.95	2,060.00	6,837.00	875.60	320.35	
00355100	D.F. VITOIK COMPANY	2,723.05	907.35	763.30	936.60	115.80	
00361200	WILLIAMSON ENERGY	3,268.83		2,631.90	418.00		218.93
00400000	WALTON PRODUCTS	4,571.01		1,003.76	2,618.00	430.75	518.50

PREV BAL	CURR CHGS	CURR PMTS	CURR ADJS	TOTAL DUE
120,531.17	39,408.67	21,276.05	966.30-	137,697.49

CURR AMOUNT	OVER 30	OVER 60	OVER 90	OVER 120
34,494.22	62,984.70	29,034.40	9,630.89	1,553.28

FIGURE 14-4 Aged Accounts Receivable Report
(courtesy of IBM Corporation)

total charges to accounts receivable, total customer payments, and total returns and adjust-ments for the current period, which is the only information needed by the general ledger. A report of this form and content is a critically important control tool and leaves a trail which allows a sales invoice to be followed completely through the accounting system as well as allowing management to closely monitor patterns of cash inflows.

3. *Billing statements* (Figures 14-5 and 14-6). This ought to be a very familiar output docu-ment to anyone with a charge account. Almost all credit customers (certainly all at the retail level) now expect to be billed monthly for amounts owed. The billing statement is an important part of the control of cash inflows because it reminds customers of the amounts owed and usually triggers payment. The statement must, of course, be accurate if goodwill and customer confidence is to be maintained. Most computer-based systems are capable of producing billing statements as frequently as desired, or even on demand, something that is simply not practical with a manual system. Of course, the more often customers are billed the greater the likelihood that cash inflows will be accelerated. Figure 14-5 is a typical billing statement and Figure 14-6 is a variation on the same idea with a slightly more personal touch. Note that in both cases the system can automatically calculate periodic finance charges on past-due amounts and add them to the billing statement.

These three documents represent the most important on-going printed output which must be generated by an accounts receivable application. Each of these computer-based system reports provides information with an accuracy and timeliness not possible from a manual system. In addition to these scheduled and recurring reports, a typical computerized receivables package can produce several special statements on-demand as the need arises. Probably the most called for of these special reports are the three listed in Figure 14-2. As accounts become seriously overdue, a business may decide to send special letters to customers emphasizing the satus of the account. Such letters can be automatically generated by the computer as specific cut-off points of delinquency are reached. Similarly, the system can be called upon to produce special detailed statements on the status and history of any particular account or set of ac-counts, or credit reports that provide information on all accounts whose balances exceed the authorized credit limit. As you might imagine these latter two statements have internal control and decision-making significance to management. This ability to use data available in the system in many different ways for different purposes is one of the major advantages of computer-based information systems over manual accounting systems.

Information Exchange

The required output of an accounts receivable application is not limited to printed reports for human consumption. The system also produces information which can be used as input for other processing applications. In fact, the information that results from the transactions processed by the receivables package is often essential to the functioning of other systems. In the financial accounting and control system discussed in Chapter 13 one of the important inputs to the general ledger comes from the sales and cash receipt transactions of the receivables package. This information may be passed from the accounts receivable application to the general ledger application in the form of a file of transactions completed and processed or as a

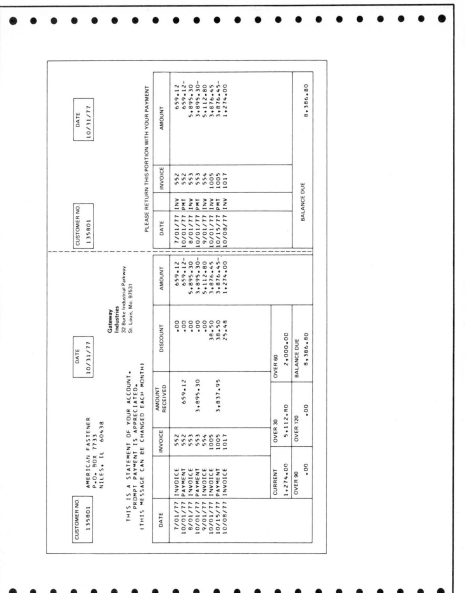

FIGURE 14-5 Customer Billing Statement
(courtesy of IBM Corporation)

```
                    PIERSOL ENTERPRISES


        DECEMBER 6,1973

        SOLD TO:                          SHIP TO:
        GARLOW'S GARAGE                   GARLOW'S GARAGE
        719 16TH ST. SW #3                719 16TH ST. SW #3
        ARAPAHOE HEIGHTS, CO 80001        ARAPAHOE HEIGHTS, CO 80001


        Dear Sir:

             Per the attached documents, please remit the following:

        Your Purchase Order Number:    357
        Invoice Number:        7002


        Price of Goods    $      12.53
        Freight                  0.00
        Service                  6.25
                                -------
        City Tax                 0.38
        State Tax                0.38
                                -------
        Total             $     19.54


        Terms: Net 30 days from date Of statement.

        Finance charge:    1.00% per month(   12.00% annual) will be added to
                           all past due accounts.


                                   Very truly yours,



                                   K.P.PIERSOL
                                   CONTROLLER
```

FIGURE 14-6 Customer Billing Statement
(courtesy of Hewlett-Packard)

series of summary totals of the events already recorded in detail and ready to be incorporated into the external reports of the business.

In addition, interaction takes place between receivables and the sales analysis and order processing packages of the sales and purchases system. Accounts receivable provides information on customer sales breakdowns to the sales analysis package and important credit limit and history information to the order processing application. Order processing, in turn, passes summary information on all sales orders processed by that application to accounts receivable. Hence, the flow is constantly two-way, with each producing information that is used by the other. Notice, however, that much of the flow represents information but not accounting transactions. This flow of nontransaction information separates information systems from accounting systems.

Before we turn our attention to the data organization and system input required for accounts receivable, notice in Figure 14-2 the curved line leading to inquiry/response. This input/output line indicates an on-line connection between a terminal(s) and the receivables package, so that questions concerning current customer account balances, credit limits, and payment histories can be immediately answered by the computer. This capability is a must for accounts receivable processing if credit-granting and order-acceptance decisions are to be made based on up-to-date and accurate information. Figure 14-7 is an example of a typical response to a terminal inquiry concerning a customer account. Note that this on-line capability allows a user to inquire into customer data files at any time and receive immediate response to questions about a specific customer or transaction, based on data stored in the system.

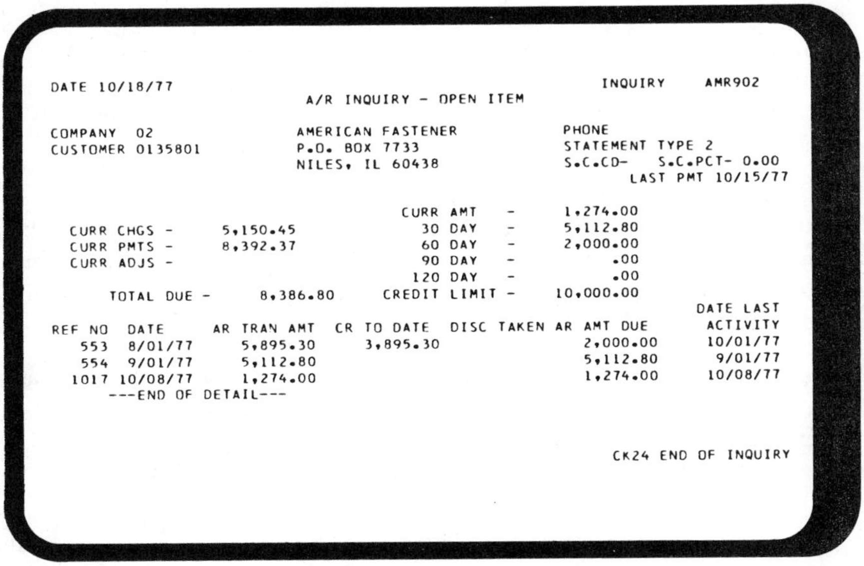

```
DATE 10/18/77                                           INQUIRY      AMR902
                               A/R INQUIRY - OPEN ITEM

COMPANY  02                    AMERICAN FASTENER          PHONE
CUSTOMER 0135801               P.O. BOX 7733              STATEMENT TYPE 2
                               NILES, IL 60438            S.C.CD-   S.C.PCT- 0.00
                                                                 LAST PMT 10/15/77

                                         CURR AMT   -      1,274.00
      CURR CHGS -     5,150.45             30 DAY   -      5,112.80
      CURR PMTS -     8,392.37             60 DAY   -      2,000.00
      CURR ADJS -                          90 DAY   -          .00
                                          120 DAY   -          .00
         TOTAL DUE -  8,386.80          CREDIT LIMIT -    10,000.00
                                                                      DATE LAST
   REF NO  DATE     AR TRAN AMT  CR TO DATE  DISC TAKEN AR AMT DUE     ACTIVITY
      553  8/01/77    5,895.30    3,895.30                 2,000.00    10/01/77
      554  9/01/77    5,112.80                             5,112.80     9/01/77
     1017 10/08/77    1,274.00                             1,274.00    10/08/77
      ---END OF DETAIL---


                                                      CK24 END OF INQUIRY
```

FIGURE 14-7 Display of Response
Information From Accounts Receivable
(courtesy of IBM Corporation)

Input Files

Finally, we come to the direct system input necessary for accounts receivable processing to function. As we discuss the required files and their content, keep in mind the basic data organization ideas discussed in Chapter 8 and briefly reviewed in Chapter 13. Following are the major files necessary for the accounts receivable application:

1. Customer master file. This file contains one record for each credit customer. Each record consists of at least the following data elements:

   a. Customer account number.

   b. Customer name.

   c. Customer address (including city and state).

   d. Credit limit.

   e. Credit history code.

   f. Current balance by age.

g.   Collections—year-to-date.

h.   Finance charges.

i.   Collections—previous year.

This file is updated with each processing and is the data base for all system inquiries. It is, like most master files, both input to and output from (updated) each processing run of accounts receivable. The customer master file is the accounts receivable subsidiary ledger in a computer-based system and provides detailed information on sales to and collections from each customer, as well as amounts owed by each customer at any time. It is the exact counterpart of the manual system subsidiary ledger of Part One.

2.   New invoices file. This transaction file is made up of all verified sales invoices created since the last processing of accounts receivable. Input data from this file is used to update the customer master file and would also be the basis for the invoice register (sales journal) which can be produced as the data is passed to the general ledger of the financial accounting and control system. This is an input file only.

3.   Cash receipts and adjustments file. Like the new invoices file above, this is a transactions file. It provides input data for the updating of the customer master file. These are the transactions that have reduced receivables balances since the last processing and, as such, are the basis for the cash receipts journal discussed in Chapter 13. This is an input file only.

In a hardware system designed to be interactive, transaction files can be created and processed as the transactions are received using an on-line device, such as a terminal. The master file, then, would be constantly updated by transactions as they occur. Alternatively, transactions can be stored (probably on a disk) as received and held until a sufficient file has been built. Then, a processing run can be made to update the master file. This second approach is more batch oriented and results in a master file which is not completely up-to-date at all times. This basic choice of approaches to the processing of transactions must be made for each of the applications we will discuss. Obviously, the interactive design is more important for some packages than for others.

You can see from the file structure and data organization that accounts receivable processing involves the basic equation depicted below.

For each Customer Account	*File*
Beginning balance	Master
+ Sales	Invoice
- Payments	Receipts and Adjustments
− Adjustments	Receipts and Adjustments
= Ending balance	Master

As these files are merged and the data processed, the equation is carried out according to programming instructions. We will find in the next section that many of the ideas introduced here as relevant to processing the accounts receivable application apply as well to accounts payable.

14.3 ACCOUNTS PAYABLE COMPONENT

The accounts receivable package we have just discussed is concerned with processing the trans-actions (sales, receipts, and adjustments) whose ultimate impact is on the cash inflows of a business. Equally important to the overall control of cash and cash flows are those transactions which affect cash outflows. These are primarily purchases of merchandise and payment of amounts due suppliers (accounts payable). The accounts payable application is designed to monitor these cash outflows and provide information which will aid in the control of the costs and expenses associated with the flows. Basically, we would like this processing package to provide information on (1) who we owe money, (2) how much, (3) for how long, and (4) if our checks are properly accounted for. The focus of this application is on cash outflows due to operations and the idea is to process payables so that cash outflows will not occur any sooner than necessary. Also, the package should provide information which will direct attention to the control of expenses associated with the purchase function. Figure 14-8 summarizes the informa-tion flow into and from an accounts payable processing application. You should take some time to become familiar with these major flows before delving into the detailed discussion of them.

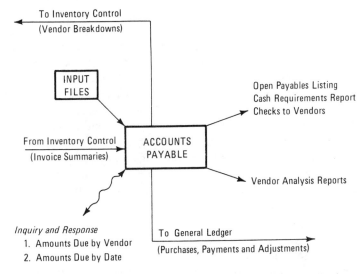

FIGURE 14-8 Information Flow in an Accounts Payable Application

Output Reports

Our starting point, as always, will be the output reports to be expected from the package. Remember that specific form, content, and frequency of reports may vary, and we are present-ing typical reports generated by this processing application.

1. *Open payables listing* (Figure 14-9). An important objective of processing payables is the careful payment of all purchase invoices in time to take advantage of discounts, but no sooner than necessary. Payment sequencing has significant impact on a business' cash position, borrowing plans, and dealings with vendors. The selection of which suppliers or

invoices (if there are several from the same supplier) to pay is a matter of cash planning and should be based on complete information about the total amounts owed each vendor, the discounts available from each, and the due dates of each amount. The open payables listing supplies all of this information for all vendors, and allows the user to select particular accounts for immediate payment and to assign a payment sequence to the other amounts due. This comprehensive listing can be generated at predetermined times or intervals for analysis prior to the writing of checks and the disbursement of cash. In the last column of this report you should notice two symbols which denote some special features of importance to users. The symbol *PP* stands for prepaid, and indicates that a particular supplier has been paid in advance for purchased goods. The system tells us that no payment will be necessary when the goods arrive. The symbol, *H2*, indicates that a halt has been placed on the payment of an invoice, perhaps because of something unusual about the invoice or some deficiency in the goods which must be followed up before payment is authorized. The computer will not pay the amount until the user removes the halt status, although the invoice will continue to appear in the listing. This effectively prevents the *accidental* payment of an amount still in question—an important feature. Other important features of this listing are highlighted in Figure 14-9.

2. *Cash requirements report* (Figure 14-10). Once the payment selection process is complete, the effect of these planned disbursements on the cash position of the business can be determined from the cash requirements report. This important report can be sequenced by the due date of invoices selected for payment or by the vendor to be paid. In either sequencing, the statement will show the cash required to cover checks written to pay accounts on a particular date. This report can also be used to answer questions from vendors on the payment status of purchase invoices. If for some reason a user reconsiders a payment selection and decides on a change, the cash requirements report can be updated based on new selections and reprinted. The cash requirements report, then, is a complete listing of all invoices and vendors to be paid during a period. As such, this statement represents critical cash control and audit trail backup to the bank statement and other cash-related documents. Other noteworthy features of this report are highlighted in Figure 14-10.

3. *Checks to vendors* (Figure 14-11). This output document should be familiar to everyone, since we all deal with checks sooner or later. This computer-produced check is really no different from the handwritten version except in the very detailed check stub which is printed along with the check itself. Like all documents in a computer-based information system, this stub is designed to fit into a chain or trail through which all payments of accounts can be traced. Notice that all of the information on the check stub can be traced back to the cash requirements report, then to the open payables listing, and ultimately (we will see in Chapter 15) to the creation of the data in the sales and purchases system. This linkage or chain of documents is absolutely critical to internal control with or without a computer-based system.

4. *Vendor analysis reports.* Several vendor reports of different format and emphasis can be generated on demand from the payables package. Reports showing purchase activity with each supplier for the current period, the year-to-date, or the previous year, as well as discounts taken and lost for the same periods are available from the data base. Also,

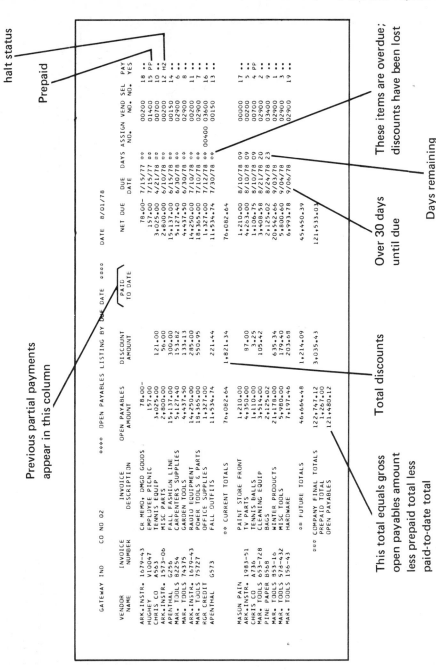

FIGURE 14-9 Open Payables Listing
(courtesy of IBM Corporation)

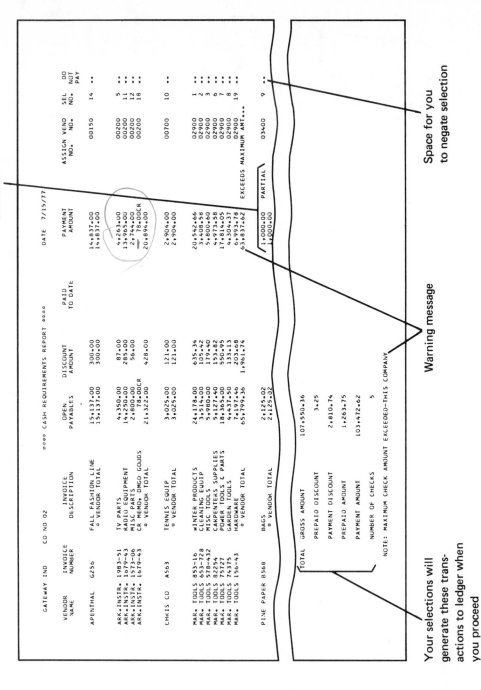

Current partial
payment against
this item

Space for you
to negate selection

Warning message

Your selections will
generate these trans-
actions to ledger when
you proceed

FIGURE 14-10 Cash Requirements Report
(courtesy of IBM Corporation)

INVOICE NUMBER	INVOICE DATE	DESCRIPTION	GROSS AMOUNT	DISCOUNT	NET AMOUNT
853-16	7/19/78	WINTER PRODUCTS	21,178.00	635.34	20,542.66
653-728	6/30/78	CLEANING EQUIP	3,514.00	105.42	3,408.58
578-432	7/03/78	MISC TOOLS	5,980.00	179.40	5,800.60
82254	5/14/78	CARPENTERS SUPPLIES	5,127.40	153.32	4,973.58
75727	9/02/78	POWER TOOLS & PARTS	18,365.00	550.95	17,814.05
74375	5/23/78	GARDEN TOOLS	4,437.50	133.13	4,304.37
156-43	7/17/78	HARDWARE	7,197.46	203.68	6,993.78
			65,799.36	1,961.74	63,837.62

103

GATEWAY IND. CO.

TO THE
ORDER OF:

MARLEY TOOLS CO.
1795 BATHGATE RD
BETHLEHEM, PA
18106

SAMPLE PRINTED
CHECK

CHECK DATE	CHECK NUMBER
7/15/78	103

PAY THIS AMOUNT
$ ✪✪✪✪✪✪63,837.62

NON-NEGOTIABLE

AUTHORIZED SIGNATURE

AUTHORIZED SIGNATURE

IBM Y08274

FIGURE 14-11 Sample Printed Check
(courtesy of IBM Corporation)

detailed vendor histories can be provided showing all of the activity since the first purchase transaction with any one vendor. Thus, an overview of all purchases for a specified time period can be obtained, or the business' historical relationship with any one supplier can be examined. Information like this can be passed along to the inventory control application (where purchasing takes place) to be used in purchasing decisions.

These are the primary management reports to be expected from an accounts payable application. It is important to realize that most payables packages can provide additional and/or different statements at the wish of the user. The processing capability and data base is there; the choice is the users.

Information Exchange

In addition to management reports, the accounts payable application also produces output which is used by other systems. Refer again to Figure 14-8, and you will notice interaction between accounts payable and the general ledger as well as accounts payable and inventory control. Specifically, the payables package passes summarized total information on purchases, payments, and adjustments to the financial accounting and control system to be included in the general ledger and in financial statements. Information is also exchanged with the inventory control package of the sales and purchases system. Data on purchase invoices created in inventory control serves as input to accounts payable, and vendor analysis information which results from processing payables is returned to inventory control to be used in future purchase decisions. These systems and applications seldom stand alone and always function more effectively when interaction possibilities are used to a maximum. Notice again, that the information flow is more than simply accounting transactions.

Like accounts receivable, some inquiry/response capability is desirable in processing accounts payable. This on-demand interaction with the system allows the user to acquire immediate information on amounts owed to specific suppliers or total amounts owed to all suppliers now or as of certain future dates specified by the user. Information of the first type would be necessary to answer vendor questions or provide instant information for purchasing decisions, while the second type of immediate response from the system is particularly useful for short-term cash disbursement planning. Figure 14-12 illustrates terminal displays of both types of information which could appear in response to specific questions by users. This inquiry/response capability is represented by the curved line in Figure 14-8.

Input Files

As in all applications, certain input is required that originates with the package rather than being passed from other processing systems. This direct input and the way it is organized will round out our discussion, of the payables package. Following are the major files necessary for the accounts payable application.

1. *Vendor master file.* This file contains one record for each vendor. Each record would contain at least the following data elements:

    a.   Vendor number.

    b.   Vendor name.

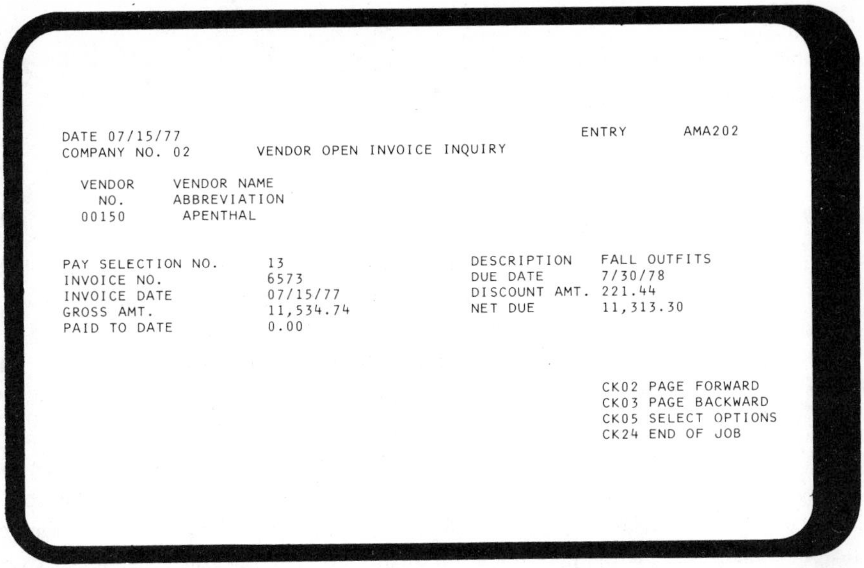

```
DATE 07/15/77                                          ENTRY      AMA202
COMPANY NO. 02        VENDOR OPEN INVOICE INQUIRY

   VENDOR      VENDOR NAME
    NO.        ABBREVIATION
   00150        APENTHAL


PAY SELECTION NO.     13            DESCRIPTION    FALL OUTFITS
INVOICE NO.           6573          DUE DATE       7/30/78
INVOICE DATE          07/15/77      DISCOUNT AMT.  221.44
GROSS AMT.            11,534.74     NET DUE        11,313.30
PAID TO DATE          0.00


                                            CK02 PAGE FORWARD
                                            CK03 PAGE BACKWARD
                                            CK05 SELECT OPTIONS
                                            CK24 END OF JOB
```

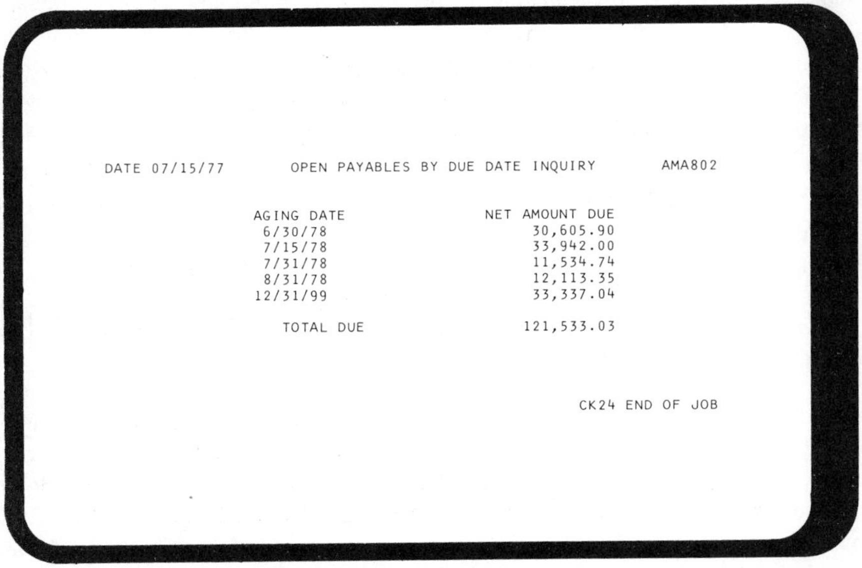

```
DATE 07/15/77        OPEN PAYABLES BY DUE DATE INQUIRY      AMA802

              AGING DATE              NET AMOUNT DUE
               6/30/78                    30,605.90
               7/15/78                    33,942.00
               7/31/78                    11,534.74
               8/31/78                    12,113.35
              12/31/99                    33,337.04

                 TOTAL DUE               121,533.03


                                     CK24 END OF JOB
```

FIGURE 14-12 Display of Response Information from Accounts Payable
(courtesy of IBM Corporation)

c. Vendor address (including city and state).

d. Vendor telephone number.

e. Name of established contact at vendor.

f. Discount provisions.

g. Payments—current period.

h. Payments—year-to-date.

i. Payments—previous year.

j. Discounts—current period.

k. Discounts—year-to-date.

l. Discounts—previous year.

m. Current balance by invoice.

This file, like all master files, is updated with each processing and is the data base for all system inquiries. It is both input and output for the accounts payable package. The vendor master file is the accounts payable subsidiary ledger in a computer-based system and provides information on purchases from and payments to each vendor as well as amounts owed to each vendor at any time. It is the exact counterpart of the manual system subsidiary ledger discussed in Part One.

2. *Open invoices file.* All open payables appear in this file with one record for each unpaid invoice. Each unpaid invoice is linked to a vendor in the vendor master file discussed above. This file allows for retrieval of any or all open payables, and together with the vendor master file makes possible the determination of the total amount owed any specific vendor. It is updated with each processing and is therefore both input and output to the application.

3. *New invoices file.* This transaction file, like the similar one in accounts receivable, is made up of all verified purchase invoices created since the last processing of accounts payable. Input from here, which represents increases in accounts payable, is the basis for updating both the vendor master file and the open invoices file. Also, this input file contains all necessary information for the production of the purchases journal in the financial accounting and control system.

4. *Cash payments and adjustments file.* Transactions which decrease payables for a given period make up this file. Data from this file completes the updating of the vendor master and open invoices files and is the basis for the cash disbursements journal discussed earlier. This, like the new invoices file, is input only.

It should be obvious that the file structure and basic processing goals and objectives of the payables and receivables packages are basically the same. This should not be surprising since these items simply represent opposite sides of the cash-flow coin. An important difference between these two applications can be traced to the essentially active role played by a business in the purchases and payments area versus the more passive position in the area of sales and receipts. A business may choose the timing and amount of purchases and payments within broad constraints, while it must wait and respond to the choices of others in sales and receipts. The open invoices file, which has no counterpart in the receivables package, provides the information for this active selection process in the purchases and payments area.

14.4 PAYROLL COMPONENT

If you remember the "big picture" of business information systems in Figure 13-1, you know that payroll is the final application of the cash receipts and disbursements system. Like the other packages of this system, payroll represents a significant and on-going cash flow and, is an important factor in the control of cash outflows. Unlike the other packages, however, many external entities have an interest in the processing of payroll and require information on the results. Governments at various levels, unions, insurance companies, and others all have a legitimate stake in this system, and the processing of this application must meet the needs of and work within certain constraints (sometimes legal) imposed by these interested parties. Payroll actually differs from the other applications discussed in this chapter in two important ways. important ways.

1. This package is probably the most "stand alone" of all the processing applications of an information system. This is not to say that payroll is completely independent because that is usually not the case. You will notice from Figure 13-1 that there is somewhat less interaction between payroll and the processing packages of other systems. From an internal information point of view, therefore, processing payroll tends to be less complex than other applications, although the information generated is just as important.

2. Payroll processing must meet the information needs of many external entities as well as provide information for the internal use of a business. These external demands on the data processing capabilities of a business are strongest in the payroll area and so the payroll application must serve several masters. The design of the package should take this into account.

Basically, payroll processing must provide information on (1) how much each employee has earned; (2) what kinds of taxes were withheld and the amounts for each employee; (3) what kinds of other deductions were withheld and the amounts for each employee; (4) if checks have been properly accounted for; and (5) if legal and reporting obligations have been met. In addition, the system should contribute to the control of the expenses associated with salary and wage payments. Figure 14-13 summarizes the information flow into and from a payroll application. Study this figure carefully and remember that the system must provide information for controlling cash outflows and expenses as well as meeting outside obligations.

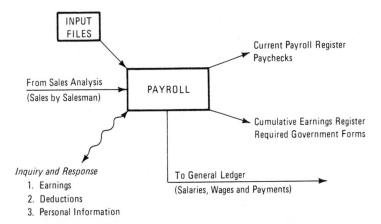

FIGURE 14-13 Information Flow in a Payroll Application

Output Reports

Typical output reports to be produced from a payroll package would at a minimum include those listed below. The choice of possible reports is very broad, and depends on the particular information needs and external requirements which must be met by a business.

1. *Current payroll register* (Figure 14-14). This statement is a complete listing of the current pay period earnings of all employees to be paid this period and all deductions (required and voluntary) from these earnings. The report reconciles gross to net earnings for each employee by itemizing all deductions and also lists total hours worked for the period. Notice that each employee's paycheck number can be printed to provide a cross-reference which allows for tracing payroll-related cash disbursements through the system and aids in bank reconciliation. If the business pays fringe benefits for employees, these payments can appear on the register and be classified as either taxable or nontaxable. The two adjustments columns immediately following "Reg/Oth Gross" allow for this classification of employer-paid benefits. Of course, any nontaxable component of gross pay would account for the difference between the columns headed "Total Gross" and "Taxable Gross." It is important to realize that these payroll registers become a permanent record of employee pay activity and can be the basis for a series of other payroll-related reports.

2. *Paychecks* (Figure 14-15). Perhaps the most familiar of all output documents is the paycheck. The paycheck is the way a payroll processing package manifests itself to employees. The only important variable in producing this "report" is the amount of information to appear on the check stub which is delivered to the employee along with the check. The stub may include information on pay rate and year-to-date earnings, but generally it reflects the current period earnings and deductions information appearing in the payroll register. Our sample printed check is comprehensive in that the stub shows information beyond that presented in the payroll register. This is, of course, a matter of user choice and can be accommodated easily.

3. *Cumulative earnings register* (Figure 14-16). This report is very much like the payroll register of Figure 14-14 except that cumulative year-to-date and quarter-to-date figures for earnings and tax deductions are substituted for the current period figures. This statement is an important permanent document when printed in its final form at the end of each calendar year. It contains basic information which must be kept and periodically reported by all businesses to federal taxing agencies (IRS and social security) as well as to state and local governments. In addition, a separate cumulative state and local register showing relevant earnings and tax information can be produced if desired. The cumulative earnings register contains most of the employee earnings information needed for meeting external reporting requirements.

4. *Required government forms* (Figure 14-17). Unique to payroll is the requirement that the application produce at the end of certain time periods, reports which are exclusively for external consumption. The generation of these quarterly and annual reports is mandatory for all businesses with employees and a payroll. Primarily, the required reports have to do with the various taxes which have been withheld from employee paychecks (and in some cases matched) and periodically remitted to the appropriate taxing authority. The two most common forms, illustrated in Figure 14-17, having to do with social security (FICA)

Vacation pay

Includes employer-paid taxable union fringes

GATEWAY IND   CO NO 02   ***** PAYROLL REGISTER *****   DATE 7/15/77

EMP NO.	EMPLOYEE NAME	HOURS	REG/OTH GROSS	TOTAL GROSS	TAXABLE NON-TAX ADJ	TAXABLE GROSS	FEDERAL TAX	FICA TAX	STATE TAX	LOCAL TAX	UNION DED	MISC DED	NET PAY	CHECK NO.
DEPARTMENT - 22														
130	EDWIN DAUM	42.00	251.45	251.45		251.45	32.70	14.71	6.28		2.50	10.00	185.26	1010
150	JUDY VANDER VEEN	42.00	239.30	239.30		239.30	42.56	14.00	8.56		2.50	165.00	6.68	1011
270	TOM RYAN	40.00	508.00	508.00		508.00	155.67	29.72	24.44				298.17	1012
		40.00	508.00	508.00		508.00	155.67	22.47	24.44			22.50	282.92	1013
1021	BOB MANKA	42.00	280.65	280.65		280.65	41.49	16.42	7.84		17.50	5.00	192.40	1014
1033	BOB JOHANNES	40.00	100.00	115.00	15.00	15.00	15.03	.88			2.50	5.00	106.62	1015
1048	JOHN GALVIN	42.50	255.68	255.68		255.68	27.74	14.96	5.78		7.50	16.00	183.70	1016
◇ DEPT 22 TOTALS		288.50	2,143.08	2,158.08	15.00	2,058.08	455.83	113.16	77.34		32.50	223.50	1,255.75	

* FINAL CONTROL TOTALS *

		HOURS			JOB		ADJUSTMENT			DEDUCTION		UNION ADJUSTMENT	
REG	OTH	VAC/HOL	SICK	TOTAL	HRS		TAXABLE	NON-TAX	SICK	ONE-TIME	PAY ADV	TAXABLE	NON TAXABLE
314.50	8.00	40.00	40.00	402.50	242.50		15.00	.00	.00	.00	155.00	.00	.00

GROSS		SICK		TAXES				MISC	UNION	NET	REVERSE	NUMBER		
TOTAL	TAXABLE	GROSS		FIT	FICA	STATE	LOCAL	DEDUCTION	DED TOT	PAY	AMOUNT	EMP	TRAN	CHEK
2,926.71	2,826.71	100.00		625.70	158.12	95.33	.00	260.72	37.50	1,749.34	.00	9	72	10

FIGURE 14-14 Current Payroll Register
(courtesy of IBM Corporation)

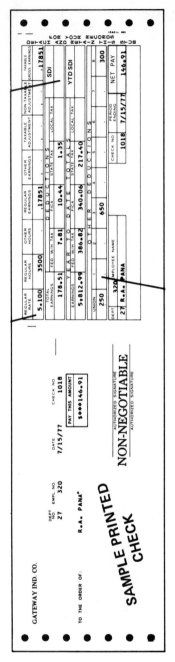

FIGURE 14-15 Sample Printed Paycheck
(courtesy of IBM Corporation)

```
GATEWAY IND    CO NO 02          *** Y-T-D / Q-T-D EARNINGS REGISTER ***          DATE 7/15/77
```

HOME EMP DEPT NO.	EMPLOYEE NAME	Y-T-D GROSS EARNINGS	Y-T-D GROSS TAXABLE	Y-T-D SICK PAY	Y-T-D FEDERAL TAX	Y-T-D FICA TAX	YTD WKS WRK	Q-T-D GROSS TAXABLE	Q-T-D FEDERAL TAX	Q-T-D FICA TAX	QTD WKS WRK
**27	75 GEORGE SPELBRINK	3,024.51	3,024.51		312.17	176.91	13				
27	100 C.M. MOODY	10,584.00	10,584.00		3,704.40	619.17	27	392.00	137.20	22.93	1
22	130 EDWIN DAUM	6,728.25	6,728.25		869.20	393.60	27	251.45	32.70	14.71	1
22	150 JUDY VANDER VEEN	6,434.50	6,434.50		1,138.85	376.42	27	239.30	42.56	14.00	1
22	270 TOM RYAN	14,224.00	14,224.00		4,358.76	824.85	28	1,016.00	311.34	52.19	2
27	320 R.A. PANA	5,812.99	5,812.99		386.82	340.06	27	178.51	7.81	10.44	1
22	1021 BOB MANKA	7,672.45	7,672.45		1,495.20	448.84	27	280.65	41.49	16.42	1
22	1033 BOB JOHANNES	4,172.20	2,472.20	1,700.00	240.14	144.63	27	15.00		.88	1
22	1048 JOHN GALVIN	6,304.68	6,304.68		652.08	368.77	26	255.68	27.74	14.96	1
27	1076 BOB WINTER	5,398.12	5,398.12		681.10	315.79	27	198.12	24.86	11.59	1

```
** CONTROL TOTALS **     70,355.70   68,655.70   1,700.00   13,838.72   4,009.04        2,826.71   625.70   158.12
** PAY PERIOD TOTALS **   2,926.71    2,826.71     100.00      625.70     158.12

CURRENT HOURS RECORDS 72    EMPLOYEE MASTER RECORDS 10                                 135100

** EMPLOYEE DID NOT WORK THIS PAY PERIOD.
```

FIGURE 14-16 Cumulative Earnings Register
(courtesy of IBM Corporation)

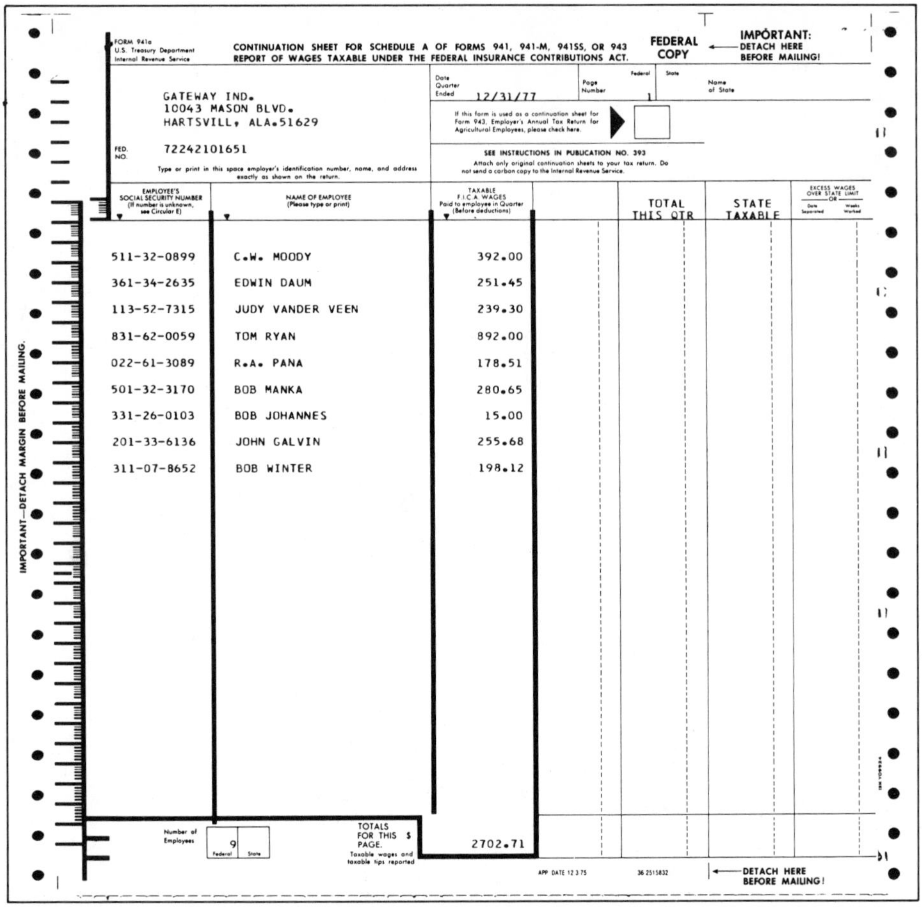
FORM 941a
U.S. Treasury Department
Internal Revenue Service

CONTINUATION SHEET FOR SCHEDULE A OF FORMS 941, 941-M, 941SS, OR 943
REPORT OF WAGES TAXABLE UNDER THE FEDERAL INSURANCE CONTRIBUTIONS ACT.

FEDERAL COPY

IMPORTANT: DETACH HERE BEFORE MAILING!

GATEWAY IND.
10043 MASON BLVD.
HARTSVILL, ALA.51629

FED. NO. 72242101651

Type or print in this space employer's identification number, name, and address exactly as shown on the return.

Date Quarter Ended 12/31/77 — Page Number 1

If this form is used as a continuation sheet for Form 943, Employer's Annual Tax Return for Agricultural Employees, please check here.

SEE INSTRUCTIONS IN PUBLICATION NO. 393
Attach only original continuation sheets to your tax return. Do not send a carbon copy to the Internal Revenue Service.

EMPLOYEE'S SOCIAL SECURITY NUMBER (If number is unknown, see Circular E)	NAME OF EMPLOYEE (Please type or print)	TAXABLE F.I.C.A. WAGES Paid to employee in Quarter (Before deductions)	TOTAL THIS QTR	STATE TAXABLE	EXCESS WAGES OVER STATE LIMIT
511-32-0899	C.W. MOODY	392.00			
361-34-2635	EDWIN DAUM	251.45			
113-52-7315	JUDY VANDER VEEN	239.30			
831-62-0059	TOM RYAN	892.00			
022-61-3089	R.A. PANA	178.51			
501-32-3170	BOB MANKA	280.65			
331-26-0103	BOB JOHANNES	15.00			
201-33-6136	JOHN GALVIN	255.68			
311-07-8652	BOB WINTER	198.12			

Number of Employees: 9 (Federal / State)

TOTALS FOR THIS PAGE. Taxable wages and taxable tips reported: $ 2702.71

IMPORTANT—DETACH MARGIN BEFORE MAILING.

APP DATE 12 3 75 — 36 2515832

DETACH HERE BEFORE MAILING!

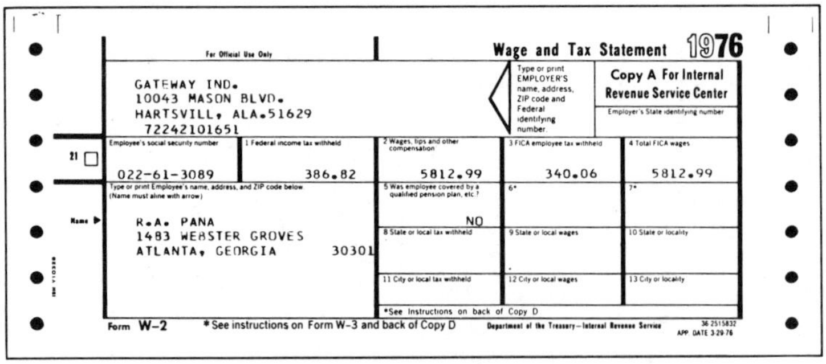
For Official Use Only

Wage and Tax Statement 1976

Copy A For Internal Revenue Service Center

Type or print EMPLOYER'S name, address, ZIP code and Federal identifying number.

GATEWAY IND.
10043 MASON BLVD.
HARTSVILL, ALA.51629
72242101651

Employee's social security number	1 Federal income tax withheld	2 Wages, tips and other compensation	3 FICA employee tax withheld	4 Total FICA wages
022-61-3089	386.82	5812.99	340.06	5812.99

5 Was employee covered by a qualified pension plan, etc.? NO

Type or print Employee's name, address, and ZIP code below (Name must aline with arrow)

Name ▶ R.A. PANA
1483 WEBSTER GROVES
ATLANTA, GEORGIA 30301

8 State or local tax withheld — 9 State or local wages — 10 State or locality
11 City or local tax withheld — 12 City or local wages — 13 City or locality

Form W-2 *See instructions on Form W-3 and back of Copy D — Department of the Treasury—Internal Revenue Service — 36 2515832 APP DATE 3-29-76

FIGURE 14-17 Required Government Forms (courtesy of IBM Corporation)

and federal income taxes, are called respectively *Form 941A* and *Form W-2.* Typically, these reports are printed by the payroll application on forms supplied by the government agencies responsible for collecting the taxes. Government agencies supply the forms, but the processing must supply the information to fill them.

The reports illustrated above are the most basic to payroll and would be fundamental to any application. Beyond these, legal requirements and user information needs would govern the exact reports produced by the package.

Information Exchange

Like all other applications in the cash receipts and disbursements system, the payroll application may receive important input information from another processing system and pass on as output, information which is essential to other packages. Once data on the expenses and cash outflows associated with payroll have been processed, these transactions are transferred in summary form to be integrated into the general ledger for financial accounting and control purposes.

Input to payroll may come from the sales analysis package, particularly if employee compensation is based on some measure of sales activity. If salesmen are paid by commission, then a breakdown of sales by salesman is absolutely necessary to the calculation of payroll. The generation of this information is one of the goals of sales analysis processing, and the sales analysis package has the data to generate such a breakdown. It makes sense to produce this information only once and transfer it to wherever it may be needed in the information system. Payroll can accept as input this and any other information from other applications which may be needed to compute salaries and wages.

All processing applications in the cash receipts and disbursements system can be improved by some kind of on-line capability. Payroll is no exception to this, however, direct human/computer interaction is not as critical here as it is in receivables and payables. Nonetheless, questions may come up concerning earnings and deductions or some personal information on an employee which require immediate answers. If so, the inquiry/response capability we have been discussing could facilitate this process. Figure 14-18 is an example of a response to an inquiry into employee files for information.

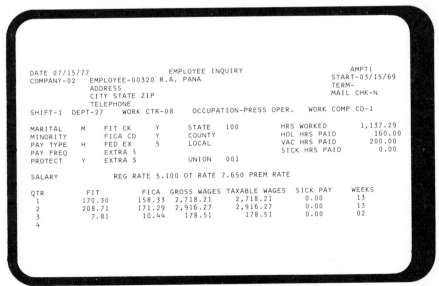

FIGURE 14-18 Display of Response Information From Payroll
(courtesy of IBM Corporation)

Input Files

Finally, payroll requires direct input in its own right in order to produce the output required. Following are the major files necessary for the payroll application:

1. *Employee master file.* This file contains one record for each employee. Each record must contain at least the following data elements:

    a. Employee number.

    b. Employee name.

    c. Employee address (including city and state).

    d. Employee social security number.

    e. Pay rate.

    f. Marital status and exemptions.

    g. Deductions information code.

    h. Cumulative gross earnings.

    i. Cumulative taxable earnings.

    j. Cumulative federal and state withholding.

    k. Cumulative social security withholding.

    l. Cumulative hours worked.

    This file is updated with each processing run and is the data base which supports all inquiries to the system. It is both input and output for the payroll package, and the cumulative earnings register and required government forms come directly from this file.

2. *Tax table and deduction table file.* This is a permanent constant file which is composed of the tax and deduction amounts or percentages necessary to determine the amounts of withholdings. When this file is merged with the earnings, exemptions, and deductions information of each employee from the employee master file, the actual deductions can be computed and net pay determined. Since the data in this file is relatively constant, the file is not affected by the normal processing of payroll. The data may be changed as external conditions (withholding rates or deduction amounts) change, but otherwise the file remains unchanged and is input to each payroll run.

3. *Current hours file.* This transactions file supplies all of the current pay period data necessary to calculate gross pay. The number of hours worked, both regular and overtime, for each employee as well as any applicable special pay rates would be a part of this input file. Also, information on where the employee worked during the period (department, job) could be provided for general ledger expense distribution. This file is used to update the employee master file and generate the payroll register.

If you will recall our discussion of the general ledger application in Chapter 13 and compare the processing problems of that package with the applications of the cash receipts and disbursements system, it should be clear that the general ledger application is certainly the most difficult area of an information system to handle and payroll is very probably the easiest.

The scope of your background in computer-based information systems for business is broadening considerably. In Chapter 13 we discussed the central and most complex processing system, the financial accounting and control system. The cash receipts and disbursements system presented in this chapter is probably the busiest system since a significant amount of information flow takes place between it and other computer systems. In the next chapter we will complete the picture of computer-based information systems (as diagrammed in Figure 13-1) with an examination of the sales and purchases system.

exercises

14-1 The information flow into and from an accounts receivable application area is depicted in Figure 14-2.

1. Give a specific example of each type of input to this application area.

2. Explain how the examples you chose are actually processed by the application.

14-2 For each of the data-items stored in the customer master file explain why such information is important in a computer-based system. Also, for each data-item, give the output report(s) in which the information is used. Which of these data-items would normally be updated with each processing run?

14-3 Two critical output reports generated by the accounts receivable package are the aged trial balance and customer billing statements.

1. Compare the aged trial balance presented in Figure 14-4 to the schedule of accounts receivable discussed in Part One. How do they differ? What do these differences indicate about the processing capabilities of computer-based versus manual systems?

2. Examine the customer billing statement presented in Figure 14-5. Notice that there are two detail lines for the customer payment made on 10/1/77. Assuming only one check for payment was sent by American Fastener on 10/1/77, why would there be two detail lines on the billing statement? What would be the summary journal entry for amounts collected from American Fastener for the period covered by the billing statement?

14-4 The information flow into and from an accounts payable application area is depicted in Figure 14-8.

1. Give a specific example of each type of input to this application area.

2. Explain how the examples you chose are actually processed by the application.

14-5 For each of the data-items stored in the vendor master file explain why such information is important in a computer-based system. Also, for each data-item, give the output report(s) in which the information is used. Which of these data-items would normally be updated with each processing run?

14-6 Two critical output reports generated by the accounts payable package are the open payables listing and the cash requirements report.

1. Compare the open payables listing presented in Figure 14-9 to the schedule of accounts payable discussed in Part One. How do they differ? What do these differences indicate about the processing capabilities of computer-based versus manual systems?

Acc/p
Cash

2. Assume all required disbursements given in the cash requirements report in Figure 14-10 are actually made. What would be the summary journal entry for vendor number 00200?

14-7 The information flow into and from a payroll application area is depicted in Figure 14-13.

1. Give a specific example of each type of input to this application area.

2. Explain how the examples you chose are actually processed by the application.

14-8 For each of the data-items stored in the employee master file, explain why such information is important in a computer-based system. Also, for each data-item, give the output report(s) in which the information is used. Which of these data items would normally be updated with each processing run?

14-9 Critical output reports generated by the payroll package include the payroll register, cumulative earnings register, and several required government forms.

1. Both the payroll register and the cumulative earnings register present earnings information by employee. How does this earnings information differ between reports?

2. What purposes are served by the required government forms presented in Figure 14-17 for (a) government, (b) employer, and (c) employee?

14-10 Edwin Daum is an employee of Gateway Industries. Trace his earnings data through the payroll output reports illustrated in the chapter. Supply the following information and state the report(s) on which it appears.

a. Employee number.

b. Weeks worked this year.

c. Take-home pay for the current pay period.

d. Gross pay for the current pay period.

e. Number of hours worked in the current pay period.

f. Union dues paid in the current pay period.

g. Year-to-date gross taxable earnings as of June 15.

h. Home address.

i. Work department.

j. Federal income tax withheld during the current pay period.

15

sales and purchases systems

outline

15.1 **Information Flow through the System**: the specific processing applications which make up the system; information flow between this and other processing systems.

15.2 **Order Processing Component**: discussion and illustration of the output reports generated by this application, input data organization and major files required; how the package works.

15.3 **Inventory Control Component**: same goals and objectives as 15.2.

15.4 **Sales Analysis Component**: same goals and objectives as 15.2.

15.5 **Information Systems and Accounting Systems**: basic distinction between these approaches to processing data; example illustrating these differences in terms of the processing applications presented in Chapters 13–15.

INTRODUCTION

The processing applications of the two systems we have discussed so far (i.e., cash receipts and disbursements and financial accounting and control) have some important characteristics in common. Before we present the final major component of a business information system, it would be helpful to summarize these fundamental ideas common to all computer-based systems. You probably have noticed that each processing package we have discussed has exhibited the following attributes.

1. *Output reports.* In each application some man-sensible output has been generated to provide information on which human action can be based. Although it is conceivable for a package to produce no printed output, this is not likely to occur very often in business processing. The ability of computer-based systems to provide man-sensible information which is not available from a manual system is one of the primary reasons for their existence. Timely and useful management reports are one of the significant advantages of a functioning information system.

2. *Interaction with other packages.* The transfer of data between applications (sometimes called *interface*) is absolutely necessary to reduce duplication and repetition in an information system. The capabilities of computer systems make this kind of interchange between processing packages relatively easy to carry out as compared to manual systems. It is unusual to find a computer-based application which is not made more efficient by accepting some organized and (at least) partially processed data from another application. By the same token, almost all packages generate some computer-sensible data which can be used elsewhere in the system.

3. *Question and response capability.* Given the inherent advantages of speed and memory possessed by computers, a good deal of the benefit of computer-based systems is lost if critical pieces of information are not available on request from the information system. Like timely and complete output reports, the ready availability of up-to-date information is one of the most significant advantages of the kinds of systems we have been discussing.

4. *Data organization into files.* The concepts of file, record (entity), and data element (item, attribute) introduced in Chapter 8 are essential to every computer-based application. Since the computer does not have intuition, judgment, or reasoning powers, the organization of input data to be processed must follow a logical design. This logical design most often results in each package having access to a permanent master file which is cumulative and updated with each processing run by a file of current transactions. Although other files may be necessary to any particular application, the basic concept of master and transaction files is common to all applications.

The sales and purchases system exhibits each of these characteristics. Keep them in mind as we discuss this final component system. You might also refer back to Figure 13-1 to reestablish in your mind the basic information flow between this and the other systems we have discussed as well as among the applications of this system.

15.1 INFORMATION FLOW THROUGH THE SYSTEM

The processing applications of this system represent the point of original data entry into the information system for many important transactions and events. As such, there is significant information flow among the individual packages which make up the sales and purchases system as well as between these packages and those of the cash receipts and disbursements system. In addition, there is limited one-way information flow from this system to the budgeting package of the financial accounting and control system. Figure 15-1 illustrates these flows and in doing so focuses on the upper left curved space of the total information system depicted in Figure 13-1. Notice that the sales and purchases system interacts significantly with the cash receipts and disbursements system. In fact, there is an important pairing of packages between these component systems with order processing–accounts receivable and inventory control–accounts payable combining to process data on sales–cash receipts and purchases–cash disbursements respectively. Recall from our discussion in Chapter 14 that sales invoice summary information is passed from order processing, where these invoices are created, to accounts receivable so that the customer master file can be updated. At the same time specific information on individual customer accounts which results from processing by the receivable package can be returned to order processing for sales order decision making. Similarly, accounts payable receives purchase invoice summaries from inventory control where they are created in order to update the vendor master file, and returns detailed vendor activity breakdowns which aid in making and analyzing purchasing decisions.

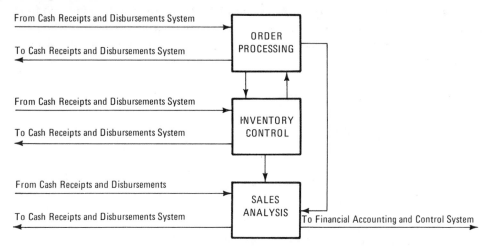

FIGURE 15-1 Information Flow in a Sales and Purchases System

Sales analysis is the only application of the sales and purchases system which directly interacts with the financial accounting and control system. Of course, data from order processing and inventory control are ultimately included in the general ledger, but only after being processed and summarized by the cash receipts and disbursements system. Output from sales analysis, however, is incorporated into the budgeting package directly, so that detailed comparisons of performance by product, territory, salesman, customer, or other basis can be readily made. Also, this sales analysis output provides a sound basis for the preparation or revision of future budgets. Sales analysis by salesman can also be used in the calculation of payroll where compensation is based on commissions. Because most detailed data on sales and collections is processed and stored in accounts receivable, important information flow takes place between the sales analysis package and accounts receivable.

Finally, you should note in Figure 15-1, the information flow within the sales and purchases system between applications. This intrasystem flow is heaviest in the sales and purchases system and is one of the most important features of the system. The sales and purchases system interacts less with other systems than does cash receipts and disbursements, however, the internal flow of information within the system is significant. We will examine the specific processing applications of the sales and purchases system in the remainder of this chapter.

15.2 ORDER PROCESSING COMPONENT

This application represents the point of original entry of sales orders, returns and adjustments from customers into the information system. The purpose of this package is to provide fast and accurate processing of orders from customers while minimizing the clerical costs and costs associated with customer dissatisfaction. Basically, we would like to know from this processing package (1) if sales orders have been properly filled, (2) if items sold have been properly priced, and (3) the status of unfilled orders. The focus of this application is on order filling and pricing, and the goal is to maximize customer service while controlling the costs associated with the processing of customer orders. Figure 15-2 summarizes the information flow into and from an order-processing application. Notice the large amount of information flow between this package and others of the sales and purchases system as well as with accounts receivable of the cash receipts and disbursements system.

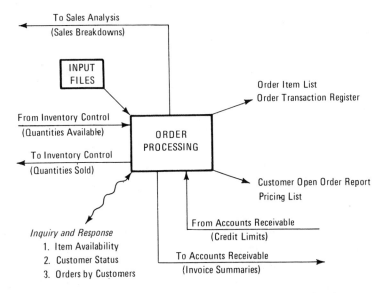

FIGURE 15-2 Information Flow in an Order Processing Application

Output Reports

Some of the important printed output related to sales orders (invoice register and bills) is produced by the accounts receivable application. Some reports, however, are generated directly by order processing and we will begin with this printed output. Typically, the following man-sensible reports would result directly from order processing.

1. *Order item list* (Figure 15-3). This report is sometimes called a *picking list*. The idea is to produce a list based on a customer order which details the items ordered by name and number so that the order can be accurately filled from inventory. This report can be quite detailed and may include the location of the items involved and packing codes as well as shipping instructions and addresses. Notice also that the list can be cross-referenced to the specific order and customer, by order and customer number. The listing can serve as a guide for filling each order and then double as a packing slip to be included in the shipment when the order is complete. Of course, one such list must be printed for each order to be filled and shipped.

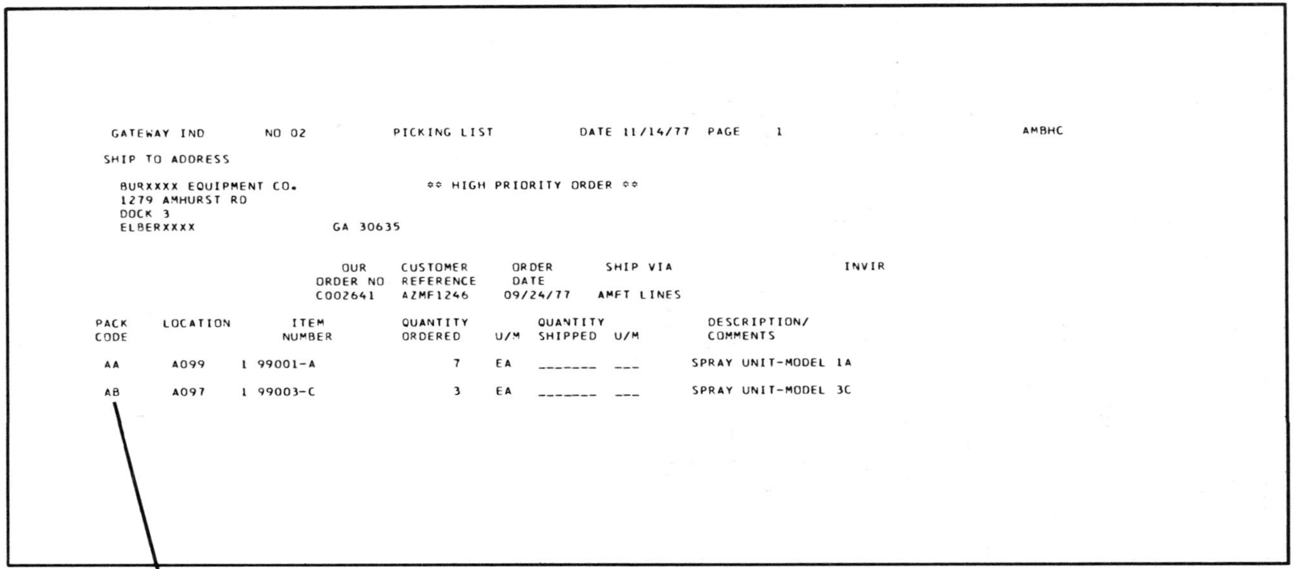

```
GATEWAY IND      NO 02         PICKING LIST              DATE 11/14/77  PAGE    1                              AMBHC

SHIP TO ADDRESS

BURXXXX EQUIPMENT CO.                        ○○ HIGH PRIORITY ORDER ○○
1279 AMHURST RD
DOCK 3
ELBERXXXX                    GA 30635

                        OUR       CUSTOMER    ORDER     SHIP VIA                    INVIR
                        ORDER NO  REFERENCE   DATE      AMFT LINES
                        C002641   AZMF1246    09/24/77

PACK    LOCATION    ITEM        QUANTITY         QUANTITY             DESCRIPTION/
CODE                NUMBER      ORDERED   U/M    SHIPPED   U/M        COMMENTS

AA      A099      1 99001-A        7      EA     -------   ---        SPRAY UNIT-MODEL 1A

AB      A097      1 99003-C        3      EA     -------   ---        SPRAY UNIT-MODEL 3C
```

Used in conjunction with
the bill of lading

Picking list shows if
customer will not
accept partial shipments
or back orders

FIGURE 15-3 Order Item List
(courtesy of IBM Corporation)

2. *Order transaction register* (Figure 15-4). Before creating transaction files for all verified and completed orders the order processing package can print a listing of these orders. This report shows all new orders accepted since the last printing as well as orders changed, and provides an audit trail for all orders which will ultimately update the various master files. The sequencing of the report is usually by order number, and codes are used to denote the status of each order with regard to invoicing, special pricing, and whether or not the order can be filled from stock. Listing all order activity for a period of time in one report allows each order to be traced to a specific customer (by customer number) and to the order's point of entry into the system by a work station identification (WSID).

3. *Customer open order report* (Figure 15-5). This listing deals with orders which are accepted but not yet filled, usually because the ordered item is not available in stock. Orders which can be filled from inventory, however, are included in this report if they are still outstanding as of the date of the printing. The open order report contains most of the same data found in the order item list (Figure 15-3) which, you will recall, is generated for those orders about to be filled. The only significant information which may appear in the open order report but would never be a part of the picking list is cost data on the items in each order. For obvious reasons, a business would not want this information included in a document which will accompany items sold as they are shipped to a customer.

4. *Pricing list* (Figure 15-6). This report serves as a source for quoting prices to customers by category of sale. Each active item of inventory is listed by number and description, a base price listed, and a mark-up (increase) or discount (decrease) percentage for each item by quantity sold. In this way quantity discounts or price breaks can be built into the report for instant referencing by those employees accepting orders and preparing them for the order processing package.

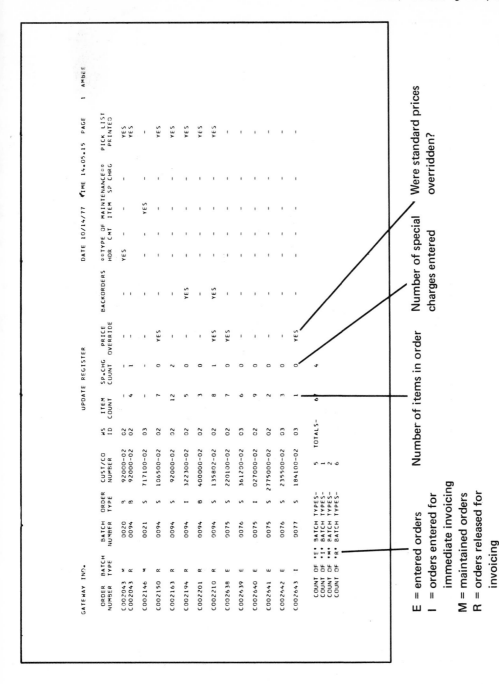

FIGURE 15-4 Order Transaction Register
(courtesy of IBM Corporation)

GATEWAY IND   NO 02   OPEN ORDERS BY CUSTOMER   DATE 10/24/77   TIME 09.14.26   PAGE   1   AMBGC3

CUSTOMER NUMBER	NAME	OUR ORDER	P.O. NUMBER	DUE DATE	HSE	WHSE LOC	ITEM NUMBER	DESCRIPTION	UM	QUANTITY	VALUE AT COST
00050500	TIOGA INDUSTRIES	00297	Z04327A	11/07/77	1	DP020	03421	HINGE ARM	EA	35	72.88
		00297	Z04327A	11/07/77	1	P120	03591-OR	WHEEL - 8 IN DIA	EA	50	37.48
		00297	Z04327A	11/07/77	1	M100	26006-20	TANK 8 X 12 INCHES	EA	10	79.08
							NUMBER ORDERS THIS CUSTOMER-	1	VALUE AT COST		189.44
00172000	SELLER ENGINEERING	00284	2763	10/28/77	1	DP095	03590	AUTO SWITCH	EA	15	18.75
		00284	2763	10/28/77	1	DP099	27003-20	PUMP ASSEMBLY	EA	1	27.33
		00284	2763	10/28/77	1	DP020	03421	HINGE ARM	EA	15	31.23
							NUMBER ORDERS THIS CUSTOMER-	1	VALUE AT COST-		77.31
00311100	ASTRO INDUSTRIES	00287	M6927F	12/10/77	1	DP020	03421	HINGE ARM	EA	25	52.06
							NUMBER ORDERS THIS CUSTOMER-	1	VALUE AT COST-		52.06
							FINAL TOTALS	ORDERS-	3	VALUE AT COST-	318.81

FIGURE 15-5 Customer Open Order Report
(courtesy of IBM Corporation)

GATEWAY IND.   ITEM PRICE LIST   DATE 10/18/77   TIME 16.20.30   PAGE   1   AMBV2

ITEM NUMBER	DESCRIPTION	BASE PRICE		1	2	3	4	5	6
26006-20	TANK TOP 8 X 12 INCHES		MARKUP %	7.000	6.000	5.000	4.000	3.000	2.000
		14.500	PRICE	15.515	15.370	15.225	15.080	14.935	14.790
26006-21	TANK TOP 10 X 12 INCHES		MARKUP %	7.000	6.000	5.000	4.000	3.000	2.000
		24.750	PRICE	24.483	26.235	25.988	25.740	25.493	25.245
26006-22	TANK TOP 12 X 24 INCHES		MARKUP %	7.000	6.000	5.000	4.000	3.000	2.000
		39.950	PRICE	42.747	42.347	41.948	41.548	41.149	40.749
99001-A	SPRAY UNIT MODEL 1A		DISCOUNT %	5.000	10.000	15.000	20.000	25.000	30.000
		155.000	PRICE	147.250	139.500	131.750	124.000	116.250	108.500
99002-B	SPRAY UNIT MODEL 2B		DISCOUNT %	7.000	12.000	17.000	22.000	27.000	32.000
		170.000	PRICE	158.100	149.600	141.110	132.600	124.100	115.600
99003-C	SPRAY UNIT MODEL 3C		DISCOUNT %	10.000	15.000	20.000	25.000	30.000	35.000
		190.000	PRICE	171.000	161.500	152.000	142.500	133.000	123.500

FIGURE 15-6 Pricing List
(courtesy of IBM Corporation)

Information Exchange

Although the output reports of this application are important, perhaps the most significant feature of order processing is the large amount of information exchange with other applications. Notice in Figure 15-2 that order processing interacts with both other applications of the sales and purchases system. A very strong tie exists between order processing and inventory control because each needs data from the other to perform its function. Orders cannot be processed without information on the quantities of each item available (inventory control) and, in turn, each order processed and quantity sold affects the inventory on hand. The flow, then, must be constant and two-way if each processing package is to work. Similarly, the relationship between order processing and accounts receivable is very close. Invoices which are created and enter the information system at the order processing application must be transferred in summary form to accounts receivable for billing and collection, and then summarized again and passed on to the financial accounting and control system for general record-keeping and financial statement purposes. Since all customer activity is processed in the receivables package and all permanent customer data held there, important information from receivables must be available to order processing as necessary input to order acceptance decisions. Most of this same sort of customer sales data is necessary for the sales analysis application and can be transferred there from order processing. All of these information exchanges can be easily accomplished in a computer-based information system with careful data base design.

If decisions are to be efficiently and effectively made on sales orders, the capacity to extract information from the system, on-demand, must be present. Employees handling orders need immediate information on inventory items and customers based on the most up-to-date data the processing system can generate. The inquiry/response capability demonstrated in Figure 15-2 gives the user access to this kind of information, something even the best designed manual system could not do. This question and answer dialogue is probably more important in order processing than in any of the other applications we have discussed so far. Figure 15-7 illustrates typical response information on item availability and customer status.

Input Files

What about the input necessary for order processing to function? Like all of the other packages, the processing of orders requires certain files of data. A word about the special requirements of processing orders would be helpful, however, before we discuss these input files. Interactive (immediate) processing is probably more important in the area of sales orders than in any of the applications of the cash receipts and disbursements or financial accounting and control systems. The importance of meeting customer demands and the competitive nature of order getting makes the interactive approach an essential in order processing. The result is that an on-line input device such as a terminal would likely find greater use in this package than in the applications discussed in earlier chapters. Figure 15-8 shows a typical order entering sequence which would occur as orders are processed interactively. Note in the sequence the give-and-take between the user and computer-stored data, with the terminal (visual screen and keyboard) as the vehicle. First, customer and order numbers are entered and the system responds with customer data from the customer master file. Then, basic data on the order is provided by the user, followed by system-requested data on the item(s) ordered. The system then provides data on the item(s) ordered from the item master file (see inventory control) including prices.

A = active
D = deleted
S = suspended (accept no
more orders from this
customer)

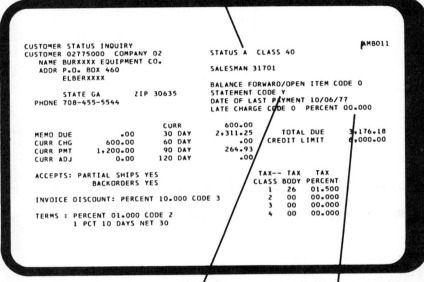

Y = customer gets
statements
N = no statement

Service charge percent if
customer is to be assessed
service charges

FIGURE 15-7 Display of Response Information From Order Processing
(courtesy of IBM Corporation)

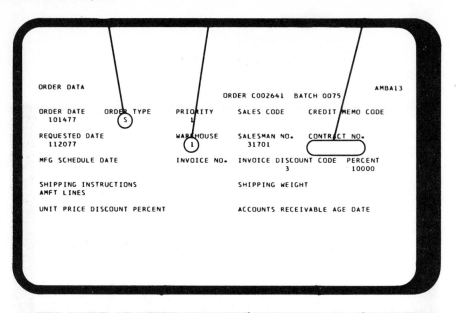

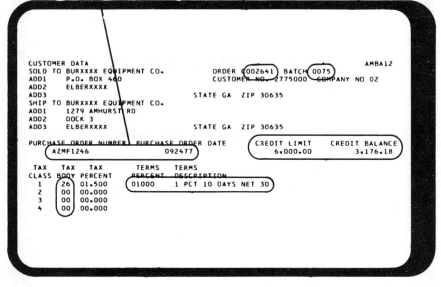

FIGURE 15-8 Display of Interactive Order Entry Sequence
(courtesy of IBM Corporation)

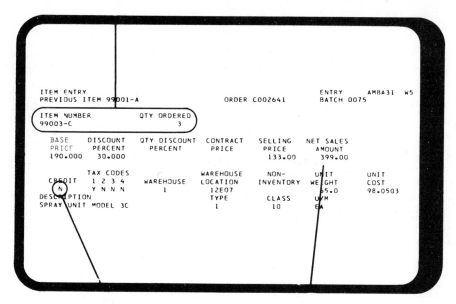

```
ITEM ENTRY                                                     ENTRY      AMBA31  W5
PREVIOUS ITEM 99001-A                  ORDER C002641           BATCH 0075

ITEM NUMBER            QTY ORDERED
99003-C                        3

   BASE      DISCOUNT   QTY DISCOUNT   CONTRACT    SELLING    NET SALES
   PRICE     PERCENT     PERCENT        PRICE       PRICE      AMOUNT
  190.000    30.000                               133.00      399.00

              TAX CODES                WAREHOUSE     NON-       UNIT       UNIT
   CREDIT     1  2  3  4   WAREHOUSE   LOCATION   INVENTORY   WEIGHT      COST
     N        Y  N  N  N       1        12E07                  25.0      98.0503
DESCRIPTION                             TYPE        CLASS       UM
SPRAY UNIT MODEL 3C                       1          10         EA
```

Figure 15-8 Display of Interactive Order Entry Sequence (Continued)

At this point the order processing is complete if the user gives the system instructions to up-date all relevant master files and produce sales invoices.

Whether or not the interactive approach is used, some input data files are necessary to order processing. This application would make use of (1) the customer master file discussed in the receivables package and, (2) the item master file to be discussed in the inventory control section of this chapter. Notice that both these master files provide important input information necessary to the processing of orders. In addition to these master files, a permanent file of relatively constant data on the prices of each item and appropriate price limits, breaks, and discount percentages would probably be used. Of course, new sales orders for a period would form a transactions file, whether or not the interactive approach is used. As these new sales orders are filled, the new invoices file used in the receivables package is created. This file construction process emphasizes the difference between sales orders and sales invoices. Sales invoices represent accounting transactions while sales orders do not.

With the order processing package you should begin to see the concept of a data base at work. Order processing makes use of the same data files used in other applications, and creates a transaction file which provides the basis for the transaction file of another package. The basic idea is that unique and distinct master files are not needed for each application to be processed. The important data of a business can be organized and stored so that it is accessible by any package within the system using the speed and memory capability of the computer. At the conclusion of this chapter, we will list each of the files discussed throughout Chapters 13-15 and connect each file to the processing application which would likely use it. It should be easier for you to appreciate this commonality of data when the entire information system is brought together.

15.3 INVENTORY CONTROL COMPONENT

In a manner similar to order processing, this application represents the point of original entry of purchase invoices, purchase returns, and adjustments into the system. The purpose of this package is to provide information which aids in the control of inventory and on which purchase decisions can be based, so that total costs associated with the purchase function are minimized. We would like for the inventory control processing package to tell us (1) if purchases have been properly timed, (2) if purchase orders have been properly filled and costed; (3) the status of unfilled purchase orders, and (4) the status of inventory on hand and item availability. The focus of this application is on maintaining appropriate levels of inventory to meet customer demands but no more than that amount, and on safeguarding the items on hand.

Figure 15-9 summarizes the flow of information into and from an inventory control processing application. Like order processing, the amount of information flow between this package and others in the sales and purchase system and, importantly, with accounts payable is significant.

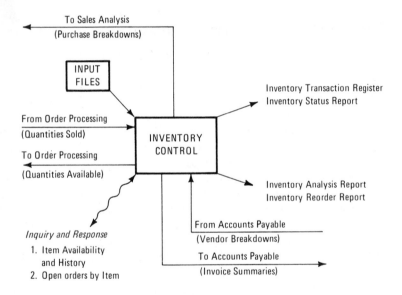

FIGURE 15-9 Information Flow in an Inventory Control Application

Output Reports

The very close relationship of inventory control with accounts payable results in several of the important reports associated with the purchase function (purchases journal and checks) being generated by the payables package. Some output reports, however, are unique to inventory control because they are directly related to the goals of this package. We will begin with these printed reports generated by inventory control.

1. *Inventory transaction register* (Figure 15-10). This is a complete listing of all transactions in inventory for the period covered by the report. The statement includes orders, receipts,

and issues of inventory items as well as adjustments to inventory. Notice that the report is sequenced by item number (although other sequencing is possible), and beginning and ending balances for each item are given. Transaction quantities and amounts which account for changes in item balances are highlighted, as is the state of completion of the inventory transaction. In this report, on-order amounts are included in the availability calculation for each item; however, the user can decide whether or not this is to be done. Since the register prints all transactions which affect relevant master files, it provides an excellent cross-reference to other documents and contributes to the traceability of transactions through the system.

2. *Inventory status report* (Figure 15-11). The focus of this statement is on quantities of each item available as of the end of a processing period. For each item a unit cost is supplied and a total cost extended. In this sample report standard cost is used, but any costing technique (average, fifo, lifo) can be applied to the items. Also, a base per unit selling price is given so that item by item profitability analysis is possible. This listing is really more than an availability report, however, because the statement summarizes all inventory activity for the period, the detail of which is given by the transaction register. Notice that for each item, the beginning balance, issues, receipts, adjustments, and ending balance is provided as well as on-order amounts as of the date of the report. A good deal of information about the status of inventory is readily available here.

Remember, the focus of the transactions register is on events, and the focus of the status report is on availability, although each report includes some summary information from the other.

3. *Management reports*. A series of decision-making and control oriented reports of almost endless variety can be delivered by the inventory control package. The two reports listed in Figure 15-9, inventory analysis and inventory reorder, are probably typical, although report format and content can be designed to meet just about any management need for information. Inventory analysis reports would highlight for management review at least the following characteristics for each item of inventory:

a. Turnover.

b. Profit.

c. Profit margin.

d. Investment required.

Reports of this sort can be sequenced in any manner desired by the user so that items of high turnover, profit, profit margin, or investment can be listed first with the report in descending order of any of the criteria. Alternatively, one report could be generated for each of these characteristics for inventory items. The basic idea of inventory analysis reports is to provide information which will allow management to determine trends and areas of success and difficulty for planning and decision-making purposes. A wealth of inventory activity data is stored in any computer-based information system; how it is channeled and used is limited only by the imagination of the system user.

A second statement, called a *reorder report*, is quite useful because decisions on when and how much to reorder are almost solely quantitative and can thus be quite easily programmed into the system. Unlike decisions on successful versus failing items which

GATEWAY IND.   INVENTORY TRANSACTION REGISTER   DATE 10/14/77   TIME 11.26.15   AM13G

BATCH NO. 146   WS ID-XX

ITEM NUMBER / TRN TRAN AC- CD DATE REC	WHSE NO. / DUE DATE	DESCRIPTION	REF. NUMBER	CUST/JOB /VEND NO	TRANS QTY	UM	TRANS AMOUNT	BEGINNING BALANCE ON-HAND	ON-ORDER	ALLOC.	ENDING BALANCE ON-HAND	ON-ORDER	ALLOC.	AVAIL.
03021 RP 10/14/77 A	1	VALVE	1362	030716	9000	EA	2,268.00	8607	9000	0	17607	0	0	17607
03385 RP 10/13/77 A	1	WRENCH	207763	072303	2000	EA	710.00	7927	6000	0	9927	4000	0	13927
RP 10/14/77 A			207792	072303	3975	EA	1411.13	9927	4000	0	13902	0	0	13902
03443 RM 10/14/77 A	1	MOTOR SUPPORT	M000742		2000	EA	10283.40	300	2000	0	2300	0	0	2300
03590 IA 10/14/77 A	1	AUTO SWITCH			25-	EA		3500	0	0	3475	0	0	3475
03591-08 CS 10/14/77 A	1	WHEEL 8 INCH DIA					0.7495	1050	2000	0	1050	0	0	3050
03593 PR 10/13/77 A	1	PIN	27737	012893	10000	EA	105.00	12666	20000	0	22666	10000	0	32666

FIGURE 15-10 Inventory Transaction Register
(courtesy of IBM Corporation)

GATEWAY IND. MONTH-END INVENTORY STOCK STATUS DATE 10/31/77 TIME 10.14.26 PAGE 1 AM16C

ALL ITEMS

ITEM CLASS	WHSE NO.	ITEM NUMBER	BEGIN BAL	ISS/SALE	RECEIPTS	VENDOR NUMBER	ITEM TYPE	ADJ.	ITEM DESCRIPTION	QTY ON-HAND	QTY ON-ORDER	QTY ALLOC.	QTY AVAIL.	U/M	STANDARD UNIT COST	EXTENDED UNIT COST	BASE PRICE
50	1	03421	509	79	0		2	0	HINGE ARM	430	150	0	580	EA	3.3310	1,423.33	.000
70	1	03590	828	235	200		4	0	*AUTO SWITCH	793	0	175	618	EA	.1140	90.40	.150
	2		1119	416	0			0		703	0	175	528	EA	.1140	80.14	.150
TOTALS-			1947	651	200			0		1496	0	350	1146			170.54	
20	1	03904-A	450	0	0		1	0	PUMP SHAFT ASSY	450	450	0	900	EA	8.8250	3,971.25	13.250
70	1	03906	365	100	0	078444	4	10	DRIVING COLLAR	275	500	100	675	EA	.2900	79.75	.450
80	1	05290	4920	1730	2600	030716	4	120-	*FERRULE	5570	3900	0	9470	EA	.1540	857.78	.200
50	1	26006-21	1225	300	150		1	0	TANK 10X18 INCHES	1075	275	135	1215	EA	12.5000	13,437.50	18.000
	2		1050	250	180			0		980	0	120	860	EA	12.5000	12,250.00	18.000
TOTALS-			2275	550	330			0		2055	275	255	2075			25,687.50	
70	1	27001-01	1280	300	600		4	380-	ADAPTER GASKET	1200	1200	685	1715	EA	.1040	124.80	.140
	2		2130	250	0			0		1880	600	750	1730	EA	.1040	195.52	.140
TOTALS-			3410	550	600			380-		3080	1800	1435	3445			320.32	

REPORT TOTAL- 32,510.47

FIGURE 15-11 Inventory Status Report
(courtesy of IBM Corporation)

require judgment and insight by management, well-established formulas can be used to determine reordering time and amount. Calculations for economic order quantity and order point can become a part of the inventory control package, and reports produced which list for management consideration the reorder decisions made by the system before they are implemented. The key to both these management-oriented reports is for the user to decide what information would be most useful and what form the information should take. Once these decisions are made, the system can deliver the data. Figure 15-12 is an example of one type of inventory analysis report, called an *A-B-C analysis report.* It focuses on the investment required in each of twenty items of inventory. In this report, investment is defined as units sold during the period multiplied by unit cost. For most businesses only a few items of inventory account for most of the sales activity, so this sort of report can be useful for management planning and control.

Information Exchange

Now to the interapplication flows for inventory control depicted in Figure 15-9. Most of these exchanges of information have been discussed in depth earlier in the context of other processing applications. The very strong two-way relationship between inventory control and order processing should be clear to you from the previous section. An equally strong tie exists between inventory control and the payables package, both of which have to do with purchases and payments. Invoices which are created and enter the system at the inventory control application must be transferred in summary form to accounts payable for payment, and then summarized again and passed on to the financial accounting and control system for general record-keeping and financial statement purposes. Since all vendor data is stored and processed in the payables application, important vendor breakdowns must be available to inventory control to aid in purchasing decisions. This inventory control–accounts payable relationship parallels that of order processing–accounts receivable. Also, like order processing, the inventory control package is capable of passing purchase analysis information (mostly cost breakdowns) on to sales analysis for the generation of profit reports.

Recall that inquiry/response capacity was critically important to the processing of sales orders because it is necessary for a business to react quickly and accurately to customer preferences in the sales area. This need for immediate response information is not so critical in the purchase function since actions by management can be more planned and deliberate. Nonetheless, some question and answer capability on the availability and recent activity of inventory items and on items currently on order can be quite useful in answering management questions as well as for short-term purchase planning. Figure 15-13 illustrates typical response information on inventory balances and current outstanding orders.

Input Files

In order to keep track of the inventory availability of each item as well as the status of new orders to vendors for inventory items, the inventory control package requires two files we have not yet discussed.

GATEWAY IND. A-B-C ANALYSIS REPORT DATE 10/31/77 TIME 11.42.17 PAGE 1 AM12G

WHSE NO.	ITEM NUMBER	ITEM TYPE	ITEM DESCRIPTION	ITEM COUNT	CUM% ITEMS	ANNUAL UNITS	UNIT COST	ANNUAL USAGE $	CUMULATIVE USAGE $	CUM% USAGE	ON-HAND VALUE	CUM% VALUE
				20	100.0			395,192		100.0	82,891	100.0
1	34250-A	1	TANK COVER ASSY	1	5.0	20,000	3.8500	77,000	77,000	19.5	25,903	31.2
2	27006-70	2	TANK BOTTOM 8 INCHES	2	10.0	35,000	1.5390	53,865	130,865	33.1	4,911	37.2
2	33480-A	4	CONTROL BOX	3	15.0	35,000	1.5370	53,795	184,660	46.7	5,687	44.0
1	03424	2	TREADLE ASSY	4	20.0	2,500	15.0000	37,500	222,160	56.2	16,125	63.5
1	03426-C	2	TUBE 12 INCH DIA	5	25.0	2,500	15.0000	37,500	259,660	65.7	14,700	81.2
2	27007-A1	1	BASE ASSEMBLY	6	30.0	2,500	9.7070	24,268	283,928	71.8	4,368	86.5
2	03905	4	WEARING COLLAR	7	35.0	35,000	.5240	18,340	302,268	76.5	555	87.2
2	03912	4	ADAPTER PLATE	8	40.0	130,000	.1380	17,940	320,208	81.0	769	88.1
2	27006-10	2	TANK TOP 10 INCHES	9	45.0	3,500	4.7390	16,797	337,005	85.3	3,527	92.3
2	27002-01	2	ADAPTER PLATE	10	50.0	60,000	.2210	13,260	350,265	88.6	151	92.5
1	03021	4	VALVE	11	55.0	45,000	.2600	11,700	361,965	91.6	201	92.8
1	03423	2	TREADLE	12	60.0	2,500	4.3000	10,750	372,715	94.3	1,849	95.0
1	3440-A	2	STAND PIPE	13	65.0	40,000	.2600	10,400	383,115	96.9	259	95.3
2	27006-20	2	TANK TOP 12 INCHES	14	70.0	2,000	4.7990	9,598	392,713	99.1	3,119	99.1
2	03023	4	DISCHARGE FERRULE	15	75.0	2,000	.3480	696	393,409	99.5	96	99.2
1	03419	4	HINGE DIN	16	80.0	48,000	.0120	576	393,985	99.7	10	99.2
1	03010	4	PLATE	17	85.0	2,500	.1720	430	394,415	99.8	136	99.4
1	34140-A	4	CLAMP WITH NUT	18	90.0	2,000	.1710	342	394,757	99.8	120	99.5
1	05290	4	FERRULE	19	95.0	2,100	.1360	286	395,063	99.9	256	99.8
1	79620-C	4	TANK TUBE	20	100.0	1,200	.1240	149	395,192	100.0	149	100.0
			TOTAL	20					395,192		82,891	

FIGURE 15-12 Inventory Analysis Report
(courtesy of IBM Corporation)

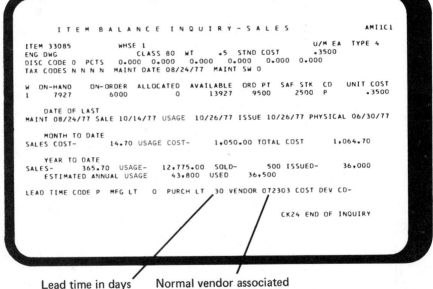

```
              O P E N   O R D E R S   I N Q U I R Y            AMI1D1

  ITEM 03385          WHSE 1   WRENCH                    U/M EA  TYPE  4
  ENG DWG                  CLASS 80  WT      .5  STND COST      .3500
  DISC CODE 0  PCTS   0.000   0.000   0.000   0.000   0.000   0.000
  TAX CODES N N N N  MAINT DATE 08/24/77  MAINT SW 0
                                                              OPERATION
  ORDER NO   VEND/JOB  STAT   ORD QTY         DUE DATE  HOURS REM  CURR  NXT
  P017943    072303     20     3000           10/20/77
  P018066    072303     10     3000           11/08/77



                                                    CK24 END OF INQUIRY
```

```
         I T E M   B A L A N C E   I N Q U I R Y - S A L E S      AMI1C1

  ITEM 33085          WHSE 1                           U/M EA  TYPE 4
  ENG DWG                  CLASS 80  WT      .5  STND COST      .3500
  DISC CODE 0  PCTS   0.000   0.000   0.000   0.000   0.000
  TAX CODES N N N N   MAINT DATE 08/24/77  MAINT SW 0

  W  ON-HAND    ON-ORDER   ALLOCATED   AVAILABLE  ORD PT   SAF STK  CD   UNIT COST
  1    7927       6000          0        13927     9500     2500   P      .3500

     DATE OF LAST
  MAINT 08/24/77  SALE 10/14/77  USAGE  10/26/77  ISSUE 10/26/77  PHYSICAL 06/30/77

     MONTH TO DATE
  SALES COST-         14.70  USAGE COST-     1,050.00  TOTAL COST      1,064.70

     YEAR TO DATE
  SALES-      365.70  USAGE-   12,775.00  SOLD-       500  ISSUED-      36,000
     ESTIMATED ANNUAL USAGE      43,800  USED      36,500

  LEAD TIME CODE P   MFG LT    0   PURCH LT   30  VENDOR 072303  COST DEV CD-

                                                    CK24 END OF INQUIRY
```

Lead time in days   Normal vendor associated
                     with this item

FIGURE 15-13 Display of Response Information From Inventory Control
(courtesy of IBM Corporation)

1. *Item master file.* This file contains one record for each individual item number in inventory. Each record would contain at least the following data elements:

   a. Item number.

   b. Item description.

   c. Unit cost.

   d. Discount provisions.

   e. Unit base price.

   f. Mark-up provisions.

   g. Current quantity on hand.

   h. Current quantity on order.

   i. Receipts—current period.

   j. Receipts—year-to-date.

   k. Receipts—previous year.

   l. Issues—current period.

   m. Issues—year-to-date.

   n. Issues—previous year.

   o. Vendor number and name.

   This file is, of course, updated with each inventory control and order processing run and is the data base for all inquiries of this system. Note that it is input and output to both the inventory control and order processing packages, since both applications require data stored in the file in order to function and both provide information necessary to update the file. This file is the interface (connection) of the inventory control and order-processing applications and thus is a pivotal master file. Note also that the item master file is linked to the vendor master file of the payable package by the data elements for vendor number and name. This link is critical because of the processing relationship of inventory control and accounts payable and the need for information from the vendor master file by the inventory control package.

2. *New purchase order file.* This transactions file is generated as new purchase orders are created in the processing of inventory. As the purchase orders themselves are filled, this file becomes the basis for the new purchase invoices file discussed in the accounts payable application in Chapter 14. Again, note the differences between purchase orders and purchase invoices.

You can see from the relationships of accounts receivable–order processing, accounts payable–inventory control and order processing–inventory control that these important processing applications all make use of the same basic group of data. Careful organization of this data base can avoid repetition and duplication, and reduce errors. All of this, of course, reduces data-processing costs and produces a better information flow.

15.4 SALES ANALYSIS COMPONENT

This is the final package of the sales and purchases system and the last processing application we will discuss. Sales analysis is an interesting package because it is wholly dependent upon output from other applications of the sales and purchases and cash receipts and disbursements systems. The goal of sales analysis is to provide information which will aid management in (1) predicting future sales activity and profitability for the business and (2) evaluating the past performance of salesmen, products, and customers. This package can generate reports which are based on any breakdowns of sales and profits specified by management. Of course, the information system can do no significant analysis of sales or profit data no matter how elaborate the breakdowns might be. The purpose of this sort of processing is to produce concise understandable reports which present the most relevant information on past performance so that management may apply judgment and analysis to the data. With such data, management should be better able to anticipate the future and make decisions accordingly, spot potential difficulties while they are correctable, and create an evaluation and reward system which will contribute to achieving the objectives of the business.

Figure 15-14 summarizes the flow of information into and from sales analysis processing. Note the significant flow of information from other packages and the fact that sales analysis does serve the payroll and budgeting applications by providing useful data which can be incorporated into their processing.

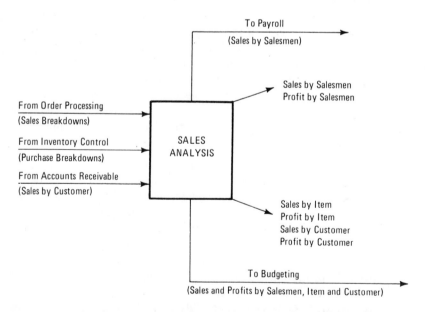

FIGURE 15-14 Information Flow in a Sales Analysis Application

Output Reports

The most important aspect of sales analysis is the management reports which can be produced for planning and control purposes. We will start with a discussion of these reports.

1. *Sales and profits by salesmen* (Figure 15-15). The usefulness of these reports and the ones to follow in both planning and control is limited only by management imagination. A breakdown of sales by salesmen, and therefore by sales territory, is a significant aid to the budgeting process which starts with the sales forecast. It is usually easier for those familiar with a territory and the people who work in it to predict future sales levels for the area than for someone to attempt prediction for the firm as a whole. These territorial sales volume "budgets" can be summed up and a sales forecast for the firm derived. A good starting point for this approach to sales forecasting is accurate, detailed information on past sales activity. *Sales by salesmen* is one of the reports which provide this information. Notice that this report shows period-to-date (in this case one month) sales and year-to-date sales for both the current and previous year together with the deviation from last year's sales performance expressed as a percentage. The focus of this statement is on sales trends, which are the basis of business budgets.

    Evaluating the performance of salesmen and territories, however, requires more than sales information. The *profit by salesmen* report is generally concerned with current period activity, although the last column of this sample profitability statement does show last year's gross profit percentages for comparison purposes. Profitability reports such as this one emphasize the measure of performance that is consistent with the achievement of company objectives. Since most businesses attempt to maximize profits (within certain broad constraints), a control system will only be effective if it encourages employees to maximize that same variable. The inclusion of costs of sales, gross profit in dollars, and gross profit percentage for each salesman allows management to structure an evaluation and reward system based on the measurement most likely to contribute to company goals. The focus of this report, then, is on evaluating performance and determining the areas in need of corrective action. Like the sales by salesmen statement, this report provides important data which can be used in the budgeting process.

2. *Sales and profits by item* (Figure 15-16). The breakdown of sales by item produces relevant budgeting information as does the sales by salesmen report. Information on units and dollars sold for each item of inventory can be used as a verification of the sales forecast which has been built (from the ground up) by salesmen and territory. Using past data on unit and dollar sales for each item, management can spot shifting demand and changing trends and incorporate this information into future sales forecasts. Since budgeting is essentially an educated guess at the future, prediction is better if more than one independent approach is used as a check on the accuracy of any one forecast. Also, sales by item provides information which helps in management decisions on sales emphasis and advertising and, very importantly, on future inventory levels. Notice that month-to-date and year-to-date unit and dollar sales are given by item in the reports illustrated.

GATEWAY IND.   NO 02

SALES ANALYSIS BY SALESMAN
FOR OCTOBER

DATE 10/31/77   TIME 10.25.00   PAGE   1   AMS32

SALESMAN NUMBER	SALESMAN NAME	M-T-D AMOUNTS			Y-T-D AMOUNTS		
		THIS YEAR	LAST YEAR	PCT. DIFF	THIS YEAR	LAST YEAR	PCT. DIFF
31701	ROBERT G. AARON	18,100.00	19,106.50	5.3-	97,315.40	90,100.00	8.0
31702	BOBBY JOE ADAMS	15,175.00	12,100.00	25.4	28,500.00	20,000.00	42.5
31705	WILLIAM E. ANDERSON	24,007.00	12,500.00	92.1	146,100.00	130,650.00	11.8
31706	CHARLES W. ARNOLD	14,000.20	13,500.00	3.7	87,150.00	80,150.00	8.7
31709	JOE DON BAKER	7,057.30	4,750.00	48.6	9,000.00	8,500.00	5.9
31901	RAY PIERCE	10,500.00	10,100.00	4.0	46,315.00	30,500.00	51.8
31999	IN-HOUSE OFFICE SALES	10,706.10	14,850.00	27.9-	77,070.00	65,230.10	18.2
	FINAL TOTALS	99,545.60	86,906.50	14.5	491,450.40	425,130.10	15.6

GATEWAY IND.   NO. 02

PROFIT ANALYSIS BY SALESMAN
FOR OCTOBER

DATE 10/31/77   TIME 09.23.19   PAGE   1   AMS32

SALESMAN NUMBER	SALESMAN NAME	M-T-D				Y-T-D				L.YR
		SALES $	COST	G.P.$	G.P.%	SALES $	COST	G.P.$	G.P.%	G.P.%
31701	ROBERT G. AARON	18,100.00	15,456.87	2,643.23	14.6	97,315.40	79,079.39	18,236.01	18.7	16.1
31702	BOBBY JOE ADAMS	15,175.00	13,093.18	2,081.82	13.7	28,500.00	24,800.20	3,699.80	13.0	10.9
31705	WILLIAM E. ANDERSON	24,007.00	20,536.00	3,471.00	14.5	146,100.00	118,070.00	28,030.00	19.2	18.1
31706	CHARLES W. ARNOLD	14,000.20	13,232.00	768.20	5.5	87,150.00	80,940.00	6,210.00	7.1	12.2
31709	JOE DON BAKER	7,057.30	6,357.93	699.37	9.9	9,000.00	9,200.00	200.00-	2.2-	9.7
31901	RAY PIERCE	10,500.00	8,973.36	1,526.64	14.5	46,315.00	39,000.00	7,315.00	15.8	15.0
31999	IN-HOUSE OFFICE SALES	10,706.10	9,851.38	854.72	8.0	77,070.00	64,300.00	12,770.00	16.6	10.2
	FINAL TOTALS	99,545.60	87,500.72	12,044.98	12.1	491,450.40	415,389.59	76,060.81	15.5	13.1

FIGURE 15-15 Sales and Profits by Salesmen
(courtesy of IBM Corporation)

GATEWAY IND. NO. 02 PROFIT ANALYSIS BY ITEM / FOR OCTOBER DATE 10/31/77 TIME 09.14.00 PAGE 1 AMS22

ITEM CL NUMBER		QUANTITIES				PROFIT		AMOUNT		PROFIT		
		SOLD M-T-D	LOST M-T-D	SOLD Y-T-D	LOST Y-T-D	G.P.$ M-T-D	G.P.% M-T-D	SALES Y-T-D	COST Y-T-D	G.P.$ Y-T-D	G.P.% Y-T-D	G.P.% L.YR
50 03423	TREADLE	1,050	130	7,636	1,031	206.74	17.9	8,400.00	7,000.00	1,400.00	16.7	17.9
50 03425	COVER	575	0	2,400	0	218.50	19.0	4,800.00	4,100.00	700.00	14.6	16.9
50 03426	TUBE - 8 INCH DIA	1,200	67	11,500	119	558.00	31.0	17,250.00	13,150.00	4,100.00	23.8	33.7
50 26006-20	TANK - 8 X 12 INCHES	1,000	0	1,200	0	51.25	4.1	1,500.00	1,600.00	100.00-	6.7-	4.1
50 26006-22	TANK - 10 X 18 INCHES	750	138	2,272	206	83.33	10.1	2,500.00	2,000.00	500.00	20.0	17.5
50 26006-22	TANK - 12 X 24 INCHES	1,500	176	4,250	319	537.00	17.9	8,500.00	7,700.00	800.00	9.4	11.0
50 27004-01	HANDLE	300	0	4,150	0	210.00	14.0	20,750.00	17,400.00	3,350.00	16.1	17.1
50 34440-A	STAND PIPE	500	0	7,780	0	100.00	8.0	19,450.00	20,000.00	550.00-	2.8-	4.0
CLASS TOTALS		6,875	511	41,188	1,675	1,964.82	14.7	83,150.00	72,950.00	10,200.00	14.0	13.0

FIGURE 15-16 Sales and Profits by Item
(courtesy of IBM Corporation)

GATEWAY IND.   NO. 02   SALES ANALYSIS BY ITEM / FOR OCTOBER   DATE 10/31/77 TIME 09.16.15 PAGE 1 AMS22

CL ITEM NO.		M-T-D QUANTITY			M-T-D AMOUNTS			Y-T-D QUANTITY			Y-T-D AMOUNTS		
		THIS YEAR	LAST YEAR	PCT. DIFF	THIS YEAR	LAST YEAR	PCT. DIFF	THIS YEAR	LAST YEAR	PCT. DIFF	THIS YEAR	LAST YEAR	PCT. DIFF
50 03423	TREADLE	1,050	1,000	5.0	1,155.00	1,100.00	5.0	7,636	6,363	20.0	8,400.00	7,000.00	20.0
50 03425	COVER 400	575	400	43.8	1,150.00	800.00	43.8	2,400	2,500	4.0-	4,800.00	5,000.00	4.0-
50 03426	TUBE - 8 INCH DIA	1,200	1,100	9.1	1,800.00	1,650.00	9.1	11,500	10,833	6.2	17,250.00	16,250.00	6.2
50 26006-20	TANK - 8 X 12 INCHES	1,000	930	7.5	1,250.00	1,162.50	7.5	1,200	1,120	7.1	1,500.00	1,400.00	7.1
50 26006-21	TANK - 10 X 18 INCHES	750	600	25.0	825.00	660.00	25.0	2,272	2,045	11.1	2,500.00	2,250.00	11.1
50 26006-22	TANK - 12 X 24 INCHES	1,500	1,600	6.3-	3,000.00	3,200.00	6.3-	4,250	4,450	4.5-	8,500.00	8,900.00	4.5-
50 27004-01	HANDLE	300	250	16.7	1,500.00	1,250.00	20.0	4,150	3,550	16.9	20,750.00	17,750.00	16.9
50 34440-A	STAND PIPE	500	380	31.6	1,250.00	950.00	31.6	7,780	5,200	49.6	19,450.00	13,000.00	49.6
CLASS TOTALS		6,875	6,260	9.8	11,930.00	10,772.50	10.7	41,188	36,061	14.2	83,150.00	71,550.00	16.2

Figure 15-16 Sales and Profits by Item (Continued)

This same sort of breakdown is provided in the *profit by item* report. Of course, the major new information contained in the profitability report is cost and gross profit (in dollars and percentage) for each item. The relative profitability of inventory items emphasizes the control of costs associated with acquiring and selling each item and (when associated with the contribution margin idea) contributes to product emphasis, product elimination, and new product decisions. These decisions are all an on-going part of the planning process.

3. *Sales and profits by customer* (Figure 15-17). The *sales by customer* report focuses on customer buying volumes and to some extent shifts in the make-up of sales. Large decreases in sales to any customer highlighted by this report can be followed up with direct customer contact, and significant increases in sales activity by a customer can signal the necessity for increased attention and service. A report of this type is a help in planning sales strategy and allocating sales time. The *profit by customer* statement follows the general format of other profit breakdown reports with absolute and relative figures for profits resulting from each customer highlighted. This report draws management attention to those customers whose buying generates substantial profit for the business, as well as to those less important to the business' future. Large profit accounts deserve extra attention and consideration (terms, discounts, special ordering, and so on), and this statement presents the data on which these special decisions can be made. Also, the reasons for particularly small absolute gross profits or gross profit percentages for a specific customer can be followed up. Information which allows management to discover and pursue unusual circumstances is critically important in planning and control.

Remember that the statements illustrated represent only one group of many possible management-oriented reports which can be generated by a sales analysis package. The wealth of information available in an information system is incredible. A package like sales analysis can, on-demand, generate reports on almost any area of company sales activity so that circumstances which require immediate analysis and action can be pinpointed. The ability to draw from a base of data and quickly and accurately produce useful management reports is one of the key advantages of computer-based information systems.

No Separate Input Files

Sales analysis also provides data, in addition to management reports, that is useful to the processing of other applications. In Chapter 13 and again in this chapter, we discussed the budgeting value of the various sales and profits breakdowns produced by sales analysis, and in Chapter 14 the necessity for sales by salesmen data in payroll commission calculations was emphasized. This kind of interchange between packages is not unusual. Unique to the sales analysis application, however, is the absence of both direct input files and inquiry/response necessity. All of the information required to provide the reports generated by sales analysis is already in the system for other processing purposes. It is only necessary for these other packages (accounts receivable, order processing, and inventory control) to transfer data on customers, sales, and purchases to sales analysis for further processing. No new files are required in this processing because of this information exchange within the system. Similarly, the need for instant response sales analysis information from the system is simply not critical. The decisions

GATEWAY IND.   NO. 02   PROFIT ANALYSIS BY CUSTOMER   DATE 10/31/77 TIME 09.18.42 PAGE   1 AMS12
FOR OCTOBER

CUSTOMER NAME CUSTOMER/SALESMAN NUMBER	SALES $	M-T-D COST	G.P.$	G.P.%	SALES $	Y-T-D COST	G.P.$	G.P.%	L-YR G.P.%
BURXXXXXXX EQUIPMENT CO. 2656000 31705	24,007.00	20,536.00	3,471.00	14.5	146,100.00	118,070.00	28,030.00	19.2	8.1
GA. HIGHWAY EXPRESS, INC. 7117000 31706	14,000.20	13,232.00	768.20	5.5	87,150.00	80,940.00	6,210.00	7.1	12.0
GOUXX TRUCKING CO. 7118000 31709	3,000.00	2,459.01	540.99	18.0	3,500.00	2,966.10	533.90	15.3	9.7
MCCXXXXX MILLS, INC. 13090000 31702	15,175.00	13,093.18	2,081.82	13.7	28,500.00	24,800.20	3,699.80	13.0	17.9
METYXXXX CORPORATION 13171000 31709	4,057.30	3,898.92	158.38	3.9	5,500.00	6,233.90	733.90-	13.3-	5.0
RONXXX NICKOLSON 13981000 31701	11,385.48	9,737.83	1,647.65	14.5	61,110.00	52,186.17	8,923.83	14.6	15.1
POSXX IRON WORKS 16185000 31901	10,500.00	8,973.36	1,526.64	14.5	46,315.00	39,000.00	7,315.00	15.8	24.1
RAY RENTS 18543000 31701	6,714.62	5,719.04	995.58	14.8	36,205.40	26,893.22	9,312.18	25.7	21.7
TAYXXX IRON WORKS 19795000 31999	10,706.10	9,851.38	854.72	8.0	77,070.00	64,300.00	12,770.00	16.6	10.2
COMPANY TOTALS	99,545.70	87,500.72	12,044.98	12.1	491,450.40	415,389.59	76,060.81	15.5	13.1

FIGURE 15-17 Sales and Profits by Customer
(courtesy of IBM Corporation)

GATEWAY IND.	NO. 02		SALES ANALYSIS BY CUSTOMER FOR OCTOBER		DATE 10/31/77 TIME 09.20.42 PAGE 1 AMS12		
			o-------- M-T-D AMOUNTS --------o			o-------- Y-T-D AMOUNTS --------o	
CUSTOMER NUMBER	SALESMAN NUMBER	CUSTOMER NAME	THIS YEAR	LAST YEAR	PCT. DIFF	THIS YEAR	LAST YEAR	PCT. DIFF
2656000	31705	BURXXXXXX EQUIPMENT CO.	24,007.00	12,500.00	92.1	146,100.00	130,650.00	11.8
7171000	31706	GA. HIGHWAY EXPRESS, INC.	14,000.20	13,500.00	3.7	87,150.00	80,150.00	8.7
7184000	31709	GOUXX TRUCKING CO.	3,000.00	3,525.00	14.9-	3,500.00	3,640.00	3.8
13090000	31702	MCCXXXXXX MILLS, INC	15,175.00	12,100.00	25.4	28,500.00	20,000.00	42.5
13171000	31709	METXXXX CORPORATION	4,057.30	1,225.00	231.2	5,500.00	4,860.00	13.7
13981000	31701	RONXXX NICKOLSON	11,385.48	12,200.00	6.7-	61,100.00	58,500.00	4.4
16185000	31901	POSXX IRON WORKS,INC.	10,500.00	10,100.00	4.0	46,315.00	30,500.00	5.2
18543000	31701	PAY RENTS	6,714.62	5,900.00	13.8-	36,205.40	31,600.00	14.6
19795000	31999	TAYXXX IRON WORKS	10,706.10	14,850.00	27.9-	77,070.00	65,230.10	18.2
		COMPANY TOTALS	99,545.70	85,900.00	14.5	491,440.40	425,130.10	15.6

Figure 15-17 Sales and Profits by Customer (Continued)

which result from sales and profit analysis information are recurring and can be programmed by management, and reports generated when needed. As we have seen, this is not always possible in other packages where nonroutine or spontaneous decisions make constant information availability necessary.

15.5 INFORMATION SYSTEMS AND ACCOUNTING SYSTEMS

In Chapter 1, as a prelude to our discussion of manual accounting systems, we introduced the fundamental distinction between information systems and accounting systems. An important factor in this distinction between systems is the treatment of accounting transactions in computer-based information systems. Much of Chapters 13–15 has been devoted to gaining an understanding of this treatment. This concluding section will review the characteristics which distinguish information systems from accounting systems and present the overall picture of the processing of accounting transactions in an information system.

Figure 15-18 presents the flow of sales and purchase information through a computer-based system. The following important points about this information flow should be understood from this diagram.

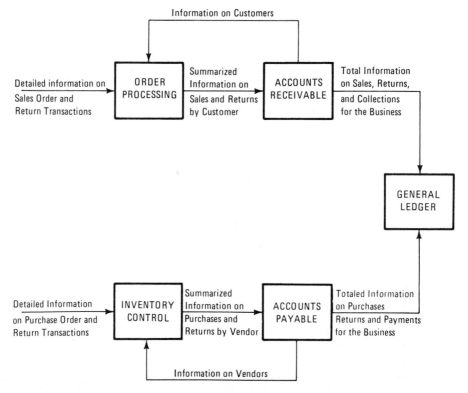

FIGURE 15-18 Information Flow and Accounting Transactions

1. Sales and purchases represent two of the most important and recurring types of transactions engaged in by most businesses. Processing these transactions in a computer-based information system requires interaction among applications from each of the processing systems we have discussed in Chapters 13-15.

2. The arrows pointing left to right in the figure indicate the flow of accounting transaction information. This flow is always toward the general ledger, which is the final resting place for all accounting events.

3. Sales and purchase transactions enter the system at the order processing and inventory control applications respectively, where substantial detail on each of these events is needed for processing. As sales and purchase information is passed to the receivables and payables applications some of this detail is summarized because these applications require only total information for each customer or vendor to carry out their processing. As this sales and purchase information is then passed to the general ledger it is further summarized since breakdowns of this information by customer or vendor are not needed for general ledger purposes. Only company totals for these transactions are necessary for general ledger and financial statement purposes.

4. As accounting transactions travel through a computer-based information system from their point of entry into the system toward the general ledger, they are summarized by each processing application and unneeded detail is dropped. Financial statements then, represent the most summarized information available from the system, while sales orders and purchase orders represent the most detailed and least summarized information available. A carefully designed system should provide a trail forward from detail to summary and backward from summary to original detail.

5. The arrows pointing from right to left in the figure indicate the flow of information, but not accounting transactions. This flow of nontransaction information, which is created by the system, is the primary distinguishing feature of information systems as compared to accounting systems.

Example

To illustrate these ideas consider a sales order for several items from a customer. In order processing, where the sales order enters the system, a good deal of detail is needed on each of the individual items ordered (price, availability, location) as well as on the customer (credit rating, shipping address). For the accounts receivable package, however, all that is needed is the total amount of the sale to the customer. Detail on each item in the sales order is not necessary for receivables to be processed and collections monitored and controlled. As a by-product of this receivables processing, however, credit information on this customer is generated and passed back to order processing for decision-making purposes. For general ledger and financial statement purposes the amount sold to this particular customer is not necessary, but rather the amount sold to all customers is required so that revenue for the income statement and accounts receivable (control) for the balance sheet can be determined. This same kind of summary takes place as all accounting transactions are processed in a computer-based information system, and new nontransaction information is always created by the system as a by-product of the processing.

In the last three chapters we have examined a total business information system. This total information system includes three component systems, each made up of three specific processing applications. Because these chapters represent a lot of material, we feel you would benefit from seeing the "big picture" one more time. Tables 15-1 and 15-2 bring together the major processing, input and output concepts presented in these chapters. Table 15-1 lists the primary output reports which should be generated by each of the processing applications we have discussed and Table 15-2 presents the major files necessary for a business information system to function, together with the packages which use these files. Table 15-2 represents, therefore, the data base of the system. These figures should cap the discussions presented in Chapters 13-15.

TABLE 15-1   PRIMARY OUTPUT REPORTS IN A BUSINESS INFORMATION SYSTEM

System and Application	Primary Output Reports
Financial Accounting and Control System	
General Ledger	General Journal
	Special Journals (4)
	General Ledger Listing
	Trial Balance
Financial Statements and Budgeting	Income Statement - past and pro-forma
	Balance sheet - past and pro-forma
	Changes in financial position worksheet
Cash Receipts and Disbursements System	
Accounts Receivable	Subsidiary Ledger
	Aged Trial Balance
	Billing Statements
Accounts Payable	Open Payables Listing
	Cash Requirements Report
	Checks to Vendors
Payroll	Current Payroll Register
	Paychecks
	Cumulative Earnings Register
	Required Government Forms
Sales and Purchases System	
Order Processing	Order Item List
	Order Transaction Register
	Customer Open Order Report
	Pricing List
Inventory Control	Inventory Transaction Register
	Inventory Status Report
	Inventory Analysis Report
Sales Analysis	Sales and Profits by Salesmen
	Sales and Profits by Item
	Sales and Profits by Customer

TABLE 15-2   MAJOR FILES IN A BUSINESS INFORMATION SYSTEM

Files	*Applications*
PERMANENT FILES	
Account Master	General Ledger, Financial Statements, and Budgeting
Customer Master	Accounts Receivable, Order Processing, and Sales Analysis
Vendor Master	Accounts Payable and Inventory Control
Employee Master	Payroll
Item Master	Order Processing, Inventory Control, and Sales Analysis
TRANSACTION FILES	
Current Accounting	General Ledger
Year-to-Date Accounting	General Ledger
New Sales Invoices	Accounts Receivable and General Ledger
Cash Receipts and Adjustments	Accounts Receivable and General Ledger
Open Purchase Invoices	Accounts Payable and Inventory Control
New Purchase Invoices	Accounts Payable and General Ledger
Cash Payments and Adjustments	Accounts Payable and General Ledger
Current Hours Worked	Payroll and General Ledger
New Sales Orders	Order Processing and Accounts Receivable
New Purchase Orders	Inventory Control and Accounts Payable
CONSTANT FILES	
Tax Table and Deduction	Payroll
Base Selling Price, Mark-Up and Discount	Order Processing

exercises

15-1 The information flow into and from an order processing application area is depicted in Figure 15-2.

1. Give a specific example of each type of input to this application area.

2. Explain how the examples you chose are actually processed by the application.

15-2 For each of the data items stored in the item master file, explain why such information is important in a computer-based system. Also, for each data-item, give the output report(s) in which the information is used. Which of these data-items would normally be updated with each processing run?

15-3 Two critical output reports generated by the order processing package are the order transaction register and the customer order report.

1. Both of these reports present order information. Why does this information differ between reports? How is any common information presented differently in each report?

2. What is the difference between a sales order and a sales invoice? Explain the accounting treatment of each in a computer-based system.

15-4 In the interactive order entry sequence displayed in Figure 15-8, a dialog occurs between the user and the information system. Specify which pieces of information in this dialog must be furnished by the user and which information is furnished by the system from stored data.

15-5 The information flow into and from an inventory control application area is depicted in Figure 15-9.

1. Give a specific example of each type of input to this application area.

2. Explain how the examples you chose are actually processed by the application.

15-6 Two critical output reports generated by the inventory control package are the inventory status report and the inventory analysis report. Supply the following information based upon the sample reports given in Figure 15-11 and Figure 15-12 and state the report from which your answer is taken.

a. The item number of a driving collar.

b. The total number of adapter gaskets on hand.

c. The total cost of valves sold (used) this year.

d. The total number of pump shaft assemblies on hand.

e. Why are there two lines of output for the adapter gasket but only one line of output for the pump shaft assembly?

f. How is each report sequenced?

g. Were more wearing collars or more treadle assemblies sold?

h. Was cost of goods sold (used) higher for wearing collars or treadle assemblies?

i. Is the markup higher on ferrules or on auto switches?

j. The three most active inventory items account for what percentages of inventory on hand and cost of goods sold?

15-7 The information flow into and from a sales analysis application area is depicted in Figure 15-14.

1. Give a specific example of each type of input to this application area.

2. Explain how the examples you chose are actually processed by the application.

15-8 The output reports of the sales analysis package are designed to be decision oriented and aid in management planning and control. For each of the following fundamental management decisions, cite the output report(s) from sales analysis which would provide necessary information for the decision.

a. Sales forecast.

b. Production planning.

c. Product emphasis.

d. Bonuses to salesmen.

e. Pricing decisions.

f. Budgeted gross margin.

g. Sales quotas for next year.

h. Elimination of a product.

i. Hiring and firing of salesmen.

j. Advertising emphasis.

15-9 Inquiry/response capability requires a dialog between the user and the system. For each of the following processing packages, specify which inquiry information must be furnished by the user and which response information would be provided by the system from stored data.

a. Accounts receivable (Figure 14-7).

b. Accounts payable (Figure 14-12).

c. Order processing (Figure 15-7).

d. Inventory control (Figure 15-13).

15-10 Most transactions enter the total information system through the sales and purchases system. This information is then summarized and passed to the cash receipts and disbursements system, which further summarizes the information and passes it to the financial accounting and control system.

1. Assume that ten sales orders are received, processed, and that sales invoices are then generated. What information would be required by the order processing application, the accounts receivable application, and the general ledger application concerning these ten orders?

2. Assume that two purchase orders are created, the goods are shipped by the vendor and a purchase invoice is received. What information would be required by the inventory control application, the accounts payable application and the general ledger application concerning these orders.

internal control in computer-based systems

INTRODUCTION

You will recall that in Chapter 3 we discussed the problem of internal control in manual systems. In computer-based systems our concern is basically the same as it was earlier: How can a system protect itself from errors, both accidental and deliberate? The difference now is simply that we have the computer to consider where we did not before.

16.1 SPECIAL PROBLEMS AND THEIR SOLUTIONS

Of course, with the introduction of the computer, we eliminate some major internal control concerns: namely, accuracy, consistency, and motivation. The computer is immeasurably more accurate than any person performing the same calculations. Similarly, once it is programmed, the computer will be consistent in its treatment of transactions. Finally, the computer will not have any dishonest or disloyal motivations, since the machine cannot profit from any misstatement.

    Along with these internal control benefits, however, there are a number of internal control problems inherent in computer use. We will discuss some of these problems in detail and offer solutions.

1. *The machine lacks judgment.* Everyone has perhaps heard various horror stories about computer systems which wrote payroll checks for $20,000 instead of $200 or which sent a truckload of magazines to a startled subscriber. In a manual system, you can see that the people doing the work will not do something completely ridiculous; they will realize that something is wrong. The machine, on the other hand, has no judgment of its own and will thus do strange things if told to do them. However, even though the machine lacks judgment, the computer system can exercise judgment by having judgment built into the computer programs. The programs should constantly test the data they are manipulating, always checking to see if the amounts are reasonable or within established limits. For example, when processing hours worked for a payroll system, the program should flag or somehow point out any people being paid for more than, say, 68 hours per week. Of course, the specific number of hours checked should be whatever is most appropriate under the particular situation; 68 is not a magic number. Similarly, the program should not process transactions outside of authorized limits. For example, in an accounts receivable system each customer is given a credit limit. The program could check all prospective sales to determine if the sale would cause the customer to exceed his credit limit; if the sale would exceed the limit, it could be rejected. Notice that this check has two purposes: to see that a customer does not charge more than he can pay and that no unreasonably large sale is processed. The computer should be programmed to constantly test its data for reasonableness.

2. *The user is in awe of the computer.* You will recall from our earlier discussion of internal control the importance of outside checks on our system's accuracy. For example, the statements of account sent to our customers were relied upon to check that our accounting records were correct. It is not uncommon, however, for people to neglect checking the computer and to simply assume that the computer is correct. One potential computer thief took advantage of that attitude by modifying the payroll deductions for the employees at his organization. He reduced everyone else's deductions by a small amount in each individual case but then added the total amount (large) to his deductions. Thus, the system was completely in balance, but he was going to get an extra-fat refund from the IRS at the expense of the other employees. He was caught only when a janitor, for an unknown reason, added up his weekly paychecks for the year and noticed the discrepancy between his totals and the amounts on his W-2. However, very few people add up the totals from their paychecks, completely check their bank statement, or completely check their credit card bill (comparing it to a file of receipts). A similar problem occurs within companies, where often the user departments do not check the output of the computer. Certainly, this is a large and growing problem and it will never be completely solved. The general solution, however, is to try to provide control totals and other information to user departments to help them check the computer output. It may even be necessary to require active checks by users of the system output rather than simply assume that if no one complains it must be all right.

3. *Duties are concentrated within the computer.* The discussion in Part one emphasized that the separation of duties is absolutely critical for effective internal control. As a particular example, the duty of journalizing transactions should be separate from the duty of posting the transaction to the ledger accounts. However, in a computer-based system, both of these

duties (along with many others) are all done by the computer. As an additional example, in a payroll system a computer might keep payroll and personal records, make the labor distribution, and prepare the payroll checks. In and of themselves, these facts are no particular cause for alarm. Unlike the human employee, the computer (since it is only a machine) cannot ever desire to divert funds or assets to itself. (Of course, computers with a will of their own, like HAL in *2001, A Space Odyssey*, are purely science fiction and will remain so.) The problem is that although the computer will not abuse its concentrated duties, others can. If a person has unauthorized control of the computer, the standard protection of separated duties will no longer be effective. Examples of this sort of problem abound in computing. In one instance a programmer modified a bank program which printed out a list of overdrawn accounts: he had the program simply omit his account from the list. He was thus able to overdraw his account without being detected. He was finally caught when a machine breakdown required that the list be prepared manually. Another instance involved a firm where a programmer instructed the computer to pay him several payroll checks. He was only caught when other employees noticed the checks piling up on his desk while he was on vacation. While we will defer a detailed discussion of appropriate preventive measures until later in this chapter, the general solution to this problem is segregation of duties and proper supervision within data processing. Ideally, data processing should involve six separate functions: (1) supervision or management, (2) systems analysts, (3) programmers, (4) operators, (5) data entry personnel, and (6) a control group to investigate and correct errors. Later we will discuss in more detail how this segregation of duties would actually work.

4. *Records and the audit trail are invisible.* Some writers like to say that with a computer system the audit trail vanishes. This is misleading, however, for even though you can no longer see the audit trail, it does exist, but in machine-readable form. This invisibility of records and the audit trail thus mean that checking accuracy, cross-checking, and the analysis of support for figures on financial statements are made more difficult. The checking and analysis cannot be done manually; it must be done utilizing the computer. The computer must be used to analyze its own records and audit trail. Because of this, the system has to be designed to incorporate the data for all necessary analysis.

5. *Information can be changed without physical traces.* One of the great protections of manual systems is that the records are in ink. If someone tries to change any information in the records, the erasures and smudge marks will make this immediately apparent. If someone removes a page, the page numbering will point this up. If someone replaces a page with a new one appropriately doctored, then the different tint of the new paper will show up. There is no similar protection for computer records: electronic information can be changed without a trace. Of course, viewed in another light, this is a tremendous advantage, since it allows the same storage media to be used over and over again. However, from an internal control viewpoint, this computer capability is a serious difficulty. Earlier we discussed the case where a programmer changed payroll deduction information to get himself an excessively large income tax refund. If that were done with manual records, the massive physical changes would be apparent to any users of the records. Since the records were on the computer, however, they could be changed without detection. In another instance, a programmer reduced individual credits to various revenue accounts by mere fractions of

dollars. The total sum was considerable, however, and to keep the system in balance, the programmer had to withdraw large amounts of cash. The reduction of individual credits simply could not have been done with manual records.

To this point, we have discussed the potential problems resulting from the changing of data. Another serious problem is the possibility of changing programs. If done properly, a program becomes operational and is used on a regular, production basis only after it has been approved, reviewed, and tested. A sophisticated embezzler could get around this either by modifying the production program directly or by replacing the production program with a new version.

Protection against this problem of change without traces is difficult but must proceed on two fronts: (1) physical controls to reduce access to the computer (in order to prevent manipulation) and (2) cross check to make sure that all data file changes are backed up by properly authorized transactions. We will go into more detail on these techniques later in the chapter.

6. *Sophisticated tampering can cause unauthorized actions.* A standard approach to data processing is to have various physical, organizational, and other internal controls on the entry of data to the computer system. Then, when the information is in the computer, the assumption is made that the transaction has been authorized. Note that if someone can surreptitiously enter information into the system by bypassing the various controls, he can, in effect, get his transactions authorized. You can see that if someone can enter information into the system that looks like an authorized transaction, then the system assumes it is an authorized transaction. For example, a California man became very familiar with the system of Pacific Telephone. He used the telephone to place orders in excess of $100,000. The company delivered the goods to various sites where he picked them up and then resold them. Another example was the programmer, irritated at being fired, who then added himself to the pension rolls. In order to combat this problem, the system must ensure that proper authorization is required for all transactions. Additionally, the system must allow the check of all authorizations—another example of the importance of a proper audit trail. Thus, if a person avoids the various controls and manipulates data on the computer, he will still not have the proper authorization. If a proper audit trail exists and if the improper transaction is checked, the tampering will come to light. However, if there is no adequate audit trail, the unauthorized transaction could only be discovered by accident or by confession (which is, in fact, how most sophisticated problems are discovered).

7. *Great speed extends one person's capabilities.* One of the protections in manual systems is the human limitation of speed: one person is only capable of doing so much. Thus, one person can alter only so many checks or change only so many records. With the use of the computer, this limitation no longer exists. An example of this problem is the computation of interest for banks. When the bank computes the appropriate interest to credit the accounts of its depositors, the computation is made to only a fixed, limited number of decimal places. Thus, there is a small difference between the interest an individual actually receives and the exact interest. The difference, of course, is always in the bank's favor. Though it is only a small amount in any individual case, with tens of thousands of depositors, the amount becomes significant in total. Programmers have taken advantage of this and have modified the interest calculation program to credit this difference to their account. The programmer would then be able to withdraw large sums from his account. Notice the difficulty of detecting this technique: the accounts all balance and nobody is in the position to

detect an error. As a result, to protect against this type of problem, the system must provide for (a) review of all programs by a supervisor and (b) physical protection of programs for unauthorized modification.

8. *Vast capabilities can create a different reality.* After a point, the information stored in the computer no longer reflects reality, it becomes the reality. Originally, the computer record simply reflected the operations of the firm. In extremely sophisticated applications, however, the computer record is the operations of the firm. For example, your bank balance is the electronic information stored in the bank's computer; in the life insurance business, an individual policy is essentially the information stored on the computer. The management at Equity Funding took the final step and created life insurance policies on their computer without any connection with real people: insurance policies without policyholders. There are immediately two basic difficulties to explain: (a) why the company would do such a thing and (b) how could the company get away with it for so many years and become a stock market favorite. First, the company created the policies because a policy can be viewed as a stream of future receipts to the company with a payment at some (uncertain) future date. Such a stream of cash receipts and disbursements has a definite present value, and there is an established reinsurance market where policies are sold for cash to reinsurers by the primary insurance company. Second, the company could get away with it because of bad auditing procedures. The procedures are somewhat understandable when you consider that a policy is essentially a liability for the insurance company (because of the payout required) and companies rarely overstate liabilities. However, whenever the auditors requested a confirmation or backup on a created policy, the Equity Funding personnel simply claimed difficulty in finding the records and then made up any necessary documents that night. In any case, with the help of their computers, the management of Equity Funding was able to create a different reality, one that only existed on their computers. But this reality was so self-consistent and so documented that it became reality. The solution to problems of this scale is effective testing of account balances. The amounts in the account balances have to be constantly checked to determine if the computer system (even if it is internally consistent) is consistent with the world outside of the computer center.

9. *Concentrated information is easier to steal.* Manual records are often so bulky that stealing them would present serious logistical problems in just moving the vast quantity of material. Of course, the loss of vast records would be immediately apparent. However, copying the records presents its own severe problems, including (a) finding time for the copying, (b) covering up a great use of reproduction facilities, and (c) equally severe or greater logistical problems with the reproduced material. This same problem no longer exists with computer-readable information: vast quantities of information are stored in a small volume and can easily be copied or physically stolen. In one recent example, investigators of the General Accounting Office (the investigative arm of the United States Congress) walked out of the Social Security System's national computer complex with a cart. The cart alone contained names, addresses, and other information of over one million beneficiaries. Another example was the insurance company which sold insurance policies by mail. The company spent a great deal of time accumulating names and addresses for a mail solicitation; there were no takers. The mailing failed because a company vice-president stole the names and addresses by copying various computer tapes. He then sold the tapes to a rival firm which made an

earlier mailing. The solution to this problem is good physical controls for the records in electronic form. Only authorized people should have access to the records and an audit trail should be available to determine who used what, when. The life insurance firm finally uncovered the man's scheme through a tape librarian who made a record that he withdrew certain tapes on a specific date.

10. *Electronic information is easy to lose.* In a manual system, the records are written in ink on substantial paper. The only way to lose the information is to lose the physical records or to have them burn in a business fire. The information written down essentially can not be erased—it is permanent. The situation is completely different with electronic information. As we discussed earlier, the information on the computer can be easily changed, leaving no trace of the earlier content. This change often happens inadvertently and huge amounts of information can be quickly lost. An example of this problem occurred during a fund-raising campaign. The pledges were recorded on a computer tape as they were phoned in; the names, addresses, and amounts were kept so that follow-up efforts would then collect the money. The information on that tape was accidentally wiped out and thus a great deal of money was never collected. The international CPA firm in charge of the system paid several million dollars to the charity to cover the loss. A somewhat different situation occurred outside of Denver, where one system kept crashing (i.e., it would stop working in a spectacular fashion) and losing information on the disk. It turned out that for over a year, one of the operators was shortcircuiting the computer and causing these crashes deliberately. When the police asked him why he did it, he said he had an "uncontrollable urge" to do it. Since electronic information can be lost so quickly and easily it is essential to provide backup capabilities for all data. This backup would begin with copying data files on a routine basis. Additionally, the system should be able to reconstruct the current status of a file based upon the transactions which have occurred since the last copy was made. For this reason, many systems have a transaction logger, a tape where every transaction is recorded or logged. If the master file were lost, the files could be reconstructed by reprocessing all of the transactions since the last backup copy was made.

11. *There are new sources and potentials for error.* Manual systems have numerous potentials for error, such as incorrect calculations and mispostings. With computer-based systems the potentials for error are generally reduced, however, new and different sources and potentials for error are created. There are basically four of these. *First*, and generally least important, are vendor-supplied errors. These errors include faulty hardware or errors in the system software, such as operating systems and compilers. These errors are usually quickly apparent and are corrected by the vendor. As a hardware control, large computers contain a parity bit for each character, which keeps the number of l's either always odd or always even; this parity bit tells the computer if a hardware error has occurred. Manufacturers of microcomputers consider their products so reliable they do not even provide a parity bit, whereas some large systems have several parity bits which can pinpoint the exact source of error. Thus, there is a wide range of hardware controls, but, in any case, you can assume the hardware is accurate. *Second* are errors in user programs. A satellite launch went out of control and had to be destroyed (at a cost of many millions of dollars) when a programmer omitted a minus sign from the control program. When the computer does some major wrong, there is generally an error in a user program. The solution is extensive and effective

testing of programs prior to their use in production. Unfortunately, this is easier to write than accomplish because of the insidious nature of many errors; they often do not become apparent until weeks, months, or even years have gone by. A *third* source of errors is user error. A user of a program is generally not intimately familiar with it and will often put in erroneous data or respond incorrectly. For example, a university hospital developed a new system for handling patient charges and billings which they wanted to check by processing the last few years of transactions of the old system. The goal was to check the results of the new system with the results of the old system. However, the new system checked for validity of the input (e.g., did the doctor code represent a valid doctor) and rejected over 20 percent of the old system's transactions. The old system assumed data would be put in properly, but it certainly was not. Thus, the results of the previous years were seriously incorrect. The solution to this problem is thorough testing of the program data being processed. All programs should be written assuming that the user will try to use the wrong disk or tape and that all data is very possibly incorrect. Some people frankly enjoy getting the computer to make mistakes. Others will simply make mistakes through inexperience or inadvertence. The *fourth* source of error is a poor design in the first place of either the program or the system. A standard problem in a computer-based system is excessive rigidity in the system; it is too difficult or impossible to handle special circumstances or situations. There have been a number of articles in newspapers and magazines about people's problems with computerized billing. The person writes concerning an error with his bill and fights for some months with the system, all the while receiving increasingly abusive letters concerning nonpayment. The solution is, of course, proper system design in the first place; the system should certainly be designed to handle unusual situations and circumstances. Chapter 11 covers the topic of system design more fully.

12. *Source documents are eliminated or reduced.* In a manual accounting system, a journal entry is made from a source document and ties to that source document. As a result, the audit trail can always go back from the journal to the original document, evidencing the original transaction authorization. In a computer-based system, a terminal operator often makes an entry directly into the computer using the terminal, without a source document. An example would be order-entry where an order is received over the phone and entered directly into the system. Another more familiar example would be the airline reservation desk, where the operator receives phone calls and makes reservations without a source document. The problem is, then, that there is no source document which indicates proper authorization and the audit trail can be lost. The solution to this problem has two aspects. The first is physical control over the terminals, so that only those who are properly authorized have access to the terminals. This will ensure that only those who are authorized to initiate transactions, in fact initiate them. The second is to tie each transaction back to the operator, terminal and time where it was initiated. This process will assign responsibility and provide a check on the authorization of transactions.

Table 16-1 provides a summary of the internal control problems specific to computer-based systems. The first column lists basic problems we discussed above. The second column then gives a typical result of this difficulty. Finally, the third column gives the general solution to the basic difficulty.

TABLE 16-1 INTERNAL CONTROL PROBLEMS SPECIFIC TO COMPUTER SYSTEMS

Control Problem	Typical Result	General Solution
The machine lacks judgment	Spectacular errors	Build in judgment with reasonableness tests
The user is in awe of the computer	User does not check computer output	Use control totals; check results of the computer
Duties are concentrated within the computer	Person in charge of computer can circumvent controls	Segregate duties within data processing
Records and the audit trail are invisible	Audit trail hard to use, if it is there	Use the computer to analyze records and audit trail.
Information can be changed without physical traces.	Change account balances without a trace	Use physical controls and cross-checks
Sophisticated tampering can cause unauthorized actions	Add name to pension rolls when fired	Ensure proper authorization
Great speed extends one person's capabilities	Accumulate round-off error in one account	Review programs, limit access to programs
Vast capabilities can create a different reality	Equity funding creates fictitious policyholders	Independent checks with "real world"
Concentrated information is easier to steal	Social Security gets over 1 million records stolen	Physical controls and proper authorization
Electronic information is easy to lose	Fund raising loses millions in pledges	Proper backup
There are new sources and potentials for error	Incorrect use of the system	Complete debugging and proper system design
Source documents are eliminated	Loss of audit trail	Physical control on access to terminals

16.2 ELEMENTS OF INTERNAL CONTROL IN A COMPUTER ENVIRONMENT

Error-detecting Features

Computer-based systems require the same basic error-detecting features introduced in our earlier discussion of manual accounting; these features are: (1) the double-entry system, (2) the audit trail, (3) bank reconciliation, (4) subsidiary ledgers, (5) customer statements, and (6) communication with vendors. Additionally, most of the specific techniques we discussed are usually applicable. You can now see how baseless are concerns that use of the computer would make auditing impossible by eliminating the audit trail. An audit trail will always be a part of a well-designed system because it is essential for management control.

Internal Control Goals/Good Control Characteristics

Controls for computer-based systems have the same goals as controls for manual systems. These goals are to help ensure that:

1. *All* transactions which should be processed are processed.
2. *Only* transactions which should be processed are processed.
3. All processing is done correctly.

In order to accomplish these goals, the system can incorporate a wide variety of controls. In our search for the proper controls in individual situations we should keep the following characteristics of good controls in mind. Good controls:

1. Identify errors at the earliest possible point in the cycle of transaction processing.
2. Prevent unauthorized use of the system and its related data files and records.
3. Are as simple as possible, while still being logical, comprehensive, and standardized.

These are ambitious goals and, of course, there is no magic group of controls which will always work in all situations. You will have to use your judgment concerning what is applicable in each particular case.

Implementation Methods

Despite the differences in internal control problems between manual and computer-based systems, the elements of internal control are the same in both situations. As you recall from Chapter 3, the elements of internal control are:

1. Honest and capable employees.
2. Clear delegation and separation of duties.
3. Proper procedures for processing of transactions.
4. Suitable documents and accounting records.
5. Adequate physical control over assets and records.
6. Independent verification of performance.

The introduction of the computer, however, changes the methods by which each of these elements is implemented. In the rest of this chapter, we will discuss the specifics of each of these elements of internal control in a computer-based system.

Honest and Capable Employees

Of course, this same element of internal control is essentially the same with computer-based systems as it was with manual systems. If employees are capable and honest, a lot can be done even in an environment of weak internal control. If employees are dishonest or incompetent, no set of internal controls will be effective. If anything, however, the importance of honest and able employees is more important in a computer environment than it is in a manual system. As we discussed earlier, the dishonest or incompetent employee can use the vast speed and electronic nature of the computer to create far more difficulties than would be possible with a manual system, with related human limitations. Thus, the *first* order of priority is to establish a climate where security is taken seriously. Many, if not most, computer centers simply do not consider the problem of security to be a serious one. As a result, the employees will share this lack of concern and will not be sensitive to potential problems or weaknesses in internal control. The *second* step is to ensure proper training on the computer. Many of the people using the computer will be unfamiliar with the machine, its capabilities and its limitations. It is essential that these people be properly introduced to the computer, so they will be capable of using it well. Even if the people were capable in the manual environment, they will not necessarily be capable in the computer environment. The *third* requirement is to check on the background of all employees and consultants. Experience has shown that many companies could have prevented problems by looking into the past history of prospective employees—they had been in trouble before and would likely be in trouble again. The *fourth* requirement is to bond critical employees because (a) it is a psychological deterrent, (b) it provides an additional check on the background of employees, and (c) it provides protection against loss in the event something does happen. The *fifth* requirement is the prompt exclusion of disgruntled employees from the computer area. Fired employees have manipulated the computer records or added errors to the system because of their anger and resentment at their firing. At the termination interview the employee should be asked to surrender keys or other means of access to the computer. *Finally*, the system should attempt to reduce temptation, so our basically honest employees will remain so. Attempts to reduce temptation should include: (a) a policy of having two people present when the computer is in use, so that one person will not be alone with his temptations; (b) control over overtime, to reduce the possibility of activities in addition to his regular job; (c) a mandatory vacation policy, to ensure that people will not be able to keep up a consistent fraud; and (d) a policy of rotating jobs, so the possibility of personal manipulation of the system will be more difficult.

Clear Delegation and Separation of Duties

This element of internal control is just as important in a computer environment as it is in manual systems. Just as in the manual system, there should be a written plan of organization, with clear assignments of authority and responsibility. As this plan is laid out, there should be a conscious effort to prevent any personnel from becoming "essential"; if one employee is unable to do his job (because of resignation, sickness, or termination) others should be able to take over. The separation of duties in a computer environment, however, will not be the same as the separation of duties in a manual system. The plan of organization must assign independent responsibility for: (a) the accuracy and timeliness of the data; (b) the appropriateness and efficiency of the systems, and (c) the correctness and integrity of the computer programs. To accomplish this assignment of responsibility, many companies separate the following duties: (a) system design or system analysis, which involves the identification of system objectives and the planning of exactly how the system will work; (b) programming, the actual coding of the programs designed by the analysts; (c) operations, the actual operation of the computer using the programs developed by the programmers; (d) data entry, which is the use of the programs to provide information to the computer either directly or from source documents; (e) library functions, which involve the custody of records, such as tapes and disks; and (f) a control group which is in charge of analyzing errors and tracking down their sources.

Next, it is important to separate people who might collude. Thus, the EDP department must be separate from operating departments. Additionally, no one in EDP should have custody of assets or should be able to authorize transactions, initiate master file changes, or reconcile output controls. Also, to the extent possible programmers and accountants should be separated, as a combination of the two skills could be disastrous for internal control.

It is also important to limit the scope of individual programmers. Programmers and system analysts should not be allowed to use programs they wrote or designed and they should not be allowed to operate the computer. Their detailed knowledge of the program and application would allow them to circumvent controls. Also, the users (with guidance and assistance, of course) should specify the functions of programs; the programmer should not be on his own. The programmer's supervisor should review each program the programmer writes and some other qualified employee should conduct the final testing of the program. Also, one programmer should not write all programs for a sensitive application.

The operators in charge of the computer should not be allowed to perform control functions such as reconciling various reports or correcting items rejected by the program. Finally, it may be a good idea to require two signatures for large checks, thus making it more difficult for embezzlers to withdraw large sums.

Proper Procedures for Processing Transactions

Certainly, procedures have to be "proper" in any system, manual or computer based. In the computer environment, however, the proper procedures will be different because the computer is used for so many procedures and does many of the procedures itself.

Authorization

As in a manual system, proper procedures begin with proper authorization of transactions. Even in a computer system, transactions often begin with "hard copy," such as a check copy or an invoice. Thus the authorization can consist of the written initials of the person authorizing the transaction. Also, special authorization for large items (such as large checks), perhaps should require two managers to approve the transaction. More sophisticated systems often originate transactions in machine-readable form only, eliminating "hard-copy." Examples of this include point-of-sale recorders and remote terminals. In these cases, proper authorization can only be assured by restricting access to the terminals to those responsible for authorizing and initiating transactions. In the case of automatic transactions (such as charges for long-distance calls), the system user authorizes the transaction, and all checking of the transaction must be built into the system.

Terminal Dialog

Since most data in the systems we discussed go into the computer *via* terminals, the next step for proper procedures must be proper design of terminal dialog. The dialog should be easy to use and should take into consideration both the operator's background and his interest. Certainly, dialog for a data-entry clerk should be written differently from dialog for analysis used by a manager. Additionally, the dialog should have appropriate response time, so that the computer responds quickly enough to keep the attention and interest of the operator. Finally, the dialog should check the entered data for error and notify the operator as soon as the error is determined. The goal should be to make the system "bulletproof"; in other words, make it impossible to enter errors into the system even deliberately.

Developing Totals/Identifying Errors

This brings up an important, pervasive goal of proper procedures: *ensure input data are properly recorded on source documents and are properly entered into the computer system.* In order to do this, the system should develop totals and identify errors as close to the source of the data as possible. Let us consider a number of examples to illustrate these ideas. First, the system should provide descriptive feedback on the data entered; for example a printout of an account name ensures that an entered account number was correct. Second, the program should check if the data is within authorized limits or is otherwise reasonable. Third, the program should check the validity of the data. For example, it should make sure the date is valid (e.g., is the month figure between one and twelve?) and that any codes are valid (e.g., does the account code exist?). Fourth, the system should ensure that a transaction is complete and consistent before it is processed. Fifth, there are a number of techniques which may or may not be appropriate in particular circumstances, such as checking an old balance prior to an update, making a record count on the transactions processed, making a control total to ensure all transactions are processed, and cross-footing distributions to ensure accuracy. (See Table 16-2).

System and Program Authorization

In addition to requiring proper authorization of transactions, we must also require proper authorization of new systems and programs. As we discussed in Part Three, any new systems need approval by the user department, an executive independent of EDP, the systems and programming management. Additionally, each new program must be completely tested and authorized. After the programmer writes the program and signs off on it, his supervisor checks the program and approves it, the control group tests it, the users test it, and only then does it come into production.

The procedures discussed above assumed the computer would keep working, but, of course, it does not always do so. The system must have procedures to use when the computer breaks down. It is important to note that the computer can break down in the middle of processing. It must be possible, even at the cost of some inconvenience, to reconstruct data lost due to a system crash.

Suitable Documents and Accounting Records

Just as in the manual system, the computer files must contain all necessary information and an effective audit trail. In addition, there are a number of requirements specific to computer systems. These requirements basically arise from the ease of losing electronic information and from the increased importance of proper documentation.

TABLE 16-2 BASIC PROGRAMMED CONTROLS

Descriptive feedback	Give name or description for items identified by code or number
Reasonableness	Test whether the amounts are within reason given the situation
Validity	Check whether numbers or codes are valid; e.g., month must be less than 13
Completeness	Determine that all elements of the transaction are given before accepting
Control total	Total meaningful amount, such as invoice amount, and compare source total to processed total
Hash total	Total meaningless amount, such as part numbers, to ensure all transactions are entered
Record count	Check of the number of records in the files so that none are added or deleted without explanation
Existence	Make sure that all account numbers refer to records actually on the file
Self-checking number	Add digit to number so that transposition errors are caught
Redundancy	Require repetition for some input data to make sure the proper account is affected
Header label	Use label at the beginning of the file to ensure the correct file is processed
Trailer label	Use label at the end of the file to ensure that file totals and record counts stay correct

Backup Files

Because the information on the computer is so easily lost, there must be proper backup files which are tested. No important information should ever exist in the computer system in only one place; for simple safety, it should always be duplicated somewhere else. Certainly, to ensure they can be relied upon, these duplicate or backup files must be periodically tested to assure that they can restore lost files. For programs, the following is essential: (a) an electronic backup, (b) a hard copy printout of the program's latest version, and (c) a set of proper documentation. For data files, the following is essential: (a) multiple copies of the file, perhaps stored off-site and (b) a planned reconstruction capability, so that the current file could be duplicated if it were lost during processing. This reconstruction capability usually begins with file dumps at regular periods, which essentially are a snapshot of the file at one point. There should then be a transaction log which records each transaction as it is processed. If a file is lost, it can be recreated by using the last file dump and any transactions which occurred since that time.

Written Procedures and Standards of Performance

The next required documents are written procedures and standards of performance. These documents should include standards for: (a) documentation, so that documentation prepared by different people at different times will be uniform and easier to understand and maintain; (b) security measures over data files, program libraries, and the computer room, so that policy will be consistent; (c) the authorization of requests for data processing, whether it is a new program, a new system, or a routine run, to ensure that order is maintained and that priorities are established in an orderly way; and (d) operation of the computer and maintenance of the files.

Documentation on Three Levels

The next requirement is for documentation on three levels: systems documentation, program documentation, and operating instructions. The system documentation provides an overall view of the system, how it works and its control features; specifically, this should include a system narrative and a system flowchart to provide the overall picture and then a discussion of the input, data files, and output of the overall system. The program documentation provides the information necessary for understanding and modifying each program, including a narrative, flowchart, and discussion of the input, data files, and output for the specific program. The operating instructions provide information necessary to use the program; this includes the purpose of the program, the source of its input, and the disposition of both the input and the program output.

Documentation is far more important in a computer environment than it is in a manual system. At least in a manual system you can see the records and their contents and visually follow the flow of information through the system—in a sense the manual system is self-documenting. This is not true in a computer system and documentation is necessary to understand the system and how it works. Documentation is required for systems analysts and programmers to understand the system they are working on. However, documentation is also necessary so a supervisor can review work and evaluate it, and also so work can be passed on to the successor in a job, to the next department, or to the next shift.

Good Forms

Just as in the manual system, our computer-based system must have good forms which are easy to use. As an example, one new system experienced an overwhelming error rate. The computer was rejecting almost 50 percent of all transactions, and the system was collapsing under the requirement of following up all the rejected transactions. The problem was corrected by simply redesigning the forms. Thus, good forms are essential for fewer errors and for easier training of new personnel. Also, the necessity of prenumbered documents is quite as important for computer-based systems. For example, the console log which shows all uses of the computer console should be prenumbered to show all transactions. Additionally, checks should be prenumbered even in computer systems. By this time you should be properly shocked to learn that many companies do not use prenumbered checks; the computer prints the check number while printing the check. The loss of internal control could be disastrous.

Additionally, there are a number of specifics which could be important in particular situations. If an account has not been used for a long period, it is probably a good idea for a manager to check into it; as discussed earlier, the account could be misused to cover defalcations. It is also a good idea to separate the master file from the related detail file or transaction file, so that the master file can be more easily reconstructed from the transaction file in case the master file is lost.

Adequate Physical Control over Assets and Records

We discussed earlier the protection of manual records against manipulation—the erasures, changes, or substitutions will generally be visually apparent unless done in an unusually expert way. Changes in computer systems can be invisible, so physical control over access to the system and records is even more important.

Protecting Programs and Data

The proper controls on access to the computer itself, the terminals, and computer records, of course, depend on the particular situation, but the following are basic elements of physical control. The first item is the importance of protecting programs as well as data. There should be a library of tapes and disks with one person accountable for them. Inventory records should be maintained and checked periodically in order to account for all file movement. Additionally, the room containing manuals, documentation, and program listings should be kept locked to protect them from the operator. At the same time, the computer room should be locked (with emergency exits for safety's sake) to restrict the access of programmers to the computer. In some situations, it may be necessary to control exposure of sensitive material by limiting access to potential security leaks such as scratch tape or disks (which might contain all copies of master files) and paper output being discarded (which might be of interest to other organizations). Finally, it is often important to regularly change keys, passwords, and combinations to ensure that access is only available to those authorized at that time, rather than to everyone who has been authorized in the past.

Further, there should be controls on access to sensitive input and output. While the input data is waiting for processing or after it is processed, the information should be protected from unauthorized access. Also, after the computer output is generated, it should be protected. It is often a good idea to log the distribution of reports, to help check that everyone who should get the reports does get them, and that only those who should get them do so.

Protection Against Catastrophic Loss/Insurance

The next item of importance is physical protection against loss from catastrophic accidents, such as a fire or flood. For example, fire protection should include a fire extinguisher and a sprinkler system. Of course, decisions on the use of further techniques should trade-off convenience and safety. In particular situations fireproof cabinets, on-site storage in vaults or off-site storage may be necessary. Finally, proper insurance coverage is essential. In all of these considerations—convenience, safety, and insurance coverage—there are two costs to keep in mind. The first is the physical loss of equipment, such as computer hardware and physical tapes and disks. The second, and often more important, cost is that of reconstructing the programs and data files.

Physical Care of Equipment

Finally, it is essential to keep proper physical care of the equipment, so that it will function properly. First, you should check that the equipment billings from the vendor match the computer equipment present; it is possible for equipment to "walk" and it is possible for the vendor to overbill. The temperature and humidity should be kept at the proper levels for the particular equipment; older equipment generally requires a lower temperature and less humidity. Also, there should be proper maintenance by qualified technicians on a regular basis; this is generally called preventive maintenance: do not wait until something breaks, but have everything reviewed on a scheduled basis.

Independent Verification of Performance

As we discussed earlier, it is possible for a computer-based system to point a balanced and consistent picture of reality which is nonetheless completely false. As a result, it is absolutely essential to have independent verification of the system picture. The basic independent verification is to periodically check asset balances: determine if the system balances of cash and inventory match with the actual amounts. Another important independent verification is for the system's users to maintain independent control totals of input and review the output of the system. Additionally, the system should periodically develop summaries for users to check. For example, does the gross margin appear reasonable based on past performance.

Determine If Proper Procedures Are Being Followed

The next important independent verification of performance is a check that the written procedures and standards of performance are, in fact, being followed. It does little good to have wonderful procedures and standards if they are widely ignored. Specifically, it is essential to check the following: (a) that security measures are followed, (b) that documentation is properly developed, (c) that there are no excessive delays in the processing of programs; (d) that error correction is accomplished expeditiously, (e) that the amount of time necessary for reruns is reasonable, and (f) that the programs do protect themselves against invalid data entry. It must be emphasized that physical controls and security measures must be checked and lax security must be disciplined if there is to be effective internal control.

System Logs

There should be system logs of both transactions and operator actions. This will allow an independent check of transactions using the audit trail. It will also allow a check if operator errors become excessive for any particular system, terminal, or operator. Excessive errors could indicate faulty system design, poor forms, poor terminal dialog, untrained operators, or attempts at unauthorized access. To accomplish these goals, the system should use suspense accounts as necessary for invalid and nonexistent accounts so that errors can be checked and so that files are kept in balance. Thus, the suspense account will collect all rejected transactions for eventual correction.

Data-processing Costs

Accounting can perform an important verification of performance by checking the way that data-processing costs are accounted for. Generally speaking, data processing is either treated as a cost center or as a profit center. If a cost center, EDP gets a budget and actual amounts are then compared to the budgeted amounts; in this case, variances should be analyzed. If a profit center, EDP bills the user departments for services rendered and revenues are matched with costs; in this case, the process by which charges are billed to user departments should be checked. Additionally, it is important to check how costs are assigned to individual development projects. In one case, a programmer was working on a personal project for the computer center director, but was charging his salary to the overhead of the department.

Independent Audit

Finally, there should be a periodic review by an independent CPA firm to get an outside perspective. This point is placed last, not because it is least important. In fact, it is very important. It is placed last because it is essential not to rely excessively on an independent audit. An independent audit is an excellent means of checking compliance with established standards and of identifying internal control deficiencies. An independent audit is of far less benefit as a means of detecting errors or fraud.

When auditing a computer-based system, there are basically two approaches: auditing "around the computer" or auditing "through the computer."

1. Auditing around the computer involves examining the input to and output from the computer, but not examining the computer's processing. This implies that the computer is not used as part of the audit to test itself, since the computer is essentially unexamined. This approach of auditing around the computer is then most useful in unsophisticated stand-alone systems. For example, suppose a payroll system merely takes timecard data and hourly rates as input and then generates payroll totals and deductions, with no connection to other systems. In this case the payroll system could be audited simply by going "around the computer" to examining only the input and output. However, in more complicated systems, this approach is simply not possible. The input is often the output of the other subsystems, and the output is the input to still other subsystems. Thus, it is not possible to treat any subsystem in isolation.

2. Auditing through the computer essentially involves the use of the computer to audit itself. As we discussed in the chapter, the data and audit trail are both in electronic form and thus cannot be read or examined directly by the auditor. Therefore, in order to examine the computer's data and to use the computer's audit trail, the computer itself has to be used.

    One use of the computer for auditing is to process test transactions in order to see whether the computer system processes them correctly. (This is often called the use of a *test deck*.) These test transactions can also determine if the programmed controls which are supposed to be in effect are actually working properly. A simple test transaction might be a request for a payroll check based upon 100 hours of overtime. This transaction should certainly be rejected as unreasonable just on the face of it. A more complicated test transaction would be an attempt to pay an invoice twice. Such a transaction would test the sophistication of the program controls, since the transaction can not be rejected simply by examining that single transaction. These test transactions are easily processed in the case of batch processing, since another copy of the files could be made and the test transaction can be processed against the file copy. Notice, however, that an on-line system can not easily be tested in this fashion—the file is being continuously updated and the computer system can not stop for testing purposes. For this reason, an *integrated test facility* (ITF) is sometimes built into an on-line system. These are separate records built into all files of the on-line system so that test transactions can be processed and not affect "live" data.

The other main use of the computer for auditing is the use of generalized audit software (GAS). This GAS is designed to work with variable file structures and data formats. Each large CPA firm has its own software to work with the files and data of their many clients. This generalized software is used to perform various tasks, such as the following:

a. Stratify accounts receivable into various levels by amount (e.g., the number and dollar amount over $1000; the number and dollar amount over $100; and the number and dollar amount under $100).

b. Print out the necessary accounts receivable confirmations (more could then be sent for those customers whose balances were over $1000 than for those under $100).

c. Test the footing of files, such as the accounts receivable file and hence check to see that the file totals truly equal those reported.

d. Summarize information in the files, (e.g., prepare an aged trial balance of the accounts receivable file).

e. Perform other tasks such as printing out all credit balances in the accounts receivable file or all debit balances in the accounts payable file, in order to check these inconsistent elements of the files.

GAS is now a standard tool. Unfortunately, its use is limited by the wide variety of incompatible equipment now used for business data processing. The GAS can work with different files, but not necessarily with all different computers.

As we discussed in the case of manual systems, it is impossible to list all the procedures, forms, and techniques which are required in all situations for effective internal control in computer-based systems. You will simply have to use your judgment in creating effective internal control in any particular situation. However, Table 16-3 gives the basic techniques for each of the six elements of internal control. These should provide a starting point for further development.

It is essential for you to realize that we are not trying to recommend an atmosphere where no one is trusted. We are simply recommending a situation where people are accountable for their actions, where the company does not depend on any particular employees, where the company is protected in the case of disastrous accidents, and where there are no excessive temptations for employees.

TABLE 16-3 ELEMENTS OF INTERNAL CONTROL IN COMPUTER-BASED SYSTEMS

Honest and capable employees	1. create climate where security is taken seriously 2. provide proper training in use of computer 3. check background and bond employees 4. promptly exclude fired employees from computer
Clear delegation and separation of duties	1. develop written plan of organization 2. do not allow any employees to be essential 3. assign responsibility for data, systems and programs 4. separate people who might collude
Proper procedures for processing of transactions	1. ensure transactions are properly authorized 2. check entered data for accuracy 3. use only authorized and tested programs 4. develop and test procedures for computer breakdown
Suitable documents and accounting records	1. provide backup files of data and programs 2. have written procedures and standards of performance 3. develop documentation of systems and programs 4. use prenumbered documents and forms
Adequate physical control over assets and records	1. control access to computer and terminals 2. protect equipment and data against loss 3. control access to sensitive input and output 4. maintain equipment on a regular basis
Independent verification of performance	1. develop overall system controls 2. check adherence to policies and procedures 3. check security and discipline lax security 4. have audit by independent CPA firm

16.3 THE FUTURE

As a final note, we would like to make some summary comments and discuss the future impact of the computer on accounting and information systems.

1. For the foreseeable future, many businesses will continue to use manual "books" and manual accounting systems. Thus, the material you covered in Part one not only provides a base for future learning, but it is also directly applicable to many small businesses.

2. Through the mid-1980s, the number of large- and medium-scale computer systems will continue to grow at a rate of approximately 10 percent per year. However, small systems should grow at a rate of over 25 percent per year.

3. As a result, the computer will affect all businesses strongly, not just the relatively large businesses affected in the 1970s.

4. Therefore, all accountants must be familiar with the computer, because the computer will affect all of them. In fact, accountants for small businesses must know more about the computer than accountants for large businesses, since there will not be a separate data-processing staff.

5. However, the development of good data-base management systems and improved programming languages will make the use of the computer much easier.

6. Thus, the impact of the computer on accounting and information systems has hardly even begun: the uses of the computer in the 1970s will be an insignificant percentage of the uses by the end of the 1980s.

7. Finally, when extensive data on the computer becomes available for analysis, the mathematical approach of management science or operations research will be much more applicable. The accountant of the 1980s will then be much more quantitative and mathematical than his 1970s counterpart.

The computer has the potential to free us from drudgery, expand our horizons, and free our creative spirit. We should pursue this opportunity to the utmost.

exercises

16-1 This chapter has stressed the internal control problems which may be part of computer-based systems. However, there are a number of internal control benefits which result from using the computer. List ten accidental or deliberate mistakes which are entirely possible in a manual system, but which are unlikely in a computer-based system.

16-2 Generally, there are two approaches to the auditing of computer-based systems: auditing "through" the system and auditing "around" the system. State five specific techniques for each of these two basic approaches.

16-3 Since a computer exercises no judgment or intuition of its own and will therefore do anything it is told to do, reasonableness tests constitute an important aspect of internal control in a computer system. Give three specific reasonableness tests for each of the following transactions.

   a. Cash is disbursed in payment of an amount owed a vendor.

   b. Credit purchase of merchandise.

   c. Payroll check for terminating employee.

16-4 A firm's data base is a critically important resource which can be damaged or destroyed in a number of different ways. Explain the basic steps you would take to safeguard a data base against each of the following occurrences.

   a. Error by terminal operator.

   b. Error in application program.

   c. Conspiracy between programmer and chief accountant.

d. Natural disaster, such as flood or fire.

e. Power failure.

16-5 Table 16-1 presents the internal control problems which are specific to computer systems, the typical result from such control problems, and a general solution for each problem. For an accounts receivable system in an organization such as Pooper Centers, give a specific example of each type of control problem and how it might arise.

16-6 Table 16-3 presents the elements of internal control and the specific steps which must be undertaken to make the element effective. For an accounts receivable system in an organization such as Pooper Centers, give a specific example of each of these steps and how each specific step might be accomplished.

16-7 The chapter suggests that the responsibilities for system development, program maintenance, and data accuracy should be separated since processing is concentrated within the computer. However, many small businesses have only one person directly responsible for all data-processing activities. Discuss five specific internal control techniques which could be used where data-processing duties and responsibilities cannot be separated.

16-8 A savings and loan association installed an on-line real-time computer system.[1] Each teller in the association's main office and seven branch offices has an on-line input-output terminal. Customer's mortgage payments and savings account deposits and withdrawals are recorded in the accounts by the computer from data input by the teller at the time of the transaction. The teller keys the proper account by account number and enters the information in the terminal keyboard to record the transaction. The accounting department at the main office has both punched-card and terminal input-output devices. The computer is housed at the main office. List the internal controls which should be in effect in such a system, classifying them as (a) controls pertaining to the input of information and (b) all other types of controls.

16-9 Your client, Lakesedge Wholesale Company, is installing an electronic data-processing system.[2] You have been asked to recommend controls for the new system. Discuss recommended controls over:

a. Program documentation

b. Program testing

c. EDP hardware

d. Data files and software.

16-10 The book began with a discussion of manual accounting systems and ended with a discussion of computer-based information systems. Clearly, the future of data processing lies in computer-based systems.

1. What role should the accountant play as these new systems evolve?

2. What skills will future accountants need to fulfill this role?

3. What training will most likely foster the development of these skills?

---

[1] Adapted from the AICPA examination.

[2] Adapted from the AICPA examination.

appendix a

sample company program development using BASIC

A.1   FILE MAINTENANCE PROGRAM

The file maintenance program has four basic purposes:

- a. To add new credit customers to the system when approved by the accountant.
- b. To delete old customer accounts when they should no longer be on the file; that is, when their accounts are no longer active due to death, relocation, etc. (Note: you cannot delete a customer account that has a nonzero balance; you will have to use the transaction program to create a zero balance).
- c. To modify the information stored on each customer, including the customer name, address, or credit limit. (Note: you cannot change a balance using this program, a balance can only be changed by the transaction program).
- d. To print out a file status report on each customer, detailing the customer name, address, credit limit, beginning balance, debits, credits, ending balance, and credit available.

When you run the program, the first question will be:

1. TYPE OF RUN (A, D, M, P, E)?

If you would like to add new customers to the file
     2. Type: A
     3. Press: RETURN
     4. Go to step 16
If you would like to delete the customer record now on file
     5. Type: D
     6. Press: RETURN
     7. Go to step 32
If you would like to modify the customer record for customers now on file:
     8. Type: M
     9. Press: RETURN
     10. Go to step 45
If you would like to print out the file status of every customer on the file
     11. Type: P
     12. Press: RETURN
     13. Go to step 1
If you would like to end the program
     14. Type: E
     15. Press: RETURN
The program will then end.
The computer will then ask you
     16. CUSTØMER NUMBER (0 TØ END)?
If you would like to stop adding customers to the file
     17. Type: O
     18. Press: RETURN
     19. Go to step 1
If you would like to add a customer to the file
     20. Type: a positive number which will uniquely identify the customer
     21. Press: RETURN
The computer will then ask
     22. CUSTØMER NAME (30 CHARACTER MAXIMUM)?
Respond by
     23. Type: name of customer, but do not use over thirty letters and spaces for the name
     24. Press: RETURN
The computer will then ask you
     25. CUSTØMER ADDRESS (30 CHARACTER MAXIMUM)?
Respond by
     26. Type: address of customer, with the same limitation as the name
     27. Press: RETURN
The computer will then ask you
     28. CREDIT LIMIT?
Respond by
     29. Type: a positive number which will give the maximum amount the customer will
                 be allowed to owe us at any one time
     30. Press: RETURN

31. Go to step 16

The computer will then ask you

32. CUSTØMER NUMBER (0 TØ END)?

If you would like to stop deleting customer records from the file

33. Type: O
34. Press: RETURN
35. Go to step 1

If you would like to delete a customer record from the file

36. Type: customer number uniquely identifying that customer
37. Press: RETURN
38. STILL WISH TO DELETE THE RECØRD (Y ØR N)?

If you decide this is not a customer you wish to delete

39. Type: N
40. Press: RETURN
41. Go to step 32

If you still wish to delete this customer record

42. Type: Y
43. Press: RETURN
44. Go to step 32

The computer will then ask you

45. CUSTØMER NUMBER (0 TØ END)?

If you would like to stop modifying customer records

46. Type: O
47. Press: RETURN
48. Go to step 1

If you would like to modify a customer record

49. Type: customer number uniquely identifying the customer to be modified
50. Press: RETURN

The computer will then print out the file status for that customer.

If the account is active, Go to step 57.

If the customer's account has been deleted, the computer will ask:

51. DO YOU WISH TO ACTIVATE THIS ACCOUNT (Y OR N)?

If you do not wish to activate this account

52. Type: N
53. Press: RETURN
54. Go to step 45

If you wish to activate this account

55. Type: Y
56. Press: RETURN

The computer will then ask you

57. LINE NUMBER FØR CØRRECTION (0 TØ END)?

If you no longer wish to modify this customer's record

58. Type: O
59. Press: RETURN
60. Go to step 45

If you would like to change the customer name
    61. Type: 1
    62. Press: RETURN
The computer will then ask you
    63. NEW CUSTØMER NAME?
Respond by
    64. Type: the name you would like on the file (remember the 30-character maximum)
    65. Press: RETURN
    66. Go to step 57
If you would like to change the customer address
    67. Type: 2
    68. Press: RETURN
The computer will then ask you
    69. NEW CUSTØMER ADDRESS?
Respond by
    70. Type: the address you would like on the file (remember the 30-character maximum)
    71. Press: RETURN
    72. Go to step 57
If you would like to change the customer credit limit
    73. Type: 3
    74. Press: RETURN
The computer will then ask
    75. NEW CUSTØMER CREDIT LIMIT?
Respond by
    76. Type: the new maximum amount of credit we will extend to this customer
    77. Press: RETURN
    78. Go to step 57

Note: the only lines which can be changed by this program are 1, 2, and 3 because balances can *only* be changed by transactions processed by the transaction processing program.

Sample Run Maintenance

```
COMMAND CODES:

    A    ADD CUSTOMER TO FILE
    D    DELETE CUSTOMER FROM FILE
    M    MODIFY CUSTOMER NAME, ADDRESS OR CREDIT LIMIT
    P    PRINT ALL INFORMATION ON ALL CUSTOMERS
    E    END EXECUTION OF PROGRAM


TYPE OF RUN (A,D,M,P,E) ?A

CUSTOMER NUMBER (0 TO END) ?11001
CUSTOMER NAME (30 CHARACTERS MAXIMUM) ?UPTOWN CONST. CO.
CUSTOMER ADDRESS (30 CHARACTERS MAXIMUM) ?FIRST ST.
CREDIT LIMIT ?75000

CUSTOMER NUMBER (0 TO END) ?11002
CUSTOMER NAME (30 CHARACTERS MAXIMUM) ?LIL' PIG LAUNDERMAT
CUSTOMER ADDRESS (30 CHARACTERS MAXIMUM) ?SECOND ST.
CREDIT LIMIT ?50000
```

Sample Run Maintenance (Continued)

```
CUSTOMER NUMBER (0 TO END) ?11007
CUSTOMER NAME (30 CHARACTERS MAXIMUM) ?WRIGLEY WRIGHT
CUSTOMER ADDRESS (30 CHARACTERS MAXIMUM) ?THIRD ST.
CREDIT LIMIT ?15000

CUSTOMER NUMBER (0 TO END) ?11019
CUSTOMER NAME (30 CHARACTERS MAXIMUM) ?AKBAR IKBAR
CUSTOMER ADDRESS (30 CHARACTERS MAXIMUM) ?FOURTH ST.
CREDIT LIMIT ?7500

CUSTOMER NUMBER (0 TO END) ?11031
CUSTOMER NAME (30 CHARACTERS MAXIMUM) ?HAROLD SHADRACK
CUSTOMER ADDRESS (30 CHARACTERS MAXIMUM) ?FIFTH ST.
CREDIT LIMIT ?5000

CUSTOMER NUMBER (0 TO END) ?0

TYPE OF RUN (A,D,M,P,E) ?M

CUSTOMER NUMBER (0 TO END) ?11081
    CUSTOMER NUMBER           11081
    ACCOUNT IS ACTIVE
1. CUSTOMER NAME            STERLING SILVER
2. CUSTOMER ADDRESS         10'TH ST.
3. CREDIT LIMIT             6000
4. BEGINNING BALANCE        0
5. DEBITS FOR PERIOD        0
6. CREDITS FOR PERIOD       0
7. ENDING BALANCE           0
8. CREDIT AVAILABLE         6000
LINE NUMBER FOR CORRECTION (0 TO END) ?2
NEW CUSTOMER ADDRESS ?TENTH ST.
LINE NUMBER FOR CORRECTION (0 TO END) ?0

CUSTOMER NUMBER (0 TO END) ?0


TYPE OF RUN (A,D,M,P,E) ?E

END OF PROGRAM
```

Program Listing File Maintenance

```
10 REM-------------------FILE MAINTANANCE PROGRAM
20 REM    THIS PROGRAM ADDS CUSTOMERS, DELETES CUSTOMERS,
30 REM    AND MODIFIES CUSTOMERS ON FILE.
40 REM
50 REM-------------------DICTIONARY OF VARIABLES
60 REM
70 REM    X$ COMMAND CODE
80 REM    C,C2,C$ CUSTOMER NUMBER
90 REM    F,F$ ACTIVITY STATUS -- 1=INACTIVE, 0=ACTIVE ACCT.
100 REM   N$ CUSTOMER NAME
110 REM   A$ CUSTOMER ADDRESS
120 REM   M,M$ CREDIT LIMIT
130 REM   B,B$ BEGINNING BALANCE
140 REM   D1,D1$ DEBITS FOR PERIOD
150 REM   C1,C1$ CREDITS FOR PERIOD
160 REM   E,E$ ENDING BALANCE
170 REM   L   LINE NUMBER TO CORRECT
180 REM   Z$ YES OR NO RESPONSE TO QUESTION
190 REM   R9 INDEX TO CUSTOMER RECORD
200 REM   R8 NUMBER OF CUSTOMERS IN CUSTOMER FILE
500 REM
510 REM-------------------MAIN PROGRAM
520 REM
530 FILES CUST.DAT$
540 PRINT"COMMAND CODES:"
550 PRINT
560 PRINT"  A    ADD CUSTOMER TO FILE"
570 PRINT"  D    DELETE CUSTOMER FROM FILE"
```

Program Listing File Maintenance (Continued)

```
580 PRINT"  M    MODIFY CUSTOMER NAME, ADDRESS OR CREDIT LIMIT"
590 PRINT"  P    PRINT ALL INFORMATION ON ALL CUSTOMERS"
600 PRINT"  E    END EXECUTION OF PROGRAM"
610 PRINT
620 REM------------------GET TYPE OF RUN
630 PRINT
640 PRINT"TYPE OF RUN (A,D,M,P,E)";
650 INPUT X$
660 IF X$="A" GOTO 720
670 IF X$="D" GOTO 1350
680 IF X$="M" GOTO 980
690 IF X$="P" GOTO 900
700 IF X$="E" GOTO 9000
710 GO TO 620
720 REM------------------ADD CUSTOMER TO FILE
730 PRINT
740 PRINT"CUSTOMER NUMBER (0 TO END)";
750 INPUT C
760 IF C <=0 GOTO 620
770 GOSUB 4000
780 IF R9 > R8 GOTO 810
790 PRINT "CUSTOMER NUMBER ALREADY IN USE --  START OVER"
800 GOTO 720
810 PRINT"CUSTOMER NAME (30 CHARACTERS MAXIMUM)";
820 INPUT N$
830 PRINT"CUSTOMER ADDRESS (30 CHARACTERS MAXIMUM)";
840 INPUT A$
850 PRINT"CREDIT LIMIT";
860 INPUT M
870 B=D1=C1=E=F=0
880 GOSUB 2000
890 GOTO 720
900 REM------------------PRINT ALL CUSTOMERS
910 FOR R9 = 1 TO INT(LOF(1)/9)
920    PRINT
930    GOSUB 3500
940    GOSUB 5000
950 NEXT R9
960 PRINT
970 GOTO 620
980 REM------------------MODIFY CUSTOMER IN FILE
990 PRINT
1000 PRINT"CUSTOMER NUMBER (0 TO END)";
1010 INPUT C
1020 IF C<=0 GOTO 620
1030 GOSUB 4000
1040 IF R9 <= R8 GOTO 1070
1050 PRINT "THAT CUSTOMER NUMBER DOES NOT EXIST"
1060 GOTO 980
1070 GOSUB 3500
1080 GOSUB 5000
1090 IF F = 0 GOTO 1160
1100 PRINT "DO YOU WISH TO ACTIVATE THIS ACCOUNT (Y OR N)";
1110 GOSUB 3000
1120 IF Z$ = "N" GOTO 980
1130 F=0
1140 GOSUB 2000
1150 GOSUB 5000
1160 PRINT"LINE NUMBER FOR CORRECTION (0 TO END)";
1170 INPUT L
1180 IF L<=0 GOTO 980
1190 IF L=1 GOTO 1230
1200 IF L=2 GOTO 1270
1210 IF L=3 GOTO 1310
1220 GOTO 1160
1230 PRINT" NEW CUSTOMER NAME":
1240 INPUT N$
1250 GOSUB 2000
1260 GOTO 1160
1270 PRINT"NEW CUSTOMER ADDRESS";
1280 INPUT A$
```

Program Listing File Maintenance (Continued)

```
1290 GOSUB 2000
1300 GOTO 1160
1310 PRINT"NEW CUSTOMER CREDIT LIMIT";
1320 INPUT M
1330 GOSUB 2000
1340 GOTO 1160
1350 REM------------------DELETE CUSTOMER FROM FILE
1360 PRINT
1370 PRINT "CUSTOMER NUMBER (0 TO END)  ";
1380 INPUT C
1390 IF C<=0 GOTO 620
1400 GOSUB 4000
1410 IF R9 <= R8 GOTO 1440
1420 PRINT "CUSTOMER NUMBER DOES NOT EXIST"
1430 GOTO 1350
1440 GOSUB 3500
1450 GOSUB 5000
1460 IF F = 1 GOTO 1350
1470 IF E=0 GOTO 1510
1480 PRINT "CANNOT DELETE RECORD - NON/ZERO BALANCE"
1490 PRINT
1500 GOTO 1350
1510 PRINT "STILL WISH TO DELETE THE RECORD (Y OR N)";
1520 GOSUB 3000
1530 IF Z$ = "N" GOTO 1350
1540 F = 1
1550 GOSUB 2000
1560 GOSUB 4500
1570 PRINT
1580 GOTO 1350
2000 REM------------------SUBROUTINE: WRITE CUSTOMER RECORD
2010 C$=STR$(C)
2020 F$=STR$(F)
2030 M$=STR$(M)
2040 B$=STR$(B)
2050 D1$=STR$(D1)
2060 C1$=STR$(C1)
2070 E$=STR$(E)
2080 SET :1, (R9-1)*9+1
2090 WRITE:1, C$,F$,N$,A$,M$,B$,D1$,C1$,E$
2100 RETURN
3000 REM------------------SUBROUTINE: ENTER YES OR NO
3010 INPUT Z$
3020 IF Z$ = "Y" GOTO 3060
3030 IF Z$ = "N" GOTO 3060
3040 PRINT "ENTER  Y OR N  -- TRY AGAIN ";
3050 GOTO 3010
3060 RETURN
3500 REM------------------SUBROUTINE: READ CUSTOMER RECORD
3510 SET :1, (R9-1)*9+1
3520 READ :1, C$,F$,N$,A$,M$,B$,D1$,C1$,E$
3530 C=VAL(C$)
3540 F=VAL(F$)
3550 M=VAL(M$)
3560 B=VAL(B$)
3570 D1=VAL(D1$)
3580 C1=VAL(C1$)
3590 E=VAL(E$)
3600 RETURN
4000 REM------------------SUBROUTINE: SET INDEX TO CUSTOMER RECORD
4010 R8 = INT(LOF(1)/9)
4020 FOR R9 = 1 TO R8
4030    SET :1, (R9-1)*9+1
4040    READ :1,C$
4050    C2 = VAL(C$)
4060    IF C2=C GOTO 4090
4070 NEXT R9
4080 R9 = R8 + 1
4090 RETURN
4500 REM------------------SUBROUTINE: PRINT ACTIVITY STATUS
4510 IF F = 1 GOTO 4540
4520 PRINT "   ACCOUNT IS ACTIVE"
```

Program Listing File Maintenance (Continued)

```
4530 GOTO 4550
4540 PRINT "    ACCOUNT IS INACTIVE"
4550 RETURN
5000 REM------------------SUBROUTINE: PRINT A CUSTOMER
5010 PRINT"    CUSTOMER NUMBER",C
5020 GOSUB 4500
5030 PRINT"1. CUSTOMER NAME",N$
5040 PRINT"2. CUSTOMER ADDRESS",A$
5050 PRINT"3. CREDIT LIMIT",M
5060 PRINT"4. BEGINNING BALANCE",B
5070 PRINT"5. DEBITS FOR PERIOD",D1
5080 PRINT"6. CREDITS FOR PERIOD",C1
5090 PRINT"7. ENDING BALANCE",E
5100 PRINT"8. CREDIT AVAILABLE",M-E
5110 RETURN
9000 REM------------------END PROGRAM
9010 PRINT
9020 PRINT "END OF PROGRAM"
9030 END
```

A.2 TRANSACTION PROCESSING PROGRAM

You will use this program to enter the credit sales, cash payments, and credit memo adjustments into the system as they occur. Each credit sale, cash payment, and credit memo adjustment for whatever customer is considered one transaction and must be entered separately. When you enter a transaction into the system, the computer will remember it. Thus, every change in a customer balance will be remembered. This is the reason you cannot change a balance with the file maintenance program. This is also the reason you cannot delete a customer with a nonzero balance: the total effect of all transactions should equal the total of all balances for customers.

When you start the program, the computer will ask

     1. TYPE ØF TRANSACTION (0 TØ END)?

If you would like to stop processing transactions

     2. Type: 0

     3. Press: RETURN

The program will then end.

If you would like to enter a transaction into the system

     4. Type: the transaction number (1 = credit sale, 2 = cash payment, 3 = credit memo, and 4 = debit memo)

     5. Press: RETURN

The computer will then ask

     6. CUSTØMER NUMBER?

Respond by

     7. Type: unique number identifying the customer for this transaction

     8. Press: RETURN

The computer will then ask

     9. DATE ØF TRANSACTION (M, D, Y)?

Respond by

    10. Type: number of the month of the transaction (e.g., January would be 1 and December would be 12)

    11. Type: ,

    12. Type: number of the day of the month of the transaction

    13. Type: ,

    14. Type: number of the year of the transaction (e.g., 1980 would be typed in 80)

    15. Press: RETURN

Note: As an example, January 12, 1980 would be typed in 1,12,80 and December 1, 1980 would be typed in 12,1,80

The computer will then ask

    16. AMØUNT ØF TRANSACTION?

Respond by

    17. Type: the dollar amount of the transaction

    18. Press: RETURN

Note: The dollar amount can be typed in with or without the decimal point. Thus, five dollars can be typed in 5 or 5. or 5.0 or 5.00. Of course, five dollars and sixty five cents would be typed in as 5.65. The computer will then print out the complete transaction, including an alphabetic description of the customer, so the correctness of the customer number can be checked.

The computer will then ask:

    19. IS THIS TRANSACTION CORRECT (Y OR N)?

If you would like the computer to process the transaction

    20. Type: Y

    21. Press: RETURN

    22. Go to step 1

If there is a mistake in the transaction or you otherwise do not want to process the transaction

    23. Type: N

    24. Press: RETURN

    25. Go to step 1

Sample Run Transaction

```
TRANSACTION TYPES:

   0    END PROGRAM
   1    CREDIT SALE
   2    CASH RECEIPTS
   3    CREDIT MEMO
   4    DEBIT MEMO


TYPE OF TRANSACTION (0 TO END) ?1
CUSTOMER NUMBER ?11001
DATE OF TRANSACTION (M,D,Y) ?12,31,78
AMOUNT OF TRANSACTION  ?50000

TRANSACTION TYPE            1
CUSTOMER NUMBER            11001
CUSTOMER NAME             UPTOWN CONST. CO.
DATE OF TRANS             12 / 31 / 78
AMOUNT                    50000
BALANCE WOULD BE          50000      CREDIT LIMIT   75000
```

Sample Run Transaction (Continued)

```
IS THIS TRANSACTION CORRECT (Y OR N) ?Y
```

```
TYPE OF TRANSACTION (0 TO END) ?4
CUSTOMER NUMBER ?11082
DATE OF TRANSACTION (M,D,Y) ?2,1,79
AMOUNT OF TRANSACTION   ?10

TRANSACTION TYPE          4
CUSTOMER NUMBER           11082
CUSTOMER NAME             CHERRY HERRING
DATE OF TRANS             2 / 1 / 79
AMOUNT                    10
BALANCE WOULD BE          810           CREDIT LIMIT   10000

IS THIS TRANSACTION CORRECT (Y OR N) ?Y

TYPE OF TRANSACTION (0 TO END) ?0


POOPER CENTERS, INC.
TOTALS OF TRANSACTIONS TO DATE

TYPE           AMOUNT

CREDIT SALES   202430
CASH RECEIPTS  51825
CREDIT MEMOS   2200
DEBIT MEMOS    1288

END OF PROGRAM
```

Program Listing Transaction

```
10 REM-------------------TRANSACTION RECORDING PROGRAM
20 REM     THIS PROGRAM RECORDS A TRANSACTION IN A TRANSACTION FILE
30 REM     AND UPDATE THE FILE OF CUSTOMER RECORDS.
40 REM
50 REM-------------------DICTIONARY OF VARIABLES
60 REM
70 REM    X,X$  TRANSACTION CODE
80 REM    C,C2,C$  CUSTOMER NUMBER
90 REM    F,F$  ACTIVITY STATUS -- 1=INACTIVE, 0=ACTIVE ACCT.
100 REM   N$   CUSTOMER NAME
110 REM   A$   CUSTOMER ADDRESS
120 REM   M,M$  CREDIT LIMIT
130 REM   B,B$  BEGINNING BALANCE
140 REM   D1,D1$  DEBITS FOR PERIOD
150 REM   C1,C1$  CREDITS FOR PERIOD
160 REM   E,E$  ENDING BALANCE
170 REM   T(1),T$(1) TOTAL OF CREDIT SALES
180 REM   T(2),T$(2) TOTAL OF CASH RECIEPTS
190 REM   T(3),T$(3) TOTAL OF ALL CREDIT MEMOES
200 REM   T(4),T$(4) TOTAL OF ALL DEBIT MEMOES
210 REM   D,D$  DATE OF TRANSACTION
220 REM   T,T$  AMOUNT OF TRANSACTION
230 REM   Z    LAST RECORD NUMBER IN THE FILE
240 REM   M6   # OF MONTH
250 REM   D6   # OF DAY
260 REM   Y6   # OF YEAR
270 REM   Z$   YES OR NO RESPONSE TO QUESTION
280 REM   R9   INDEX TO CUSTOMER RECORD
500 REM
510 REM-------------------MAIN PROGRAM
520 REM
530 FILES CUST.DAT$, TRANS.DAT$
540 PRINT "TRANSACTION TYPES:"
```

Program Listing Transaction (Continued)

```
550 PRINT
560 PRINT "  0    END PROGRAM"
570 PRINT "  1    CREDIT SALE"
580 PRINT "  2    CASH RECEIPTS"
590 PRINT "  3    CREDIT MEMO"
600 PRINT "  4    DEBIT MEMO"
610 PRINT
620 REM-----------------CREATE TRANSACTION FILE
630 IF LOF(2) > 1 GOTO 690
640 T$(1)=T$(2)=T$(3)=T$(4)=STR$(0)
650 SET :2,1
660 WRITE :2,T$(1),T$(2),T$(3),T$(4)
670 GOTO 690
680 PRINT "   TRANSACTION NOT PROCESSED"
690 REM-----------------GET TRANSACTION TYPE
700 PRINT
710 PRINT "TYPE OF TRANSACTION (0 TO END)";
720 INPUT X
730 X = INT(X)
740 IF X<0 GOTO 1040
750 IF X>4 GOTO 1040
760 IF X=0 GOTO 1250
770 REM-----------------GET TRANSACTION INFORMATION
780 PRINT "CUSTOMER NUMBER";
790 INPUT C
800 IF C <= 0 GOTO 1020
810 GOSUB 4000
820 IF R9 > R8 GOTO 1020
830 GOSUB 3500
840 IF F = 1 GOTO 1000
850 PRINT "DATE OF TRANSACTION (M,D,Y)";
860 INPUT M6,D6,Y6
870 IF M6> 12 GOTO 980
880 IF M6< 1  GOTO 980
890 IF D6> 31 GOTO 980
900 IF D6< 1  GOTO 980
910 IF Y6< 77 GOTO 980
920 D = Y6*10000+M6*100+D6
930 PRINT "AMOUNT OF TRANSACTION ";
940 INPUT T
950 IF T <= 0 THEN 1060
960 GOTO 1100
970 REM-----------------ERROR MESSAGES
980 PRINT"INVALID DATE - VERIFY AND REENTER CORRECTLY"
990 GOTO 690
1000 PRINT "    ACCOUNT IS INACTIVE"
1010 GOTO 690
1020 PRINT"INVALID CUSTOMER NUMBER - VERIFY AND REENTER CORRECTLY"
1030 GOTO 690
1040 PRINT"INVALID TRANSACTION TYPE - VERIFY AND REENTER CORRECTLY"
1050 GOTO 690
1060 PRINT "INVALID AMOUT - VERIFY AND REENTER CORRECTLY"
1070 GOTO 690
1080 REM-----------------CHECK TRANSACTION INFORMATION
1090 REM                 AND ACCEPT OR REJECT
1100 GOSUB 2500
1110 PRINT
1120 PRINT "TRANSACTION TYPE",X
1130 PRINT "CUSTOMER NUMBER",C
1140 PRINT "CUSTOMER NAME",,N$
1150 PRINT "DATE OF TRANS",,M6;"/";D6;"/"Y6
1160 PRINT "AMOUNT",,T
1170 PRINT "BALANCE WOULD BE",E,"CREDIT LIMIT",M
1180 PRINT
1190 PRINT "IS THIS TRANSACTION CORRECT (Y OR N)";
1200 GOSUB 3000
1210 IF Z$ = "N" GOTO 680
1220 GOSUB 2000
1230 GOSUB 6500
1240 GOTO 690
1250 REM-----------------PRINT TOTALS
1260 Z = LOF(2)
```

Program Listing Transaction (Continued)

```
1270 SET :2,Z-3
1280 READ :2,T$(1),T$(2),T$(3),T$(4)
1290 FOR I = 1 TO 4
1300 T(I) = VAL(T$(I))
1310 NEXT I
1320 PRINT
1330 PRINT
1340 PRINT "POOPER CENTERS, INC."
1350 PRINT "TOTALS OF TRANSACTIONS TO DATE"
1360 PRINT
1370 PRINT "TYPE","AMOUNT"
1380 PRINT
1390 PRINT"CREDIT SALES",T(1)
1400 PRINT"CASH RECEIPTS",T(2)
1410 PRINT"CREDIT MEMOS",T(3)
1420 PRINT"DEBIT MEMOS ",T(4)
1430 GOTO 9000
2000 REM-----------------SUBROUTINE: WRITE CUSTOMER RECORD
2010 C$=STR$(C)
2020 F$=STR$(F)
2030 M$=STR$(M)
2040 B$=STR$(B)
2050 D1$=STR$(D1)
2060 C1$=STR$(C1)
2070 E$=STR$(E)
2080 SET :1, (R9-1)*9+1
2090 WRITE:1, C$,F$,N$,A$,M$,B$,D1$,C1$,E$
2100 RETURN
2500 REM-----------------SUBROUTINE: UPDATE CUSTOMER RECORD
2510 REM                        WITH A TRANSACTION
2520 IF X=1 THEN 2580
2530 IF X=2 THEN 2610
2540 IF X=3 THEN 2610
2550 IF X=4 THEN 2580
2560 PRINT"CAN NOT RECOGNIZE TRANSACTION"
2570 GOTO 2630
2580 D1=D1+T
2590 E=E+T
2600 GOTO 2630
2610 C1=C1+T
2620 E=E-T
2630 RETURN
3000 REM-----------------SUBROUTINE: ENTER YES OR NO
3010 INPUT Z$
3020 IF Z$ = "Y" GOTO 3060
3030 IF Z$ = "N" GOTO 3060
3040 PRINT "ENTER  Y OR N  -- TRY AGAIN ";
3050 GOTO 3010
3060 RETURN
3500 REM-----------------SUBROUTINE: READ CUSTOMER RECORD
3510 SET :1, (R9-1)*9+1
3520 READ :1, C$,F$,N$,A$,M$,B$,D1$,C1$,E$
3530 C=VAL(C$)
3540 F=VAL(F$)
3550 M=VAL(M$)
3560 B=VAL(B$)
3570 D1=VAL(D1$)
3580 C1=VAL(C1$)
3590 E=VAL(E$)
3600 RETURN
4000 REM-----------------SUBROUTINE: SET INDEX TO CUSTOMER RECORD
4010 R8 = INT(LOF(1)/9)
4020 FOR R9 = 1 TO R8
4030    SET :1, (R9-1)*9+1
4040    READ :1,C$
4050    C2 = VAL(C$)
4060    IF C2=C GOTO 4090
4070 NEXT R9
4080 R9 = R8 + 1
4090 RETURN
4500 REM-----------------SUBROUTINE: PRINT ACTIVITY STATUS
4510 IF F = 1 GOTO 4540
```

Program Listing Transaction (Continued)

```
4520 PRINT "    ACCOUNT IS ACTIVE"
4530 GOTO 4550
4540 PRINT "    ACCOUNT IS INACTIVE"
4550 RETURN
6500 REM-----------------SUBROUTINE: ADD NEW TRANSACTION
6510 REM                      TO THE TRANSACTION FILE
6520 Z=LOF(2)
6530 SET :2, Z-3
6540 READ :2, T$(1),T$(2),T$(3),T$(4)
6550 T(X)=VAL(T$(X))
6560 T(X)=T(X)+T
6570 T$(X)=STR$(T(X))
6580 SET :2, Z-3
6590 X$=STR$(X).
6600 C$=STR$(C)
6610 D$=STR$(D)
6620 T$=STR$(T)
6630 WRITE :2, X$,C$,D$,T$
6640 WRITE :2, T$(1),T$(2),T$(3),T$(4)
6650 RETURN
9000 REM-----------------END PROGRAM
9010 PRINT
9020 PRINT "END OF PROGRAM"
9030 END
```

A.3 AGED TRIAL BALANCE PROGRAM

The aged trial balance program simply prints out an aged trial balance of accounts receivable. The aged trial balance as printed out is current as of the last transactions processed by the transaction processing program. You will use this aged trial balance printout for three basic reasons:

- the printout totals the amount due from all our customers. This amount should balance to (i.e., equal) the total in the General Ledger Control account for Accounts Receivable.
- the printout apportions the balance owed by each customer into the amount that is current, the amount that is over 30 days old, and the amount that is over 60 days old. This breakdown will pinpoint customers whose balances (and payments) are starting to slip—these customers can then be contacted to urge payment.
- the aging of customer balances mentioned above serves an additional purpose. It provides information necessary for making decisions concerning write-offs of accounts receivable. These decisions include the individual decision to write-off a particular customer account and the overall decision on how much to debit to bad debt expense and credit to the allowance for bad debits. This information is important in determining if the allowance is inadequate, is proper, or is excessive.

The computer will only ask one question
     1. DATE ØF RUN (M, D, Y)?
Respond by
     2. Type: the number of the month for the date of run (e.g., January would be 1 and December would be 12)
     3. Type: ,
     4. Type: the number of the day of the month for the date of run
     5. Type: ,
     6. Type: the number of the year for the date of run (e.g., 1980 would be 80)
Note: This date of run is used by the computer program as a base for determining how old the various customer balances are. As a result, you may not use exactly the real day you are running the programming, but the day you wish to age from.

Sample Run Aged Trial Balance

```
DATE OF RUN (M,D,Y) ?2,1,79


AGED TRIAL BALANCE
POOPER CENTERS, INC.
1000 CANAL STREET
NEW ORLEANS, LA.    70000
```

NAME	TOTAL	CURRENT	OVER 30	OVER 60
UPTOWN CONST	42500	22500	20000	0
LIL' PIG LAU	17712	1812	15900	0
WRIGLEY WRIG	2310	1310	1000	0
AKBAR IKBAR	500	500	0	0
HAROLD SHADR	709	9	700	0
MARVIN MESHA	0	0	0	0
BRUCE ABENDI	862	12	850	0
IONA CARR	1015	15	1000	0
I.M. WOMAN	1662	512	1150	0
STERLING SIL	558	8	550	0
CHERRY HERRI	810	10	800	0
MAJOR CREDIT	48355	48355	0	0
TRIP THE LIT	10000	10000	0	0
HOUSE OF PLE	14000	14000	0	0
WO FAT CONST	8200	8200	0	0
SUNBEAM	500	500	0	0
TOTALS	149693	107743	41950	0

```
END OF PROGRAM
```

Program Listing Aged Trial Balance

```
10 REM------------------AGED TRIAL BALANCE PROGRAM
20 REM    THIS PROGRAM AGES THE AMOUNT OWED BY EACH CUSTOMER
30 REM
40 REM------------------DICTIONARY OF VARIABLES
50 REM
60 REM   X,X$  COMMAND CODE
70 REM   C,C2,C$ CUSTOMER NUMBER
80 REM   F,F$ ACTIVITY STATUS -- 1=INACTIVE, 0=ACTIVE ACCT.
90 REM   N$ CUSTOMER NAME
100 REM   A$ CUSTOMER ADDRESS
110 REM   M,M$ CREDIT LIMIT
120 REM   B,B$ BEGINNING BALANCE
130 REM   D1,D1$ DEBITS FOR PERIOD
140 REM   C1,C1$ CREDITS FOR PERIOD
150 REM   E,E$ ENDING BALANCE
160 REM   D,D$  DATE OF TRANSACTION
170 REM   T,T$ AMOUNT OF TRANSACTION
180 REM   M6 # OF MONTH
190 REM   D6 # OF DAY
200 REM   Y6 # OF YEAR
210 REM   D9 DATE OF RUN
220 REM   D8 DATE ONE MONTH PRIOR TO RUN
230 REM   D7 DATE TWO MONTHS PRIOR TO RUN
240 REM   E8 # OF TRANSACTIONS
250 REM   I,J INDEX VARIABLES
260 REM   T9 TOTAL OF TRANS FOR 1 FIRM THAT ARE CURRENT
270 REM   T8 TOTAL OF TRANS FOR 1 FIRM THAT ARE OVER 30
280 REM   T7 TOTAL OF TRANS FOR 1 FIRM THAT ARE OVER 60
290 REM   A9 TOTAL OF TRANS FOR ALL FIRMS THAT ARE CURRENT
300 REM   A8 TOTAL OF TRANS FOR ALL FIRMS THAT ARE OVER 30
310 REM   A7 TOTAL OF TRANS FOR ALL FIRMS THAT ARE OVER 60
320 REM   R9 INDEX TO CUSTOMER RECORD
330 REM   R8 NUMBER OF CUSTOMERS IN CUSTOMER FILE
500 REM
510 REM------------------MAIN PROGRAM
520 REM
530 REM------------------GET DATE OF RUN
```

Program Listing Aged Trial Balance (Continued)

```
540 FILES CUST.DAT$, TRANS.DAT$
550 PRINT "DATE OF RUN (M,D,Y)";
560 INPUT M6,D6,Y6
570 D9=Y6*10000+M6*100+D6
580 REM-----------------DEVELOP AGE BREAKS
590 D5 = D9 - 100
600 GOSUB 5500
610 D8 = D5
620 D5 = D8 - 100
630 GOSUB 5500
640 D7 = D5
650 REM-----------------PARAMETERS AND HEADING
660 R8 = INT(LOF(1)/9)
670 E8 = INT((LOF(2)-4)/4)
680 PRINT
690 PRINT
700 PRINT "AGED TRIAL BALANCE"
710 PRINT "POOPER CENTERS, INC."
720 PRINT "1000 CANAL STREET"
730 PRINT "NEW ORLEANS, LA.     70000"
740 PRINT
750 PRINT "NAME","TOTAL","CURRENT","OVER 30","OVER 60"
760 PRINT
770 REM-----------------BEGIN OUTER LOOP:
780 REM                   ONCE THROUGH LOOP PER CUSTOMER
790 FOR R9 = 1 TO R8
800    GOSUB 3500
810    IF F = 1 GOTO 1040
820    C2 = C
830    T7=T8=T9=0
840    REM---------------BEGIN INNER LOOP:
850    REM                 READ ALL TRANSACTIONS
860    FOR J = 1 TO E8
870       GOSUB 6000
880       IF C <> C2 GOTO 960
890       IF D>D8 GOTO 950
900       IF D>D7 GOTO 930
910       GOSUB 7000
920       GOTO 960
930       GOSUB 7050
940       GOTO 960
950       GOSUB 7090
960    NEXT J
970    REM---------------END OF INNER LOOP
980    REM
990    REM                 PRINT AGED TOTALS FOR EACH CUSTOMER
1000   PRINT LEFT$(N$,12),T9+T8+T7,T9,T8,T7
1010   A9=A9+T9
1020   A8=A8+T8
1030   A7=A7+T7
1040 NEXT R9
1050 REM-----------------END OF OUTER LOOP
1060 REM
1070 REM                    PRINT AGED TOTALS FOR ALL CUSTOMERS
1080 PRINT
1090 PRINT "TOTALS",A9+A8+A7,A9,A8,A7
1100 GOTO 9000
3500 REM-----------------SUBROUTINE: READ CUSTOMER RECORD
3510 SET :1, (R9-1)*9+1
3520 READ :1, C$,F$,N$,A$,M$,B$,D1$,C1$,E$
3530 C=VAL(C$)
3540 F=VAL(F$)
3550 M=VAL(M$)
3560 B=VAL(B$)
3570 D1=VAL(D1$)
3580 C1=VAL(C1$)
3590 E=VAL(E$)
3600 RETURN
5500 REM-----------------SUBROUTINE: SHIFT MONTHS
5510 Y6 = INT(D5/10000)
5520 M6 = INT((D5-Y6*10000)/100)
5530 IF M6 > 0 GOTO 5550
```

Program Listing Aged Trial Balance (Continued)

```
5540 D5 = D5 -10000+1200
5550 RETURN
6000 REM------------------------READ TRANSACTIONS
6010 SET :2, (J-1)*4+1
6020 READ :2,X$,C$,D$,T$
6030 X=VAL(X$)
6040 C=VAL(C$)
6050 D=VAL(D$)
6060 T=VAL(T$)
6070 RETURN
7000 REM------------------SUBROUTINE: UPDATE BALANCES
7010 IF X = 2 THEN 7130
7020 IF X = 3 THEN 7130
7030 T7=T7+T
7040 GOTO 7240
7050 IF X = 2 THEN 7130
7060 IF X = 3 THEN 7130
7070 T8=T8+T
7080 GOTO 7240
7090 IF X = 2 THEN 7130
7100 IF X = 3 THEN 7130
7110 T9=T9+T
7120 GOTO 7240
7130 IF T7=0 GOTO 7180
7140 T7=T7-T
7150 IF T7 >= 0 GOTO 7240
7160 T = -T7
7170 T7 = 0
7180 IF T8=0 GOTO 7230
7190 T8=T8-T
7200 IF T8 >=0 GOTO 7240
7210 T=-T8
7220 T8=0
7230 T9=T9-T
7240 RETURN
9000 REM------------------END PROGRAM
9010 PRINT
9020 PRINT "END OF PROGRAM"
9030 END
```

A.4 STATEMENT OF ACCOUNT PROGRAM

The statement of account program prints out customer bills. The statement of account begins with the customer name and address. Then a line is printed for each transaction which has affected this customer account. The bill ends with the balance owed by the customer to us and a request for payment.

You will use this program at the end of every month to generate customer statements. The statements also provide a written audit trail which backs up every balance in the customer master file.

When you run the program, the computer will ask only one question
     1. DATE ØF RUN (M, D, Y)?
Respond by
     2. Type: number of the month for the date of run (e.g., January would be 1 and December would be 12)
     3. Type: ,
     4. Type: number of the day of month for the date of run
     5. Type: ,
     6. Type: number of the year of the date of run (e.g., 1980 would be 80)

Sample Run Billing Statement Program

```
DATE OF RUN (M,D,Y) ?2,1,79

*-*************************************************************************
                        POOPER CENTERS, INC.
                         1000 CANAL STREET
                       NEW ORLEANS, LOUISIANA

                        STATEMENT OF ACCOUNT
                          AS OF 2/1/79


UPTOWN CONST. CO.                      ACCOUNT # 11001
FIRST ST.


DATE            TRANS TYPE    DEBIT         CREDIT       BALANCE

                BEG BALANCE                              0
12/31/78        PURCHASES     50000                      50000
1/5/79          PURCHASES     10000                      60000
1/10/79         PAYMENTS                    15000        45000
1/18/79         PAYMENTS                    15000        30000
1/19/79         PURCHASES     12000                      42000
2/1/79          DEBIT MEMO    500                        42500


                    SUMMARY OF ACTIVITY

BEGINNING BALANCE          0
PLUS TOTAL CHARGES         72500
LESS TOTAL CREDITS         30000
EQUALS NEW BALANCE         42500

NEW BALANCE IS PAYABLE IN FULL WITHIN 25 DAYS OF STATEMENT DATE

**************************************************************************
```

Program Listing Billing Statement Program

```
10 REM-------------------BILLING PROGRAM
20 REM    THIS PROGRAM PRINTS A SEPARATE BILL FOR EACH CUSTOMER
30 REM
40 REM-------------------DICTIONARY OF VARIABLES
50 REM
60 REM    X,X$  TRANSACTION CODE
70 REM    C,C$ CUSTOMER NUMBER
80 REM    F,F$ ACTIVITY STATUS -- 1=INACTIVE, 0=ACTIVE ACCT.
90 REM    N$ CUSTOMER NAME
100 REM    A$ CUSTOMER ADDRESS
110 REM    M,M$ CREDIT LIMIT
120 REM    B,B$ BEGINNING BALANCE
130 REM    D1,D1$ DEBITS FOR PERIOD
140 REM    C1,C1$ CREDITS FOR PERIOD
150 REM    E,E$ ENDING BALANCE
160 REM    D,D$  DATE OF TRANSACTION
170 REM    T,T$ AMOUNT OF TRANSACTION
180 REM    T4 RUNNING BALANCE OF TRANSACTIONS
190 REM    M6 # OF MONTH
200 REM    D6 # OF DAY
210 REM    Y6 # OF YEAR
220 REM    D9$ DATE OF TRANSACTION
230 REM    R8 # CUSTOMERS
240 REM    E8 # OF TRANSACTIONS
250 REM    J    INDEX VARIABLES
260 REM    R$ DATE OF RUN
270 REM    R9 INDEX TO CUSTOMER RECORD
```

Program Listing Billing Statement Program (Continued)

```
500 REM------------------MAIN PROGRAM
510 REM
520 REM------------------GET DATE
530 FILES CUST.DAT$, TRANS.DAT$
540 PRINT "DATE OF RUN (M,D,Y)";
550 INPUT M6,D6,Y6
560 R$ = STR$(M6)+"/"+STR$(D6)+"/"+STR$(Y6)
570 REM------------------PARAMETERS
580 R8 = INT(LOF(1)/9)
590 E8 = INT((LOF(2)-4)/4)
600 REM------------------BEGIN OUTER LOOP:
610 REM                  ONCE THROUGH LOOP PER CUSTOMER
620 FOR R9 = 1 TO R8
630    GOSUB 3500
640    C2 = C
650    PRINT
660    REM---------------SKIP CUSTOMER WITH NO ACTIVITY
670    IF B  > 0  GOTO  720
680    IF C1 > 0  GOTO  720
690    IF D1 > 0  GOTO  720
700    IF E  > 0  GOTO  720
710    GOTO 1350
720    FOR J = 1 TO 70
730       PRINT "*";
740    NEXT J
750    REM---------------PRINT HEADING
760    PRINT
770    PRINT TAB(21);"POOPER CENTERS, INC."
780    PRINT TAB(22);"1000 CANAL STREET"
790    PRINT TAB(18);"NEW ORLEANS, LOUISIANA"
800    PRINT
810    PRINT TAB(21);"STATEMENT OF ACCOUNT"
820    PRINT TAB(25);"AS OF ";R$
830    PRINT
840    PRINT
850    PRINT N$;TAB(35);"ACCOUNT #";C
860    PRINT A$
870    PRINT
880    PRINT
890    PRINT"DATE","TRANS TYPE","DEBIT","CREDIT","BALANCE"
900    PRINT
910    PRINT ,"BEG BALANCE",,,B
920    T4 = B
930    REM---------------BEGIN INNER LOOP:
940    REM                  READ ALL TRANSACTION
950    FOR J = 1 TO E8
960       GOSUB 6000
970       Y6 = INT(D/10000)
980       M6 = INT((D-Y6*10000)/100)
990       D6 = D - Y6*10000 - M6*100
1000      D9$ = STR$(M6)+"/"+STR$(D6)+"/"+STR$(Y6)
1010      IF C <> C2 GOTO 1150
1020      REM-------------PRINT EACH TRANSACTION
1030      ON X GOTO 1040,1070,1100,1130
1040      T4=T4+T
1050      PRINT D9$,"PURCHASES",T,,T4
1060      GOTO 1150
1070      T4=T4-T
1080      PRINT D9$,"PAYMENTS",,T,T4
1090      GOTO1150
1100      T4=T4-T
1110      PRINT D9$,"CREDIT MEMO",,T,T4
1120      GOTO 1150
1130      T4=T4+T
1140      PRINT D9$,"DEBIT MEMO",T,,T4
1150   NEXT J
1160   REM---------------END OF INNER LOOP
1170   REM---------------PRINT SUMMARY TOTALS FOR CUSTOMER
1180   PRINT
1190   PRINT
1200   PRINT TAB(25)"SUMMARY OF ACTIVITY"
1210   PRINT
```

Program Listing Billing Statement Program (Continued)

```
1220      PRINT"BEGINNING BALANCE",B
1230      PRINT"PLUS TOTAL CHARGES",D1
1240      PRINT"LESS TOTAL CREDITS",C1
1250      PRINT"EQUALS NEW BALANCE",E
1260      PRINT
1270      PRINT"NEW BALANCE IS PAYABLE IN FULL WITHIN 25 DAYS OF STATEMENT DATE"
1280      PRINT
1290      FOR J= 1 TO 70
1300       PRINT "*";
1310      NEXT J
1320      PRINT
1330      PRINT
1340      PRINT
1350      REM----------------END OF OUTER LOOP
1360 NEXT R9
1370 GOTO 9000
3500 REM------------------SUBROUTINE: READ CUSTOMER RECORD
3510 SET :1, (R9-1)*9+1
3520 READ :1, C$,F$,N$,A$,M$,B$,D1$,C1$,E$
3530 C=VAL(C$)
3540 F=VAL(F$)
3550 M=VAL(M$)
3560 B=VAL(B$)
3570 D1=VAL(D1$)
3580 C1=VAL(C1$)
3590 E=VAL(E$)
3600 RETURN
6000 REM------------------READ TRANSACTIONS
6010 SET :2, (J-1)*4+1
6020 READ :2,X$,C$,D$,T$
6030 X=VAL(X$)
6040 C=VAL(C$)
6050 D=VAL(D$)
6060 T=VAL(T$)
6070 RETURN
9000 REM------------------END PROGRAM
9010 PRINT
9020 PRINT "END OF PROGRAM"
9030 END
```

appendix b

sample company program
development using COBOL

B.1 FILE MAINTENANCE PROGRAM

The maintenance program has several functions:

    a. To add customers to the customer file;

    b. To modify the name, address, or credit limit of an existing customer;

    c. To delete a customer account that has a zero ending balance or activate an account that is presently inactive;

    d. To print the entire contents of the customer file.

The maintenance program uses input commands to maintain the customer master file. The customer master file is an indexed sequential file and is organized according to customer numbers. Thus, it is impossible to add a customer using an existing customer number or to modify or delete a customer number that does not exist.

The edit listing is a printed output listing the successful and unsuccessful operations of the maintenance program. When a customer is added, modified, or deleted, a list of the new information stored in the customer record is printed. If a command is not accepted, then an error message is printed. Included in the error message is the entire input command.

The input commands are created by the user. These commands have a very rigid structure. Usually, the information is keypunched which makes it easy to place the data in the correct columns. Placing the data in the correct columns is very important because the maintenance program looks for information in only six places (i.e., fields). These six fields are the command field, customer number field, customer name field, customer address field, credit limit field, and reactivation field.

There are two general kinds of fields: numeric fields and alphanumeric fields. The *numeric fields* are the customer number field and the credit limit field. The information placed in these fields must be right justified (i.e., placed to the right), so that any spaces in the field are on the left. The other four fields are alphanumeric and the information should start on the left side of the field in the usual manner. Altogether the six fields use seventy-six (76) columns. The last four columns on the keypunch card are unused.

The following is a description of the input command fields:

Columns	Data
1	Command code (A, M, D, or P)
2-8	Customer number, right justified
19-38	Customer name
39-68	Customer address
69-75	Credit limit in dollars, right justified
76	Command code R to reinstate, else leave blank
77-80	Blank

To add a customer use Command code A in Column 1. Then, put the proper information in the next four fields.

To modify a customer record use Command code M in Column 1. An existing customer number must be used in the second field. Then, leaving the fields blank for which the file contains the correct information, place the corrected information in the appropriate field.

To delete a customer record, use Command code D in Column 1. Again, an existing customer number must be used in the second field. If that customer is active and presently has a zero-ending balance, it will be deleted; otherwise, an error message will be generated and the customer will not be deleted. Once a customer is deleted, the transaction program will not process transactions for that customer number until that customer is reactivated.

To reactivate a customer record, use Command code M in Column 1, the customer number in the second field, and an R in column 76. Modifications can be made in other fields at the same time the customer is activated.

To print the contents of the customer master file, use Command code P in Column 1. The rest of the card is ignored.

Sample Input File Maintenance

```
A   11001UPTOWN CONST. CO.          FIRST. ST.               75000
A   11002LIL' PIG LAUNDERMAT        SECOND 9T.               50000
A   11007WRIGLEY WRIGHT             THIRD ST. '              15000
A   11019AKBAR IKBAR                FOURTH ST.                7500
A   11031HAROLD SHADRACK            FIFTH ST.                 5000
A   11044MARVIN MESHACK             SIXTH ST.                 4000
A   11045BRUCE ABENDIGO             SEVENTH ST.               7000
A   11046IONA CARR                  EIGHTH ST.                9000
A   11069I.M. WOMAN                 NINTH ST.                11000
A   11081STERLING SILVER            10'TH ST.                 6000
A   11082CHERRY HERRING             11'TH ST.                10000
M   11081                           TENTH ST.
D   11082
D   11082
M11082
M
M   11082                                                         R
M   11082                                                         R
A   11083MAJOR CREDIT CARDS         12'TH ST.                95000
A   11084TRIP THE LITE DISCO        13'TH ST.                45000
A   11085HOUSE OF PLEASURE APTS.    14'TH ST.                45000
A   11086WO FAT CONSTRUGTION CO.    15'TH ST.                50000
A   11087SUNBEAM                    16'TH ST.                  500
P
```

Sample Output File Maintenance

```
*****************************************************************************
CUSTOMER ADDED TO CUSTOMER FILE:
    CUSTOMER NUMBER            11001
    ACTIVITY STATUS            ACTIVE
    CUSTOMER NAME              UPTOWN CONST. CO.
    CUSTOMER ADDRESS           FIRST. ST.
    CREDIT-LIMIT               $75000.00
    BEGINNING BALANCE          $0.00
    DEBITS FOR THE PERIOD      $0.00
    CREDITS FOR THE PERIOD     $0.00
    ENDING BALANCE             $0.00
    CREDIT-AVAILABLE           $75000.00
*****************************************************************************
CUSTOMER ADDED TO CUSTOMER FILE:
    CUSTOMER NUMBER            11002
    ACTIVITY STATUS            ACTIVE
    CUSTOMER NAME              LIL' PIG LAUNDERMAT
    CUSTOMER ADDRESS           SECOND ST.
    CREDIT-LIMIT               $50000.00
    BEGINNING BALANCE          $0.00
    DEBITS FOR THE PERIOD      $0.00
    CREDITS FOR THE PERIOD     $0.00
    ENDING BALANCE             $0.00
    CREDIT-AVAILABLE           $50000.00
*****************************************************************************
CUSTOMER ADDED TO CUSTOMER FILE:
    CUSTOMER NUMBER            11007
    ACTIVITY STATUS            ACTIVE
    CUSTOMER NAME              WRIGLEY WRIGHT
    CUSTOMER ADDRESS           THIRD ST.
    CREDIT-LIMIT               $15000.00
    BEGINNING BALANCE          $0.00
    DEBITS FOR THE PERIOD      $0.00
    CREDITS FOR THE PERIOD     $0.00
    ENDING BALANCE             $0.00
    CREDIT-AVAILABLE           $15000.00
*****************************************************************************
CUSTOMER ADDED TO CUSTOMER FILE:
    CUSTOMER NUMBER            11019
    ACTIVITY STATUS            ACTIVE
    CUSTOMER NAME              AKBAR IKBAR
    CUSTOMER ADDRESS           FOURTH ST.
    CREDIT-LIMIT               $7500.00
    BEGINNING BALANCE          $0.00
    DEBITS FOR THE PERIOD      $0.00
    CREDITS FOR THE PERIOD     $0.00
    ENDING BALANCE             $0.00
    CREDIT-AVAILABLE           $7500.00
*****************************************************************************
CUSTOMER ADDED TO CUSTOMER FILE:
    CUSTOMER NUMBER            11031
    ACTIVITY STATUS            ACTIVE
    CUSTOMER NAME              HAROLD SHADRACK
    CUSTOMER ADDRESS           FIFTH ST.
    CREDIT-LIMIT               $5000.00
    BEGINNING BALANCE          $0.00
    DEBITS FOR THE PERIOD      $0.00
    CREDITS FOR THE PERIOD     $0.00
    ENDING BALANCE             $0.00
    CREDIT-AVAILABLE           $5000.00
*****************************************************************************
CUSTOMER INFORMATION BEFORE MODIFICATION:
    CUSTOMER NUMBER            11081
    ACTIVITY STATUS            ACTIVE
    CUSTOMER NAME              STERLING SILVER
    CUSTOMER ADDRESS           10'TH ST.
    CREDIT-LIMIT               $6000.00
    BEGINNING BALANCE          $0.00
    DEBITS FOR THE PERIOD      $0.00
    CREDITS FOR THE PERIOD     $0.00
```

Sample Output File Maintenance (Continued)

```
    ENDING BALANCE                    $0.00
    CREDIT-AVAILABLE               $6000.00
CUSTOMER INFORMATION AFTER MODIFICATION:
    CUSTOMER NUMBER                  11081
    ACTIVITY STATUS                 ACTIVE
    CUSTOMER NAME                   STERLING SILVER
    CUSTOMER ADDRESS                TENTH ST.
    CREDIT-LIMIT                   $6000.00
    BEGINNING BALANCE                $0.00
    DEBITS FOR THE PERIOD            $0.00
    CREDITS FOR THE PERIOD           $0.00
    ENDING BALANCE                   $0.00
    CREDIT-AVAILABLE               $6000.00
***********************************************************************
```

```
***********************************************************************
    PRINT-COMMANDS                        1
RECORDS ADDED                    16
RECORDS MODIFIED                  2
RECORDS DELETED                   1
TOTAL RECORDS WRITTEN                    19
INPUT COMMAND ERRORS                      4
 TOTAL COMMANDS READ                     24
```

Program Listing of the Maintenance Program MAINT

```
00010 IDENTIFICATION DIVISION.
00020 PROGRAM-ID.      MAINT.
00030 AUTHOR.          ROB JENNINGS.
00040 INSTALLATION.    UNIVERSITY OF NEW ORLEANS.
00050 DATE-COMPILED.   TODAY.
00060 REMARKS.
00070 *
00080 *
00090 ENVIRONMENT DIVISION.
00100 *
00110 CONFIGURATION SECTION.
00120 SOURCE-COMPUTER. DECSYSTEM-10.
00130 OBJECT-COMPUTER. DECSYSTEM-10.
00140 SPECIAL-NAMES.
00150     CHANNEL(1) IS TOP-OF-PAGE.
00160 *
00170 INPUT-OUTPUT SECTION.
00180 FILE-CONTROL.
00190     SELECT CUSTOMER-INDEX-FILE  ASSIGN TO DSK
00200         ACCESS MODE IS INDEXED
00210         SYMBOLIC KEY IS CUSTOMER-IDX-SYMBOLIC-KEY
00220         RECORD KEY IS CUSTOMER-NUMBER-KEY
00230         RECORDING MODE IS ASCII.
00240     SELECT MAINTENANCE-COMMAND-FILE  ASSIGN TO DSK
00250         RECORDING MODE IS ASCII.
00260     SELECT LOG-FILE  ASSIGN TO DSK
00270         RECORDING MODE IS ASCII.
00280 *
00290 *
00300 DATA DIVISION.
00310 *
00320 FILE SECTION.
00330 *
00340 FD  CUSTOMER-INDEX-FILE
00350     BLOCK CONTAINS 12 RECORDS
00360     RECORD CONTAINS 120 CHARACTERS
00370     VALUE OF ID IS "CUSTOMIDX".
00380 01  CUSTOMER-INDEX-RECORD.
00390     02  CUSTOMER-NUMBER-KEY                    PIC 9(7).
00400     02  FILLER                                 PIC X(113).
```

Program Listing of the Maintenance Program MAINT (Continued)

```
00410 FD  MAINTENANCE-COMMAND-FILE
00420     RECORD CONTAINS 80 CHARACTERS
00430     VALUE OF ID IS "CUSTOMINP".
00440 01  MAINTENANCE-COMMAND-RECORD                PIC X(80).
00450 FD  LOG-FILE
00460     RECORD CONTAINS 120 CHARACTERS.
00470     VALUE OF ID IS "CUSTOMLOG".
00480 01  LOG-RECORD                                PIC X(132).
00490 *
00500 WORKING-STORAGE SECTION.
00510 *
00520 01  CUSTOMER-IDX-SYMBOLIC-KEY                  PIC 9(7).
00530 01  READ-COUNTER          VALUE IS ZERO        PIC 9(5).
00540     88  NO-RECORDS-READ     VALUE IS ZERO.
00550 01  WRITE-COUNTER         VALUE IS ZERO        PIC 9(5).
00560     88  NO-RECORDS-WRITTEN  VALUE IS ZERO.
00570 01  ERROR-COUNTER         VALUE IS ZERO        PIC 9(5).
00580     88  NO-ERRORS-FOUND     VALUE IS ZERO.
00590 01  ADD-COUNTER           VALUE IS ZERO        PIC 9(5).
00600     88  NO-RECORDS-ADDED    VALUE IS ZERO.
00610 01  MODIFY-COUNTER        VALUE IS ZERO        PIC 9(5).
00620     88  NO-RECORDS-MODIFIED VALUE IS ZERO.
00630 01  DELETE-COUNTER        VALUE IS ZERO        PIC 9(5).
00640     88  NO-RECORDS-DELETED  VALUE IS ZERO.
00650 01  PRINT-COUNTER         VALUE IS ZERO        PIC 9(5).
00660     88  NO-PRINTS           VALUE IS ZERO.
00670 01  COMMAND-FILE-STATUS   VALUE IS ZERO        PIC 9.
00680     88  END-OF-COMMAND-FILE VALUE IS 1.
00690 01  COMMAND-FILE-END      VALUE IS 1           PIC 9.
00700 01  ACTIVE-CUSTOMER       VALUE IS "0"         PIC X.
00710 01  INACTIVE-CUSTOMER     VALUE IS "1"         PIC X.
00720 01  ACTIVE                VALUE IS "ACTIVE"    PIC X(8).
00730 01  INACTIVE              VALUE IS "INACTIVE"  PIC X(8).
00740 01  ERROR-STATUS                               PIC 9.
00750     88  NO-ERROR-YET      VALUE IS ZERO.
00760     88  ERROR-EXISTS      VALUE IS 1.
00770 *
00780 01  CUSTOMER-RECORD.
00790     02  CUSTOMER-NUMBER                        PIC 9(7).
00800     02  CUSTOMER-ACTIVITY-STATUS               PIC X.
00810         88  CUSTOMER-IS-ACTIVE    VALUE IS "0".
00820         88  CUSTOMER-IS-INACTIVE  VALUE IS "1".
00830     02  CUSTOMER-NAME                          PIC X(30).
00840     02  CUSTOMER-ADDRESS                       PIC X(30).
00850     02  CREDIT-LIMIT                           PIC 9(7).
00860     02  BEGINNING-BALANCE                      PIC S9(7)V99.
00870         88  NO-BEGINNING-BAL  VALUE IS ZERO.
00880     02  DEBITS-FOR-PERIOD                      PIC 9(6)V99.
00890         88  NO-DEBITS         VALUE IS ZERO.
00900     02  CREDITS-FOR-PERIOD                     PIC 9(6)V99.
00910         88  NO-CREDITS        VALUE IS ZERO.
00920     02  ENDING-BALANCE                         PIC S9(7)V99.
00930         88  NO-ENDING-BAL     VALUE IS ZERO.
00940     02  CREDIT-AVAILABLE                       PIC S9(7).
00950     02  FILLER                                 PIC X(4).
00960 *
00970 01  INPUT-RECORD.
00980     02  COMMAND-CODE                           PIC X.
00990         88  COMMANDED-TO-ADD-CUSTOMER        VALUE IS "A".
01000         88  COMMANDED-TO-MODIFY-CUSTOMER     VALUE IS "M".
01010         88  COMMANDED-TO-DELETE-CUSTOMER     VALUE IS "D".
01020         88  COMMANDED-TO-PRINT-CUSTOMERS     VALUE IS "P".
01030     02  CUSTOMER-NUMBER-IN                     PIC 9(7).
01040         88  CUSTOMER-NUMBER-IS-ZERO          VALUE IS ZERO.
01050     02  CUSTOMER-NAME-IN                       PIC X(30).
01060         88  CUSTOMER-NAME-IS-EMPTY           VALUE IS SPACES.
01070     02  CUSTOMER-ADDRESS-IN                    PIC X(30).
```

Program Listing of the Maintenance Program MAINT (Continued)

```
01080            88  CUSTOMER-ADDRESS-IS-EMPTY          VALUE IS SPACES.
01090        02  CREDIT-LIMIT-IN                        PIC X(7).
01100            88  CREDIT-LIMIT-IS-EMPTY              VALUE IS SPACES.
01110        02  FILLER                                 PIC X.
01120            88  REACTIVATE-ACCOUNT                 VALUE IS "R".
01130            88  REACTIVATE-COL-IS-EMPTY            VALUE IS SPACES.
01140        02  FILLER                                 PIC X(4).
01150 *
01160 01  CUSTOMER-PRINT-RECORDS.
01170        02  CUST-NUMB.
01180            03  FILLER       VALUE IS SPACES        PIC X(4).
01190            03  FILLER                              PIC X(27)
01200                VALUE IS "CUSTOMER NUMBER".
01210            03  CUST-NUMB-OUT                       PIC Z(6)9.
01220        02  ACTIVITY-STATUS.
01230            03  FILLER       VALUE IS SPACES        PIC X(4).
01240            03  FILLER                              PIC X(27)
01250                VALUE IS "ACTIVITY STATUS".
01260            03  ACT-STAT-OUT                        PIC X(8).
01270        02  CUST-NAME.
01280            03  FILLER       VALUE IS SPACES        PIC X(4).
01290            03  FILLER                              PIC X(27)
01300                VALUE IS "CUSTOMER NAME".
01310            03  CUST-NAME-OUT                       PIC X(30).
01320        02  CUST-ADDRESS.
01330            03  FILLER       VALUE IS SPACES        PIC X(4).
01340            03  FILLER                              PIC X(27)
01350                VALUE IS "CUSTOMER ADDRESS".
01360            03  CUST-ADD-OUT                        PIC X(30).
01370        02  CREDIT-LIM.
01380            03  FILLER       VALUE IS SPACES        PIC X(4).
01390            03  FILLER                              PIC X(27)
01400                VALUE IS "CREDIT-LIMIT".
01410            03  CR-LIM-OUT                          PIC $(7)9.99.
01420        02  BEGINNING-BAL.
01430            03  FILLER       VALUE IS SPACES        PIC X(4).
01440            03  FILLER                              PIC X(27)
01450                VALUE IS "BEGINNING BALANCE".
01460            03  BEG-BAL-OUT                         PIC $(7)9.99-.
01470        02  DR-PERIOD.
01480            03  FILLER       VALUE IS SPACES        PIC X(4).
01490            03  FILLER                              PIC X(27)
01500                VALUE IS "DEBITS FOR THE PERIOD".
01510            03  DR-PERIOD-OUT                       PIC $(7)9.99.
01520        02  CR-PERIOD.
01530            03  FILLER       VALUE IS SPACES        PIC X(4).
01540            03  FILLER                              PIC X(27)
01550                VALUE IS "CREDITS FOR THE PERIOD".
01560            03  CR-PERIOD-OUT                       PIC $(7)9.99.
01570        02  ENDING-BAL.
01580            03  FILLER       VALUE IS SPACES        PIC X(4).
01590            03  FILLER                              PIC X(27)
01600                VALUE IS "ENDING BALANCE".
01610            03  END-BAL-OUT                         PIC $(7)9.99-.
01620        02  CR-AVAILABLE.
01630            03  FILLER       VALUE IS SPACES        PIC X(4).
01640            03  FILLER                              PIC X(27)
01650                VALUE IS "CREDIT-AVAILABLE".
01660            03  CR-AVAIL-OUT                        PIC $(7)9.99-.
01670 01  PRINT-RECORDS.
01680        02  BLANK-LINE              VALUE IS SPACES  PIC X(100).
01690        02  BREAK-LINE              VALUE IS ALL "*" PIC X(100).
01700        02  ADD-CUST-MESSAGE            PIC X(100)  VALUE IS
01710            "CUSTOMER ADDED TO CUSTOMER FILE:".
01720        02  MODIFY-CUST-MESSAGE        PIC X(100)  VALUE IS
01730            "CUSTOMER INFORMATION BEFORE MODIFICATION:".
01740        02  CUST-ACCT-ACTIVE           PIC X(100)  VALUE IS
01750            "*****  THIS ACCOUNT IS NOW ACTIVE  *****          ".
```

Program Listing of the Maintenance Program MAINT (Continued)

```
01760      02   MODIFIED-CUST-MESSAGE        PIC X(100)  VALUE IS
01770           "CUSTOMER INFORMATION AFTER MODIFICATION:".
01780      02   DELETE-CUST-MESSAGE          PIC X(100)  VALUE IS
01790           "CUSTOMER RECORD TO BE DELETED:".
01800      02   CUSTOMER-DELETED             PIC X(100)  VALUE IS
01810           "***** CUSTOMER RECORD IS NOW DELETED *****".
01820      02   PRINT-MESSAGE                PIC X(100)  VALUE IS
01830           "THE FOLLOWING IS A LISTING OF THE CUSTOMER FILE".
01840 01   PRINT-ERROR-MESSAGES.
01850      02   ERROR-MESSAGE                            PIC X(132).
01860      02   ERROR-LINE                   PIC X(100)  VALUE IS
01870           "--------- ERROR ON FOLLOWING INPUT ---------".
01880      02   COMMAND-ERROR                PIC X(100)  VALUE IS
01890           "THE COMMAND CODE IN COL. 1 IS IN ERROR".
01900      02   CUST-NUMB-ERR                PIC X(100)  VALUE IS
01910           "CUSTOMER NUMBER IS NOT IN LEGAL FORM".
01920      02   CUST-NUMB-ALREADY-EXISTS     PIC X(100)  VALUE IS
01930           "CUSTOMER NUMBER ALREADY EXISTS IN THE CUSTOMER FILE".
01940      02   CUST-NUMB-NONEXISTENT        PIC X(100)  VALUE IS
01950           "CUSTOMER NUMBER DOES NOT EXIST IN CUSTOMER FILE".
01960      02   CUSTOMER-ALREADY-ACTIVE      PIC X(100)  VALUE IS
01970           "***** CUSTOMER ACCOUNT ALREADY ACTIVE *****".
01980      02   REACTIVATE-ERROR             PIC X(100)  VALUE IS
01990           "ONLY AN A CAN BE USED TO ACTIVATE AN ACCOUNT".
02000      02   CANT-DEL-INACTIVE-CUST       PIC X(100)  VALUE IS
02010           "***** CAN NOT DELETE AN INACTIVE CUSTOMER".
02020      02   CANT-DEL-NONZERO-BAL         PIC X(100)  VALUE IS
02030           "***** CANNOT DELETE RECORD - NON/ZERO BALANCE".
02040 01   CLOSING-PRINTS.
02050      02   PRINTS-OUT.
02060           03  FILLER     PIC X(40)  VALUE IS
02070               "PRINT-COMMANDS".
02080           03  PRINTS-O              PIC ZZZZ9.
02090      02   ADDS-OUT.
02100           03  FILLER     PIC X(30)  VALUE IS
02110               "RECORDS ADDED".
02120           03  ADDS-O                PIC ZZZZ9.
02130      02   MODIFY-OUT.
02140           03  FILLER     PIC X(30)  VALUE IS
02150               "RECORDS MODIFIED".
02160           03  MODIFY-O              PIC ZZZZ9.
02170      02   DELETE-OUT.
02180           03  FILLER     PIC X(30)  VALUE IS
02190               "RECORDS DELETED".
02200           03  DELETE-O              PIC ZZZZ9.
02210      02   WRITES-OUT.
02220           03  FILLER     PIC X(40)  VALUE IS
02230               "TOTAL RECORDS WRITTEN".
02240           03  WRITES-O              PIC ZZZZ9.
02250      02   ERRORS-OUT.
02260           03  FILLER     PIC X(40)  VALUE IS
02270               "INPUT COMMAND ERRORS".
02280           03  ERRORS-O              PIC ZZZZ9.
02290      02   READS-OUT.
02300           03  FILLER     PIC X(40)  VALUE IS
02310               "TOTAL COMMANDS READ".
02320           03  READS-O               PIC ZZZZ9.
02330 *
02340 PROCEDURE DIVISION.
02350 *
02360 MAIN-PARAGRAPH.
02370      OPEN INPUT MAINTENANCE-COMMAND-FILE
02380           OUTPUT LOG-FILE
02390           INPUT-OUTPUT CUSTOMER-INDEX-FILE.
02400      WRITE LOG-RECORD FROM BLANK-LINE
02410           BEFORE ADVANCING 2 LINES.
02420      PERFORM READ-COMMAND-FILE.
02430      PERFORM MAIN-LOGIC-PARA UNTIL END-OF-COMMAND-FILE.
```

Program Listing of the Maintenance Program MAINT (Continued)

```
02440        PERFORM CLOSING-STATEMENT.
02450        CLOSE MAINTENANCE-COMMAND-FILE
02460             LOG-FILE
02470               CUSTOMER-INDEX-FILE.
02480        STOP RUN.
02490 READ-COMMAND-FILE.
02500        READ MAINTENANCE-COMMAND-FILE INTO INPUT-RECORD
02510             AT END MOVE COMMAND-FILE-END TO COMMAND-FILE-STATUS.
02520        IF NOT END-OF-COMMAND-FILE
02530             ADD 1 TO READ-COUNTER
02540             EXAMINE CUSTOMER-NUMBER-IN REPLACING LEADING " " BY "0".
02550             MOVE ZERO TO ERROR-STATUS
02560             WRITE LOG-RECORD FROM BREAK-LINE
02570                BEFORE ADVANCING 2 LINES
02580             IF CUSTOMER-NUMBER-IN IS NOT NUMERIC
02590                MOVE CUST-NUMB-ERR TO ERROR-MESSAGE
02600                PERFORM INPUT-ERROR-PARA
02610                GO TO READ-COMMAND-FILE
02620             ELSE
02630                MOVE CUSTOMER-NUMBER-IN TO CUSTOMER-IDX-SYMBOLIC-KEY
02640                CUSTOMER-NUMBER.
02650 *
02660 INPUT-ERROR-PARA.
02670        WRITE LOG-RECORD FROM ERROR-LINE.
02680        WRITE LOG-RECORD FROM INPUT-RECORD.
02690        WRITE LOG-RECORD FROM ERROR-MESSAGE
02700             BEFORE ADVANCING 3 LINES.
02710        ADD 1 TO ERROR-COUNTER.
02720 *
02730 MAIN-LOGIC-PARA.
02740        IF COMMANDED-TO-ADD-CUSTOMER     PERFORM ADD-CUSTOMER.
02750        IF COMMANDED-TO-MODIFY-CUSTOMER PERFORM MODIFY-CUSTOMER.
02760        IF COMMANDED-TO-DELETE-CUSTOMER PERFORM DELETE-CUSTOMER.
02770        IF COMMANDED-TO-PRINT-CUSTOMERS PERFORM PRINT-CUSTOMERS.
02780        IF NOT (COMMANDED-TO-ADD-CUSTOMER OR
02790             COMMANDED-TO-MODIFY-CUSTOMER OR
02800             COMMANDED-TO-DELETE-CUSTOMER OR
02810             COMMANDED-TO-PRINT-CUSTOMERS)
02820             MOVE COMMAND-ERROR TO ERROR-MESSAGE
02830             PERFORM INPUT-ERROR-PARA.
02840        PERFORM READ-COMMAND-FILE.
02850 *
02860 ADD-CUSTOMER.
02870        MOVE ACTIVE-CUSTOMER TO CUSTOMER-ACTIVITY-STATUS.
02880        MOVE CUSTOMER-NAME-IN TO CUSTOMER-NAME.
02890        MOVE CUSTOMER-ADDRESS-IN TO CUSTOMER-ADDRESS.
02900        MOVE CREDIT-LIMIT-IN TO CREDIT-LIMIT
02910             CREDIT-AVAILABLE.
02920        MOVE ZEROES TO BEGINNING-BALANCE   DEBITS-FOR-PERIOD
02930             CREDITS-FOR-PERIOD  ENDING-BALANCE.
02940        WRITE CUSTOMER-INDEX-RECORD FROM CUSTOMER-RECORD
02950             INVALID KEY  MOVE 1 TO ERROR-STATUS.
02960        IF NO-ERROR-YET
02970             WRITE LOG-RECORD FROM ADD-CUST-MESSAGE
02980                BEFORE ADVANCING 2 LINES
02990             PERFORM PRINT-CUSTOMER-INFO
03000             ADD 1 TO ADD-COUNTER WRITE-COUNTER
03010          ELSE
03020             MOVE CUST-NUMB-ALREADY-EXISTS TO ERROR-MESSAGE
03030             PERFORM INPUT-ERROR-PARA.
03040 *
03050 PRINT-CUSTOMER-INFO.
03060        MOVE CUSTOMER-NUMBER TO CUST-NUMB-OUT.
03070        WRITE LOG-RECORD FROM CUST-NUMB.
03080        IF CUSTOMER-IS-ACTIVE
03090             MOVE ACTIVE TO ACT-STAT-OUT
03100          ELSE
```

Program Listing of the Maintenance Program MAINT

```
03110          MOVE INACTIVE TO ACT-STAT-OUT.
03120       WRITE LOG-RECORD FROM ACTIVITY-STATUS.
03130       MOVE CUSTOMER-NAME TO CUST-NAME-OUT.
03140       WRITE LOG-RECORD FROM CUST-NAME.
03150       MOVE CUSTOMER-ADDRESS TO CUST-ADD-OUT.
03160       WRITE LOG-RECORD FROM CUST-ADDRESS.
03170       MOVE CREDIT-LIMIT TO CR-LIM-OUT.
03180       WRITE LOG-RECORD FROM CREDIT-LIM.
03190       MOVE BEGINNING-BALANCE TO BEG-BAL-OUT.
03200       WRITE LOG-RECORD FROM BEGINNING-BAL.
03210       MOVE DEBITS-FOR-PERIOD TO DR-PERIOD-OUT.
03220       WRITE LOG-RECORD FROM DR-PERIOD.
03230       MOVE CREDITS-FOR-PERIOD TO CR-PERIOD-OUT.
03240       WRITE LOG-RECORD FROM CR-PERIOD.
03250       MOVE ENDING-BALANCE TO END-BAL-OUT.
03260       WRITE LOG-RECORD FROM ENDING-BAL.
03270       MOVE CREDIT-AVAILABLE TO CR-AVAIL-OUT.
03280       WRITE LOG-RECORD FROM CR-AVAILABLE
03290          BEFORE ADVANCING 3 LINES.
03300 *
03310 MODIFY-CUSTOMER.
03320       PERFORM READ-CUSTOMER-FILE.
03330       IF NO-ERROR-YET
03340          WRITE LOG-RECORD FROM MODIFY-CUST-MESSAGE
03350             BEFORE ADVANCING 2 LINES
03360          PERFORM PRINT-CUSTOMER-INFO
03370          PERFORM MOVE-CHANGES
03380          WRITE LOG-RECORD FROM MODIFIED-CUST-MESSAGE
03390             BEFORE ADVANCING 2 LINES
03400          PERFORM PRINT-CUSTOMER-INFO.
03410 *
03420 READ-CUSTOMER-FILE.
03430       READ CUSTOMER-INDEX-FILE INTO CUSTOMER-RECORD
03440          INVALID KEY MOVE 1 TO ERROR-STATUS.
03450       IF ERROR-EXISTS
03460          MOVE CUST-NUMB-NONEXISTENT TO ERROR-MESSAGE
03470          PERFORM INPUT-ERROR-PARA.
03480 *
03490 MOVE-CHANGES.
03500       ADD 1 TO MODIFY-COUNTER  WRITE-COUNTER.
03510       IF CUSTOMER-NAME-IS-EMPTY
03520          NEXT SENTENCE
03530        ELSE
03540          MOVE CUSTOMER-NAME-IN TO CUSTOMER-NAME.
03550       IF CUSTOMER-ADDRESS-IS-EMPTY
03560          NEXT SENTENCE
03570        ELSE
03580          MOVE CUSTOMER-ADDRESS-IN TO CUSTOMER-ADDRESS.
03590       IF CREDIT-LIMIT-IS-EMPTY
03600          NEXT SENTENCE
03610        ELSE
03620          EXAMINE CREDIT-LIMIT-IN REPLACING ALL SPACES BY ZEROES
03630          MOVE CREDIT-LIMIT-IN TO CREDIT-LIMIT.
03640       IF (REACTIVATE-ACCOUNT AND CUSTOMER-IS-ACTIVE)
03650          SUBTRACT 1 FROM MODIFY-COUNTER  WRITE-COUNTER
03660          ADD 1 TO ERROR-COUNTER
03670          WRITE LOG-RECORD FROM CUSTOMER-ALREADY-ACTIVE
03680             BEFORE ADVANCING 2 LINES.
03690       IF (REACTIVATE-ACCOUNT AND CUSTOMER-IS-INACTIVE)
03700          MOVE ACTIVE-CUSTOMER TO CUSTOMER-ACTIVITY-STATUS
03710          WRITE LOG-RECORD FROM CUST-ACCT-ACTIVE
03720             BEFORE ADVANCING 2 LINES.
03730       IF (NOT (REACTIVATE-ACCOUNT OR REACTIVATE-COL-IS-EMPTY))
03740          MOVE REACTIVATE-ERROR TO ERROR-MESSAGE
03750          SUBTRACT 1 FROM MODIFY-COUNTER  WRITE-COUNTER
03760          PERFORM INPUT-ERROR-PARA.
03770       REWRITE CUSTOMER-INDEX-RECORD FROM CUSTOMER-RECORD
03780          INVALID KEY PERFORM NOTHING.
```

Program Listing of the Maintenance Program MAINT (Continued)

```
03790 *
03800 NOTHING.
03810 *
03820 DELETE-CUSTOMER.
03830     PERFORM READ-CUSTOMER-FILE.
03840     IF NO-ERROR-YET
03850         PERFORM DELETE-1.
03860 *
03870 DELETE-1.
03880     WRITE LOG-RECORD FROM DELETE-CUST-MESSAGE
03890     BEFORE ADVANCING 2 LINES.
03900     PERFORM PRINT-CUSTOMER-INFO.
03910     IF  (CUSTOMER-IS-ACTIVE AND NO-ENDING-BAL)
03920         MOVE INACTIVE-CUSTOMER TO CUSTOMER-ACTIVITY-STATUS
03930         WRITE LOG-RECORD FROM CUSTOMER-DELETED
03940             BEFORE ADVANCING 2 LINES
03950         ADD 1 TO DELETE-COUNTER   WRITE-COUNTER
03960         REWRITE CUSTOMER-INDEX-RECORD FROM CUSTOMER-RECORD
03970             INVALID KEY PERFORM NOTHING
03980       ELSE
03990         ADD 1 TO ERROR-COUNTER
04000         IF CUSTOMER-IS-INACTIVE
04010             WRITE LOG-RECORD FROM CANT-DEL-INACTIVE-CUST
04020           ELSE
04030             WRITE LOG-RECORD FROM CANT-DEL-NONZERO-BAL.
04040 *
04050 PRINT-CUSTOMERS.
04060     ADD 1 TO PRINT-COUNTER.
04070     CLOSE CUSTOMER-INDEX-FILE.
04080     OPEN INPUT-OUTPUT CUSTOMER-INDEX-FILE.
04090     MOVE LOW-VALUES TO CUSTOMER-IDX-SYMBOLIC-KEY.
04100     WRITE LOG-RECORD FROM PRINT-MESSAGE
04110         BEFORE ADVANCING 2 LINES.
04120     PERFORM PRINT-ALL UNTIL ERROR-EXISTS.
04130 *
04140 PRINT-ALL.
04150     READ CUSTOMER-INDEX-FILE INTO CUSTOMER-RECORD
04160         INVALID KEY MOVE 1 TO ERROR-STATUS.
04170     IF NO-ERROR-YET  PERFORM PRINT-CUSTOMER-INFO.
04180 *
04190 CLOSING-STATEMENT.
04200     WRITE LOG-RECORD FROM BREAK-LINE
04210         BEFORE ADVANCING 3 LINES.
04220     IF NOT NO-PRINTS
04230         MOVE PRINT-COUNTER TO PRINTS-O
04240         WRITE LOG-RECORD FROM PRINTS-OUT.
04250     MOVE ADD-COUNTER     TO ADDS-O.
04260     MOVE MODIFY-COUNTER TO MODIFY-O.
04270     MOVE DELETE-COUNTER TO DELETE-O.
04280     MOVE WRITE-COUNTER   TO WRITES-O.
04290     MOVE ERROR-COUNTER   TO ERRORS-O.
04300     MOVE READ-COUNTER    TO READS-O.
04310     WRITE LOG-RECORD FROM ADDS-OUT.
04320     WRITE LOG-RECORD FROM MODIFY-OUT.
04330     WRITE LOG-RECORD FROM DELETE-OUT.
04340     WRITE LOG-RECORD FROM WRITES-OUT.
04350     WRITE LOG-RECORD FROM ERRORS-OUT
04360         BEFORE ADVANCING 2 LINE.
04370     WRITE LOG-RECORD FROM READS-OUT.
```

B.2 TRANSACTION PROCESSING PROGRAM

The second program in the accounts receivable system is the transaction processing program which: updates the customer record in the customer master file; writes an accepted transaction file recording the transactions; merges this file with a transaction history file of all previous transactions; and generates an edit listing giving the accepted and rejected transaction commands. The last four records of the transaction history file contain the totals of each of the four different kinds of transactions.

The transaction program makes use of three data files. The customer master file is updated by each transaction so that it always contains current balances. An accepted transaction file is generated containing just those transactions that were currently processed. After all of the current transactions have been processed, the accepted transaction file is closed as an output file and opened as an input file. It is then merged with the transaction history file and output as an updated transaction history file containing all transactions for the period.

The input transactions are coded and keypunched by the user prior to the execution of the transaction processing program. The input transactions contain four fields, all of which are numeric and are, therefore, right justified. The four fields are the transaction type field, the customer field, the date field, and the transaction amount field. The date field may not have any spaces in it. The amount field may not have a decimal.

There are four types of transactions:

> 1 = Credit sale
> 2 = Cash receipt
> 3 = Credit memo
> 4 = Debit memo

The following is a description of the transaction-processing program input transactions:

Columns	Data
1	Transaction type (1, 2, 3, or 4)
2-8	Customer number
9-14	Transaction date (MMDDYY format)
15-21	Amount of transaction (in cents)

All four fields must contain numeric data. The transaction type must have a value from one to four. The customer number field must contain an existing active customer number. The date field must be in a six-digit form with no spaces. There are two digits each for the month, day, and year. June 1, 1949 would be 060149 for example. The amount field may not contain a decimal; therefore, all transactions are recorded in cents. Fifty dollars would be 0005000 or 5000 with three leading spaces.

The edit listing is the printed output, listing the successful and unsuccessful operations of the transaction program. A rejected transaction will be printed as an error. An accepted transaction will show the transaction type, customer number and name, date, amount, credit limit, and ending balance. At the end of the edit listing the number of accepted and rejected transactions, totals for the currently processed transactions, and cumulative totals for all transactions of the period will be printed.

This edit listing could be used as part of the internal control system. One use would be to add the cumulative totals of the previous execution to the totals currently processed to confirm the new cumulative totals. Another use could be to compare the invoices to the customer name on the edit listing to verify that the correct customer number was used in the input data.

Sample Input Transaction

```
100110011231785000000
1  110021231782120000
1  11007123178 100000
1  11019123178  70000
1  11031123178  90000
1  11044123178  50000
1  11045123178 120000
1  11046123178 150000
1  11069123178 120000
1  11081123178  80000
1  11082123178 100000
2  110440103790050000
2  11002010479 530000
1  11019010579  70000
1  110010105791000000
1  110830105791377500
2  11082010879  20000
3  11019010879  20000
2  11069010879   5000
2  110010110791500000
2  11046011179  50000
2  11045011279  35000
1  110840112791000000
1  11002011279 160000
1  110830112791548500
2  11031011279  20000
2  11019011779  70000
2  110010118791500000
1  110010119791200000
1  11007011979  50000
1  110830119791339500
2  11081012579  25000
1  11069012679  30000
1  110830126791045000
1  110850126791600000
2  110830129791377500
3  11085013179 200000
4  11087013179  50000
1  11007020179  80000
1  11069020179  20000
1  11086020179 820000
1  11083020179 902500
4  11001020179  50000
4  11002020179  21200
4  11007020179   1000
4  11031020179    900
4  11045020179   1200
4  11046020179   1500
4  11069020179   1200
4  11081020179    800
4  11082020179   1000
```

Sample Output Transaction

```
TRANSACTION LOG FOR POOPER CENTERS
TRANSACTION CODES:
1  CREDIT SALE
2  CASH RECEIPTS
3  CREDIT MEMO
4  DEBIT MEMO
************************************************************************
   TRANSACTION CODE          1
   CUSTOMER NUMBER           11001
   CUSTOMER NAME             UPTOWN CONST. CO.
   TRANSACTION DATE          12/31/78
   TRANSACTION AMOUNT        $50000.00
   BALANCE WOULD BE          50000.00   CREDIT LIMIT IS    75000.00
************************************************************************
```

Sample Output Transaction (Continued)

●

●

●

●

```
****************************************************************************
       TRANSACTION CODE          4
       CUSTOMER NUMBER           11082
       CUSTOMER NAME             CHERRY HERRING
       TRANSACTION DATE          02/ 1/79
       TRANSACTION AMOUNT        $10.00
       BALANCE WOULD BE          810.00    CREDIT LIMIT IS     10000.00
****************************************************************************
****************************************************************************
     TOTAL ACCEPTED                       51
TOTAL REJECTED                             0
TOTAL COMMANDS READ                       51
****************************************************************************
              CREDIT SALES    CASH RECEIPTS   CREDIT MEMOS   DEBIT MEMOS
TOTALS       202430.00        51825.00        2200.00        1288.00


****************************************************************************
CUMMULATIVE TOTALS FOR THE ENTIRE TRANSACTION FILE
****************************************************************************
              CREDIT SALES    CASH RECEIPTS   CREDIT MEMOS   DEBIT MEMOS
TOTALS       202430.00        51825.00        2200.00        1288.00
```

Program Listing of Transaction Program TRANS

```
00010 IDENTIFICATION DIVISION.
00020 PROGRAM-ID.     TRANS.
00030 AUTHOR.         ROB JENNINGS.
00040 INSTALLATION.   UNIVERSITY OF NEW ORLEANS.
00050 DATE-COMPILED.  TODAY.
00060 REMARKS.
00070 *
00080 *
00090 ENVIRONMENT DIVISION.
00100 *
00110 CONFIGURATION SECTION.
00120 SOURCE-COMPUTER. DECSYSTEM-10.
00130 OBJECT-COMPUTER. DECSYSTEM-10.
00140 SPECIAL-NAMES.
00150     CHANNEL(1) IS TOP-OF-PAGE.
00160 *
00170 INPUT-OUTPUT SECTION.
00180 FILE-CONTROL.
00190     SELECT CUSTOMER-INDEX-FILE   ASSIGN TO DSK
00200          ACCESS MODE IS INDEXED
00210          SYMBOLIC KEY IS CUSTOMER-IDX-SYMBOLIC-KEY
00220          RECORD KEY IS CUSTOMER-NUMBER-KEY
00230          RECORDING MODE IS ASCII.
00240     SELECT TRANSACTION-COMMAND-FILE   ASSIGN TO DSK
00250          RECORDING MODE IS ASCII.
00260     SELECT LOG-FILE   ASSIGN TO DSK
00270          RECORDING MODE IS ASCII.
00280     SELECT TRANS-INPUT-FILE  ASSIGN TO DSK
00290          RECORDING MODE IS ASCII.
00300     SELECT TRANS-TEMP-FILE    ASSIGN TO DSK
00310          RECORDING MODE IS ASCII.
00320     SELECT SORT-FILE  ASSIGN TO DSK,DSK,DSK,DSK,DSK
00330          RECORDING MODE IS ASCII.
00340 *
00350 *
00360 DATA DIVISION.
```

Program Listing of Transaction Program TRANS (Continued)

```
00370 *
00380 FILE SECTION.
00390 *
00400 FD  CUSTOMER-INDEX-FILE
00410     BLOCK CONTAINS 12 RECORDS
00420     RECORD CONTAINS 120 CHARACTERS
00430     VALUE OF ID IS "CUSTOMIDX".
00440 01  CUSTOMER-INDEX-RECORD.
00450     02  CUSTOMER-NUMBER-KEY                 PIC 9(7).
00460     02  FILLER                              PIC X(113).
00470 FD  TRANSACTION-COMMAND-FILE
00480     RECORD CONTAINS 80 CHARACTERS
00490     VALUE OF ID IS "TRANS INP".
00500 01  MAINTENANCE-COMMAND-RECORD              PIC X(80).
00510 FD  LOG-FILE
00520     RECORD CONTAINS 120 CHARACTERS
00530     VALUE OF ID IS "TRANS LOG".
00540 01  LOG-RECORD                              PIC X(132).
00550 FD  TRANS-INPUT-FILE
00560     RECORD CONTAINS 23 CHARACTERS
00570     VALUE OF ID IS "TRANSACTS".
00580 01  TRANS-INPUT-REC                         PIC X(23).
00590 FD  TRANS-TEMP-FILE
00600     RECORD CONTAINS 23 CHARACTERS
00610     VALUE OF ID IS "TRANS TMP".
00620 01  TRANS-TEMP-REC                          PIC X(23).
00630 SD  SORT-FILE
00640     RECORD CONTAINS 23 CHARACTERS.
00650 01  SORT-REC.
00660     02  SORT-DATE                           PIC X(6).
00670     02  FILLER                              PIC X(17).
00680 *
00690 WORKING-STORAGE SECTION.
00700 *
00710 01  CUSTOMER-IDX-SYMBOLIC-KEY               PIC 9(7).
00720 01  READ-COUNTER          VALUE IS ZERO     PIC 9(5).
00730     88  NO-RECORDS-READ   VALUE IS ZERO.
00740 01  ACCEPT-COUNTER        VALUE IS ZERO     PIC 9(5).
00750     88  NO-RECORDS-ACCEPTED VALUE IS ZERO.
00760 01  ERROR-COUNTER         VALUE IS ZERO     PIC 9(5).
00770     88  NO-ERRORS-FOUND   VALUE IS ZERO.
00780 01  INPUT-FILE-END        VALUE IS 1        PIC 9.
00790 01  INPUT-FILE-STATUS     VALUE IS ZERO     PIC 9.
00800     88  END-OF-INPUT-FILE VALUE IS 1.
00810 01  ERROR-STATUS                            PIC 9.
00820     88  NO-ERROR-YET      VALUE IS ZERO.
00830     88  ERROR-EXISTS      VALUE IS 1.
00840 01  TRANS-AMOUNT-TEMP                       PIC 9(7).
00850 *
00860 01  CUSTOMER-RECORD.
00870     02  CUSTOMER-NUMBER                     PIC 9(7).
00880     02  CUSTOMER-ACTIVITY-STATUS            PIC X.
00890         88  CUSTOMER-IS-ACTIVE   VALUE IS "0".
00900         88  CUSTOMER-IS-INACTIVE VALUE IS "1".
00910     02  CUSTOMER-NAME                       PIC X(30).
00920     02  CUSTOMER-ADDRESS                    PIC X(30).
00930     02  CREDIT-LIMIT                        PIC 9(7).
00940     02  BEGINNING-BALANCE                   PIC S9(7)V99.
00950         88  NO-BEGINNING-BAL     VALUE IS ZERO.
00960     02  DEBITS-FOR-PERIOD                   PIC 9(6)V99.
00970         88  NO-DEBITS            VALUE IS ZERO.
00980     02  CREDITS-FOR-PERIOD                  PIC 9(6)V99.
00990         88  NO-CREDITS           VALUE IS ZERO.
01000     02  ENDING-BALANCE                      PIC S9(7)V99.
01010         88  NO-ENDING-BAL        VALUE IS ZERO.
01020     02  CREDIT-AVAILABLE                    PIC S9(7).
01030     02  FILLER                              PIC X(4).
01040 *
01050 01  INPUT-RECORD.
```

Program Listing of Transaction Program TRANS (Continued)

```
01060      02   COMMAND-CODE                              PIC X.
01070           88   LEGAL-COMMAND              VALUE IS 1 THRU 4.
01080      02   CUSTOMER-NUMBER-IN                        PIC X(7).
01090      02   TRANSACTION-DATE-IN.
01100           03   MONTH-IN                             PIC X(2).
01110           03   DAY-IN                               PIC X(2).
01120           03   YEAR-IN                              PIC X(2).
01130      02   TRANSACTION-AMOUNT-IN                     PIC X(7).
01140           88   TRANS-AMOUNT-IS-ZERO       VALUE IS ZERO.
01150      02   FILLER                                    PIC X(59).
01160 01   TRANS-REC.
01170      02   TRANS-DATE.
01180           03   TRANS-YEAR                           PIC 99.
01190           88   LEGAL-YEAR        VALUES ARE 77 THRU 99.
01200           03   TRANS-MONTH                          PIC 99.
01210           88   LEGAL-MONTH       VALUES ARE 1 THRU 12.
01220           03   TRANS-DAY                            PIC 99.
01230           88   LEGAL-DAY         VALUES ARE 1 THRU 31.
01240           88   MONTH-IS-ZERO     VALUE IS ZERO.
01250      02   TRANS-CODE                                PIC 9.
01260           88   CREDIT-SALE-COMMAND        VALUE IS 1.
01270           88   CASH-RECEIPT-COMMAND       VALUE IS 2.
01280           88   CREDIT-MEMO-COMMAND        VALUE IS 3.
01290           88   DEBIT-MEMO-COMMAND         VALUE IS 4.
01300           88   LEGAL-TRANS-CODE           VALUE IS 1 THRU 4.
01310      02   TRANS-CUSTOMER-NUMBER                     PIC 9(7).
01320      02   TRANS-AMOUNT                              PIC 9(7)V99.
01330 *
01340 01   TRANSACTION-PRINT-RECORDS.
01350      02   TRANS-NUMB-O.
01360           03   FILLER       VALUE IS SPACES         PIC X(4).
01370           03   FILLER                               PIC X(27)
01380                VALUE IS "TRANSACTION CODE".
01390           03   TRANS-OUT                            PIC 9.
01400      02   CUST-NAME.
01410           03   FILLER       VALUE IS SPACES         PIC X(4).
01420           03   FILLER                               PIC X(27)
01430                VALUE IS "CUSTOMER NAME".
01440           03   CUST-NAME-OUT                        PIC X(30).
01450      02   CUST-NUMB.
01460           03   FILLER       VALUE IS SPACES         PIC X(4).
01470           03   FILLER                               PIC X(27)
01480                VALUE IS "CUSTOMER NUMBER".
01490           03   CUST-NUMB-OUT                        PIC Z(6)9.
01500      02   TRANS-DATE-O.
01510           03   FILLER       VALUE IS SPACES         PIC X(4).
01520           03   FILLER                               PIC X(27)
01530                VALUE IS "TRANSACTION DATE".
01540           03   MONTH-OUT                            PIC 99.
01550           03   FILLER       VALUE IS "/"            PIC X.
01560           03   DAY-OUT                              PIC Z9.
01570           03   FILLER       VALUE IS "/"            PIC X.
01580           03   YEAR-OUT                             PIC 99.
01590      02   TRANS-AMOUNT-O.
01600           03   FILLER       VALUE IS SPACES         PIC X(4).
01610           03   FILLER                               PIC X(25)
01620                VALUE IS "TRANSACTION AMOUNT".
01630           03   AMOUNT-OUT                           PIC $(8)9.99.
01640      02   UPDATE-BAL.
01650           03   FILLER       VALUE IS SPACES         PIC X(4).
01660           03   FILLER                               PIC X(26)
01670                VALUE IS "BALANCE WOULD BE".
01680           03   UPDATE-BAL-OUT                       PIC Z(7)9.99.
01690           03   FILLER                               PIC X(21)
01700                VALUE IS "    CREDIT LIMIT IS".
01710           03   CRED-LIM-OUT                         PIC Z(7)9.99.
01720 01   PRINT-RECORDS.
01730      02   BLANK-LINE            VALUE IS SPACES  PIC X(100).
01740      02   BREAK-LINE            VALUE IS ALL "*"  PIC X(70).
```

Program Listing of Transaction Program TRANS (Continued)

```
01750      02  HEADING-1              PIC X(100)  VALUE IS
01760          "TRANSACTION LOG FOR POOPER CENTERS".
01770      02  HEADING-2              PIC X(100)  VALUE IS
01780          "TRANSACTION CODES:".
01790      02  HEADING-3              PIC X(100)  VALUE IS
01800          "  1   CREDIT SALE".
01810      02  HEADING-4              PIC X(100)  VALUE IS
01820          "  2   CASH RECEIPTS".
01830      02  HEADING-5              PIC X(100)  VALUE IS
01840          "  3   CREDIT MEMO".
01850      02  HEADING-6              PIC X(100)  VALUE IS
01860          "  4   DEBIT MEMO".
01870      02  CUMM-TOTALS          PIC X(100)  VALUE IS
01880          "CUMMULATIVE TOTALS FOR THE ENTIRE TRANSACTION FILE".
01890 01  PRINT-ERROR-MESSAGES.
01900      02  ERROR-MESSAGE                         PIC X(132).
01910      02  ERROR-LINE            PIC X(100)  VALUE IS
01920          "--------- ERROR ON FOLLOWING INPUT ---------".
01930      02  COMMAND-ERROR         PIC X(100)  VALUE IS
01940          "THE COMMAND CODE IN COL. 1 IS IN ERROR".
01950      02  CUST-NUMB-ERR         PIC X(100)  VALUE IS
01960          "CUSTOMER NUMBER IS NOT IN LEGAL FORM".
01970      02  CUST-NUMB-NONEXISTENT    PIC X(100)  VALUE IS
01980          "CUSTOMER NUMBER DOES NOT EXIST IN CUSTOMER FILE".
01990      02  TRANS-DATE-ERROR      PIC X(100)  VALUE IS
02000          "ERROR IN DATE FOR TRANSACTION".
02010      02  TRANS-AMOUNT-ERROR    PIC X(100)  VALUE IS
02020          "ERROR IN AMOUNT OF TRANSACTION".
02030 01  TOTALS-STORAGE.
02040      02  TOTAL-CREDIT-SALES     VALUE IS ZERO   PIC 9(7)V99.
02050      02  TOTAL-CASH-RECEIPTS    VALUE IS ZERO   PIC 9(7)V99.
02060      02  TOTAL-CREDIT-MEMOS     VALUE IS ZERO   PIC 9(7)V99.
02070      02  TOTAL-DEBIT-MEMOS      VALUE IS ZERO   PIC 9(7)V99.
02080 01  TOTALS-TABLE REDEFINES TOTALS-STORAGE.
02090      02  TOTALS      PIC 9(7)V99 OCCURS 4 TIMES.
02100 01  TOTALS-OUT-REC.
02110      02  TOTALS-HEADING.
02120          03  FILLER          VALUE IS SPACES    PIC X(9).
02130          03  FILLER             PIC X(16)  VALUE IS
02140              "CREDIT SALES".
02150          03  FILLER             PIC X(16)  VALUE IS
02160              "CASH RECEIPTS".
02170          03  FILLER             PIC X(16)  VALUE IS
02180              "CREDIT MEMOS".
02190          03  FILLER             PIC X(16)  VALUE IS
02200              "DEBIT MEMOS".
02210      02  TOTALS-OUT.
02220          03  FILLER             PIC X(9)   VALUE IS
02230              "TOTALS".
02240          03  TOTAL-SALES-O                PIC Z(6)9.99.
02250          03  FILLER          VALUE IS SPACES    PIC X(6).
02260          03  TOTAL-RECEIPTS-O             PIC Z(6)9.99.
02270          03  FILLER          VALUE IS SPACES    PIC X(6).
02280          03  TOTAL-CREDIT-M-O             PIC Z(6)9.99.
02290          03  FILLER          VALUE IS SPACES    PIC X(6).
02300          03  TOTAL-DEBIT-M-O              PIC Z(6)9.99.
02310 01  CLOSING-PRINTS.
02320      02  ACCEPTED-OUT.
02330          03  FILLER     PIC X(40)  VALUE IS
02340              "TOTAL ACCEPTED".
02350          03  ACCEPT-O               PIC ZZZZ9.
02360      02  ERRORS-OUT.
02370          03  FILLER     PIC X(40)  VALUE IS
02380              "TOTAL REJECTED".
02390          03  ERRORS-O               PIC ZZZZ9.
02400      02  READS-OUT.
02410          03  FILLER     PIC X(40)  VALUE IS
02420              "TOTAL COMMANDS READ".
```

Program Listing of Transaction Program TRANS (Continued)

```
02430        03   READS-O              PIC ZZZZ9.
02440 *
02450 PROCEDURE DIVISION.
02460 *
02470 MAIN-PARAGRAPH.
02480     OPEN INPUT TRANSACTION-COMMAND-FILE
02490          OUTPUT LOG-FILE    TRANS-TEMP-FILE
02500          INPUT-OUTPUT CUSTOMER-INDEX-FILE.
02510     WRITE LOG-RECORD FROM BLANK-LINE
02520          BEFORE ADVANCING 2 LINES.
02530     PERFORM REPORT-HEADINGS.
02540     PERFORM READ-COMMAND-FILE.
02550     PERFORM MAIN-LOGIC-PARA UNTIL END-OF-INPUT-FILE.
02560     PERFORM CLOSING-STATEMENT.
02570     CLOSE TRANSACTION-COMMAND-FILE
02580           TRANS-TEMP-FILE
02590           CUSTOMER-INDEX-FILE.
02600     SORT SORT-FILE
02610          ASCENDING KEY SORT-DATE
02620          INPUT PROCEDURE SORT-INPUT
02630          OUTPUT PROCEDURE SORT-OUTPUT.
02640     STOP RUN.
02650 *
02660 REPORT-HEADINGS.
02670     WRITE LOG-RECORD FROM HEADING-1
02680          BEFORE ADVANCING 3 LINES.
02690     WRITE LOG-RECORD FROM HEADING-2.
02700     WRITE LOG-RECORD FROM HEADING-3.
02710     WRITE LOG-RECORD FROM HEADING-4.
02720     WRITE LOG-RECORD FROM HEADING-5.
02730     WRITE LOG-RECORD FROM HEADING-6
02740          BEFORE ADVANCING 3 LINES.
02750 *
02760 READ-COMMAND-FILE.
02770     READ TRANSACTION-COMMAND-FILE INTO INPUT-RECORD
02780          AT END MOVE INPUT-FILE-END TO INPUT-FILE-STATUS.
02790     IF NOT END-OF-INPUT-FILE
02800          ADD 1 TO READ-COUNTER
02810          EXAMINE CUSTOMER-NUMBER-IN REPLACING LEADING " " BY "0".
02820          MOVE ZERO TO ERROR-STATUS
02830          WRITE LOG-RECORD FROM BREAK-LINE
02840               BEFORE ADVANCING 2 LINES
02850          IF CUSTOMER-NUMBER-IN IS NOT NUMERIC
02860               MOVE CUST-NUMB-ERR TO ERROR-MESSAGE
02870               PERFORM INPUT-ERROR-PARA
02880               GO TO READ-COMMAND-FILE
02890          ELSE
02900               MOVE CUSTOMER-NUMBER-IN TO CUSTOMER-IDX-SYMBOLIC-KEY.
02910     IF NOT END-OF-INPUT-FILE
02920          EXAMINE INPUT-RECORD REPLACING ALL SPACES BY ZEROES
02930          MOVE COMMAND-CODE TO TRANS-CODE
02940          MOVE CUSTOMER-NUMBER-IN TO TRANS-CUSTOMER-NUMBER
02950          MOVE YEAR-IN TO TRANS-YEAR
02960          MOVE MONTH-IN TO TRANS-MONTH
02970          MOVE DAY-IN TO TRANS-DAY
02980          MOVE TRANSACTION-AMOUNT-IN TO TRANS-AMOUNT-TEMP
02990          DIVIDE 100 INTO TRANS-AMOUNT-TEMP GIVING
03000               TRANS-AMOUNT ROUNDED
03010          PERFORM ERROR-CHECK
03020          IF (ERROR-EXISTS)  GO TO READ-COMMAND-FILE.
03030 *
03040 ERROR-CHECK.
03050     IF NOT LEGAL-COMMAND
03060          MOVE COMMAND-ERROR TO ERROR-MESSAGE
03070          PERFORM INPUT-ERROR-PARA.
03080     IF (NO-ERROR-YET AND NOT(LEGAL-DAY OR LEGAL-MONTH
03090          OR LEGAL-YEAR))
03100          MOVE TRANS-DATE-ERROR TO ERROR-MESSAGE
```

Program Listing of Transaction Program TRANS

```
03110        PERFORM INPUT-ERROR-PARA.
03120     IF  (NO-ERROR-YET AND
03130         (( TRANS-AMOUNT-IS-ZERO) OR
03140         (TRANS-AMOUNT IS NOT NUMERIC)))
03150         MOVE TRANS-AMOUNT-ERROR TO ERROR-MESSAGE
03160         PERFORM INPUT-ERROR-PARA.
03170 *
03180 INPUT-ERROR-PARA.
03190     MOVE 1 TO ERROR-STATUS.
03200     WRITE LOG-RECORD FROM ERROR-LINE.
03210     WRITE LOG-RECORD FROM INPUT-RECORD.
03220     WRITE LOG-RECORD FROM ERROR-MESSAGE
03230         BEFORE ADVANCING 3 LINES.
03240     ADD 1 TO ERROR-COUNTER.
03250 *
03260 READ-CUSTOMER-FILE.
03270     READ CUSTOMER-INDEX-FILE INTO CUSTOMER-RECORD
03280         INVALID KEY MOVE 1 TO ERROR-STATUS.
03290     IF ERROR-EXISTS
03300         MOVE CUST-NUMB-NONEXISTENT TO ERROR-MESSAGE
03310         PERFORM INPUT-ERROR-PARA.
03320 *
03330 MAIN-LOGIC-PARA.
03340     PERFORM READ-CUSTOMER-FILE.
03350     IF NO-ERROR-YET
03360         PERFORM DECISION-MAKING-PARA.
03370     PERFORM READ-COMMAND-FILE.
03380 *
03390 DECISION-MAKING-PARA.
03400     IF CREDIT-SALE-COMMAND PERFORM DEBIT-ACCOUNT.
03410     IF CASH-RECEIPT-COMMAND    PERFORM CREDIT-ACCOUNT.
03420     IF CREDIT-MEMO-COMMAND     PERFORM CREDIT-ACCOUNT.
03430     IF DEBIT-MEMO-COMMAND      PERFORM DEBIT-ACCOUNT.
03440     REWRITE CUSTOMER-INDEX-RECORD FROM CUSTOMER-RECORD
03450         INVALID KEY PERFORM NOTHING.
03460     WRITE TRANS-TEMP-REC FROM TRANS-REC.
03470     MOVE TRANS-CODE TO TRANS-OUT.
03480     MOVE CUSTOMER-NUMBER TO CUST-NUMB-OUT.
03490     MOVE TRANS-MONTH TO MONTH-OUT.
03500     MOVE TRANS-DAY TO DAY-OUT.
03510     MOVE TRANS-YEAR TO YEAR-OUT.
03520     MOVE TRANS-AMOUNT TO AMOUNT-OUT.
03530     MOVE CUSTOMER-NAME TO CUST-NAME-OUT.
03540     MOVE ENDING-BALANCE TO UPDATE-BAL-OUT.
03550     MOVE CREDIT-LIMIT TO CRED-LIM-OUT.
03560     WRITE LOG-RECORD FROM TRANS-NUMB-O.
03570     WRITE LOG-RECORD FROM CUST-NUMB.
03580     WRITE LOG-RECORD FROM CUST-NAME.
03590     WRITE LOG-RECORD FROM TRANS-DATE-O.
03600     WRITE LOG-RECORD FROM TRANS-AMOUNT-O.
03610     WRITE LOG-RECORD FROM UPDATE-BAL
03620         BEFORE ADVANCING 3 LINES.
03630     ADD 1 TO ACCEPT-COUNTER.
03640 *
03650 DEBIT-ACCOUNT.
03660     ADD TRANS-AMOUNT TO DEBITS-FOR-PERIOD
03670         TOTALS(TRANS-CODE) ON SIZE ERROR PERFORM NOTHING.
03680     PERFORM RETOTAL-CUST-REC.
03690 *
03700 CREDIT-ACCOUNT.
03710     ADD TRANS-AMOUNT TO CREDITS-FOR-PERIOD
03720         TOTALS(TRANS-CODE) ON SIZE ERROR PERFORM NOTHING.
03730     PERFORM RETOTAL-CUST-REC.
03740 *
03750 RETOTAL-CUST-REC.
03760     MOVE BEGINNING-BALANCE TO ENDING-BALANCE.
03770     ADD DEBITS-FOR-PERIOD TO ENDING-BALANCE.
03780     SUBTRACT CREDITS-FOR-PERIOD FROM ENDING-BALANCE.
03790     SUBTRACT ENDING-BALANCE FROM CREDIT-LIMIT GIVING
03800         CREDIT-AVAILABLE ROUNDED.
03810 *
03820 CLOSING-STATEMENT.
03830     MOVE ACCEPT-COUNTER TO ACCEPT-O.
```

Program Listing of Transaction Program TRANS (Continued)

```
03840      MOVE ERROR-COUNTER TO ERRORS-O.
03850      MOVE READ-COUNTER TO READS-O.
03860      WRITE LOG-RECORD FROM BREAK-LINE
03870          BEFORE ADVANCING 3 LINES.
03880      WRITE LOG-RECORD FROM ACCEPTED-OUT.
03890      WRITE LOG-RECORD FROM ERRORS-OUT.
03900      WRITE LOG-RECORD FROM READS-OUT
03910          BEFORE ADVANCING 3 LINES.
03920      PERFORM LAST-PRINTOUT.
03930 *
03940 LAST-PRINTOUT.
03950 MOVE TOTAL-CREDIT-SALES TO TOTAL-SALES-O.
03960 MOVE TOTAL-CASH-RECEIPTS TO TOTAL-RECEIPTS-O.
03970 MOVE TOTAL-CREDIT-MEMOS TO TOTAL-CREDIT-M-O.
03980 MOVE TOTAL-DEBIT-MEMOS TO TOTAL-DEBIT-M-O.
03990 WRITE LOG-RECORD FROM BREAK-LINE BEFORE
04000      ADVANCING 3 LINES.
04010 WRITE LOG-RECORD FROM TOTALS-HEADING.
04020 WRITE LOG-RECORD FROM TOTALS-OUT
04030      BEFORE ADVANCING 3 LINES.
04040 *
04050 NOTHING.
04060 *
04070 SORT-INPUT.
04080      OPEN INPUT TRANS-INPUT-FILE  TRANS-TEMP-FILE.
04090      MOVE ZERO TO INPUT-FILE-STATUS.
04100      PERFORM READIN-OLD-FILE UNTIL (NOT LEGAL-MONTH OR
04110          END-OF-INPUT-FILE)
04120      MOVE ZERO TO INPUT-FILE-STATUS.
04130      PERFORM READIN-TEMP-FILE UNTIL END-OF-INPUT-FILE.
04140      CLOSE TRANS-TEMP-FILE  TRANS-INPUT-FILE.
04150 *
04160 READIN-OLD-FILE.
04170      READ TRANS-INPUT-FILE  INTO TRANS-REC
04180          AT END MOVE INPUT-FILE-END TO INPUT-FILE-STATUS.
04190      IF (LEGAL-MONTH AND NOT END-OF-INPUT-FILE)
04200          RELEASE SORT-REC FROM TRANS-INPUT-REC.
04210 *
04220 READIN-TEMP-FILE.
04230      READ TRANS-TEMP-FILE
04240          AT END MOVE INPUT-FILE-END TO INPUT-FILE-STATUS.
04250      IF NOT END-OF-INPUT-FILE
04260          RELEASE SORT-REC FROM TRANS-TEMP-REC.
04270 *
04280 SORT-OUTPUT.
04290      OPEN OUTPUT TRANS-INPUT-FILE.
04300      MOVE ZERO TO INPUT-FILE-STATUS.
04310      MOVE ZEROES TO TOTALS-STORAGE.
04320      PERFORM WRITE-NEW-FILE UNTIL END-OF-INPUT-FILE.
04330      PERFORM WRITE-TOTALS.
04340      CLOSE TRANS-INPUT-FILE  LOG-FILE.
04350 *
04360 WRITE-NEW-FILE.
04370      RETURN SORT-FILE INTO TRANS-REC
04380          AT END MOVE INPUT-FILE-END TO INPUT-FILE-STATUS.
04390      IF NOT END-OF-INPUT-FILE
04400          ADD TRANS-AMOUNT TO TOTALS(TRANS-CODE)
04410          WRITE TRANS-INPUT-REC FROM TRANS-REC.
04420 *
04430 WRITE-TOTALS.
04440      MOVE ZEROES TO TRANS-REC.
04450      MOVE 999999 TO TRANS-DATE.
04460      PERFORM WRITE-NEW-TOTAL VARYING TRANS-CODE
04470          FROM 1 BY 1 UNTIL NOT LEGAL-TRANS-CODE.
04480      WRITE LOG-RECORD FROM BREAK-LINE
04490          BEFORE ADVANCING 3 LINE.
04500      WRITE LOG-RECORD FROM CUMM-TOTALS
04510          BEFORE ADVANCING 3 LINES.
04520      PERFORM LAST-PRINTOUT.
04530 *
04540 WRITE-NEW-TOTAL.
04550      MOVE TOTALS(TRANS-CODE) TO TRANS-AMOUNT.
04560      WRITE TRANS-INPUT-REC FROM TRANS-REC.
```

B.3   AGED TRIAL BALANCE PROGRAM

The third program in the accounts receivable system is the aged trial balance program. This program accepts a date as an input and outputs a listing of aged accounts.

There are two data files. The customer master file and the transaction history file are used to create the printout of aged accounts. This printout is then used in the manual accounting system.

The operator must input only one piece of information: a date. This date uses only one field that must contain six digits with no spaces. There are two digits each for the month, day, and year. June 1, 1949 would be 060149 for example.

The following is a description of the input fields:

Columns   Data

1-6   Date to be used to compute aged trial
balances (MMDDYY format)

The printout will list on one line, for each customer in the customer master file, the total balance for the customer, the amount due over 60 days, over 30 days, and the amount that is current. After all the customers have been aged and printed, totals are printed for each category.

020179

Sample Input Aged Trial Balance

```
DATE OF RUN (M,D,Y) ?   2, 1,79
  AGED TRIAL BALANCE
POOPER CENTERS, INC.
1000 CANAL STREET
NEW ORLEANS, LA.    70000
  NAME              TOTAL           CURRENT         OVER 30         OVER 60
 UPTOWN CONST      42500.00        22500.00        20000.00           0.00
LIL' PIG LAU       17712.00         1812.00        15900.00           0.00
WRIGLEY WRIG        2310.00         1310.00         1000.00           0.00
AKBAR IKBAR          500.00          500.00            0.00           0.00
HAROLD SHADR         709.00            9.00          700.00           0.00
MARVIN MESHA           0.00            0.00            0.00           0.00
BRUCE ABENDI         862.00           12.00          850.00           0.00
IONA CARR           1015.00           15.00         1000.00           0.00
I.M. WOMAN          1662.00          512.00         1150.00           0.00
STERLING SIL         558.00            8.00          550.00           0.00
CHERRY HERRI         810.00           10.00          800.00           0.00
MAJOR CREDIT       48355.00        48355.00            0.00           0.00
TRIP THE LIT       10000.00        10000.00            0.00           0.00
HOUSE OF PLE       14000.00        14000.00            0.00           0.00
WO FAT CONST        8200.00         8200.00            0.00           0.00
SUNBEAM              500.00          500.00            0.00           0.00

TOTALS            149693.00       107743.00        41950.00           0.00
```

Sample Output Aged Trial Balance

```
00010 IDENTIFICATION DIVISION.
00020 PROGRAM-ID.     BILL.
00030 AUTHOR.         ROB JENNINGS.
00040 INSTALLATION.   UNIVERSITY OF NEW ORLEANS.
00050 DATE-COMPILED.  TODAY.
00060 REMARKS.
00070 *
```

Program Listing of the Aged Trial Balance Program AGETS (Continued)

```
00080 *
00090 ENVIRONMENT DIVISION.
00100 *
00110 CONFIGURATION SECTION.
00120 SOURCE-COMPUTER. DECSYSTEM-10.
00130 OBJECT-COMPUTER. DECSYSTEM-10.
00140 SPECIAL-NAMES.
00150     CHANNEL(1) IS TOP-OF-PAGE.
00160 *
00170 INPUT-OUTPUT SECTION.
00180 FILE-CONTROL.
00190     SELECT CUSTOMER-INDEX-FILE  ASSIGN TO DSK
00200         ACCESS MODE IS INDEXED
00210         SYMBOLIC KEY IS CUSTOMER-IDX-SYMBOLIC-KEY
00220         RECORD KEY IS CUSTOMER-NUMBER-KEY
00230         RECORDING MODE IS ASCII.
00240     SELECT BILL-COMMAND-FILE  ASSIGN TO DSK
00250         RECORDING MODE IS ASCII.
00260     SELECT LOG-FILE  ASSIGN TO DSK
00270         RECORDING MODE IS ASCII.
00280     SELECT TRANS-INPUT-FILE  ASSIGN TO DSK
00290         RECORDING MODE IS ASCII.
00300 *
00310 *
00320 DATA DIVISION.
00330 *
00340 FILE SECTION.
00350 *
00360 FD  CUSTOMER-INDEX-FILE
00370     BLOCK CONTAINS 12 RECORDS
00380     RECORD CONTAINS 120 CHARACTERS
00390     VALUE OF ID IS "CUSTOMIDX".
00400 01  CUSTOMER-INDEX-RECORD.
00410     02  CUSTOMER-NUMBER-KEY                PIC 9(7).
00420     02  FILLER                             PIC X(113).
00430 FD  BILL-COMMAND-FILE
00440     RECORD CONTAINS 80 CHARACTERS
00450     VALUE OF ID IS "BILL   INP".
00460 01  BILL-COMMAND-RECORD                    PIC X(80).
00470 FD  LOG-FILE
00480     RECORD CONTAINS 120 CHARACTERS
00490     VALUE OF ID IS "BILL   LOG".
00500 01  LOG-RECORD                             PIC X(132).
00510 FD  TRANS-INPUT-FILE
00520     RECORD CONTAINS 23 CHARACTERS
00530     VALUE OF ID IS "TRANSACTS".
00540 01  TRANS-INPUT-REC                        PIC X(23).
00550 *
00560 WORKING-STORAGE SECTION.
00570 *
00580 01  CUSTOMER-IDX-SYMBOLIC-KEY              PIC 9(7).
00590 01  READ-COUNTER           VALUE IS ZERO   PIC 9(5).
00600     88  NO-RECORDS-READ    VALUE IS ZERO.
00610 01  ACCEPT-COUNTER         VALUE IS ZERO   PIC 9(5).
00620     88  NO-RECORDS-ACCEPTED VALUE IS ZERO.
00630 01  ERROR-COUNTER          VALUE IS ZERO   PIC 9(5).
00640     88  NO-ERRORS-FOUND    VALUE IS ZERO.
00650 01  INPUT-FILE-END         VALUE IS 1      PIC 9.
00660 01  INPUT-FILE-STATUS      VALUE IS ZERO   PIC 9.
00670     88  END-OF-INPUT-FILE  VALUE IS 1.
00680 01  ERROR-STATUS                           PIC 9.
00690     88  NO-ERROR-YET       VALUE IS ZERO.
00700     88  ERROR-EXISTS       VALUE IS 1.
00710 01  TOTALS                 VALUE IS "TOTALS"  PIC X(6).
00720 01  DATES-FOR-COMPARISONS.
00730     02  TEMP-DATE.
00740         03  TEMP-YEAR                      PIC 99.
00750         03  TEMP-MONTH                     PIC 99.
00760         03  TEMP-DAY                       PIC 99.
00770     02  DATE-30-DAYS-AGO                   PIC 9(6).
00780     02  DATE-60-DAYS-AGO                   PIC 9(6).
```

Program Listing of the Aged Trial Balance Program AGETS (Continued)

```
00790 *
00800 01  CUSTOMER-RECORD.
00810     02   CUSTOMER-NUMBER                               PIC 9(7).
00820     02   CUSTOMER-ACTIVITY-STATUS                      PIC X.
00830          88   CUSTOMER-IS-ACTIVE    VALUE IS "0".
00840          88   CUSTOMER-IS-INACTIVE  VALUE IS "1".
00850     02   CUSTOMER-NAME-ALL.
00860          03   CUSTOMER-NAME                            PIC X(12).
00870          03   FILLER                                   PIC X(18).
00880     02   CUSTOMER-ADDRESS                              PIC X(30).
00890     02   CREDIT-LIMIT                                  PIC 9(7).
00900     02   BEGINNING-BALANCE                             PIC S9(7)V99.
00910          88   NO-BEGINNING-BAL      VALUE IS ZERO.
00920     02   DEBITS-FOR-PERIOD                             PIC 9(6)V99.
00930          88   NO-DEBITS             VALUE IS ZERO.
00940     02   CREDITS-FOR-PERIOD                            PIC 9(6)V99.
00950          88   NO-CREDITS            VALUE IS ZERO.
00960     02   ENDING-BALANCE                                PIC S9(7)V99.
00970          88   NO-ENDING-BAL         VALUE IS ZERO.
00980     02   CREDIT-AVAILABLE                              PIC S9(7).
00990     02   FILLER                                        PIC X(4).
01000 *
01010 01  INPUT-RECORD.
01020     02   TRANSACTION-DATE-IN.
01030          03   MONTH-IN                                 PIC 9(2).
01040          88   LEGAL-MONTH-IN   VALUES 1 THRU 12.
01050          88   MONTH-IS-ZERO    VALUE IS ZERO.
01060          03   DAY-IN                                   PIC 9(2).
01070          88   LEGAL-DAY-IN   VALUES ARE 1 THRU 31.
01080          03   YEAR-IN                                  PIC 9(2).
01090          88   LEGAL-YEAR-IN  VALUES ARE 77 THRU 99.
01100     02   FILLER                                        PIC X(74).
01110 01  TRANS-REC.
01120     02   TRANS-DATE.
01130          03   TRANS-YEAR                               PIC 99.
01140          88   LEGAL-YEAR     VALUES ARE 77 THRU 99.
01150          03   TRANS-MONTH                              PIC 99.
01160          88   LEGAL-MONTH    VALUES ARE 1 THRU 12.
01170          03   TRANS-DAY                                PIC 99.
01180          88   LEGAL-DAY      VALUES ARE 1 THRU 31.
01190     02   TRANS-CODE                                    PIC 9.
01200          88   CREDIT-SALE-COMMAND     VALUE IS 1.
01210          88   CASH-RECEIPT-COMMAND    VALUE IS 2.
01220          88   CREDIT-MEMO-COMMAND     VALUE IS 3.
01230          88   DEBIT-MEMO-COMMAND      VALUE IS 4.
01240          88   LEGAL-TRANS-CODE        VALUE IS 1 THRU 4.
01250     02   TRANS-CUSTOMER-NUMBER                         PIC 9(7).
01260     02   TRANS-AMOUNT                                  PIC 9(7)V99.
01270 *
01280 01  PRINT-RECORDS.
01290     02   BLANK-LINE           VALUE IS SPACES  PIC X(100).
01300     02   BREAK-LINE           VALUE IS ALL "*" PIC X(70).
01310     02   HEADING-1.
01320          03   FILLER                  PIC X(22)  VALUE IS
01330               "DATE OF RUN (M,D,Y) ?".
01340          03   MONTH-OUT                          PIC Z9.
01350          03   FILLER                  PIC X      VALUE IS ",".
01360          03   DAY-OUT                            PIC Z9.
01370          03   FILLER                  PIC X      VALUE IS ",".
01380          03   YEAR-OUT                           PIC Z9.
01390     02   HEADING-2               PIC X(100) VALUE IS
01400          "AGED TRIAL BALANCE".
01410     02   HEADING-3               PIC X(100) VALUE IS
01420          "POOPER CENTERS, INC.".
01430     02   HEADING-4               PIC X(100) VALUE IS
01440          "1000 CANAL STREET".
01450     02   HEADING-5               PIC X(100) VALUE IS
01460          "NEW ORLEANS, LA.    70000".
01470     02   HEADING-6.
01480          03   FILLER                  PIC X(20)  VALUE IS
01490               "NAME".
01500          03   FILLER                  PIC X(15)  VALUE IS
01510               "TOTAL".
```

Program Listing of the Aged Trial Balance Program AGETS (Continued)

```
01520           03  FILLER                    PIC X(15)    VALUE IS
01530               "CURRENT".
01540           03  FILLER                    PIC X(15)    VALUE IS
01550               "OVER 30".
01560           03  FILLER                    PIC X(15)    VALUE IS
01570               "OVER 60".
01580 01   PRINT-ERROR-MESSAGES.
01590      02   ERROR-MESSAGE                            PIC X(132).
01600      02   ERROR-LINE            PIC X(100)  VALUE IS
01610           "--------- ERROR ON FOLLOWING INPUT ---------".
01620      02   AGETB-DATE-ERROR         PIC X(100)  VALUE IS
01630           "ERROR IN DATE FOR EXECUTION OF AGETB.CBL".
01640 01   OVERALL-TOTALS-STORAGE.
01650      02   OVERALL-TOTAL-TOTAL      VALUE IS ZERO  PIC S9(7)V99.
01660      02   OVERALL-TOTAL-CURRENT    VALUE IS ZERO  PIC S9(7)V99.
01670      02   OVERALL-TOTAL-OVER-30    VALUE IS ZERO  PIC S9(7)V99.
01680      02   OVERALL-TOTAL-OVER-60    VALUE IS ZERO  PIC S9(7)V99.
01690 01   CUSTOMER-TOTALS-STORAGE.
01700      02   CUSTOMER-TOTAL-TOTAL     VALUE IS ZERO  PIC S9(7)V99.
01710      02   CUSTOMER-TOTAL-CURRENT   VALUE IS ZERO  PIC S9(7)V99.
01720      02   CUSTOMER-TOTAL-OVER-30   VALUE IS ZERO  PIC S9(7)V99.
01730      02   CUSTOMER-TOTAL-OVER-60   VALUE IS ZERO  PIC S9(7)V99.
01740 01   TOTALS-OUT-REC.
01750      02   NAME-OUT                              PIC X(15).
01760      02   TOTALS-OUT                            PIC Z(8)9.99-.
01770      02   FILLER              VALUE IS SPACES   PIC X(2).
01780      02   CURRENT-OUT                           PIC Z(8)9.99-.
01790      02   FILLER              VALUE IS SPACES   PIC X(2).
01800      02   OVER-30-OUT                           PIC Z(8)9.99-.
01810      02   FILLER              VALUE IS SPACES   PIC X(2).
01820      02   OVER-60-OUT                           PIC Z(8)9.99-.
01830 *
01840 PROCEDURE DIVISION.
01850 *
01860 MAIN-PARAGRAPH.
01870      OPEN INPUT AGED-TRIAL-BAL-COMMAND-FILE
01880           OUTPUT LOG-FILE
01890           INPUT-OUTPUT CUSTOMER-INDEX-FILE.
01900      WRITE LOG-RECORD FROM BLANK-LINE
01910           BEFORE ADVANCING 2 LINES.
01920      PERFORM READ-COMMAND-FILE.
01930      PERFORM REPORT-HEADINGS.
01940      MOVE LOW-VALUES TO CUSTOMER-IDX-SYMBOLIC-KEY.
01950      PERFORM READ-CUSTOMER-FILE.
01960      PERFORM MAIN-LOGIC-PARA UNTIL ERROR-EXISTS.
01970      MOVE TOTALS TO NAME-OUT.
01980      MOVE OVERALL-TOTALS-STORAGE TO CUSTOMER-TOTALS-STORAGE.
01990      WRITE LOG-RECORD FROM BLANK-LINE.
02000      PERFORM PRINT-LINE.
02010      STOP RUN.
02020 *
02030 REPORT-HEADINGS.
02040      WRITE LOG-RECORD FROM HEADING-1
02050           BEFORE ADVANCING 3 LINES.
02060      WRITE LOG-RECORD FROM HEADING-2.
02070      WRITE LOG-RECORD FROM HEADING-3.
02080      WRITE LOG-RECORD FROM HEADING-4.
02090      WRITE LOG-RECORD FROM HEADING-5
02100           BEFORE ADVANCING 2 LINES.
02110      WRITE LOG-RECORD FROM HEADING-6
02120           BEFORE ADVANCING 2 LINES.
02130 *
02140 READ-COMMAND-FILE.
02150      READ AGED-TRIAL-BAL-COMMAND-FILE INTO INPUT-RECORD
02160           AT END MOVE 1 TO ERROR-STATUS.
02170      IF NO-ERROR-YET  PERFORM ERROR-CHECK.
02180      IF NO-ERROR-YET
02190           MOVE MONTH-IN TO MONTH-OUT
02200           MOVE DAY-IN   TO DAY-OUT
02210           MOVE YEAR-IN  TO YEAR-OUT
02220           PERFORM BACK-ONE-MONTH
02230           MOVE TEMP-DATE TO DATE-30-DAYS-AGO
02240           PERFORM BACK-ONE-MONTH
```

Program Listing of the Aged Trial Balance Program AGETS (Continued)

```
02250          MOVE TEMP-DATE TO DATE-60-DAYS-AGO
02260 *
02270 ERROR-CHECK.
02280      IF NOT(LEGAL-YEAR-IN OR LEGAL-MONTH-IN OR LEGAL-DAY-IN)
02290          MOVE AGETB-DATE-ERROR TO ERROR-MESSAGE
02300          PERFORM INPUT-ERROR-PARA.
02310 *
02320 INPUT-ERROR-PARA.
02330      MOVE 1 TO ERROR-STATUS.
02340      WRITE LOG-RECORD FROM ERROR-LINE.
02350      WRITE LOG-RECORD FROM INPUT-RECORD.
02360      WRITE LOG-RECORD FROM ERROR-MESSAGE
02370          BEFORE ADVANCING 3 LINES.
02380 *
02390 READ-CUSTOMER-FILE.
02400      READ CUSTOMER-INDEX-FILE INTO CUSTOMER-RECORD
02410          INVALID KEY MOVE 1 TO ERROR-STATUS.
02420 *
02430 BACK-ONE-MONTH.
02440      SUBTRACT 1 FROM MONTH-IN.
02450      IF MONTH-IS-ZERO
02460          MOVE 12 TO MONTH-IN
02470          SUBTRACT 1 FROM YEAR-IN.
02480      MOVE YEAR-IN TO TEMP-YEAR.
02490      MOVE MONTH-IN TO TEMP-MONTH.
02500      MOVE DAY-IN TO TEMP-DAY.
02510 *
02520 MAIN-LOGIC-PARA.
02530      MOVE ZERO TO INPUT-FILE-STATUS.
02540      MOVE ZEROES TO CUSTOMER-TOTALS-STORAGE.
02550      OPEN INPUT TRANS-INPUT-FILE.
02560      READ TRANS-INPUT-FILE INTO TRANS-REC
02570          AT END MOVE INPUT-FILE-END TO INPUT-FILE-STATUS.
02580      PERFORM TOTAL-CUSTOMER-TRANSACTIONS
02590          UNTIL NOT LEGAL-MONTH.
02600      CLOSE TRANS-INPUT-FILE.
02610      ADD CUSTOMER-TOTAL-TOTAL TO OVERALL-TOTAL-TOTAL.
02620      ADD CUSTOMER-TOTAL-CURRENT TO OVERALL-TOTAL-CURRENT.
02630      ADD CUSTOMER-TOTAL-OVER-30 TO OVERALL-TOTAL-OVER-30.
02640      ADD CUSTOMER-TOTAL-OVER-60 TO OVERALL-TOTAL-OVER-60.
02650      MOVE CUSTOMER-NAME TO NAME-OUT.
02660       PERFORM PRINT-LINE.
02670      PERFORM READ-CUSTOMER-FILE.
02680 *
02690 TOTAL-CUSTOMER-TRANSACTIONS.
02700      IF (CUSTOMER-NUMBER=TRANS-CUSTOMER-NUMBER)
02710          PERFORM TOTAL-TRANSACTIONS.
02720      READ TRANS-INPUT-FILE INTO TRANS-REC
02730          AT END MOVE INPUT-FILE-END TO INPUT-FILE-STATUS.
02740 *
02750 TOTAL-TRANSACTIONS.
02760      IF (CREDIT-SALE-COMMAND OR DEBIT-MEMO-COMMAND)
02770          PERFORM DEBIT-ENTRY.
02780      IF (CASH-RECEIPT-COMMAND OR CREDIT-MEMO-COMMAND)
02790          PERFORM CREDIT-ENTRY.
02800 *
02810 DEBIT-ENTRY.
02820      ADD TRANS-AMOUNT TO CUSTOMER-TOTAL-TOTAL.
02830      IF (TRANS-DATE IS GREATER THAN DATE-30-DAYS-AGO)
02840          ADD TRANS-AMOUNT TO CUSTOMER-TOTAL-CURRENT
02850          ELSE
02860          IF (TRANS-DATE IS GREATER THAN DATE-60-DAYS-AGO)
02870              ADD TRANS-AMOUNT TO CUSTOMER-TOTAL-OVER-30
02880             ELSE
02890              ADD TRANS-AMOUNT TO CUSTOMER-TOTAL-OVER-60.
02900 *
02910 CREDIT-ENTRY.
02920      SUBTRACT TRANS-AMOUNT FROM CUSTOMER-TOTAL-TOTAL.
02930      IF (CUSTOMER-TOTAL-OVER-60 IS GREATER THAN TRANS-AMOUNT)
02940          SUBTRACT TRANS-AMOUNT FROM CUSTOMER-TOTAL-OVER-60
02950          MOVE ZERO TO TRANS-AMOUNT
```

Program Listing of the Aged Trial Balance Program (Continued)

```
02960      ELSE
02970         SUBTRACT CUSTOMER-TOTAL-OVER-60 FROM TRANS-AMOUNT
02980         MOVE ZERO TO CUSTOMER-TOTAL-OVER-60.
02990      IF (CUSTOMER-TOTAL-OVER-30 IS GREATER THAN TRANS-AMOUNT)
03000         SUBTRACT TRANS-AMOUNT FROM CUSTOMER-TOTAL-OVER-30
03010         MOVE ZERO TO TRANS-AMOUNT
03020      ELSE
03030         SUBTRACT CUSTOMER-TOTAL-OVER-30 FROM TRANS-AMOUNT
03040         MOVE ZERO TO CUSTOMER-TOTAL-OVER-30.
03050      SUBTRACT TRANS-AMOUNT FROM CUSTOMER-TOTAL-CURRENT.
03060 *
03070 PRINT-LINE.
03080      MOVE CUSTOMER-TOTAL-TOTAL TO TOTALS-OUT.
03090      MOVE CUSTOMER-TOTAL-CURRENT TO CURRENT-OUT.
03100      MOVE CUSTOMER-TOTAL-OVER-30 TO OVER-30-OUT.
03110      MOVE CUSTOMER-TOTAL-OVER-60 TO OVER-60-OUT.
03120      WRITE LOG-RECORD FROM TOTALS-OUT-REC.
```

B.4 BILLING STATEMENT PROGRAM

The fourth program in the accounts receivable system is the billing program. This program accepts a date as an input and outputs a list of billing statements suitable for mailing.

There are two input files. The customer master file and the transaction history file used to create a printout of billing statements. Each billing statement contains the activity of the customer for the period and the present balance.

The operator must input only one piece of information: a date. This date uses only one field that must contain six digits with no spaces. There are two digits each for the month, day, and year. June 1, 1949 would be 060149 as an example.

The following is a description of the input field:

Column   Data

1-6   Date of billing (MMDDYY format)

The log file will be a list of billing statements. One statement will be printed for each customer in the customer file. A statement will contain the vendor's name and address, the statement date, name and address of customer, and the customer activity. Each transaction for the period will be listed with a running customer balance. At the end of the statement will be a summary of the activity of the customer for the period.

Sample Input Billing Statement

```
020179
```

Sample Output Billing Statement

```
DATE OF RUN (M,D,Y) ?  2, 1,79
*******************************************************************
                    POOPER CENTERS, INC.
                    1000 CANAL STREET
                 NEW ORLEANS, LOUISIANA
                   STATEMENT OF ACCOUNT
                      AS OF  2/ 1/79
  UPTOWN CONST. CO.                 ACCOUNT #    11001
FIRST. ST.
   DATE           TRANS TYPE        DEBIT        CREDIT       BALANCE
```

Sample Output Billing Statement (Continued)

	BEG BALANCE			0.00
12/31/78	PURCHASES	50000.00		50000.00
1/ 5/79	PURCHASES	10000.00		60000.00
1/10/79	PAYMENTS		15000.00	45000.00
1/18/79	PAYMENTS		15000.00	30000.00
1/19/79	PURCHASES	12000.00		42000.00
2/ 1/79	DEBIT MEMO	500.00		42500.00

```
                 SUMMARY OF ACTIVITY
   BEGINNING BALANCE              0.00
PLUS TOTAL CHARGES           72500.00
LESS TOTAL CREDITS           30000.00
EQUALS NEW BALANCE           42500.00
NEW BALANCE IS PAYABLE IN FULL WITHIN 25 DAYS OF STATEMENT DATE
*************************************************************
```

Program Listing of the Billing Program BILL

```
00010 IDENTIFICATION DIVISION.
00020 PROGRAM-ID.      AGETB.
00030 AUTHOR.          ROB JENNINGS.
00040 INSTALLATION.    UNIVERSITY OF NEW ORLEANS.
00050 DATE-COMPILED.   TODAY.
00060 REMARKS.
00070 *
00080 *
00090 ENVIRONMENT DIVISION.
00100 *
00110 CONFIGURATION SECTION.
00120 SOURCE-COMPUTER. DECSYSTEM-10.
00130 OBJECT-COMPUTER. DECSYSTEM-10.
00140 SPECIAL-NAMES.
00150     CHANNEL(1) IS TOP-OF-PAGE.
00160 *
00170 INPUT-OUTPUT SECTION.
00180 FILE-CONTROL.
00190     SELECT CUSTOMER-INDEX-FILE  ASSIGN TO DSK
00200         ACCESS MODE IS INDEXED
00210         SYMBOLIC KEY IS CUSTOMER-IDX-SYMBOLIC-KEY
00220         RECORD KEY IS CUSTOMER-NUMBER-KEY
00230         RECORDING MODE IS ASCII.
00240     SELECT AGED-TRIAL-BAL-COMMAND-FILE  ASSIGN TO DSK
00250         RECORDING MODE IS ASCII.
00260     SELECT LOG-FILE  ASSIGN TO DSK
00270         RECORDING MODE IS ASCII.
00280     SELECT TRANS-INPUT-FILE  ASSIGN TO DSK
00290         RECORDING MODE IS ASCII.
00300 *
00310 *
00320 DATA DIVISION.
00330 *
00340 FILE SECTION.
00350 *
00360 FD  CUSTOMER-INDEX-FILE
00370     BLOCK CONTAINS 12 RECORDS
00380     RECORD CONTAINS 120 CHARACTERS
00390     VALUE OF ID IS "CUSTOMIDX".
00400 01  CUSTOMER-INDEX-RECORD.
00410     02  CUSTOMER-NUMBER-KEY                 PIC 9(7).
00420     02  FILLER                              PIC X(113).
00430 FD  AGED-TRIAL-BAL-COMMAND-FILE
00440     RECORD CONTAINS 80 CHARACTERS
00450     VALUE OF ID IS "AGETB INP".
00460 01  MAINTENANCE-COMMAND-RECORD              PIC X(80).
00470 FD  LOG-FILE
00480     RECORD CONTAINS 120 CHARACTERS
00490     VALUE OF ID IS "AGETB LOG".
00500 01  LOG-RECORD                              PIC X(132).
00510 FD  TRANS-INPUT-FILE
00520     RECORD CONTAINS 23 CHARACTERS
```

Program Listing of the Billing Program BILL (Continued)

```
00530       VALUE OF ID IS "TRANSACTS".
00540 01    TRANS-INPUT-REC                                 PIC X(23).
00550 *
00560 WORKING-STORAGE SECTION.
00570 *
00580 01    CUSTOMER-IDX-SYMBOLIC-KEY                        PIC 9(7).
00590 01    READ-COUNTER              VALUE IS ZERO          PIC 9(5).
00600       88  NO-RECORDS-READ       VALUE IS ZERO.
00610 01    ACCEPT-COUNTER            VALUE IS ZERO          PIC 9(5).
00620       88  NO-RECORDS-ACCEPTED   VALUE IS ZERO.
00630 01    ERROR-COUNTER             VALUE IS ZERO          PIC 9(5).
00640       88  NO-ERRORS-FOUND       VALUE IS ZERO.
00650 01    INPUT-FILE-END            VALUE IS 1             PIC 9.
00660 01    INPUT-FILE-STATUS         VALUE IS ZERO          PIC 9.
00670       88  END-OF-INPUT-FILE     VALUE IS 1.
00680 01    ERROR-STATUS                                    PIC 9.
00690       88  NO-ERROR-YET          VALUE IS ZERO.
00700       88  ERROR-EXISTS          VALUE IS 1.
00710 01    RUNNING-BALANCE                                 PIC S9(7)V99.
00720 *
00730 01    CUSTOMER-RECORD.
00740       02  CUSTOMER-NUMBER                             PIC 9(7).
00750       02  CUSTOMER-ACTIVITY-STATUS                    PIC X.
00760           88  CUSTOMER-IS-ACTIVE    VALUE IS "0".
00770           88  CUSTOMER-IS-INACTIVE  VALUE IS "1".
00780       02  CUSTOMER-NAME                               PIC X(30).
00790       02  CUSTOMER-ADDRESS                            PIC X(30).
00800       02  CREDIT-LIMIT                                PIC 9(7).
00810       02  BEGINNING-BALANCE                           PIC S9(7)V99.
00820           88  NO-BEGINNING-BAL      VALUE IS ZERO.
00830       02  DEBITS-FOR-PERIOD                           PIC 9(6)V99.
00840           88  NO-DEBITS             VALUE IS ZERO.
00850       02  CREDITS-FOR-PERIOD                          PIC 9(6)V99.
00860           88  NO-CREDITS            VALUE IS ZERO.
00870       02  ENDING-BALANCE                              PIC S9(7)V99.
00880           88  NO-ENDING-BAL         VALUE IS ZERO.
00890       02  CREDIT-AVAILABLE                            PIC S9(7).
00900       02  FILLER                                      PIC X(4).
00910 *
00920 01    INPUT-RECORD.
00930       02  TRANSACTION-DATE-IN.
00940           03  MONTH-IN                                PIC 9(2).
00950               88  LEGAL-MONTH-IN  VALUES 1 THRU 12.
00960               88  MONTH-IS-ZERO   VALUE IS ZERO.
00970           03  DAY-IN                                  PIC 9(2).
00980               88  LEGAL-DAY-IN  VALUES ARE 1 THRU 31.
00990           03  YEAR-IN                                 PIC 9(2).
01000               88  LEGAL-YEAR-IN  VALUES ARE 77 THRU 99.
01010       02  FILLER                                      PIC X(74).
01020 01    TRANS-REC.
01030       02  TRANS-DATE.
01040           03  TRANS-YEAR                              PIC 99.
01050               88  LEGAL-YEAR      VALUES ARE 77 THRU 99.
01060           03  TRANS-MONTH                             PIC 99.
01070               88  LEGAL-MONTH     VALUES ARE 1 THRU 12.
01080           03  TRANS-DAY                               PIC 99.
01090               88  LEGAL-DAY       VALUES ARE 1 THRU 31.
01100       02  TRANS-CODE                                  PIC 9.
01110           88  CREDIT-SALE-COMMAND    VALUE IS 1.
01120           88  CASH-RECEIPT-COMMAND   VALUE IS 2.
01130           88  CREDIT-MEMO-COMMAND    VALUE IS 3.
01140           88  DEBIT-MEMO-COMMAND     VALUE IS 4.
01150           88  LEGAL-TRANS-CODE       VALUE IS 1 THRU 4.
01160       02  TRANS-CUSTOMER-NUMBER                       PIC 9(7).
01170       02  TRANS-AMOUNT                                PIC 9(7)V99.
01180 *
01190 01    TRANS-TYPE-LIST.
01200       02  FILLER  VALUE IS "PURCHASES"                PIC X(11).
01210       02  FILLER  VALUE IS "PAYMENTS"                 PIC X(11).
01220       02  FILLER  VALUE IS "CREDIT MEMO"              PIC X(11).
01230       02  FILLER  VALUE IS "DEBIT MEMO"               PIC X(11).
```

Program Listing of the Billing Program BILL (Continued)

```
01240 01  TRANS-TYPE-TABLE REDEFINES TRANS-TYPE-LIST.
01250     02  TRANS-TYPE-NAME  PIC X(11)  OCCURS 4 TIMES.
01260 *
01270 01  PRINT-RECORDS.
01280     02  BLANK-LINE              VALUE IS SPACES   PIC X(100).
01290     02  BREAK-LINE              VALUE IS ALL "*"  PIC X(70).
01300     02  HEADING-1.
01310         03  FILLER                 PIC X(22)     VALUE IS
01320             "DATE OF RUN (M,D,Y) ?".
01330         03  MONTH-OUT                            PIC Z9.
01340         03  FILLER                 PIC X         VALUE IS ",".
01350         03  DAY-OUT                              PIC Z9.
01360         03  FILLER                 PIC X         VALUE IS ",".
01370         03  YEAR-OUT                             PIC Z9.
01380     02  HEADING-2               PIC X(100)  VALUE IS
01390         "                    POOPER CENTERS, INC.".
01400     02  HEADING-3               PIC X(100)  VALUE IS
01410         "                     1000 CANAL STREET".
01420     02  HEADING-4               PIC X(100)  VALUE IS
01430         "                 NEW ORLEANS, LOUISIANA".
01440     02  HEADING-5               PIC X(100)  VALUE IS
01450         "                 STATEMENT OF ACCOUNT".
01460     02  HEADING-6.
01470         03  FILLER                 PIC X(30)     VALUE IS
01480             "                      AS OF ".
01490         03  MONTH-O                              PIC Z9.
01500         03  FILLER                 PIC X         VALUE IS "/".
01510         03  DAY-O                                PIC Z9.
01520         03  FILLER                 PIC X         VALUE IS "/".
01530         03  YEAR-O                               PIC 99.
01540     02  HEADING-7.
01550         03  NAME-OUT                             PIC X(35).
01560         03  FILLER                 PIC X(9)      VALUE IS
01570             "ACCOUNT #".
01580         03  NUMBER-OUT                           PIC Z(8).
01590     02  HEADING-8.
01600         03  ADDRESS-OUT                          PIC X(40).
01610     02  HEADING-9               PIC X(100)  VALUE IS
01620         "DATE          TRANS TYPE            DEBIT          CREDIT
01630 -"       BALANCE".
01640     02  HEADING-10.
01650         03  FILLER                 PIC X(57)     VALUE IS
01660             "                      BEG BALANCE".
01670         03  BEG-BAL-OUT                          PIC Z(7)9.99.
01680 01  DETAIL-LINE.
01690     02  FILLER.
01700         03  TRANS-MONTH-OUT                      PIC Z9.
01710         03  FILLER                 PIC X         VALUE IS "/".
01720         03  TRANS-DAY-OUT                        PIC Z9.
01730         03  FILLER                 PIC X         VALUE IS "/".
01740         03  TRANS-YEAR-OUT                       PIC 99.
01750     02  FILLER                  VALUE IS SPACES PIC X(6).
01760     02  TRANS-TYPE                           PIC X(15).
01770     02  COL-1                                PIC Z(8).ZZ.
01780     02  COL-2                                PIC Z(11).ZZ.
01790     02  COL-3                                PIC Z(11).ZZ.
01800 01  REPORT-FOOTINGS.
01810     02  FOOTING-1.
01820         03  FILLER                 VALUE IS SPACES PIC X(25).
01830         03  FILLER                 PIC X(30)     VALUE IS
01840             "SUMMARY OF ACTIVITY".
01850     02  FOOTING-2.
01860         03  FILLER                 PIC X(29)     VALUE IS
01870             "BEGINNING BALANCE".
01880         03  BEG-BAL-O                            PIC Z(7)9.99-.
01890     02  FOOTING-3.
01900         03  FILLER                 PIC X(29)     VALUE IS
01910             "PLUS TOTAL CHARGES".
01920         03  PER-DR-OUT                           PIC Z(7)9.99-.
01930     02  FOOTING-4.
01940         03  FILLER                 PIC X(29)     VALUE IS
```

Program Listing of the Billing Program BILL (Continued)

```
01950            "LESS TOTAL CREDITS".
01960      03  PER-CR-OUT                         PIC Z(7)9.99-.
01970    02  FOOTING-5.
01980      03  FILLER               PIC X(29)    VALUE IS
01990            "EQUALS NEW BALANCE".
02000      03  END-BAL-OUT                        PIC Z(7)9.99-.
02010    02  FOOTING-6              PIC X(100)  VALUE IS
02020        "NEW BALANCE IS PAYABLE IN FULL WITHIN 25 DAYS OF
02030  -"STATEMENT DATE".
02040 *
02050 01  PRINT-ERROR-MESSAGES.
02060    02  ERROR-MESSAGE                       PIC X(132).
02070    02  ERROR-LINE            PIC X(100)  VALUE IS
02080        "--------- ERROR ON FOLLOWING INPUT ---------".
02090    02  BILL-DATE-ERROR          PIC X(100)  VALUE IS
02100        "ERROR IN DATE FOR EXECUTION OF BILL.CBL".
02110 *
02120 PROCEDURE DIVISION.
02130 *
02140 MAIN-PARAGRAPH.
02150     OPEN INPUT BILL-COMMAND-FILE
02160          OUTPUT LOG-FILE
02170          INPUT-OUTPUT CUSTOMER-INDEX-FILE.
02180     WRITE LOG-RECORD FROM BLANK-LINE
02190          BEFORE ADVANCING 2 LINES.
02200     PERFORM READ-COMMAND-FILE.
02210     WRITE LOG-RECORD FROM HEADING-1
02220          BEFORE ADVANCING 2 LINES.
02230     MOVE LOW-VALUES TO CUSTOMER-IDX-SYMBOLIC-KEY.
02240     PERFORM READ-CUSTOMER-FILE.
02250     PERFORM MAIN-LOGIC-PARA UNTIL ERROR-EXISTS.
02260     STOP RUN.
02270 *
02280 READ-COMMAND-FILE.
02290     READ BILL-COMMAND-FILE INTO INPUT-RECORD
02300          AT END MOVE 1 TO ERROR-STATUS.
02310     IF NO-ERROR-YET  PERFORM ERROR-CHECK.
02320     IF NO-ERROR-YET
02330        MOVE MONTH-IN TO MONTH-OUT   MONTH-O
02340        MOVE DAY-IN    TO DAY-OUT    DAY-O
02350        MOVE YEAR-IN   TO YEAR-OUT   YEAR-O.
02360 *
02370 ERROR-CHECK.
02380     IF NOT(LEGAL-YEAR-IN OR LEGAL-MONTH-IN OR LEGAL-DAY-IN)
02390        MOVE BILL-DATE-ERROR TO ERROR-MESSAGE
02400        PERFORM INPUT-ERROR-PARA.
02410 *
02420 INPUT-ERROR-PARA.
02430     MOVE 1 TO ERROR-STATUS.
02440     WRITE LOG-RECORD FROM ERROR-LINE.
02450     WRITE LOG-RECORD FROM INPUT-RECORD.
02460     WRITE LOG-RECORD FROM ERROR-MESSAGE
02470        BEFORE ADVANCING 3 LINES.
02480 *
02490 READ-CUSTOMER-FILE.
02500     READ CUSTOMER-INDEX-FILE INTO CUSTOMER-RECORD
02510        INVALID KEY MOVE 1 TO ERROR-STATUS.
02520 *
02530 MAIN-LOGIC-PARA.
02540     MOVE ZERO TO INPUT-FILE-STATUS.
02550     PERFORM PRINT-HEADINGS.
02560     OPEN INPUT TRANS-INPUT-FILE.
02570     READ TRANS-INPUT-FILE INTO TRANS-REC
02580        AT END MOVE INPUT-FILE-END TO INPUT-FILE-STATUS.
02590     PERFORM PRINT-EACH-TRANSACTION
02600        UNTIL NOT LEGAL-MONTH.
02610     CLOSE TRANS-INPUT-FILE.
02620     PERFORM PRINT-FOOTINGS.
02630     PERFORM READ-CUSTOMER-FILE.
02640 *
02650 PRINT-HEADINGS.
```

Program Listing of the Billing Program BILL (Continued)

```
02660        WRITE LOG-RECORD FROM BREAK-LINE.
02670        WRITE LOG-RECORD FROM HEADING-2.
02680        WRITE LOG-RECORD FROM HEADING-3.
02690        WRITE LOG-RECORD FROM HEADING-4
02700            BEFORE ADVANCING 2 LINES.
02710        WRITE LOG-RECORD FROM HEADING-5.
02720        WRITE LOG-RECORD FROM HEADING-6
02730            BEFORE ADVANCING 3 LINES.
02740        MOVE CUSTOMER-NAME TO NAME-OUT.
02750        MOVE CUSTOMER-NUMBER TO NUMBER-OUT.
02760        MOVE CUSTOMER-ADDRESS TO ADDRESS-OUT.
02770        WRITE LOG-RECORD FROM HEADING-7.
02780        WRITE LOG-RECORD FROM HEADING-8
02790            BEFORE ADVANCING 3 LINES.
02800        WRITE LOG-RECORD FROM HEADING-9
02810            BEFORE ADVANCING 2 LINES.
02820        MOVE BEGINNING-BALANCE TO BEG-BAL-OUT   RUNNING-BALANCE.
02830        WRITE LOG-RECORD FROM HEADING-10.
02840 *
02850 PRINT-FOOTINGS.
02860        WRITE LOG-RECORD FROM BLANK-LINE
02870            BEFORE ADVANCING 2 LINES.
02880        WRITE LOG-RECORD FROM FOOTING-1
02890            BEFORE ADVANCING 2 LINES.
02900        MOVE BEGINNING-BALANCE TO  BEG-BAL-O.
02910        MOVE DEBITS-FOR-PERIOD TO PER-DR-OUT.
02920        MOVE CREDITS-FOR-PERIOD TO PER-CR-OUT.
02930        MOVE ENDING-BALANCE TO END-BAL-OUT.
02940        WRITE LOG-RECORD FROM FOOTING-2.
02950        WRITE LOG-RECORD FROM FOOTING-3.
02960        WRITE LOG-RECORD FROM FOOTING-4.
02970        WRITE LOG-RECORD FROM FOOTING-5
02980            BEFORE ADVANCING 2 LINES.
02990        WRITE LOG-RECORD FROM FOOTING-6
03000            BEFORE ADVANCING 2 LINES.
03010        WRITE LOG-RECORD FROM BREAK-LINE
03020            BEFORE ADVANCING 4 LINES.
03030 *
03040 PRINT-EACH-TRANSACTION.
03050        IF (CUSTOMER-NUMBER=TRANS-CUSTOMER-NUMBER)
03060            PERFORM PRINT-DETAIL.
03070        READ TRANS-INPUT-FILE INTO TRANS-REC
03080            AT END MOVE INPUT-FILE-END TO INPUT-FILE-STATUS.
03090 *
03100 PRINT-DETAIL.
03110        MOVE ZEROES TO COL-1  COL-2  COL-3.
03120        IF (CREDIT-SALE-COMMAND OR DEBIT-MEMO-COMMAND)
03130            PERFORM DEBIT-ENTRY.
03140        IF (CASH-RECEIPT-COMMAND OR CREDIT-MEMO-COMMAND)
03150            PERFORM  CREDIT-ENTRY.
03160 *
03170 DEBIT-ENTRY.
03180        ADD TRANS-AMOUNT TO RUNNING-BALANCE.
03190        MOVE TRANS-AMOUNT TO COL-1.
03200        MOVE RUNNING-BALANCE TO COL-3.
03210        MOVE TRANS-TYPE-NAME(TRANS-CODE) TO TRANS-TYPE.
03220        MOVE TRANS-MONTH TO TRANS-MONTH-OUT.
03230        MOVE TRANS-DAY TO TRANS-DAY-OUT.
03240        MOVE TRANS-YEAR TO TRANS-YEAR-OUT.
03250        WRITE LOG-RECORD FROM DETAIL-LINE.
03260 *
03270 CREDIT-ENTRY.
03280        SUBTRACT TRANS-AMOUNT FROM RUNNING-BALANCE.
03290        MOVE TRANS-AMOUNT TO COL-2.
03300        MOVE RUNNING-BALANCE TO COL-3.
03310        MOVE TRANS-TYPE-NAME(TRANS-CODE) TO TRANS-TYPE.
03320        MOVE TRANS-MONTH TO TRANS-MONTH-OUT.
03330        MOVE TRANS-DAY TO TRANS-DAY-OUT.
03340        MOVE TRANS-YEAR TO TRANS-YEAR-OUT.
03350        WRITE LOG-RECORD FROM DETAIL-LINE.
```

index

Q

R

S